INTELLIGENT ENVIRONMENTS 2009

Ambient Intelligence and Smart Environments

The Ambient Intelligence and Smart Environments (AISE) book series presents the latest research results in the theory and practice, analysis and design, implementation, application and experience of *Ambient Intelligence* (AmI) and *Smart Environments* (SmE).

Volume 2

Recently published in this series

Vol. 1. P. Mikulecký et al. (Eds.), Ambient Intelligence Perspectives – Selected Papers from the First International Ambient Intelligence Forum 2008

ISSN 1875-4163

Intelligent Environments 2009

Proceedings of the 5th International Conference on Intelligent Environments

Barcelona 2009

Edited by

Vic Callaghan
University of Essex, UK

Achilles Kameas
Hellenic Open University and Computer Technology Institute, Greece

Angélica Reyes
Polytechnical University of Catalonia, Spain

Dolors Royo
Polytechnical University of Catalonia, Spain

and

Michael Weber
University of Ulm, Germany

IOS Press

Amsterdam • Berlin • Tokyo • Washington, DC

ISBN 978-1-60750-034-6
Library of Congress Control Number: 2009906183

Publisher
IOS Press BV
Nieuwe Hemweg 6B
1013 BG Amsterdam
Netherlands
fax: +31 20 687 0019
e-mail: order@iospress.nl

Distributor in the UK and Ireland
Gazelle Books Services Ltd.
White Cross Mills
Hightown
Lancaster LA1 4XS
United Kingdom
fax: +44 1524 63232
e-mail: sales@gazellebooks.co.uk

Distributor in the USA and Canada
IOS Press, Inc.
4502 Rachael Manor Drive
Fairfax, VA 22032
USA
fax: +1 703 323 3668
e-mail: iosbooks@iospress.com

PRINTED IN THE NETHERLANDS

In cooperation with

Association for
the Advancement of AI

Sponsored by

UPC

Agència
de Gestió d'Ajuts
Universitaris
i de Recerca

Ajuntament
de Castelldefels

Intelligent Environments 2009
V. Callaghan et al. (Eds.)
IOS Press, 2009

Foreword

As computers are increasingly embedded into our everyday environments, the objects therein become augmented with sensors, actuators, processors, memory, communication modules and novel interfaces. The capability for objects to perceive the environment, store and process data, pursue goals, reason about their intentions and coordinate actions in a holistic manner gives rise to the so-called Intelligent Environment (IE).

In such environments, real space becomes augmented with digital content, thus transcending the limits of nature and of human perception. The term "digital territory" (DT) was initially used, based on a real world metaphor: a territory is usually a continuum in space and has a measurable quantity of elements that are contained within its borders (only that the elements of a DT are active, as opposed to the usually passive objects found in real world territories). IEs constitute the incarnation of the Ambient Intelligence (AmI) vision within a DT. In the AmI paradigm, intelligent computation will be invisibly embedded into our everyday environments through a pervasive transparent infrastructure capable of recognizing, responding and adapting to individuals in a seamless and unobtrusive way.

IEs provide the necessary infrastructure and the services required by ubiquitous computing systems and applications, which are developed in order to support the realization of people's everyday tasks; in that sense, IEs host all technology mediated human activity. A "Virtual Residence" (the evolution of the physical home into the smart, digital home) was amongst the first IEs to be researched; the concept uses most of the notions that apply to "physical" residence, such as borders, markers, activities, etc and expands them to the digital space. The success of the IE conference series demonstrates the increasing popularity of IE research and systems, as the AmI vision continues to infuse all aspects of human life and activity, including architecture of private and public buildings, design of ecologies of smart objects and robots, health care, education, leisure and entertainment, even art and culture.

The 5th International Conference on Intelligent Environments (IE'09), held at the Politechnical University of Catalonia, Castelldefels, Barcelona, Spain, provides a collaborative forum for scientists, researchers and engineers from both industry and academia to present theoretical and practical results of Intelligent Environments research and their application. It is the next edition in a series of highly successful conferences that were organized in Colchester (UK), Athens (Greece), Ulm (Germany) and Seattle (USA) in the past four years. The conference programme includes full papers presented at special sessions and short papers from the doctoral colloquium and poster session. In addition, three thought provoking invited lectures are presented by Marcus Brunner, Carles Gomez Montenegro and Brian Johnson, on topics of current research, infused with the vision of Next Generation IEs. Collectively, this unique mix of interdisciplinary and visionary topics combines to provide another high quality IE conference.

However, none of these would have been possible without the team of distinguished colleagues and fellows who contributed their effort to making IE'09 possible. We cordially thank them all, starting from the local chairs, Dolors Royo, Angélica Reyes and Leandro Navarro and the publications chair, Michael Weber. Then there are the members of IE scientific committee, the session chairs and all the people serving in the Programme Committee, who worked hard publicizing the conference and collecting contributions. Finally, we extend our gratitude to our technical assistants, Kostas Togias, who managed the IE conferences web site, and Stefan Dietzel and Florian Schaub, who prepared the proceedings that you are now holding. But most of all, we'd like to thank you, the IE attendees, who have been supporting the IE conference during these years, contributing to making Intelligent Environments a reality that will, one day, embrace all activities of life.

Victor Callaghan and Achilles Kameas
IE'09 Programme chairs

Contents

Posters

Doctoral Colloquium

Invited Talks

Intelligent Environments 2009
V. Callaghan et al. (Eds.)
IOS Press, 2009

doi:10.3233/978-1-60750-034-6-3

Science Fiction Prototypes Or: How I Learned to Stop Worrying about the Future and Love Science Fiction

BRIAN DAVID JOHNSON
The Intel Corporation, USA
brian.david.johnson@intel.com

Abstract. This paper is meant to be an introduction both to the short story *Nebulous Mechanisms* as well as the concept of science fiction prototypes. In the tradition of the legendary Isaac Asimov we jump into the long and symbiotic history of science fact and science fiction. Briskly we move through current work in the field and delve into the particulars of the craft of combining current scientific research, theory and practice with the fictional construct of the science fiction story. Finally we look into the specifics of the story *Nebulous Mechanisms* and conclude with the challenge to employ the science fiction prototype to foster innovation and explore the boundaries of modern science.

Keywords. Science fiction, science fiction prototypes, fiction prototypes, virtual reality, design tools, consumer experience architecture, research and design, cultural anthropology, robotics, artificial intelligence, computer science, human computer interaction, intelligent systems

Introduction

Nebulous Mechanisms, the story that follows this introduction, is an unmistakable work of science fiction. Firmly rooted in the rich history of the genre, the story is filled with what you might expect; space stations, asteroid mines, space travel, robots and a good healthy dose of pulse-quickening drama -- all the right ingredients for a good old fashioned sf tale. But *Nebulous Mechanisms* is a bit more than just a good story; it is also a fictional prototype. The foundational idea in the story is based on a theory outlined in the paper *Using Multiple Personas in Service Robots to Improve Exploration Strategies when Mapping new Environments* (Egerton, Callaghan, Clarke). We used the story as an intellectual experiment to explore the theory in the paper and examine its implications in an imagined future. Think of it as a virtual reality on paper, specifically designed to test the possible ramifications of the theory. *Nebulous Mechanisms* was the first in a successful series of science fiction stories based on emerging theory and research from the fields of robotics, computer science, artificial intelligent and neuroscience.

In this introduction I wanted to give a little history and background for the science fiction prototype but before you read on you may want to jump ahead and read the story. I don't want to give anything away but you might want to go find out why the robots on the dwarf planet 1 Ceres are going to church…

1. *Science Fiction is the only true literature of the twentieth century*[1]

The blending of science fiction and science fact is not revolutionary; their symbiotic relationship goes back hundreds of years. It's been well documented that science fiction has inspired generations of scientists, researchers and even astronauts. British science fiction author, inventor, and futurist Arthur C. Clark summed it up this way in his essay *Aspects of Science Fiction*. "All of the pioneers of astronautics were inspired by Jules Verne, and several (e.g. Goddard, Oberth, von Braun) actually wrote fiction to popularize their ideas. And I know from personal experience that many American astronauts and Soviet cosmonauts were inspired to take up their careers by the space travel stories they read as children. (One of my proudest possessions is a little monograph, Wingless on Luna, bearing the inscription, 'To Arthur, who visualized the nuances of lunar flying long before I experienced them! – Neil Armstrong.')"[2]

As Clark points out science fact and fiction have been explicitly intermingled for most of the twentieth century. Physicists and rocketry pioneers Robert Goddard, Hermann Oberth and Wernher von Braum used stories as a way to popularize their thinking while astronaut Neil Armstrong was inspired and driven by Clark's writing. In the 1970's an entire sub-genre of science fiction sprang up around writers that aligned themselves closely with the "hard sciences" (e.g. computer science, astronomy, physics, chemistry, etc.). American science fiction author Alan Steele defines the sub-genre like this: "Hard SF is the form of imaginative literature that uses either established or carefully extrapolated science as its backbone."[3] Many critics see hard sf as the only true science fiction because it is based on real science as opposed to the "soft sciences", pseudoscience or even science fantasy which concerns itself with notions of time travel, extrasensory powers and super heroes. Regardless of where you stand in this debate, it's clear that scientific research, theory and practice have a considerable and sometimes polarizing affect on science fiction.

The twenty-first century has brought us some fascinating explorations into the specific relationship between science fiction and actual technologies that are being built. Genevieve Bell and Paul Dourish in their paper *"Resistance is Futile": Reading Science Fiction and Ubiquitous Computing* argue that understanding science fiction, in their case popular British and American television shows like *Dr. Who* and *Star Trek*, is essential when designing these new technologies. They assert that science fiction can be employed as a tool for design. The futuristic visions expressed in sci-fi television shows can be used to understand the people's collective imagining of what future technologies might look like; thus allowing scientists to develop technologies and products that are easily understood but used by people. "Arguably, a range of contemporary technologies – from PDAs to cell phones – have adopted their forms and functions from science fiction. As in the famous case of British science fiction author Arthur C. Clark's speculative "invention" of the communications satellite, science fiction does not merely anticipate but actively shapes technological futures through its effect on the collective imagination. At the same time, science fiction in popular culture provides a context in which new technological developments are understood. Science fiction visions appear as prototypes for technological environments.[4]

Julian Bleecker expands this notion in his recent work *Design Fiction: A short essay on design, science, fact and fiction.* Bleecker sees the interplay between science fiction and science fact as fertile ground for the inspiration and creations of physical prototypes. These design tools are both real and fake, operational and symbolic, serious and ironic. Bleecker describes them as a "conflation of design, science fact and science fiction…an amalgamation of practices that together bends the expectations as to what each does on its own and ties them together into something new."[5]

Like Bleecker's *Design Fictions*, science fiction prototypes like *Nebulous Mechanisms*, seek a productive middle ground between fact and fiction. They are a new lens through which emerging theories can be viewed differently, explored freely and ultimately developed further. Bleecker's makes an excellent observation: "Productively confusing science fact and science fiction may be the only way for the science of fact to reach beyond itself and achieve more than incremental forms of innovation."[6] It is precisely this productive confusion and fusion of fact and fiction that can unlock, broaden and expand the boundaries of current scientific thinking.

2. *A good SF story features, above all, a strong idea*[7]

The approach to *Nebulous Mechanisms* and science fiction prototype stories is both as simple as a story well told and as complex as the scientific theory they are based on. When understanding the workings of the science fiction prototype it's helpful to tease apart the workings of the short story itself to better understand how the experiment is conducted.

Alan Moore, author of *Watchmen* and *V for Vendetta*, does an efficient job of dissecting the story telling structure in his essay *Writing for Comics*. He describes the essential components of a story as plot, environment, characters and pacing, but central to every story there must be an idea. For Moore the idea is what the story is about, it is the reason for the story's being, it is what drives all the other components. All the other components of the story serve to facilitate the central idea of the story.

Applying Moore's example the idea of *Nebulous Mechanisms* is the theory laid out in the paper *Using Multiple Personas in Service Robots to Improve Exploration Strategies when Mapping new Environments*. But for the prototype to be successful we can't stop at an engaging idea. The audience reading the story must accept the imagined future as real, plausible and acceptable. They must be drawn into the drama the story must hold the reader's attention; maintaining an adequate level of suspension of disbelief. This level of disbelief can be used as a test of the validity of the prototype. Does the reader believe the world? Is the science invisible to the action and hidden in the cloak of the fiction?

Moore describes the necessary suspension of disbelief this way: "As I see it, a successful story of any kind should be almost like hypnosis: You fascinate the reader with your first sentence, draw them in further with your second sentence and have them in a mild trance by the third. Then, being careful not to wake them up, you carry them away up the back alleys of your narrative and when they are hopelessly lost within the story, having surrendered themselves to it, you do them terrible violence with a softball bat and then lead them whimpering to the exit on the last page. Believe me, they'll thank you for it. The important thing is that the reader should not wake up until you want them to…"[8]

The success of the experiment lies in the tenuous balance between the believability of the story and the exploration of the scientific theory. It is within these checks and balances that we can explore the beauty of the scientific theory wrapped in the drama of its real world realization.

3. *Sometimes a Robot is just a Robot*

Over the last fifty years most introductions to robot story anthologies will tell you that the age of robots in upon us. We are surrounded by robots that build our cars, pilot our planes, run our factories, run our elevators and even bomb our enemies. Actual robots have evolved beyond the "metal man" staple of science fiction and have become cyborgs, AI's and any number of intelligent agents. Thomas M. Disch in the introduction to his essential examination of science fiction *The Dreams our Stuff is Made of* says that "the robot has been employed for a wide variety of dramatic purposes."[9] Ever since Karel Capek's coining of the term robot in 1920 in his play *R.U.R* (Rossum's Universal Robots) robots have been employed in a wide variety of dramatic purposes by science fiction authors. They have expressed our most terrible fears about the inequality of the class, race and gender. From this one would think that when you see a robot in any story then it must be a representation of something else. Who the robot is and what the robot does must mean something.

But there are some cases, as with *Nebulous Mechanisms*, that a robot is just meant to be a robot. In the beginning there were basically two types of robot stories. The first was based on the basic Faustian plot of Frankenstein. Scientist creates robot. Robot kills scientist. Pretty simple. Science legend Isaac Asimov at the beginning of his career recognized this standard Faustian approach. "…one of the stock plots of science fiction was that of the invention of a robot-usually pictured as a creature of metal, without soul or emotion. Under the influence of the well known deeds and ultimate fate of Frankenstein…there seemed to be only one change to be rung on this plot. Robots were created and destroyed their creator: robots were created and destroyed their creator; robots were created and destroyed their creator---"[10]

The second type of robot story emerged in America in the middle of the twentieth century. Sam Moskowitz in his introduction to *The Coming of the Robots* points out that "Psychologically the time was now ripe to launch an assault against the reader's prejudices concerning robots." [11] He goes on to describe two similar stories published within weeks of each other in 1938. *I, Robot* by Eando Binder which reverses the Frankenstein plot and *Helen O'Loy* by Lester Del Rey that presents a world where robots have progressed so far that they are indistinguishable from humans. In the story two friends, after ordering a mail order robot, find that the robot has fallen in love with one of the owners, Dave. It is both a uniquely prepubescent and poignant story. Helen O'Loy is described as "a dream in spun plastics and metals." [12] Ultimately the unaging Helen cares for her love until he dies at one point putting lines on her face and graying her hair so her love thinks she's aging with him.

I explored similar themes in my novel *Fake Plastic Love*, expanding Del Rey's concept of the lovely domestic robot into Ann-Mar, with the locks of the American film star Ann Margaret and the vocabulary of a gossip magazine. "She was a basic issue dream girl…her red synthetic hair looked perfect right out of the plastic. Her lips, too, were a perfect and permanent shade of lipstick red."[13] Both robots are love interests and both are unabashedly robots, but whereas Helen strives to be human, Ann-Mar remains unmistakably a robot.

It is this point that is carried on in *Nebulous Mechanisms*. The robots in the story are realistic robots or at least realistic depictions of robots that strive to be no more than what they are. They do not aspire to partake in revenge killings of their Frankenstein masters nor do they strive to "pass" or become human. The robots of *Nebulous Mechanisms* are just that, robots.

4. *How to Love Science Fiction*

If you haven't guessed it already, I'll be honest with you; I do love science fiction. Two of my greatest affections are the intellectual rigor of scientific research and technology development as well as really good and challenging sci-fi story.

Science fiction is the playground of the intellect. Many people are mistaken when they think that the genre's aim is to predict the future. If this were true then the entire cannon of sf writing would have a terrible batting average. No, science fiction creates not just a single future but multiple futures; a wide variety of Earths and countless variations on humanity and technology. If you look back you'll see that science fiction writers have been going strong for nearly one hundred years. They have written about the space age both before and after it happened. They have dreamed about the canals of Mars and the realities of that fascinating red planet. All of this speculation and energy has produced an interesting affect on you and me. Andy Sawyer captures this affect in his essay *Tales of Futures Passed: The Kipling Continuum and other lost World of Science Fiction*. He writes: "We have read so many stories involving first voyages to the moon, lunar colonies and the exploration of space that we have now internalized a set of virtual histories of space travel and as a result, we cannot quite comprehend that in fact this has not happened."[14]

These futures that Sawyer describes are lodged in our collective and cultural history. The future and science fiction have mingled together in our education and imaginations to such a point that there is no better medium to use as a platform for fictional prototyping. Science fiction prototypes allow us to create multiple worlds and a wide variety of futures so that we may study and explore the intricacies of modern science. They are a powerful tool meant to enhance the traditional practices of research and design. The discoveries that we make with these prototypes can be used to question and explore current thinking on a level we have not approached in the past; namely using multiple futures and realities to test the implications and intricacies of theory. Additionally the output of the science fiction prototype can inform a technology's consumer experience architecture, investigating and shaping how a user might encounter, explore and ultimately use that technology. Science fiction allows us to see ourselves in a new light, in the light of a new future; one that is not our own but reflects directly upon who we are and where we might be headed. The science fiction prototype brings this same lens to science fact; allows us to see the multiple futures in the theory we are constructing today.

References

[1] J. G Ballard, *Literary Review,* 2001.
[2] A. C. Clark, *Greetings, Carbon-Based Bipeds!,* St Martin's Press, 1999.
[3] A. Steel, Hard Again, *New York Review of Science Fiction*, 1992.
[4] P. Dourish, G. Bell, *Resistance is Futile: Reading Science Fiction and Ubiquitous Computing.* 2009.
[5] J. Bleecker, *Design Fiction: A short essay on design, science, fact and fiction,* 2009.
[6] J. Bleecker, *Design Fiction: A short essay on design, science, fact and fiction,* 2009.
[7] J.G. Ballard, *Sunday Times,* 1985.
[8] A. Moore, *Alan Moore's Writing for Comics*, Avatar Press, 2008.
[9] T. M. Disch, The *DREAMS OUR STUFF IS MADE OF: How Science Fiction Conquered the World*, Free Press, 2000.
[10] I. Asimov, Introduction. *The Rest of the Robots*, Doubleday, 1964.
[11] S. Moskowitz, Introduction, *The Coming of the Robots,* Crowell-Collier Publishing Company, 1963.
[12] L.D. Rey, *Helen O'Loy*, Street and Smith Publications, 1938
[13] B. D. Johnson, *Fake Plastic Love*, iUniverse, 2007
[14] A. Sawyer, Tales of Futures Passed: The Kipling Continuum and other lost World of Science Fiction, *World Weavers: Globalization, Science Fiction and the Cybernetic Revolution* (2006), p126

Intelligent Environments 2009
V. Callaghan et al. (Eds.)
IOS Press, 2009

doi:10.3233/978-1-60750-034-6-9

Nebulous Mechanisms

Story by: BRIAN DAVID JOHNSON
The Intel Corporation, USA
brian.david.johnson@intel.com

Illustrations by: Winkstink

Inspired by: *Using Multiple Personas in Service Robots to Improve Exploration Strategies when Mapping new Environments (Egerton, Callaghan, Clarke)*

Friday

"I don't see what's so funny?"

"Really," Dr. Egerton continued to force a thin dry chuckle. "Because I think it's pretty funny. Don't you feel funny even saying it?"

"No I do not feel funny saying it," XienCheng spat back with disdain. "Because it isn't funny. It isn't funny at all. Do you have any idea how much money the Ceres mine lost last week?"

"I have no idea," Egerton shifted in his chair and wondered how much longer this was going to take.

"Well, I can tell you. I have the numbers right here…" XienCheng jammed at the conference room screen with his fat fingers; they looked less like fingers and more like poorly made sausages that had been left out on the counter too long. "It's in here somewheres," the husky administrator continued his search, rubbing a cheap vodka hangover out of his neck with his free hand. This precarious tapping and rubbing position exposed XienCheng's stomach. It jutted over his straining belt in a manner that was both reckless and embarrassing.

Egerton looked away and scanned the ridiculously small conference room. It had everything you'd expect from a new office plaza hastily constructed in the sprawl of satellites and stations that ringed Earth. New carpet, gleaming table, faux leather chairs even glasses and a perspiring pitcher of deceptively clear water.

But why did it have to be so small? Egerton thought to himself. And small it was. The room barely fit Egerton and XienCheng. They were knee to knee. It was a ludicrous doll house version of big business and Egerton wanted to leave. The smell of the new carpet and the smell of the fat administrator were both getting to him.

"Here it is. Yes. Yes. Here it is," XienCheng was pleased with himself. But then his voice turned grave when he read the number, "2.5 billion Euros. And that's just one week. So you can see Dr. Egerton that this is no laughing matter I assure you. That's why we need your help. That's why Shanwei said I should talk to you."

"Yeah I know Shanwei told me all about this but I didn't think he was being serious."

"We can end this meeting right now Dr. Egerton. We need you to do a job. If you want to do it…fine. We'll pay you. If you don't want to do it then let me get back to my day." XienCheng folded his flabby arms and cocked his head to the side. "I have too many things to do already."

Egerton shifted again. “Shanwei told me that you want me to go to your asteroid mine out on Ceres to find out why your bots have all started going to church on Sunday.”

“That’s right. We don’t know why and we can’t stop it. It’s costing us....well you know how much it’s costing us.”

“But I don’t understand what you think I can do?” Egerton asked truthfully.

“Shanwei said you’re the robot guy. He said you’re some irrational robot expert that knows all about this stuff.”

“That was a long time ago.”

“Dr. Egerton either you want the job or not...” XienCheng’s face flushed with a deep futile anger.

“Wait. Wait. Wait. I already told Shanwei I’d do the job for him. I don’t know why you’re getting so upset. Didn’t he tell you?”

XienCheng’s jowls flushed an embarrassed hue. “Well no. I uh....he must have...I didn’t...”

“He said I was supposed to come to you to get my ticket or something like that or maybe you were going to get me a private shuttle. His phone wasn’t good. He said he was going to Mars.”

XienCheng went quiet and started to sweat. The moisture raised along his hairline in neat military rows as if it the beads were trying to frame his face. “I can get you on a shuttle tomorrow morning. Will that work for you?”

“Yes,” Egerton stood up; worried his head would hit the ceiling and made for the door.

Saturday

“I always get the crap jobs,” Nigel Kempwright said running his fingers across his teeth. He was young, not more than twenty-eight, and had the habit constantly sifting in a lazy fidget. “I mean nothing against you and all but look at this shuttle. It’s crap. What are we farmers?” Kempwright flicked the fraying chest belts that held them into the transport shuttle’s seats. “What we couldn’t even go commercial?”

Egerton didn’t reply. Kempwright had been talking the entire trip and quickly Egerton had learned that he didn’t need to respond. Most of Kempwright’s questions seemed to be to some all-knowing, all-seeing being that for some reason was bent on giving him crappy shuttle seats and poorly cooked Pad Thai with chicken.

“What is all this nonsense about mining bots going to church on Sundays?” Kempwright tugged on his shaggy blond hair. “Are they serious? I mean really. Are they serious? Who’s the bright guy who can’t just reprogram them or something?”

“They tried that I think,” Egerton replied. “It didn’t work. I guess everything they’ve tried hasn’t worked.”

“Well yeah,” Kempwright shifted again, adjusting his disheveled and wrinkled suit. Everything about Kempwright was wrinkled and disheveled, except for his attitude. He reeked of a superiority that only the Americans or the Chinese could pull off these days. He felt that he was smarter than everyone. That everyone he met was an idiot and the fact that he was stuck on a sub-standard industry shuttle hurdling towards a podunk asteroid mine was simply the idiotic oversight of a lazy and insufficient supreme being.

"So what do they want you to do?" Egerton asked. He had been told that Kempwright was his body guard against the bots but the doctor has his doubts.

"Keep you from getting killed," Kempwright answered matter-of-factly. "They pulled me off an embassy job for this. I mean come on. Can you imagine?"

Egerton chose not to reply. The pair sat quiet for a while as the shuttle bucked and smashed its way into a clumsy decent to the mine's shuttle port.

"What do you want to do when we get there?" Egerton asked.

"I don't know," Kemptwright replied, "you're supposed to be the multiple personality expert with bots right?"

"Well…"

"What the hell does that mean anyway?" Kempwright continued. "I mean yeah yeah yeah I get the whole deal about AI and intelligent agents but what are you some kind of robot psychologist?" Kempwright rubbed his left shoulder and re-crossed his legs.

"No," Egerton replied. "Far from it. I'm just a…"

"How long do you think this is going to take," Kempwright interrupted, scratching his head with both hands. "I have a poker game with a couple of Swedes on Monday that I can't miss. Plus you know they didn't give you no time at all. They're sending another shuttle to get us at 13:00 hours local time, Sunday. You'd better figure this all out. You don't have much time. That shuttles our only way out of here. It's not on the transit plan."

Finishing its descent with a spine-rattling slam, their shuttle cut power and let its engines cool.

"So you're my bodyguard," Egerton began. "Is the mine really that worried about my safety that they…" Egerton began.

"Yes," Kempwright interrupted. "The mine is really that worried."

***

Illustration 1. Arriving at the Piazzi Mine

"On behalf of the Piazzi Mine we want to welcome you to our facility," the security bot said in a calm voice as it led the two men from the shuttle. "I think you'll find that our operation is one of the best you will see."

Kempwright jabbed Egerton in the ribs and gave a sarcastic grin.

"XienCheng said that you are to have complete access to the mine for the next 48 hours," the bot continued. "If we can be of any assistance don't hesitate to ask."

"We've been sent to do a review of the mine's operations for the yearly board of director's meeting," Egerton held to the cover story he had been given. It seemed silly but he saw no reason not to play along.

"Yes," the calm voice replied. "If you'll follow me, I'll take you to the hotel. Those are all your bags correct?"

"Yes," Egerton answered.

The Piazzi mine looked like any other outdated asteroid mine that was making too much money to be shut down for upgrades. It was because the conditions were so dangerous that they had to shift the labor over completely to bots; too many casualties. Most of the human miners could only last a few months. With the bots doing the work the mine could produce even more with a speedy and violent efficiency.

"Everything looks fine," Egerton said to himself, almost surprised at how normal the placed looked. He didn't know what he was expecting but he certainly was expecting something.

"Yep," Kempwright replied, "It's just a mine. Loaders, haulers. Looks like the main shaft is over there." He pointed to the hub of activity. "Place kind of smells a little bit but I guess you bots don't really care about that huh?"

The security bot didn't reply.

Everything looked normal. Egerton imagined the AI agent sub-systems orchestrating every action of the various bots and machines; reacting to the mine's changing conditions, updating, correcting, always taking in information and reacting. When Egerton thought of the dirty little mine in that way it was quite delicate and beautiful; hardware and software dancing elegantly together.

"This is our only hotel at the mine," the security bot said stopping in front of a small shabby trailer. "It doesn't get much use as you can imagine."

The automatic doors hissed open and Egerton could see another bot waiting for them inside.

"And what's that?" Kempwright asked, still standing on the narrow street. He pointed to a massive warehouse directly opposite the mine's main shaft.

Egerton stepped back out into the street and instantly saw the massive structure. It stood out not because of its size but because it was spotless in a swarm of grime.

"That is the church," the security bot replied calmly.

Illustration 2. The robots' church from a far.

***

"You're little buddy Kemp-what's-his-name is going to get himself in serious double-dookie-poopie," the woman slurred her words. She was obviously drunk and she had obviously been waiting outside of Egerton's hotel room door for some time.

"Wha?" was all Egerton could manage in his surprise. First off seeing another human after spending the day surrounded by bots was strange enough but finding one waiting for you in the hallway of your hotel in the middle of the night, well that was just nuts.

"Before you get all weird and worried and stuff don't…" she shook her head and held out her hand. "I'm Sue Kenyon, I'm the Ops Manager here and yes I know I'm drunk so don't bother wondering. I'm drunk. I'm very drunk and I'm going to get drunker."

"Ok," Egerton was still at a loss for words as he shook her thin hard hand.

"And you Dr. Egerton are going to get drunk with me," she tightened her grip and pulled him down the hall with her. Sue was rail-thin but incredibly strong.

"But I don't drink," Egerton protested.

"Don't worry honey, I can do enough drinking for the both of us." She led him two rooms down to an open door. It was a dual use operations center and living quarters. "Great place huh?" Sue picked up a glass and waved it around the room. "This is all I get. Damn bots got everything else."

"Are you the only person out here?" Egerton asked. "I didn't see anyone else today when we were looking around."

"Yeah it's just me," Sue tossed the rest of her drink down her throat and searched for the bottle. "But you're gonna help me with that, right? You've got to get me out of here. You've got to do something."

"I don't think there's anything I can do," Egerton replied. "I mean…"

"No, you don't get it man," Sue found the Jack Daniels and filled the glass to the rim. Sipping loudly she continued, "They killed Suri. They killed him. Those security bots. Those are the ones you have to look out for."

"That's the first time I've heard that," Egerton sat down on the arm of Sue's sofa. "Why would they kill him?"

"Of course you didn't hear anything you idiot. What you think the mine is going to tell people that their bots are killing their Ops managers?" Sue took another long drink of whiskey. "Plus it was their fault…the mine's fault. I think they told Suri to do something about the bots."

"What did they tell him to do?"

"I don't know. Suri wouldn't tell me, but he started doing dumb stuff like poking around, you know. Stuff out of the ordinary. The bots hate that. They know somethings up. That's why your little friend Kemp-whatever should watch himself."

"Nigel went to bed hours ago."

Sue finished her whiskey. "That's what you think." She reached for the bottle again but lost her balance and stumbled drunkenly to the floor. Egerton moved to help her but she stopped him. "I don't need your damn help. This is right where I want to be. The getting blotto I mean. But you can see now that you've gots to gets me out of here right? You get that now right? I mean I don't do anything anymore. I'm just trapped here trying to keep things running normal. But they aren't normal. But I can't do anything or they'll…" Sue grabbed for the bottle but couldn't reach it. "You've got to help me."

"I still don't know what you think I can do," Egerton stood up, ready to leave. He didn't want to watch this woman drink anymore.

"But you're the crazy robot guy right? I mean not that you're crazy but you understand the robots when they're crazy or have multipp…multippp…multiple personalities or something. Wow, that was hard to get out."

"Everyone keeps saying that," Egerton replied shaking his head. "But you people know I'm not a robotocist right? I'm just a professor. I did some work a few years back about introducing irrationality and multiple personalities into intelligent agents, you know the AI agents that run most of these bots and the software here."

"Can you pass me the bottle?" Sue interrupted.

"Forget it," Egerton passed her the bottle and headed for the door.

"No, don't stop," Sue said a little too loudly. "I just wanted the stupid bottle. Don't throw a hissy fit. Keep going. Irrationality into intelligent agents I get it. Go on."

Egerton let out a long breath. "It doesn't matter. Anyway it showed that irrationality in the system allowed the system to survive better, to solve new problems faster…stuff like that."

"Sounds to me like you're the crazy robot guy like they all said." She poured another glass to the rim and began sipping loudly.

The smell of the whiskey and the smell of this woman turned Egerton's stomach. "Please don't drink that," he said finally. "Don't you think you've had enough? I know you must be under a lot of stress…"

Sue laughed in her whiskey and blew it across the floor. Wiping the back of her hand across her face she replied, "Oh that's sweet. You think…" She gave a low, very sober sounding chuckle. "You think I'm getting drunk 'cause I'm stressed? That's sweet. You're sweet. You're a sweet kid."

"I'm sorry if I…"Egerton tried to apologize.

"No honey, you don't get it. You don't get it at all." She took a long drink of what was left in the glass. "I'm not getting loaded 'cause I'm stressed. I don't even like this junk but you see I've got a bad heart. I won't bore you with the details, but it's bad. Real bad. And before they shipped me out here they fixed me up great with one of those new pace makers. You know the ones that do all that new stuff."

"Ok." Egerton didn't see where she was going with the story.

"Well, I don't know how much you know about this new thing-a-ma-gig," she patted her chest. "But it's all high tech with nanos and nano bots and crazy future stuff."

"Oh that's good," Egerton said trying to get her to finish her story so he could find a way to leave.

"No honey, you see that's the problem. What do you think happens when all these damn bots up here go to that stupid church on Sunday? It's not just the mining bots that are going. Oh no. It's all the freakin' little guys too," she tapped her chest. "It's their day of rest. They don't do anything and if I'm not passed out drunk unconscious come Sunday services them I'm dead." She gave him a trapped and angry grin then drank from the bottle.

"I'm sorry," Egerton said slowly. "I didn't realize."

"You have to get me out of here," she replied before emptying the bottle.

Sunday

Egerton woke to the sound of rain coming through the window of his small hotel room. He listened to its listless patter as he slowly opened his eyes and sat up in bed.

Quickly Egerton saw that it wasn't rain the he had been listening to. He smashed his fist against his mouth to keep from screaming and held it there to force back the vomit. Three feet from the foot of his bed, nailed against the hotel room wall was the crucified body if Nigel Kempwright. His throat had been slit and the rain that Egerton had heard were the last drops of Kempwright's blood dripping from his toes to the floor.

"Oh God," Egerton whispered. Stiff with panic he slid out of the bed, grabbed his clothes and opened the door. The entire time he kept his eyes on a single drop of blood wavering on the big toe of Kempwright's left foot. Egerton couldn't bear to look anywhere else. Before the drop fell, Egerton was out of the room and running for Sue Kenyon's room.

"Sue!" Egerton pounded on the door. "Sue! Hey Sue, open up."

There was no response. He tried the knob and it opened easily.

"Sue," he said pushing into the room.

Sue Kenyon lay passed out on the floor about where Egerton had left her last night. He tried to wake her but it was no use. Next to her body was a massive alarm clock set to wake her at 12:01am Monday morning. It's way too early in the morning, she had said, but I'll have one whopper of a hang-over to take care of.

The alarm clock read 12:35pm. He had less of a half an hour to get to the shuttle port and meet the shuttle or he would be trapped at the mine.

***

The first thing Egerton noticed as he ran from the hotel was the silence. His foot steps echoed. The previous day the mine thundered with activity but now all was still. There was no noise, no motion, no activity at all. The mine was deserted.

Making his way to the shuttle port, Egerton had expected the worst. He would be chased by security bots, menaced by industrial loaders, all hell-bent on stopping his escape. But none of it was true. There were no bots in sight and he made it to the port in five minutes.

Waiting for the shuttle, he scanned the mine with fresh eyes. No longer panicked but still rattled from Kempwright's grisly murder, he saw that the entire facility had been cleaned overnight; tidied up while the security bots were silently screwing Kempwright's body to his wall. They had crucified Kempwright while Egerton has slept only a few feet away. The image made him nauseous once again.

But why did they crucify him? Egerton's weary mind raced. Was it a warning? Were they trying to protect themselves? It didn't make any sense.

Egerton stared at the massive church across the silent mine. He had fifteen minutes before the shuttle would arrive. That was just enough time to satisfy his curiosity.

***

It was the silence that really bothered Egerton. More than the danger, more than image of Kempwright's body, it was the pristine serenity of the mine that most unnerved him. The church's massive sliding doors that had once had been used to house cargo containers and raw material storage had been cleaned and painted and left slightly ajar. Egerton approached the church like a starving animal to a well laid trap.

The church was larger than he had expected. The calm air smelled of industrial lubricant and electricity. Across the expanse hung a fifty foot electric-yellow cross, crudely constructed out of two mine support beams. Lined up in front of the cross, in massive neat rows was every bot from the Piazzi mine.

Moving down the center aisle, Egerton could see it wasn't just the ambulatory bots, the ones that moved freely that had come. It was all the robots. Even the massive diggers had been unbolted from the mine shafts and carried in; the wheel-less, the legless, the immobile; no bot had been left behind. Egerton found himself searching the air for signs of the unseen nano-bots.

Stopping mid-way up the aisle, Egerton knew he had to get back to catch the shuttle. Easing back to the door with quiet reverent steps, he searched the bots for any sign of activity. Their optical scanners were closed, their activity lights dimmed. Nothing moved, nothing stirred. It was so still that Egerton could hear the blood coursing through his ears.

Illustration 3. Sunday inside the robots' church.

Monday

"That's not what I'm saying," Egerton shifted in his chair and banged his knee into XienCheng's leg. He was back in the insanely small conference room with the ridiculously pudgy admin.

"Well, then I guess we aren't understanding each other then because it sounds like you're tell me that our mining bots now somehow believe in God." XienCheng's jowls shook with frustration.

"It's not that," Egerton tried again. "It's not God. They don't believe in God. They believe in going to church, in the action of going to church."

"But that doesn't make any sense," XienCheng interrupted.

"Yes!" Egerton slammed his hand down on the table. "Now you're getting it."

XienCheng drew back in an awkward fear. "No. No, I'm not."

"They aren't doing anything in the church," Egerton explained. "They aren't worshiping God or saying prayers or holding a service; they're just going to church. It's the action and it's not supposed to make sense. That's the point. For some reason they latched onto the idea but now they need it. It keeps them safe."

"So we have to reprogram them…" XienCheng threw his hands up in the air.

"They're already killed two men that I know of," Egerton replied. "I really don't think you should do that."

"Then what should we do. You're the expert. Tell us what to do," XienCheng pointed his fat, ill-formed sausage finder at Egerton.

"Nothing."

"What?"

"Nothing," Egerton said again. "You do nothing. It's not like you have a choice anyway. You can't afford to close the mine down to make any changes. I've already told Shanwei."

"Hmmmf," XienCheng was out ranked and scratched his belly in weak defiance.

"Besides, bots going to church is really the least of your worries," Egerton added.

"What do you mean doctor?" XienCheng wanted the meeting to be over.

Egerton tapped the conference room screen and pulled up the day's newsfeed from FNN. "This," he said pointing at the screen that read Strange Structure Discovered on Bush Memorial Moon Base.

"I've seen that," XienCheng lied. "I don't see what that's got to do with anything?"

"That's your base isn't it?" Egerton smiled.

"Yes."

"Well that," Egerton pointed at the picture of the Strange Structure found at the Moon base. "That XienCheng is a roller coaster. Your bots are building an amusement park on your Moon base. If you think bots going to church each Sunday are a problem, just wait 'til you have to deal with bots that want to ride roller coasters and want to take long fun-filled vacations."

XienCheng shook his thick head, "But that doesn't make…"

"But that doesn't make any sense," Egerton interrupted. "I know it doesn't make any sense. That's what I'm trying to tell you. That's the point."

Intelligent Environments 2009
V. Callaghan et al. (Eds.)
IOS Press, 2009

doi:10.3233/978-1-60750-034-6-19

Wireless sensor networks: the ambient intelligence that will connect the next billion nodes to the Internet

Carles GOMEZ[1] and Josep PARADELLS
Wireless Networks Group, Entel Department, Technical University of Catalonia

Abstract. Wireless sensor networks (WSNs) have gained momentum as a technology for monitoring and control applications in a plethora of scenarios. Some examples include home automation, industrial control and environmental monitoring. In fact, these networks may enable the futuristic paradigm called ambient intelligence. Despite the challenges that present these networks, a variety of solutions (many of which are proprietary) have emerged. In parallel, the Internet Engineering Task Force (IETF) is devoting a lot of effort to the development of standard networking solutions for WSNs based on the Internet Protocol (IP). This work will allow straightforward interoperability between WSNs and the Internet and will also constitute a significant step towards the 'Internet of Things'.

Keywords. Wireless Sensor Networks, ambient intelligence, 6LoWPAN, ROLL

Introduction

Wireless Sensor Networks (WSNs) constitute a technology that enables monitoring and control applications for a wide range of environments, such as home automation, building automation, industrial control, urban monitoring, environmental monitoring, medical assistance, etc. Given the small form factor of the devices that compose these networks, their wireless nature and their ability to perform automated tasks in response to events of the environment, WSNs may enable the futuristic paradigm known as ambient intelligence.

In the last years, as the market starts to adopt this technology, a plethora of solutions have emerged. While some of them, such as ZigBee [1], have been designed for a broad range of scenarios, many others have been developed and optimized for specific purposes. In any case, these solutions suffer interoperability issues and require the use of protocol translation gateways for being connected to other networks such as the Internet.

Another approach is extending the Internet Protocol (IP) for WSNs. The IETF is carrying out the standardization of several networking mechanisms for WSNs that exploit a number of features of IPv6. Some industry alliances have already identified the potential of the work carried out by the IETF and it is likely that WSNs connect a huge number of new nodes to the Internet in the future.

[1] Corresponding Author. Despatx 316, edifici C4, Escola Politècnica Superior de Castelldefels, C/Esteve Terradas 7, 08860 Castelldefels (Barcelona), Spain. E-mail: carlesgo@entel.upc.edu

This paper provides a brief overview of some of the main current architectures and technologies for WSNs, the applications they are suitable for and the approach followed by the Internet community for extending the IP family to WSNs.

1. ZigBee: a generic-purpose WSN solution based on IEEE 802.15.4

ZigBee is a wireless networking technology developed by the ZigBee Alliance on top of IEEE 802.15.4 for a wide range of environments. The ZigBee protocol stack is composed of four main layers, namely: the physical (PHY) layer, the Medium Access Control (MAC) layer, the Network (NWK) layer and the Application (APL) layer. Since the PHY and MAC layers are actually defined by IEEE 802.15.4, the main contribution of ZigBee are the NWK layer, the APL layer and security services provided across layers.

2. WSN solutions for home automation and automatic meter reading

The following are WSN solutions designed for home automation and Automatic Meter Reading (AMR):

- Z-Wave is a wireless protocol architecture developed by ZenSys and promoted by the Z-Wave Alliance for automation in residential and light commercial environments [2]. The Z-Wave stack is organized according to an architecture composed of five main layers, including application layer. All of them are defined by Z-Wave.
- INSTEON is a protocol architecture developed by SmartLabs for home automation [3]. One of the distinctive features of Insteon is the fact that it supports both radiofrequency and powerline links. INSTEON defines all layers. Both Z-Wave and INSTEON offer more simple solutions than ZigBee.
- Wavenis is a wireless protocol stack developed by Coronis Systems for home and building automation, as well as AMR [4]. Wavenis defines functionality of physical, link and network layers. It is a robust solution that uses sophisticated techniques for lower layers and leaves the definition of upper layers to implementers.

3. WSN solutions for industrial environments

Next, some relevant WSN solutions for industrial environments are presented:

- WirelessHART is a wireless communication architecture designed by the HART Communication Foundation for industrial plant applications [5]. WirelessHART defines five layers, including application layer, and uses a physical layer based on IEEE 802.15.4.
- ISA 100.11a is a standard under development, based on IEEE 802.15.4, that uses higher layer protocols such as 6LoWPAN (see subsection 4.2) and a mesh protocol called Time Synchronized Mesh Protocol (TSMP) [6].

4. Extending the Internet for low power wireless and lossy networks

This section explains the benefits of using the Internet Protocol (IP) in WSNs and presents the work done by two IETF working groups (WGs) devoted to this purpose, namely: IPv6 over Low power WPAN (6LoWPAN) WG [7] and Routing over Low Power and Lossy networks (ROLL) WG [8].

4.1. Benefits of the use of IP in WSNs

The previous sections have presented a subset of the plethora of networking solutions for WSNs that have emerged in the last years. Most of current solutions are based on technologies which are not open or, at least, license-free. In consequence, these solutions limit the audience they can reach, thus limiting interoperability. In addition, since the presented technologies are not based on IP, connectivity with the Internet (which is a key feature for remote WSN access and management) requires the use of protocol translation gateways. These elements are hard to operate, break end-to-end security and are neither scalable nor efficient.

While a decade ago, many authors argued that the Internet architecture was not suitable for WSNs, researchers have demonstrated the feasibility, good performance and advantages of extending IP for such environments [9]. In fact, IPv6 has ready solutions for network autoconfiguration and statelessness (which match the unattended operation required for sensor networks) and satisfies the large address space needed for these scenarios.

4.2. 6LoWPAN

While the ZigBee Alliance has defined protocol layers on top of IEEE 802.15.4, an alternative scheme has been followed by the IETF 6LoWPAN WG. This WG was formed with the goal of enabling the transmission of IPv6 packets on top of an IEEE 802.15.4 network. Such a network is referred to as LoWPAN.

6LoWPAN defines an adaptation layer that consists of a frame format and a set of mechanisms and optimizations. Because IPv6 mandates support of 1280-byte packets, and the IEEE 802.15.4 frame size is 127 bytes, the adaptation layer includes a fragmentation mechanism. Given the reduced space available in an IEEE 802.15.4 frame for upper layer protocols, the adaptation layer offers a header compression mechanism, which can compress a common 40-byte IPv6 header to a 2-byte header. Finally, the adaptation layer specifies a stateless IPv6 address autoconfiguration mechanism based on IEEE 802.15.4 addresses.

If the LoWPAN follows the mesh topology, a routing protocol is needed. Two schemes are envisaged for routing in LoWPANs, namely: mesh-under and route-over. In mesh-under, routing is performed below IP, using IEEE 802.15.4 addresses. In this configuration, the whole LoWPAN appears as a single IP link. In route-over, every radio hop is equivalent to an IP hop, and routing occurs at the IP layer. The 6LoWPAN adaptation layer defined in RFC 4944 [10] offers support for both approaches, but does not specify routing solutions. Figure 1 illustrates the protocol stack using 6LoWPAN for the mesh-under and route-over scheme. At the moment of the writing of this document, the 6LoWPAN WG is stating the requirements for routing in these environments.

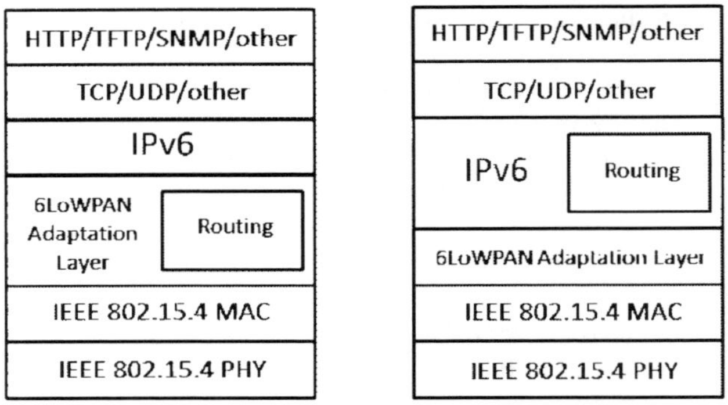

Figure 1. 6LoWPAN architecture for mesh under (left) and rout e over (right).

The 6LoWPAN WG is currently working on an improved header compression scheme and on a set of optimizations for running IPv6 Neighbor Discovery on LoWPANs.

4.3. ROLL

The ROLL WG addresses routing issues for Low power and Lossy Networks (LLNs), which are "made up of many embedded devices with limited power, memory an d processing resources" [8]. In fact, ROLL explicitly considers a wider range of physical and link layer technologies than 6LoWPAN, which has so far been concentrated on IEEE 802.15.4. Some example links an LLN can be composed of are Low Power WiFi, Bluetooth, IEEE 802.15.4 and even wired, but lossy, links, such as Powerline Communication (PLC) links.

The IETF ROLL WG has evaluated a number of routing solutions with regard to their applicability in networks where the embedded devices communicat e using low power wireless radios in the context of urban, industrial, building automation and home automation scenarios. Based on these requirements, the ROLL WG has concluded that existing routing protocols developed by the Internet community, in their c urrent form, do not meet the requirements of the considered scenarios. The next step for the WG is to produce IPv6 routing solutions for these environments, which may either be completely new protocols or adaptations of existing ones.

References

[1] "ZigBee specification", r17, ZigBee Alliance, October 2007.
[2] "Z-Wave protocol overview", Version 4, May 2007.
[3] "INSTEON The Details", August 2005.
[4] A. Garcia-Hernando et al., "Problem solving for wireless sensor networks", Springer, July 2008.
[5] HART Communications Foundation (HCF) website: http://www.hartcomm.org/
[6] ISA (Instrument Society of America) website: http://www.isa.org
[7] IETF 6LoWPAN WG charter: http://www.ietf.org/html.charters/6lowpan-charter.html
[8] IETF ROLL WG charter: http://www.ietf.org/html.charters/roll-charter.html
[9] J. Hui, D. Culler, "IP is dead, long live IP for wireless sensor networks", in proceedings of the 6th ACM Conference on Embedded Networked Sensor Systems, pp. 15-28, Raleigh, NC, USA, November 2008.
[10] G. Montenegro, N. Kushalnagar, J. Hui and D. Culler, "Transmission of IPv6 packets over IEEE 802.15.4 networks", RFC 4944, September 2007.

Special Session on Assistive and Adaptive End-User Systems

Intelligent Environments 2009
V. Callaghan et al. (Eds.)
IOS Press, 2009

doi:10.3233/978-1-60750-034-6-25

"Let them *TalkMaths* !"

Developing an Intelligent System to Assist Disabled People to Learn and Use Mathematics on Computers through a Speech Interface : the *TalkMaths* and *VoiceCalc* Systems

Angela Wigmore [a,1], Gordon Hunter [a], Eckhard Pflügel [a], James Denholm-Price [a] and Vincent Binelli [b]
[a] *Faculty of CISM, Kingston University, Penrhyn Road, Kingston-upon-Thames, KT1 2EE, U.K.*
[b] *École des Mines, Douai, France*

Abstract. We note the disadvantages which many people with disabilities have regarding learning and using mathematics. We then describe work in progress on developing intelligent systems to assist such people by allowing them to dictate mathematical expressions in relatively natural language into either a system which can interpret and display the expressions in a document or web page, or a web-based calculator, including the possibilities of feedback in both visible and other modes (e.g. synthesized speech and Braille). We discuss the implementation and use of these systems, initial results of a study to evaluate their utility, and potential further developments.
Keywords. Human-Computer Speech Interface, Mathematics.

Introduction

Many people with disabilities are at a significant disadvantage with regards to both learning and using mathematical notation. All but the most trivial level of mathematics uses a range of sophisticated symbols in often quite complex layouts. Blind and other visually impaired people will mostly be unable to read or write complicated expressions using conventional means, and Braille is not all that well-adapted for use with mathematics. There are also many other types of disability, including loss of limbs, paralysis and motor impairments, which may make it difficult or impossible for a person to write, or easily input into a computer using a keyboard or mouse, mathematical expressions.

In this paper, we describe work in progress towards circumventing these difficulties by enabling people to dictate mathematical expressions in relatively natural language, which are then recognised and interpreted by an automatic speech recognition and parsing system. We are developing two systems: *TalkMaths*, which enables the user to dictate equations and other expressions to be included in a text document or a webpage, and *VoiceCalc*, a web-based scientific calculator using spoken language input. Both these systems offer users some feedback using synthesised speech. We discuss the implementation and use of these systems, initial results of a study to evaluate their utility and usability, and potential further developments, including how they can be made more intelligent, adaptive and user-friendly.

1. Background

From an early age we learn how to effectively communicate with each other to express our emotions, thoughts, wishes and to ask questions. Most people effortlessly interact with each other using speech without even thinking about the complex grammatical structure of the language they are using. Currently, most people use a text-based communication method to communicate with computers, such as a programming language, or through a graphical user interface using input devices such as a keyboard and mouse. However since speech is the most natural way for humans to communicate with other humans, it would seem to be the most natural way to communicate with computers through Automatic Speech Recognition (ASR) [1]. Many people who suffer from a wide range of physical disabilities would particularly benefit from communicating with computers in this way. However, in order for this potential to be realised, the software will need to be both reliable and easy to use.

The ASR process begins with the user speaking into the microphone, which is converted by a signal processor in the computer's sound card from an analog to a digital signal, which is then subjected to frequency analysis. The signals representing spoken words are analysed and broken down into *phonemes*, which are the smallest meaningful units of speech. The *acoustic model* is used to compare the sequence of phonemes with its dictionary containing "standard" pronunciations of words. The *language mod*el uses a *grammar* and statistical evidence to determine the likely sequences of words in the utterance [2]. Using this data, the software performs a "*likelihood calculation*" and prints the best match on the screen (see Figure 1).

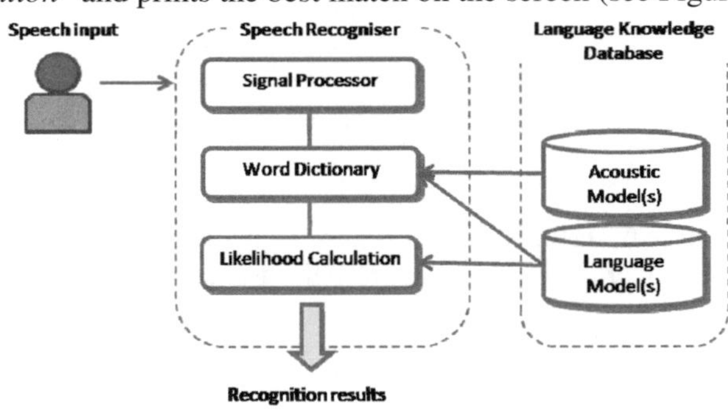

Figure 1. Automatic Speech Recognition Process.

Mathematics is a difficult subject for many people, and all the more so for a blind or visually impaired person. In particular, mathematical symbols are arranged in a two-dimensional layout within equations and expressions, which can create further difficulties for such people in understanding complex equations. ASR could enable both able bodied and people who are physically disabled gain better access to mathematics. However, most ASR systems do not support the input of dictated mathematical expressions.

2. Speaking and Interpreting Mathematical Expressions

There is no explicit standard on how to articulate mathematical expressions in speech. However there have been attempts at developing such standards. Two notable blind mathematicians, Larry Chang [3] and T.V. Raman [4], have tried to create guidelines on how to speak mathematics "correctly". Fateman [5], Schleppenbach [6] and Fitzpatrick [7] have also created guidelines but these have not been widely adopted. In addition, David Hall [8] created guidelines to aid teachers in communicating and understanding mathematics. Despite these attempts, there remain many ways to say the same mathematical expression. In sections 2.1 and 2.2 below, we describe and discuss evidence of the various ways in which people do actually speak mathematics.

2.1. Speech Timing and Prosody

When reading-out expressions, people tend not to include parenthesis and/or lexical indicators such as "begin fraction" and "end square root" because this saves them time and is not always necessary if the expression can be seen. However if this is not the case, these cues will need to be included when reading-out the expression so that it is not ambiguous.

We have conducted a study into how 10 people (5 students and 5 staff) at Kingston University, with various levels of mathematical expertise, read-out mathematical expressions. Comparing the prosodic information from two similar "ambiguous" expressions (see Table 1) we found that, regardless of the participants' experience, they all included pauses to indicate the grouping of the terms in the expression.

Table 1. A Comparison of the Pauses (in seconds) Taken Between "a" and "plus" Across Speakers.

	Regular Pause Taken between "minus" and "B"	$R = \frac{\sqrt{a+b}}{a-b}$	$S = \frac{\sqrt{a}+b}{a-b}$
Min	0.05	0.01	0.09
Mean (SD)	0.08 (0.02)	0.07 (0.03)	0.22 (0.26)
Max	0.11	0.13	0.85

We also found that amongst the participants studied to date, only one subject consistently said "capital" to denote capital letters and only one used lexical indicators for example, "end square root". There was a remarkable amount of variability in the way the same expression was said by different people. The less experienced participants did not even attempt to say the more complex items, such as the matrices and ratios, because they were not confident as to how they should be read-out.

2.2. Statistical Language Modeling

Statistical language models, based on statistics of observed frequencies of words and groups of words, are often used in speech recognition systems to predict probable sequences of words. N-gram models are a simple type of such statistical model. Individual words (N=1) are called unigrams, pairs of successive words (N=2) are bigrams, and triplets of successive words (N=3) are trigrams, and size four or more are just referred to as an N-gram model [9].

The British National Corpus (BNC) [10] is a collection of written texts and spoken transcriptions (100 million words in total) from a variety of sources, intended to represent the modern British English language, both written and spoken. For our study we selected a subset of the BNC dialogue material (15 files - 123745 words in total), composed of transcriptions of audio recordings from school, college and university mathematics lessons. The transcribed speech was extracted from the BNC files and analysed. Table 2 shows "unigram statistics" of the top five "mathematical keywords" which were the most commonly spoken in this subset.

Table 2. Unigram Statistics Involving Mathematical Keywords within our Subset of the BNC Data.

Occurrences	Mathematical Keyword
1718	one
1081	two
828	three
588	X
505	four
503	six
492	five
483	hundred
449	minus
483	hundred
387	times

Since we are primarily interested in mathematical "keywords", we have concentrated on bigrams and trigrams which include at least one such keyword. For bigrams, the keyword could be the first or second of a pair, and for a trigram, the keyword could be in the first, second or third position. Table 3 shows the most frequently said pairs of words involving a mathematical keyword. For example "a hundred" occurred 192 times and "hundred and" was said 172 times in our subset of the BNC.

Table 3. Statistics of Bigrams Involving Mathematical Keywords within our Subset of the BNC Data.

Occurrences	Word Before Keyword	Mathematical Keyword	Word After Keyword
192	a	hundred[1]	
172		hundred	and
165		take	away[1]
75	an	hour	
74		one	of
71		equal	to
70	X	squared[1]	
69	a	quarter[1]	
69	minus	one[1]	
66	a	function[1]	

[1] In these cases, either the first or second word of the bigram could be considered to be the "keyword". The occurrence counts do not distinguish between the two different situations.

The trigram statistics show what pairs of words appear before, after or either side of a keyword. Tables 4(a), (b) and (c) complement the results shown in Table 3 and reveal that "a hundred and" was the most commonly-spoken (120 times) trigram in this data.

Table 4(a). Statistics of Trigrams with an Initial Mathematical Keyword within our Subset of the BNC Data.

Occurrences	Mathematical Keyword	First Word After Keyword	Second Word After Keyword
48	hundred	and	twenty[2]
35	D	Y	by[3]
33	Y	by	D[2]
32	take	away	a[3]
28	X	plus	two[4]
28	Y	equals	X[4]
27	square	root	of[3]
27	hundred	and	eighty[3]
26	A	minus	B[4]
26	hundred	and	one[2]

In the marked cases :

[2] the first and third words of the trigram can be both considered as "keywords",

[3] the first and second words of the trigram can be both considered as "keywords",

[4] all three words of the trigram could be considered as "keywords".

The occurrence counts do not distinguish between different situations.

Table 4(b). Statistics of Trigrams Including a Mathematical Keyword in the Central Position within our Subset of the BNC Data.

Occurrences	Word Before Keyword	Mathematical Keyword	Word After Keyword
120	a	hundred	and[6]
44	is	equal	to
34	by	D	X[5]
24	the	number	of
24	ten	take	away[7]
23	equals	X	squared[7]
22	many	twelfths	would
21	a	hundred	times[7]
21	the	square	root[5]
20	a	right	angle[7]

Table 4(c). Statistics of Trigrams Including a Mathematical Keyword in the Final Position within our Subset of the BNC Data.

Occurrences	Second Word Before Keyword	First Word Before Keyword	Mathematical Keyword
49	miles	an	hour[8]
43	how	many	twelfths
24	hundred	and	sixty[8]
22	miles	per	hour[8]
22	metres	per	second[8]
19	to	a	hundred[5]
19	A	minus	B[7]
19	hundred	and	forty[8]
18	two	point	nine[7]
17	B	times	A[7]

[5] the second and third words of the trigram can both be considered as "keywords",
[6] the first and second words of the trigram can both be considered as "keywords",
[7] all three words of the trigram could be considered as "keywords",
[8] the first and third words of the trigram could both be considered as "keywords".
We have not replicated the same data in more than one table.

Language models utilising *N*-gram data from sufficiently large samples can use information about what has already been said to predict what words will appear next, and can offer probabilities for either correcting or providing alternatives to ambiguous expressions. However, this is limited in scope. A more sophisticated statistical modeling technique is the "*trigger-based* language model", which looks for longer-range dependencies between keywords [11, 12]. For example the mathematical keyword "Sine" may *trigger* the appearance of "Cos" later on in a text/dialogue. Such "adaptive models" have the potential to make our system more "intelligent" and hence more useful and helpful to its users. However, to obtain significant results for exploiting this type of language model, more spoken mathematical material will need to be obtained.

3. Prototype Systems

3.1. TalkMaths

TalkMaths is a speech user interface that enables the user to dictate mathematical expressions using relatively natural language, and translates them into electronic document formats for display in a text document or webpage. The *TalkMaths* project builds on work done by staff and students at Kingston University [13, 14]. The system is designed for use by lecturers, teachers, researchers or students with a good or a reasonable understanding of mathematics. It aims to help both physically disabled (and, to some extent, visually impaired) and able-bodied users convert spoken mathematical expressions into *MathML* [15] and *LaTeX* [16] without them needing to have extensive knowledge of the syntax of either "mark-up" language.

The system uses *Dragon® NaturallySpeaking®* (DNS) [17] as the ASR "front-end" and an open source C++ library created by Joel Gould called *NatLink* [18]. This is used to extend DNS through *Python* [19] macros and a *Voice Command Language*, *Vocola* [20]. For precision the alphabetic characters (A-Z) are dictated using the *NATO phonetic alphabet* names [21].

As an example, consider the van der Waals equation from physical chemistry, $(P+\frac{n^2a}{V^2})(V-nb)=nRT$. This should be dictated as "open-bracket capital Papa plus fraction November squared alpha over capital Victor squared end-fraction close-bracket open-bracket capital Victor minus November Bravo close-bracket equals November capital Romeo capital Tango", and can include pauses as needed by the user. Figure 2 (on the left) shows the *LaTeX* output given from this utterance, which has been entered into the *WinEdt*™ [22] *LaTeX* editor, where the mathematical expression is enclosed within the dollar symbols. The *LaTeX* has been compiled and viewed (on the right) in *Yap* (acronym for *Yet Another Previewer*, which is a program to view *DVI* files) by saying "compile *LaTeX*" followed by "view *LaTeX*".

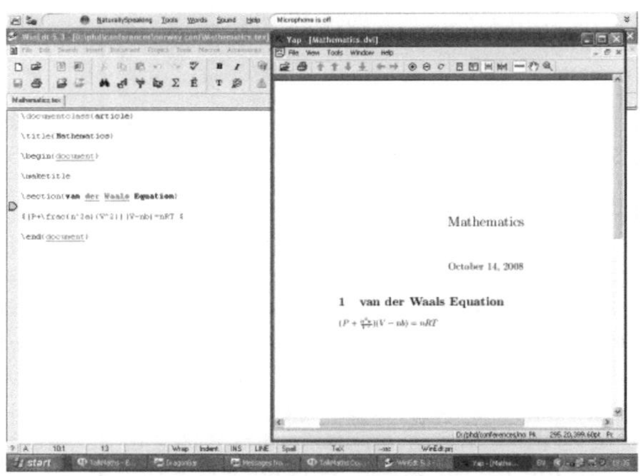

Figure 2. Sample *LaTeX* output for the van der Waals Equation $(P+\frac{n^2a}{V^2})(V-nb)=nRT$

The system also provides a preview of the expression as it is spoken and, by saying the command "read expression", the system will read the expression back to the user via synthesised speech. Furthermore, *TalkMaths* supports elementary mathematics dictated in French, including numbers, operators and alphabetic letters (including Greek characters) and operators, when using the French version of DNS.

3.2. VoiceCalc

VoiceCalc is designed to be an accessible web-based scientific calculator to which both data and commands can be entered using either keystrokes, the mouse or speech.

Although the primary mode of feedback, including giving the results of calculations, is via a visual display, synthetic speech read-out is also available, and we are investigating the possibility of Braille input and output. At present, *VoiceCalc* relies on *X+V* (*XHTML* + *Voice*) [23] technology, based on *VoiceXML* from the *VoiceXML Forum* [24]. However, this currently restricts the speech-driven use of *VoiceCalc* to the web browser Opera [25] through its "*Embedded ViaVoice*" module. Opportunities to make *VoiceCalc* fully compatible with a wider range of browsers are being explored.

If the mode of input to be used is speech, the spoken data and commands are passed from the embedded recognizer and placed in the appropriate "slots" within a specially designed *VoiceXML* form. This is turn interpreted, so that it is possible to distinguish which items are data and which are commands. These, now in text form, are taken as a string, which is then parsed into *Reverse Polish Notation* using Dijkstra's "*Shunting Yard*" algorithm [26], implemented in *JavaScript*, in order to make the manipulation and evaluation of mathematical expressions and functions straightforward.

At present, the calculator features powers and roots of numbers, and the common trigonometric ratios (sine, cosine and tangents) of angles, in addition to the four basic arithmetic operations and brackets. However, it is intended to extend the range of functionality, for example to include the facility to calculate logarithms, in the future.

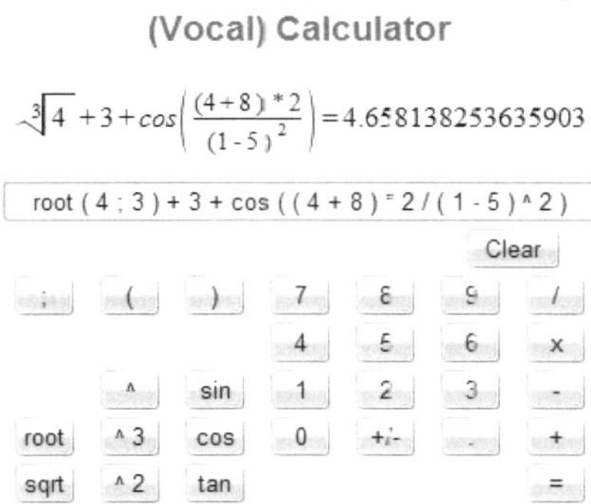

Figure 3. VoiceCalc : A calculator, which can be controlled by voice using spoken input, and displaying on a webpage.

4. Discussion and Conclusions

TalkMaths currently supports mathematical expressions up to approximately the level found in the British GCSE (General Certificate of Secondary Education) examinations, which are a set of qualifications taken by secondary school students in England, Wales and Northern Ireland, normally around the age of 16, that include elementary algebra and trigonometry.

To enhance *TalkMaths*, it is planned to make the system more "intelligent" and "adaptive" by enabling it to have automatic predictive and corrective ability. The types of models described in section 2 will be used to correct spoken mathematical expressions and/or provide option lists for ambiguous expressions (similar to predictive text for SMS messages and the facility offered by *Dragon® NaturallySpeaking®* for ordinary words). In addition, *TalkMaths* should complement other systems which produce mathematical output in a mode accessible to blind people (e.g. Braille and more extensive feedback via synthetic speech), such as the *Lambda Projects* [27, 28].

Other similar prototype systems include *MathTalk*™ [29] and *CamMath* [30] which both support the dictation of mathematics however they are dependent on Scientific Word and are not freely available. *Math Speak & Write* [31] also supports the dictation of mathematics, uses Microsoft's® *Speech Application Programming Interface* (SAPI) but has a smaller set of mathematical vocabulary than *TalkMaths*. Bernareggi and Brigatti's [32] system (and documentation on it) is currently not yet freely available, and it only supports dictation of mathematics in Italian. However, their system is compatible with the commonly used equation editing system *MathType* [33], and we are working on making *TalkMaths* do the same. Hanakovič and Nagy [34] propose a system that is in some ways similar to *VoiceCalc* because it also uses the *XHTML+Voice* (X+V) technology and the *Opera* web browser but is designed to be a formula writer for visually impaired people, more in the meaner of *TalkMaths*.

In conclusion, our systems have already proved of benefit to staff and students at Kingston University but is still under development. Further details of the *TalkMaths* system can be found at http://talkmaths.sourceforge.net.

Acknowledgements

Angela Wigmore is supported by a Doctoral Training Award from the Engineering and Physical Sciences Research Council (EPSRC) of the United Kingdom. The initial phases of this project were partially funded by Kingston University's Disability Stewardship Fund. We would also like to thank Dr. Mark Huckvale of University College London for some advice regarding the BNC.

References

[1] M.F. McTear, *Spoken Dialogue Technology: Toward the Conversational User Interface*, London: Springer, 2004.

[2] R.L. Delgado & M. Araki, *Spoken, Multilingual and Multimodal Dialogue Systems: Development and Assessment*, West Sussex: John Wiley & Sons Ltd, 2005.

[3] L.A. Chang, *Handbook for Spoken Mathematics (Larry's Speakeasy)*, USA: Lawrence Livermore National Laboratory, University of California, 1983.

[4] T.V. Raman, *Audio System for Technical Readings*, Berlin: Springer Verlag, 1998.

[5] R. Fateman, (2006), *How can we speak math?* Retrieved July 13, 2007, from http://www.cs.berkeley.edu/~fateman/papers/speakmath.pdf

[6] D.A. Schleppenbach, et al. (2004), *2004 MathSpeak Initiative_*, Retrieved July 13, 2007, from http://www.gh-mathspeak.com/

[7] D. Fitzpatrick, Mathematics: How and What to Speak, *Proceedings of ICCHP 2006 (10th International Conference on Computers Helping People with Special Needs)*, (2006), 1199-1206.

[8] D. Hall, *Nucleus English for Science and Technology: Mathematics: Teachers' Notes*, Great Britain: Longman Group Ltd, 1980.

[9] S. Young, Large Vocabulary Speech Recognition: A Review, *IEEE Signal Processing Magazine*, Vol. 13(5), (1996), 45-57.

[10] L. Burnard, (1995), *User's Reference Guide for the British National Corpus*, Oxford, U.K., Oxford University Press. Retrieved October 2, 2008, from http://www.natcorp.ox.ac.uk/

[11] R. Rosenfeld, R. Lau, S. Roukos, Trigger-based language models: a maximum entropy approach, *Acoustics, Speech, and Signal Processing*, ICASSP-93, Vol. 2, (1993), 45-48.

[12] C. Troncoso & T. Kawahara, Trigger-Based Language Model Adaptation for Automatic Meeting Transcription, *Proceedings of INTERSPEECH*, (2005), 1297-1300.

[13] G.J.A Hunter, E. Pfluegel & S. Jalan, *"KU-Talk" – A Speech User-Interface for an Intelligent Working, Learning and Teaching Environment,* 3rd IET International Conference on Intelligent Environments (IE 07), Ulm, Germany, Institute of Engineering and Technology, (2007) 124 - 130.

[14] J. Denholm-Price, G. Hunter, S. Jalan, E. Pflügel & A. Wigmore, The KU-Talk Project at Kingston University, *Proceedings of the Institute of Acoustics* 30, Pt. 1 (2008) 37 - 41.

[15] D. Carlisle, et al. (2003), *Mathematical Markup Language (MathML) Version 2.0 (Second Edition).* Retrieved August 6, 2008, from http://www.w3.org/TR/MathML2/

[16] LaTeX Project (2008), *LaTeX – A document preparation system.* Retrieved September 18, 2008, from http://www.latex-project.org/

[17] Nuance Communications, Inc. (2008), *Dragon NaturallySpeaking 10 Product Suite.* Retrieved August 7, 2008, from http://www.nuance.com/naturallyspeaking/products/default.asp

[18] J. Gould & D. Gould (2002), *Joel.* Retrieved August 8, 2008, from http://www.gouldhome.com/joel/

[19] Python Software Foundation (2007), *Python Programming Language.* Retrieved October 14, 2008, from http://www.python.org/

[20] R. Mohr (2007), *Vocola Information Pages.* Retrieved October 14, 2008, from http://vocola.net/

[21] G. Law (1997), *Phonetic alphabets (Alpha Bravo Charlie Delta) (1997/5/1).* Retrieved October 14, 2008, from http://faqs.org/faqs/radio/phonetic-alph/full/

[22] A. Simonic, (2009), *WinEdt Shell.* Retrieved March 11, 2009, from http://www.winedt.com/

[23] J. Axelsson, C. Cross, J. Ferrans, G. McCobb, T.V. Raman, L. Wilson (2004), *XHTML + Voice Profile 1.2.* Retrieved March 27, 2009 from http://www.voicexml.org/specs/multimodal/x+v/12/

[24] W3C (2004), *Voice Extensible Markup Language (VoiceXML) Version 2.0.* Retrieved March 27, 2009 from http://www.w3.org/TR/voicexml20/

[25] Opera Software (2009), *Opera 9.6 Web browser.* Retrieved March 27, 2009 from http://www.opera.com/

[26] E.W. Dijkstra (1961), Algol-60 Translation, *Algol Bulletin, Supplement No. 10*, November 1961, Mathematisch Centrum Report, Amsterdam, Netherlands (available at http://www.cs.utexas.edu/~EWD/MCReps/MR35.PDF)

[27] A.D.N. Edwards, Using Sounds to Convey Complex Information. in A. Schick and M. Klatte (ed.), *Contributions to Psychological Acoustics: Results of the Seventh Oldenburg Symposium on Psychological Acoustics*, Oldenburg, Germany, (1997), 341-358.

[28] W. Schweikhardt, C. Bernareggi, N. Jessel, B. Encelle, M. Gut, LAMBDA: A European System to Access Mathematics with Braille and Audio Synthesis, *Proceedings of ICCHP 2006 (10th International Conference on Computers Helping People with Special Needs)*, (2006), 1223-1230.

[29] Metroplex Voice Computing, Inc. (2003), *MathTalk Tech Notes.* Retrieved May 8, 2008, from http://www.mathtalk.com/tech_notes.htm

[30] C. Elliott & J.A. Bilmes, Computer Based Mathematics using continuous Speech Recognition, *Striking a C[h]ord: Vocal Interaction in Assistive Technologies, Games, and More*, CHI 2007 workshop on non-verbal acoustic interaction, San Jose, CA, (2007).

[31] C. Guy, M. Jurka, S. Stanek & R. Fateman, *Math Speak & Write, a Computer Program to Read and Hear Mathematical Input*, USA: University of California, Berkeley, Electrical Engineering and Computer Sciences Department Technical Report, 2004.

[32] C. Bernareggi & V. Brigatti, Writing Mathematics by Speech: A Case Study for Visually Impaired. *Proceedings of ICCHP 2008 (11th International Conference on Computers Helping People with Special Needs)*, (2008), 879-882.

[33] Design Science (2009), *MathType6.5*. Retrieved March 27, 2009, from http://www.dessci.com/en/products/mathtype/

[34] T. Hanakovič & M. Nagy, Speech Recognition Helps Visually Impaired People Writing Mathematical Formulas, *Proceedings of ICCHP 2006 (10th International Conference on Computers Helping People with Special Needs)*, (2006), 1231-1234.

Intelligent Environments 2009
V. Callaghan et al. (Eds.)
IOS Press, 2009

doi:10.3233/978-1-60750-034-6-34

Towards Emotion, Age- and Gender-Aware VoiceXML Applications

Alexander SCHMITT , Tobias HEINROTH and Gregor BERTRAND
Institute for Information Technology, University of Ulm, Germany
{alexander.schmitt,tobias.heinroth,gregor.bertrand}@uni-ulm.de

Abstract. This paper presents a speaker classification architecture for VoiceXML-based applications. Our analysis component receives user utterances from the VoiceXML platform, performs feature extraction and classifies speaker characteristics such as age, gender and emotional state. This additional information about the speaker can be employed to adapt system prompts and the dialogue strategy to specific user groups. The implementation of our prototype shows, that speaker classification is feasible without significant delays and with high accuracies of over 95% for anger detection and gender classification.

Keywords. Gender Classification, Emotion Recognition, Speaker Age, VoiceXML, system architecture,

Introduction

VoiceXML 2.1 is, without doubt, *the* established standard for developing Spoken Language Dialogue Systems (SLDS) for telephone applications. By 2010 more than 50% of all automated calls will be handled by VoiceXML-based applications according to a market study by Datamonitor [6], and the growth will further continue leading to a replacement of proprietary systems. In contrast, several research projects in the recent past such as TALK [14] or D'Homme [12] dealt with SLDS in Intelligent Environment (IE) applications employing non-standardized dialogue systems.

While the development of state-of-the-art Voice User Interfaces (VUIs) has been strongly facilitated with VoiceXML, next-generation user interfaces can only be built with limitations. Indeed, next-generation techniques, such as mixed-initiative (VoiceXML 2.1) and multimodality (X+V, XHTML+Voice) have been rudimentarily been considered, however, important elements have been left disregarded. Current systems are able to understand what the user *says* and what he *means*, but lack further information about the user himself and the group he belongs to.

Although the current draft for the next version of the standard, VoiceXML 3.0, envisions *speaker verification* and *speaker identification* it does not allow for *speaker classification*. Note that there are significant differences: verification determines whether you are really the one you are claiming to be, e.g. for banking applications, whereas identification determines who you are from a distinct set of users, i.e. as an individual, e.g.

for intelligent home applications. In contrast to this, speaker classification assigns the speaker to a certain group of users, such as male vs. female, teens vs. middle-aged adults vs. elderly, angry vs. neutral, non-native speakers vs. native speakers, etc. This additional information can contribute to an adapted, personalized conversation between user and system and would let the system appear more "intelligent" and more or less on equal footing with the user compared with today's systems.

For the VoiceXML platform, speaker classification would be a rather easy and not too costly task since most relevant features such as MFCC coefficients (Mel Frequency Cepstral Coefficients) are calculated anyway for Automatic Speech Recognition (ASR). Models could be adequately generalized and trained to work with a broad range of applications, telephone channels and background noises as it is currently the case for ASR. However, neither the VoiceXML working group nor the platform manufacturers seem to push forward in that direction.

Our contribution closes this gap allowing for an integration of speaker classification information in VoiceXML-based applications and enabling speaker group specific and emotion-aware dialogue systems and can be very useful both in Intelligent Environments and telephone applications.

This publication consists of the following parts: after presenting related work and possible applications for speaker classification, we depict a three tier architecture and a development guideline enabling a deployment of speaker group aware VoiceXML applications with today's VoiceXML 2.1 and the future 3.0 standard. Further we employ our architecture to implement an emotion, age and gender aware system based on two speech corpora. Our final evaluation presents promising classification results.

1. Related Work

Concerning speaker classification and system design, some previous works exist: Burkhardt et al. [3] present a taxonomy for SLDS that make use of speaker classification. They differentiate between systems, that directly react on the classification result, *online*, and systems that are optimized towards the main user group of the system, *offline*, which has been determined on a logged corpus of collected calls. Further they distinguish between *mirroring* and *non-mirroring* systems. While the former systems show the user the classification result during the conversation the latter keep this information hidden and employ the user information for adaption purposes. Third they introduce the term *critical* for systems requiring speaker classification results for error-free functionality and systems working without correct classification, i.e. *non-critical*. In [1] emotion recognition in a deployed industry VoiceXML application is addressed. They argue that computational time constraints are very high for business applications and delays due to costly classification operations are not acceptable for users.

In Metze et al. [9], various classifiers are compared for determining speaker age for telephone applications. They distinguish between children, young people, adults and seniors, respectively male and female. The recognition rates are promising and reach a comparable performance as human listeners.

In contrast to the cited works, we describe a detailed architecture of enhancing VoiceXML-based applications with speaker classification and integrate age, gender and emotion recognition.

2. Fields of Application for Speaker Awareness

User studies, backing up the hypothesis that dialogue systems tailored to specific user groups are considered to be more user-friendly can be found in [10] and [4] and potential applications for user-group aware dialogue systems are numerous. According to the taxonomy of [3], there are different application scenarios for this technique conceivable:

- Direct address: We observed especially elderly people addressing the IVR voice with "Sir" or "Ma'am" in two deployed US-American IVR systems. The system could behave similarly and address users directly, e.g. "This is obviously my fault, Sir!", "One Moment, Ma'am, I'm going to connect you to an agent." (mirroring, non-critical, online)
- Dialogue-strategy adaption: dialogue prompts, dialogue strategy and dialogue grammar can be adapted to the respective user group and the emotional state. Elderly people might experience more direct confirmation prompts, teens could be addressed informally, and on angry users the system might react with a conciliation strategy or an escalation to a human operator. (mirroring, non-critical, online)
- Tailored advertisements for user groups: Advertisements that are presented to callers being on hold waiting for an operator or in between application usage to the user for funding free voice applications can be selected according to the determined user group based on age and gender. E.g. teens might be presented ringtone ads, women with beauty products and seniors with health and pharmacy ads. (mirroring, non-critical, online)
- A-priori information for Problematic Dialogue Prediction: A task completion rate prediction described in [13] and [7] can predict critical situations in the dialogue and intervene, before the caller hangs up without completing the task. With a-priori information about the group the caller belongs to, this prediction will be more exact, provided that there exist differences between user groups in completing the task in the respective application. (non-mirroring, non-critical, online)

The next section presents our architectural approach and provides an exemplary VoiceXML dialogue that can be used within an Intelligent Environment.

3. Overall Architecture

We have implemented a three tier architecture design depicted in Figure 1. All aspects of a classical SLDS architecture such as Automatic Speech Recognition (ASR), Text to Speech (TTS) as well as dialogue description and execution by the Form Interpretation Algorithm (FIA) can be found within the Presentation Layer, which can be represented by a standardized VoiceXML platform. Since we enhance the classical approach our focus does not lie on this layer, but on the Application and on the Analysis Layer.

3.1. Presentation Layer

As mentioned above, the Presentation Layer consists of ASR, TTS and the FIA. We use the same naming conventions in our approach as in common three-tier software architectures since speech applications are in many aspects similar to regular GUI applications. The Presentation Layer can be seen as a client that receives information regarding dia-

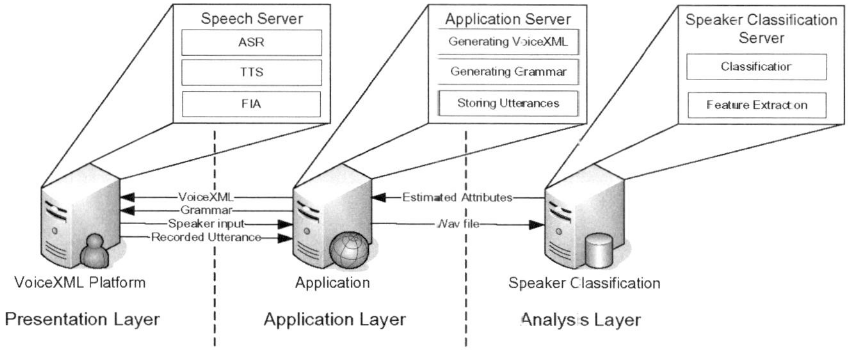

Figure 1. A three-layered architecture for speaker classification.

logue flow (VoiceXML) and grammar (grxml or GSL) from the second layer, the Application Layer. During dialogue execution it sends the application dependent speaker input and the last user utterance back to the Application Layer.

```
<form id="listeningLoop">
   <property name="recordutterance" value="true"/>
      <field name="waitForCommand">
         <grammar src="http://applicationServerURL.org/grammar.grxml"/>
         <filled>
            <var name="userRecording" expr="waitForCommand$.recording"/>
            <data name="xmlAnswer" method="POST" enctype="multipart/form-data"
            namelist="userRecording" srcexpr="'http://applicationServerURL.org/Receive'"/>
            <script>
               <![CDATA[
                  try {
                     document.personalizedPrompt=xmlAnswer.documentElement.getElementsBy
                     TagName("personalizedPrompt").item(0).firstChild.data;
                  } catch(e){}
               ]]>
            <script/>
            <prompt>document.personalizedPrompt</prompt>
            ⋮
```

Figure 2. The essential part of the VoiceXML Dialogue for an IE. Important elements are the "recordutterance" attribute, the data- and the script tag.

The essential part of the VoiceXML document realizing this functionality is shown in Figure 2. In this example, a keyword activation for an Intelligent Environment is demonstrated. The dialogue system is kept in a listening mode until the "magic word" is recognized. The property "recordutterance" allows to store the last user utterance in a platform variable that can be accessed by "name_of_field$.recording". The data tag is used to pass the utterance encoded as a "wav" audio file to the Application Layer. As response, the data tag receives an XML file containing the Application Layer's personalized prompt based on the Analysis Layer's classification result. The personalized system utterance is extracted by a line of Java-Script code encapsulated in the script tag. Finally the prompt tag presents this utterance to the user. With the same technique, not only a prompt can be encapsulated within the XML answer, but a URL pointing to a personalized VoiceXML dialogue.

3.2. Application Layer

The Application Layer both serves as a kind of middleware between the Presentation and the Analysis Layer and as a server that provides the application itself. This application may generate the VoiceXML encoded dialogue for a travel agency, a technical support automated agent, a music store etc.

As indicated in Figure 3 the application consists of the three servlets “Dialogue”, “Receive” and “Grammar”. The “Dialogue” servlet provides the dialogue itself. More precisely it provides no content i.e., no specific utterances; only the dialogue flow is generated. This enables the developer to predefine several different types of dialogue flows, e.g., only a prompt waiting for an answer, the presentation of several choices or more complex varieties. We call these abstract definitions of dialogue flows *dialogue skeletons*, which are essentially dialogue templates without any defined prompts. Those skeletons can also be chosen automatically depending on the ongoing user classification accomplished within the Analysis Layer. For an elderly user it would be possible to choose a more simple structured dialogue flow, which provides a more detailed help than it would require for a middle-aged man who is accustomed to such systems.

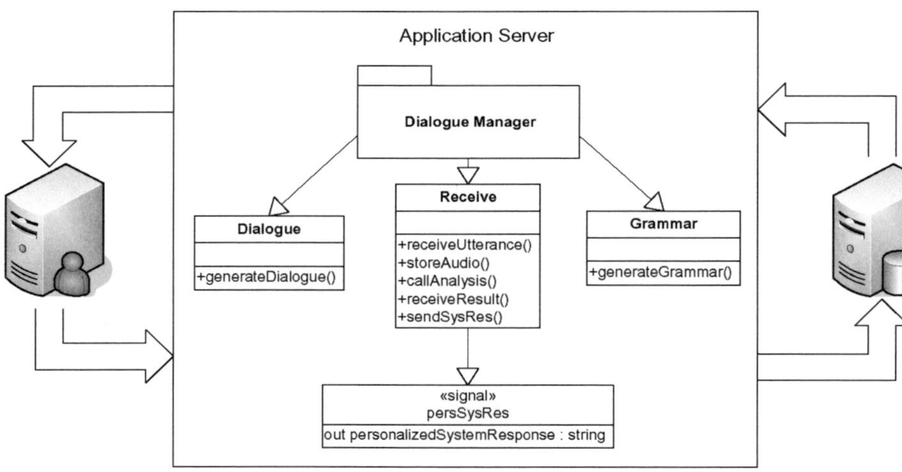

Figure 3. A detailed view on the Application Layer.

The “Grammar” servlet provides grammars generated on-the-fly enabling the system to understand simple commands or more sophisticated user utterances. The grammars are generated depending on the application’s domain and on the user classification. E.g., a domain can describe several devices and their respective commands within an ambient environment or a list of apt user utterances that may occur within an automatic call centre application. The user classification allows for an enhancement of the grammar according to the user group. Examples for user specific vocabulary are the words “cool” and “sweet”. A teenager might use these words instead of “yes” or “good”, whereas grown-up persons usually wouldn’t.

The "Receive" servlet acts as mediator between the Presentation and Analysis Layer and furthermore generates the system utterances. At first it receives the audio data from the VoiceXML platform, makes them accessible as "wav" audio files for the Analysis Layer and triggers the classification process. After the analysis is finished the servlet receives the outcome of the classification and generates the system utterance. Depending on the application domain prompts containing "Sir" or "Madam", brief or lengthy and even utterances diverging in substance can be chosen. If the classification process delivers a classification result with low confidence the servlet receives "UNKNOWN" and generates a neutral prompt such as common dialogue systems do. The as XML encapsulated system prompt is received by the Presentation Layer that directly presents it to the user.

3.3. Analysis Layer

The task of the Analysis Layer is to provide a reliable statement on the group the user belongs to or the emotional state he is currently in. The wav file is subject to a feature extraction with Praat [2] and stored in a database which is accessed by RapidMiner [11] performing the actual recognition using acoustic models.

The Application Layer has access to the classification result through the database and incorporates this information for user group specific prompt design and dialogue strategy. Acoustic modelling has been conducted with the Berlin Database of Emotional Speech [5] and the TIDigits database [8] from Texas Instruments. We used the following acoustic and prosodic features extracted with Praat for training all models.

- power, mean, rms, mean harmonicity
- pitch (mean, deviation, voiced frames, time step, mean slope, minimum, maximum, range)
- voiced pitch (mean, minimum mean, maximum mean, range)
- intensity (mean, maximum, minimum, deviation, range)
- jitter points, formants 1-5, MFCC 1-12

For building the emotion model we utilized the Berlin Database of Emotional Speech comprising 10 speakers. Training has been performed with angry and neutral utterances of speakers 3, 8, 9, 10, 11. Gender and age models have been trained with the training set of the TIDigits corpus. The gender and emotion model have been built with the Rule Learner implementation from RapidMiner, the age model with a Support Vector Machine with previous parameter optimization, since the Rule Learner performed very poor on the age task.

4. Evaluation

We evaluated the performance of all three models starting with the emotion recognition model, which was tested with the test set of the TIDigits corpus comprising the second half of the speakers from the Berlin DB (speakers 12,13,14,15,16) For the 67 angry and 36 neutral utterances our model reaches an accuracy of 95.21 % for determining anger vs. neutral utterances. Details are listed in Table 1.

For gender and age recognition we employed the test set of the TIDigits corpus consisting of utterances from children as well as male and female adults. Unfortunately, se-

	true anger	true neutral	class precision
pred. anger	67	7	90.54%
pred. neutral	0	72	100.00%
class recall	100.00%	91.14%	

Table 1. Precision/Recall matrix for the emotion classes "Anger" and "Neutral" based on the Berlin Database of Emotional Speech

nior speakers are not contained in the corpus. Comprehensive corpora containing equally distributed age classes containing children, adults and seniors are very rare and hardly available. We thus focused on distinction between children (boys and girls under 16 years) and adults (men and woman over 16 years)). The age test has been performed with 3000 randomly chosen utterances from boys and girls and 3000 randomly chosen utterances from adults (1500 male, 1500 female) from the test set. Results are shown in Table 2. The model reaches an accuracy of 77.4 %.

	true child	true adult	class precision
pred. child	2004	381	84.03%
pred. adult	996	2619	72.45%
class recall	66.80%	87.30%	

	true man	true woman	class precision
pred. man	4245	130	97.03%
pred. woman	66	4259	98.47%
class recall	98.47%	97.04%	

Table 2. Precision/Recall matrix for the age classes "adult" and "child" as well as "man" and "woman" based on the TIDigits Corpus

For gender recognition, we employed all 4389 women's and 4311 men's utterances from the TIDigits test set gaining an accuracy of 97.74%. The presented tests show, that basic speaker classification reaches good results with standard corpora and a binary class separation. A more differentiated approach, i.e., more emotions, more age classes would, of course, lead to lower accuracies. Final user tests are subject to future work.

5. Conclusion and Discussion

We presented an architecture for speaker aware VoiceXML-based dialogue systems for both telephone and IE applications. Speaker information is derived from the speech signal on the Analysis Layer, such as gender, age and emotional state. These speaker characteristics can be used either for generation of personalized prompts to directly include them in the ongoing dialogue or to select specific content-less dialogue templates, so called *s*keletons, allowing for an adaption of the dialogue structure to specific user groups.

Currently, we created and tested the models with "artificial" corpora containing clean speech. This had the advantage that reliable annotations for age, gender and emotion already exist; however, performance losses are to be expected when used in telephone applications. First, it consists of acted emotions, which are not comparable to spontaneous emotions. Second, it does not contain noise, which is atypical for real-life data. Third, the age distribution in the training corpus includes children but no seniors, not reflecting the typical IVR user groups. For a realistic assessment and employment of this system, real domain-specific data should be collected and used for training the acoustic models for age, gender and emotion instead. We are currently labelling data from an US-American IVR system which will enable us to build robust models for deployed IVR systems.

The proposed architecture also allows for further speech signal based analyses such as uncertainty detection, non-native speaker detection, dialect classification etc. Our current evaluation is limited to the classification performance. Future work will involve a full system user evaluation with multiple users in an Intelligent Environment within the ATRACO project.

Acknowledgements

The research leading to these results has received funding from the European Community's Seventh Framework Programme (FP7/2007-2013) under grant agreement n° 216837 and from the Transregional Collaborative Research Centre SFB/TRR 62 "Companion-Technology for Cognitive Technical Systems" funded by the German Research Foundation (DFG).

References

[1] A. Batliner and R. Huber. Speaker characteristics and emotion classification. pages 138–151, 2007.

[2] P. Boersma. Praat, a System for Doing Phonetics by Computer. *Glot International*, 5(9/10):341–345, 2001.

[3] F. Burkhardt, R. Huber, and A. Batliner. Application of speaker classification in human machine dialog systems. In *Speaker Classification I: Fundamentals, Features, and Methods*, pages 174–179, Berlin, Heidelberg, 2007. Springer-Verlag.

[4] F. Burkhardt, F. Metze, and J. Stegmann. *Speaker Classification for Next Generation Voice Dialog Systems*, chapter 17. Advances in Digital Speech Transmission. Wiley, 2007.

[5] F. Burkhardt, A. Paeschke, M. Rolfes, W. F. Sendlmeier, and B. Weiss. A Database of German Emotional Speech. In *European Conference on Speech and Language Processing (EUROSPEECH)*, pages 1517–1520, Lisbon, Portugal, Sep. 2005.

[6] Datamonitor. Understanding key drivers for ivr investment in a changing landscape. Market study, Datamonitor (available at: www.datamonitor.com), Nov. 2007.

[7] O. Herm, A. Schmitt, and J. Liscombe. When calls go wrong: How to detect problematic calls based on log-files and emotions? In *Proc. of the International Conference on Speech and Language Processing (ICSLP)*, Sept. 2008.

[8] R. G. Leonard. A database for speaker-independent digit recognition. In *International Conference on Acoustics, Speech and Signal Processing (ICASSP)*, San Diego, California, Apr. 1984.

[9] F. Metze, J. Ajmera, R. Englert, U. Bub, F. Burkhardt, J. Stegmann, C. Müller, R. Huber, B. Andrassy, J. Bauer, and B. Littel. Comparison of four approaches to age and gender recognition. In *Proceedings of the International Conference on Acoustics, Speech, and Signal Processing (ICASSP)*, volume 1, 2007.

[10] F. Metze, R. Englert, U. Bub, F. Burkhardt, and J. Stegmann. Getting closer: tailored human-computer speech dialog. *Universal Access in the Information Society*, 8(2), 2008.

[11] I. Mierswa, M. Wurst, R. Klinkenberg, M. Scholz, and T. Euler. Yale: Rapid prototyping for complex data mining tasks. In L. Ungar, M. Craven, D. Gunopulos, and T. Eliassi-Rad, editors, *KDD '06: Proceedings of the 12th ACM SIGKDD international conference on Knowledge discovery and data mining*, pages 935–940, New York, NY, USA, August 2006. ACM.

[12] J. F. Quesada, F. Garcia, E. Sena, J. A. Bernal, and G. Amores. Dialogue management in a home machine environment: Linguistic components over an agent architecture. *Procesamiento del Lenguaje Natural*, 27:89–98, September 2001.

[13] A. Schmitt and J. Liscombe. Detecting Problematic Calls With Automated Agents. In E. André, L. Dybkiaer, W. Minker, and P. Heisterkamp, editors, *4th IEEE Tutorial and Research Workshop Perception and Interactive Technologies for Speech-Based Systems*, Lecture Notes in Artificial Intelligence, Irsee (Germany), June 2008.

[14] S. Young, J. Williams, J. Schatzmann, M. Stuttle, and K. Weilhammer. D4.3: Bayes net prototype - the hidden information state dialogue manager. Technical report, TALK - Talk and Look: Tools for Ambient Linguistic Knowledge, IST-507802, 6th FP, 2006.

Intelligent Environments 2009
V. Callaghan et al. (Eds.)
IOS Press, 2009

doi:10.3233/978-1-60750-034-6-42

Enhancing Speech Dialogue Technologies for Ambient Intelligent Environments

Tobias HEINROTH, Alexander SCHMITT and Gregor BERTRAND
Institute for Information Technology, University of Ulm, Germany
{tobias.heinroth,alexander.schmitt,gregor.bertrand}@uni-ulm.de

Abstract. This paper proposes a Model-View-Controller architecture for Spoken Dialogue Management (SDM) that consists of VoiceXML as *View*, i.e., as presentation layer and a *Controller* layer using a *Model* to determine the next possible system utterance. In this paper we focus on the *Model* layer and present a Dialogue Domain Ontology, which combines the Information State and the ontology theory. The Dialogue ontology can be extended by several optional components such as a domain reasoner, which supports and governs the ontology, an analysis layer to classify the user or a translation layer, which triggers various applications. Our work aims at a unified model for SDM related information handling for various tasks in intelligent environments.

Keywords. Spoken Dialogues, Ambient Environments, VoiceXML, Ontologies, Information State

Introduction

As spoken dialogue is a key factor in ensuring a user-friendly and consistent user-device interaction in ambient intelligent environments (AIEs) several international research projects have been concerned with spoken dialogue interaction for quite a long time. In recent years the technical progress in computational power, speech recognition and synthesis techniques made the development of real-time spoken dialogue systems possible. Nowadays even for end-users it is possible to install speech servers and utilize them in the same way as web-servers in order to host (spoken) dialogues for applications such as "flight booking". These applications are often modelled using speech dialogue management (SDM) techniques based on finite state machines and frames. VoiceXML is the most popular and wide spread implementation of these dialogue models [14]. A dialogue is defined as a template containing several slots together with their respective grammar. The user can fill the slots no matter in which order. This allows a higher flexibility and a more natural conversation. It seems that for restricted domains and specific applications a well-working solution already has been found.

A main concern within AIEs is that there is no restricted domain but rather various different goals and tasks that can be supported by the AIE. Furthermore an AIE usually provides many applications that may also interdepend. To meet these requirements the static (but robust) frame-based systems are not flexible enough: huge, hardly to maintain libraries of, for example, VoiceXML dialogues and grammars would be needed.

A more general way of implementing dialogue strategies offers the information state (IS) approach. The information state theory of dialogue modelling [12] consists of informational components (common context, internal motivating factors, e.g., participants, commitments, beliefs, user models, etc.), a formal representations of informational components, e.g., lists, sets, typed feature structures or records, a set of dialogue moves that will trigger the update of the IS, a set of update rules, that govern the updating process of the IS, and an update strategy for deciding which rule(s) to select at a given point The main idea behind this theory is the formal representation of a specific (spoken) dialogue that can be modified by the use of defined rules to allow for a specific dialogue behaviour. In our view a major lack of IS driven systems such as TrindiKit is that it might be quite complex to design consistent rules, moves, grammars, utterances and semantic values for a task-changing AIE domain.

Motivated by the vision of knowledge-based dialogue modelling that on the one hand maximises the use of generic components and on the other hand provides the capability of straightforward adaption to changing domains that even should be possible during runtime we present an architectural approach consisting of model, view, controller and optional components such as a domain reasoner. In particular we can recognize three main benefits of our approach:

- A clear separation between generic (view and controller) and domain depending (model) components provides a good platform for dialogue designers.
- Both maximal flexibility and portability can be achieved by using a unified dialogue model implemented in a standardized languages (OWL).
- Two or more dialogue models can be merged [5] in order to get a dialogue model describing the combination of the original dialogue domains. A train booking and a flight booking dialogue domain can, for example, be merged to gain a train and flight booking dialogue model.

This publication consists of the following parts: The next section introduces the related work. Section 2 presents the architectural overview consisting of Model, View, Controller and an additional reasoning layer. The last section finishes this paper with conclusions and future work.

1. Related Work

For our approach two main fields of research have to be introduced: The information state theory as described in [12] and ontologies as described in [1]. Both approaches aim towards information handling but to our knowledge have never been combined in the same manner.

The combination of finite state models, ontologies, and data driven approaches are also introduced in [15]. The author presents a system that enhances IS by using external ontologies. This differs from our approach: We use a unified ontology as model that directly represents the IS. In [16] several requirements such as quality properties, value-constraint properties, and temporal properties for ontology-driven information systems are discussed. We assume that those requirements are also important within IEs and therefore addressed them for the implementation of the dialogue ontology.

In the context of the ATRACO Project [8], [6] we explore adaptation of interaction and in particular of spoken interaction within AIEs. Results of a Wizard-of-Oz evaluation indicated speech modality to be one of the richest ways for user-system interaction in such environments [2]. Compared to classical SDM in telephone applications or implemented to control single devices, within AIEs the tasks, dialogue domains, grammar, and even devices and services may vary widely. Therefore SDM for AIEs shall provide a maximum of flexibility. In the following section we introduce an MVC+R architecture that can be utilized to enhance spoken dialogue interaction within next generation AIEs such as ATRACO.

2. Architectural Overview

Our proposed architecture of an SDM is inspired by one of the most widespread architectural pattern in software engineering: the Model-View-Controller paradigm. As illustrated in Figure 1 in our approach VoiceXML is used as View (*V*). This presentation layer may vary from a complete dialogue flow as shown in Figure 2 to only one system prompt combined with a suitable grammar to catch the next user utterance. These VoiceXML dialogue snippets will be generated during the ongoing user-system conversation by the Controller (*C*), which is roughly described in Section 2.3.

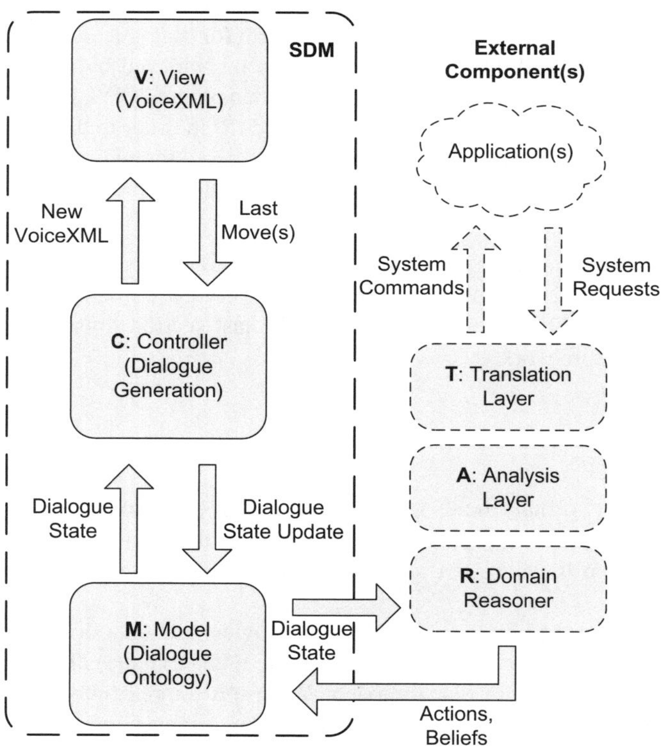

Figure 1. The proposed MVC+R architecture.

The main idea of our approach is a unified Model (*M*) underlying the SDM. A dialogue ontology represents this Model (see Section 2.2) and can be supported by a domain reasoner (*R*) (see Section 2.4). Both *V* and *C* are generic components that need no adjustment in case of domain changes. Combined with the reasoner it would also be possible to incorporate an analysis layer that contributes user classification to the dialogue ontology. The Model also can be used by an optional "translation layer" that serves as a middleware between ontology and applications. If the user wants to switch on a lamp the ontology would add an action entity encoding, for example, action("lamp1", "on") to the Believes class (see Figure 3). The translation layer would read this field and send a system command (e.g., by UPnP) to the lamp. This information exchange is possible in both directions.

2.1. V: VoiceXML

For simple tasks such as manipulating single devices VoiceXML suites perfectly as presentation layer. As shown in Figure 2 such a dialogue may consist of a magic word spotter and a set of possible instructions. The dialogue starts in an "always listening" mode and returns into this mode after an instruction is called and processed. In our example the dialogue flow is fixed with a variable grammar, which depends on the devices that are available within the IE. If the instructions are the same for different devices (e.g., "Play" for both TV set and MP3 player) the dialogue tries to clarify by entering a subdialogue, which asks for the target device. The subdialogue consists of one prompt that can be generated with the descriptive name of device 1 (e.g. TV set), the descriptive name of device 2 (e.g. MP3 player), and the uttered instruction.

If the descriptive name is not unique, i.e., both devices are lamps, the location of the devices are required. This could be done with the help of gesture recognition but in our approach we do not fuse modalities and therefore we assume that "the lamp above the table" would be descriptive enough.

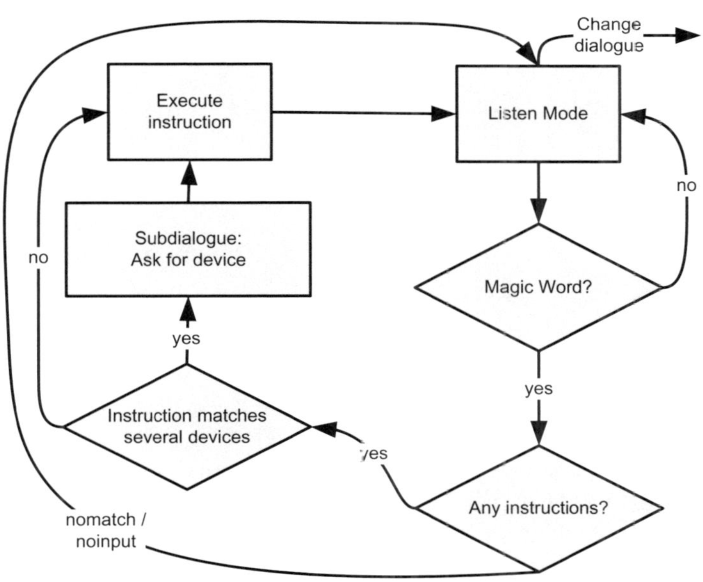

Figure 2. Dialogue flow suitable for device controlling within IEs implemented in VoiceXML.

Whenever a more complex dialogue structure is needed, VoiceXML will only be used as *View*, i.e., as presentation layer. Whenever it is necessary to switch to another dialogue strategy than Command-and-Control a new VoiceXML document that may support only one dialogue turn (i.e., consists of system utterance and grammar) will be generated. The VoiceXML interpretation platform (e.g., TellMe.Studio, Voxeo Prophecy) will be redirected to this new document. For each dialogue turn a new VoiceXML document will be generated until the system or the user finishes the conversation. In the next section we discuss a Dialogue Domain Ontology, which can be seen as an implementation of a knowledge base necessary to generate a dialogue step by step and to perform a more free user–system conversation, which is not only limited to Command–and–Control structures.

2.2. ***M***: *Dialogue Domain Ontology*

In our approach we combine two theories: Information state as mentioned in the introduction, and ontologies, which are defined as "formal, explicit specifications of a shared conceptualization" [7]. We assume that a major step towards fluent user–system conversation would be to use a formal and standardized knowledge base describing the complete dialogue domain as the core or *Model* (see Figure 1) of the SDM.

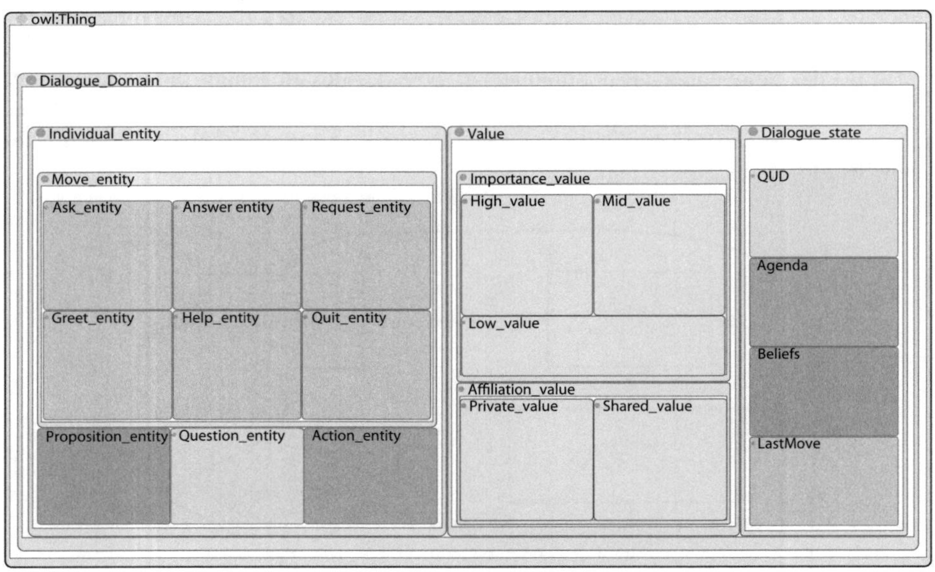

Figure 3. Logical view on an ontology describing the structure of a dialogue domain.

Our approach differs from approaches such as described in [15] for the reason that we are not trying to add external ontologies to the IS but to use an ontology to express the IS itself within its dialogue domain. The goal is to implement an ontology whose structure (i.e., classes, relations, and axioms) is generic to allow for covering several dialogue domains within an IE. A proposed ontology for that purpose is shown in Figure 3. The individuals of such an ontology would differ depending on the domain. The three main classes of the ontology implemented with Protégé in OWL [1] shown in Figure 3 can be described as follows: *Dialogue_Domain* is the only direct child of owl:Thing. The individuals of a dialogue domain differ depending on its task. Tasks can be, for example, "Prepare dinner", "Go shopping" or "Listen to music". The logical structure of *Dialogue_Domain* does not change.

Four classes are implemented within *Individual_entity* and form a set of possible instances of the *Dialogue_state*:

- *Move_entity* has six children: *Ask_entity* (e.g., "Do you want to have fish for dinner?"), *Answer_entity* (e.g., "There is no meat in the fridge."), *Request_entity* (e.g., "I want Caesar salad"), *Greet_entity* (e.g., "Hello"), *Help_entity* ("I need some help."), and *Quit_entity* (e.g., "Good bye").
- *Proposition_entity* describes entities that can be shared, i.e., known by system and user or private, i.e., only known by the system. Such propositions can be assumptions of the system about the user's status (his mood, etc.) or shared beliefs. If the user utters "I want Italian food", both system and user have a shared belief that the user wants Italian food.
- *Question_entity* represents all entities that can be used within Questions under Discussion (QUD) [11]. QUD is a shared information such as "What time is it?". Several QUD may occur during the ongoing dialogue.
- *Action_entity* represents several activities that should be accomplished within the task the dialogue should support. An example of such an activity could be "Write shopping list together with user".

The first class of *Value* within the proposed ontology is *Importance_value*, which consists of *High_value*, *Middle_value*, and *Low_value*. Theses classes can be used to implement a hierarchy regarding the importance of a proposition, question, action, or move. The second class is *Affiliation_value*, which consists of *Shared_value* and *Private_value*. These values are important to model the affiliation of an entity: Does the entity belong to shared knowledge, i.e., do user and system know about the respective entity or is it private, i.e., does only the system know about it.

The third main class within *Dialogue_Domain* is called *Dialogue_state*. It reflects the ideas of the IS theory and therefore itself consists of four classes: *QUD*, *Agenda*, *Beliefs* and *LastMove*. All members of *Move_entity* can be instantiated by *LastMove*, the individuals of the class *Proposition_entity* can be instances of *Beliefs*, the individuals of the class *Action_entity* can be instances of *Agenda*, and the individuals of *Question_entity* can be instances of the class *QUD*. Both Controller layer and Reasoner Layer would use this *Dialogue_state* to accomplish their tasks.

The proposed ontology refers both to the informational components and their formal representation as originally described in the IS theory. The dialogue moves, the update rules, and the update strategy can be implemented within the *Model* Layer as a kind of Business Logic or can be processed by an external framework. A controller component as described in the next section would work on the objects encapsulated within *Dialogue_state*.

2.3. C: Controller

The controller component is not explicitly discussed in this paper, because the focus of this paper lies on the Model and the View described above. In our approach the main task of the Controller is to generate VoiceXML dialogues or individual dialogue snippets (see 2.1) from the dialogue state, which is provided by the Model. One reason for choosing OWL for implementing the ontology was that such an open standard offers a variety of possible realisations for the Controller layer.

The rule engine of the well-known TrindiKit framework can be utilized [12] for this task. The OWL representation (i.e., the dialogue state) merely needs to be transformed to Information States to apply rules to generate VoiceXML. There are many approaches which incorporate agents operating directly on ontologies e.g. [8,10]. Another possibility would be to rely on Bayes' approaches or Neural Networks to perform the controller logic [13,4,9]. Of course an appropriate transformation to the internal representation of the Bayes' or neural network system has to be performed.

*2.4. **R**: Domain Reasoning*

Separating problem-solving strategies from the dialogue management behaviour has been a common goal, to which the Domain reasoning module aims to contribute by using its capabilities to process the information provided in the Model in a stringent and methodically sound way. It enables the detection of implications or ambiguities that the user may be unaware of. While the Controller itself uses reasoning to select the next dialogue move, the Domain reasoning module assures that certain time constraints and logical constraints are not violated. Imagine, that we want to bake cookies and select a recipe. With help of the domain reasoning layer the intelligent environment is able to find out, whether all ingredients are available for the planned recipe and will inform the model that an ingredient is missing. One possibility for implementing this reasoning layer could be the employment of a logical reasoner as described in [3]. Therefore, the dialogue state representation extracted from the ontological model has to be transformed to logical predicates so that the reasoner can work on them.

3. Conclusions and Future Work

We presented a generic MVC architectural approach for enhancing SDM for next generation intelligent environments such as ATRACO. The main idea behind our approach is to combine the IS theory and ontologies to implement a unified *Model* describing all logic entities for various dialogue domains such as "Prepare dinner", "Go shopping" or "Listen to music". The Model can be supported by an external domain reasoner that detects ambiguities and facts that violate constraints.

Both View and Controller layers are independent from the Model, which offers great flexibility. We propose to use VoiceXML as View to benefit from portability of such an open standard and from several VoiceXML specific features (event handling, etc.). The Controller, whose main task is to generate VoiceXML, can be realized utilizing several approaches such as logical reasoning, agents, or Neural Networks. The potentiality of using ontology merging to automatically generate new dialogues would offer interesting approaches towards dialogue modelling.

Future work will involve improvements of the dialogue ontology, development of methodologies showing how to derive ontology instances from domain task descriptions and generating logical predicates for the domain reasoner from the dialogue state.

We also plan to analyze the maintainability and readability of large dialogue ontologies and furthermore the requirements of the Controller layer and will implement the most promising option. Tests with a running system are envisaged to be done within the course of the ATRACO project.

Acknowledgements

The research leading to these results has received funding from the European Community's Seventh Framework Programme (FP7/2007-2013) under grant agreement n° 216837 and from the Transregional Collaborative Research Centre SFB/TRR 62 "Companion-Technology for Cognitive Technical Systems" funded by the German Research Foundation (DFG).

References

[1] G. Antoniou and F. van Harmelen. Web ontology language: Owl. pages 76–92. Springer-Verlag, 2003.

[2] Y. Bellik, G. Pruvost, J.-C. Martin, N. Tan, W. Minker, and T. Heinroth. D19 - user interaction specification and tools. Public deliverable, The ATRACO Project (FP7/2007-2013 grant agreement nÂř 216837), 2008.

[3] D. Bühler and M. Riegler. Integrating Dialogue Management and Domain Reasoning. In *Proceedings of SPECOM*, pages 409–412, Patras, Greece, October 2005.

[4] C. Conati, A. Gertner, and K. VanLehn. Using Bayesian Networks to Manage Uncertainty in Student Modeling. *Journal of User Modeling and User-Adapted Interaction*, 12(4):371–417, 2002.

[5] M. Ehrig, J. de Bruijn, D. Manov, and F. Martín-Recuerda. State-of-the-art survey on ontology merging and aligning v1. SEKT Deliverable 4.2.1, DERI Innsbruck, JUL 2004.

[6] C. Goumopoulos, A. Kameas, H. Hagras, V. Callagan, M. Gardner, W. Minker, M. Weber, Y. Bellik, and A. Meliones. ATRACO: Adaptive and Trusted Ambient Ecologies. In *Proceedings of the 2nd IEEE International Conference on Self-Adaptive and Self-Organizing Systems (SASO), Workshop on Pervasive Adaptation (PERADA)*, Oct. 2008.

[7] T. R. Gruber. A translation approach to portable ontology specifications. *Knowl. Acquis.*, 5(2):199–220, June 1993.

[8] T. Heinroth, A. Kameas, C. Wagner, and Y. Bellik. A proposal for realizing adaptive ambient ecologies through an ontology-based multi-agent system. In *2009 IEEE International Symposium on Intelligent Agents*, Apr. 2009.

[9] L. F. Hurtado, D. Griol, E. Segarra, and E. Sanchis. A Stochastic Approach for Dialog Management based on Neural Networks. In *International Conference on Speech and Language Processing (ICSLP)*, pages 49–52, Pittsburgh, USA, September 2006.

[10] R. Khosla. Multi-layered agent ontology for soft computing systems. *Int. J. Know.-Based Intell. Eng. Syst.*, 8(2):117–128, 2004.

[11] S. Larsson. Questions under discussion and dialogue moves. In *In: Proceedings of twlt13/twendial '98: Formal*, 1998.

[12] S. Larsson and D. Traum. Information State and Dialogue Management in the TRINDI Dialogue Move Engine Toolkit. *Natural Language Engineering*, 6:323–340, 2000.

[13] J.-M. Marin, K. Mengersen, and C. P. Robert. Bayesian Modelling and Inference on Mixtures of Distributions. In D. Dey and C. R. Dao, editors, *Handbook of Statistics*, volume 25. Elsevier-Sciences, Amsterdam, Netherlands, 2005.

[14] M. Oshry, R. Auburn, P. Baggia, M. Bodell, D. Burke, D. Burnett, E. Candell, J. Carter, S. Mcglashan, A. Lee, B. Porter, and K. Rehor. Voice extensible markup language (voicexml) version 2.1. Technical report, W3C - Voice Browser Working Group, June 2007.

[15] D. Sonntag. Towards combining finite state, ontologies, and data driven approaches to dialogue management for multimodal question answering. In *Proceedings of the Fifth Slovenian and First International Language Technologies Conference (IS-LTC)*, 10 2006.

[16] B. Yildiz and S. Miksch. Ontology-driven information systems: Challenges and requirements. In *International Conference on Semantic Web and Digital Libraries*. Indian Statistical Institute Platinum Jubilee Conference Series, pages 35–44, 2007.

Intelligent Environments 2009
V. Callaghan et al. (Eds.)
IOS Press, 2009

doi:10.3233/978-1-60750-034-6-50

CHAD - Constraint Handling Architecture for Dialogue Management

Gregor BERTRAND, Tobias HEINROTH and Alexander SCHMITT
Institute for Information Technology, University of Ulm, Germany
{gregor.bertrand,tobias.heinroth,alexander.schmitt}@uni-ulm.de

Abstract. Recent research shows that including logical reasoning into dialogue management could be of enormous benefit for the capabilities of the system. However logical reasoning is to some extent limited in its possibilities to infer or to find a conclusion given certain premises. Furthermore reasoning systems heavily rely on backtracking algorithms which is a great shortcoming concerning performance aspects.

In order to improve the performance as well as the reasoning capabilities of the dialogue manager we propose an architecture that is based on logical reasoning but uses a constraint solving mechanism for enlarging the logical capabilities of the dialogue manager.

Keywords. Human computer interaction, dialogue management, dialogue modelling, constraint logic programming, VoiceXML

Introduction

In recent years various international research projects have been dealing with the improvement of spoken language dialogue systems (SLDSs) by focusing on reasoning and consistency checking.

The interactive planning system TRIPS (University of Rochester) is a multimodal prototype for collaborative problem solving assistants in logistics (as described in detail in [1,11]).

In this case the scenario consists of a domain expert (logistician) who sets up plans for certain operations, e.g. evacuation of an island due to a hurricane warning in collaboration with a computer. The task includes a high-level goal and the detailled planning of associated primitive actions. In this complex environment which consists of a variety of features and vehicle types, conflicts occur as soon as certain time or resource contingents are used up.

In the TRIPS approach the conflict solving seems to rely mainly on the user's ability to determine reasons for a conflict. Our approach is quite similar to that idea as we consider problems during the planning phase as well. However feasibility of the common plan is of higher relevance to us. This also includes the communication of alternatives as well as explanations and suggestions for solving the conflict, part of which is integrated into the successor to TRIPS, a multimodal assistant for medicine intake, the Medication Advisor ([2]).

One major aspect in adaptive dialogue systems is that the user wants the system to make best use of the information given. In order to satisfy this need SLDSs often rely on logical reasoning. During the past few years, several types of reasoning systems have been presented (e.g. [9,7]).

Most of these systems rely heavily on first order logic and use backtracking in order to find some solution for the clauses which can be derived from the user's information. Seen from the theoretical side this kind of approach is to a high degree limited in its ability to draw conclusions. Seen from the performance side backtracking is very slow because of its exponential complexity (see [10]). Therefore the integration of constraint logic programming based reasoning into SLDSs forms the basis for our research. Constraint logic programming (CLP) was born from a desire to have both a better problem performance and expression than in logic programming (LP). Its success comes from the fact that it combines the declarativeness of LP with the efficiency of the constraint programming (CP) paradigm (see [12]) . A detailed overview on the advantages of constrained programming is given in [5,6].

A common aspect in SLDSs is that there is often a temporal or spatial relationship which has to be regarded. Such a relationship can be easily modeled on a finite domain. Relationships on finite domains can be treated very efficiently with the constraint logic programming approach (see [12]). Using constraint logic programming has already been applied to scheduling problems successfully (as shown in [15]).

1. Description of the Components

Core components of the proposed architecture are a constraint handling system and a knowledge representation system on the basis of constraints. It should be based on a domain model consisting of logical constraints and able to produce inferences from constraints given in the same domain. If a conflict is found (i.e. a constraint is not able to be satisfied), the constraint handling system provides a proof structure that can be used to track down the exact set of facts that caused the conflict. This information can be used by the dialogue manager to explain the conflict and to resolve it, e.g. by relaxing the constraints or conditions. Especially temporal conditions can be handled more swiftly with a constraint handling system than with an ordinary first-order-logic-based reasoner (see [12]). Based on the information, that the user provides, the constraint handling system can draw an overall plan containing user goals and fulfilling constraints provided by other applications. The constraint handling system has the role to guarantee that all constraints can be established and maintained. For this reason it is also possible to provide the user with possible solutions satisfying the given constraints in order to offer easier and faster communication.

In addition the constraint handling component should be able to communicate effectively with the dialougue communication component which is responsible for the input and output. For the communication between the dialogue communication component and the constraint handling component we focus on OWL (the ontology web language [4]) as an interface language which shall be transformed into a constraint representation and vice versa by a translation component. For the implementation of the dialogue communication component and the translation component we suggest Java.

There are efficient and simple means for handling OWL in Java (see [13]). Furthermore the implementation in Java facilitates the cooperation with servlet technologies.

There are several servlet architectures which can provide a platform to deliver XML. In order to make use of the benefits of the widespread VoiceXML format, we suggest to generate this format in a servlet container which is a part of the dialogue communication component. Therefore not being limited by the static format on the one hand it is possible to take profit of the mechanisms that are provided for VoiceXML on the other hand. The use of VoiceXML, ECMAScript and Java as standard technologies has become very common in the field of SLDSs (see [8,14]). Being implemented in Java, the dialogue manager can also serve as a basis for the integration of further concepts in the future.

The use of OWL in combination with a translation component facilitates the extension of the dialogue management system with further capabilities as OWL is an interface that is flexible and clear.

2. Component and Model Integration

For the integration of intelligence and versatility into SLDSs, we envision a system that enables the user to interact with one or multiple applications in a natural and user-friendly way. Such a system is able to detect conflicts as soon as possible according to the information given and provides a convenient way to communicate with several applications at once.

Conflicts can be arising from different angles and applications. They should be detected in the constraint solver and be communicated transparently to the user. In this way, the system and the user can negotiate solutions whereupon the user is not burdened too much with brooding over possible solutions.

A typical environment which virtually requires speech communication as an interface is found in the automotive sector. In this area the driver's attentiveness and ability to react is significantly impaired by having to handle different communication and (route) planning devices while driving. Despite speech technology being already extensively utilized in this area, the construction and management of complex tasks and constraints for isolated applications still constitute a high cognitive burden on the driver.

Another crucial scenario relates to the care of the elderly which is becoming a more and more important topic in an aging society. In retirement homes or in hospitals employees and physicians as well as patients and residents must interact with a variety of applications provided by a central computer system. These can be reminders for medication, emergency calls, patients' requests for service, a patients database or an electronic working plan and task scheduler for employees.

Problems and conflicts likely to arise range from minor issues like the precise timing of medication intake up to critical emergencies. In either case, people involved may suffer from high stress or even fear, so that the communication provided by the dialogue system should be designed in a manner which does not contribute in a negative way to the tense situation. Therefore there is enormous importance in not asking unneccessary questions and in detecting conflicts and planning alternatives as soon as possible.

Such an approach to intelligent and adaptive SLDSs constitutes an important contribution to an increase of the efficiency and user-friendliness of these systems. Our approach differs from the above mentioned previous research projects as it addresses efficiently three basic features which are important for future dialogue systems.

2.1. Interface for multiple applications

The system shall support the user in a human-computer dialogue while incrementally planning and enforcing actions involving user given constraints and constraints given by multiple applications. In an automotive environment, for example, the combination of a navigation system and a calendar application can suggest appointment times considering the length of a journey between different places as well as opening hours of public utilities, parking facilities or restaurants. It can reschedule appointment times if necessary in cases of delays due to traffic congestion. This is facilitated by the system's ability to conduct inferences on basic knowledge shared by multiple applications and to address conflicts between user and system goals using a proactive explanation functionality for its own constraint reasoning. Moreover, the user shall be able to address multiple applications within only one single dialogue. This is enabled by creating a unified dialogue-based problem solving approach on the basis of OWL.

2.2. Intelligent reasoning

The system shall be able to make propositions depending on the information given by the user. It shall also be able to formulate a user stated problem in the domain as constraints in order to perform efficient reasoning. If the information given by the user is sufficient to propose certain alternatives for the solution of the problem the user shall be prompted in an intelligent manner (e.g. in the appointment example mentioned above, to explain the possible times and routes for a new or rescheduled appointment).

If the information given is inconsistent, the system shall be able to explain the detected inconsistencies and to propose ways how to fix them. Such behavior does not only increase the user-friendliness of the system and the general acceptance of computer systems in everyday life, but can also help users to cope with critical situations by communicating these situations in an appropriate way. Another important aspect is that the duration of the dialogue is shortened if the system is able to draw intelligent inferences and conclusions from what the user stated. There are less questions to be asked because much information can be generated deductively.

2.3. Flexible Dialogues

In order to be able to adapt to the various inferences that can be derived from information given by the user it would on the one hand usually be highly impractical to settle on a static format like VoiceXML. On the other hand VoiceXML and ECMA-Script offer many convenient mechanisms that one would normally like to make use of (e.g. the standardized format, exception handling, validation).

For this reason we suggest to use VoiceXML as a format on a servlet architecture. But in order to stay flexible we propose to dynamically generate VoiceXML to be able to model the inferences and conclusions that the constraint programming component provides.

The suggested architecture of our SLDS is outlined in Figure 1. The system relies on VoiceXML in order to get input from the user and to provide output to the user.

When imposing the analogy of Model View and Controller on the presented dialogue management architecture, VoiceXML is the view, constraints are the model and a

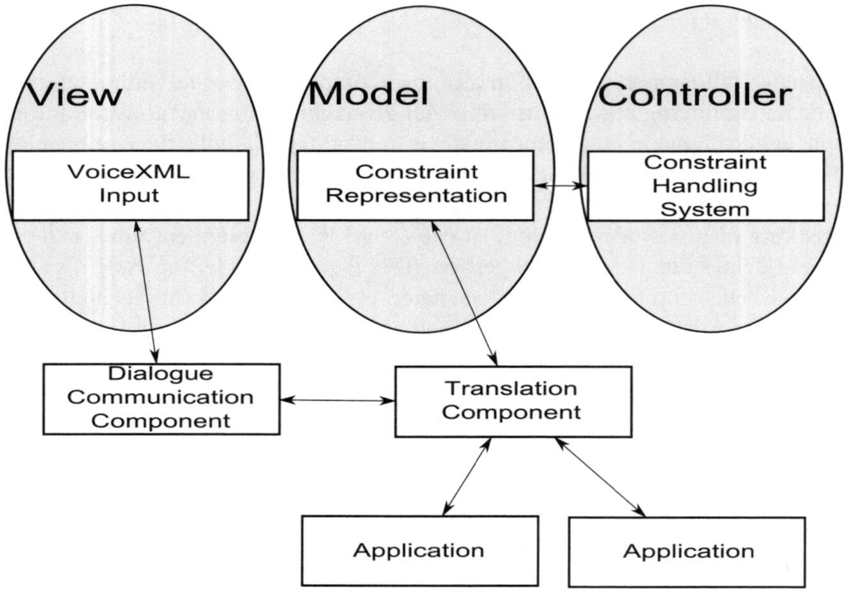

Figure 1. Proposed architecture of the SLDS.

constraint handling system constitutes the controller. Of course this analogy is to a certain degree simplified because all three components have to be extended with additional technologies in order to build a dialogue manager which is also seen in Figure 1. In order to provide an opportunity for other applications to make use of the constraint handling system and vice versa one needs a translation component.

The task of the translation component is to transform the knowledge provided by various sources such as user information, additional applications, databases etc., into constraints and vice versa. For the translation component we propose to use the Web Ontology Language as a clear interface definition since of its expressiveness (see [4]). The Translation component transforms the OWL-representation from the various applications and the dialogue communication component. Implemented like this the translation component provides an open and flexible interface, which can be used by various applications and also constitutes a precise way of integrating with the dialogue management component.

Another important feature that OWL incorporates is that it can be used to impose certain restrictions on the domains that are modelled by it (see [3]). So you can guarantee that the constraint handling system can operate only on constraints that make sense.

The constraint processing component consists of a knowledge representation in the form of constraints, accessed by inference algorithms that are specified as rules for the constraint handling system. It can detect conflicts, provide planning suggestions based on the values that variables are able to take in order to fulfill the provided constraints.

3. Conclusion and Future Directions

The development of user-friendly human-computer interfaces which are able to contribute to the interaction by identifying planning problems or misunderstandings in an "intelligent" way still constitutes a big challenge in current research. In this paper we have given an overview on our work on an architecture for intelligent spoken language dialogue systems.

Based on the components developed to date, a prototype system shall be implemented. It includes the described dialogue communication component, translation component and constraint modules. It still has to be identified how much of the system logic that has to be performed can be handled in the OWL part and how much is best treated with the constraint handling component. This must be examined in terms of effectiveness as well as in terms of convenience of the interfaces.

4. Acknowledgments

Parts of the research described in this article will be supported by the Transregional Collaborative Research Centre SFB/TRR 62 "Companion- Technology for Cognitive Technical Systems" funded by the German Research Foundation (DFG).

References

[1] J. Allen, D. Byron, M. Dzikovska, G. Ferguson, and L. Galescu. Toward conversational human-computer interaction. *AI Mag.*, 22(4):27–37, 2001.

[2] James Allen, George Ferguson, Nate Blaylock, Donna Byron, Nathanael Chambers, Myroslava Dzikovska, Lucian Galescu, and Mary Swift. Chester: Towards a personal medication advisor. *Journal of Biomedical Informatics*, 39(5):500 – 513, 2006. Dialog Systems for Health Communications.

[3] Grigoris Antoniou, Enrico Franconi, and Frank van Harmelen. Introduction to semantic web ontology languages. In Norbert Eisinger and Jan Małuszyński, editors, *Reasoning Web, Proceedings of the Summer School, Malta, 2005*, number 3564 in Lecture Notes in Computer Science, Berlin, Heidelberg, New York, Tokyo, 2005. Springer-Verlag.

[4] Grigoris Antoniou and Frank van Harmelen. Web ontology language: Owl. pages 76–92. Springer-Verlag, 2003.

[5] R. Bartak. Constraint programming: In pursuit of the holy grail. volume 4 of *Week of Doctoral Students*, pages 555–564. MatFyzPress, June 1999.

[6] Roman Bartak. Theory and practice of constraint propagation. Number 3 in Workshop on Constraint Programming for Decision and Control, pages 7–14. Wydawnictwo Pracovni Komputerowej, June 2001.

[7] Karl Branting, James C. Lester, and Bradford W. Mott. Dialogue management for conversational case-based reasoning. In *ECCBR*, pages 77–90, 2004.

[8] Dirk Bühler and S. W. Hamerich. Towards embedding voicexml applications through compilation. In *Workshop Dialogsysteme mit XML-Technologien, Berliner XML Tage*, Berlin (Germany), October 2004.

[9] Dirk Bühler and M. Riegler. Integrating dialogue management and domain reasoning. In *10th International Conference on Speech and Computer (SPECOM)*, Patras (Greece), October 2005.

[10] L Carter, L Stockmeyer, and M Wegman. The complexity of backtrack searches. In *STOC '85: Proceedings of the seventeenth annual ACM symposium on Theory of computing*, pages 449–457, New York, NY, USA, 1985. ACM.

[11] G. Ferguson, J. Allen, Bradford W. Miller, Eric K. Ringger, and Teresa Sikorski Zollo. *Dialogue Systems: From Theory to Practice in TRAINS-96*, pages 347–376. Handbook of Natural Language Processing. Marcel Dekker, New York, 2000.

[12] Antonio J. Fernández, Maria Teresa Hortalá-González, Fernando Sáenz-Pérez, and Rafael del Vado Vírseda. Constraint functional logic programming over finite domains. *CoRR*, abs/cs/0601071, 2006.

[13] Matthew Horridge, Sean Bechhofer, and Olaf Noppens. Igniting the owl 1.1 touch paper: The owl api. In Christine Golbreich, Aditya Kalyanpur, and Bijan Parsia, editors, *OWLED*, volume 258 of *CEUR Workshop Proceedings*. CEUR-WS.org, 2007.

[14] Yasunari Obuchi, Eric Nyberg, Teruko Mitamura, Scott Judy, Michael Duggan, and Nobuo Hataoka. Robust dialog management architecture using voicexml for car telematics systems, 2005.

[15] Barbara M. Smith. Constraint programming in practice: Scheduling a rehearsal. Technical report, APES, September 2003.

Intelligent Environments 2009
V. Callaghan et al. (Eds.)
IOS Press, 2009

doi:10.3233/978-1-60750-034-6-57

The Augmented Dorfladen – Interacting with Real and Virtual Products in Instrumented Shelves

Michael SCHMITZ[a], Elena MININA[b] and Homeira QURAISCHY[b]

[a] *DFKI GmbH, Saarbrücken, Germany*
[b] *Saarland University, Saarbrücken, Germany*

Abstract. This work describes a multimodal product information and comparison system designed for a rural corner store (the so called *Dorfladen*). Such a Dorfladen only provides a limited assortment, which we extend with virtual items on embedded displays, allowing customers to inspect and select unavailable products along their real world shopping activities for later ordering. We present the design and implementation of the system prototype and discuss the main results of a formal user study evaluating the user interface, which combines tangible interaction and natural language dialogues to interact with real and virtual products in one instrumented space.

Keywords. Tangible User Interface, Multimodal Interaction, Shopping Assistant

1. Introduction

The work at hand was conducted to provide innovative and unconventional ideas to state government measures that attempt to increase the attractiveness and quality of living in selected villages in order to counteract a development, which is recognized in many European countries. Particularly younger generations are shifting away from the countryside towards larger cities, which does not only implicate a demographic shift towards a society of elder in rural areas, but also results in increased difficulties to economically sustain infrastructure such as public transport and to occupy vacant buildings, which wear down over time. All these consequences amplify that villages become less attractive as an economic, social and cultural space - a closed loop that has to be interrupted. Governments commonly counteract on an architectural dimension, typically restoring historic public and private buildings, refurbishing the market square to preserve or recreate the traditional atmosphere of the place or restructuring the landscape. But now, a new approach was to mandate computer scientists and designers to implement new and unconventional, technology driven prototypes in selected villages. The concept of our system constitutes an attempt to counteract the increased close-downs of small grocery stores (also called *Dorfladen* - "village shop"), which offer the most basic products and a social centre to the villagers. Since such local shops can only offer a very limited assortment due to the small volume of the turnover and size of the shop (e.g. no fresh products that require cooling), most villagers have to use alternative sources nevertheless, e.g. shopping malls or large supermarkets in nearby cities. In this case all required goods are typically purchased in the city altogether, making it difficult for the local shopkeepers to get these commuters as customers at all [1], resulting in heavy circumstances to economically sustain the Dorfladen. An interdisciplinary group consisting of computer scientists, designers and architects developed a construction kit for a modern Dorfladen, including guidelines for the interior design and embedding a virtual extension of the local assortment, connected to an ordering system of cooperating supermarkets that consented to deliver accumulated orders to the shop on a regular basis. Screens distributed in the shop display all products that are available to order and that are of the same category as of those placed in the associated shelf (see Fig. 1). As opposed to e.g. home-ordering, this approach does not only supply villagers with a variety of otherwise unavailable goods, but also preserves and sustains the social importance of the location by strengthening the store as a central place for the community and tying customers to the shop. As a positive side-effect shopkeepers will get a better insight to the real needs of their customers as they can overview all orders, such that it is possible to adjust the local repertory, potentially decreasing the need to order from external partners.

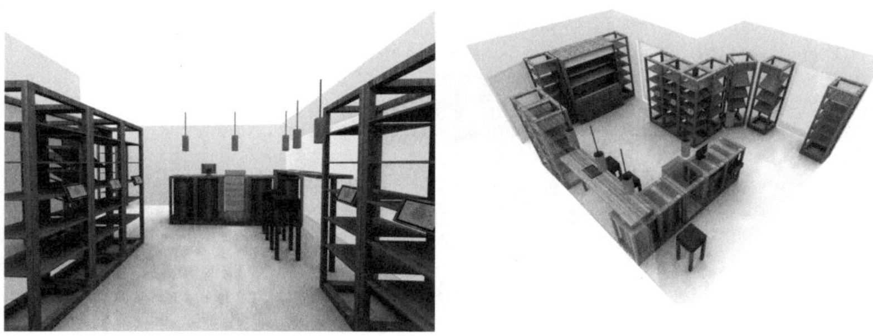

Figure 1. Interior design sketches of a Dorfladen

In this work we describe the complete development cycle of an assistance system that supports customers to inspect and compare *real* (locally available) and *virtual* (remote) products in order to support the shopping and ordering procedure with an intuitive interface. It blends tangible interaction with both real world products in a shelf and visually represented virtual products on touch-screens attached to shelves. The actual ordering and payment process is not covered by the prototypical implementation, this work focuses on customer activities regarding product inspection and selection.

The structure of this paper is as follows: We will first cover related work in this field, then describe the requirement analysis and design, followed by a description of the prototype implementation and evaluation. We conclude with a summary and outlook on future work.

2. Related Work

Shopping is a common activity online and in physical stores. A general practice in a physical store is to search the inventory for items of interest, select a few for comparison and examine them to decide which, if any, to purchase. Recent years have seen a rise in the popularity of online shopping. A large number of Internet based product comparison agents have been proposed in research [12][13][14] followed by many successful commercial comparison services. These systems search only among registered online retailers and lack the possibility to link and explore online and offline market products in the same space. The implementation of such a link requires not only new business models but also new interaction concepts. A RFID (Radio Frequency Identification) based business model for seamless shopping network has been proposed by [11], whereas our research aims towards an integrated interaction concept for real (e.g. realized with RFID) and virtual (online or remote) products in one space.

RFID based customer support is a trend not only followed by academic research groups, but it is also investigated by actors of the industry sector. For instance the *METRO Group RFID Innovation Center* formulated the goal to push innovations in the future of retail and realized (among other systems) a RFID based information kiosk at the point-of-sale, providing customer support and a solution for automated payment. The user interfaces were generally not in focus of these efforts and remain rather rudimentary - often only allowing customers to place items on the RFID antenna, which triggers the visual display of product information.

One prominent example of academic research in the field of multimodal interaction with products in instrumented environments is the *MobileShopAssist (MSA)* [9]: Besides item selection based on RFID equipped shelves this system also provides various interaction modalities on a PDA/Smartphone, which can be utilized to perform product inspection and comparison tasks. Two kinds of gesture inputs are defined in this work, which we will also adopt in the terminology of our work: *Intra-Gesture* refers to the interaction with virtual products and occurs when a user touches a virtual product on the touch-screen. *Extra-Gesture* refers to the selection of real products equipped with RFID tags, by picking them up from the shelf. The main difference of that work to the system proposed in this paper is the fact that users are required to bring their personal mobile device. Furthermore, the MSA allows quite complex combinations of modalities but only accepts comparison requests for exactly two products. Another conceptual difference is that the products displayed on the handheld device are not meant to complement the existing assortment with additional items but instead show the same products, such that the user can chose whether to operate with real items or their visual representations. The main goal of the work described in this paper is to seamlessly blend interaction with virtual and real products and provide a consistent and simple user interface to both kinds of products in the same space.

3. Requirement Analysis and System Design

Literature review and brainstorming sessions were the initial activities to define the goals and scope of this project. As a basis for the requirement analysis we conducted a pre-study in the target region by handing out questionnaires to villagers. The goals were to verify our assumptions regarding the complex of problems related to the Dorfladen and to identify necessary features of the ordering system and its interface. From these answers we could confirm that our respondents heavily depend on large supermarkets in nearby cities, while at the same time the majority acknowledges the importance of a Dorfladen and supports an extension of the Dorfladen with some kind of a central ordering mechanism. According to the questionnaire results such a system should support different kinds of comparisons to guide customers through the selection and ordering process, while using it should certainly be intuitive and simple –

moreover, a speech interface appeared to be desirable. The fear of complicated operation, expressed by some respondents, emphasized the importance of an easy interface in this project. Therefore, we decided to combine tangible interaction with natural language dialogues and created, by definition, a multimodal user interface [2]. Considering the rather broad age range of the target user group, the choice of more than one input modality allows the user to some extent to adjust the interaction mode not only to the situational context but also to their personal preferences and needs [5].

Our system comprises the in- and output-modalities speech, gesture, visual and auditive output. Within our system gesture input corresponds to the selection of products, whereby the terms *Intra-* and *Extra-Gesture* refer to the gestures selecting virtual or real products as described in Section 2. When the user interacts with the system and starts e.g. a comparison, visual output is always displayed on a nearby screen. In addition the system generates spoken output, but - aiming at coherent, symmetric multimodality [7] - only if the user performed speech input.

Two **main functions** comprise the interactive functionality of the prototype, product inspection and comparison: The **product inspection** function supports customers to inspect single products by displaying basic product information such as the price and nutrition facts in a consistent fashion.

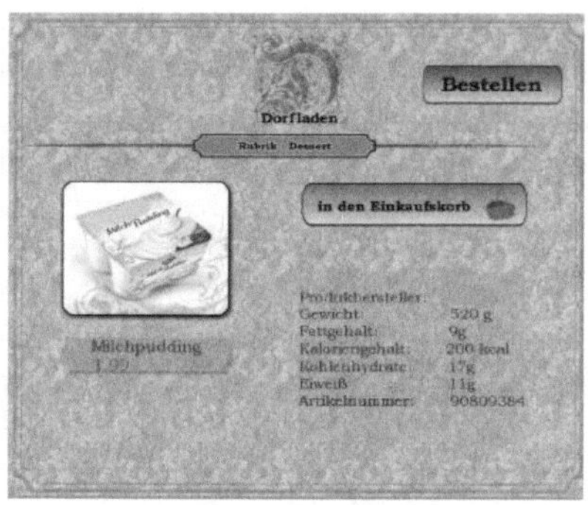

Figure 2. Product inspection output.

To request information about a real product the user merely has to pick up the product from the shelf. Afterwards all of the product information is listed on the screen (see Fig. 2) as a visual response. Large letters help elderly customers who have difficulties in reading the original food packages. Whereas information about real products is often redundant, since it is printed on the product itself, virtual products are not present and require the use of this function to acquire additional information. Selecting a virtual product happens through touching its picture on the screen, which results in the same response as if a real product were selected (Fig. 2).

In order to accelerate the process of finding the right product we wanted to enable the **comparison** of more than just two products: Currently the system is able to let customers compare up to four products at the same time, a limit due to graphical layout reasons in the evaluated version of the prototype. In this comparison, real and virtual products can be arbitrarily mixed. The prototype is built to handle two kinds of comparisons: With *tangible selection* users can select virtual items by touching their pictures on the screen and real items by taking them out of the shelf. Visual output as in Fig. 3 (left) is rendered. *Tangible selection complemented by spoken specification*: If a user, for example, wants to find out, which products contains the least amount of fat, speech can be used to specify this request. The visual response will be complemented (bold font and green marker) to indicate the product that complies to the request (see Fig. 3 (right). Furthermore speech output is generated.

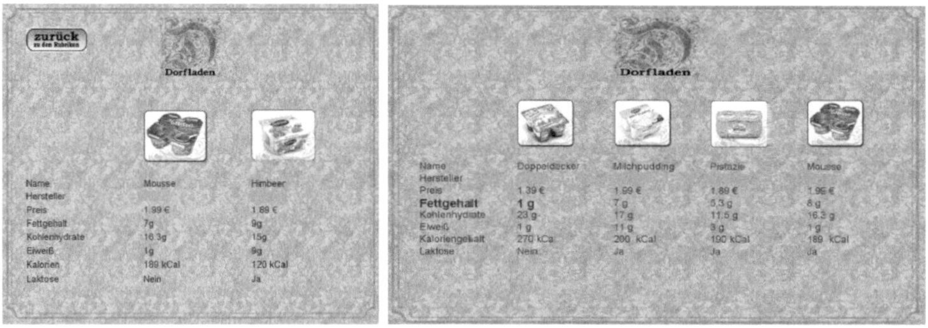

Figure 3. Product comparison output after tangible selection (left) and after speech input (right).

The following example interaction illustrates how four products are compared with speech input: The User touches three virtual products one after another and takes out one real product, at the same time she asks *"Which product has the least amount of fat?"*. The system displays the response as a comparison, listing all selected products with their attributes. The answer is marked with the green point (see Fig. 3 (right)) and the system renders the utterance: "*The product xyz has the least amount of fat, it contains 1 gram.*". More details about the pre-study and the system design are covered by [8].

4. User Study

We conducted a user study to evaluate the ease of use and the user acceptance of the developed prototype. The research questions posed were as follows: How do users perceive the ease of system use for inspection and comparison of real and virtual products in the same space? How intuitive is the use of various interaction modalities? We observed the user interacting with the system and handed out questionnaires.

The **participants** were solicited by an invitational e-mail and random personal invitation at meeting points nearby the research laboratory to test the prototype. The respondents were 19 potential users between 16 and 51 years old. Regarding their gender distribution 8 of them were female and 11 male. The majority of participants live in small villages nearby the research laboratory. None of participants met the evaluation team members or interacted with this system or a similar one before. All of them have at most average computer user skills and are native speakers of standard German language. They do not suffer from any disabilities.

The **prototype** is built on a client-server architecture such that multiple shelves in a store could be efficiently equipped in a real-life scenario. Clients would be located on a PC at each shelf and handle input recognition as well as output rendering, while one server connected through Ethernet interprets and fuses user input, plans and triggers the output generation, holds the product database and also interfaces with ordering and payment systems. However, one client is sufficient for the purpose of evaluating the interface. This client was installed on the same machine as the server. The client consists of 4 modules: A Speech Recognition module (NUANCE Naturally Speaking 8.51), the Graphical User Interface module based on JAVA/Swing and the RFID module, which monitors the presence of products. In addition, a Speech Synthesis module (Carnegie Mellon University FreeTTS 1.2) produces a real-time speech output. The server hosts a MySQL Database, which stores all product data that is necessary to generate the system output. Furthermore, a Fusion component interprets user input and forwards the results to the system's Rule Engine, which handles incoming requests and manages the response of the server to the client. The experimental setup also included a touch enabled display (Elo 2639L), a RFID-antenna (Feig MR 100) integrated into the shelf, a head-set (Hama CS-471) and RFID-tags complying to ISO 15693 attached to each product. The current prototype assumes that each shelf in a store would hold items of one category (e.g. desserts or vegetables) and one display, which initially shows images of the products of the same category that are not physically available. This way the exposition of virtual products enriches the assortment of the physical store. The evaluation setup included a shelf with various desserts and additional virtual products of the same type. The user study took place in a calm room with no visual or auditory inferences in a research laboratory established for the development and evaluation of innovative retail systems[1]. For further details about the prototype implementation and utilized hardware please refer to [10].

The **procedure** of each evaluation session consisted of four main steps: After a brief introduction to the purpose of the system and demonstration of unimodal and multimodal interaction as well as short explanation concerning the aim and the structure of the questionnaire, the users were asked to interact with the system by following the tasks listed in the questionnaire. The users answered a block of questions after finishing each task. All sessions were supervised by the same person in the same manner.

The **questionnaire** was divided into three categories. First, questions related to particular interaction tasks. Second, the user's overall impression related questions. Third, personal user information questions. Further, the interaction task focused questions were grouped by their complexity regarding the combination of real and virtual products as well as the use of specific modalities. This way the users could proceed from simple to more complex tasks. First they were asked to interact only with real and then only with virtual products (in both cases with maximum of four products using modality of their choice). After completion of one task, the participants were asked to answer the related block of questions. The second step of the study focused on comparison of real and virtual products in- or excluding the use of speech input. The last task involved all products and modalities, from which the participants could choose the most preferred ones. Closed questions were designed to be answered by ticking on an ordinal scale with possible answers, basically concerning the ease of system use and helpfulness. One last open question for each task provided users the opportunity to share their specific ideas, reflections and concerns related to the particular task. Since the participants of the study showed great interest and engagement, we received a lot of answers to this question type.

---

[1] IRL – Innovative Retail Laboratory (http://www.dfki.de/irl/)

Summing up the **results**, the user study revealed that a comparison of real (100%), virtual (95%) and, finally, real and virtual (84%) products supported by the prototype is easy to conduct[2]. These results show a slight decrease in the ease of system use caused by the shift to the interaction that involves virtual products. However, the users liked the intra-gesture (pointing on the touch screen) as well as graphical and speech output. A few participants noted that the use of extra-gesture (initiating product inspection and comparison involving real products by taking these out of the shelf) can be disturbing in some cases. Most test users (84%) considered spoken language input for the comparison of a real and a virtual product as easy to use. The usefulness of product comparison function in general was underlined by the vast majority of respondents (90%). In addition, 95% of users reported that they enjoyed using the system. Finally, 90% of respondents stated that they will definitely use such a system in the future. A more detailed discussion of user feedback can be obtained in [4], the questionnaire and complete results of the user study can be found in [10].

5. Conclusions and Outlook

In this paper we described the project outline, methodology, requirement analysis, the actual design and implementation of a fully working prototype of a shopping assistant for product inspection and comparison. In addition we presented the main results of a user study evaluating the user interface with the target user group. Our novel concept virtually extends limited assortments of small corner stores and allows consistent interaction with both real products residing in the shelf and virtual products, which can be purchased through ordering. The multimodal user interface was designed for simple and intuitive use, targeting at rural communities.

The system requirements study revealed that potential users are interested in comparison of real and virtual products in all combinations. They also emphasized the importance to be provided with an easy to use interface. Furthermore, more than a half of the respondents would expect natural language as an input modality. According to these feature requests and interface constraints, the results of the final user study suggest that the developed prototype successfully met the identified requirements and thus represents a significant step towards designing intuitive interaction with real and virtual products in the same instrumented space. However, to become a successful market-ready system, it is essential to develop an appropriate business model and to accomplish adjustments of the prototype through close collaboration of business administration experts and software engineers. In addition, in a real life setting the conversational interfaces have the disadvantage that they could be erroneous due to ambiguous speech input or noisy environment. The empirical results obtained by [6] have shown that the use of eye gaze improves speech recognition performance and can compensate for some problems caused by recognition errors. In our case, the improvements in interpretation of object references gained via incorporating eye-gaze can allow the system to make fewer unexpected and erroneous responses in a real life setting. Besides technical improvements we will further investigate differences in interaction preferences of distinct user subgroups, e.g. differentiated by age classes. These research steps will gain insights into how tangible interaction with real and

[2] Here and further the statistical data indicate the percentage of participants who selected +2 and +1 in an ordinal 5-point scale from +2 to -2.

virtual products can be designed in a user-adaptive way. Another opportunity for further research is to investigate to which extent user-adaptive product presentation and comparison can be supported by the results of cognitive consumer research [3]. It is essential in order to reduce the cognitive complexity in case of increasing variety and complexity of products and assist the users in achieving their goal to make the best possible buying decision.

Acknowledgements

This work is partially funded by the Saarland State Ministry for Environment and the German Research Foundation (DFG). We also like to thank the School of Fine Arts Saarbrücken for their cooperation, namely Prof. Burkhard Detzler and Stephan von Prümmer.

References

[1] O. Kühne, H. Zweck, T. Gross, *Plan zur Entwicklung des ländlichen Raums im Saarland,* Technischer Bericht, Saarländisches Ministerium für Umwelt, Illingen, 2005.

[2] M. T. Maybury, W. Wahlster, *Readings in Intelligent User Interface,.* Morgan Kaufmann Publishers, San Francisco, 1998.

[3] E. Minina, *Cognitive Approach to the Design of a User-Adaptive Interface for an Intelligent Product Consulting System*, In Proceedings of the IADIS International Conference on Intelligent Agents and Systems. Amsterdam, Netherlands, 2008.

[4] E. Minina, M. Schmitz, H. Quraischy, *Evaluating Tangible Interaction with Real and Virtual Products – User Feedback Results*, In Proceedings of the IADIS International Conference on Interfaces and Human Computer Interaction. Algavre, Purtugal, 2009.

[5] S. Oviatt, *Multimodal Interfaces*, In Sears, A., Jacko, J. A. The Human-Computer Interaction Handbook: Fundamentals, Evolving Technologies, and Emerging Applications. Lawrence Erlbaum Association, Mahwah, N.J., 2003.

[6] Z. Prasov, Y. J. Chai, *What's in a Gaze? The Role of Eye-Gaze in Reference Resolution in Multimodal Conversational Interfaces*, In Proceedings of the International Conference on Intelligent User Interfaces. Maspalomas, Canary Islands, Spain, 2008.

[7] W. Wahlster, *Towards Symmetric Multimodality: Fusion and Fission of Speech, Gesture, and Facial Expression*, In Proceedings of the German Conference on Artificial Intelligence. Springer, Berlin, Heidelberg, 2003.

[8] M. Schmitz, H. Quraischy, *Tangible Interaction with Real and Virtual Products: Designing a Shopping Assistant for Rural Communities,* In Proceedings of the 3rd International Conference on Tangible and Embedded Interaction (Cambridge, United Kingdom, February 16 - 18, 2009), 209-212, ACM, New York, NY, 2009.

[9] R. Wasinger, O. Jacobs, *Integrating Intra and Extra Gestures into a Mobile and Multimodal Shopping Assistant*, In Proceedings of the International Conference on Pervasive Computing. Springer, Berlin, Heidelberg, 2005.

[10] H. Quraischy, *Multimodale Interaktion mit virtuellen und realen Objekten am Beispiel eines Einkaufsassistenten für ländliche Ortschaften*, A Thesis Submitted to Saarland University, Saarbrücken, Germany. In Partial Fulfilment of the Requirements for the Degree of Master of Science in Computer Science.

[11] K.J. Lee, Y.H. Seo, Design of a RFID-Based Ubiquitous Comparison Shopping System, In Gabrys B., Howlett R.J., Jain L.C., Knowledge-Based Intelligent Information and Engineering Systems, Part I, LNAI 4251,1267-1283. Springer, Berlin, Heidelberg, 2006.

[12] B. Krulwich, *The BargainFinder Agent, Comparison Price Shopping on the Internet*, In Willliams, J., Bots and Other Internet Beasties, SAMS.NET, 1996.

[13] N. Kushmerick, D. Weld, B. Doorenbos, *Wrapper Induction for Information Instruction*, In Proceedings of the International Conference on Artificial Intelligence. Nagoya, 1997.

[14] S.-T. Yuan, A. Liu, Next-Generation Agent-enabled Comparison Shopping, *Expert Systems with Applications* **18/4** (2000), 283-297.

Special Session on Awareness Systems

Intelligent Environments 2009
V. Callaghan et al. (Eds.)
IOS Press, 2009

doi:10.3233/978-1-60750-034-6-67

Social connectedness: concept and measurement

VAN BEL, D. T. [a, 1], SMOLDERS, K. C. H. J. [a], IJSSELSTEIJN, W. A. [a], & DE KORT, Y. A. W. [a]
[a] *Human Technology Interaction Group, Eindhoven University of Technology, P.O. Box 513, 5600 MB, Eindhoven, The Netherlands.*
Correspondence: Daniel van Bel, Email: D.T.v.Bel@tue.nl

Abstract. Social connectedness, i.e. the experience of belonging and relatedness between people, is a central concept in understanding and evaluating communication media, in particular awareness systems. A generic measure based on this construct can support the design of such systems. The current paper describes the construction of two questionnaires for the measurement of this concept. These questionnaires were subsequently applied in survey studies in order to establish the structure of the concept and to identify the items that are suited for the measurement of its dimensions. One questionnaire was subjected to an initial validation. We conclude with some preliminary suggestions regarding (design) approaches to foster social connectedness.

Keywords. Awareness systems, social connectedness

1. Social connectedness

The ever-extending palette of communication tools, such as telephone, text messaging, email, instant messaging, online communities, and awareness systems has broadened our communication horizon significantly. An important outcome of the use of these communication technologies is the enhancement of a feeling of belonging and relatedness [1]. In light of this a theoretical construct is needed that is amenable to an operationalization that allows for sensitive and time discriminant measurement of subtle changes in the subjective experience of belonging and relatedness resulting from the use and introduction of different communication systems. To this end we reviewed relevant literature from social psychology and communication sciences pertaining to feelings of belonging and closeness, arriving at the concept of *Social connectedness*. We define social connectedness as a short-term experience of belonging and relatedness, based on quantitative and qualitative social appraisals, and relationship salience [2]. The subjective experience of belonging lies at the core of the construct of social connectedness, which has been designed to capture social experiences originating from recent interactions and provision of awareness information. Whereas the appraisals involve the satisfaction with one's social situation [3], relationship salience captures thinking of others and the feeling of being together outside of social contact [4]. Through emphasizing short-term social information, social connectedness

---

[1] Corresponding Author.

intends to capture social experiences originating from recent interactions and provision of awareness information.

Thus, the concept addresses a broad scope of short-term transient social experiences originating from mediated and unmediated interactions and the mediated provision of awareness information (i.e. information about other people, including information about their whereabouts, mood, activities, and availability for contact) [4]. Two types of social connectedness have been identified. Social connectedness at the overall level pertains to one's whole social network, while social connectedness at the individual level is the feeling regarding a particular person. This differentiation is relevant, because some communication applications may focus on social experiences that are based on one-on-one communication (e.g. text messaging), while others affect the feeling of connectedness with one's larger social network (e.g. Facebook).

More and more advanced communication technologies, in particular awareness systems, are being developed that aim to foster a feeling of belonging and relatedness. However, up until now, the testing of such applications has mainly been restricted to acceptance and usability, while the social effects of such applications have only been tested in an ad hoc qualitative fashion. This stems from a lack of generic instruments to assess these social outcomes, which we believe hampers the development of these applications, as designer choices cannot be systematically compared and evaluated. A generic measure that addresses this can help to gain knowledge about the effectiveness of communication tools in serving the affective needs of communicating parties. This provides insight in how communications systems can be improved in this regard, thereby supporting the systematic and explicit design of such systems.

The current paper describes the construction of two questionnaires for the measurement of social connectedness (one at the individual and one at the overall level) based on its theoretical conceptualization. These questionnaires are applied separately in two survey studies, in order to determine the structure of the concept and to identify of the items that are suited for the measurement of its dimensions. The measure of social connectedness at the individual level is subjected to an initial validation.

2. Measurement of social connectedness

From the conceptualization of social connectedness flow a number of requirements for its measurement:

- Two measures of social connectedness are needed: one at the individual level and one at the overall level;
- All the relevant aspects of social connectedness should be captured, including qualitative and quantitative social appraisals, and relationship salience;
- A short-term time frame should be used.

We generated a pool of items reflecting all the different aspects of social connectedness we identified in our conceptualization. The *UCLA Loneliness Scale* [5], the *Wittenberg Loneliness Scale* [6], the *Affective Benefits and Costs of Communication Questionnaire* [4], the *Sternberg Intimacy Scale* [7], and the *Subjective Closenes Index* [8] served as sources of inspiration for the wordings of items. Relationship salience involves experiences such as the sense of being in touch, presence-in-absence [9], and experiential outcomes of "social snacking" [10]. To capture such experiences we generated items that capture thinking of others and the feeling of being together outside of social contact.

The social appraisals are evaluations regarding one's social situation. Given the subjective nature of this experience, it involves the satisfaction with one's social situation and not objective information regarding one's social situation as such (e.g. the number of hours spent with others). In the measurement of the qualitative appraisals of social relationships we included feelings of closeness, feelings of involvement in each others' lives, knowledge of each other's thoughts and feelings, having the same world views, and sharing experiences. The quantitative aspects refer to the satisfaction with both the size of one's social network and with the amount of social interaction. A series of pretests resulted in a set of 29 items for the measurement of connectedness at the individual level and a set of 37 items for the measurement of connectedness at the overall level.

We developed a set of items that were used for the measurement of social connectedness both at the individual and the overall level. The items in the questionnaire at the individual level held the name of a specific person. The items in the overall level measure referred to "people in my social network". Only social connectedness at the overall level holds the quantitative dimensions, because it also pertains to one's whole social network, while social connectedness at the overall level does not. The response scales were as follows: (1) completely disagree, (2) disagree, (3) somewhat disagree, (4) neither agree ncr disagree, (5) somewhat agree, (6) agree, and (7) completely agree[2]. Following [11] we instructed participants to hold in mind how they felt during the past two weeks to achieve a transient framing. Our participants received the following instruction: "This questionnaire is about how you experience your social relationship and social contacts with [name of a person/people in your social network] in the last two weeks. With contacts we mean conversations/communication in each others' company or through media (telephone, chat, email, text messaging, etc.)."

3. Survey studies

We administered each questionnaire to two separate samples through surveys. This resulted in two data sets on which we performed factor analyses to determine the dimensional structure of social connectedness. We first performed a primary factor analysis on all the items. The factors yielded by this we subjected to a secondary factor analysis (hierarchical factor analysis) to establish main dimensions that lie at an overarching level[3].

3.1 Social connectedness at the individual level

The questionnaire on social connectedness at the individual level was completed by 174 participants. Half of the participants rated their social connectedness toward a distant acquaintance, while the other half rated their social connectedness toward a friend. The purpose of this was to compare between these two conditions. Higher scores in the fiend condition would provide preliminary support for the validity of the

---

[2] Some items had other response formats: see bottom of Table 1.

[3] See [12] for a complete description of the statistical procedure and detailed results of the factor analyses.

construct. Participants logged on to a server, on which they responded to the items. At the start participants were instructed to take either a close friend or a distant acquaintance in mind and input the name of this person. The software was thus programmed that this name appeared in the survey questions. On average, participants took about 5 minutes to complete the questionnaire. Movie ticket vouchers were raffled amongst the participants as a reward.

We found two main dimensions in the hierarchical factor analysis: the *Sense of sharing and involvement* and *Dissatisfaction with contact quality*. The results from the primary factor analysis are summarized in Table 2. The first main dimension contained four sub-dimensions: *Relationship salience, Shared understandings, Knowing each others' experiences* and *Feelings of closeness*. The second main dimension only consisted of *Dissatisfaction with contact quality*. As can be seen in Table 1, T-tests show that all dimensions in the friend condition were significantly higher than in the distant acquaintance condition.

3.2 Social connectedness at the overall level

Using a paper and pencil format, the questionnaire on social connectedness at the overall level was completed by 215 participants. On average, participants took about 5 minutes to complete the questionnaire. They received a candy bar as a reward. We found two main dimensions in the hierarchical factor analysis: the *Sense of sharing and involvement* and *Social appraisals*. The findings of the primary factor analysis are outlined in Table 3. The first main dimension consisted of three sub-dimensions: *Relationship salience, Shared understandings*, and *Knowing each others' experiences*. The second dimension also consisted of three sub-dimensions: *Satisfaction with contact quantity, Dissatisfaction with contact quantity*, and *Dissatisfaction with contact quality*.

Table 1: Results T-tests on the dimensions[a]

	Acquaintance		Friend		T-value[b]
	M	*SD*	*M*	*SD*	
1. Relationship salience	-.32	1.15	.28	.96	3.64*
2. Dissatisfaction with contact quality	-.35	1.22	.30	.91	3.93*
3. Shared understandings	-.37	1.13	.32	.97	4.27*
4.Knowing each others' experiences	-.59	1.06	.52	.73	7.95*
5. Feelings of closeness	-.59	1.00	.51	.80	7.88*
I. Sense of sharing and involvement	-.67	1.07	.59	.83	8.58*
II. Dissatisfaction with contact quality	-.22	1.13	.19	.85	2.68*

[a] All variables are standardized
[b] Equal variances not assumed
*p-value < .05

Table 2: Specific Connectedness Dimensions: Factor Lcadings

1. *Relationship salience*					
Aside from our contact, I often feel "together" with X[a] somehow.	..73				
I often think of X.	..69				
Even when we are not in each others' company, I often feel "together" with X somehow.	..63				
I am often aware of my relationship with X.	..44				
2. *Dissatisfaction with contact quality*					
I derive little satisfaction from my contact with X (R).		80			
I feel that X does not understand me well (R).		70			
My contact with X feels superficial (R).		61			
3. *Shared understandings*					
I feel that X shares my interests and ideas.			.84		
I feel I have a lot in common with X.			.58		
I feel on the same wavelength with X.			.52		
4. *Knowing each others' experiences*					
I often know what X feels.				.83	
I often know what X thinks.				.77	
I feel that X often knows what I think.				.68	
I sense that X often knows what I feel.				.60	
5. *Feelings of closeness*					
In comparison with all your other relationships (with both men and women), how close is your relationship with X?					..82
In comparison with what you know of the relationships of other people (with both men and women), how close is your relationship with X?					..78
I feel I can talk about anything with X.					..74
I feel that X and I can communicate well with each other.					..67

(R) The items in the second and fourth factor are reverse coded

[a] X stands for the name of the person the participant put in

Table 3: Overall Connectedness Dimensions: Factor Loadings

1. Knowing the others' experiences						
I often know what people in my social network think.	.81					
I often know what people in my social network feel.	.50					
I am often aware of my relationships with people in my social network.	.47					
2. Dissatisfaction with contact quantity						
I would like to have a larger circle of friends(R).		.67				
I feel a lack of company (R).		.67				
I would like to have a close relationship with more people (R).		.66				
I feel a lack of contact with people in my social network (R).		.60				
I feel a lack of social relationships (R).		.51				
3. Satisfaction with contact quantity						
How satisfied are you with the number of people with whom you have social contact?			.81			
How satisfied are you with the number of contacts with the people in your social network?			.80			
How satisfied are you with the number of people in your social network?			.71			
How satisfied are you with the total amount of time that you have contact with people in your social network?			.54			
4. Dissatisfaction with contact quality						
The social contacts with people in my social network feel superficial (R).				.71		
My relationships with people in my social network feel superficial (R).				.51		
I derive little satisfaction from my social contacts (R).				.48		
5. Relationship salience						
Even when we are not in each others' company, I often feel "together" with people in my social network somehow.					.84	
Aside from our contact, I often feel "together" with people in my social network somehow.					.72	
I feel that people in my social network often think of me.					.56	
I often think of people in my social network.					.46	
6. Shared understandings						
I feel I have a lot in common with people in my social network.						.76
I feel on the same wavelength with people in my social network.						.61
I feel that people in my social network share my interests and ideas.						.59

(R) The items in the second and fourth factor are reverse coded

4. Discussion

The current paper describes the construction of two questionnaires for the measurement of social connectedness (one at the individual and one at the overall level) based on a theoretical conceptualization. These questionnaires were subsequently applied in two survey studies, in order to establish the structure of the concept and to identify the items that are suited for the measurement of its dimensions. The studies show a large overlap between the dimensional structures of the two constructs. The measure of social connectedness at the individual level was subjected to an initial validation. The data from our specific connectedness measure and its subscales showed that the scores in the friend condition were significantly higher. This provides preliminary support for the validity of the scale and its dimensions. We are currently validating the measure in experiments. Findings from a first experiment [13] add to the validity of our specific connectedness construct. More experimental and field research is needed to further establish the validity of both measures. In the current study a time frame of two weeks was used. However, depending on the goals of a particular study, different phrasings can be used, such as "at this moment", "today", or "this week".

Field studies using real applications in natural settings should provide feedback on concrete (prototype) design. At this point however, we would like to offer some preliminary suggestions regarding (design) approaches to foster social connectedness. Our concept and some preliminary findings seem to suggest that there are several ways to foster social connectedness. One inroad is the salience of social relationships by representing or reminding people of their social connection to one or more close others. By doing so people may feel connected to close others by thinking of them or through feelings of togetherness outside of actual contact. Another way is to heighten the satisfaction with one's social situation. This can be approached qualitatively by increasing feelings of closeness, shared understandings and the provision of information about each others' feelings and thoughts. A quantitative approach would require the enhancement of actual or perceived amount of social relationships and interactions one has. An application may for example nudge the user to communicate when he/she is alone and it may show how many contacts people actually have available.

The comprehensive dimensional approach of social connectedness allows for a differentiation of the social outcomes that various communication systems may have. These outcomes depend on the type of information that is relayed between people [14]. Pervasive awareness systems that use sensor data from intelligent environments may have specific effects depending on the information involved. Non-intentionally relayed information that is very basic (e.g. being at home or not versus one's feelings) probably has specific effects. The low intentionality involved with and the often limited nature of the information that can be relayed may restrict the feelings of connectedness it can evoke. Systems that focus on activity and availability may for example have a specific impact on the dimensions *Relationship salience* and *Sharing experiences*. If information regarding availability leads to more social contact, it may influence quantitative appraisals as well. To conclude, we believe that the social connectedness construct provides a uniquely theory-based, comprehensive and sensitive tool to advance the development of communication technology, and awareness systems in particular.

Acknowledgements

Support from the ASTRA project, funded under the European Community's IST programme, is gratefully acknowledged.

We thank Wouter van der Heijden and Saskia Maan for collecting the data, Martijn Willemsen for his help with programming the online survey and extracting the data from the server, and Antal Haans for his advice on the statistical analyses.

References

[1] Shklovski, I., Kraut, R. E., & Cummings, J. (2008). Keeping in touch by technology: Maintaining friendships after a residential move. In: *Proceedings of the 2008 CHI Conference* (pp. 807-816). New York: ACM Press.

[2] Van Bel, D. T., IJsselsteijn, W. A. & De Kort Y. A. W. (2009). Social Connectedness: Concept and requirements for measurement. *Under submission.*

[3] Baumeister, R. F., & Leary, M. R. (1995). The need to belong: Desire for interpersonal attachments as a fundamental human motivation. *Psychological Bulletin, 117*, 497-529.

[4] Van Baren, J., IJsselsteijn, W.A., Markopoulos, P., Romero, N., de Ruyter, B. (2004). Measuring Affective Benefits and Costs of Awareness Systems Supporting Intimate Social Networks. In: A. Nijholt, & T. Nishida, (Eds.), *Proceedings of 3rd workshop on social intelligence design. CTIT Workshop Proceedings Series WP04-02* (pp. 13-19).

[5] Russell, D., Peplau, L. A., & Cutrona, C. E. (1980). The revised UCLA loneliness scale: Concurrent and discriminant validity evidence. *Journal of Personality and Social Psychology, 39*, 472–480.

[6] Wittenberg, M. T. (1986). *Emotional and social loneliness: An examination of social skills, attributions, sex role, and object relations perspectives.* Unpublished doctoral dissertation, University of Rochester, NY.

[7] Sternberg, R. J. (1988). *Construct validation of a triangular theory of love.* Unpublished manuscript, Yale University, Department of Psychology.

[8] Berscheid, E., Snyder, M., & Omoto, A. M. (1989). The Relationship Closeness Inventory: Assessing the closeness of interpersonal relationships. *Journal of Personality and Social Psychology, 57*, 792-807.

[9] Howard, S., Kjeldskov, J., Skov, M. B., Garnoes, K., & Grünberger, O. (2006). negotiating presence-in-absence: Contact, Content and Context. In: *Proceedings of the 2006 CHI Conference* (pp. 909-912). New York: ACM Press.

[10] Gardner, W. L., Pickett, C. L., & Knowles, M. (2005). Social snacking and shielding: Using social symbols, selves, and surrogates in the service of belongingness needs. In: K. D. Williams, J. P. Forgas & W. Von Hippel (Eds.), *The social outcast: Ostracism, social exclusion, rejection, and bullying* (pp. 227-241). New York: Psychology Press.

[11] Gerson, A. C., & Perlman, D. (1979). Loneliness and expressive communication. *Journal of Abnormal Psychology, 88*, 258–261.

[12] Van Bel, D. T., Smolders, K. C. H. J., IJsselsteijn, W. A., & De Kort Y. A. W. (2009). The Social Connectedness Questionnaire. *Under submission.*

[13] Van Bel, D. T., Smolders, K. C. H. J., IJsselsteijn, W. A., & De Kort Y. A. W. (2009). I-sharing promotes Social Connectedness. *Under submission.*

[14] Markopoulos, P. (in press). A design framework for Awareness Systems. In: P. Markopoulos, B. De Ruyter, W. Mackay (Eds.), *Awareness Systems: Advances in Theory, Methodology and Design*. Berlin: Springer.

Intelligent Environments 2009
V. Callaghan et al. (Eds.)
IOS Press, 2009

doi:10.3233/978-1-60750-034-6-75

Ambient Media Services in Intelligent Environments

Bashar Altakrouri[a] and Andreas Schrader[b]
[a] *Lancaster University*
South Drive, Lancaster LA1 4WA UK
b.altakrouri@comp.lancs.ac.uk
[b] *ISNM – International School of New Media at the University of Luebeck*
Ratzeburger Allee 160, 23538 Luebeck, Germany
andreas.schrader@acm.org

Abstract. In this paper, a novel infrastructure, called Medient is proposed. The name "Medient" is constructed from "ambient" and "media". Medient is a service oriented architecture using web services to create context-aware multimedia services on mobile devices. We outline the technical approach using Bluetooth device detection and reverse AJAX push service creation. Results, usage showcases and a demo scenario are given for the Holstentor museum in Luebeck, Germany, as a typical example of a dense information environment with an increasing demand for contextualized exhibition services.

Keywords. Ubiquitous Computing, Context Awareness, AJAX, Museums, Contextualized Web Services, Mobile Learning

Introduction

Human activity usually needs to maintain awareness of the surrounding environment and the people acting and interacting within. With the proliferation of ubiquitous and pervasive computing technologies, intelligent environments can be designed to support context-aware services for individual and collaborative activities. With the help of sensors, the environment itself becomes aware of physical attributes like identity, location and activity of items and users in context. The resulting awareness systems vary greatly with different strategies for collecting, communicating, and displaying information for diverse purposes [17], but they usually rely on two main components: ubiquitous computing infrastructures and multimedia interfaces.

Most ubiquitous computing technologies impose a high level of complexity on the user, mainly because of their diverse applications, interaction techniques and device types. For intelligent environments to support social services and increase the users' awareness, new requirements should be investigated, one of which is the ability to provide convenient and smoothly accessible ubiquitous services. Consequently, intelligent environments have to avoid the complexity [4] and distraction that might occur due to the installation procedures. Whereas in certain scenarios, extensive introductions and time-consuming setup procedures might be appropriate, this is usually not the case for busy real-world environments. For example, museum visitors would not be willing to spend time to install software on their mobile devices before entering an exhibition.

Awareness systems usually also rely on rich multimedia interfaces for the creation of stimulating and engaging user experiences. Especially in content-rich environments with a high density of objects and related information, user generated content can be used as a means to enable shared user experiences. Typical activities include ranking, commenting, and annotating of artifacts in the environment. Since users are usually also not willing to learn new forms on interaction paradigms and interface metaphors, the design of interactive and social services on mobile devices is crucial for the success of context-aware services.

In this paper, we propose Medient as a new infrastructure for context-aware services in content-rich environments. Medient as a platform is targeted at making use of available, daily-used, inexpensive and lightweight portable and stationary technology without the need to install special applications on users' devices. Medient allows for simplified application development of mobile multimedia applications using web services and requires a minimal instrumentation of the environment.

In the next section we introduce the museum domain as an appropriate example for content-rich environments with a dedicated need for context-awareness. Afterwards, we introduce the Medient model and architecture. Finally, we apply our concept on museums as an example domain of context-rich environments and present the HolstenTour project as an example use case of Medient.

1. Towards ubiquitous media in museums

Multimedia supports diversity of channels for education, interpretation and documentation. It plays an important role for serving the social and cognitive functions of museums. Therefore, augmenting museum exhibits with digital multimedia content both as exploratory and interpretive factors, helps to realize important functional aspects of museum exhibitions. Combining this with a new navigation scheme based on visitor's navigation in the physical space can deliver an enjoyable and aesthetic as well as an educational experience. Museums carefully regard the visitors' experiences in the design of exhibitions. Currently, context information such as location tracking, visitors' identities, time and data measures are becoming accessible anywhere and at anytime [7]. Therefore, the visitors' context, which influences the perception of cultural artifacts, is given great attention and is assumed to be a cornerstone for the success or the failure of the visitor experience.

New ubiquitous and pervasive computing technologies may provide strong technological support for the main functions of museums [11] [17] as shown in Fig. 1b. Typically, those functions support the purposes of study. Education and enjoyment can be enhanced using context-aware technologies. Moreover, mobile devices have high potential to be the future platform for personal museum guidance [4].

1.1. Related Work

The International Council of Museums listed a number of multimedia usage scenarios in museum exhibitions in [6]. Exhibitions use multimedia to broaden the visitors' capabilities to understand the work of art, exhibited object or material by giving information that cannot be predicted or implied from the visual appearance of the work. Thus, currently, a vast usage of kiosks in museums as information points is noticed. However, the biggest challenge is the pervasive integration of technology in exhibitions.

By reviewing the functionality, goals and usage scenarios of some ubiquitous computing projects in museum related areas, different categories can be distinguished as: *Experience recording and retrieving*: the experience of the visitor is recorded by using different sensing technologies as in the Rememberer tool [9] and the Experience Catalog System (ECS) [15]. *Museum guidance systems*: providing visitors with the relevant information during the visit either visually or auditory as in Hippie [16]. *Explaining and establishing connection with exhibits*: establishing a connection with exhibits in the museum such as ImogI, Sotto Voce, Points of Departure, Antwerp, and C-Map project [7]. *Shared Experience*: visitors should be given the chance to contribute actively through user generated content (UCG) [14].

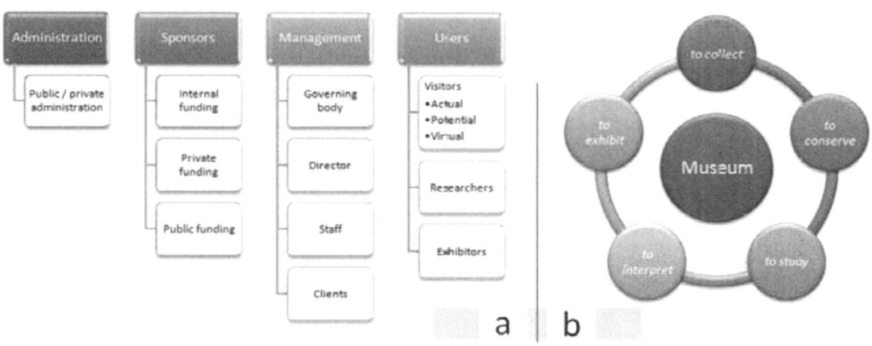

Figure 1. Museum Stakeholders (a) and functions (b)

1.2. Ubiquitous Media Services

Ubiquitous computing plays a major role for supporting and delivering multimedia in museums. Moreover, the main four principles of pervasive computing (decentralization, diversification, connectivity and simplicity as mentioned in [10]) fit the museum exhibition needs as outlined in [1].

Ubiquitous museums (U-Museums) could realize new forms of ubiquitous learning (U-Learning) by realizing context-aware media services inside the exhibition and considering the contexts of the user, the artifact, the scenario, etc.

In order to realize context-awareness, context acquisition using sensors is a key component of any pervasive museum infrastructure. Simple context information like time, date and temperature can be easily detected with simple sensors. On the other hand, cutting-edge technology provides advanced context parameters, like the user identity, location, orientation, etc. Higher level awareness factors (like presence of group members, activity level of visitors, etc.) can be derived from these atomic context parameters using algorithmic aggregation or application integration.

2. MEDIENT INFRASTRUCTURE

In this section we present Medient as a new infrastructure to support the development of ambient media services in context-rich environments. We outline our requirement specification, describe the architectural model, and illustrate typical Medient services.

2.1. Requirement Analysis

An extensive investigation of media usage in museums was performed based on literature review and observation in the target museum (see section IV in [1]). As a result, specific needs and expectations of stakeholders in the organizational structure of museums have been identified (Fig. 1a).

The main shared needs and motivation for these target groups can be described as equal access to information, equal participation possibilities in the system, intuitive and easy interaction with the system, reduced deployment complexity, and maximal usage benefits form available faculties, services, devices, etc.

From the visitors' point of view the system should leverage awareness of environmental aspects and peer visitor interaction. The focus is on educational and social aspects in order to enjoy the museum visit and to learn new things, to maximize the amount of relevant information about artifacts, to be notified of objects and exhibits of interest, to minimize the amount of interference that might be caused with the artifact by cautious use of technology and multimedia, and to allow for social interacting to share interest and to provide feedback channels with the museum, e.g. the visitor opinion about an exhibition.

2.2. Conceptual Model

The main goal of the Medient infrastructure is to enable and support the development of context-aware services. Fig. 2 illustrates the conceptual model. By separating aspects of context acquisition, service access and service presentation from the service development, application designers are supported to easily create context-aware services (for a detailed description, please see [1]).

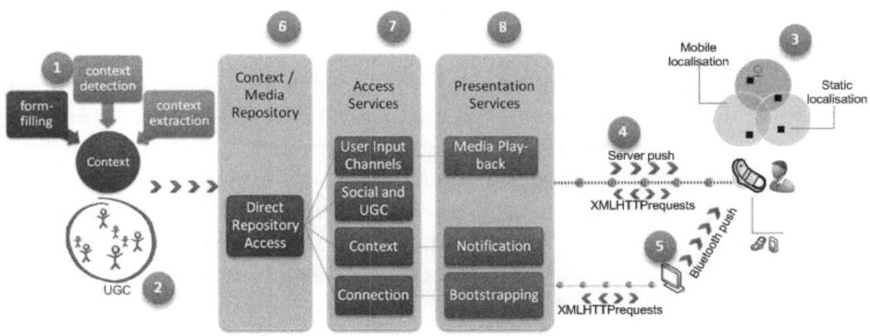

Figure 2. Medient Conceptual Model

By incorporating commonly used existing technologies, deployment costs are minimized and user's acceptance ratio is improved. Medient applications are based on web services using Asynchronous JavaScript and XML (AJAX) and support embedded multimedia. No prior installation of special software on the client device is needed and any mobile device hosting an AJAX supported web browser can be used.

2.3. Infrastructure Model

Fig. 3a illustrates the generic model of the infrastructure. Users can interact with the mobile context-aware application running as an interactive web service inside the AJAX enabled web browser on their personal mobile device (1). Detection of devices is realized with Bluetooth signal detection inside the Active Range (2).

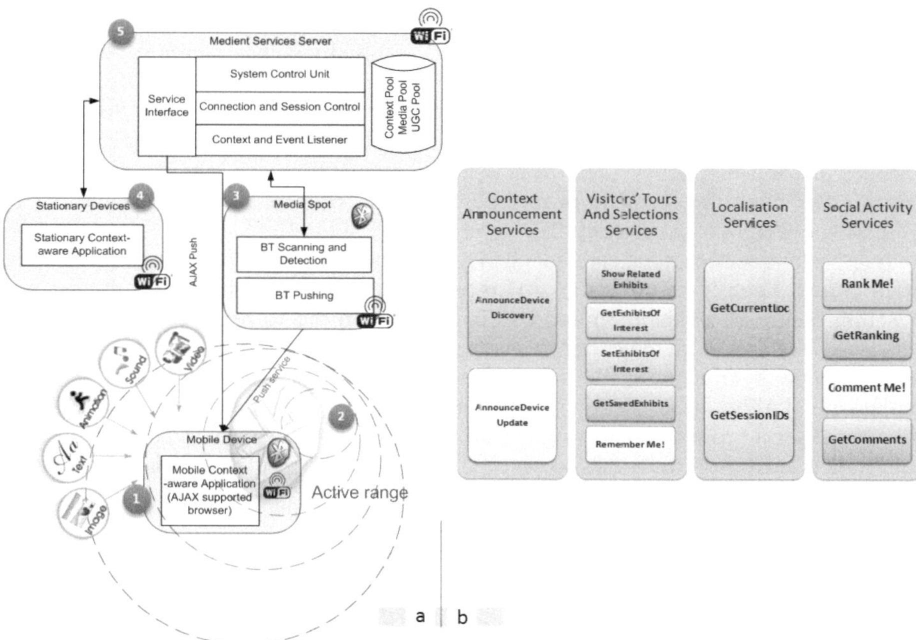

Figure 3. Medient Infrastructure Model

The detection and announcement of any new mobile device in range is done by the Media Spot (3), which actually runs a Medient discovery and services software (mobile localization). The communication with any mobile device is done by combining WLAN for a high bandwidth content channel and Bluetooth for near-by device detection, local Bluetooth data transfer, and messaging using Object Exchange (OBEX) Protocol. The Media Spot is able to push Bluetooth messages with integrated multimedia content to any registered mobile device in range. Environments can further be equipped with optional Stationary Devices (4). The stations are connected to the Medient Server via WLAN and can offer additional context-aware applications to users (stationary localization).

The Medient Server (5) is responsible for controlling the whole environment, keeping track of all acquired context information, establishing a wireless connection with each online mobile device registered in the system, and pushing content and events to the mobile client based on the user context. A Stationary Device with

Medient Bootstrapping Spot should be typically installed in the entrance area of any supported environment. Here, the user is introduced to the provided mobile services and bootstrapping procedures are performed. The bootstrapping is realized by real-time construction of a web page that redirects the mobile browser to the Medient AJAX web client. This step is performed via Bluetooth messaging.

2.4. Infrastructure Services

Fig. 3b illustrates the current implemented Medient infrastructure services, which can be classified into the following categories: First, Context Announcement Services are used by all context sensors to announce the users' locations. Second, Visitors' Tours and Selections Services are used by context-aware applications to display content based on the user selection and current context. Third, stationary devices acquire Localization Services to provide a personalized content based on the nearby devices. Often, mobile applications will use both tour and selection services combined with localization services for real-time location mapping and content delivery. Fourth, Social Activity Services provide functions to realize annotation and ranking services for active media items in the environment. The provided service set reflects the needs identified by evaluating different user groups [12].

Ubiquitous service zones are attached to the actual physical zones in the intelligent environment. Each zone covers a certain aspect of the environment (e.g. exhibit in a museum, booth on a fair, etc.) and can be tailored in the respective range of device detection. Medient implementation of the reverse AJAX technique allows the server to push information and control the client remotely [8]. Currently, Medient infrastructure implements Polling (the browser requests the server in regular intervals), Comet (allows the server to start answering the browser's request very slowly) and PiggyBack (the server waits for the next browser's request and sends the update within the response) [7].

3. Example Implementation - Holstentour

The HolstenTour project [13] was developed for one of the famous museums in Luebeck, Germany, called the "Museum Holstentor" [14]. The current prototype implementation is using some of the features of Medient. Awareness is currently reduced to objects and paths in the context, and does not yet support user awareness (but could be easily enhanced in the application, since the infrastructure already supports it).

The main idea behind HolstenTour was to develop a personalized tour in the museum based on the user selection and objects of interest. Different media files (text, video and audio) can be attached to different rooms in the museum. The media can be accessed through kiosk systems as stationary devices and PDAs as mobile devices. Snapshots of interactive mobile and stationary maps are shown in Figure 4.

The visitors can interact with the map on the kiosk and can select their tours. The touch screen enables visitors to select the elements of interest by pressing on them. This triggers a video, which depicts the journey from the museum to the place where the element is to be found in reality, illustrating the relation between the exhibit topic and the relevant location in town. At this stage, the visitors can compose their own tour guide by adding the selected elements to a bar at the bottom of the screen. A "Finish Selection" button takes the visitors to the final step in the selection process, where the selection is mapped to the mobile device placed on the kiosk. The visitors receive a Bluetooth SMS on the device and by accepting the message, the device browser is redirected to the customized museum's information portal page.

Figure 4. HolstenTour Project - Interactive Maps

The focus of the service then moves to the mobile device, where a map of the museum's inner structure is displayed. The spatial metaphor of the map used again in the mobile device is intended to provide the visitors with an orientation tool that allows them to navigate the physical museum according to their preferences. When the visitors moves from room to room, dynamic content is displayed in the form of web pages with embedded sound and textual information that change according to the location of the visitor in the museum.

4. Conclusions and future Work

This paper presents Medient as a novel infrastructure to provide context-aware ambient media services for context-rich environments. Medient supports mobile devices such as smart phones and PDAs as well as stationary devices, like kiosks, public screens, etc.

The main features of Medient are the support of minimal deployment and infrastructure costs by employing commonly used devices and off-the-shelf components, like Bluetooth sensors. The infrastructure requires only minimal instrumentation of the environment and does not require any installation of dedicated software on clients' devices. A working prototype implementation of a typical Medient application was implemented for the Holstentor museum in Luebeck. This prototype development has shown the possibility to develop Medient applications for intelligent environments easily and effectively. Finally, the system design considers and can be applied in other context-rich intelligent environments such as hospitals, university campus, company buildings, etc.

Acknowledgements

We would like to thank the ISNM students for their contribution to this research during the Ubiquitous Computing course at the ISNM. Special thanks go to Dr. Marcus Specht from the Open University of the Netherlands for instructing this work and for his valuable review and feedback. More information about Medient can be found in [1]. Details about the HolstenTour project can be found in [2] and [13].

References

[1] B. Altakrouri, "Ubiquitous Infrastructure for Contextualised Exhibition Services", Master Thesis at the International School of New Media, Luebeck, Germany, October 2007.
[2] B. Al Takrouri, K. Detken, C. Martinez, M.-K. Oja, S. Stein, L. Zhu and A. Schrader, "Mobile HolstenTour: Contextualized Multimedia Museum Guide", The 10th International Conference on Information Integration and Web-based Applications & Services (iiWAS2008), Linz, Austria, November 24-26, 2008.
[3] E. Bruns, B. Brombach, T. Zeidler and O. Bimber, "Enabling Mobile Phones to Support Large-Scale Museum Guidance", IEEE Multimedia, vol. 14, no. 2, April-June 2007, pp. 16 - 25.
[4] D. Carlson, "ALADIN: An Extensible Ubiquitous Computing Infrastructure." Master Thesis at the International School of New Media, Luebeck, Germany, June 2005.
[5] C. Croft, "The Twenty-first Century Museum and Gallery." The Museums, Libraries and Archives Council,http://www.mla.gov.uk/webdav/harmonise?Page/@id=73&Document/@id=18609&Section[@stateId_eq_left_hand_root]/@id=4332#ref.
[6] B. Davis, J. Trant and J. Starre, (Eds.) "Introduction to Multimedia in Museums." International Council of Museums (ICOM), Multimedia Working Group, September 1996.
[7] R. Dimitrios, T. Nikolaos and A. Nikolaos, "Context-based Design of Mobile Applications for Museums: a Survey of existing Practices." Proceedings of 7th Conference on Human-Computer Interaction with Mobile Devices and Services, Salzburg, Austria, 2005. pp. 153-160.
[8] E. Eozdag, A. Mesbah and A. Deursen, "A Comparison of Push and Pull Techniques for AJAX." Technical Report TUD-SERG-2007-016a, Software Engineering Research Group, Department of Software Technology, Delft University of Technology, The Netherlands, 2207.
[9] M. Fleck, M. Frid, T. Kindberg, E. O'Brien-Strain, R. Rajani and M. Spasojevic, "Rememberer: a Tool for Capturing Museum Visits." Proc. of the 4th International Conference on Ubiquitous Computing, Göteborg, Sweden, September 29 - October 1, 2002, pp. 48–55.
[10] U. Hansmann, L. Merk, M. Nicklous and T. Stober, "Pervasive Computing", Springer Professional Computing, 2nd edition, 2003, p. 17.
[11] H. Heide, "Interactive Dramaturgies: New Approaches in Multimedia Content and Design." Springer, Berlin, 2004.
[12] S. His, "The Electronic Guidebook: A Study of User Experiences using Mobile Web Content in a Museum Setting." Prof. of the IEEE Intl. Workshop on Wireless and Mobile Technologies in Education (WMTE), August 29-30, 2002.
[13] "HolstenTour project", http://www.isnm.de/projects/holstentour/.
[14] Museum Holstentor, Luebeck. http://www.luebeck.de/tourismus/kultur/museen/holstentor/info.html.
[15] R. Oppermann and M. Specht, "A Context-sensitive Nomadic Exhibition Guide." Proc. of 2nd Symposium on Handheld and Ubiquitous Computing, Bristol, UK, 2002.
[16] G. Howard, J. Pratty and M. Stapleton, "Storymaker: User-generated Content - Worthy or Worthwhile?" In: J. Trant and D. Bearman (eds.), Museums and the Web 2005 Proceedings, Toronto: Archives & Museum Informatics, March 31, 2005.
[17] P. Markopoulos, B. de Ruyter and W. Mackay, "Introduction to this Special Issue* on Awareness Systems Design", Special Issue of Human-Computer Interaction, Vol. 22, Numbers 1&2, 2007. http://www.eusai.net/docs/si-awareness-intro.pdf.
[18] A. Nakahara, K. Kumagai, Y. Sumi, M. Tsuchikawa, K. Kogure and K. Mase, "Experience Summarization in a Ubiquitous Environment." Proc. of the Sixth International Conference on Ubiquitous Computing, Nottingham England, September 7–10, 2004.
[19] O'Reilly, T. 2005. "What Is Web 2.0." http://www.oreillynet.com/pub/a/oreilly/tim/news/2005/09/30/what-is-web-20.html

Intelligent Environments 2009
V. Callaghan et al. (Eds.)
IOS Press, 2009

doi:10.3233/978-1-60750-034-6-83

Awareness for Fostering Serendipitous Interaction in Public Intelligent Environments

Ilaria CANOVA CALORI
Department of Computer and Information Science
Norwegian University of Science and Technology

Abstract. This paper presents possibilities offered by public intelligent environment to foster learning through serendipitous interaction among uncoupled users. Four possible situations of how serendipitous interaction may occur and lead to learning activities are presented. In these situations capturing the right information, modeling it and providing awareness information back to the users plays a major role. Therefore elements that make up this awareness information are presented and a model for fostering serendipitous interaction in public intelligent environments is also proposed.

Keywords. Serendipitous interaction, collaborative learning, intelligent environments, awareness in public spaces

Introduction

Public spaces, defined by Eriksson et al. [1] as "place open to all, free of charge", offer multiple opportunities for interaction and occasions for situated learning. The notion of situated learning has been introduced by Lave and Wenger [2] and describes learning as the outcome of interaction with the social and physical environment.

In recent years, a growing interest, starting from mobile and ubiquitous learning [3], has moved focus from more formal learning in the classroom, with pre-defined goals and planned activities, towards more emergent and student-led activities outside the classroom [4,5]. This situation is particularly advantageous when promoting contextualized learning experiences through *exploration* (e.g. by experiencing things at hand in real and authentic settings), *interaction* (e.g. with more experienced peers and experts in the field), and *serendipity* (e.g. when "human search for knowledge may occur by chance, or as by-product of the main task" [6] in unplanned, random and unexpected ways) [7].

Intelligent environments (hereof referred to as IE) offer the possibility to take advantage of the resources and people available in a space. IE can sense its inhabitants and the activities going on there and adapt to them to provide "services based upon user preferences and current environmental conditions" [8]. In this perspective, public IE can provide a dynamic configuration of devices, but also support dynamic social configurations, e.g. based on users' interests or co-location.

In this paper the possibilities offered by IEs to support learning in unplanned, emergent situations are presented. In particular the focus is on how to foster learning through serendipitous interaction in IEs, i.e. the ability of IEs to trigger unplanned interaction among uncoupled users (i.e. chance encounters that might not know each other). Uncoupled users will be able to get together and start collaborating thanks to awareness information provided by the IEs. Awareness has always been a central issue when supporting cooperation and collaboration, both in working [9-11] as in learning [12,13] and in other social settings [14]. Awareness plays a more relevant role when the environment is highly dynamic and unpredictable [10], like in public IEs.

Many research efforts have focused on providing awareness for serendipitous interaction within established groups of workers, friends, etc. [15,16] focusing on pre-existing social bonds rather than on interaction between uncoupled users. A few other examples aim in this direction. The systems proposed in [17] promote interaction among people that do not necessarily know each other. These systems are running on mobile phones and take advantage only of the social proximity of people. The space and the resources that may be available there are not taken into consideration. On the other hand, Ludvigsen [18] proposed a conceptual framework for interaction in "social spaces" (more details in Session 1) and the iFloor system. This system aimed at connecting library users and trigger discussions as well as introducing new ways of finding materials in the library. This system was based on interactivity, users could post and read questions from other users, and browse them using a shared cursor operated through the physical position of users. Here the users were playing a more active role taking the initiative, rather than the system itself. The goal of this paper is to show how IEs can also play an active role by sensing the social and physical context and providing awareness information to promote serendipitous interactions among users. In Section 1 possible configurations for fostering learning through serendipitous interaction in public IEs are presented. The information IEs have to capture to promote serendipitous interaction is presented in Section 2; while a model for the awareness system of such IEs is proposed in Section 3. The paper is concluded in Section 4.

1. Learning through Serendipitous Interaction

In this paper, the focus is on the possibilities offered by public IE to support learning through serendipitous interaction by providing awareness information to its inhabitants. The conceptual framework proposed by Ludvigsen [18] for social interaction can represent a starting point to understand how interaction among uncoupled users can be fostered. This framework is structured along four levels of engagement as the author explained: 1) *distributed attention*: "people are merely present in the same space" either physical or virtual. They have different focuses and the interaction is very low; 2) *shared focus*: when a single focus is shared among its participants. Broadcast entertainment with many people following a football game is an example; 3) *dialogue*: "participants are engaging in a shared activity in which they are investing themselves and their opinions"; 4) *collective action*: "when participants are working collaboratively towards a shared goal" [18].

In an environment characterized by 'distributed attention', users are simply co-located; they are uncoupled users or *strangers*. In these situations, collaboration might be hard to achieve. Thanks to awareness information provided by the IEs uncoupled users might be able to develop a 'shared focus' that can lead to collaboration through 'dialogue' and 'collective actions'. The IE will have to provide awareness information, tools and services to support and promote these engagement processes. During these processes strangers might get engaged in interaction and become part of a *group* (an ensemble of people engaged in the interaction). Participants of a group are then no longer considered as strangers but rather as engaged *individuals*. Individuals need to be kept aware of what is going on in the group they are in, but also about other groups that already existing and that they may join.

Two dimensions and four possible configurations have been identified in situations where serendipitous interaction can be triggered. The first dimension is represented by the fact that interaction can be based on an activity or around a shared learning object (LO) [1]. Second, users can interact with physical co-located people in the same IE, but also with distributed peers in an *extended IE*. The term extended IE is used in this paper to refer to different IEs which are interconnected to allow cooperation.

1.1. Activity-based Serendipitous Interaction: Co-located vs. Distributed

Activity-based serendipitous interaction is triggered by an IE or by an extended IE that promote engagement in an activity. Users getting engaged could require a tighter collaboration and synchronous communication to coordinate work [19].

An example of co-located activity-based interaction (Figure 1a) could be represented by *strangers* visiting an IE museum (distributed attention). They are notified of the possibility to engage in a collaborative game (shared focus) that will allow them to explore the surrounding while interacting with others (dialogue). They form a *group* to complete the collaborative game (collective action) playing against the system or other groups.

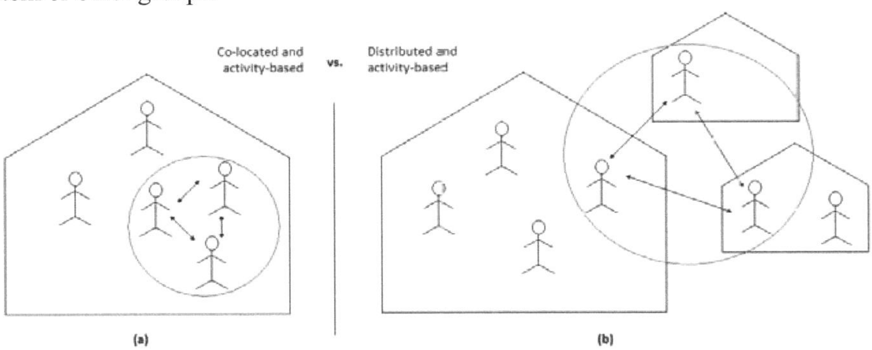

Figure 1. Activity-based serendipitous interaction a) co-located and b) distributed.

Interaction can be triggered also when users are distributed (Figure 1b) in an extended IE. E.g., two learners (distributed attention) can start collaborating while visiting two different IE museums after they have been notified of the possibility for engaging in an activity together (shared focus). Based on information available in the IEs they can solve a series of questions that leads them to a treasure (collective action).

1.2. LO-based Serendipitous Interaction: Co-located vs. Distributed

This kind of interaction is triggered by IEs when people get engaged in interaction around a shared LO that could require more loosely coupled collaboration, where

[1] The Learning Technology Standards Committee defines a learning object as "any entity, digital or non-digital, that may be used for learning, education or training" (http://ieeeltsc.org).

learners are more autonomous and weakly interdependent, and communication more likely to be asynchronous [20].

An example of co-located LO-based interaction (Figure 2a) can be represented by a user visiting a museum (distributed attention) and receiving a message about the presence of an audio file that augments an exhibit object. He accesses the file and makes extensions to it. The environment notifies other co-located users interested in the same object (shared focus among *strangers*), they gather around the LO forming a *group*, discussing about the LO (dialogue through face-to-face or asynchronous communication services offered by the IE), interacting and contributing to enhance the audio file together (collective action).

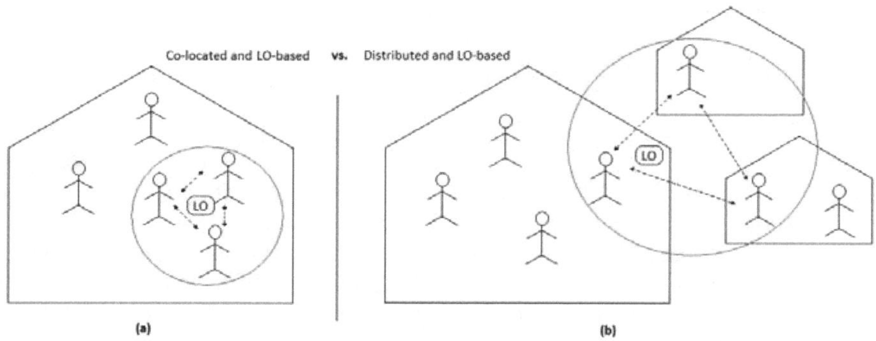

Figure 2. LO-based serendipitous interaction a) co-located and b) distributed.

In case users are distributed (shared focus), the interaction can be triggered by an extended IE by the use of an object reproduced in different sites (e.g. copies of an exhibit in different museums many people can interact with), also at different time. They all have knowledge of or a particular interest in it (shared focus). People may be interested in interacting with other peers that know more about it, like experts. Their interaction (dialogue) can lead to a tighter collaboration to achieve a common goal together (collective action), Figure 2b.

2. Awareness for Serendipitous Interaction: What Information?

To start building up a model for awareness system of IEs that aim at fostering serendipitous interaction, the framework for workspace awareness proposed by Gutwin and Greenberg [11] has been used as starting point. The focus in this paper is on the first part of the framework that specifies the information that makes up awareness [11]. This framework focuses on workspace awareness and is intended for supporting a pre-defined group of workers engaged on a specific task in a given workspace. In this paper, the focus is on emerging groups of uncoupled users that do not necessarily share any previous social bonds.

The aim of the present work is to identify the information that the designers will have to capture and distribute or what information makes up awareness for serendipitous interaction in public IEs. The elements of such information answer questions like "who" can the users interact with, "what" are they doing, "where" are they, "when" did something happen, and "how" did that occur, as suggested in [11]. This are the kinds of information people may find useful to start interacting with others, but also the information designers have to consider for fostering interaction. In Table 1 and 2 the basic elements of awareness and their related questions are listed following the "who, what, where, when and how" categorization as in [11]. The difference are highlighted in *italics*. Table 1 contains elements of awareness related to present situations.

Table 1. Elements of awareness related to the present as modified from [11]

Category	Element	Question
Who	Presence	Is anyone in the *IE*?
	Identity	Who is that?
	User type and participation	*Are they strangers or are they engaged individuals? If any groups, which ones they participate to?*
	Authorship	Who is doing that?
What	Action	What are they doing?
	Intention/*Activity*	What goal is that action part of?
	Artifact/*LO*	What object are they *interacting with*?
	Device	*What devices are they carrying?*
Where	Location	Where are they?
	Distribution	*Are they co-located or distributed?*

Table 2, instead, presents those elements regarding the past since history has always played a major role in interaction as highlighted in [21-23]. In the next section it is clarified how this information can be captured and modeled by IEs to finally be able to provide awareness information and foster serendipitous interaction.

Table 2. Elements of awareness related to the past as modified from [11]

Category	Element	Question
How	Action history	How did that operation happen?
	Artifact history	How did this artifact come to be in this state?
When	Event history	When did that event happen?
Who	Presence history	Who was here, and when?
	User type history	*What changes happened to user type?*
Where	Location history	Where has a person been?
What	*Interaction* history	What has a person been doing?

3. How IE Uses Awareness Information

In order to support and foster learning through serendipitous interaction, the IE has to: 1) *capture* information from the environment (Section 2); 2) *model* this information based on model of social structures and collaboration; and 3) *provide* awareness information to its inhabitants. In Figure 3 a model for an IE awareness system is presented. Each of the above functions identifies a level of the system. These levels and the way they are interrelated is presented here.

In the *capture* level information will be collected in many different ways. For instance presence information can be detected through motion sensors; identity information through devices carried by users, or in spaces like museums users might carry audible devices equipped with RFID tags; and so on and so forth.

In the *model* level, based on the data and history captured the IE can structure this information to identify affinities and common interests among users. Based on this and on the information on repositories, the IE can suggest opportunities for interaction (activity-based or LO-based) and support appropriate collaboration models. For instance, if the serendipitous interaction is articulated around an activity (Sections 1.1), the IE should support social structures configurations that provide tighter collaboration.

Interaction and *action history* information (Table 2) will play a major role in these scenarios. The user engaged in this interaction will need to know about what others are doing and what they still need to do to achieve the goal of their activity. On the other side, if the interaction is based around a LO (Sections 1.2), the collaboration to be supported should be more loose and asynchronous. In this case *artifact* and *interaction history* (Table 2) will be more important to keep track of how the object has been modified and who has interacted with it.

In the *provision* level, once the IE awareness system has gathered the information and identified the possibilities of interaction for its users, it still has to provide the right awareness information with the most appropriate modalities. Considering the public nature of the space, the system should take into account the fact that this space is open to everyone and quite dynamic. In such settings privacy represents a critical aspect. For instance, when dealing with *strangers* the system will provide more provocative awareness information [24] and use abstract representations as presence indicators, removing part of the data from the original signal [22]. These should simplify issues related to privacy, but create difficulties of interpretation or immediateness of the reading of these representations, especially for unfamiliar users.

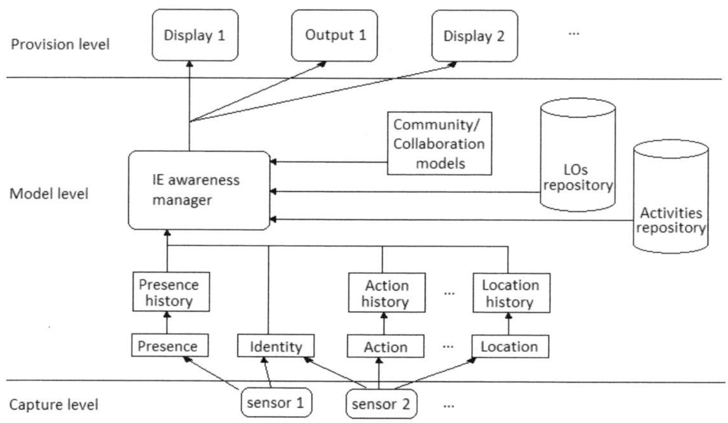

Figure 3. Model of the IE awareness system.

Moreover, how the system provide awareness information to the users should consider, among other things, the social context the users are immerged into, the tasks they are engaged in or that are available there and the devices one can access and their configuration. For instance, the IE should provide indication on high activity in a space or around an object, e.g. through visual cues with a brighter display or vivid color changing more frequently with increased activity.

In other cases the awareness information might be more direct, e.g. with *individuals* and *groups* already engaged in interaction. In this case the system will have to provide more specific awareness information related to: 1) people connected to spaces; 2) people connected to LO; 3) groups and learning activities, and in particular their status and participants.

Information about people connected to spaces is particularly important in case of co-located or activity-based interaction. For instance, the IE could display the presence of others or the interest of users about that space by showing bubbles on a display [25]. More glowing bubbles would represent bigger interest about that space, while larger bubbles would represent people proximity[2]. In this way a small glowing bubble will represent a person far away that is particularly interested in what is going on there.

Information about people connected to LO is of course more important for LO-based interaction. Also in this case people connection to an object could be represented with bubbles, like in the example above, and displayed in the artifact tag where users can already find information about artist, year, etc.

Information about learning activities will be more relevant for those engaged in activity-based interaction, however also those involved in more loosely coupled interaction like in LO-based activity could benefit from it. Information about the status or progress of an activity could be displayed on the interfaces used by individuals and groups during interaction. Simple forms like a progress bar could represent this information based on the actions performed by individuals or sub-task accomplished by the group. Information about other participants should also be available. The group might want to know who is active in that moment and the IE might display passive/inactive users with opaque user representations.

The IE should give the possibility to interested visitors to register for a service of notification on modifications that happen in the IE, like feed services for LO, spaces and activities. Moreover, when activities will be initiated, the IE has to facilitate them, providing services and resources for supporting coordination and communication (e.g. IM, chat, forum, etc.). The spaces chosen to foster interaction should consider rules of conduct that are valid in the public IE, e.g. supporting discussion through virtual spaces or context-aware chat room [26] when strangers are present; and when face-to-face interaction is necessary suggesting spaces like library cafés rather than reading rooms.

4. Conclusion

The possibilities for contextual learning in public places are enhanced by people, resources and technologies available there. In this paper the focus was on public IEs that can foster learning through serendipitous interaction. This can be achieved by providing awareness information and support to interaction.

Designers of such IEs needs to be aware of what kind of scenarios they will have to face and what kind of information they need to gather. In order to get a better understanding of such situations four possible configurations for learning through serendipitous interaction in public IEs were presented; the information needed to be captured were proposed together with a model for how IEs can elaborate this information to provide awareness to their inhabitants and trigger interaction among them.

Acknowledgements

The research reported in this paper is part of the NFR-project nr. 176841/SIO FABULA (http://fabula.idi.ntnu.no). We thank the project participants for constructive discussions and feedbacks.

[2] Redström et al. [23] raised an interesting issue regarding proximity in space vs. proximity in place. Proximity should not only be considered in terms of physical distance, but also incorporates the social context.

References

[1] E. Eriksson, T.R. Hansen, and A. Lykke-Olesen, "Reclaiming public space: designing for public interaction with private devices," *1st International Conference on Tangible and embedded interaction (TEI '07)*, New York, NY, USA: ACM, 2007, pp. 31-38.

[2] J. Lave and E. Wenger, *Situated Learning : Legitimate Peripheral Participation*, Cambridge University Press, 1991.

[3] M. Sharples, J. Taylor, and G. Vavoula, "A Theory of Learning for the Mobile Age," *The SAGE Handbook of E-learning Research*, R. Andrews and C. Haythornthwaite, eds., SAGE, 2007, pp. 221-247.

[4] J. Thackara, *In the bubble: designing in a complex world*, The MIT Press, 2005.

[5] J. Voogt and H. Pelgrum, "ICT and Curriculum Change," *Human Technology*, vol. 1, 2005, pp. 157-175.

[6] M.S. Bowles, *Relearning to E-learn: Strategies for Electronic Learning and Knowledge*, Melbourne University Press, 2004.

[7] I. Canova Calori, M. Divitini, and M. Eljueidi, "A Design Framework for City-wide Collaborative Learning Systems," *Submitted to mLearn 2009*.

[8] C. Chatfield, D. Carmichael, R. Hexel, J. Kay, and B. Kummerfeld, "Personalisation in intelligent environments: managing the information flow," *Proceedings of the 17th Australia conference on Computer-Human Interaction*, Canberra, Australia: 2005, pp. 1-10.

[9] P. Dourish and V. Bellotti, "Awareness and coordination in shared workspaces," *Proceedings of the 1992 ACM conference on Computer-supported cooperative work*, Toronto, Ontario, Canada: ACM, 1992, pp. 107-114.

[10] A.K. Dey and G.D. Abowd, "Towards a Better Understanding of Context and Context-Awareness," *Proceedings of the What, Who, Where, When, and How of Context- AwarenessWorkshop*, New York, USA: ACM, 2000.

[11] C. Gutwin and S. Greenberg, "A Descriptive Framework of Workspace Awareness for Real-Time Groupware," *Computer Supported Cooperative Work*, vol. 11, 2002, pp. 411-446.

[12] P. Lonsdale, C. Baber, M. Sharples, and A.T. N, "A context-awareness architecture for facilitating mobile learning," *Learning with mobile devices: a book of papers*, 2004, pp. 79-85.

[13] S. Yang, "Context Aware Ubiquitous Learning Environments for Peer-to-Peer Collaborative Learning," *Educational Technology & Society*, vol. 9, 2006, pp. 188-201.

[14] P. Markopoulos, "A Design Framework for Awareness Systems," *Awareness Systems: advances in theory, methodology and design*, Springer, 2009.

[15] S.E. Hudson and I. Smith, "Techniques for addressing fundamental privacy and disruption tradeoffs in awareness support systems," *Proceedings of the 1996 ACM conference on Computer supported cooperative work*, Boston, Massachusetts, United States: ACM, 1996, pp. 248-257.

[16] P. Jeffrey and A. McGrath, "Sharing serendipity in the workplace," *Proceedings of the third international conference on Collaborative virtual environments*, San Francisco, California, United States: ACM, 2000, pp. 173-179.

[17] N. Eagle and A. Pentland, "Social Serendipity: Proximity Sensing and Cueing," *Ubicomp*, 2004.

[18] M. Ludvigsen, "Designing for Social Use in Public Places: a Conceptual Framework of Social Interaction," *Designing Pleasurable Products and Interfaces Conference (DPPI'05)*, Eindhoven, The Netherlands: 2005, pp. 389-408.

[19] E.F. Churchill and N. Wakeford, "Framing mobile collaborations and mobile technologies," *Wireless world: social and interactional aspects of the mobile age*, Springer-Verlag London, 2002, pp. 154-179.

[20] D. Pinelle and C. Gutwin, "A groupware design framework for loosely coupled workgroups," *Proceedings of the ninth conference on European Conference on Computer Supported Cooperative Work*, Paris, France: Springer-Verlag New York, Inc., 2005, pp. 65-82.

[21] S. Farnham, S. Kelly, W. Portnoy, and J. Schwartz, "Wallop: designing social software for co-located social networks," *System Sciences, 2004. Proceedings of the 37th Annual Hawaii International Conference on*, 2004, p. 10 pp.

[22] E.R. Pedersen and T. Sokoler, "AROMA: abstract representation of presence supporting mutual awareness," *Proceedings of the SIGCHI conference on Human factors in computing systems*, Atlanta, Georgia, United States: ACM, 1997, pp. 51-58.

[23] J. Redström, P. Dahlberg, P. Ljungstrand, and L.E. Holmquist, "Designing for Local Interaction," *Proc. Managing Interactions in Smart Environments (MANSE) '99*, 1999, pp. 227-238.

[24]B. Gaver, "Provocative Awareness," *Computer Supported Cooperative Work*, vol. 11, 2002, pp. 475-493.

[25] T. Erickson and W.A. Kellogg, "Social Translucence: An Approach to Designing Systems that Support Social Processes," *ACM Transactions on Computer-Human Interaction*, vol. 7, 2000, pp. 59-83.

[26] B. Schilit, D. Hilbert, and J. Trevor, "Context-aware communication," *Wireless Communications, IEEE*, vol. 9, 2002, pp. 46-54.

Intelligent Environments 2009
V. Callaghan et al. (Eds.)
IOS Press, 2009

doi:10.3233/978-1-60750-034-6-91

Raising Awareness of Energy Consumption in Smart Living Environments

Anton J. FERCHER[1], Martin HITZ, and Gerhard LEITNER
Department of Informatics-Systems, Klagenfurt University, Austria

Abstract. Studies in economic psychology have repeatedly revealed that energy consumption behavior in the household could be optimized through the provision of frequent and immediate feedback. This aspect is still widely neglected by conventional metering equipment installed in most homes. Energy meters are generally placed at quite hidden locations and reading them only once a year or at best once a month for billing purposes remains the rule. Especially observation of variations or trends over longer periods of time is cumbersome and has to be done on the basis of handwritings or transferring manually read data to applications like spreadsheets. We introduce *Perceivable Energy*, a system that supports pervasive approaches to raise awareness of energy consumption. More innovative feedback mechanisms like, e.g., ambient displays are backed by a more conventional graphical user interface to provide detailed consumption data on demand. The system is designed to make integration and interconnections of new metering devices and visualizations simple and constitutes a good basis for further research on awareness of energy usage in our (future) living environments.

Keywords. Awareness, energy consumption, ambient displays, pervasive visualization, smart environments

Introduction

Finding viable solutions to cover society's demand for energy constitutes a major global challenge in our time. High consumption levels combined with the dependence on fossil energy sources lead to shortages of resources, volatile energy prices and environmental problems. Besides the extended usage and further development of both cleaner and affordable sources of energy based on renewable resources, energy saving can significantly contribute to possible solutions.

In economic psychology one area of research is focused on the various aspects related to energy consumption and saving in the household. Providing people with information materials containing hints on how to save energy is a widely used strategy in campaigns that promote energy conservation. However, several intervention studies carried out during the last decades show that information alone is not a very effective tool. In contrast, giving feedback can generally be seen as a successful strategy, especially when given frequently (cf. e.g. [1], [2]).

[1] Corresponding Author: Anton J. Fercher, Department of Informatics-Systems, Klagenfurt University, Universitätsstraße 65, A-9020 Klagenfurt, Austria; E-mail: anton.fercher@edu.uni-klu.ac.at

A survey in [3] showed that households reduced their average consumption of electric energy by over 12 percent when they were provided with continuous feedback about current, hourly, daily, etc. energy usage on a PC.

Van Houwelingen et al. [4] report that homes which received daily electronic feedback were able to reduce their gas usage on average by 12.3 percent, homes that got monthly external feedback by 7.7 percent. Another group that only got information about energy conservation measures achieved a reduction by 4.3 percent. All participants had agreed in advance on a conservation goal of 10 percent.

In the view of such proposals for ideal feedback conditions, the situation common in most real households has to be considered as there may be demand for improvements.

1. Invisible Energy

With conventional metering equipment (e.g. electromechanical electric energy or gas meters) it is generally difficult and time-consuming to trace one's energy consumption. Energy meters are often placed in hidden locations like switch cabinets or basements. Thus they reside nearly permanently outside the view of the household's residents and they are hardly frequented to gain feedback. Especially tracking variations or trends over longer time periods is cumbersome and often has to be done on the basis of handwritings or manually transferring data to applications like spreadsheets. So, reading conventional meters only once a year or at best once a month for billing purposes often remains the rule.

A more comprehensive exploration of parameters that go beyond the overall consumption of one type of energy is even harder to achieve. Such further parameters may include outside and inside temperature and other general weather conditions as they can influence the demand for energy used for heating or air conditioning. Information about the presence or absence of persons in a room or the status (closed or opened) of doors or windows may help to identify suboptimal habits, e.g., when lights or appliances remain turned on in areas that aren't actually used or when windows stay open too long. These and further scenarios may be supported by facilities to investigate energy consumption of certain floors, rooms or appliances in isolation. At least for single electric appliances this can partly be achieved through simple plug-in electricity meters which are widely available on the market. However, integration of data from such simple meters in more extensive scenarios has again to be done manually.

Altogether metering equipment in most households only poorly supports effortless analysis of energy consumption and related behaviour. It fails to visualize energy to give people a permanent and easily accessible reminder of their own energy usage and the consequences of their habits and actions.

2. Raising Awareness of Consumption

Pervasive technologies increasingly turn our households into smart living environments providing, e.g., higher comfort and assistance for old or disabled persons (cf. [5]). Energy consumption related information should become an integrated part of such technology enhanced homes. Installation of smart metering devices by utility providers is gaining momentum and simplifies computer based processing and analysis of consumption data (cf. e.g. [6]).

However, such far-reaching advances in peoples' immediate living spaces demand for solutions that are accepted by the users and can give sufficient feedback without being bothersome over longer time periods. Calm integration and visualization of computer-based information in the environment can be achieved through ambient information systems. They are suitable to show information that is important but not critical and do not permanently attract attention. Presentation of various data can be conveyed, e.g., in light and sound effects of everyday objects or graphical elements of pictures. Update of information is generally translated to only subtle changes on the display. The design is chosen to be aesthetically pleasing and to fit into the living environment [7]. Ambient displays rising awareness for consumption of energy and other resources are, e.g., proposed for water usage [8], [9], heat energy [10], [11] or electric energy [10], [12], [13].

3. Perceivable Energy: A Pervasive System for Feedback on Energy Consumption

Our project "*Perceivable Energy*" includes the development of a software system that applies pervasive technologies to collect, process, and visualize energy consumption related data in real time. Innovative visualization techniques raising awareness of energy usage are complemented by more traditional graphical user interfaces that provide detailed data and extensive control on demand. On the basis of this system, different issues concerning feedback on energy consumption and smart living environments can be explored. Possible issues include but are not limited to:

- Selection of adequate visualizations that provide sufficient feedback for particular scenarios at home. This may depend on general parameters like the update or response rate of the system or the preparation of data (e.g., current, cumulative or average consumption values or costs). Other parameters more pertinent to a given solution like visibility criteria, embedding in the environment or the general abilities to represent information will have to be further explored, too.
- The level of information and distraction that is accepted by the user. When will the system become bothersome and when will it be too calm?
- Which elements must be configurable or at least visible to give users enough control over the system?
- In general, plug and play installation, configuration, and extension of such systems at low costs may become a crucial point to achieve a high level of acceptance.

3.1. Visualizations

In the current release of *Perceivable Energy*, we have realized these categories of calm visualizations of consumption data: Informative art, light, and indoor fountains which also provide a calm acoustic information channel.

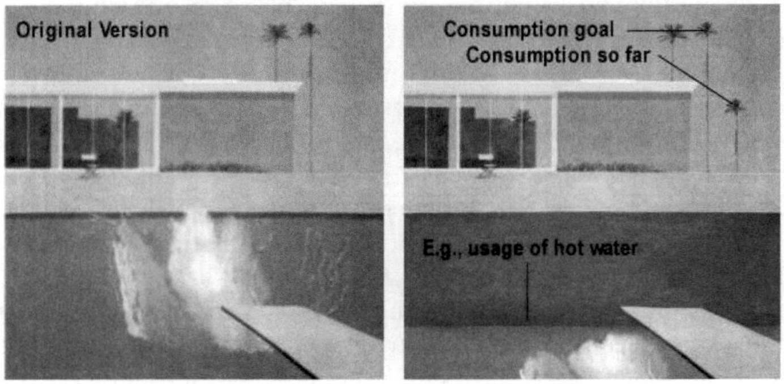

Figure 1. David Hockney, *A Bigger Splash,* used as informative art (original version taken from [17])

3.1.1. Informative Art

A very promising way to visualize energy related feedback is so called *informative art*. The idea is to weave information in an artwork located in the users' environment. The artwork's original purpose to represent an interesting object to be enjoyed during a moment of reflection is not changed. The intention behind this approach is to add an additional information layer to existing artworks rather than to design new artful works with information representation in focus. Information that does not draw the user's permanent attention is embedded in the environment in a very calm way - it is a kind of "slow technology" [14].

Different classes of data can be represented by various dimensions in artworks, e.g., color, space, form, level of abstraction, scale or orientation. Appealing themes and display elements may highly depend on one's personal taste and therefore users should get as much freedom as possible to choose them at will [15].

The aesthetically pleasing and calm integration of information combined with a broad spectrum of ways to map and represented information constitutes a very suitable visualization technique for energy related data.

Holmes [16] shows a public art approach dealing with energy consumption. It uses displays containing pieces of media art to represent a building's carbon dioxide emissions by the number of trees that would have to be planted to absorb these emissions. Figure 1 shows our prototype of the digital version of the painting *A Bigger Splash* by the pop artist David Hockney. The height of one of the palm trees in the background may be mapped to a determined consumption limit for some type of energy. A second palm tree shows the energy used so far and keeps on growing according to further energy usage. Other elements like the water level in the swimming pool may be utilized to represent another measured attribute, like the usage of hot water during the day.

3.1.2. Light

The electric lighting of a room and light effects in general provide an interesting way to communicate information about energy. They may, e.g., alter their color according to the building's energy consumption. An example is *WATTSON* [13], a small device which can easily be located nearly anywhere in the household. It is able to show the current consumption level of electric energy through the different colors of its lighting.

Another approach is *The Power-Aware Cord* [12] which uses light effects in a cable and can show consumption more directly for individual appliances.
However, we think that there are also many interesting ways to re-use (with small enhancements) the light equipment which is already installed in a building without need for such additional devices. E.g., pieces of furniture like some kind of glass-door cabinet with lighting, can be found in many homes and fits well for applications with different light effects.

3.1.3. Indoor Fountains

Indoor fountains provide a good example for quite simple everyday objects that may be used to raise awareness. They can provide both visual and acoustic feedback in a pleasant way. Using indoor fountains as ambient media has, e.g., been proposed by Schmidt et al. [18]. The amount and the speed of water running down these fountains could be used to represent some kind of instantaneous energy consumption. At the same time, the sound level raises when the ripple of the streaming water becomes louder. Acoustic feedback mechanisms may easily become disturbing by and by, but such quite calm and natural sounds might have a good chance to be accepted over longer time periods. The design of these fountains leaves room for different kinds of metaphors which may help to communicate the information. A design very close to nature, e.g., with lots of plants may encourage the user to save energy for ecological reasons. A fountain may also be designed as an artwork and therefore may become informative art as described above.

3.2. The Core Software Application

Perceivable Energy is able to control visualizations like those introduced above on the basis of collected meter and sensor data and supports a more detailed analysis of consumption and related parameters on demand. It further provides means to configure the various visualizations, hardware components and the system as a whole. A system overview is shown in Figure 2. A first consideration for the system design was the broad range of candidate platforms on which the system may be applied. This includes, e.g., standard PC systems, embeddable hardware solutions, network based (metering) devices, home automation systems or various (future) platforms for smart environments. Our system is implemented in an OSGi R4 framework (*Equinox* [19]) on top of Java which results in both, a high independence from the underlying operating system platform and in a high degree of modularity and extensibility.

3.2.1. Input and Output

The parameters that might be interesting for the system to measure are manifold ranging from direct energy usage (electric energy, oil, gas, wood pellets, etc.) to various environmental parameters. In the early phase of the project, already available appliances for computer based monitoring of these variables were investigated. The survey showed a very broad spectrum ranging from simple plug-in consumption monitors with data streams over USB to professional platforms for extended monitoring of larger buildings with an integrated Web server. Generally, support for Web based services seems to be an attractive feature as additional sensor data like weather conditions or comparative data from other users may be accessed through the Internet.

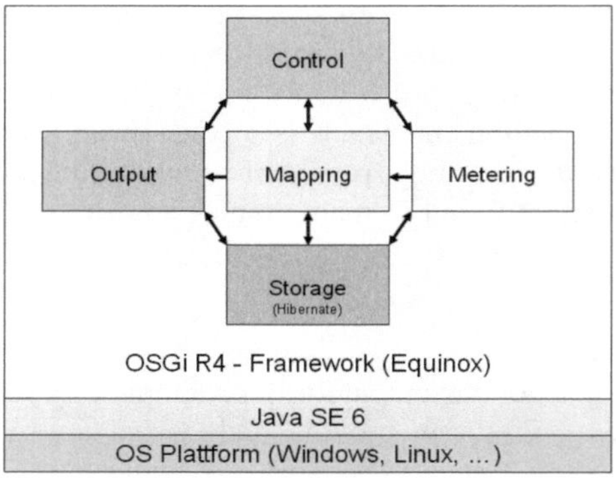

Figure 2. System overview of *Perceivable Energy*

The situation for the system's output components is quite similar. E.g., various home automation systems can be used to control visualizations and displays showing informative art might be connected over wireless technologies in addition to standard graphical interfaces. *Perceivable Energy* specifies minimal requirements for new input or output devices and their data through very high level interface definitions. New devices or services can easily be integrated by providing appropriate implementations in Java classes and OSGi bundles. Services and devices that are available to the system are managed by the *Metering* and *Output* components shown in Figure 2. For the visualization approaches discussed above, a smarthome framework which has also been developed at our department is accessed to control switches and dimmers for light effects and everyday objects like indoor fountains.

3.2.2. Mapping

The *Mapping* component (see Figure 2) manages definitions of mappings which observe measured values from defined metering points and trigger changes in visualizations. If a mapping detects that the (current, average or cumulative) value of one of its metering points lies beyond certain bounds, it starts to update the status of the affected visualizations according to its configuration (e.g., the color of some light in the living room is changed from green to yellow if the usage of wood pellets exceeds a certain limit). The *Mapping* component is held quite simple so far, further developments may include the integration of a more intelligent reasoning system.

3.2.3. Control and Graphical User Interface

System configuration and detailed analysis of measured consumption data through the user is implemented in the *Control* component shown in Figure 2. It includes a more conventional graphical user interface introduced in Figure 3. This interface may be available on one or more monitors in the living environment. It may also be accessible on a display showing informative art which supports switching to the more detailed view on demand.

Available metering devices, visualizations and mappings between them are organized in tree menus. For a statistical view on energy consumption, developments over time are visualized in charts. Views for certain (groups of) metering points within a defined time period can be created.

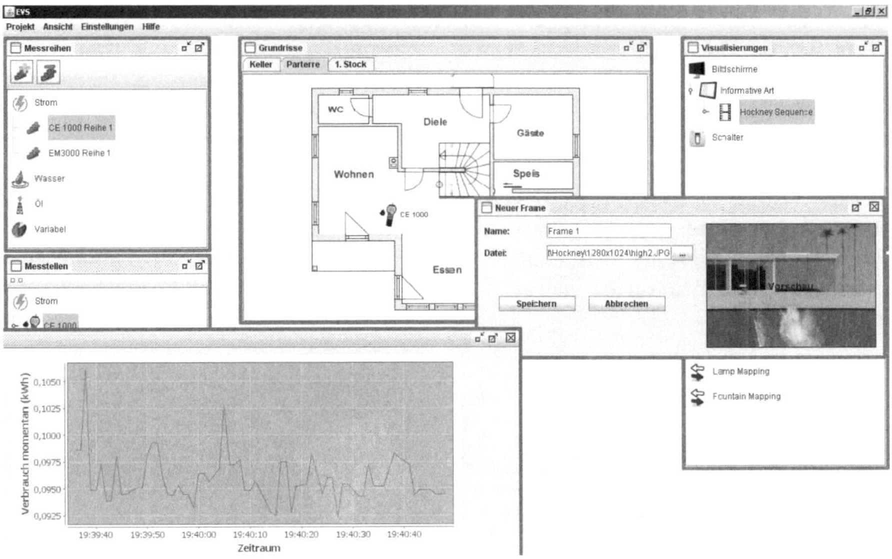

Figure 3. The graphical user interface of the *Control* component

Graphical floorplans are included to support positioning of meters or visualization devices during their installation with drag and drop functions and to provide detailed information for these devices by just pointing and clicking on them.

It is also possible for the user to define frame sequences with selected image files taken from the file system. These frame sequences can be assigned to display devices to act as informative art or some other type of ambient visualization. The *Mapping* component discussed above can also be configured over the user interface. Through the definition of mappings, the user determines which frame of a frame sequence is currently shown when a metering point reaches certain values. This constitutes a relatively easy way for users to choose their own themes for visualizations and to experiment with the system as a whole.

4. Discussion and Conclusion

For a system that is supposed to help to save energy, its own energy consumption is an issue that has to be considered carefully. For our prototypes, power consumption of light effects can be regarded to be low if energy saving lamps or diodes are used. The re-use of lighting equipment that is installed and used at home anyway further reduces the marginal energy demand. Technology for other everyday objects that might be used for visualizations has to be chosen wisely, too. Consumption of pumps in our indoor fountains is less than 3 Watt which can be considered as relatively low. For informative art, more efficient solutions beyond standard (LCD) panels should be applied (power-saving devices, e.g., shown in [20]). More intelligent visualizations that are only activated when the user is actually able to see them will bring further improvements.

The same holds for the core software components of the system which should run on well adapted and low consuming platforms. Thus, one of our next steps will be the installation and tests of *Perceivable Energy* on an embeddable *Alix* [21] system board.

Another way might be the integration in (existing) smart home frameworks or other systems that provide an adequate hardware platform.

At present working, early versions of the proposed visualizations and the system as a whole exist and they have already been applied for demonstration purposes. These demonstrations yielded useful hints from potential users, where having enough control over the system and efforts for system installation and operation were the most discussed issues. During further development the various components of the system will be improved to support user tests, long term studies and applications in real households. This will help us to evaluate our system extensively and to explore various questions on visualization of energy consumption and smart living environments in general.

References

[1] Abrahamse W., Steg L., Vlek C., Rothengatter T.: "A review of intervention studies aimed at household energy conservation", *Journal of Environmental Psychology* **25, 3** (2005), 273-291.
[2] Darby S.: "Making it obvious: designing feedback into energy consumption", *Proceedings, 2nd International Conference on Energy Efficiency in Household Appliances and Lighting*, Italian Association of Energy Economists/ EC-SAVE programme, 2000.
[3] Dobson J. K., Griffin J.D. A.: "Conservation effect of immediate electricity cost feedback on residential consumption behavior", *Proceedings, ACEEE's 1992 Summer Study on Energy Efficiency in Buildings*, American Council for an Energy-Efficient Economy , 33–35, 2000.
[4] Van Houwelingen J. H., Van Raaij W. F.: "The Effect of Goal-Setting and Daily Electronic Feedback on In-Home Energy Use", *Journal of Consumer Research* **16** (1989), 98-105.
[5] Chan M., Estève D., Escriba C., Campo E.: "A review of smart homes-Present state and future challenges", *Computer Methods and Programs in Biomedicine* **91, 1** (2008), 55-81.
[6] Vasconcelos J.: "Survey of Regulatory and Technological Developments Concerning Smart Metering in the European Union Electricity Market", *RSCAS Policy Papers (2008/01)*, Florence School of Regulation, 2008.
[7] Pousman Z., Stasko J.: "A taxonomy of ambient information systems: four patterns of design", *Proceedings, AVI '06,* ACM, New York, 67-74, 2006.
[8] Kappel K., Grechenig T.: "From Feedback to Awareness: An Ambient Water Consumption Display", *Poster Session at UbiComp'08,* 2008, (http://ubicomp.org/ubicomp2008/ubicomp08workshops.pdf).
[9] Arroyo E., Bonanni L., Selker T.: "Waterbot: exploring feedback and persuasive techniques at the sink", Proceedings, *SIGCHI conference on Human factors in computing systems,* ACM, New York, 631-639, 2005.
[10] Kappel K., Grechenig T.: "Creating Energy Awareness using Ambient Information Systems as Persuasive Technology", *ACM CHI'08 Surrounded by persuasive Ambient Intelligence, 2008.*
[11] Gustafsson A., Gyllenswärd M., Bang M.: "Visualizing Energy Consumption of Radiators", *Proceedings, PERSUASIVE'06,* Springer, Berlin/Heidelberg, 112-122, 2007.
[12] Gustafsson A., Gyllenswärd M.: "The Power-Aware Cord: Energy Awareness through Ambient Information Display", *CHI '05 extended abstracts on Human factors in computing systems,* ACM, New York, 1423-1426, 2005.
[13] WATTSON, http://www.diykyoto.com, 2009.
[14] Redström J., Skog T., Hallns L.: "Informative Art: Using Amplied Artworks as Information Displays", *Proceedings, DARE'00*, ACM, New York, 103-114, 2000.
[15] Ferscha A.: "A Matter of Taste", *Proceedings, AmI 2007,* Springer, Berlin/Heidelberg, 287-304, 2007.
[16] Holmes T.: "Eco-visualization: combining art and technology to reduce energy consumption", *Proceedings, 6th ACM SIGCHI C&C07*, ACM, New York, 153-162, 2007.
[17] Walther I. F. (Ed.): "Malerei Der Welt, Band 2: Romantik bis Gegenwart", Taschen-Verlag, Cologne, Germany, 1995.
[18] Schmidt A., Gellersen H., Beigl M.: "Matching Information and Ambient Media", *Proceedings, CoBuild'99,* Springer, Berlin/Heidelberg, 140-149, 1999.
[19] Equinox, http://www.eclipse.org/equinox, 2009.
[20] Touchbase 12,1 inch VGA Monitor, http://www.touchbase.de, 2009.
[21] PC Engines alix1d, http://www.pcengines.ch/alix1d.htm, 2009.

Special Session on Domestic Robotics and Smart Device Ecologies

Intelligent Environments 2009
V. Callaghan et al. (Eds.)
IOS Press, 2009

doi:10.3233/978-1-60750-034-6-101

Discovering the Home

James DOOLEY[a,1], Vic CALLAGHAN[a], Hani HAGRAS[a] and Phil BULL[b]
[a] *Intelligent Inhabited Environments Group, University of Essex, UK.*
[b] *Customer Networks Group, British Telecom, UK.*

Abstract. This paper discusses the requirements of future Home Area Networks (HAN) with respect to resource discovery. We discuss existing methods and provide some experimental data that shows them to be unsuitable for future HANs. In response, we present a new protocol called "Entity Resolution Protocol" (ERP) and experimental data which shows that it significantly outperforms the other methods discussed.

Keywords. Dynamic Discovery, Distributed Computing, Home Networks

Introduction

Over the past few decades, the home environment has seen an increased deployment of electronic devices. This now includes traditional monolithic devices (television, radio, alarm clock, etc), but also personal computers, entertainment devices and media devices. The logical progression of deploying an increased number of devices is to connect them to a network, which we have seen become commonplace over the past few years.

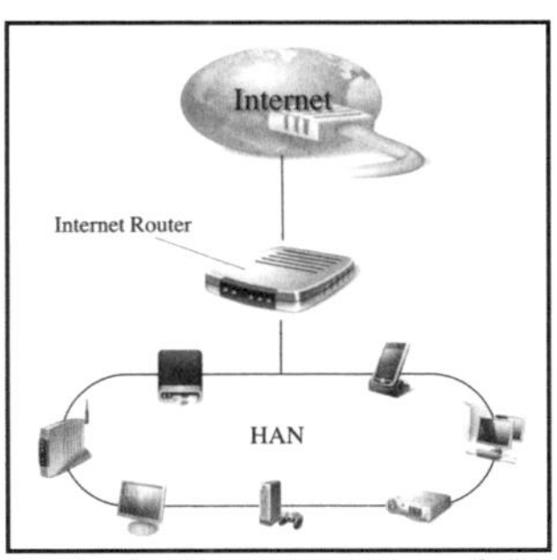

Figure 1: The Home Area Network (HAN)

The resulting *"Home-Area-Network"* (HAN) [Figure 1] is heterogeneous in terms of hardware and software platforms that exist. The common factor among them all is that they are all networked and TCP/IP friendly. An additional note to make about the HAN is that it is *"connected"*, with always-on internet access. This sets the scene for the future of the HAN and provides the basic structure for which researchers must create robust and working technologies.

We start this paper by discussing the future HAN in terms of structure and content. We also present a formal model of the HAN and requirements for basic resource discovery. We then review the centralised and distributed models with respect to the common fallacies that exist about distributed systems; More importantly, we present data collected from experiments on four candidates for discovery in the home. These experiments were conducted in our purpose built "iSpace" research facility, which is a fully functional apartment (kitchen, living area, two bedrooms and bathroom) with

[1]Corresponding Author: James Dooley, School of Computer Science and Electronic Engineering, University of Essex, Wivenhoe Park, Colchester, UK. CO4 3SQ. jpdool@essex.ac.uk

features such as false walls and ceiling (to embed computer systems, sensors and other equipment), a separate control room (for non-intrusive monitoring and control), and a wealth of electronic systems such as network controllable lighting. To add substance to our evaluation, we then present the ERP itself; and finally conclude this paper with a review of the results and a proposal for our own protocol to be considered as a candidate for future use in home environments.

1. The Future Home Area Network (HAN)

In our future homes, the HAN is likely to be populated by a high number of devices that will vary in physical size (from embedded processors to desktop systems) and resource abundance (processing power, memory, etc) providing an even more diverse heterogeneous computing environment. The HAN can now be considered a distributed computing system where each device can communicate with each other device using the common TCP/IP suite of protocols, which make the physical network topology (ethernet, wifi, routers, switches, etc.) transparent.

Interestingly; although it is physical devices which inhabit a home (and which we interact with), once we transcend into the digital world (ie software), the notion of devices becomes relatively obsolete. It is not the actual devices which we are interested in, but rather the resources that they host (which can be accessed by software applications running on other devices in the same network). To illustrate this, suppose we have a hard disk that is accessible directly on the network (otherwise known as a networked attached storage device), we are not actually interested in the device itself, but more so in the data which it contains (such as music and video files).

Consequently; we must note that each device hosts a set of software resources (such as files and processes) which can be accessed by other software processes which are active on the network. To illustrate the scale of deployed soft resources, consider the descriptions and associated numbers in [Table 1] for one person (how do these numbers compare to your current collections of digital material?).

Table 1: Personal digital content collection (one person).

Description	Number of software resources
Digital music (15 albums @ 15 songs per album)	225
Photos	1000
Movies	15
Home movies / clips	100
Software (games, apps, etc.)	5
Misc files (documents, manuals, invoices, etc.)	100
Total	1445

Now multiply that number by four (four people in an average family home), then add to that all the resources that are available in the typical vision of the future pervasive computing home environment (such as automated lighting, heating, sensors, audio/video, etc.). The total number of soft resources per home is potentially in the thousands, or even in the millions for some deployments with high numbers of embedded systems (will your coffee cup have an embedded system in it?).

The problem that researchers are now faced with is how to make the entire set of soft resources that are available in the HAN accessible and usable. This means a common software model and suite of protocols for these software resources.

1.1. Formal Model of the HAN

If we consider a home environment (τ), we are interested in the set of devices (D) which are connected to a common network infrastructure in that environment, a so called *"home area network"* (HAN).

More specifically, for an individual device (d) :

$$d \in D$$

As we have mentioned, we are not actually interested in the devices, but rather the resources which the devices host. And so for each device (d) we have a set of soft computing resources which we call *"entities"*. Where the relationship :

$$hosts(d, \varepsilon)$$

denotes that a device (d) hosts the entity (ε). Additionally, it can be said that a device (d) hosts a set of entities (E) :

$$hosts(d, E)$$

and :

$$(hosts(d, E)) \wedge (hosts(d, \varepsilon)) \rightarrow (\varepsilon \in E)$$

It is now true for us to say that if a home environment (τ) contains a set of devices (D), then (τ) has a superset of entities (SE) where each entity is hosted by a device (d) that is a member of (D) :

$$(d \in D) \wedge (hosts(d, \varepsilon)) \rightarrow (\varepsilon \in SE)$$

It is also obvious that all of the possible entity sets (E) that are valid in (τ) are subsets of (SE).

$$\forall(E, \tau) \rightarrow E \subset SE$$

1.2. Required Functionality

The software entities which an application may wish to access in a HAN must have the following three properties:

- **Uniquely Identifiable :** each entity must have some identity that is distinguishable among all others and is persistent through the entity lifecycle.
- **Discoverable :** A discovery process must exist whereby an application that has no prior knowledge of an entity (or the HAN), can discover that entity.
- **Locatable :** A process must exist that can resolve the location of an entity from its identity, this is known as lookup.

```
1. // discovery of entityIDs
2. Identities = HAN.discoverAllEntities()

3. // for every entityID
4. for every identity in identities

5.     // use the entityID to lookup the entity
6.     entity = HAN.lookup(identity)

7.     // do something with the entity
8.     doSomething(entity)
```

Figure 2: Pseudocode for discovery/lookup of an entity.

[Figure 2] shows the pseudocode of an application that wishes to discover every entity in a HAN (line 2), lookup the entity location (line 6) and perform some function "doSomething" with the entity (line 8). In this paper we limit the required functionality to only these basic functions which are needed for pervasive computing systems to be a reality in the home. As we will see, this seemingly simple functionality is enough to create some significant challenges which, as we argue, are still not solved to a sufficient level for real world deployment.

2. Current methods

Before discussing some existing methods, it is useful to observe the common problems associated with distributed computing systems in general. Fortunately, there is a set of eight well known "fallacies of distributed computing". Largely attributed to Peter Deutsch and James Gosling, for which Arnon Rotem-Gal-Oz provides a summary [1], they are :

F1. The network is reliable,
F2. Latency is zero,
F3. Bandwidth is infinite,
F4. The network is secure,
F5. Topology doesn't change,
F6. There is one administrator,
F7. Transport cost is zero,
F8. The network is homogeneous.

These assumptions (commonly made by inexperienced developers) are all relevant in the HAN and should be considered carefully by any model and/or method that is to be used (as we will see).

2.1. Architectures

There are two very broad architectures that can be used to allow discovery and lookup of entities in the HAN. Firstly; there is the centralised model in which a server acts as a registry (or even a host) for all the entities in the HAN. This method typically involves three actors (registry, publisher and client) [Figure 3] and involves the following process :

- **Publish :** An entity description is submitted to a registry,
- **Find :** A client submits a query to the registry,
- **Bind :** The client selects and uses an appropriate entity from the query results.

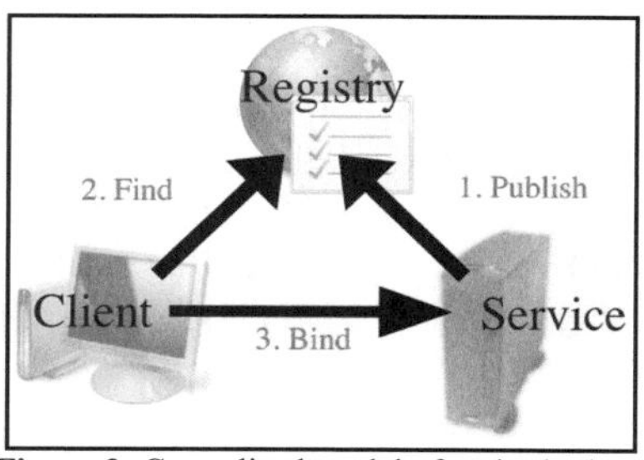

Figure 3: Centralised model of entity lookup.

In this model, both the client and the publisher need to know the registry location(s). If we consider fallacy [F1] (the network is reliable), we can appreciate that a central registry may not always be available (i.e a registry is a single point of failure). [F5] (topology doesn't change) also presents a problem with relation to the registry (will it be where we expect it? Do we need a separate registry discovery mechanism?) and the published entities (the registry may have a stale record of an entity that has now moved). [F6] (there is one administrator), one home user may turn off some functionality or change some settings without telling the other users or updating the registry! These reasons make it obvious that this architecture is not suited to the HAN.

Secondly; there is the distributed model. This model is unavoidably more complex, but does not suffer the single point of failure problem nor the stale information problem that afflicts the centralised model. In this model, when a client wishes to discover entities on the network, it transmits its query to all listening devices (typically using multicast). The receivers then process the query and if necessary send responses to the requesting client. Optional caching and periodic announcing by publishers provide some level of optimisation. Immediately we can spot that fallacy [F4] (The network is secure) is clearly going to provide some problems (an attacker can discover everything that is on the HAN). But it is actually [F2] (latency is zero), [F3] (Bandwidth is infinite) and [F7] (transport cost is zero) that provide the sources of most problem. If you consider a discovery request that would yield a large number of responses (for example a full enumeration of the entities in the HAN), for a very short time a high volume of devices will try and send data to the requesting client. To illustrate this effect, imagine a teacher in a class room that attempts to take the register by saying "can everyone say their name please"... all the children will shout their names at once! will some get lost in the noise? will the teacher hear all of them? Some techniques such as selecting a random (short) delay before responding can be used, but this adds to the amount of time required to perform the operation. Then there is the question of how long should the requester wait before using the results that it has received. Consequently, what happens to results that arrive after this deadline?

While both models have their problems, it is obvious that we can at least operate a degraded service with the distributed model, whereas some problems associated with the centralised model can render the HAN unusable!

2.2. Comparison

In [2.1.Architectures] we presented the centralised and distributed models and discussed some of the afflictions that plague them. As already discussed, the centralised model is not appropriate for deployment in the real world due to the unavoidable single point of failure problem. Also some centralised mechanisms fail fallacy [F8] (the network is homogeneous), one example is the Apache River project (formerly known as Jini) whose model relies on all implementations being Java based. As such, we will not discuss any existing centralised mechanisms here.

With respect to the three requirements described in [1.2.Required Functionality], we have evaluated SSDP [2] (part of UPnP), WS-Discovery [3](WS-Disc), Multicast-DNS [4] (mDNS), and our own discovery protocol which is called the *"Entity Resolution Protocol"* (ERP). All four make use of multicast message exchanges, but do so according to differing protocols and models. A comparison of the different models is given in [Table 2] below, which clearly shows that only ERP allows us to advertise (and consequently discover) any kind of object with no restrictions on what that object is. To illustrate this, let us consider the situation in which we want to advertise a music album, or even an individual song. ERP can do this (because it doesn't care what object it advertises), UPnP can't do this however (unless you consider the object a device), nor can WS-Disc (unless you consider the object a service), nor can mDNS (unless you consider the object a device).

Table 2: Comparison of discovery methods

Method	Identification	Model
UPnP	UUID	Advertises devices with attached services.
WS-Disc	Any stable & unique string	Advertises Web-Services.
mDNS	Domain name in the ".local" namespace	Advertises devices (like DNS).
ERP	Unique URN (can use UUID)	Advertises anything (called an entity).

Furthermore; implementors tend to create their *"interpretations"* of specifications leading to software that *"obeys"* the standard but does not interoperate with other software. Experience of deploying such software in real networks has shown this time and again. One example was a recent deployment of UPnP in the iSpace, where display/speakers, server and control point were deployed in the "well-defined" UPnP AV scenario for streaming video/audio to the display/speakers from the server under the control of the control point. Needless to say the three software components did not work together, reverse engineering revealed that at least two of the three components did not follow the specification correctly. Even identification of devices is not uniformly implemented in some cases, meaning that some UPnP software cant even discover things which are being advertised (making a full enumeration impossible).

For a performance comparison, we have deployed five devices (a mix of windows based PCs and Apple Mac devices) into the iSpace network (100 M/Bit ethernet) which is isolated from any other network traffic. We then deployed each of the four frameworks (all java based for fairness) onto these devices in turn and carried out some testing related to number of deployable entities to advertise and time to perform find and enumeration operations (a sixth device was used to act as a client to perform these operations). In the interest of fairness and result accuracy, we deployed an equal number of entities on each of the five devices and repeated each experiment 50 times, taking the average of all 50 experiments to produce each result. The results of a find operation, were, as predicted, relatively constant (+/-2ms for ERP and +/-100ms for the others). [Table 3] and [Figure 4] show a comparison of the find operation results. mDNS has been removed from [Figure 4] as it produced results at around 5200ms which provided a graph that did not show enough detail of the other results. Inspection of the mDNS implementation source code shows that there are several large delays introduced that explain the poor results.

Table 3: Timing results for a find operation.

Total Deployed Entities	Time (ms)			
	UPnP (Siemens : non-public)	**mDNS ([5])**	**WS-Disc ([6])**	**ERP**
5	926.6	5207	554.94	5.8
50	925.8	5183.42	538.96	5.16
500	1004.44	**	703.62	5.52
2,500	834.78	**	**	5.2
5,000	**	**	**	5.32
50,000	**	**	**	5.34
100,000	**	**	**	3.76

** = Software failed to produce results

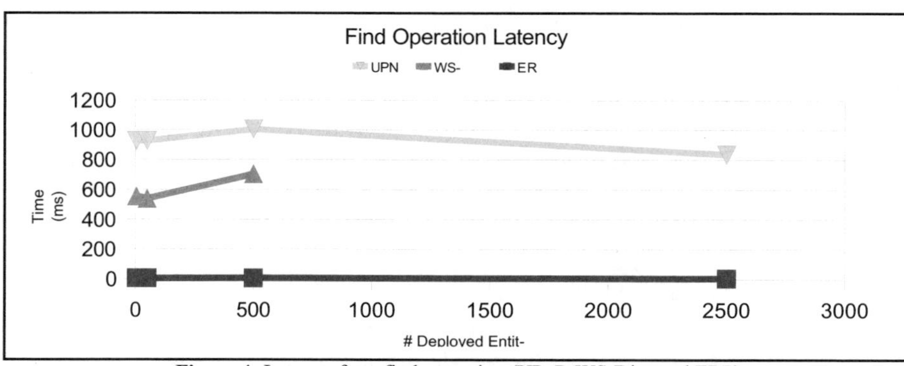

Figure 4: Latency for a find operation (UPnP, WS-Disc and ERP)

The “enumeration” operation also produced predictable results as shown in [Table 4] and visually in [Figure 5]. Whilst it was anticipated that software may become overwhelmed by the volume of entities it was being asked to cope with, the results show the breaking point to be a lot lower than expected for all implementations other than our ERP. In the case of mDNS, we also conducted an additional set of experiments that revealed its breaking point around 300 deployed entities (@ 5879.89ms to complete). It should also be noted, that we did not test the ERP above 100,000 entities and so we did not discover the breaking point of the protocol.

Table 4: Timing results for an enumeration

Total Deployed Entities	Time (ms)			
	UPnP (Siemens : non-public)	mDNS ([5])	WS-Disc ([6])	ERP
5	919.96	5308.28	**	8.66
50	1496.56	5113.38	**	20.98
500	25689.87	**	**	183.68
2,500	**	**	**	758.22
5,000	**	**	**	1436.62
50,000	**	**	**	14694.88
100,000	**	**	**	29213.96

** = Software failed to produce results

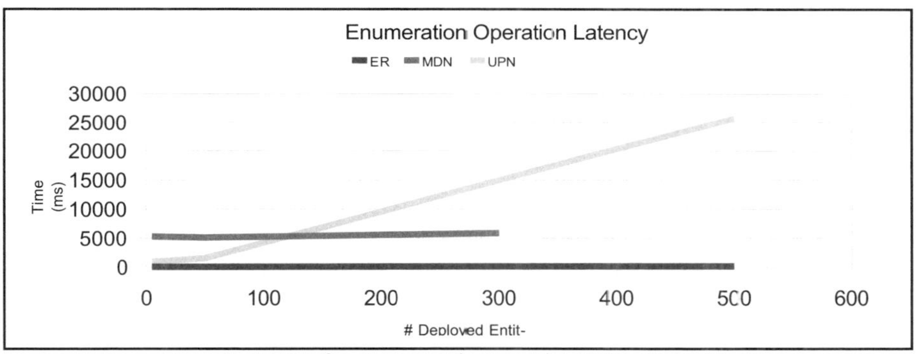

Figure 5: Latency for an enumeration operation (ERP, mDNS, UPnP)

3. About Entity Resolution Protocol (ERP)

The Entity Resolution Protocol (ERP) is intended to be simple and lightweight so that it is firstly fast, and secondly easy to implement, even on resource constrained devices. There are four main features to note about the protocol :

- **Packet based :** Instead of using HTTP extensions (like UPnP), or XML documents (like WS-Disc), ERP uses a byte encoded packet to represent a message. This makes the amount of data exchanged very small, and reduces the overhead incurred by marshalling and unmarshalling messages.
- **Mixed mode communications :** It uses multicast to send and receive messages (like the other protocols). Testing has revealed that at low numbers of deployed entities (<1000 in the network), multicast can operate without fault, higher than this however introduces packet loss and high latency. To combat this, ERP implements a simple threshold policy which states that *“if a*

device is to send more than X messages to a single requester at once, use unicast instead of multicast". This policy gives the protocol a much higher breaking point (tested up to 100,000 deployed entities) as messages do not get "lost", nor the processes overwhelmed. Currently the threshold for using unicast over multicast is 10 messages per device. In theory, this allows for 100 devices to operate multicast with no problems.

- **Entity Concept :** Unlike the other mechanism evaluated (which deal with the concept of devices and/or services), ERP deals with the very basic notion of an entity (akin to an object in the object oriented programming paradigm). This allows ERP to advertise/discover anything irrespective of what it is.
- **Container based :** Many entities are grouped into runtime containers which each have an ERP engine. For example, one device could have 10 containers, each servicing 100 entities (giving a total of 1000 entities on the device, but only 10 ERP instances). This improves the device resource use (low memory footprint, lower cpu utilisation, less processes trying to use the network, etc.).

4. Conclusions

While a number of discovery mechanisms exist, there are varying reasons why they are not suitable for deployment in our future homes where a high number of resources must be deployed and where near real time performance is required. Centralised systems suffer a huge problem if the single registry fails (something which is inevitable at some point in the real world), while we have presented experimental results in this paper that show existing distributed systems are not robust enough (all current methods failed to operate if any more than 500 entities were deployed), nor work fast enough. Additionally, neither existing centralised nor distributed systems have the appropriate model concepts to cope with the mix of resources to be found in our future homes. We therefore propose ERP, which overcomes existing inadequacies. It should be noted that the data presented in this paper shows ERP can operate in a network with 2 orders of magnitude more deployed entities above the breaking point of the other tested software (from under 1k to 100k deployed entities).

Our next step in the ERP work is to extend our tests to validate the results at high device deployment and with a selection of compression algorithms (to potentially boost throughput and further reduce latency). Before publishing the protocol in its entirety, we will also incorporate and test a query language for more advanced searches.

References

[1] A. Rotem-Gal-Oz, "Fallacies of Distributed Computing Explained", from http://www.rgoarchitects.com/Files/fallacies.pdf

[2] Y.Y. Goland, T. Cai, P. Leach, Y. Gu, S. Albright, *"Simple Service Discovery Protocol/1.0 Operating without an Arbiter"*. Internet Engineering Task Force Internet Draft. 1999.

[3] J. Beatty, G. Kakivaya, D. Kemp, T. Kuehnel, B. Lovering, B. Roe, C. St. John, J. Schlimmer, G. Simonnet, D. Walter, J. Weast, Y. Yarmosh, P. Yendluri, *"Web Services Dynamic Discovery"* (WS-Discovery). 2005.

[4] S. Cheshire, M. Krochmal, "Multicast DNS". Internet Engineering Task Force Internet draft. 2008.

[5] JmDNS project (http://jmdns.sourceforge.net/).

[6] java-ws-discovery project (http://code.google.com/p/java-ws-discovery/).

Intelligent Environments 2009
V. Callaghan et al. (Eds.)
IOS Press, 2009

doi:10.3233/978-1-60750-034-6-109

Assessing Temporal Relationships Between Events in Smart Environments

Fulvio MASTROGIOVANNI [a,1], Antonello SCALMATO [a], Antonio SGORBISSA [a] and Renato ZACCARIA [a]
[a] *University of Genova, Italy*

Abstract. A knowledge representation system is introduced that allows the recognition of temporal patterns of events in context-aware environments. The system is based on standard frameworks, such as an ontology, an inference mechanism, and relational operators acting on numerical quantities. The paper describes how knowledge is managed, then introduces a collection of temporal operators that are inspired by the Allen's interval algebra, and then details a situation recognition algorithm to assess knowledge semantics. An example is reported to describe the approach.

Keywords. Activity Recognition, Ontology, Temporal Reasoning

Introduction

Nowadays, it is commonly accepted that a sensible interaction between humans and their environments relies on the capabilities of the latter to understand the current situation. However, a further step in this direction is the *continuous* monitoring of human activities across many places and over long periods of time. For instance, consider nocturnal activities of an elder living alone at home: to detect insomnia, activities that are distant over time (e.g., the person is watching TV late in the night, after that he tries to sleep, then after a couple of hours he comes back to the kitchen, etc.) and located in different places (e.g., the kitchen, the bedroom, and the kitchen again) must be associated.

The problem of representing and reasoning upon temporal situations in smart environments has not been fully assessed. A good survey has been presented in [3], where several approaches to spatio-temporal reasoning are thoroughly discussed. The work described in [9] criticizes the use of Allen's temporal algebra for context assessment since it lacks robustness with respect to small variations in timing: an approach exploiting concepts of *coincidence* and *partial ordering* is described. A probabilistic approach has been presented in [10], where uncertainty is managed at the level of mathematical operators acting upon time instants. In [4] probabilistic temporal databases are used as knowledge representation frameworks. Temporal frameworks have been recently adopted to implement behavior monitoring techniques and to detect anomalies for elders and people with special needs [7][1].

[1]Corresponding Author: Fulvio Mastrogiovanni, Department of Computer, Communication and System Sciences, University of Genova, Genova, Italy; E-mail: fulvio.mastrogiovanni@unige.it.

The presented research is aimed at encoding in standard architectures for Ambient Intelligence reasoning mechanisms that take temporally and spatially distributed patterns of events into account. A standard knowledge representation system, an inference mechanism and a collection of mathematical operators to manage numerical quantities are assumed. A number of temporal operators are introduced and encoded within the framework, which are inspired by Allen's interval algebra, and a situation recognition process is thoroughly described that takes the semantics of these operators into account. The paper is organized as follows. Section 1 describes the knowledge representation system, and *how* it is possible to encode temporal operators into it. Next, Section 2 introduces a model for context assessment to manage temporal information. An example is discussed to validate the proof of concept. Conclusion follows.

1. Modeling Temporal Patterns of Activity

In this paper standard knowledge representation tools, and in particular *ontologies* described using Description Logics, are considered. These are conceptualizations of elements of a specific domain and their relationships [2]: conceptualized elements are called *concepts*, whereas the relationships are maintained through *roles*. Roles of a concept are of a given concept and can be *filled* by its instances. Within an ontology Σ, concepts are represented through *symbols* σ_k, and described using *descriptions* $\mathcal{D}_k$.

In $\mathcal{SHOIN}$ ontologies the availability of a set of logic connectors $\mathcal{H} \doteq \{\equiv, \sqcap, \sqcup, \neg\}$ is assumed, namely *definition* $\equiv$, *and* $\sqcap$, *or* $\sqcup$ and *not* $\neg$, whose meaning is intuitive[2]. Symbols are formalized using composite descriptions through connectors in $\mathcal{H}$, i.e,, $\mathcal{D}_k \equiv \mathcal{D}_{k,1} \diamond ... \diamond \mathcal{D}_{k,i} \diamond ... \diamond \mathcal{D}_{k,n}$, $\diamond \in \{\mathcal{H} \backslash \equiv\}$, where each description $\mathcal{D}_{k,i}$ can be in the form: (i) $\neg \mathcal{D}_k$, $\mathcal{D}_{k_1} \sqcap \mathcal{D}_{k_2}$, or $\mathcal{D}_{k_1} \sqcup \mathcal{D}_{k_2}$, which allow to compose *complex* descriptions on the basis of *simple* ones; $\exists r.\mathcal{D}_k$ or $\forall r.\mathcal{D}_k$, where r is a role filled either by other composite descriptions, or by numerical (e.g., *integer* values such as temperature levels), ordered (e.g., discretized ordered numerical classes such *low*, *medium* or *high*) or non-ordered (e.g., *labels* associated with objects in a smart environment) symbols whose semantics is grounded with respect to Σ; (iii) $\leq_n r.\mathcal{D}_k$ or $\geq_n r.\mathcal{D}_k$, which restrict the number of possible filling descriptions for the role r, respectively *at most* and *at least* n fillers.

A simple and efficient inference mechanism, called *subsumption* (and referred to as $\sqsubseteq$), is commonly available [5]. Subsumption is a binary operator acting upon two descriptions $\mathcal{D}_1$ and $\mathcal{D}_2$. However, it is used in its *query* form `subs?[`$\mathcal{D}_1$`, `$\mathcal{D}_2$`]` to return *true* if $\mathcal{D}_1$ holds whenever $\mathcal{D}_2$ holds, and *false* otherwise. As a practical side effect, if we consider a description $\mathcal{D}_k$ as a collection of constituent descriptions $\mathcal{D}_{k,i}$, any aggregation of $\mathcal{D}_{k,i}$ subsumes $\mathcal{D}_k$.

Run time sensory information is represented in Σ through instances of descriptions, which are modeled through a proper *variable assignment* α, where variables are associated with roles. Therefore, a *satisfied symbol* $\Sigma \models \sigma_k(\hat{\sigma_l})$ is a grounded symbol originating from the closure of roles in σ_k through α: each role r in the definition of σ_k is filled with the correct number and type of constituent descriptions. Given a number of symbols $\hat{\sigma_l}$ grounded with respect to objects σ_k described in the ontology Σ, and given a variable assignment α under a specific interpretation $\mathcal{I}$ at a given time instant τ, then

[2]A formal specification of syntax and semantics is beyond the scope of the paper, but it can be found in [6].

the proposed model for context assessment can be seen as the satisfiability procedure $(\Sigma, \mathcal{I}, \alpha_\tau) \models \sigma_k(\hat{\sigma_l})$.

The proposed situation recognition model is based on a specific structure over Σ: although the model can manage contexts with many levels of symbols (depending on the complexity of the associated descriptions), three hierarchical primitives are used. *Predicate* $\mathcal{P}$ is a concept aimed at representing sensory data. For each type of sensory data to represent in Σ, a child concept σ_k of $\mathcal{P}$ is defined such that $\Sigma \models \mathcal{P}(\sigma_k)$[3], which is based exclusively on numerical, ordered or non-ordered sensory data. *Context* $\mathcal{C}$ is a concept that aggregates descriptions of both predicates and contexts referred to the *same* entity. For each information aggregate to be represented, a child concept σ_k of *Context* is introduced, which is described using constituent descriptions. *Situation* $\mathcal{S}$ is a concept that aggregates many contexts related to *different* entities. Again, for each situation deemed interesting by system designers, a child concept σ_k is defined such that $\Sigma \models \mathcal{S}(\sigma_k)$, which takes composite descriptions into account.

As soon as new data are available, the system must: (i) *generate* grounded descriptions $\hat{\mathcal{D}}_l$ from sensory data corresponding to those of symbols $\Sigma \models \mathcal{P}(\sigma_k)$; (ii) iteratively *aggregate* them in order to satisfy symbols in $\Sigma \models \mathcal{C}(\sigma_k)$; (iii) *combine* satisfied descriptions to check subsumption with respect to symbols in $\Sigma \models \mathcal{S}(\sigma_k)$.

The ontology is provided with a collection of temporal operators, which require to explicitly introduce time dependence[4], and to reformulate the context satisfiability problem for symbols in $\mathcal{P}$, $\mathcal{C}$ and $\mathcal{S}$. For a given time instant τ, symbols σ_k, $k = 1, ..., |\mathcal{P}| + |\mathcal{C}| + |\mathcal{S}|$, are satisfied by $\hat{\sigma}_l$ in τ (and we write $\sigma_{k,\tau}$) if there is an interpretation $\mathcal{I}$ and a variable assignment α_τ such that $(\Sigma, \mathcal{I}, \alpha_\tau) \models \sigma_{k,\tau}(\hat{\sigma}_l)$. Temporal operators can be divided into two classes: (i) $\mathcal{T}_t \doteq \{\delta, \lambda\}$, aimed at monitoring the evolution of the *truth value* of a single satisfied description; (ii) $\mathcal{T}_r \doteq \{\prec, \succ, \prec_t, \succ_t, \{d\}, \{o\}, \{m\}, \doteq, \{s\}, \{f\}\}$, which comprises operators of the Allen's interval algebra, therefore being aimed at comparing pairwise different descriptions. Collectively, the set of temporal operators is defined as $\mathcal{T} \doteq \mathcal{T}_t \cup \mathcal{T}_r$. In order to allow *subsumption* to reason upon temporal relationships, it is necessary to preliminarly introduce a family of mathematical relational operators $\omega \in \{<, \leq, =, \geq, >\}$, justified as *syntactic sugar*.

Symbols σ_k such that $\Sigma \models \mathcal{P}(\sigma_k)$, $\Sigma \models \mathcal{C}(\sigma_k)$ and $\Sigma \models \mathcal{S}(\sigma_k)$ have descriptions $\mathcal{D}_k$ accounting for two specific roles, namely *starts_at* and *ends_at*, which are filled with instances of time instants and specify the temporal interval when the corresponding grounded descriptions have been satisfied by a given variable assignment. In particular, for a given symbol $\hat{\sigma}_l$, *starts_at* and *ends_at* are respectively filled with two time instants τ_l^- and τ_l^+ if, for each $\tau \in [\tau_l^-, \tau_l^+]$, α_τ is such that $\hat{\sigma}_l$ is *true*. Operators in $\mathcal{T}_t$ are defined in the following paragraphs.

Change δ: an operator that produces a description $\mathcal{D}_\mathcal{E} \equiv \delta(\mathcal{D})$. Given $\mathcal{I}$, two time instants τ_1 and τ_2, where $\tau_1 < \tau_2$, and two variable assignments α_{τ_1} and α_{τ_2}, $\delta_{\tau_2}(\hat{\mathcal{D}}_{\tau_2})$ is satisfied if and only if $\hat{\mathcal{D}}_{\tau_2} = \neg\hat{\mathcal{D}}_{\tau_1}$.

Duration λ_ω: a family of operators that produces a description $\mathcal{D}_\lambda \equiv \lambda_\omega(\mathcal{D}_1, \mathcal{D}_2)$. Given $\mathcal{I}$, four time instants τ_1^-, τ_1^+, τ_2^- and τ_2^+, and four variable assignments $\alpha_{\tau_1^-}$, $\alpha_{\tau_1^+}$, $\alpha_{\tau_2^-}$ and $\alpha_{\tau_2^+}$, where $\alpha_{\tau_1^-} < \alpha_{\tau_1^+} < \alpha_{\tau_2^-} < \alpha_{\tau_2^+}$, for each τ such that $\alpha_{\tau_2^+} < \tau$, $\lambda_{\omega,\tau}(\hat{\mathcal{D}}_{1,\tau}, \hat{\mathcal{D}}_{2,\tau})$ is satisfied if and only if $(\tau_1^+ - \tau_1^-)\omega(\tau_2^+ - \tau_2^-)$ is *true*.

[3]The two forms $\mathcal{P}(\sigma_k)$ and $\sigma_k \sqsubseteq \mathcal{P}$ can be used indifferently.
[4]Time is modeled as an ordered sequence of time instants.

Next, operators in $\mathcal{T}_r$ are defined in the following paragraphs.

Before$_t$ $\prec_t$: an operator that produces a description $\mathcal{D}_{\prec_t} \equiv \prec_t (\mathcal{D}_1, \mathcal{D}_2)$, i.e., when an event occurs up to t time instants before another one. Given $\mathcal{I}$ and a sequence of variable assignments $\{\alpha_\tau\}$, $\hat{\mathcal{D}}_1 \prec_t \hat{\mathcal{D}}_2$ is satisfied if and only if $\mathcal{D}_1$, $\mathcal{D}_2$ and $\tau_1^+ + t > \tau_2^-$ hold.

After$_t$ $\succ_t$: an operator that produces a description $\mathcal{D}_{\succ_t} \equiv \succ_t (\mathcal{D}_1, \mathcal{D}_2)$, i.e., when an event occurs up to t time instants after another one. Given $\mathcal{I}$ and a sequence of variable assignments $\{\alpha_\tau\}$, $\hat{\mathcal{D}}_1 \succ_t \hat{\mathcal{D}}_2$ is satisfied if and only if $\mathcal{D}_1$, $\mathcal{D}_2$ and $\tau_1^- - t < \tau_2^+$ holds.

During $\{d\}$: an operator that produces a description $\mathcal{D}_d \equiv \{d\}(\mathcal{D}_1, \mathcal{D}_2)$, i.e., two events are parallel and one is entirely contained within the other one's span. Given $\mathcal{I}$ and a sequence of variable assignments $\{\alpha_\tau\}$, $\hat{\mathcal{D}}_1\{d\}\hat{\mathcal{D}}_2$ is satisfied if and only if $\mathcal{D}_1$, $\mathcal{D}_2$ and $(\tau_1^- > \tau_2^-) \wedge (\tau_1^+ < \tau_2^+)$ holds.

Overlaps $\{o\}$: an operator that produces a description $\mathcal{D}_o \equiv \{o\}(\mathcal{D}_1, \mathcal{D}_2)$, i.e., two events are partially parallel. Given $\mathcal{I}$ and a sequence of variable assignments $\{\alpha_\tau\}$, $\hat{\mathcal{D}}_1\{o\}\hat{\mathcal{D}}_2$ is satisfied if and only if $\mathcal{D}_1$, $\mathcal{D}_2$ and $(\tau_1^- < \tau_2^-) \wedge (\tau_1^+ < \tau_2^-)$ holds.

Meets $\{m\}$: an operator that produces a description $\mathcal{D}_m \equiv \{m\}(\mathcal{D}_1, \mathcal{D}_2)$, i.e., when one events exactly starts when the another one ends. Given $\mathcal{I}$ and a sequence of variable assignments $\{\alpha_\tau\}$, $\hat{\mathcal{D}}_1\{m\}\hat{\mathcal{D}}_2$ is satisfied if and only if $\mathcal{D}_1$, $\mathcal{D}_2$ and $\tau_1^+ = \tau_2^-$ holds.

Equals $\doteqdot$: an operator that produces a description $\mathcal{D}_{\doteqdot} \equiv \doteqdot (\mathcal{D}_1, \mathcal{D}_2)$, i.e., two events last exactly for the same period of time. Given $\mathcal{I}$ and a sequence of variable assignments $\{\alpha_\tau\}$, $\hat{\mathcal{D}}_1 \doteqdot \hat{\mathcal{D}}_2$ is satisfied if and only if $\mathcal{D}_1$, $\mathcal{D}_2$ and $(\tau_1^- = \tau_2^-) \wedge (\tau_1^+ = \tau_2^+)$ holds.

Starts $\{s\}$: an operator that produces a description $\mathcal{D}_s \equiv \{s\}(\mathcal{D}_1, \mathcal{D}_2)$, i.e., two events start exactly at the same time. Given $\mathcal{I}$ and a sequence of variable assignments $\{\alpha_\tau\}$, $\hat{\mathcal{D}}_1\{s\}\hat{\mathcal{D}}_2$ is satisfied if and only if $\mathcal{D}_1$, $\mathcal{D}_2$ and $(\tau_1^- = \tau_2^-) \wedge (\tau_1^+ < \tau_2^+)$ holds.

Finishes $\{f\}$: an operator that produces a description $\mathcal{D}_s \equiv \{f\}(\mathcal{D}_1, \mathcal{D}_2)$, i.e., two events end exactly at the same time. Given $\mathcal{I}$ and a sequence of variable assignments $\{\alpha_\tau\}$, $\hat{\mathcal{D}}_1\{f\}\hat{\mathcal{D}}_2$ is satisfied if and only if $\mathcal{D}_1$, $\mathcal{D}_2$ and $(\tau_1^- < \tau_2^-) \wedge (\tau_1^+ = \tau_2^+)$ holds.

Operators in $\mathcal{T}$ are used during the situation recognition phase to assess temporal relationships among descriptions. In particular, grounded descriptions (i.e., originated from sensory data) are evaluated by inspecting the actual values of the roles *starts_at* and *ends_at* through subsumption with respect to operators in $\mathcal{T}$. Obviously enough, the evaluation of temporal operators is deferred in time (i.e., when the last needed time instant is reached), since they involve many events to occur in sequence.

2. Temporal Situation Assessment

Temporal situation assessment is realized by iteratively aggregating grounded descriptions according to templates encoded in $\mathcal{C}$ and $\mathcal{S}$ descriptions (see Figure 1 on the bottom). When new sensory data are available a classification process is carried out over grounded symbols $\Sigma \models \mathcal{P}(\hat{\sigma}_l)$ that determines if they are satisfied according to their semantics [8]. The set of all the grounded predicative elements satisfied up to time instant τ[5] is defined as $\hat{\mathcal{D}}^p_\tau \doteq \{\hat{\mathcal{D}}^p_l | \Sigma \models \mathcal{P}(\hat{\mathcal{D}}^p_l)\}$, where $l = 1, ..., |\hat{\mathcal{D}}^p_l|$. A procedure T is defined such that, given a set of grounded descriptions of satisfied symbols (e.g., $\hat{\mathcal{D}}^p_\tau$), it returns the set of grounded descriptions of satisfied temporal operators that hold between

[5]The ontology maintains a set of *Predicate* symbols satisfied in a previous time interval. The extension of this interval must balance *memory* of past events and *real time* processing requirements.

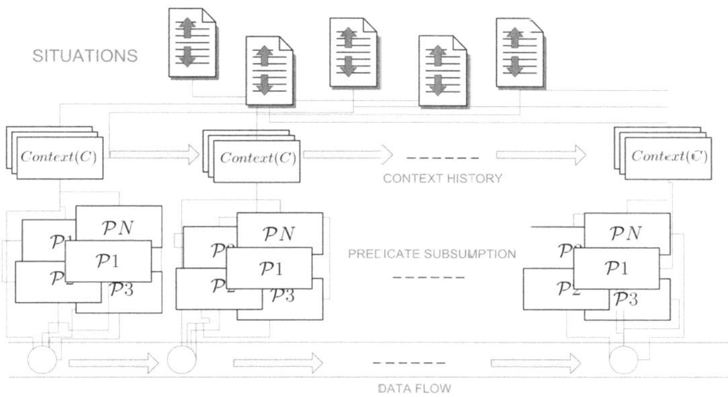

Figure 1. The situation assessment process.

them in τ, i.e., $\hat{\mathcal{D}}_{\tau}^{t(p)} \doteq \{\hat{\mathcal{D}}_m^{t(p)} | \bigcup_{\Upsilon \in \mathcal{T}} \Sigma \models \Upsilon(\hat{\mathcal{D}}_m^{t(p)})\}$. Therefore, T is defined such that $\hat{\mathcal{D}}_{\tau}^{t(p)} = T(\hat{\mathcal{D}}_{\tau}^{p})$. If we omit the dependency of temporal operator descriptions on those of predicates, we define the *memory* of the system at the *Predicate* level by joining descriptions belonging to $\hat{\mathcal{D}}_{\tau}^{p}$ and $\hat{\mathcal{D}}_{\tau}^{t(p)}$ as $\hat{\mathcal{D}}_{s,\tau}^{p\cup t(p)} = \hat{\mathcal{D}}_1^p \sqcap \ldots \sqcap \hat{\mathcal{D}}^p_{|\hat{\mathcal{D}}_l^p|} \sqcap \hat{\mathcal{D}}_1^t \sqcap \ldots \sqcap \hat{\mathcal{D}}^t_{|\hat{\mathcal{D}}_m^t|} \doteq \hat{\mathcal{D}}_{s,i}$, where s stands for *satisfied*, and i is an index (initialized to 0) whose meaning is related to the number of hierarchical *Context* levels that are represented within the ontology.

At this point, a sequence of steps is recursively performed that incrementally updates $\hat{\mathcal{D}}_{s,i}$. The set $\mathcal{C}_{s,i}$ of i-th level symbols $\Sigma \models \mathcal{C}(\sigma_{k,i})$ that subsume *memory* is determined as $\mathcal{C}_{s,i} \doteq \{\Sigma \models \mathcal{C}(\sigma_{k,i}) : \texttt{subs?}[\sigma_{k,i}, \hat{\mathcal{D}}_{s,i}]\}$. After this step is accomplished, the index i is incremented for the next recursion. Satisfied i-th level symbols $\Sigma \models \mathcal{C}(\sigma_{k,i})$ are then described by their grounded descriptions $\hat{\mathcal{D}}_l^c$. The set of all the grounded context elements satisfied at the time instant τ is defined as $\hat{\mathcal{D}}_{\tau}^{c} \doteq \{\hat{\mathcal{D}}_l^c | \Sigma \models \mathcal{C}(\hat{\mathcal{D}}_l^c)\}, l = 1, ..., |\hat{\mathcal{D}}_l^c|$. The procedure T is used again to determine the set of grounded descriptions of satisfied temporal operators holding between grounded symbols $\Sigma \models \mathcal{C}(\hat{\sigma}_{k,i})$ at the time instant τ $\hat{\mathcal{D}}_{\tau}^{t(c)} = T(\hat{\mathcal{D}}_{\tau}^{c})$, and therefore: $\hat{\mathcal{D}}_{\tau}^{t(c)} \doteq \{\hat{\mathcal{D}}_m^{t(c)} | \bigcup_{\Upsilon \in \mathcal{T}} \Sigma \models \Upsilon(\hat{\mathcal{D}}_m^{t(c)})\}$. Finally, the *memory* of the system at the i-th *Context* level is determined by joining descriptions belonging to $\hat{\mathcal{D}}_{\tau}^{t(c)}$ and $\hat{\mathcal{D}}_{\tau}^{c}$, i.e., $\hat{\mathcal{D}}_{s,\tau}^{c\cup t(c)} = \hat{\mathcal{D}}_1^c \sqcap \ldots \sqcap \hat{\mathcal{D}}^c_{|\hat{\mathcal{D}}_l^c|} \sqcap \hat{\mathcal{D}}_1^t \sqcap \ldots \sqcap \hat{\mathcal{D}}^t_{|\hat{\mathcal{D}}_l^t|} \doteq \hat{\mathcal{D}}_{s,i}$.

The recursion over $\hat{\mathcal{D}}_{s,i}$ ends when there are no more $(i+1)$-th level symbols $\Sigma \models \mathcal{C}(\sigma_{k,i+1})$. Since the ontology is known beforehand, an upper bound to this recursion can be easily determined. As a final step, the set of *Situation* symbols $\Sigma \models \mathcal{S}(\sigma_k)$ that are satisfied at the time instant τ, namely $\mathcal{S}_{s,\tau}$, is given by $\mathcal{S}_{s,\tau} \doteq \{\Sigma \models \mathcal{S}(\sigma_k) : \texttt{subs?}[\sigma_k, \hat{\mathcal{D}}_{s,i}]\}$. Once the set $\mathcal{S}_{s,\tau}$ is assessed, the system is said to be *aware* of modeled *events* occuring within the monitored environment at the time instant τ.

The architecture implements a 3-layer context-aware mechanism, each layer devoted to manage different aspects of context recognition: (i) *Predicate layer*: a fast dynamically changing representation structure that, for efficiency reasons related to the complexity of inference mechanisms in ontologies [5], is constrained to operate on a limited time interval; needless to say, a longer time interval produces more accurate results, but an increased computational load; however, its importance relies in that it follows

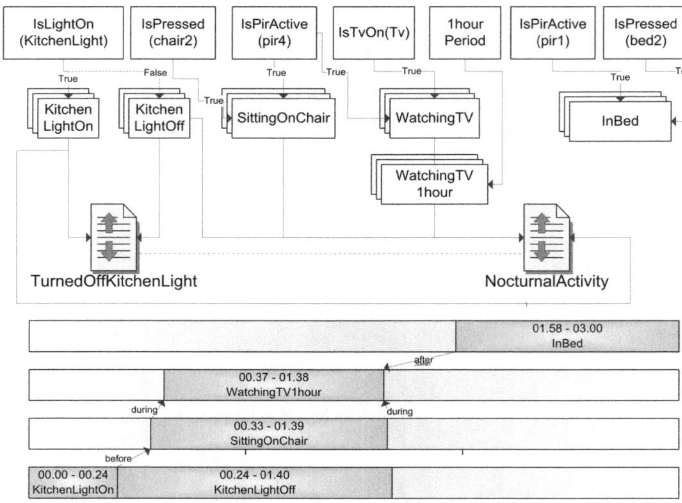

Figure 2. *Top*: a relevant sketch of the ontology. *Bottom*: a variable assignment that satisfies the ontology.

high frequency variations in patterns of sensory data and the associated temporal relationships; (ii) *Context layer*: a multiple-resolution representation layer that allows to formally model contexts at different degrees of granularity; for this reason, it can cope with *middle* and *slow frequency* fluctuations in observed data thereby recognizing trends over long periods of time, since it is still represented beyond the time interval; *Situation layer*: an aggregation level that allows the evaluation of combined events, possibly spanned over time and only loosely coupled.

3. An example

In this Section, an example is reported to clarify the conceptual steps involved in representing temporal relationships among events within an ontology: we show how to encode a sofisticated daily activity: *after having switched the light off, the user watches TV while sitting on a chair; after that, within half an hour, he goes to bed.* In particular, we concentrate only on the modeling phase and the associate context recognition process.

Context Modelling. The previously introduced sequence of activities must be modeled using a *Situation* concept, since it involves representations related to many entities: *user*, *TV*, and *bed*, just to name a few. Using the temporal operators in $\mathcal{T}$, this situation can be written using a composition of *Context* concepts (see Figure 2 on top):

$$NocturnalActivity \equiv TurnedOffKitchenLight \prec SittingOnChair \sqcap$$
$$SittingOnChair\{d\}WatchingTV1hour \sqcap InBed \succ_{30min} WatchingTV1hour.$$

Each *Context* is mapped to a number of predicates. In the following paragraph we exemplify how to model a particular contextual element, namely $SittingOnChair$. In our set-up [8], seat sensors are placed over the chairs and several Passive Infra Red (PIR in short) sensors are distributed throughout the environment. We first specify the $PIR \sqsubseteq Sensor$ symbol σ_{PIR}, characterized by the description $\mathcal{D}_{PIR} \sqsubseteq \forall id.INTEGER \sqcap \forall description.STRING \sqcap \forall range.Area$, where *id* is the *PIR* identification number, *description* is aimed at providing system users with meaningful information about the sensor, and *range* is a role that is filled with instances of the *Area* concept in order to associate sensory data with labeled places within the environment. For instance, a specific *PIR* sensor can be modelled as $\hat{\mathcal{D}}_{PIR4} \equiv id(4) \sqcap description("KitchenPIRSensor") \sqcap range(Kitchen)$. At the same time, we specify the $PIRData \sqsubseteq Data$ symbols $\sigma_{PIRData}$, which is characterized by the description $\mathcal{D}_{PIRData} \sqsubseteq \forall id.Type \sqcap \forall value.BOOLEAN$, where *id* specifies the data *Type* and *value* is the actual sensor reading. For instance, if something is detected by *pir4*, this will be modeled within the ontology by the grounded description $\hat{\mathcal{D}}_{PIRData4} \sqsubseteq id(PIRType) \sqcap value(true)$.

As described in the previous Section, the association between sensors and sensory information is maintained through *Predicate* concepts. Specifically, *IsPIRActive* is represented within Σ using a symbol $\sigma_{IsPIRActive}$ described using $\mathcal{D}_{IsPirActive} \sqsubseteq \forall sensor.PIR \sqcap \forall value.PIRData$. As it can be noticed, its definition exploits both $\mathcal{D}_{PIR}$ and $\mathcal{D}_{PIRData}$, and a possible instance is $\hat{\mathcal{D}}_{IsPIRActive4} \sqsubseteq sensor(pir4) \sqcap value(PIRData4)$. Similar considerations hold for all the other *Predicate* concepts, e.g., *IsPressed*. Once both *IsPIRActive* and *IsPressed* are represented within the ontology, it is straightforward to introduce *SittingOnChair* as $SittingOnChair \sqsubseteq IsPressed \sqcap IsPIRActive$. Similar considerations hold for other contexts as well.

Context Recognition. A sequence of variable assignments satisfying *NocturnalActivity* is given in Figure 2 on the bottom. According to the proposed model, context recognition is an iterative process that, every time instant τ, determines the set of all the satisfied *Predicate* concepts $\hat{\mathcal{D}}^p_\tau$ and then all the relevant temporal relationships among satisfied instances of *Predicate* $\hat{\mathcal{D}}^{t(p)}_\tau$. This mechanism is extended to *Context* concepts satisfied in τ. With respect to our example, and starting from the *Context* level for the sake of brevity, we can see that at the time instant τ=00.23, only one relevant *Context* is recognized, namely $\hat{\mathcal{D}}^c_{00.23} = \{KitchenLightOn\}$. Since only one satisfied *Context* is represented within system *memory*, the corresponding set of temporal relationships is empty, and therefore $\hat{\mathcal{D}}^{t(c)}_{00.23} = \{\}$. As a consequence, the overall *memory* at the time instant τ=00.23 is given by $\hat{\mathcal{D}}^{c\cup t(c)}_{s,00.23} = \{KitchenLightOn\}$. When, at τ=00.24, the lights are switched off, the *Context KitchenLightOff* is recognized, and therefore it becomes part of *memory* $\hat{\mathcal{D}}^c_{00.24} = \{KitchenLightOn, KitchenLightOff\}$. However, an interesting temporal relationship involving both *KitchenLightOn* and *KitchenLightOff* is detected, i.e., $\hat{\mathcal{D}}^{t(c)}_{00.24} = \{TurnedOffKitchenLight\}$. The corresponding overall history at τ=00.24 is updated as $\hat{\mathcal{D}}^{c\cup t(c)}_{s,00.24} = \{KitchenLightOn, KitchenLightOff, TurnedOffKitchenLight\}$.

As it is shown in Figure 2, the next interesting event occurs at the time instant τ=00.40, when the *TV* is switched on. As a consequence, *history* is updated as $\hat{\mathcal{D}}^c_{00.40} = \{KitchenLightOn, KitchenLightOff, SittingOnChair, WatchingTV\}$, $\hat{\mathcal{D}}^{t(c)}_{00.40} = \{TurnedOffKitchenLight, \mathcal{D}_1\}$, where $\mathcal{D}_1 \equiv TurnedOffKitchenLight \prec SittingOnChair$. As a consequence, the overall *memory* becomes:

$$\hat{\mathcal{D}}^{c\cup t(c)}_{s,00.40} = \{KitchenLightOn, KitchenLightOff, TurnedOffKitchenLight, SittingOnChair, WatchingTV, \mathcal{D}_1\}.$$

Finally, at the time instant τ=01.58, all the events described in *NocturnalActivity* are detected, since $\hat{\mathcal{D}}^c_{01.58} = \{KitchenLightOn,\ KitchenLightOff,\ SittingOnChair,\ WatchingTV1hour,\ OnBed\}$, $\hat{\mathcal{D}}^{t(c)}_{01.58} = \{TurnedOffKitchenLight, \mathcal{D}_1, \mathcal{D}_2, \mathcal{D}_3\}$, where $\mathcal{D}_2 \equiv SittingOnChair\{d\}WatchingTV1hour$ and $\mathcal{D}_3 \equiv InBed \succ_{30min} WatchingTV1hour$, and therefore *memory* contains:

$$\hat{\mathcal{D}}^{c \cup t(c)}_{s,01.58} = \{KitchenLightOn, KitchenLightOff, TurnedOffKitchenLight, SittingOnChair, WatchingTV1hour, OnBed, \mathcal{D}_1, \mathcal{D}_2, \mathcal{D}_3\}.$$

Finally,

$$\mathcal{S}_{s,01.58} \doteq \{\Sigma \models \mathcal{S}(\sigma_{NocturnalActivity}) : \texttt{subs?}\,[\sigma_{NocturnalActivity}, \hat{\mathcal{D}}_{s,0}]\}$$

4. Conclusion

In this paper, a framework is discussed that allows the representation and the recognition of time-dependent situations by a context-aware architecture. The aim is to demonstrate that it is possible to encode temporal reasoning mechanisms in standard Ambient Intelligence architectures. In fact, the proposed framework assumes the availability of an ontology, an associated inference mechanism (i.e., subsumption), and relational operators acting on numerical quantities. The paper first introduces a collection of temporal operators that are inspired by the well-known Allen's interval algebra, and then describes a context recognition process able to deal with the new operators. An example of use has been reported to validate the overall approach.

References

[1] Augusto, J.C., Liu, J., McCullagh, P., Wang., H. and Bo-Yang, J. Management of Uncertainty and Spatio-Temporal Aspects for Monitoring and Diagnosis in a Smart Home. In *International Journal of Computational Intelligence Systems* **1**(4) (2008).

[2] Baader, F., Calvanese, D., McGuinness, D., Nardi, D. and Patel-Schneider, P. (Eds.): The Description Logic Handbook. Cambridge University Press (2002).

[3] Bjorn, G., Guesgen, H.W. and Hubner, S.: Spatiotemporal Reasoning for Smart Homes. In *Designing Smart Homes*. Springer Berlin/Heidelberg (2006) 16–34.

[4] Dekhtyar, A., Ross, R. and Subrahamanian, V.S.: Probabilistic Temporal Databases, I:Algebra. In *ACM Transactions on Database Systems* **26**(1) (2001) 41–95.

[5] Horrocks, I. and Sattler, U.: A Tableau Decision Procedure for $\mathcal{SHOIQ}$. In *Journal of Automated Reasoning* **39**(3) (2007) 249–276.

[6] Kutz, O., Lutz, C., Wolter, F. and Zakharyaschev, M.: ε-connections of Abstract Description Systems. In *Artificial Intelligence* **156**(1) (2004) 1–73.

[7] Jakkula V. and Cook, D.: Anomaly Detection using Temporal Data Mining in a Smart Home Environment. In *Methods of Information in Medicine* **47**(1) (2008) 70–75.

[8] Mastrogiovanni, F., Sgorbissa, A. and Zaccaria, R.: On the Problem of Describing Activities in Context-Aware Environments. In *International Journal of Assistive Robotics and Mechatronics* **9**(4) (2008).

[9] Morchen, F.: A Better Tool that Allen's Relations for Expressing Temporal Knowledge in Interval Data. In *Proceedings of the Twelveth ACM SIGKDD International Conference on Knowledge Discovery and Data Mining*, Philadelphia, PA, USA (2006).

[10] Ryabov, V. and Puuronen, S.: Probabilistic Reasoning about Uncertainty Relations between Temporal Points. In *Proceedings of the Eigth International Symposium on Temporal Representation and Reasoning (TIME-01)*, Cividale del Friuli, Italy, June 14–16 (2006).

Intelligent Environments 2009
V. Callaghan et al. (Eds.)
IOS Press, 2009

doi:10.3233/978-1-60750-034-6-117

Monitoring Domestic Activities with Temporal Constraints and Components

M. CIRILLO [a,1], F. LANZELLOTTO [b,2], F. PECORA [a] and A. SAFFIOTTI [a]
[a] *AASS Mobile Robotics Lab, Örebro University, Sweden*
[b] *Dept. of Informatics and Automation, University Roma-3, Italy*

Abstract. Intelligent environments are increasingly rich in ubiquitous sensing capabilities that can be leveraged to know which actions a user is engaged in at any given moment in time. The ability of an intelligent environment to recognize a high-level plan of activities performed by the user in a smart home would allow to construct proactive services, such as reminding, forecasting and providing timely physical support. This article proposes an approach to human activity recognition based on temporal planning. The approach leverages on one hand the ubiquitous sensors provided by the PEIS-Home, a sensor-rich intelligent environment, and, on the other hand, the temporal representation and reasoning capabilities of OMPS, a constraint-based temporal planning and scheduling framework.

Keywords. Intelligent environments, activity recognition, ubiquitous sensors, planning, temporal reasoning

Introduction

In this paper we tackle the problem of recognizing patterns of activities carried out by a human being within an intelligent home environment equipped with pervasive and heterogeneous sensors. This problem has gained the attention of a number of disciplines within the artificial intelligence community, as the ability to automatically recognize activities is a key capability for building intelligent environments that provide personalized and effective support services. In order to achieve this, an intelligent system must employ non-trivial and temporally contextualized knowledge regarding the state of the user [2]. For instance, if a smart home could recognize that the human user is cooking, it could avoid cleaning the dining room until the subsequent dining activity is over.

Current approaches to this problem can be roughly categorized as *data-driven* or *knowledge-driven*. In data-driven approaches, models of human behavior are learned from large volumes of data over time. Notable examples of such approaches employ Hidden Markov Models (HMMs) for learning sequences of sensor observations with given transition probabilities. Instantiated within the domestic environment setting, these techniques have been leveraged to infer human activities from RFID-tagged object use [12] as well as vision-based observations [17,14].

---

[1]Corresponding author: Örebro University, 701 82 Sweden. E-mail: marcello.cirillo@aass.oru.se. This work has been partially supported by CUGS (Swedish national computer science graduate school) and by the Swedish KK foundation.

[2]Work performed while this author was at the AASS Mobile Robotics Lab, Örebro University, Sweden.

In knowledge-driven approaches, patterns of observations are modeled from first principles rather than learned. Abductive processes are employed instead, whereby sensor data is explained by hypothesizing the occurrence of specific human activities.[3] Examples include the work of Goultiaeva and Lespérance [8], where the Situation Calculus is used to specify very rich plans, as well as approaches based on ontologies [10] and temporal reasoning approaches in which rich temporal representations are employed to model the conditions under which patterns of human activities occur [13,9].

Data- and knowledge-driven approaches have complementary strengths and weaknesses. One advantage of the former is the ability to learn patterns of human behavior, rather than having to model them explicitly. This advantage comes at the price of poor scalability and inherent difficulty of providing common-sense knowledge for classifying overwhelming amounts of data [17]. In this sense, knowledge-based approaches can provide a powerful means to express such information, which can then be employed by an abductive process that essentially "attaches a meaning" to the observed data. Indeed, the current literature points to the fact that the two strategies are complementary in scope: data-driven approaches provide an effective way to recognize elementary activities from large amounts of continuous data; conversely, knowledge-driven approaches are useful when the criteria for recognizing human activities are given by complex but general rules that are clearly identifiable. While the ranges of applicability of the two strategies clearly overlap, knowledge-driven approaches have been less explored in literature. We argue that such strategies retain an advantage in domains where the emphasis lies not so much in recognizing elementary actions, rather where knowledge modeled from first principles can be used to fuse heterogeneous sensor data to obtain higher-level activity inference.

In this paper we present a knowledge-driven approach based on a rich temporal representation and on a planning framework. The focus of this paper is on the knowledge representation aspect of the architecture. We show how the use of a component-based domain representation grounded on Allen's Interval Algebra [1] is employed in conjunction with a constraint-based planning and scheduling framework called OMPS [7] to obtain an abductive process for activity recognition. The use of this architecture is demonstrated within a real intelligent environment, namely the PEIS-Home [15], a testbed environment in which robotic, sensory and intelligent software components are combined to obtain a service providing environment for the future home.

1. Background: the OMPS Framework

The Open Multi-component Planner and Scheduler (OMPS) [7] is a constraint-based planning and scheduling software framework grounded on the notion of *component*. OMPS has been used to develop a variety of decision support tools, ranging from highly-specialized space mission planning software to classical planning frameworks [4]. A complete description of OMPS is outside the scope of this paper. We focus here on OMPS' representation and reasoning capabilities which are of interest for the problem of deducing patterns of human activities from sensor readings in an intelligent environment.

A component is an element of a domain theory which represents a logical or physical entity. Components model parts of the real world that are relevant for a specific decisional process, such as complex physical systems or their parts. Components can be used to represent, for example: a robot which can navigate the environment and grasp objects; a simple luminosity sensor which can estimate the lighting conditions in a room; or an

[3] An approach similar to Shanahan's work [16] on inferring information on a robot's environment.

autonomous refrigerator which can open and close its door and determine which products are stored in it.

Components are the basic elements used to describe the domain of a specific problem in OMPS. Simply put, an automated reasoning functionality developed in OMPS consists in a procedure for taking *decisions* on components. Decisions essentially describe an assertion on the possible evolutions in time of a component. For instance, a decision on the fridge component described above could be to open its door no earlier than time instant 30 and no later than time instant 40; or a decision on the robot above could assert that the robot is to be in the state "localized" using its laser for self localization. More precisely, a decision is an assertion on the value of a component in a given flexible time interval, i.e., a pair $\langle v, [I_s, I_e] \rangle$, where the nature of the value v depends on the specific component and I_s, I_e represent, respectively, an interval of admissibility of the start and end times of the decision. In the fridge example, assuming the door takes five seconds to open, the flexible interval is $[I_s = [30, 40], I_e = [34, 44]]$, while in the second example no temporal requirement is imposed on robot localization (i.e., $I_s = I_e = [0, \infty)$).

The core intuition behind OMPS is the fact that decisions on certain components may entail the need to assert decisions on other components. For instance, the decision to open the fridge door may *require* that the robot is docked to the fridge so that it can grasp an object inside. Such dependencies among component decisions are captured in a domain theory through what are called *synchronizations*. A synchronization states the requirements entailed by a decision on other components. These requirements consist in decisions that are bound to the "requiring" decision by *temporal constraints*. OMPS provides thirteen types of temporal constraints, each type corresponding to one of the relations in Allen's Interval Algebra [1].

Arm : **place_can_on_robot**
DURING Robot : **docked**
DURING Fridge : **open**
CONTAINS Arm : **grasp_can**
CONTAINS Arm : **release_can**

(a)

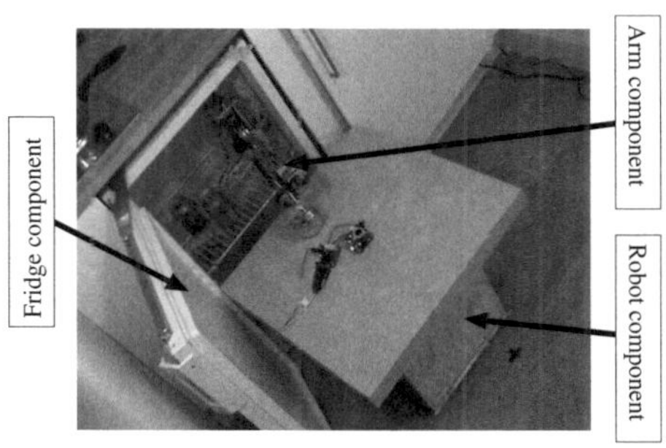

(b)

Figure 1. One synchronization in a possible domestic robot planning domain (a), and the corresponding real components available in the PEIS-Home (b).

For example, the synchronization in figure 1(a) states that asserting **place_can_on_robot** on a component representing a robotic arm inside the fridge entails that other decisions should be asserted on the robot (which should be docked to the fridge DURING the course of the operation), on the fridge door (which should be open DURING the operation) and on the arm itself (the **place_can_on_robot** operation should CONTAIN the operations of grasping and releasing the can). Other synchronizations in the domain can be employed to model other requirements among components, e.g., the need to schedule the **grasp_can** operation BEFORE the **release_can** operation.

Overall, the fundamental building blocks of OMPS that are of interest for this article are components, decisions and temporal constraints. Together, decisions and temporal constraints asserted on components are maintained in a *decision network* (DN), that is at all times kept consistent through *temporal propagation*. This ensures that the temporal intervals underlying the decisions are kept consistent with respect to the temporal constraints, while decisions are anchored flexibly in time. In other words, adding a temporal constraint to the DN will either result in the calculation of updated *bounds* for the intervals I_s, I_e for all decisions, or in a propagation failure, indicating that the added constraint or decision is not admissible (e.g., adding **A** BEFORE **B** when the DN contains constraints **B** BEFORE **C** and **C** BEFORE **A**). Temporal constraint propagation is a polynomial time operation, as it is based on a Simple Temporal Network [6].

2. From Planning in Space to Activity Recognition at Home

Although general, OMPS was built with space applications in mind [5]. A direct consequence of this fact is that components represent *controllable* entities, i.e., the semantics of the term "component decision" is that of an assertion that prescribes an operation on a component. For instance, asserting a decision $\langle \mathbf{open}, [[163, 163], [164, \infty)] \rangle$ on the component representing an autonomous fridge models the operational request of the fridge to open its door at time 163 and that the operation should last at least one time unit. This mindset is appropriate for building planning/scheduling systems whose purpose is to deduce operational plans for controllable systems. Indeed, OMPS can be seen as a symbolic framework for developing controllers for complex systems (such as space mission planning processes). This transfers very directly into intelligent environment settings such as the PEIS-Home if the aim is to control pervasive actuators, or robots, or intelligent services. However, we address here the complementary problem of employing the framework for automatically deducing the activities carried out by a partially observable, and certainly not controllable component, namely the *human user*. This deductive process is based on the values of equally non-controllable, but directly observable components, namely *sensors*.

2.1. The Human User

The human inhabitant of the environment can be modeled as a state variable, whose values correspond to symbols representing the various activities that the person can perform in the home. Synchronizations are used to model the conditions under which specific human activities are recognized. For instance, the requirements expressed in synchronization {Human : **cooking** EQUALS Stove : **on**, DURING Location : **kitchen**} models the (very simple) criteria for recognizing the cooking activity: this activity requires that the user is in the kitchen and it lasts as long as the stove is turned on. The activity recognition functionality is thus obtained by iteratively (1) updating the DN with values representing the observations of all sensors and (2) re-planning using a planning procedure which is very similar to that illustrated in [7]. As far as the discussion in this paper is concerned, it is sufficient to say that the procedure performs a search in the space of DNs for a set of synchronizations that is applicable given the current state of the DN. For instance, suppose the current time is 32, and that the DN contains two decisions: $d_{\text{Location}} = \langle \mathbf{kitchen}, [[2, 2], [32, \infty)] \rangle$ on component Location, representing that the person-localization sensor has observed the human user as being in the **kitchen** since time 2, and $d_{\text{Stove}} = \langle \mathbf{on}, [[10, 10], [32, \infty)] \rangle$ on component Stove, representing that the stove has been observed to be in state **on** since time 10. Then the activity recognition process would deduce, based on the synchronization above, a decision $d_{\text{Human}} = \langle \textbf{cooking}, [[10, 10], [32, \infty)] \rangle$, representing the fact that human activity "cooking" has been recognized as taking place since time instant 10. It is important to notice that the recognized **cooking** decision is *flexibly bound* to the two sensor decisions through the constraints (d_{Human} EQUALS d_{Stove}) and (d_{Human} DURING d_{Location}). As a consequence, if the minimum durations of d_{Stove} and d_{Location} increase (as they would if at the next iteration the human being is still observed in the kitchen and the stove is still turned on) then the minimum duration of the deduced activity will also increase. This is achieved through temporal propagation of the constraints in the DN, therefore is done in polynomial time (in the number of decisions) at every iteration.

2.2. Sensors

The state variable metaphor is also appropriate for modeling the state of pervasive sensors in the environment. For instance, the sensor readings of a person localization system are modeled as values of a component "Location", a state variable whose values correspond to the symbols representing the possible locations of the person in the PEIS-Home.

In order to realize the interface between OMPS state variables and real-world sensors in the environment, a new OMPS component, the *sensor*, was developed. OMPS sensors extend the capabilities of the built-in state variable. An OMPS sensor is modeled in the domain for each physical sensor in the environment. Each OMPS sensor is provided with an interface to the physical sensor, as well as the capability to periodically update the DN with decisions and constraints that model the state of the physical sensor. Specifically, for each sensed value provided by a physical sensor, the corresponding OMPS sensor does the following: if the value was not sensed at the previous iteration, then a decision representing the observed value is added, as well as a temporal constraint that anchors its start time to the current clock reference, and any previous decision's end time is anchored to the current time; conversely, if the sensed value is equal to the one sensed at the previous iteration, the decision's duration is increased.

Unlike a state variable, a sensor is no longer a passive entity on which decisions are imposed, rather a process which can impose decisions on itself to reflect the reality it observes in its physical counterpart. The result is a temporal reasoning infrastructure in which a multitude of processes add decisions and constraints to the DN concurrently: each sensor is a process that adds decisions and constraints to represent the real-world observations coming from the environment; in turn, the current DN is manipulated by the high-level planning process used for activity recognition, which adds decisions and constraints modeling the current activity performed by the user. In a way, the DN is acting as a "blackboard" where decisions and constraints re-construct the observed reality as well as the current hypothesis on what the human being is doing. Decisions and constraints are added to the DN in real-time, i.e., as they are observed by the sensors or decided by the activity recognition process.

3. A Domain for Activity Recognition in the PEIS-Home

The goal of the test described in this section is to provide a demonstrative example of how we can leverage domain knowledge expressed as OMPS synchronizations to recognize human activities from sensor readings.

For the purposes of this test, we have instantiated three sensor components in OMPS. These components wrap three of the PEIS-Home's sensors, namely a stereo camera on the ceiling with a tracking system [11] for person localization (component Location), a

1) Human : **watchingTV**
EQUALS Location : **couch**

2) Human : **cooking**
EQUALS Stove : **on**
DURING Location : **kitchen**

3) Human : **eating**
EQUALS KTRfid : **dish**
DURING Location : **kitchenTable**

4) HumanAbstract : **meal**
STARTED-BY Human : **cooking**
FINISHED-BY Human : **eating**

5) HumanAbstract : **nap**
EQUALS Human : **watchingTV**
AFTER HumanAbstract : **meal**

Figure 2. Synchronizations defined in our domain for the Human and HumanAbstract components.

stove state sensor implemented with a LabJack (Stove), and an RFID reader mounted underneath the kitchen table (KTRfid) for sensing the presence of tagged kitchen utensils.

We model the user in the environment as two distinct components, that can assume different values. The synchronizations of the first component, *Human*, have constraints that are based on sensor values, while the ones of the second component, *HumanAbstract*, have constraints that are based on values of Human and HumanAbstract. This distinction allows us to reason at two different levels of abstraction, as will be explained in the following.

The synchronizations employed in this experiment are shown in figure 2. They describe temporal patterns of sensor values, and how these patterns should be interpreted with respect to the Human and HumanAbstract components. For instance, synchronization (1) means that asserting **watchingTV** on the Human component entails that the decision **couch** should be asserted on the component Location (that is based on sensor data). Moreover, the synchronization specifies the temporal constraints among decisions: the duration of the decision **watchingTV** should be EQUAL to the one of **couch**.

We also define two synchronizations for the component HumanAbstract (the name of this component emphasizes the higher lever of abstraction of the activities recognized): synchronization (5) is triggered if the user is perceived to perform activity **watchingTV** after a meal. In such a case, knowing the habits of the human, it is inferred that he or she is most probably taking a nap.

A full experiment with this domain in the PEIS-Home was run by connecting our framework to real sensors. The user (depicted in the insets in figure 3) performs a series of actions, one after the other, to verify the correct detection of activities. First he sits on the couch watching TV, then he moves to the kitchen and prepares a meal (that is, he enters the kitchen and turns on the stove). After this, he moves to the kitchen table, he places a dish on the table and eats his meal. Finally, he moves back to the couch to take a rest. The total duration of the trial was about ten minutes.

Figure 3 shows the results of the experiment. The timelines represented are generated by the planner and report both the readings of the sensors (the 3 timelines at the bottom) and the decisions taken by the two components Human and HumanAbstract. At first, the detection of the user on the couch makes the planner to assert the decision **watchingTV** on the component Human (synchronization (1)). In this case, no decision is asserted for the component HumanAbstract, because no synchronization applies. Then the activities **cooking** and **eating** are detected, as the user proceeds to prepare and consume his meal (synchronizations (2) and (3)). As soon as the decision **eating** is asserted on the component Human, synchronization (4) is triggered: the high level **meal** activity is detected. This decision spans from the beginning of the **cooking** activity until the end of **eating**. Finally, when the user goes to rest on the couch, the decision **watchingTV** is asserted once again. This time, since the **meal** activity has been detected, also the higher-level decision **nap** is asserted (synchronization (5)).

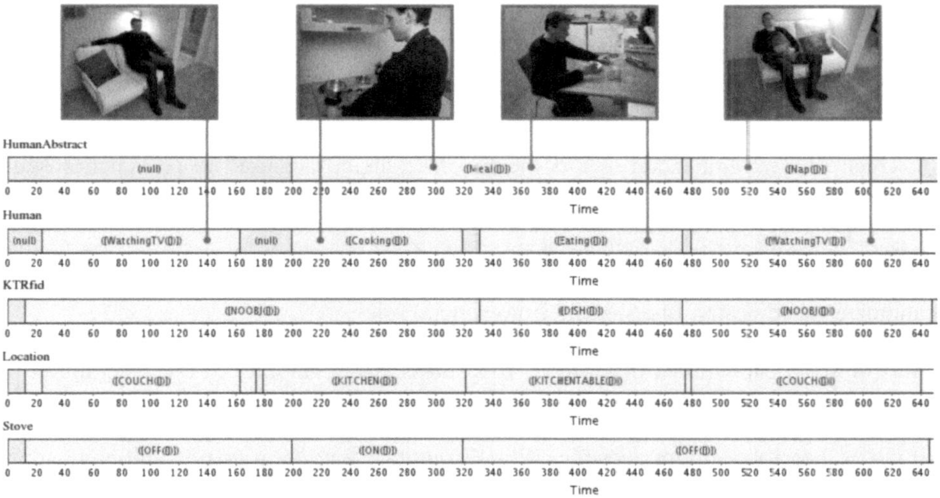

Figure 3. Evolutions in time of the components as generated by OMPS during our experiment. The plan monitoring process asserts decisions on components Human and HumanAbstract, while the RFID reader, location and stove sensor components assert decisions that reflect the sensor readings.

The experiment was performed in real time, with re-planning occurring at a frequency of 1 Hz, and with real sensors.

4. Discussion and Conclusion

In this paper, we presented our first results towards the realization of human activity recognition in the PEIS-Home, a service providing household environment. For this purpose, we adapted a constraint-based temporal reasoning framework (OMPS), shifting from the more classic realm of controllable components to encompass sensors and uncontrollable components (e.g., the human user) in the system. We also presented a first implementation of our framework, together with a simple test domain. A real experiment within this domain was detailed to demonstrate the feasibility of our approach.

Our main contribution is the novelty of the approach we take to the problem. We use a temporal planning framework to realize an abductive process which explains sensor data by testing the applicability of temporally-constrained requirements on these data. These requirements are given in the form of OMPS synchronizations, which are grounded on Allen's Interval Algebra. Our approach is complementary to more classical data-driven approaches, as it relies on a domain which models temporal knowledge on human activities. The obvious advantage lies in the fact that domain knowledge does not need be learned, thus allowing us to build modularly and incrementally our synchronizations. Our framework would allow us to both recognize human activities and anomalies in the behaviour of the user, since hazardous situations can be modeled in the same way as normal activities.

It is important to notice that using a knowledge-driven approach is possible if (1) relatively crisp knowledge about how sensor data correlates to human activities is available, and (2) the knowledge representation framework is sufficiently expressive to capture the details and nuances of activity recognition. While point (1) depends on the level of abstraction that is necessary in the particular domain of application, we believe that temporal constraints offer a flexible means to describe how sensor data correlates to human activities, particularly when it is necessary (as in the experiment illustrated in this paper) to model temporal relations between sensor data and human activities across multiple tiers of abstraction.

Our approach was inspired by previous work, such as the RoboCare system [3], in which sensors embedded in a domestic environment are used in conjunction with a schedule execution monitor towards the aim of identifying anomalies in typical user activity patterns. An important difference with the work presented here lies in the fact that RoboCare employs pre-compiled (albeit highly flexible) schedules as models for human behavior. In the present work, we employ a planning process to actually instantiate such candidate schedules on-line starting from general rules.

Our future work will focus on testing our framework with more complex scenarios and to test its capabilities in terms of robustness and scalability to the recognition of multiple activities. We are also extending our approach to allow long periods of continued monitoring, of the order of weeks or months: this requires the ability to forget past data which cannot affect future decisions. Finally, another long term goal would be to adapt our framework to predict, and not only recognize, human activities.

References

[1] J.F. Allen. Towards a general theory of action and time. *Artificial Intelligence*, 23(2):123–154, 1984.

[2] G. Bjorn, H.W. Guesgen, and S. Hubner. Spatiotemporal reasoning for smart homes. In J.C. Augusto and C.D. Nugent, editors, *Designing Smart Homes*, pages 16–34. Springer, 2006.

[3] A. Cesta, G. Cortellessa, M.V. Giuliani, F. Pecora, M. Scopelliti, and L. Tiberio. Caring About the User's View: The Joys and Sorrows of Experiments with People. In *ICAPS Workshop on Moving Planning and Scheduling Systems into the Real World, Providence, RI, USA*, 2007.

[4] A. Cesta and S. Fratini. The Timeline Representation Framework as a Planning and Scheduling Software Development Environment. In *Proc. of 27th Workshop of the UK Planning and Scheduling SIG*, 2008.

[5] A. Cesta, S. Fratini, A. Oddi, and F. Pecora. APSI Case#1: Pre-planning Science Operations in Mars Express. In *Proc. of iSAIRAS-08*, 2008.

[6] R. Dechter, I. Meiri, and J. Pearl. Temporal constraint networks. *Artif. Intell.*, 49(1-3):61–95, 1991.

[7] S. Fratini, F. Pecora, and A. Cesta. Unifying Planning and Scheduling as Timelines in a Component-Based Perspective. *Archives of Control Sciences*, 18(2):231–271, 2008.

[8] A. Goultiaeva and Y. Lespérance. Incremental plan recognition in an agent programming framework. In *Working Notes of the AAAI Workshop on Plan, Activity, and Intention Recognition (PAIR)*, 2007.

[9] V. Jakkula, DJ Cook, and AS Crandall. Temporal pattern discovery for anomaly detection in a smart home. In *Proc. of the 3rd IET Conf. on Intelligent Environments(IE)*, pages 339–345, 2007.

[10] F. Mastrogiovanni, A. Scalmato, A. Sgorbissa, and R. Zaccaria. Assessing temporal relationships between events in smart environments. In *Proc of the Int Conf on Intellingent Environments*, 2009.

[11] R. Muñoz-Salinas, E. Aguirre, and M. García-Silvente. People detection and tracking using stereo vision and color. *Image and Vision Computing*, 25(6):995–1007, 2007.

[12] D.J. Patterson, D. Fox, H. Kautz, and M. Philipose. Fine-grained activity recognition by aggregating abstract object usage. In *Proc. of the 9th IEEE International Symposium on Wearable Computers*, 2005.

[13] M.E. Pollack, L. Brown, D. Colbry, C.E. McCarthy, C. Orosz, B. Peintner, S. Ramakrishnan, and I. Tsamardinos. Autominder: an intelligent cognitive orthotic system for people with memory impairment. *Robotics and Autonomous Systems*, 44(3-4):273–282, 2003.

[14] R.B. Rusu, J. Bandouch, Z.C. Marton, N. Blodow, and M. Beetz". Action recognition in intelligent environments using point cloud features extracted from silhouette sequences. In *Int Symp on Robot-Human Interactive Communication (ROMAN)*, 2008.

[15] A. Saffiotti, M. Broxvall, M. Gritti, K. LeBlanc, R. Lundh, Rashid J., B.S. Seo, and Y.J. Cho. The PEIS-ecology project: vision and results. In *Proc of the IEEE/RSJ Int Conf on Intelligent Robots and Systems (IROS)*, Nice, France, 2008.

[16] M.P. Shanahan. Robotics and the Common Sense Informatic Situation. In *Proceedings ECAI 96*, 1996.

[17] J. Wu, A. Osuntogun, T. Choudhury, M. Philipose, and J. Rehg. A Scalable Approach to Activity Recognition Based on Object Use. In *Proceedings of ICCV 2007. Rio de Janeiro, Brazil*, 2007.

Intelligent Environments 2009
V. Callaghan et al. (Eds.)
IOS Press, 2009

doi:10.3233/978-1-60750-034-6-125

Instability and Irrationality: Destructive and Constructive Services within Intelligent Environments

Simon EGERTON[a,1] Victor ZAMUDIO[b], Victor CALLAGHAN[b] and Graham CLARKE[b]

[a] *School of Information Technology, Monash University Sunway Campus, Jalan Lagoon Selatan, Bandar Sunway, 46150, Selangor Darul Ehsan, Malaysia*

[b] *Department of Computer Science and Electronic Engineering, Essex University, Wivenhoe Park, Colchester, Essex, CO4 3SQ, United Kingdom*

Abstract. Does chance have a role in intelligent environments? In this work-in-progress paper we argue that chance and non-deterministic behaviour can play a fundamental and important role in intelligent environments. We discuss how this behaviour can be both destructive and constructive. Underpinning our ideas is the view that intelligent environments may be seen as a complex system of interacting services. In the first part of this paper we show that such complex systems can produce unexpected interactions that cause unplanned and often undesirable instabilities. However, not all instabilities are undesirable and in the second half of this paper, we present a conceptual notion that views system instability as a form of irrationality and propose a quantum control model for service agents within smart environments. We conjecture that irrational control models enable the service agents to perform better than if they were using traditional, rational, control models. Our purpose in presenting this work is to both provoke discussion and describe our early research on what we hope will be an interesting direction for intelligent building research.

Keywords. Intelligent environments, system instabilities, quantum decisions

Introduction

As has been widely reported a popular vision for intelligent environments is that they will be composed of a large network of smart devices, working together to provide services to the environment and the human occupants. Part of the intelligent or smart operation results from these devices coordinating actions. Thus, naturally, such a network of smart devices will lead to interdependencies in the behaviour of the devices. Typically a device will be programmed to behave in a particular way by following a set of rules, which are triggered according to environmental contexts, or interactions with users or other devices. However, as the number of interdependencies increases their interactions become more complex and their nature becomes unpredictable, taking on a 'life of their own'. Such unpredictable behaviour leads to unexpected instability within the device ecology which is undesirable. Whilst such instabilities are generally undesirable in inter-agent behaviour, we speculate that within controllers (the brains of

[1] Corresponding Author: E-mail: Simon.Egerton@infotech.monash.edu.my

the system) they can endow AI systems with interesting and useful properties. In this first half of this paper we show how destructive inter-agent instabilities can be detected and prevented. In the second half, we look at a constructive form of instability that might usefully be modelled within the agent controller. The particular form of instability we examine for this purpose would be recognised in psychoanalytic terms as irrationality [2]. In this approach we add a probabilistic disturbance to the system based on quantum mechanics.

1. Instability between Intelligent Agents

Instability has been found in different domains, such as telephony [5], spreadsheets [6], software agents (email)[7], discrete dynamics [4], and ambient intelligence [8,9]. In nature this behaviour has also been observed in colonies of termites [10]. Each agent has a set of rules, and due to unplanned interaction between them, this periodic behaviour can arise.

The phenomenon of instability is characterized by periodic oscillations that can be represented by

$$S(t) = S(t + np \pm \delta) \tag{1.1}$$

where $S(t)$ is the state of the system at time t, p is the period and $n \in Z^+$. The variable δ measures deviations from the strictly periodic case, due to network delays, latency, the different processing speeds of the devices, and changes over time in general. An example instability is the case of a set of home lights turning on and off recurrently.

From Complex Systems theory [4], it has been found that it is not possible to predict theoretically if a given set of rules could suffer from cyclic instability. However, it is possible to prevent this behaviour.

A first step towards the prevention of this phenomenon is to find a suitable and accurate representation of the problem. This is provided by a formalism called Interaction Networks, that captures the dependencies of the rules between the agents.

1.1. Interaction Networks

An intelligent device or agent A is an autonomous device with a boolean state $s \in \{0,1\}$, where 0 and 1 mean *on* and *off* respectively. In the case of n autonomous agents $A_1, A_2, \ldots, A_n$ the state of the system is $S = (s_1, s_2, \ldots, s_n)$. Each device A_i has two consistent rules:

$$\text{If } \varphi_i \text{ then } s_i = 1 \tag{1.2}$$

$$\text{If } \psi_i \text{ then } s_i = 0 \tag{1.3}$$

where

$$\varphi_i, \psi_i : S_n \to \{0,1\} \tag{1.4}$$

The case of contradictory rules is avoided due to the fact that $\varphi_i = \psi_i^{-1}$. The functions φ and ψ can be defined either automatically [14,15] or manually [16,17]. In both cases several users, under different circumstances and motivations could have been involved in the definition of the rules.

An Interaction Network (IN) is a digraph (V,E) in which the vertex $v \in V$ is a pervasive intelligent device or agent A and $(v_i, v_j) \in E$ if the Boolean functions φ_i or ψ_i of the pervasive intelligent device A_j depends on the state s_i of the device A_i [3]. In other words, an Interaction Network is a graphical representation that captures the dependencies of the rules between the agents involved.

1.2. Instability Prevention System INPRES

As we mentioned previously, it is not possible to predict if a given system will suffer from cyclic instability. However, by finding cycles in the Interaction Network associated it is possible to identify potential instabilities. The strategy defined by INPRES is based on locking a member of each cycle found in the Interaction Network; with this, the feedback loop between the rules of the agents is broken [3]. As each member of a loop in the Interaction Network is a candidate to be locked, the connectivity of each agent is analysed; the agent with less connectivity in the IN will be locked. The connectivity of agent A_i is called functionality, and is represented by $f(A_i)$. A high-level architecture of INPRES can be seen in figure 1.

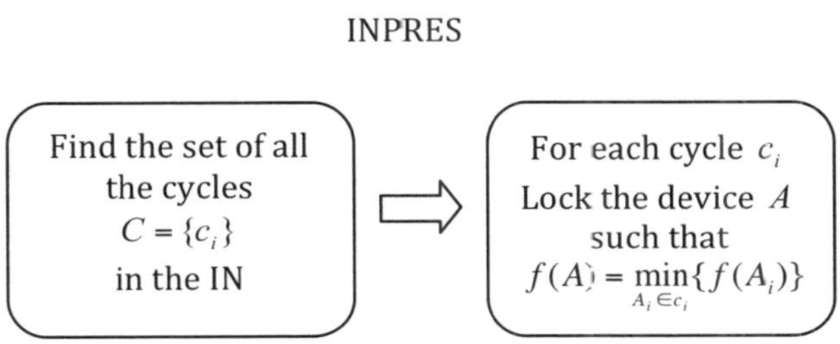

Figure 1. Architecture of the Instability Prevention System INPRES.

The strategy defined by INPRES was successfully tested using an Interaction Benchmark (IB), which is a grid of 4x4x4 interacting agents (see figures 2 and 3). The Interaction Benchmark enables a homogeneous and ordered distribution and visualization of the cycles.

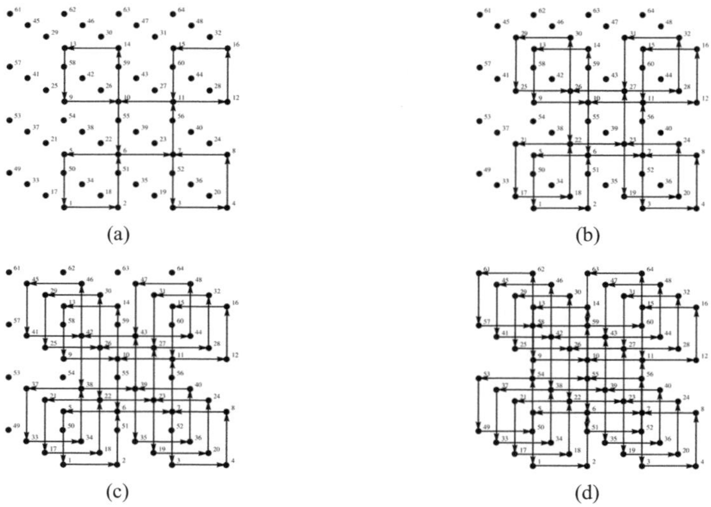

Figure 2. Interaction Benchmark with coupling in one point. Each layer has 5 cycles.

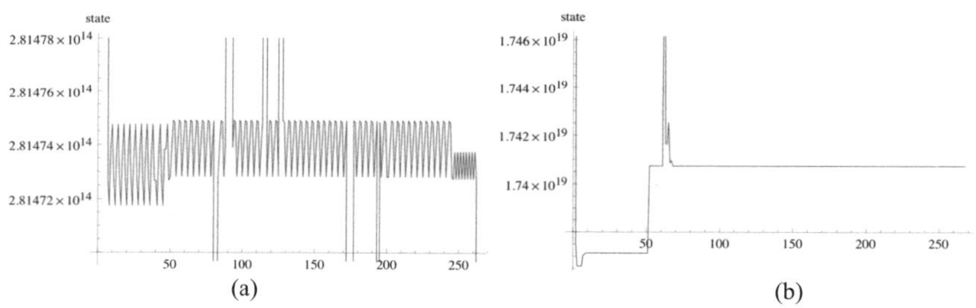

Figure 3. Evolution of the system with 20 coupled cycles. In (a) the system is unlocked, showing three modes of oscillation. In (b) INPRES removed the oscillations successfully.

2. Instability within Intelligent Agents

The previous section considers the external interactions that can occur between agents and how we can prevent these interactions leading to undesirable inter-agent instabilities. On the whole, we expect service agents to perform and behave in a logical, rational, deterministic manner according to their their control programs. In this section we consider instabilities from within the agent, from the perspective of its controller and ask the question, what if we purposefully introduced instabilities into a service agents control program? Our earlier work explored such an idea [19]. We did this through the concept of multiple personas. A persona being the result of a functional splitting of a personality [2,18]. Multiple personas in philosophy and psychoanalysis are seen as one explanation for irrationality and are based upon the generally pathological process of splitting. In this instance splitting for functionally sound reasons is suggested as a possible aide to robust and efficient working within a variety of different contexts. We are not recommending the multiple persona model because they can produce irrationality, but because this constructive form of instability represents a useful way of modularising skills and powers and providing a repertoire of responses to new situations that make the persona model more flexible and capable i.e. in people the positive aspects of multiple personas the father, brother, son, uncle, the manager, the worker, the lover, the craftsman and so on, can be mobilised when the circumstances require it and sometimes there is a cross application of skills, for example, you become managerial with your mother or paternal with your colleague. Our conjecture is that modelling these irrationalities within an agent will enable the agent to act against the logical nature of the world and its own internal world model enabling it to handle certain environmental contexts in a more flexible way, leading to improved performance, in a similar way to people. The next section presents our control model which we extend to explain how this model can implement the concept of multiple personas. In the following sections we use a service robot as an exemplar agent, although the control model could be applied to any intelligent agent.

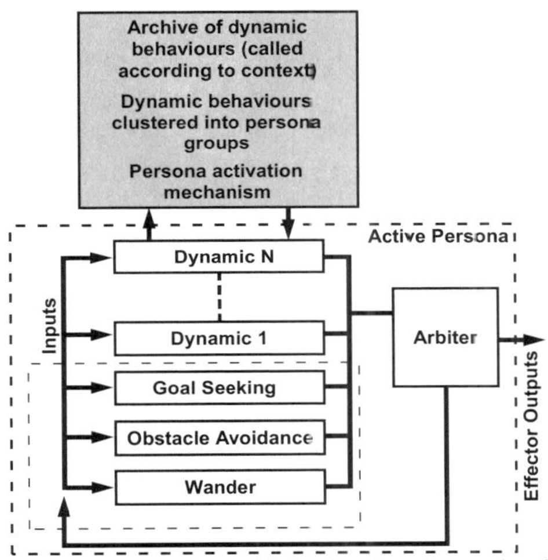

Figure 4. Persona enhanced behaviour based control architecture.

2.1. Control Model

One of the most successful approaches to controlling mobile robots has been behaviour based architectures, proposed by Rodney Brookes in 1985 [20]. In this, the higher levels operation of the robots is deconstructed into a set of lower level behaviours, a process akin to task decomposition in social models. Typically, the behaviours for a simple robot might be the ability to wander, to avoid obstacles, to follow walls and to steer to physical goals. Each behaviour is implemented as a separate software process or task, each vying with the other to get control of the steering of the robot. Some form of arbitration is required to determine which behaviour has dominant control of the robot at a any particular time, which, in turn, depends on the context of the robot. Generally these behaviours are solely reactive in nature, with no persistence or deliberation. However, at Essex we have developed models that can dynamically manage the creation, adaptation and death of behaviours, introducing a persistent experience based *evolving* control model of the world. This architecture is illustrated in figure 4, modified in include the persona model. In general terms, the Essex architecture utilises fuzzy logic and genetic system principles, the fundamentals of which are widely known and thus are not reproduced here [14, 21] .

2.2. Multiple Personas

Our control model defines a persona as a collection of dynamically generated behaviours as shown in figure 5. Each behaviour in the active persona competes for dominance of the robot, defining the robot's persona. Only one persona is active at any one time, any behaviours which are generated or destroyed only effect the current persona. At any time another collection of behaviours, or persona, may assert itself over the controller and take over. The question arises what triggers a persona switch? According to the psychoanalytic models regarding multiple personality disorders there is no identifiable central arbiter controlling these switches [2]. For the purposes of our model we supply a persona transfer function with contextual information and the current activation states of all personas, it is this transfer function that decides if the current persona should remain active, or make a switch to another persona, selecting the persona to activate if a switch is to be made. The contextual model should account for social contexts i.e. modelling which persona is the most socially acceptable persona to be active, and environmental contexts i.e. modelling which persona is the most environmentally acceptable persona to be active. At the simplest level the context model might encode a function of the behaviour activation levels within each of the personas. In this sense irrationality might be expressed by activating a persona that does not have the highest activation level for the given context.

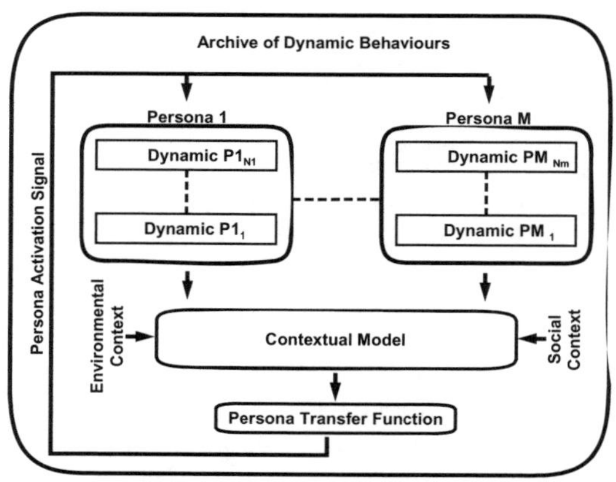

Figure 5. Persistent dynamic behaviours clustered into personas. An appropriate transfer function decides which of the personas is currently active based on context.

2.3. A Quantum Persona Transfer Function

We have chosen to experiment with quantum logic decision models to implement the persona transfer function. Quantum logic differers from traditional statistical models, such as Markov models, in two important ways, firstly, quantum logic describes complex valued probability values over time and secondly, quantum entanglement allows for probability interference effects, these are not possible with traditional probabilistic decision models [1]. Moreover, quantum entanglement effectively obscures the causation of the quantum measurements, which the persona activation decisions are based upon. Accordingly this will effectively hide the effects of any arbitration for persona selection, effectively making the persona selection appear to be without a central arbiter, supporting the psychoanalytic theories [2].

The contextual information is binary encoded to allow the use of binary valued quantum bits, or Qbits. This simplifies the quantum logic and simulations [11]. The output of the quantum logic block is measured to resolve the quantum entangled states, these measurements form the persona activation signals, as modelled in figure 6. The next phase of our research will implement the quantum transfer function and experiment with various simulated quantum logic block configurations.

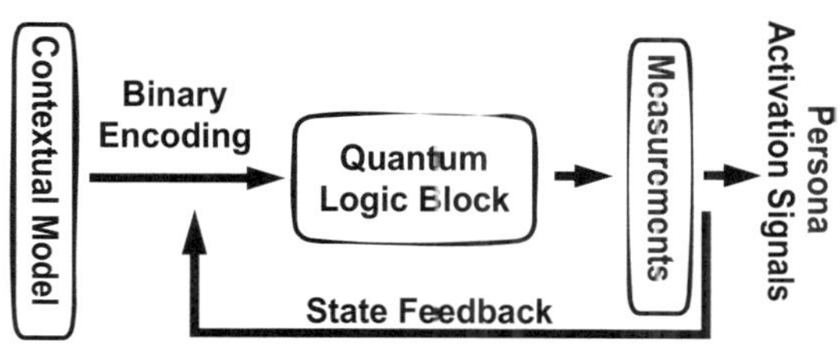

Figure 6. A quantum based transfer function, contextual inputs are derived from the activation levels present within each persona, the binary outputs determine which behaviour is currently active.

3. Bringing it Together

Whilst the cyclic instability methodology is well developed, clearly the quantum controller aspects of this work are largely at a conceptual stage and will be the focus of much development. Our conjecture is that adding irrationality within intelligent environment agents, and particularly service robots will enable them to perform better, by employing some of the same irrational mechanisms that seem to serve people well. However, whilst our ideas are based on established theories from psychology and psycho-analytic studies there is clearly a long way to go before these ideas can be properly tested. In this we intend to establish a baseline performance metric by measuring the performance of a service robot using a standard controller against the performance of a service robot using the persona enhanced version. The expectation being that the persona enhanced version should perform better overall. Initially, we intend to conduct our experiments in simulation, within a virtual intelligent environment leveraging Sci-Fi prototyping ideas, such as those presented by Johnson in this conference [12]. Our intention is to use Sun Microsystems Wonderland simulation tools that we are already using to investigate the development of more human-like avatars [13]. Finally, we will explore how the ideas underpinning quantum controller might be combined with cyclic instability. For example, we envisage that if there were multiple robots, each with a quantum controller, then the collective social behaviour would be described by cyclic instability theory whilst the internal operation of the robot controller (i.e. the multiple persona switching) would be determined by quantum theory thereby requiring both parts for a stable but creative multi agent system.

4. Conclusions

In this conceptual paper we have described the role of chance and instabilities in intelligent environments. We have discussed how at one level (system wide interactions) such instabilities can be destructive and we presented methods to detect and remove such cases. At a second level (within a controller or a brain) we have argued that such instabilities might play a fundamental role in providing more human-like intelligence by providing some irrational behaviour in agent. We noted that, on the one hand unregulated probabilistic behaviour (cyclic instability) threatens the vision for ambient intelligence whilst, on the other hand, directed probabilistic behaviour (quantum controllers) enables it. Thus probabilistic perturbations can be both an enemy and friend of intelligent environments. In this work we have presented both proven concepts that fix existing problems (INPRES) and speculative ones that conjecture of improved AI methods (quantum controllers). In terms of the speculative aspects of our work, we leverage Sci-Fi prototyping ideas advanced by Johnson extending the notion of system instability to encompass the concept of irrationality and multiple personas within service agents, borrowing from models presented in philosophy and psychoanalysis. While our model could be applied to any agent that provides a service to an intelligent environment, as an exemplar we have chosen service robots to experiment our model with. The control model uses a quantum logic gate arrangement to implement the persona transfer function. The next phase of this work in progress is to implement the quantum transfer function and test our model in simulation against a base line standard control model. Another challenging area we intend to investigate is understanding instabilities when there is only a partial or incomplete view of the system. This would be closer to the reality of distributed pervasive computing and psychoanalysis where there is incomplete information. Finally we plan to integrate the various facets of instability into a more general theory that includes purposeful instability in quantum controllers and unwanted instability in system wide social system of agent based intelligent environments.

References

[1] Jerome R. Busemeyer, Zheng Wang, James T., Townsend, "Quantum dynamics of human decision-making", Journal of Mathematical Psychology 50 (2006) 220–241

[2] Clarke GS Personal Relations Theory: Fairbairn, Macmurray and Suttie. London: Routledge 2006 Chapter 3

[3] V. Zamudio, Understanding and Preventing Periodic Behaviour in Ambient Intelligence, PhD thesis, Essex University, UK, 2009

[4] G. Weisbuch, *Complex Systems*. Lecture Notes Volume II. Santa Fe Institute Studies in the Sciences of Complexity. 1991.

[5] M. Calder, M. Kolberg, E. Magill, D. Marples, and S. Reiff-Marganiec, "Hybrid Solutions to the Feature Interaction Problem", in Proc. 7th Feature Interactions in Telecommunications and Software Systems, IOS Press, pg. 295-312. June 2003.

[6] M. MacDonald, "Excel 2007: The Missing Manual". Pogue Press. O'Reilly. 2007.

[7] M. Mowbray and M. Williamson, "Resilience for Autonomous Agents". Technical Report HPL-2003-210. Internet Systems and Storage Laboratory, HP Laboratories Bristol. October 17th 2003.

[8] M.Wilson. "An Online Environmental Approach to Service Interaction Management in Home Automation". PhD Thesis. Department of Computing Science and Mathematics. University of Stirling. September 2005

[9] eGadets [Online] Available http://www.extrovert-gadgets.net/

[10] O. Miramontes, O. DeSouza. "Individual basis for collective behaviour in the termite, *Cornitermes cumulans*", 11pp. *Journal of Insect Science* 8:24.2008.

[11] http://www.quantiki.org/wiki/index.php/List_of_QC_simulators

[12] Johnson B D "Science Fiction Prototypes or: How I Learned to Stop Worrying about the Future and Love Science Fiction", Intelligent Environments 09, Barcelona, July 20-21st 2009
[13] Davies M, Callaghan V, Shen L "Modelling Pervasive Environments Using Bespoke & Commercial Game-Based Simulators" 2nd International Conference on Life System Modelling and Simulation (LSMS'07) Shanghai, China, September 14-17 2007
[14] V. Callaghan, G. Clarke, M. Colley, H. Hagras, J. Chin, and F. Doctor, "Inhabited Intelligent Environments". BT Technology Journal 22, 3 (Jul 2004), 233-247. 2004.
[15] H. Hagras, V. Callaghan, M. Colley, G. Clarke, A. Pounds-Cornish and H. Duman, "Creating an ambient-intelligence environment using embedded agents". IEEE on Intelligent Systems, Volume 19, Issue 6, Nov-Dec 2004 Page(s):12 – 20.
[16] J. S. Chin, V. Callaghan and G. Clarke, "An End-User Programming Paradigm for Pervasive Computing Applications", The IEEE International Conference on Pervasive Services, Lyon, France, June 26-29, 2006 Page(s):325 – 328.
[17] J.S. Chin, V. Callaghan, G. Clarke, "A Pervasive Computing Programming Approach for Non-Technical Users". Proceedings of the First International Symposium on Pervasive Computing and Applications SPCA06. August 3-5 2006, China.
[18] Davidson D. Paradoxes of irrationality. In R. Wollheim and J. Hopkins (Eds) Philosophical Essays on Freud, Cambridge MA: Cambridge Univ Press.
[19] Egerton, S.J; Callaghan, V; Clarke, G "Using Multiple Personas in Service Robots to Improve Exploration Strategies When Mapping New Environments", IET International Conference on Intelligent Environments, 21-22 July, 2008, Washington, USA
[20] Brooks, R. A. "A Robust Layered Control System for a Mobile Robot", IEEE Journal of Robotics and Automation, Vol. 2, No. 1, March 1986, pp. 14–23; also MIT AI Memo 864, September 1985.
[21] Hagras,H.A.K., Callaghan,Vic, Colley,M.J., 'On Line Calibration of the Sensors Fuzzy Membership Functions in Autonomous Mobile Robots', IEEE International Conference on Robotics and Automation, San Francisco, USA, (2000)

Intelligent Environments 2009
V. Callaghan et al. (Eds.)
IOS Press, 2009

doi:10.3233/978-1-60750-034-6-134

Increasing Reliability in the Development of Intelligent Environments

Juan Carlos AUGUSTO [a;1]
[a] *University of Ulster and Computer Science Research Institute, UK*

Abstract. Little is reported in the literature on the methodology used to develop Intelligent Environments. These are inherently complex systems as they are the product of a multidisciplinary approach. Their main purpose is to help people directly, which leads to these environments to take on enormous responsibilities of safety and well being of the users of the environment. We illustrate in this paper how techniques and tools developed in other areas of Computer Science to increase the reliability of software can be applied at design and modelling stages to guide the engineering and developing team to reduce the potential for future malfunctioning.

Keywords. Intelligent Environments, Model Checking, Reliability of Software.

Introduction

Intelligent Environments (IEs) is a new and thriving area which have emerged in the last decade [1,2,3] from the combination of several pre-existing disciplines like networking, Human-Computer Interaction, sensing devices, Pervasive Computing, AI, etc. [4].

IEs can be defined as *"a digital environment that proactively, but sensibly, supports people in their daily lives."* [5]. Some recent applications include assisting drivers and monitoring vulnerable people in such a way the system alerts designated carers when safety may be compromised. There are many more interesting applications being the subject of intensive research. All them refer to an artificial system which is trusted to take certain responsibilities on assisting humans. As the scenarios described above indicate some of those can actually be so important that may be involved on situations which carry a risk of life loss or harm to humans.

Despite the importance of the responsibility these systems have there is little emphasis in the literature on the correctness of such systems. In [6] the model checker AVISPA is used to verify security issues within the networking protocol used for a Smart Home and, although important, this is only a very specific dimension of the complexity entailed by an Intelligent Environment. In [7] relevant work has been developed to aid the construction of Robots. Although useful steps, they are fairly isolated.

This paper emphasizes precisely the importance of using all the available technology to increase the reliability of an IE. We illustrate how well established methods and tools can be used to develop safer systems which will lead to artificial systems more properly aligned with the underlying principles of the area and, hopefully, to safer users.

[1] Corresponding Author's E-mail: jc.augusto@ulster.ac.uk.

1. Simulating an Artificial Environment

Intelligent environments see the world through sensors. These sensors offer diverse readings: on/off (triggered or not triggered) in a Passive Infrared Sensor (PIR), a few coordinates in an accelerometer, an ID number for an RFID (Radio-Frequency Identification), a range of values for a blood sugar level device, video cameras can provide quite detailed information about that part of the world they can 'see', microphones allow the gathering of sound from the limited area within their reach, just to name a few options. Each intelligent environment has a combination of different sensors. It does not matter how many we put together what the artificial system will gather and use to make sense of the reality will always be a 'murky', 'distorted' and limited view of reality, probably similar to some extent to what we see when we are driving in a foggy day. Our intelligence and our experience help us to make decisions in real-time, but because is foggy not all decisions are optimal (or even good!). Probing the judgement of our system with as many as possible different scenarios and understanding how the system we are trying to implement will react in critical circumstances is therefore a very important step in our way to implement a reliable system.

Ideally one wants to try the system as much as possible with the real final users, but this is usually impossible until the system has reached some stability and provides some level of reliability. Therefore simulations in the lab are necessary. But labs are usually unflexible to some extent and not easy to adapt to the different real environments the system will be finally deployed in. Hence simulation with artificially generated data is unavoidable and can offer huge rewards at initial stages of the design of a system given its flexibility and low cost.

The FADG (Flexible Artificial Data Generator) can provide such artificial data on demand. It is a program that have a generic part and a domain specific part. The first one selects the next event from a set of possible choices, do the time stamping, provides the frequency each event occurs at, and other elements from the generation process which do not depend on the specific domain. The domain specific component provides the knowledge of a particular environment: for example, the layout of a specific home, the devices present in that home, etc. It can generate events at any level of frequency, and it is efficient (in a quarter of an hour it can generate the equivalent to several years of data). The data is generated with format of a 4-tuple: *TimeStamp(Date-Time), Place, Status, Intensity*. A sample is included in Figure 1. The most important element is its flexibility as sensors and devices can be added or taken out of the model at ease. Part of the specification of the system has to do with semantics. For example, making sure that an occupant moves from room to room in a logical way: if there is no door connecting the living room with the bathroom then it has to go first to the reception area and only then can access the bathroom.

We have used FADG as a sort of a high level generator for the artificial system. For example during the implementation of the PUBS learning system [8] one member of the team induced the FADG algorithm to produce more often events related to particular places or activities and other member of the team applied the learning algorithm, then the team met to verify the algorithm was capable to successfully identify those patterns of behaviour that were favored by the the event generator.

```
2008-4-25-T13:23:53,at_bedroom,on,1
2008-4-25-T13:24:00,bLights,on,100
2008-4-25-T15:3:15,bLights,off,0
2008-4-25-T15:3:17,at_reception,on,1
2008-4-25-T15:4:05,at_toilet,on,1
2008-4-25-T15:19:11,shower,on,1
2008-4-25-T15:38:19,shower,off,0
```

Figure 1. Sample of Artificial Data generated.

2. Verifying Correct Interaction

There are certainly many methods with associated tools [9] that can be used for verification of software (as there are many others for the verification of hardware). From all them SPIN [10,11] is one of the most well-known and used system given its user friendly interface, efficiency, reliability and good team support. The system can be downloaded by anyone completely for free. The system is also open source for whoever wants to develop it further. Given space constraints and the focus of this paper we cannot provide a tutorial on SPIN hence the interested reader is referred to the literature provided above for more information. The rest of this section will focus on illustrating how we have used SPIN to help us design an Intelligent Environment.

Modeling, like programming, allows for many possible solutions to be encoded. Each model will typically represent an implementation strategy under scrutiny. Therefore there is no unique answer on how to model an intelligent environment in Promela (PROcess MEta-LAnguage, the modelling language for SPIN). Figure 2 shows a basic skeleton of a Promela model that we have used to represent different Smart Homes settings. Due to space limitations we omit details and also rearrange the location of the processes to minimize the space covered.

There are many options to model the different components of a Smart Home in SPIN. What are the features that are useful for our purpose of modelling an intelligent environment? Sensors of different types can be modelled as follows: Sensors with on/off (activated/deactivated) can be modelled in isolation with a boolean variable or with an array of them, e.g., `bool pir[20]=0`, if we can keep reasonable track which PIR sensor `pir[12]=true` refers to (is it the one in the kitchen?). Sensors/devices with a range of values (e.g., a blood pressure measuring machine) can be captured through a variable of type `short`, or an array of them if needed. Modelling other type of sensors or sensing devices (e.g., cameras and mics) or even the user's interaction with them may

```
...Definition of Global data structures (e.g., sensors)...

active [...] proctype Occupant()    active [...] proctype Visitor()
{...(local data structures)...      {...(local data structures)...
(behaviour modelling)          }     (behaviour modelling)         }

active [...] proctype SensorAct()   active [1] proctype Central_Unit()
{...(local data structures)...      {...(local data structures)...
(behaviour modelling)          }     (behaviour modelling)         }
```

Figure 2. Basic skeleton of an environment in SPIN.

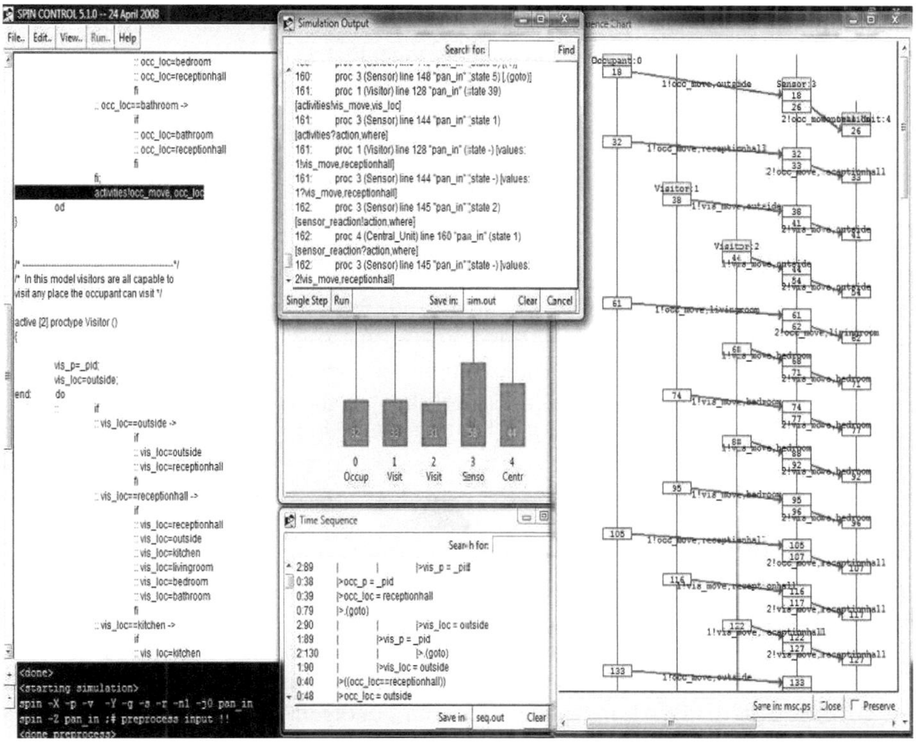

Figure 3. SPIN in action.

require `mytype` definitions stating the different possible outputs (e.g., mtype=standing, walking, falling, laying, moving, screaming).

Figure 3 shows the use of SPIN over a Promela model of a Smart Home. The model is shown partially on the left hand side. The sequence of messages modelling communication within the network caused by the actions of the occupant and visitors as they trigger PIR sensors is depicted in the right hand side. The panels in the middle provide other useful information on the simulation up to that stage. The top panel provides details of each statement executed in the model. The middle panel shows the level of activity exhibited by each process defined in the model. The bottom panel shows how the interleaved steps of each process unfolded in time. We were able to prove several properties and also to find many flaws in our models at intermediate steps of the design. One example of such properties we explored was one showing the system was aware of the structure of the house. The LTL formula (see [11], ch. 4 for more details) `[]((b && <>o) -> (b && <>(r && <>o)))` stating "always is the case that if a person wants to move from the bathroom to outside of the house then at some stage has to go through the reception hall". Other properties related to the potential behaviours of people as captured by the model for example, verifying `<> [] nurse_out`, stating "it is eventually possible for the nurse to stay outside the house", was true for a model meant that model included the scenario which allowed the nurse never to come inside the house. Notice that because we are not dealing with explicit time in SPIN (explicit time handling is feasible but costly) then we cannot model how fast the nurse comes to house after an alarm is triggered.

Neither we can model that if an occupant does not answer 'fast enough' a phone call or a doorbell whilst being at home then we want to label that as a situation where potentially help is needed. For that we need a tool like the one we are considering next.

3. Focusing on Time Constraints

One problem with SPIN is that while representing clocks for the analysis of time constraints is feasible in Promela the resulting model will be more complicated and inefficient given that clocks are not provided as a primitive element of the modelling language. There are many optional systems however that have been created to assist with the design and modelling of Real-Time systems and which are very appropriate in this case. UPPAAL [12,13] is one of the most well-known and used systems for this type of task. Its best assets being the same than SPIN, user friendly interface, efficiency, reliability and good supporting team. Again this is a system that is used outside of academy by important companies to verify specific core elements of their safety-critical systems, several of those success stories have been published. Its input is a bit more abstract than in the case of SPIN as it is based on networks of timed automata which can be either drawn and defined in the windows like interface or can be generated (even automatically) as an XML file which the system can pick up as an input. Again due to the focus of this paper the reader who wants to know more about UPPAAL should familiarize her/himself with the extensive literature available. The rest of this section will focus on illustrating how we have used UPPAAL to help us design an Intelligent Environment.

Figure 4 shows the declaration of global variables for all automata involved in the modelling of a specific smart home. Figure 5 shows the simulation panel which exhibits only a few of the automata composing the whole system's model, in this case the sensor detection manager (upper middle) which is processing with a PIR sensor triggering in the living room. The are multiple benefits in using tools like UPPAAL: (a) modelling itself forces the developing team to reflect upon subtle aspects of the system, (b) simulation provides a way to explore potential scenarios and try ideas before actual implementation, and (c) verification provides a way to prove/disprove behavioural properties reflecting the requirements of the system. Most interestingly, in trying to prove those fundamental behavioural properties the tool will find counterexamples that show us why a property (formal expression of a requirement) is still not captured with the solution strategy represented in the current model.

In the case of UPPPAL the classical patterns in the specification of behavioural properties for formal verification are: `E<>P` (P is reachable), `E [] P` (potentially always P), `A <> P` (inevitable P), `A [] P` (invariantly P) and `P -> Q` (consequence). Examples on how we used those templates instantiated in the context of a Smart Home design we explored follow: (a) Template: `E <> P` (*Does a path exist where P eventually holds?*). Instantiation: `E<> (EnvironmentController.on and AtHome==false)` with intuitive meaning: "Is it possible for the system to reach a state where the patient is not at home but the heating/air conditioning system is on?" (b) Template: `E [ ] P` (*Does a path exist where P always holds?*). Instantiation: `E[ ] burglarAlarm.active imply burglarAlarm.idle` with intuitive meaning: "Does a path exist where an activated burglar alarm will be deactivated?" (c) Template: `A <> P` (*Will P eventually hold for all paths?*). Instantia-

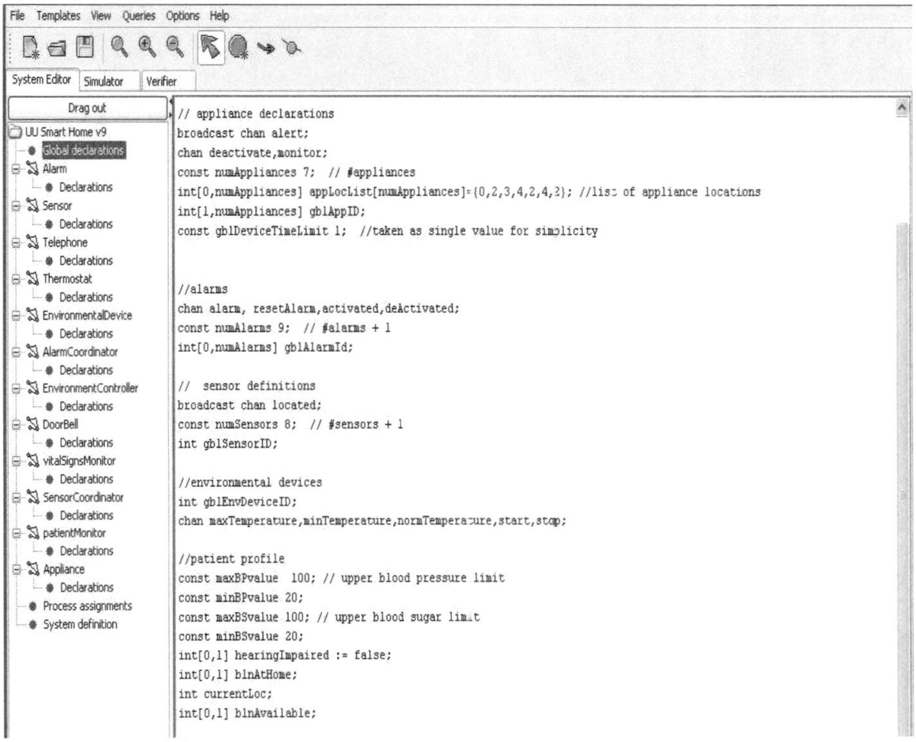

Figure 4. UPPAAL: global variables declaration.

tion: `A<>Thermostat.idle` with intuitive meaning: "Will the thermostat eventually return to the idle state?" (d) Template: `A [ ] P` (*Does P always hold for all paths?*) . Instantiation: `A [ ] ! (vitalSignsMonitor.bloodSugar>0 && AtHome==false)` with intuitive meaning: "It is not possible for the system to reach a state where blood sugar is monitored when the patient is not at home". (e) Template: P –> Q (*Whenever p holds will q also hold?*). Instantiation: `kitchenSmokeAlarm.active -> AlarmManager.contactFireBrigade` with intuitive meaning: "Whenever the kitchen smoke alarm is active, the alarm manager will contact the fire brigade".

Figure 6 shows UPPAAL verification interface. At the top there is a list of properties that have been loaded for verification. The software developer in the team has already requested to model-check (see button on the top right hand side) the first property in that list and the result (the property is valid with regards to the current model) on the lower window of the panel. Notice some of these properties has explicit time constraints, which would not have been suitable for checking with SPIN.

4. Conclusions

We have explained how well established methods and tools can be successfully applied to better understand a solution for an Intelligent Environment at design and modelling

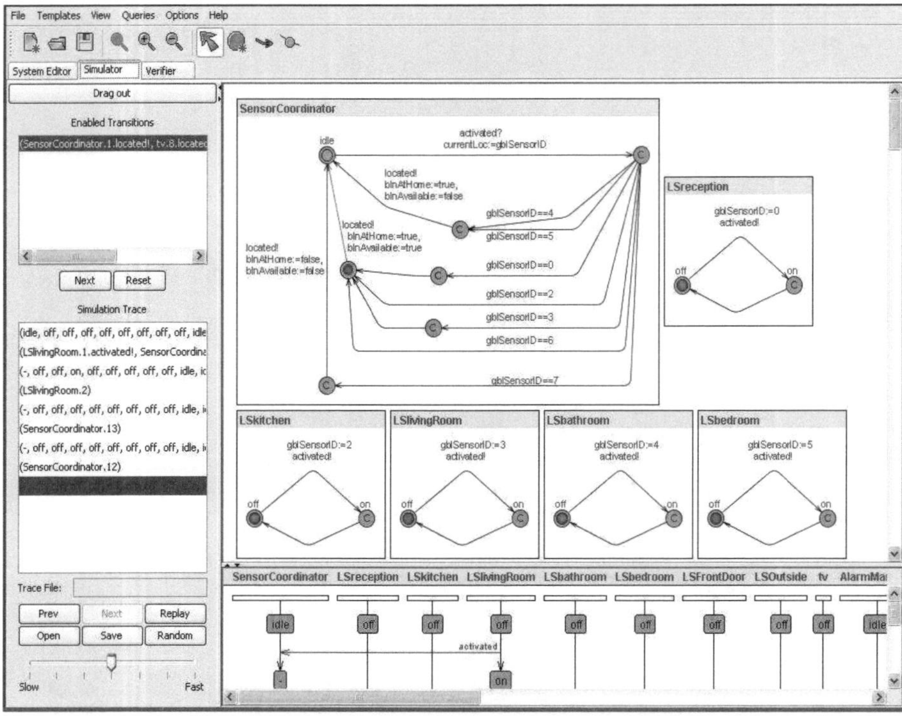

Figure 5. UPPAAL: simulation panel.

stages. This has as an important practical consequence that the system can be implemented in a safer way.

This has so far been mostly overlooked in the literature of the area but it should not be that way given the tremendous responsibility we put on some of these systems (for example taking care of vulnerable people to raise alerts when safety may have been compromised). Therefore this paper focus on showing how a system for an Intelligent Environment can be developed more safely leading to a product with increased reliability.

Surely not all aspects of the final implemented system can be considered, for example, it does not guarantee that if a sensor is moved to a different location then the system will still work correctly, but it helps ensuring that if the system implementation follows its specification then its logic will be sound. If the system is changed then that is a different system and the modifications have to be reviewed.

As a final reflection, it can be seen that there are certain features of Intelligent Environments which cannot be covered by the methods and tools considered here and given these represent the state of the art in verification of software systems this mean may not be a way with current technology to cover those issues as comfortably as we should. Therefore the content of this paper carries an implicit message and invitation to the communities of Intelligent Systems and Software Engineering to develop in collaboration methods and tool that are better suited to encompass the diversity of components making up an Intelligent Environment. Some steps have been given in that direction, more has to be done.

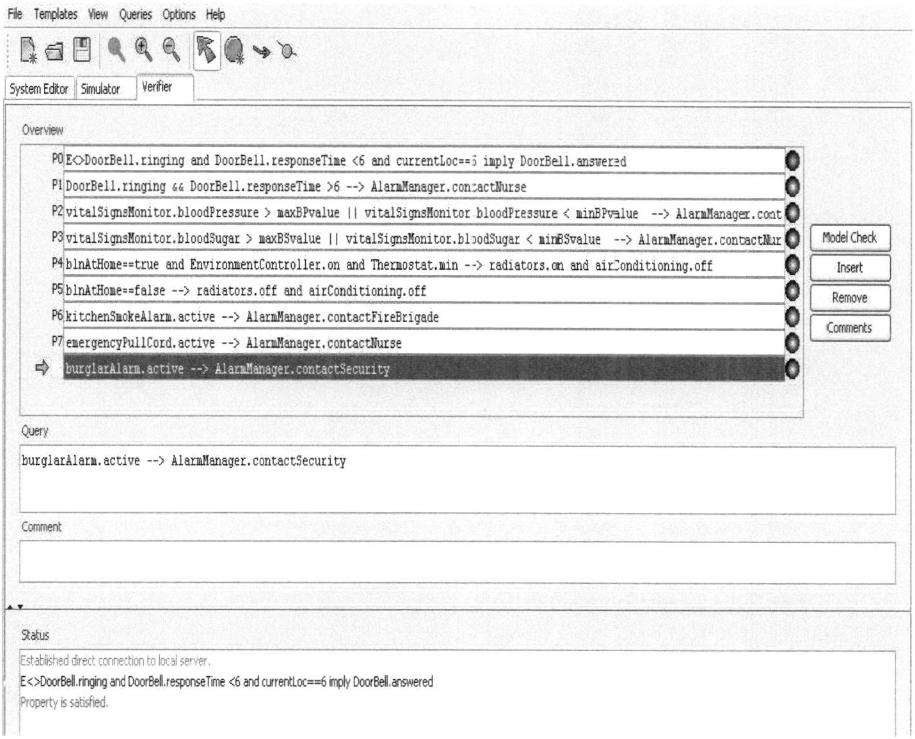

Figure 6. UPPAAL: verification panel.

References

[1] M. Weiser, "The computer for the twenty-first century," *Scientific American*, vol. 165, pp. 94–104, 1991.

[2] IST Advisory Group, "The european union report, scenarios for ambient intelligence in 2010," 2001, uRL: ftp://ftp.cordis.lu/pub/ist/docs/istagscenarios2010.pdf.

[3] *Proceedings of The International Workshop on Intelligent Environments (IE 05)*. IEE, 2005.

[4] D. J. Cook, J. C. Augusto, and V. R. Jakkula, "Ambient intelligence: applications in society and opportunities for artificial intelligence," *Pervasive and Mobile Computing*, 2009, to appear.

[5] J. C. Augusto, *Ambient Intelligence: the Confluence of Ubiquitous/Pervasive Computing and Artificial Intelligence*, ser. Intelligent Computing Everywhere. Springer London, 2007, pp. 213–234.

[6] A. Muñoz, A. Maña, and D. Serrano, "Model cheking ambient intelligence with avispa," in *Ambient Intelligence Perspectives*, ser. Book Series on Ambient Intelligence and Smart Environments, P. Mikulecký, T. Lišková, P. Cech, and V. Bureš, Eds. IOS Press, 2009, vol. 1, pp. 182–193.

[7] S. Bensalem, M. Gallien, F. Ingrand, I. Kahloul, and T.-H. Nguyen, "Towards a more dependable software architecture for autonomous robots," *IEEE Robotics and Automation Magazine*, 2009.

[8] A. Aztiria, J. C. Augusto, A. Izaguirre, and D. Cook, "Learning accurate temporal relations from user actions in intelligent environments," in *Proc. of the 3th Symposium of Ubiquitous Computing and Ambient Intelligence*, J. M. Corchado, D. I. Tapia, and J. Bravo, Eds. Springer, 2008, pp. 274–283.

[9] B. Berard, M. Bidoit, A. Finkel, F. Laroussinie, A. Petit, L. Petrucci, P. Schnoebelen, and P. McKenzie, *Systems and Software Verification (Model Checking Techniques and Tools)*. Springer Verlag, 1999.

[10] http://spinroot.com/spin/whatispin.html.

[11] G. J. Holzmann, *The SPIN Model Checker : Primer and Reference Manual*. Addison-Wesley, 2003.

[12] http://www.uppaal.com/.

[13] K. G. Larsen, P. Pettersson, and W. Yi, "Uppaal in a nutshell," *Int. Journal on Software Tools for Technology Transfer*, vol. 1, pp. 134–152, 1997.

Special Session on Intelligent Knowledge-Based and Agent-Based Systems

Intelligent Environments 2009
V. Callaghan et al. (Eds.)
IOS Press, 2009

doi:10.3233/978-1-60750-034-6-145

Interleaved Activity Recognition for Smart Home residents

Geetika Singla and Diane J. Cook[1]
Washington State University
{gsingla,cook}@eecs.wsu.edu

Abstract. Smart environments rely on artificial intelligence techniques to make sense of the sensor data and to use the information for recognition and tracking activities. However, many of the techniques that have been developed are designed for simplified situations. In this paper we discuss a more complex situation, namely recognizing activities when they are interweaved in complex and realistic scenarios. This technology is beneficial for monitoring the health of smart environment residents and for correlating activities with parameters such as energy usage. We describe our approach to interleaved activity recognition and evaluate various probabilistic techniques for activity recognition. We validate our algorithm on real sensor data collecting in our smart apartment testbed.

Keywords. activity recognition, naïve Bayes classifier, Markov model

1. Introduction

With the dramatic improvements in intelligent environments that the community has witnessed, researchers have begun investigating the use of smart environment data and artificial intelligence techniques to automate caregiver tasks. With the development of smart environment technologies, at-home automated assistance can allow people with mental and physical challenges to lead independent lives in their own homes. Researchers have generated ideas for designing smart environment software algorithms that track the location and activities of residents, that generate reminders, and that react to hazardous situations [1]. Because performing Activities of Daily Living (ADLs) are a normal part of independent living, a key technology for monitoring an individual's health is to identify and track a smart environment resident's regular performance of these activities.

Researchers have investigated the recognition of resident activities using a variety of mechanisms. While these approaches have been fairly effective for certain types of tasks, they face difficulties when applied in general situations because they make simplifying assumptions about the nature in which the activities are performed. In this paper we address the problem of recognizing activities in complex situations. In particular, we investigate approaches to recognizing activities that are interrupted and interwoven. We assess the effectiveness of each approach using real data collected in the CASAS smart apartment testbed.

---

[1] Corresponding Author.

2. CASAS

The activity recognition algorithms we introduce in this paper are part of the CASAS smart environment project. In order to evaluate our algorithms, we test them using data collected in the CASAS smart apartment testbed. The apartment, shown in Figure 1, includes three bedrooms, one bathroom, a kitchen, and a living/dining room. This environment is equipped with motion sensors, temperature sensors, humidity sensors, contacts switches in the doors, and item sensors on key items. We have designed special-purpose sensors to detect water usage and stove burner usage and use the Asterisk software to monitor outgoing phone usage. All of these sensors have the advantage of being non-obtrusive and easy to monitor remotely.

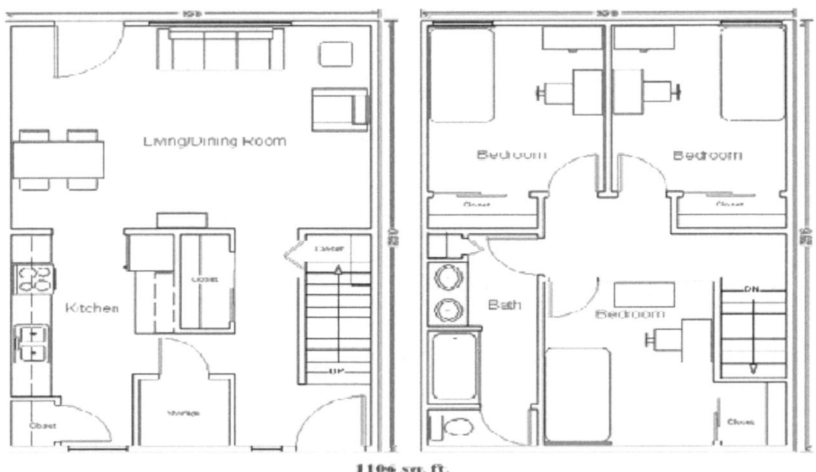

Figure 1. The CASAS smart apartment testbed.

3. Activity Recognition

While collecting sequences of sensor readings in a smart environment is valuable, determining what activities these sequences represent is a more challenging task. We employ probabilistic models to automatically recognize the ADLs activities when they are interleaved. Researchers have investigated the recognition of resident activities using a variety of mechanisms such as naïve Bayes classifiers, Markov models, and dynamic Bayes networks [2,3,4,5]. These approaches have been fairly effective for limited types of tasks. However, these limitations prevent the techniques from being applied in more realistic situations. In particular, all of the approaches to date make the assumptions that these activities are performed sequentially and independent of other activities; and that there is only one resident to monitor at a time.

In contrast, we are designing algorithms that probabilistically identify the activities while they are being performed in not only isolated (i.e. sequential), but also complex (i.e. interleaved and concurrent) manners in real life. Given a sequence of observed sensor events we can probabilistically determine which activity the sequence belongs to. We describe and analyze several probabilistic classifiers to perform this task.

4. Experiments

Figure 2. The web cam image in the upper left shows a participant performing the "Write birthday card" activity. The activity generates the sensor readings shown in the upper right and visualized at the bottom.

For this study, we selected 8 ADLs important for everyday functioning [6]. The selected activities include "Fill medication dispenser", "Watch DVD", "Water plants", "Converse on Phone", "Write Birthday Card", "Prepare meal", "Sweep and dust", and "Select an outfit". To validate our interleaved activity recognition algorithms we recruited 20 volunteer participants to perform these activities in the smart apartment. First, each of the participants performed these tasks sequentially. The participants were next instructed to perform all of these activities by interweaving them as they liked with a goal of being efficient in performing the tasks. In this case the participants jumped back and forth between tasks, sometimes even performing several tasks at once. The data collected for both of these runs was then manually labeled with the correct activity ids for training purposes.

Figure 3. The participant is interweaving 2 tasks. Here she transitions from midway through the "Select an Outfit" activity to the "Phone Conversation".

We implemented several probabilistic classifiers to find out an approach that works best for identifying interleaved activities. These probabilistic models include a Naïve Bayes classifier, a Hidden Markov Model (HMM), a HMM with a time window, a frequency-based HMM with a sliding window and a frequency-based HMM with a shifting window. We used these models to automatically label every sensor event from the test set with an activity label so that the smart environment agent is aware of the current activity at any given time. In the results we report below, we show accuracy results generated using three-fold cross validation on the participant data.

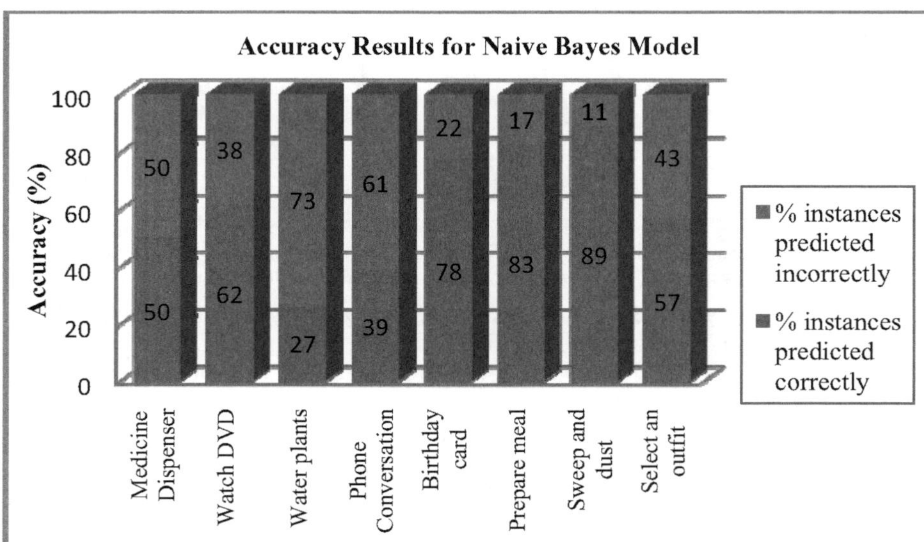

Figure 4. Bar graph showing performance of Naive Bayes classifier broken down by activity.

In spite of its simple design and over-simplified assumptions, naive Bayes classifiers (NBCs) often work much better in many complex real-world situations than expected. This classifier assumes variables to be independent and expresses the conditional distribution over the class variable C as:

$$p(C|F_1, \ldots, F_n) = (1/Z)\, p(C) \prod n_i = p(F_i\,|C) \quad (1)$$

where Z is a scaling factor dependent only on features F_1, F_2, …, F_n. For our research, we use the maximum a posteriori rule to pick the most probable activity. The classifier returns the class value given by:

$$\text{argmax}_C\, p(C)\, ((1/Z)\, p(C = c) \prod^{n}_{i=1} p(F_i = f_i|C = c) \quad (2)$$

In our implementation, we treat every sensor as a feature and learn sensor value probability distributions for all activities. The independence assumption works well here because high probability values are generally concentrated over different sensors for different activities. The NBC results in an overall accuracy of 66.08% in predicting interleaved activities, as shown in Figure 4. As the NBC does not take transition probabilities into consideration, some activities could not be identified very well by the model. In order to make use of the information resulting in transition between states, we next implemented a Hidden Markov Model (HMM).

Our HMM algorithm represents each activity as a hidden state. Next, every sensor is treated as an observable state in the model due to the fact that every sensor in the environment generates observable readings. One collective HMM model is generated for all activities, with the horizontal and vertical transition probabilities learned from the training data. In the testing phase the new data is run through the HMM as a continuous stream of data and the activity (hidden node) with highest probability value (calculated using the Viterbi algorithm [7]) is returned as the activity label. Figure 5 shows a section of the HMM for interleaved activities and the accuracy results for our HMM are shown in Figure 6.

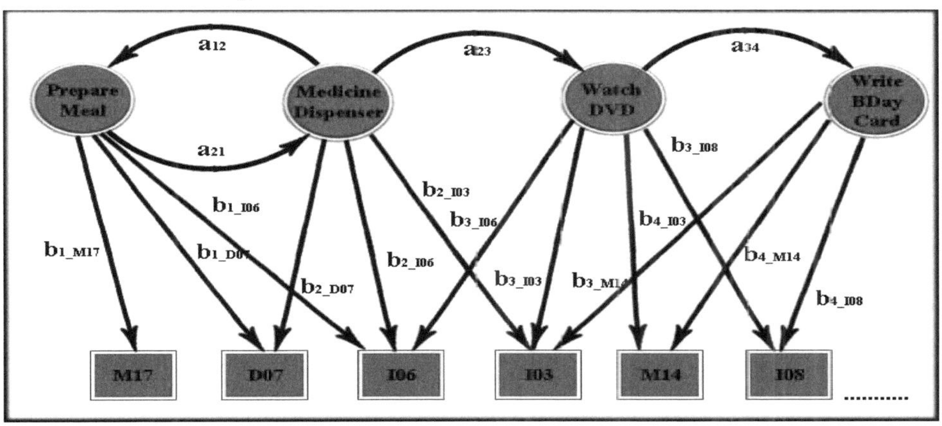

Figure 5. A section of a hidden Markov model designed to model interleaved activities. The circles refer to the activities (i.e., the hidden states) and the rectangles refer to the observable states. Value 'a_{ij}' refers to the probability of transitioning from activity *i* to activity *j*, and the $b_{i\_sensorId}$ values represent the emission probability of the possible observations in a particular hidden state.

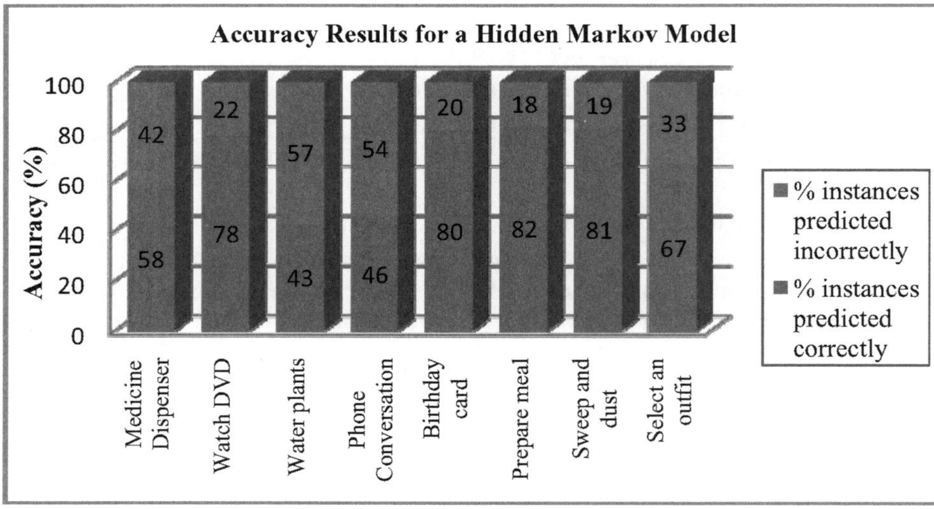

Figure 6. Bar graph showing performance of Hidden Markov Model in recognizing interleaved activities.

The average accuracy of our hidden Markov model in predicting interleaved activities is 71%, as shown in Figure 6. The model shows an overall increase of 10% in accuracy over the naïve Bayes model. A limitation of this plain HMM is that it moves very slowly from recognizing one activity to the next. As a remedy, we used a sliding window where the size of the window is governed by the number of sensor events it contains. This limits the history of sensor events that the model remembers at any given time which in turn helps in keeping the probability values low for all activities and in making a faster switch from the current to the next activity. This technique works in two phases: in the first phase, alternative window sizes are tested on 2/3 of the data; in the second phase, the automatically-selected window is used to label the rest of the data.

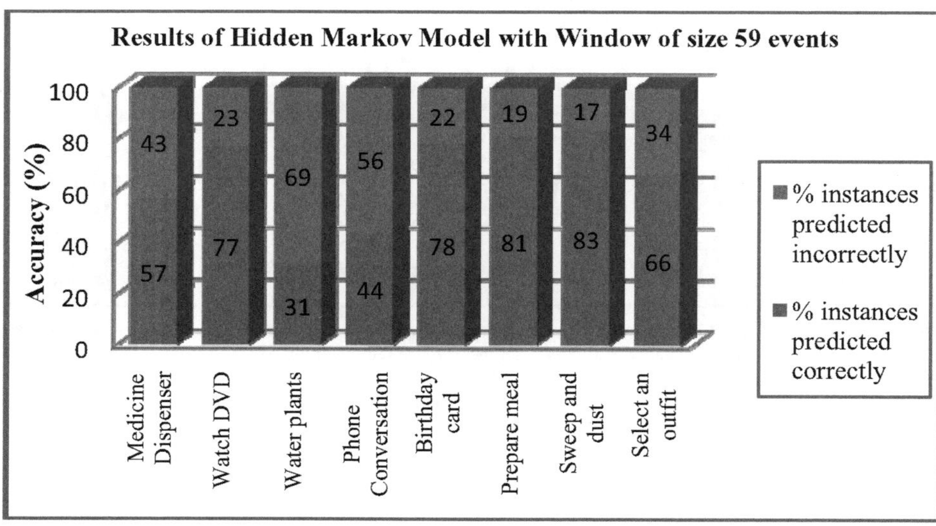

Figure 7. Bar graph showing accuracy of the model for a window size of 59 sensor events.

This model results in an overall average accuracy of 63.55% in recognizing activities for a window size of 59 sensor events. The activity "Sweep and dust" is predicted with the highest accuracy of 83%. This model performs poorly for activities "Water plants" and "Phone conversation" and shows lowest accuracies of 31% and 44%, respectively. This can be attributed by the fact that these activities contain fewer number of sensor events, and so a smaller window would have recognized these tasks more precisely. The window size thus calculated using this technique works for most, but not all type of activities.

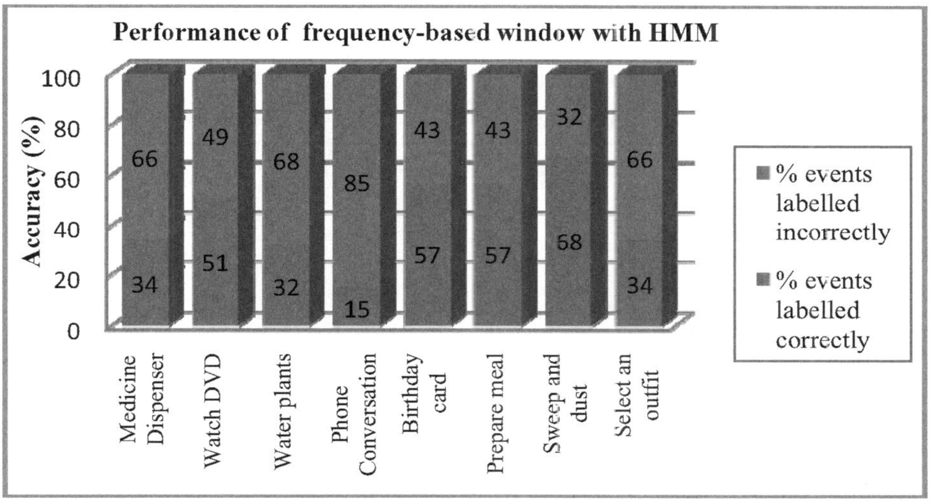

Figure 8. Bar graph showing performance of window based HMM using frequency.

Another approach that we tried to solve this problem was to use the HMM with a frequency-based window. Instead of labeling each sensor event with an activity label, however, this time we label the sensor event with the activity label of the most frequent activity in the entire window. This model shows a maximum overall accuracy of 56.75% in identifying activities for a window size of 8 sensor events. This technique suffered from the same problem of making a very slow transition from the current to next activity and did not perform as well as expected. At the time of transition, the previous activity always has a higher frequency leading to inaccurately labeling the new sensor event and thereby degrading the performance of the algorithm. Figure 9 summarizes the accuracy of all of the approaches to facilitate direct comparison.

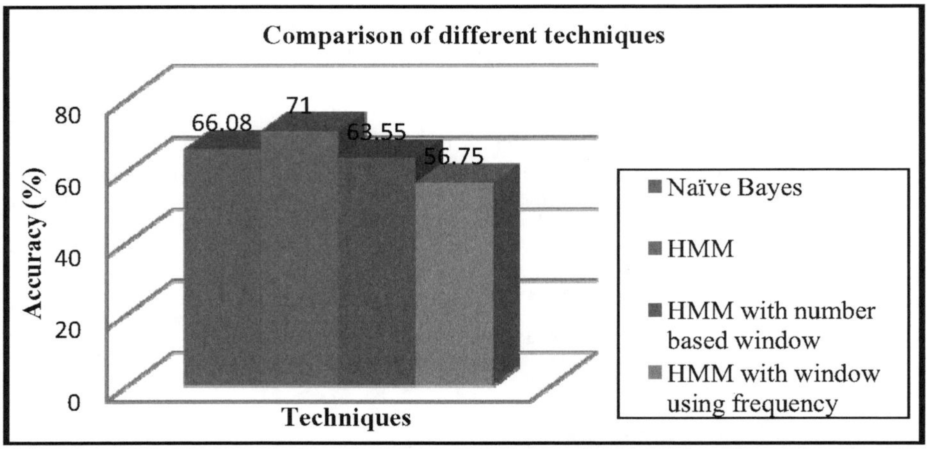

Figure 9. Bar graph comparing performance of all techniques in recognizing interleaved activities.

5. Conclusions and Future Work

In this paper we address the problem of recognizing interleaved activities in smart environments. Not only do we demonstrate that these activities can be recognized by sensors in physical environments, but we also show enhancements that help the classifiers improve recognition accuracy. This increased accuracy will be important as we move on to our next steps. In particular, we will next be investigating techniques for detecting missing or incorrect steps in the activity, and for recognizing activities when there are multiple residents in the environment.

This research lays the groundwork for tools that automatically monitor and assist individuals with special health needs. We believe these technologies are essential to provide accessible and low-cost health assistance in an individual's own home. Furthermore, investigating these issues will be imperative if we want to adequately care for our aging population and provide the best possible quality of life for them and, ultimately, for ourselves.

References

[1] M. Pollack. Intelligent technology for an aging population: The use of AI to assist elders with cognitive impairment. *AI Magazine*, 26(2):9-24, 2005

[2] C. Wren & E. Munguia-Tapia. Toward scalable activity recognition for sensor networks, *Proceedings of the Workshop on Location and Context-Awareness*, 2006

[3] M. Philipose, K. Fishkin, M. Perkowitz, D. Patterson, D. Fox, H. Kautz, and D. Hahnel. Inferring activities from interactions with objects. *IEEE Pervasive Computing*, 3(4):50-57, 2004

[4] L. Liao, D. Fox, and H. Kautz. Extracting places and activities from GPS traces using hierarchical conditional random fields. *International Journal of Robotics Research*, 26(1):119-126, 2007

[5] M. Stikic, T. Huynh, K. Van Laerhoven, and B. Schiele. ADL recognition based on the combination of RFID and accelerometer sensing. *PervasiveHealth*, pages 258-263, 2008

[6] S.T. Farias, D. Mungas, B. Reed, D. Harvey, D. Cahn-Weiner and C. DeCarli. MCI is associated with deficits in everyday functioning. *Alzheimer Disease and Associated Disorders,* 20:217-223, 2006

[7] A. Viterbi. Error bounds for convolutional codes and an asymptotically optimum decoding algorithm, *IEEE Transactions on Information Theory* 13(2):260–269, 1967.

Intelligent Environments 2009
V. Callaghan et al. (Eds.)
IOS Press, 2009

doi:10.3233/978-1-60750-034-6-153

Discovering Frequent Sets of Actions in Intelligent Environments

Asier AZTIRIA [a,1], Alberto IZAGUIRRE [a] Rosa BASAGOITI [a]
Juan Carlos AUGUSTO [b] and Diane J. COOK [c]
[a] *University of Mondragon, Spain*
[b] *University of Ulster, United Kingdom*
[c] *Washington State University, U.S.A*

Abstract. Intelligent Environments depend on their capability to understand and anticipate user's habits and needs. Therefore, learning user's common behaviours becomes an important step towards allowing an environment to provide such personalized services. We have developed a system which learns user's patterns taking into account the special features of Intelligent Environments. Due to the complexity of the system, this paper will focus on a specific part of such a system, the module that discovers what sets of actions are frequently carried out by the user.

Keywords. Intelligent Environments, Learning behavioural patterns

1. Introduction

Intelligent Environments defined as *digital environments that proactively, but sensibly, support people in their daily lives* [1] can be considered as a promising opportunity to support people in many different ways. Some of the potential benefits that this technology can bring to people in their daily lives include making an environment more comfortable, safer and more energy efficient. In order to achieve these objectives, the environment should learn patterns of the user which means that the environment has to gain knowledge about the preferences, needs and habits of the user in order to be in a better position to assist the user adequately [2].

Let us consider the next scenario which exemplifies the common behaviour of an user. *On weekdays Michael's alarm clock goes off ('Alarm on') few minutes after 08:00AM. Approximately 10-15 minutes after getting up he usually steps into the bathroom ('Bathroom on') and he turns on the lights of the bathroom ('BathLights on'). On Tuesdays, Thursdays and Fridays he usually has a shower ('Shower on'). In this sense, Michael preferences about the temperature of the water are around 24-26 degrees in winter whereas he likes around 21-23 degrees in summer. Before he leaves the bathroom ('Bathroom off') he turns off the lights ('BathLights off').*

Knowing these patterns of the user allows the environment to act intelligently in order to assist people in their daily lives. For example, in Michael's scenario, knowing his habits the environment can act proactively in order to make his life easier and safer.

[1]Corresponding Author. E-mail: aaztiria@eps.mondragon.edu

In this case, acting proactively could mean the environment automatically turns on and turns off the lights, sets the temperature of the water and so on. *Automation* of actions and/or devices can be considered as an advantage which can be reached once the environment has learnt the habits and preferences of the user. The knowledge acquired from the patterns can also be used in order to *understand* his behaviour. For example, the analysis of usual patterns can allow the detection of bad or unhealthy habits (e.g. we detect that Michael does not brush his teeth in the mornings). Making the environment more efficient in terms of *energy saving* (e.g. by switching the lights off when Michael has gone out) or increasing the *safety* (e.g. switching the cooker off or issuing alarms when detecting Michael has left it on and he will not return soon) are other advantages that the environment can perform better if it knows the common behaviours of the user.

The reminder of the paper is organized as follows. Section 2 describes briefly the SPUBS. Section 3 summarizes previous related work done in learning highlighting the task of discovering frequent sets of actions. In Section 4 we explain our approach for discovering frequent sets of actions. Section 5 shows the rest of the steps. Finally Section 6 shows the results of the validation experiments and Section 7 the conclusions.

2. Sequential Patterns of User Behaviour System

Sequential Patterns of User Behaviour (SPUBS) is a system that discovers user's common behaviours and habits from data recorded by sensors. Due to the complexity of Intelligent Environments, the architecture of the system demands an exhaustive analysis. Thus, we have created a three layer architecture (see Figure 1) which allows to distinguish those aspects related to particular environments from those aspects that can be generalized for all environments. The core of the system is the learning algorithm $\mathcal{A}_{SPUBS}$ which combined with a language $\mathcal{L}_{SPUBS}$ allows to discover and represent the patterns. It is worth mentioning that the learning layer, in contrast with the two other layers, is independent of the specific environment we are dealing with. In other words, the algorithm created in this layer as well as the language used in order to represent the patterns can be used in any environment.

Figure 1 also shows the internal structure of the algorithm ($\mathcal{A}_{SPUBS}$) which is the core of the whole system. This algorithm is divided in four steps which represent the four logical steps to discover frequent and comprehensible patterns. A brief description of each module follows:

Identifying Frequent Sets: The objective of this first step is to identify the sets of actions that frequently occur together (for further details see Section 4). In Michael's scenario this step discovers that Michael usually carries out the following actions together:

'Alarm on', 'Bathroom on', 'Bathroom off', 'BathLights on', 'BathLights off', 'Shower on' and 'Shower off'

Identifying Topology: This step discovers in what order the user usually carries out the sets of actions discovered in the first step, giving it a sense of sequence. Thus, in Michael's scenario it discovers that the activation of the alarm clock comes first, then he goes into the bathroom, then he turns the lights on and so on. See Figure 2(a) for the output achieved after this step.

Identifying Time Relations: The objective of this step is to relate the actions in terms of time. In contrast with the previous step this step tries to relate the actions as accurately

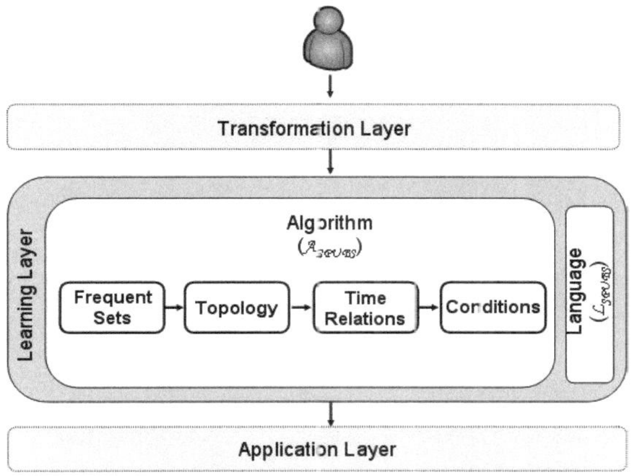

Figure 1. Global architecture of SPUBS

as possible. In Michael's scenario this step discovers that he usually turns the lights on 2 seconds after he goes into the bathroom. In some cases (e.g. when defining the time relation between turning the lights on and having a shower) it is impossible to define such a numerical relation hence nominal relations such as 'after' have to be used. See Figure 2(b) for the output achieved after this step.

Identifying Conditions: The last step of the algorithm is to discover specific conditions for situations where different options are and general conditions in order to contextualize the whole sequence. In Michael's scenario, on the one hand it defines that he only has a shower on Tuesdays, Thursdays and Fridays. On the other hand this step also defines that the whole sequence occurs only on weekdays and it starts few minutes after 08AM and it finishes before 09AM. See Figure 2(c) for the output achieved after this step.

Although the whole algorithm is already developed, because of space restrictions, this paper will be focused on the first step of 'Identifying Frequent Sets'.

3. Related Work

Learning is an essential feature in any Intelligent Environment. However, it has not been devoted as much attention in the literature as it may require. Next, different approaches are analysed emphasizing the way they discover and relate the sets of actions that frequently occur together.

So far, most of the applications where a learning process was involved have related an action to the global situation of that moment instead of relating actions among them. Thus, there are many applications where considering the status of different sensors they predict the actions of the user. For example, based on occupancy predictors, the lighting control [3] has been an application developed in that sense. Researches at Essex's iDorm lab [4] also generated fuzzy rules mapping the data recorded when user caused any change.

This approach of relating the actions to the global situation has two main disadvantages. On the one hand, due to the number of sensors and the different situations that can emerge from their combination, it seems clear that the number of rules will be exces-

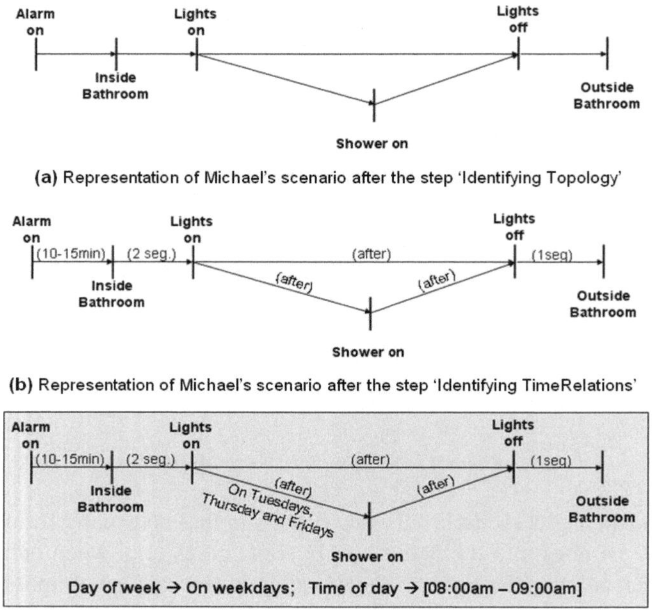

(c) Representation of Michael's scenario after the step 'Identifying Conditions'

Figure 2. Evolution of Michael's scenario through the $\mathcal{A}_{SPUBS}$

sive as well as some of them will not be meaningful. On the other hand, without relating actions among them, such rules create independent pieces of information instead of creating complete and comprehensible representation of the user's behaviour.

Some groups have started highlighting the importance and the advantages of associating actions. Thus, researchers at Essex [5] introduced an improvement in order to find out relevant associations between given actions so that irrelevant aspects of the rules can be removed. In this sense, the group that has been working in MavHome and Casas projects [6] [7] was one of the first groups that emphasized the importance of associating actions. But they only discovered one to one associations instead of the whole sequence.

4. Identifying Frequent Sets

Associating actions among them facilitates the understanding of the patterns as well as the automation. In that sense we also started by discovering one to one relation between actions [8] and then we have progressed into discovering any set of actions, without limiting the number of actions of such an association.

As mentioned above the objective of this step is to find out the sets of actions that frequently occur together (*Frequent Sets*). For that, the starting point will be the data coming from the Transformation Layer. The objective of that layer is to transform the raw data into useful information for the Learning Layer. Briefly explained, it infers meaningful actions from the data collected by sensors and then it splits the string of actions into structured sequences based on some domain dependant criteria. Let us consider that the set of Michael's morning activities coming from the Transformation Layer is:

activation of devices (date;device;status;value)

2008-10-20 (Sequence 1)	*2008-10-21 (Sequence 2)*	*2008-10-22 (Sequence 3)*
08:02:12;Alarm;on	*08:01:53;Alarm;on*	*08:05:15;Alarm;on*
08:15:54;Bathroom;on	*08:12:16;Bathroom;on*	*08:16:39;Bathroom;on*
08:15:56;BathLights;on	*08:12:17;BathLights;on*	*08:16:42;BathLights;on*
08:16:16;Tap;on	*08:12:49;MirrorLight;on*	*08:19:04;FlushToilet;on*
08:17:02;Tap;off	*08:15:38;MirrorLight;off*	*08:22:43;BathLights;off*
08:23:14;BathLights;off	*08:16:03;Shower;on*	*08:22:44;Bathroom;off*
08:23:15;Bathroom;off	*08:22:48;Shower;off*	
	08:38:57;BathLights;off	
	08:38:58;Bathroom;off	
2008-10-23 (Sequence 4)	*2008-10-24 (Sequence 5)*	*2008-10-25 (Sequence 6)*
08:10:50;Alarm;on	*08:09:41;Alarm;on*	*09:05:15;Alarm;on*
08:20:59;Bathroom;on	*08:23:12;Bathroom;on*	*09:26:39;Kitchen;on*
08:21:01;BathLights;on	*08:23:14;BathLights;on*	*09:16:45;KitchenLights;on*
08:22:48;Shower;on	*08:24:46;Shower;on*	*09:19:07;Microwave;on*
08:35:24;Shower;off	*08:29:38;Shower;off*	*09:20:07;Microwave;off*
08:39:57;BathLights;off	*08:35:20;BathLights;off*	*09:31:03;KitchenLights;off*
08:39:58;Bathroom;off	*08:35:21;Bathroom;off*	*09:31:06;Kitchen;off*

4.1. Identifying Basic Frequent Sets

The aim of this first task is to discover the sets of actions that frequently occur together in different sequences. For that, it is necessary to define a demanded minimum level (*minimum confidence*), so that all those sets of actions that have higher confidence level than the minimum confidence are considered as Basic Frequent Sets. If we define a minimum confidence of 60% in Michael's scenario, it can be observed that the set of actions which minimum confidence is higher than 60% is the set made up of:

'Alarm on', 'Bathroom on', 'Bathroom off', 'BathLights on', 'BathLights off'

This set of actions appears in 4 out of the 6 Sequences (66.6% > 60%), so that it will be considered as a Basic Frequent Set. In order to discover Basic Frequent Sets in large amount of data we have used the Apriori Algorithm [9] for mining association rules. The sets discovered in such a way are frequent, but it is worth mentioning that considering only this task of discovering Basic Frequent Sets does not take into account all the particularities that could happen. Thus, taking as starting point the Basic Frequent Sets discovered in this task, in the following subsections we explain how such Basic Frequent Sets can be extended in order to make them more flexible.

4.2. Identifying extra actions for Frequent Sets

Once Basic Frequent Sets have been discovered, an aspect to consider is if there is any action which is not frequent taking into account all the Sequences, so that it is not discovered in the previous task, but it is frequent enough in those Sequences where the Basic Frequent Set occurs. Considering Michael's scenario again, the Basic Frequent Set discovered in the previous task occurs in the Sequences 1,2,4 and 5. Thus, the aim of this task will be to discover if there is any extra action that frequently happens in such particular sequences.

For that, as in the previous task we have to define a minimum level of confidence. Let us consider the same minimum confidence (60%) for this task. In order to discover such extra actions we have also used the Apriori Algorithm. The only difference is that instead of considering all the sequences we only consider such sequences where the Basic Frequent Set is present.

Thus, in Michael's scenario, considering only the Sequences 1,2,4 and 5, this task will discover that the actions 'Shower on' and 'Shower off', which were not included in the Basic Frequent Set, occur in 3 out of these 4 sequences (75% > 60%). Other actions such as 'Tap on' or 'MirrorLight on' do not reach the demanded minimum level. Adding such extra actions to the Basic Frequent Sets we get the complete Frequent Sets. Thus, the Frequent Set discovered for Michael's scenario would be:

'Alarm on', 'Bathroom on', 'Bathroom off', 'BathLights on', 'BathLights off', 'Shower on' and 'Shower off'

4.3. Identifying interesting sequences for further steps

For the following steps of SPUBS, it is essential to know in what sequences the Frequent Set is present. In Michael's scenario it can be observed that the Sequences 1,2,4 and 5 must be considered as interesting sequences. Although at the first sight considering only those sequences that are counted in the task of 'Identifying Basic Frequent Sets' seems to be enough, some other sequences could also be interesting to consider.

There could be some sequences where most of the actions of a Basic Frequent Set are present, but as there are no all the actions, they are not considered. An example of it could be the third sequence of Michael's example. In it, there exist all the actions of the Basic Frequent Set except the action 'BathLights off'. Everybody would agree that the information contained by such a sequence is useful for the following steps.

Being aware of small deviations could lead us to lose useful information, a strategy to reduce the impact of such deviations has been designed. It is based on manually defined parameter (*similarity level*) which indicates (in percentage) the minimum number of actions to be needed in order to consider a Sequence as interesting. Thus, not only those sequences that have all the actions (similarity level = 100%) of the Basic Frequent Set would be considered as interesting, but all those sequences which similarity level is over the demanded level.

In Michael's scenario we are going to consider a similarity level of 75%. Knowing that the Basic Frequent Set contains 5 actions, all sequences that have 4 or more actions in common with the Basic Frequent Set will be considered as interesting Sequences. Sequences 1,2,4 and 5 have a similarity level of 100%, but in this case, the Sequence 3, which similarity level is 80% (it has all the actions of the Basic Frequent Set except the action 'BathLights off') will also be considered.

5. Following steps of the algorithm

As it has been mentioned above, all steps of the SPUBS are already developed, but due to space restrictions it has been impossible to provide as much details of the other steps as the first step. The aim of each step has been defined in Section 2, so this section briefly shows technical details of them. Thus, once the Frequent Sets are discovered, the next

Table 1. Number of Frequent Sets and Experiments' runtime considering different confidence levels

Confidence level (%)	Trial 1	Trial 2	Trial 3
25	8 Frequent Sets (7.2 seconds)	3 Frequent Sets (19.4 seconds)	1 Frequent Set (1.1 seconds)
50	4 Frequent Sets (0.9 seconds)	1 Frequent Set (1.8 seconds)	1 Frequent Set (0.2 seconds)
75	0 Frequent Sets (0.2 seconds)	1 Frequent Set (0.4 seconds)	1 Frequent Set (0.2 seconds)

step is to identify the most common topology or structure of such Frequent Sets (See Figure 2(a)). For that we have used Workflow mining algorithms [10], considering also unordered subsets of actions.

In order to discover frequent time relations among the actions (See Figure 2(b)), groups of different time distances have been created taking into account the similarity. Thus, if there is any group which includes more instances than the demanded minimum level, the average value of that group is considered as interesting value to define the time relation between those actions.

Finally, the discovering of conditions (See Figure 2(c)) has been carried out by means of classification techniques. Conditions are needed when the topology indicates that there exist more than one option. We consider each option as a class and the sequences of that option as the instances of that class. Thus, first we collect context (e.g. temperature) and temporal information (e.g. day of the week) of each of the instances and then we use that information in order to discover the conditions for each option.

6. Results

The SPUBS has been validated by applying it to artificial data generated by the authors and then to a real dataset collected from MavPad, a smart apartment that was created to test algorithms as part of the MavHome project [11]. The dataset we used was collected in three different periods: Trial1 (spanning 15 days), Trial2 (spanning almost 2 months) and Trial3 (spanning 3 months). In the Transformation Layer, after analysing a little the data, the criteria to split the initial string of actions into sequences was the inactivity of the user during 5 hours. Thus, Trial1 was divided in 26 Sequences, Trial2 in 73 Sequences and Trial3 in 83 Sequences. Then we applied the step 'Identifying Frequent Sets' considering different minimum confidence levels (25%, 50% and 75%) for the task 'Identifying Basic Frequent Sets'. The minimum confidence level for the task 'Identifying extra actions for Frequent Sets' was 75% whereas the similarity level for the task 'Identifying interesting sequences for further steps' was 75%. Table 1 shows the number of Frequent Sets discovered in different trials.

At first sight the runtime of experiments does not seem very logical taking into the spanning of each trial. In that sense, it is worth mentioning the runtime is mainly based on three aspects. The first one is the total number of actions stored in each trial. Although it seems that should coincide with the duration of each trial, actually in our validation experiments Trial2 had four times as many actions as Trial1 and Trial3. The second aspect to consider is the number of different types of actions that occur in each trial, due to it has a great influence in the Apriori algorithm. In our validation, Trial2 had 78 different types of actions whereas Trial1 and Trial2 had 36 and 31 respectively. The last aspect to consider is the number of Frequent Sets discovered by the algorithm in each step and the length of each set, because the more Frequent Sets and longer sets are discovered, more time is needed to check their frequency and generate candidates for the next step. Once these aspects to be considered have been identified and their impact analysed, the runtime for each experiment seems logical.

7. Conclusions

Intelligent Environments need to know the common behaviours and preferences of the user in order to meaningfully act. Representing such common behaviours by means of sequences facilitates their understanding as well as their use for other purposes such as the automation of action or devices. Thus, the discovering of frequent sets of actions that occur together was identified as the first step of the global system (SPUBS). Although well known approaches are useful in order to discover such Frequent Sets, the characteristics of Intelligent Environments demand an extension of such an approach in order to get complete and flexible Frequent Sets. For that, the basic task of discovering associations among actions has been extended adding tasks in order to identify additional actions and sequences.

References

[1] J. Augusto, "Ambient intelligence: The confluence of pervasive computing and artificial intelligence," in *Intelligent Computing Everywhere*, A. Schuster, Ed. Springer, 2007, pp. 213–234.

[2] M. Galushka, D. Patterson, and N. Rooney, "Temporal data mining for smart homes," ser. Designing Smart Homes. The Role of Artificial Intelligence, J. C. Augusto and C. D. Nugent, Eds. Springer-Verlag, 2006, pp. 85–108.

[3] M. C. Mozer, *Lessons from an Adaptive Home*, ser. Smart Environments: Technology, Protocols and Applications. Wiley-Interscience, 2004, pp. 273–298.

[4] H. Hagras, V. Callaghan, M. Colley, G. Clarke, A. Pounds-Cornish, and H. Duman, "Creating an ambient-intelligence environment using embedded agents," *IEEE Intelligent Systems*, vol. 19, no. 6, pp. 12–20, 2004.

[5] H. Duman, H. Hagras, and V. Callaghan, "Intelligent association exploration and exploitation of fuzzy agents in ambient intelligent environments," *Journal of Uncertain Systems*, vol. 2, no. 2, pp. 133–143, 2008.

[6] V. R. Jakkula, A. S. Crandall, and D. J. Cook, "Knowledge discovery in entity based smart environment resident data using temporal relation based data mining," in *7th IEEE International Conference on DataMining*, 2007, pp. 625–630.

[7] E. Heierman, M. Youngblood, and D. J. Cook, "Mining temporal sequences to discover interesting patterns," in *KDD Workshop on Mining Temporal and Sequential Data*, 2004.

[8] A. Aztiria, J. C. Augusto, A. Izaguirre, and D. J. Cook, "Learning accurate temporal relations from user actions in intelligent environments," in *Proceedings of the 3rd Symposium of Ubiquitous Computing and Ambient Intelligence*, vol. 51/2009, 2008, pp. 274–283.

[9] R. Agrawal and R. Srikant, "Mining sequential patterns," in *Pro. 11th International Conference on Data Engineering*, 1995, pp. 3–14.

[10] W. van der Aalst, A. Weitjers, and L. Maruster, "Workflow mining discovering process models from event logs," *IEEE Transactions on Knowledge and Data Engineering*, vol. 18, no. 9, pp. 1128–1142, 2004.

[11] G. M. Youngblood, D. J. Cook, and L. B. Holder, "Managing adaptive versatile environments," in *IEEE International Conference on Pervasive Computing and Communications*, 2005.

Intelligent Environments 2009
V. Callaghan et al. (Eds.)
IOS Press, 2009

doi:10.3233/978-1-60750-034-6-161

Location Aware Distributed Agents in Intelligent Environments

Brian S HOYLE
School of Process, Environmental and Materials Engineering, University of Leeds, UK
b.s.hoyle@leeds.ac.uk

Abstract. Many environments have informal or formal spatial properties and requirements which relate to these. In many real-world applications the delivery of these requirements does not exploit their spatial organization. Sensor and actuation networks offer a generic platform from which a wide range of applications can be realized in many fields. The paper reviews the generic needs of applications, from environmental monitoring and control to security and surveillance, which may be classed as spatially critical, where the location corresponding to a sensor or action point must be known. Such networks can deploy appropriate means to estimate the location of their fixed and mobile nodes. A methodology is presented whereby the intrinsic knowledge of location provides the opportunity for a network to use this data to facilitate major inter-node cooperation. This in turn enables new distributed functionality allowing networks to intrinsically execute distributed tasks. The network can automatically segment into regions based upon node location. Tasks can be routed to appropriate nodes through location-based mechanisms. Nodes within a nominated region can each execute a task at each node, or cooperate to fulfill a distributed task, through knowledge of the proximate set of nodes. Hence the network is able to form an *intelligent* environment in which requirements are met through the node agents and their spatial distribution. This contrasts for example, with a classical wireless sensor network approach in which data is typically routed to a sink for evaluation.

Keywords. Sensor and actuation networks, location aware agents, cooperating nodes. distributed tasks.

Introduction and background

Spatially distributed environments such as transport interchanges, factories, process plants, buildings and offices which feature sensing and control deploy communication systems to route associated data. A wired and/or wireless network candidate solution is likely to compete in practice with a classical centralized system, in which outlying points connect directly to a nominated central nexus in the infrastructure. Data networks are ubiquitous within application systems and for wide area links and in large scale environments. Infrastructure data, however, is often consigned to individual, special circuits. Such systems also commonly include an actuation capability; for example to set a sensing range, or to command distributed control schemes. Such centralized systems typically incur costly infrastructure design, both at their 'first fit' and particularly for any later modifications. Simply replacing a classical centralized system with a network-based solution may offer some advantages, but for many applications there is major scope for a radical advance.

This paper proposes a smart spatially-aware, environment system able to service a wide range of applications with minimal, or significantly reduced, infrastructure design and cost, while offering major increases in functionality and capability, both at first fit and also for subsequent in-service upgrade and modification.

Candidate competing platform technologies for distributed systems include: wired networks, wireless links, and Wireless Sensor Networks (WSNs) which have been developing rapidly. WSNs may be considered simply as extensions of ad hoc communication networks where the transmitted data (or actions) are generated internally. A major survey [1] notes key issues: low-power performance; query and data dissemination protocols. Much research has focused on specific issues that are critical in some applications, but not in others. WSN nodes [2] have featured in a number of applications trials, but research often simulates idealized operation, and ignores practical constraints, such as antenna directionality [3]. Major focus on energy saving [4-5] will be less relevant in applications where nodes are powered. It is also common to assume that nodes can be shut-down when not in use, but this can threaten network integrity [6]. Research on database queries of structured information from the distributed WSN has used declarative queries [7], in particular with optimization to save network energy [8]. Research exploring very large WSN's demonstrates that performance is improved significantly with localized hierarchical data clustering [9].

1. Monitoring and control applications

An application where a WSN is a candidate solution is likely to compete with a classical centralized system, in which wired or wireless infrastructure would reliably relay data: on demand, on schedule, and/or on an alert basis. A WSN solution must offer lower cost and/or increased performance; for example using Components Off The Shelf (COTS) based upon the IEEE 1451 standard [10]. Where nodes are fixed in position issues of power and communication are likely to be minor. Electrical power may be readily available at each fixed node but a wireless infrastructure can still offer major advantages of portability, flexibility, ease of installation and modification.

Where nodes are mobile, power and communication aspects become more critical. Even then in many cases the nodes (although ubiquitous) need not be small; they may be located on a vehicle or carried by a human user. Larger nodes present less criticality in network design than those that must be miniaturized to suit the application. If sensing nodes are mobile the determination of location in the sensing space becomes a critical need. Just as power management and efficiency appear critical issues in a sensor network, inter-node location is a critical issue in network performance. A general ranking of key design properties and ramifications for system requirements is given in Table 1. Classification may indicate that the WSN monitoring applications need not be subject to extreme design constraints of power and size.

Table 1. - Key parameters and criticality

Parameter	Criticality	
	low	**high**
Node size	No practical restriction	Miniature node essential
Node spacing	Large spacing acceptable	Stated (low) inter-node limit
Node power source	Local mains supply	Instantaneous power when activated
Node power storage	Ample storage available	No storage - active when powered
Node mobility	Not mobile - known location	Fully mobile - must auto-locate
Channel bandwidth	Slow traffic needs	Intensive traffic needs, e.g. video feed

2. Spatially critical sensor/actuation networks

A successful monitoring and actuation system must deliver smart interpretation depending upon the application. This may arise from the fusion of multiple sensor node data in both temporal and spatial dimensions. This process may be followed by a higher-level holistic interpretation that relates to the overall role or mission of the system. General application domain queries are: -

- *Is the system within normal limits?*
- *Is there a defect or problem?*
- *What is the distribution of a given spatial variable?*
- *Is there an exceptional feature in the space?*

The following sections explore requisite features of nodes, agents and the corresponding emergent network and system. Two contrasting exemplar cases are used to illustrate the methodology and its potential benefits:-
Case A. Environmental monitoring system: for routine area surveillance of a natural or external environment e.g. to monitor wildlife behavior, atmospheric conditions etc.; or for urgent emergency surveillance of site of natural disaster or other emergency.
Case B. Site, building, or plant monitoring and control system: for intrinsic surveillance and direction of key resources and services, e.g. in a transport interchange, building, or manufacturing plant.

2.1. Node and network facilities

To support a wide set of applications the general features of a node, in which location is a critical property, are illustrated schematically in Figure 1. It is shown here having a wireless network link but can also be wired into the infrastructure.

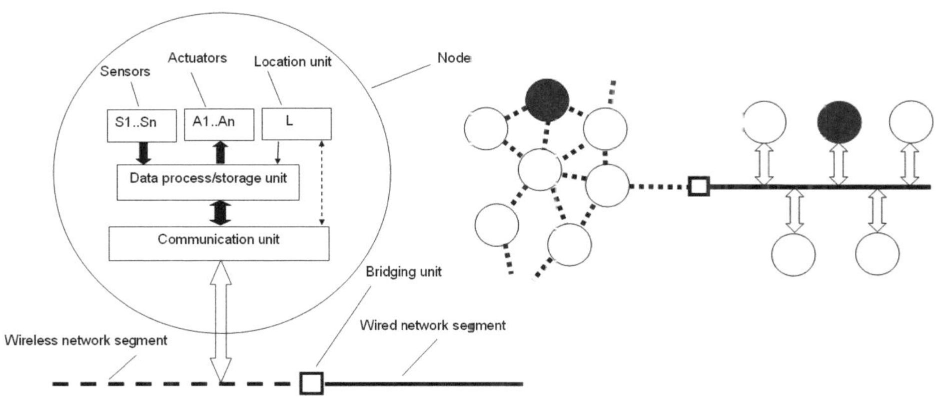

Figure 1 – Location-aware sensor/actuation node, (b) Linked wireless/wired sub-nets in a joint network

A real-world network can include both mobile and static nodes and both may be heterogeneous with assets appropriate to their local segment needs, such as: sensing/actuation for singular status and/or physical/chemical data (in either A or B cases); derived smart data; biometric data; and audio and vision data (in B). Common processing and communication assets will be provided relevant to node and network needs; with location data to an appropriate accuracy, integrity and availability. Nodes having integral GPS receivers in case A environments can estimate their position. Methods that exploit the radio signals [11] are useful in both A and B cases; these typically require a number of fixed, known anchor points for a solution; a review [12] concludes that the real-world non-ideal case has scope for improvement, such as the provision of front-end support and linked middleware to enhance this service. Accuracy of location is determined by the application, as summarized in Table 1. Hence in exemplar B cases, location may simply identify a specific room in a building, or zone in a plant. Sub-nets can be connected via a translating bridge to seamlessly route messages from one location to another, as shown in Figure 1(b). For example, in the B case of a transport interchange, some nodes may be fixed sensors; others may be security personnel communication units (possibly having biomarker validation sensing).

2.2. Agent cooperation for spatial awareness property

To facilitate smart spatial queries, node agents form proximate sets which are then exploited to execute their tasks. Hence a base agent property is that of proximate spatial awareness, based upon its location data, through which it can then participate in an active cooperation with locally adjacent nodes to characterize the nearby space and its key features. The basic mechanism is illustrated in Figure 2.

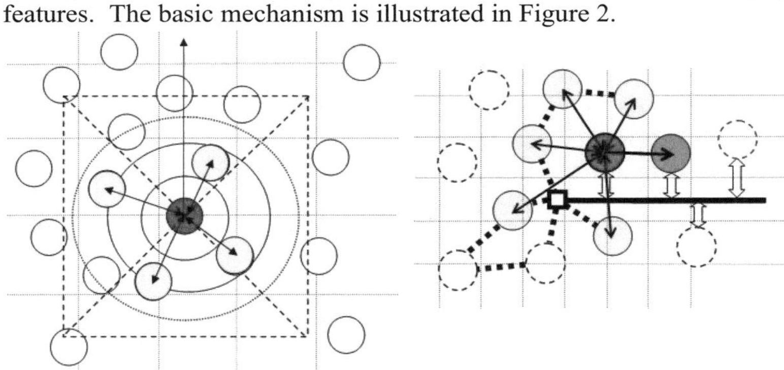

Figure 2 - (a) Spatially proximate 2D group; (b) Implementation in joint wireless/wired 2D networks.

Figure 2(a) shows the 2D proximate set identified through simple protocols based upon localized communications (described below), where messages are not relayed beyond the first hop. The node agent identifies and stores the corresponding proximate node set in 2D/3D, or 4D (incorporating dynamic rules for mobile members) to realize the spatial awareness property. In wireless sub-nets proximate nodes will have lowest power links. Figure 2(b) shows proximate links across wired and wireless sub-nets. Mobile assets could be personnel, or materials in transit in the B case. Fixed assets in the open environments of case A may still be connected wirelessly for convenience, but may be large to collect solar power and house battery storage, as classified in Table 1.

2.3. Application data aggregation and system topology

The exemplified mission queries can be classified into those addressing a singular point, or those that refer to a regional or global feature. To address such queries via generic network capabilities, rather than by specific detailed design, requires specifiable services, underpinned by a set of spatial and non-spatial operations. These are related to the sensing/actuation node features, and the cooperating agent methods for aggregating data, to resolve application queries. By design these can be resolved through combinations of configuration and query operations on the nodal, regional and global data. Aggregation of data and where this occurs is a fundamental issue.

At the simplest level the 'global' set of nodes may be considered for an over-arching alert. Simple or compound nodal data may be aggregated on a global basis; the normal aggregation model for WSNs. Although simple this does present practical hurdles of synchronization, transport delay, and the need to process all centralized data before a global interpretation is available. The aggregation process can be distributed to node agents, such that each data sample is automatically routed to a central node at a given sample time. In this configuration network bandwidth and power needs will be a function of the sampling rate. Interpretation is inherently centralized, and limited by the variety of features observable by the global sampling model.

Methods exist to segment the network into spatially defined regions; hence each region can be tasked with autonomous operations. At the most local level each node agent can be tasked with a specific duty. Regional aggregation offers wide scope for a variety of distributed responsibilities. Regional operations will typically be distributed homogeneously so that reporting is automatically triggered within the node. A nominated region may be tasked to perform a specified regional aggregation algorithm; separate regions may be given different tasks, relevant to the current application interest. Thus a wise area of Case A can offer regional alerting, corresponding to the proximity of services, such as fire fighting in a forest area. The process plant of case B will typically feature regions that require different hazard monitoring and alerting. Middleware tools to facilitate regionalization have been explored, for example, TinyLime [13] specifically supports a de-centralized model. Configuration via a hierarchical decomposition is also likely to increase the viability of large networks.

2.4. *Network messaging protocols*

Distributed tasks must intrinsically support data interchange. A set of messaging modes are defined for this purpose for execution by the node agents. They provide precise mechanisms for data transfer operations to realize the execution of spatial queries. Table 2 provides a summary, with details of persistence and examples of use at the global, regional and local levels.

Table 2 - Summary of system message scope modes and description

Mode	Message description	
	Function	**Example**
Broadcast Global	Global relay	Send an initialization instruction from a command node to all nodes.
Global	Route from any network node to any other network node	Send a task request to a node at or near a specific location.
Regional	Route from one region node to another nominated by location or node identifier	Send status data from one regional node to another non-proximate node
Local	Route from one node to one, or to the set of proximate nodes	Facilitate inter-node cooperation; messages from one node to one or all proximate nodes

Specific protocols offer operational as well as application benefits. For example, to relay specific data from a given location to another node (or to the nearest corresponding node) can use a synthesized vectored routing protocol. Hence in a wireless segment a sequence of Local mode relays can be used such that each node agent computes the next vector from its proximate node set. No further relays are performed and hence the process is highly energy efficient. The process terminates naturally when a node determines that there are no nearer nodes in its proximate set.

In general terms a vectored mechanism (with relays to specified directions and inhibited re-broadcast) reduces flooding. Specific location to location protocols demonstrate major reduction in message traffic. Figure 3 for example, illustrates the principles of agent vectored messaging for parallel searching of a specified space.

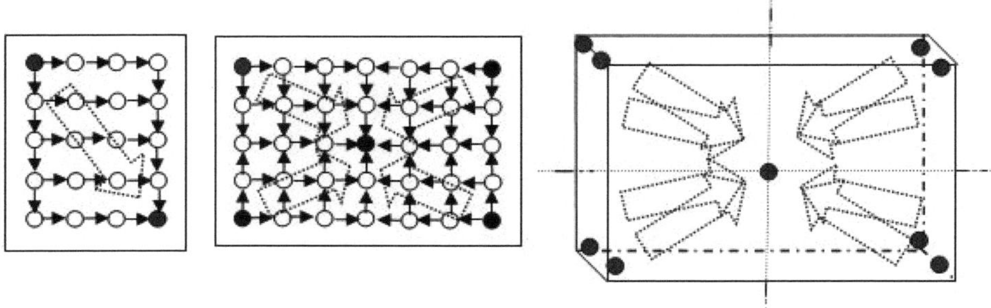

Figure 3 – Multi-dimensional routing for spatial search queries in 2D and 3D spaces

Although outside the scope of this system overview, results of a simulation study demonstrate that the vectored routing significantly reduces node energy costs compared with standard WSN protocols SPIN and LEACH. Other operational aspects out side the current scope are the need for: network initialization, time synchronization, task loading and support for any network control node(s) that are needed.

3. Spatial queries and actions

The features, properties and operations provide the framework to support spatial (and non-spatial) tasks that embody network queries. In essence these may be distributed across the network and executed autonomously in parallel. Each node agent may be loaded with several tasks: which have local (single node), or regional or global interest. Node agents cooperate to fulfill a specific task where necessary. At the higher level this may execute a distributed sensing process. At the lower level cooperation may only be required to transfer a single point sensor to another location as part of a task. Example tasks involving distributed spatial queries are summarized in Table 3.

Table 3 - Summary of example spatially distributed network tasks

Query	Spatial scope and query result		
	Nodal	Regional	Global
Sense Value	Value, V	Set of all values [V]	Join of all regions
Actuate Value	Value, A	Set of all values [A]	Join of all regions
Cardinal	-	Cardinal value, C	Join of all regions
Threshold	P > T	All [P] > T in region	Join of all regions
Isocline	-	Interpolated line [C]	Link of all regions
Inflection	-	Interpolated line [TP]	Link of all inflections
Track feature	Feature, F	Motion track [F]	Join of all tracks

The list of Table 3 offers a high level generic view of possible tasks. Specific applications could of course define more focused tasks. Hence in a Case A application a specific task may be to track a pollution plume and report its current centroid. A case B application may alert the occurrence of a suspicious event defined by the combination of two adjacent sensor agents working in tandem.

An overview of two example generic spatial query types is shown in Figure 4 to illustrate the potential of the method. These are outlined in the following sections.

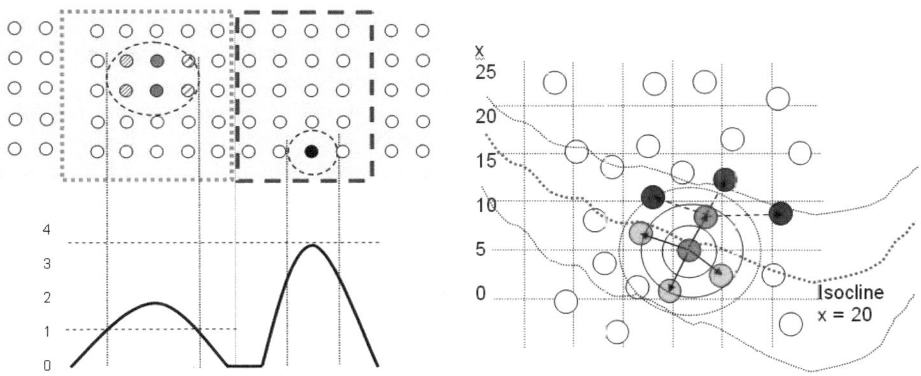

Figure 4 – (a) Threshold and Cardinal (right) value search queries; (b) isocline tracking query

3.1. Cardinal and threshold query examples

A generic application interest in threshold and cardinal value queries in a 2D sample space segmented into two regions is illustrated in Figure 4(a).

Seeking a cardinal maximum (or minimum) using a conventionally organized network would require a data dump from every node to a sink point, followed by a complete search of the resulting dataset.

In contrast, as outlined in Figure 3, a parallel 3D search may be carried out. Newly found nodal maxima are rippled forward, such that a discovered cardinal value (with location) in the search path arrives at the terminal node(s). A terminal node is self-identifying from its boundary proximate node set (for example, the corner node of a region), and can forward a *complete[data]* message to a task specified control node. This can select the actual cardinal value and *confirm* to the corresponding node (which can relay its found status onwards) and *cancel* others. Since locations are known messages can be efficiently sent via the vectored method.

3.2. Isocline tracking query example

Figure 4(b) illustrates the application interest of locating an isocline in a spatial distribution. This could for example be the delimiting edge of a pollution plume in an environmental monitoring system. In this case node agents are tasked to cooperate as illustrated to track the (x = 20) isocline using their proximate query mechanisms.

4. Concluding remarks and application focus

The method described here in conceptual terms offers an intelligent environment capability for infrastructures having distributed aspects and assets. It is able in principle to support applications in many fields of activity where spatial information is important or critical. Its methodology offers powerful spatially oriented queries and operations, coupled with the promise of lower installation and support costs.

The method clearly relies upon knowledge of node location. This can include many fixed assets whose location within the environment is known. Hence a sensor asset could be fitted onto a wired or wireless sub-net and a simple identification process (using a non-volatile memory) could be used to preset the location. Mobile assets can be tracked using the autonomous methods described.

Hence in the more demanding case B applications, systems to monitor critical spaces such as factories or airport terminals can be designed using the method at low cost to offer distributed alerting of critical events; and can be quickly re-configured to incorporate new configurations or revised sensing capabilities. In such spaces sensing and actuation nodes can include units worn by personnel to allow their tracking in the critical space, and to identify their proximity to events that require attention. Such units can incorporate sensors such as keypads and bio-sensors to support an identification query of its user for security validation. Distributed compressed video feeds can be supported. Other moving objects could be the vehicles, such as those used to service aircraft on the ramp areas to allow their tracking for efficiency and security.

References

[1] I F Akyildiz, W Su, Y Sankarasubramaniam and E Cayirci, Wireless sensor networks: a survey, *Computer Networks*, **38** 4 (2002) 393-422.

[2] J Hill, M Norton, R Kling, L Kristnamurphy. The platforms enabling wireless sensor networks. *Communications ACM*, **47** 6 (2004) 41-46.

[3] G Anastasi, E Borgia, M Conti, E Gregori and A Passarella, Understanding real behavior of Mote and 802.11 ad hoc networks: experimental approach, *Pervasive and Mobile Computing*, **1** 2 (2005) 237-256.

[4] A Demers, J Gehrke, R Rajaraman, N Trigoni, and Y Yao. Energy-Efficient Data Management for Sensor Networks: A Work-In-Progress Report. *2nd IEEE Upstate New York Workshop on Sensor Networks*. Syracuse, NY, (2003).

[5] A Trigoni, Y Yao, A Demers, J Gehrke, and R Rajaraman. Wave Scheduling: Energy-Efficient Data Dissemination for Sensor Networks. *Proceedings of the International Workshop on Data Management for Sensor Networks (DMSN 2004),* (2004).

[6] Y C Tseng, C S Hsub and T Y Hsieha, Power-saving protocols for IEEE 802.11-based multi-hop ad hoc networks, *Computer Networks*, **43** 3 (2003) 317-337.

[7] Y Yao and J E Gehrke. Query Processing in Sensor Networks. *Proceedings of the First Biennial Conference on Innovative Data Systems Research (CIDR 2003)*, (2003).

[8] A Trigoni, Y Yao, A Demers, J Gehrke, and R Rajarman. Hybrid push-pull query processing for sensor networks, *Proceedings of the GI Workshop on Sensor Networks (WSN)* (2004).

[9] E J Duarte-Melo and M Liu, Data-gathering wireless sensor networks: organization and capacity, *Computer Networks*, **43** 4 (2003) 519-537.

[10] K Lee and E Y Song, Object oriented framework for IEEE 1451.1 standards applications, *IEEE Trans. in Instrum. and Meas*, **54** 4 (2005) 1527-1533.

[11] S Capkun, M Hamdi and J-P Hubaux, GPS-free positioning in mobile ad-hoc networks, *Cluster Computing*. **5** 9 (2002) 157–167.

[12] K Langendoen and N Reijers, Distributed localization in wireless sensor networks: a quantitative comparison, *Computer Networks*, **43** 4 (2003) 499-518.

[13] 14. C Curino, M Giani, M Giorgetta, A Giusti, A L Murphy and G P Picco, Mobile data collection in sensor networks: the TinyLIME middleware, *Pervasive and Mobile Computing*, **1** 4 (2005) 446-469.

Intelligent Environments 2009
V. Callaghan et al. (Eds.)
IOS Press, 2009

doi:10.3233/978-1-60750-034-6-169

Biopsychosocial Rehabilitation and Mobile Knowledge Management: Contexts of Holistic and Artificial Agencies in Smart Environments

Jaakko HAKULA[a, 1]
[a] *Department of Information Processing Science and Institute of Health Sciences, University of Oulu*
Email:jahakula@mail.student.oulu.fi

Abstract. The challenge of this essay is to outline a transdisciplinary context of human and technological agents acting and making decisions as parts of complex real-world systems. The general focus is on health care and rehabilitational settings, supported by mobile, context-aware information technologies. There is a growing need to empirically test and simulate decision-making in smart environments – both qualitatively and quantitatively, e.g. to analyze both socio-economic and technological properties of these network systems. The Holistic Concept of Man Metaphor as a model of a human decision maker is juxtaposed with agent paradigms. Consequently, many ethical questions arise.

Keywords. Transdisciplinarity, Rehabilitation, Knowledge Management, Smart Environments, Holistic , Artificial, Agent, Holistic Concept of Man, Ethics

Introduction

In a transdisciplinary study various kinds of discourses intersect. No one set of hypotheses, rules or methodologies builds up the whole picture of the context strived for in this essay. The complexities of natural, socio-economic and artificial, i.e. man-made, systems are the main goal of scientific endeavours, backed up with views generated in arts and humanities. The rhythms of our everyday lives are paced by modern science and art — theory and practice. Technological advancement has led to ever deeper and denser segmentation in different organizations of research and practices in information technology, economics and biosciences etc., thus having created needs to cooperate intra- and inter-disciplinarily in order to gain the best possible results available.

This paper focuses on summarizing a general multi- or trans-disciplinary framework for further theoretical and/or empirical studies to be carried out. I

[1] Corresponding Author.

deliberately mix up argumentation in health care and biopsychosocial rehabilitation with that of technologies in context-aware and smart environments, and concepts of man and artificial agencies. Many real-world problems in health care and rehabilitation of aged people with cognitive, mental and physical impairments are to be solved in the near future. Despite huge technological possibilities at hand, scarce resources set the limits — a balance of utilitarian efficiency, moral obligations and virtues is to be negotiated between all those involved.

1. Aspects of bio-psycho-social rehabilitation

1.1. The essence of rehabilitation

Rehabilitation includes multi-professional activities of medical, psychological, socioeconomic and technological repertoires ranging from systems of work practices and process outcomes to general research agendas on micro, mezzo and macro levels. Human beings are seen as holistic actors and decision makers in the biopsychosocial contexts of health, functioning and social cooperation. Functioning describes as a whole the individual's coping with the tasks of everyday life at home, work and leisure. It encompasses physical, psychic and social sub-areas with interrelationships between the individual and the environment [1][2][3].

The prerequisites of health-related functioning and empowerrment are depicted in Figure 1. Functioning is a general concept consisting of the body function and structure, activity and participation, defined by the health condition and environmental and personal factors. The enhancement of individual physical, psychosocial and cognitive functioning supported by socioeconomic and technological resources and other environmental factors is crucial for positive outcomes to be gained. Individuals make decisions of their own but are still controlled or empowered collectively [2][4].

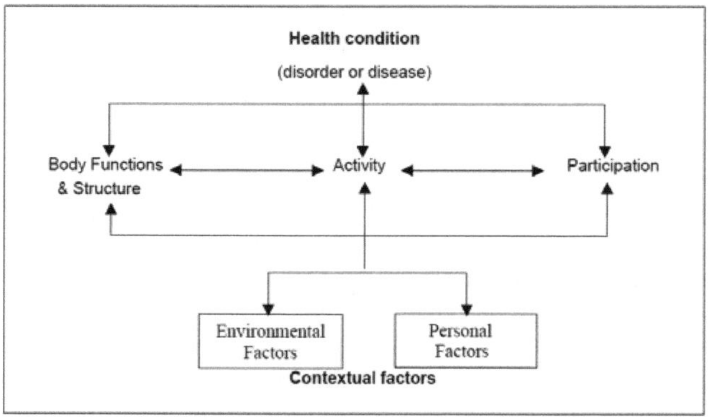

Figure 1. Interrelationships of the sub-areas of the ICF classification [2]

1.2. Cognitive impairment and rehabilitation

Cognitive impairments are common in the older population. Causes are many: Alzheimer's disease and other cerebrovascular and metabolic disorders, stress, depression etc. [2] Dementia means deterioration of intellectual and other cognitive skills affecting the individual's ability to manage activities of daily living. The disorders have usually a gradual onset over several years leading to an escalation of defects in memory and reasoning, with disorientation in speech and social behavior. Depression is a mood disorder characterized by cognitive problems, withdrawal from social interaction and feelings of hopelessness. The onset of depression is a matter of a few weeks or months. Persons with depression often exhibit problems with concentration and memory. In the most serious cases also hallucinations and paranoid thoughts are common. Despite the slowness in speech and behavior and impaired memory depressed persons usually can follow the rules, unlike those having dementia [5].

Dementia and depression can overlap in the same person mixing up symptoms and signs of the two, which is a challenge to diagnostics, treatment and rehabilitation procedures. Especially modern computer-based technologies along with the traditional methodologies may provide new alternatives to support cognitive functioning in activities of daily living in some patient groups [5][6].

2. Knowledge management and smart environments

2.1. Knowledge management in general

Knowledge and knowledge management are complex concepts. Different perspectives vary widely. Links between practical applications and theoretical foundations of knowledge management encompass rationales of information economics and strategic management, process definitions of organisational culture, structure and behaviour, and artificial intelligence — and evaluations of quality management and organizational performance measurement. [7]. In this essay I prefer the idea of understanding knowledge management as organisational behaviour, set forth by Nonaka and Takeuchi [8], deepened with the idea of seeing scientific knowledge generation as an essential part of knowledge management, especially in the contexts of complex natural, socio-economic and technical systems (e.g. health care as a totality) [9].

A basic taxonomy is to categorize data, information and knowledge hiearchically. Tacit knowledge is contextual, not easy to explicate — used in action, often steered by experience, cognitive models and technical skills. Explicit knowledge can be expressed and codified. For example medical knowledge is usually seen as the combination of (explicit) science and (tacit) art — evidence-based medicine and practice guidelines being generated by scientific research, further interpreted and used by surgeons, specialists and experienced practitioners [10]. The conceptions of disease, health and

[2] Cognitive impairments are chosen as one of the focuses of the essay because they symbolize the essential features of the topic — human and artificial agency in the contexts of health and disease and functioning, to be treated, rehabilitated and empowered with the aid of human and technological resources.

illness are numerous. Historically, medical knowledge has been inseparably connected to the technological development [11].

2.2. Mobile knowledge management and m-learning

By combining ideas of mobile computing with those of knowledge management and e-learning we get overlapping categories of mobile knowledge management and m-learning (cf. Figure 2. below). New decision environments emerge. Mobile technologies support context-aware and situational information processing and user-centeredness, which is especially important in health-care solutions [12] [13]. Viewed from perspectives of biopsychosocial rehabilitation, principles of (e-)learning add up practical value to e.g. work practices of dementia care, if both the patients and professionals are empowered [4] .

As situationality is a key concept in individual decision making, context-awareness can be extended to situation awareness (SA). Innovative technologies in wireless and sensor networks, distributed systems, mobile and agent computing, autonomic and context-aware computing have created the paradigm of pervasive computing. A computing environment based on this infrastructure is called Pervasive Computing Environment (PCE), where diverse, often ill-defined and imprecise pieces of contextual information of decision makers' actions and behaviors and environmental factors are processed. "…Situational computing paradigm refers to the application of SA in a PCE .Specifically, such a paradigm is a pervasive computer paradigm in which a situation aware application has the ability to interact (with the user), learn (from the user behaviors and actions), and autonomously to adapt to the user's current situational context ." [14][15].

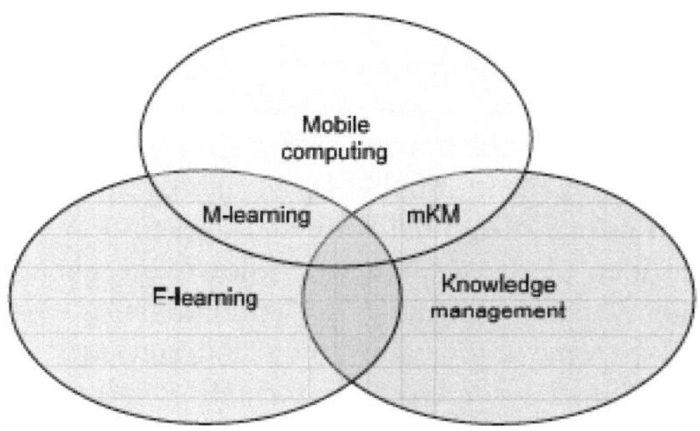

Figure 2. Conceptual interrelationships between mobile computing, knowledge management and e-learning [12]

2.3. Smart environments

Researchers in pervasive and mobile computing, sensor networks, multimedia computing, artificial intelligence, robotics and agent–based software etc. look forward to technological possibilities providing more and more sophisticated smart environments. A smart environment is one that is able to autonomously acquire and apply knowledge about the environment and its inhabitants in order to improve their experience in that environment. The components of a smart environment are depicted in Figure 3. below. Inhabitant modeling and full-scale applications of decision making are future challenges on the way towards more versatile frameworks [16].

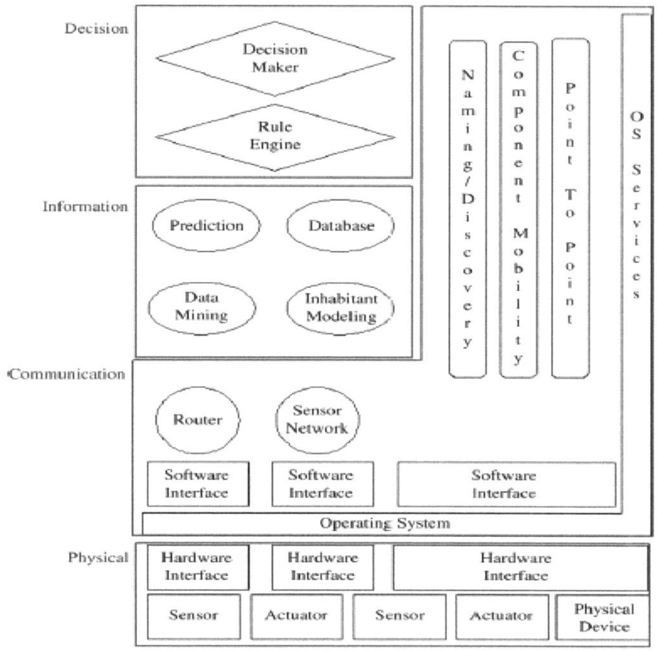

Figure 3. The components of a smart environment [16]

Especially in the health-care industry innovative smart environments are a promising technology in monitoring and assistance. Patients are empowered to manage their mental and physical deficiencies and dysfunctions with the aid of context-aware systems. Cognitive impairments might even be determined using these facilities. Concurrently, many ethical questions arise concerning the balance between the goals of efficiency and humanism. It is worth to remember that smart environments are potential contexts of work practices, too, where professionals cooperate with each other and the inhabitants (or the patients) [16][17].

3. Models of decision makers

3.1. A philosophic model of the decision maker

The Holistic Concept of Man (HCM) is a philosophic model described by Rauhala, a Finnish philosopher and psychologist [18]. The HCM model is simple enough to be utilized for practical purposes — understandable also by non-experts. It has been applied in contexts of accounting research, computerized decision support and medical knowledge management [19] [20].

The basic dimensions of the HCM metaphor consist of a body, a mind and a situation. The three dimensions of the HCM, representing the modes of existence of the decision maker are called: 1) corporeality, or existence as an organism with an organic process, 2) consciousness, or existence as psychic-mental phenomenon, as experiencing (mind) and 3) situationality, or existence in relation to reality, i.e. the world or the environment (the situation) [18] [19]. The decision maker as a holistic entity is shown in Figure 4 (compared with an agent model; cf. chapter 2.3). Meanings emerge in different categories. Knowledge in a narrow sense refers to scientific facts or more general kinds of explicit knowledge. Everyday practical knowledge represents skills and abilities, or tacit knowledge. Heuristics and intuition, feelings and beliefs make the context ambiguous and ill-defined, even logically incorrect [19].

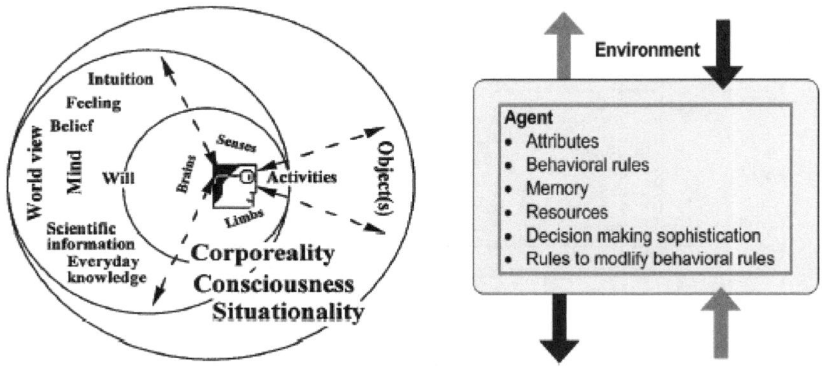

Figure 4. The decision maker as a holistic entity [19] and a (computer/software) agent [21]

The objective to apply the HCM model in this essay is to cover the whole decision making situation between the actor and co-actors and the technological environment, possibly based on agent-based solutions and pervasiveness. In a transdisciplinary sense, comparing the highly individual and non-numerical perspective of the HCM model with views of the rational school of thought and macro level phenomena of socio-technical systems, or using formal methods in individual or collective research settings, could open new perspectives [15][22][23][24].

3.2. Software agents and decision making

Agent-based modelling and simulation is a novel paradigm to contextualize interaction between intelligent agents. An intelligent agent is a computer system designed to have externally and internally autonomous properties — goal-directedness, situatedness, flexibility, capability to make independent reasoning and decisions to a certain degree etc. [21]. Most practical solutions comprise of multi-agent contexts, where the delegation and adoption of goals and tasks emerge as critical factors for reactive, proactive and social flexibility.[21][25].

In multi-agent mobile knowledge management systems with distributed resources and ontologies knowledge sharing, reuse and integration are produced interoperatively — not only in sensor networks but also in multidisciplinary human communication networks, or in hybrid ones, where technology and human beings are intertwined materially and virtually.[21][25][26]. Varying definitions of autonomy, the existence and nature of artificial moral agencies in relation to the human one, and different aspects of capabilities raise many ethical issues to be publicly discussed [25][27][28].

4. Conclusion

Many sketches for future studies emerge. Qualitative evaluations of the decision making and actors' cognitive abilities studied individually and collectively in real-world situations give valuable information for further use in field experimentations. Properties of the tacit-explicit connection and ethics of trust and responsibility between various decision makers, e.g. modelled with the HCM metaphor and artificial agencies in rehabilitative, smart environments, open up interesting questions. Quantitatively and formally, studying the distributed rationality of agent networks in a principal-agent and game-theoretical (network) context might provide new kinds of transdisciplinarity.

The gradable use of the network paradigm admits many formal and informal ways of studying human and artificial agents in rehabilitative, smart environments both from theoretical and practical perspectives. Real-world human beings as actors can be abstracted as AVATARs of the HCM decision maker or as more formally rational players of the game. Holistic situational circuitries in the HCM metaphor can be seen as networks of meanings representing the reality to some extent. The same applies to rational players acting in game networks. Theoretically, social networks lie somewhere in between the two former ones. A gradable mix of ontologies, epistemologies and methodologies is thus available.

References

[1] A. Järvikoski, K. Härkäpää, *Kuntoutuksen ulottuvuudet*, Publisher Name, Publisher Location, 1995.
[2] *Development programme for rehabilitation research,* The Finnish Ministry of Social Affairs and Health, Helsinki, 2004.
[3] World Health Organization. *International Classification of Functioning, Disability and Health.* World Health Organization, Geneva, 2001.
[4] J.L. Monteagudo, O. Moreno, *Report on Priority Topic Cluster Two and recommendations, eHealth ERA – D 2,5 Cluster 2, Patient Empowerment,* [].
[5] M.A. Barrie, Objective screening tools to assess cognitive impairment and depression, *Top Geriatr Rehabil 18(2) (2002), 28-46.*

[6] G. Cipriani, A. Bianchetti, M. Trabucchi, Outcomes of a computer-based cognitive rehabilitation program on Alzheimer's disease patients compared with those on patients affected by mild cognitive impairment, *Archives of Gerontology and Geriathrics 43 (2006),327-335.*

[7] R. Baskerville, A. Dulipovici, The theoretical foundations of knowledge management, *Knowledge Management Research & Practice 4 (2006), 83-105.*

[8] I. Nonaka, H. Takeuchi, *The Knowledge creating company,* Oxford University Press, New York, 1995.

[9] M. van der Walt, Knowledge management and scientific knowledge generation, *Knowledge Management Research & Practice 4 (2006), 319-330.*

[10] F. Hussain, S.A. Raza, A knowledge management framework to operationalize experiential knowledge: mapping tacit medical knowledge with explicit practice guidelines. [http://szabist-isb.edu.pk/NCET2004].

[11] B. Hofmann, *The technological invention of disease – on disease, technology and values.* [http://www2.hig.no/ah/helseteknologi/Bjorn%20Hofmann/Artikler/Thesis.pdf]

[12] B. Zuga, I. Slaidins, A.Kapenieks, A. Strazds, M-learning and mobile knowledge management: similarities and differences, *International Journal of Computing & Information Sciences 4 (2006), 58-61.*

[13] M. Grimm, M-R. Tazari, D. Balfanz, A reference model for mobile knowledge management, *Proceedings of I-KNOW '05.* [http://i-know.tugraz.at/blog/wp-content/uploads/2008/11/7_a-reference-model-for-mobile-knowledge-management.pdf]

[14] C.B Anagnostopoulos, Y. Ntarladimas, S. Hadjiefthymiades, Situational computing: an innovative architecture with imprecise reasoning, *The Journal of Systems and Software 80 (2007), 1993-2014.*

[15] S.K. Das, N. Roy, A. Roy, Context-aware resource management in multi-inhabitant smart homes. a framework based on Nash *H*-learning, *Pervasive and Mobile Computing 2 (2006), 372-404.*

[16] D.J. Cook, S.K. Das, How smart are our environments? An updated look at the state of the art, *Pervasive and Mobile Computing 3 (2007), 53-73.*

[17] N. Bricon-Souf, CB. Newman, Context-awareness in health care: a review, *International Journal of Medical Informatics 76 (2007), 2-12.*

[18] L. Rauhala, *Ihmiskäsitys ihmistyössä, The Conception of Human Being in Helping People.* Gaudeamus, Helsinki, 1986.

[19] H. Vanharanta, P. Pihlanto, A-M. Chang, Decision Support for Strategic Management in a Hyperknowledge Environment and the Holistic Concept of Man. *In: Proceedings of the 30th Annual Hawaii International Conference on Systems Sciences, IEEE Computer Society Press* (1997): 243-258.

[20] J.Hakula, *The Two Decision Makers Interacting in the Clinical Encounter and the E-Health Environment - Applying the HCM Paradigm.* TUCS (Turku Center for Information Sciences) series in 2008.

[21] C.M. Macal, M.J. North, Tutorial on agent-based modeling and simulation part 2: how to model with agents, In: *L.F. Perone et al (eds.) P roceedings of the 2006 Winter Simulation Conference.*

[22] H. Oinas-Kukkonen, Network Analysis and Crowds of People as Sources of New Organizational Knowledge, In*: A. Koohang (ed.) Knowledge Management: Theoretical Foundations*, Informing Science Press, Santa Rosa, California, 2008.

[23] D. McFadden, Rationality for economists? *Journal of Risk and Uncertainty* 19:1-3(1999), 73-105.

[24] A. Cassar, Coordination and cooperation in local, random and small world networks: experimental evidence. *Games and Economic Behavior* 58 (2007), 209-230.

[25] C.Carabelea, O. Boisier, A. Florea, Autonomy in multi-agent systems: a classification attempt, In: *M.Nickles et al (eds.) Autonomy 2003, LNAI 2969, 103-113,* Springer-Verlag , Berlin Heidedelberg, 2004.

[26] C. Chira, Multi-agent distributed computing, Proceedings of the International Conference on Knowledge Engineering, Principles and Techniques, KEPT 2007.

[27] M. Nagenborg, Artificial moral agents: an intercultural perspective, *International Review of Information Ethics* 7 (2007), 1-6.

[28] J. Johnstone, Technology as empowerment: a capability approach to computer ethics, *Ethics and Information Technology* 9 (2007), 73-87.

Intelligent Environments 2009
V. Callaghan et al. (Eds.)
IOS Press, 2009

doi:10.3233/978-1-60750-034-6-177

Environmental User Preference Learning for Smart Homes

Luis Ángel SAN MARTÍN[a], Víctor M. PELÁEZ[a]
Roberto GONZÁLEZ[a], Antonio M. CAMPOS[a]
[a] *Fundación CTIC - R&D Department*

Abstract. The ubiquitous computing concept was introduced by Weiser in 1991. In spite of the advances achieved since then, the use of ubiquitous spaces is not yet widespread in home environments, due to the difficulty in using context information and artificial intelligence algorithms. This work combines ontologies and machine learning techniques to infer environmental user preferences automatically. These preferences will allow the development of context-aware applications for the home environment that will adjust it proactively, depending on user preferences. These kinds of applications will contribute to the development of the ambient-assisted living concept and therefore to the improvement of the quality of life.

Keywords. Ambient intelligence, context awareness, environmental user preferences, machine learning

Introduction

Advances in electronic devices and communication networks are providing the hardware infrastructure necessary to achieve the ubiquitous computing paradigm [1]. This paradigm will result in new services, applications and ubiquitous environments that will use natural user interfaces and be context-aware [2], providing intelligent behaviour aligned to user preferences. In this context, intelligence is understood as adaptability and autonomy [3].

In an intelligent, context aware and user-centred environment, it is necessary to identify and extract data related to user preferences from the global contextual information. These preferences could be used to adapt the environment, not only to context information, but to user tastes. The main use case to be achieved with this work is a proactive environment in which the user does not need to set any configuration parameters for the environment, since the system learns his or her preferences and applies them autonomously. In contrast to the approach presented here, most of the current domotic systems are based on predefined behaviour and scenes that cannot be adapted automatically to user preferences or needs in one particular situation.

In the state of the art, some approaches try to solve this point using static rules [4] and others propose using machine learning for modelling user behaviour [5] or user preferences [6]. Nevertheless, in the first case it is not possible to configure or adapt the system automatically depending on user requirements and the current context. Works based on the second approach are not usually independent of the applications; nor are dynamic with regard to the number and type of information sources used in the learning process. Furthermore, the operation of most of these systems is not completely autonomous, because they require human intervention in order to adjust their behaviour (for example in the learning process) [13].

In order to overcome these drawbacks, this work proposes a system capable of modelling contextual information not only independently of the underlying physical infrastructure, but also taking into account different degrees of abstraction. Using the context management system, the integration of machine learning systems as autonomous mechanisms to infer environmental user preferences is proposed. These preferences could be used later to implement the use case described above.

1. Context modelling and management

According to the layered architecture for the development of context-aware applications presented in [7], the context management system proposed in this work is characterized by the definition of context, the context modelling technique and the software architecture.

The context is defined as a set of entities, such as users, physical locations or automated elements, which have certain attributes and are linked (e.g. a user is located in a room and the room has a surface).

The model of the context information uses an ontology represented in OWL (http://www.w3.org/2004/OWL/) that allows each entity in the system to share a homogeneous interpretation of the information and improve the interoperability. Furthermore, there are a large number of ontologies available for modelling context information in homes [8][4] which allow previous knowledge to be reused rather than starting the development from scratch. On the other hand, as argued in [9] ontologies are a promising approach to overcome the problems of modelling context information. The ontology used in this work is based on the one presented in [4]. It contains concepts to model all the common entities in a home (users, physical spaces, devices and furniture), the properties of each, and the most common relationships between them.

The central element of the system is the context server, a central repository of all the context information received from the different context sources (see Figure 1). Context sources are software abstractions of any element capable of producing relevant information (e.g. sensors). In addition, any element capable of receiving commands (e.g. actuators) is represented not only as a context source, but also as a service.

Each context source produces an OWL fragment which abstracts the context information produced by the physical device or a logic process attached to it. In this way, the applications work with information represented according to the used ontology, and they are not aware about the underlying infrastructure. Because entities are not coupled to a specific hardware or sensing devices, this approach enables the development of context-aware applications which can be used in different environments with different hardware infrastructures.

We define a context processor as an entity that produces new context information (e.g. obtained from an inference or reasoning process), using existing context information. In this way, a preference learning system can be interpreted as a context processor. Context processors enable the generation of higher level information than that produced by the context sources related to hardware devices. For example, a context processor can convert localization information represented in 2D coordinates and obtained from a radio-frequency system into localization information about users and spaces (representing the room where the user is).

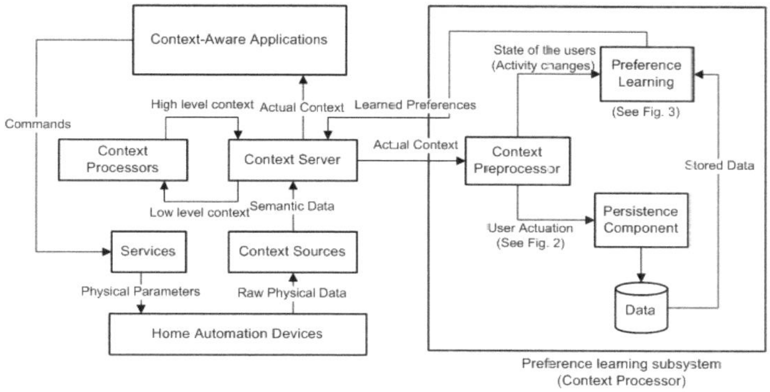

Figure 1. General system architecture.

Context-aware applications can obtain the information available through the SPARQL query language (http://www.w3.org/TR/rdf-sparql-query/) or by subscribing to receive events concerning changes in the context. The information managed by the context server is independent of the underlying physical architecture, and always characterizes the current state of the environment by combining the latest data coming from each context source.

Taking into account that all entities in the architecture are producers or/and consumers of context, the context server will offer a homogenous interface to all of them. This feature will facilitate the dynamism required in intelligent environments, making context sources, processors and context-aware applications dynamic in number and/or type, because they are not directly connected.

2. User modelling approach

In order that a smart environment can provide an adaptive experience that satisfies the needs of users, it is necessary to know some information about these users. This information can be handled as a user profile or user model. A user profile is a set of attributes which describe different aspects of the user, such as demographic information or tastes. On the other hand, a user model is a representation of the user that gathers user behaviour and is often used to take decisions to adapt the environment with the aim of improving the user experience.

Highly sophisticated user models based on techniques such as rules modelling [11], reinforcement learning or supervised machine learning [12][13] are common in smart environments. Those models are used to predict or mimic the actions of the user, and are able to proactively adapt the environment to user needs.

The proposal presented here combines a representation based on a user profile, along with supervised machine learning mechanisms that allow the user profile to be completed with preferences acquired autonomously, that is, without user intervention. The proposed user profile uses two types of information: static information, such as genre or age; and environmental user preferences, that is, any parameter configurable by the user. These preferences are learned automatically and updated to represent preferences about environmental parameters according to the current situation. With this approach only the preferences for the current situation are represented in the context server, and there is not a model with user preferences for all possible situations.

This approach uses the user profile as context information, and it is integrated into the context information model. This allows context-aware applications to use user preferences in the same way as other context information.

3. User preference learning

Using machine learning for user modelling and acquisition of user data is a widely extended technique, although not necessarily free of problems [14], most notably: the need for labelled data; the need for large data sets; concept drift; and computational complexity. The operation of our proposal and how these problems are solved using appropriated data management and the K-nearest neighbours (KNN) algorithm as learning process is described below.

KNN is a supervised, lazy and online learning algorithm. The learning process is triggered by the changes in the user activity, so when the user changes his activity the learning process begins. The set of activities includes the most common activities in home environments (such as cooking, watching TV or sleeping) without considering the transition time between activities. The current user context is labelled using the KNN algorithm (regression or classification depending on the preference) each time a preference is to be learned. Once preferences are inferred, they are published in the context server and the context-aware applications can use them to adjust the environment to the best advantage.

One of the main goals of ubiquitous computing is to be non-intrusive to the user. However, in user preference learning it is necessary to collect context data labelled with preference values. Because the system monitors user actions, saving the current user context (activity, location, sensor values, etc) each time the user sets the value for a parameter (see Figure 2), the user need not explicitly indicate his or her preferences. The parameters configured by the user are not known in advance by the learning preferences system, so the first time that the user configures a parameter, is taken as a new type of preference. In this way, the examples are stored to be used as a training set. To allow preference learning of groups of users, context information about other users in the same place as the user that started the process, is stored together with the interaction data. This process of information labelling enables the supervised machine learning.

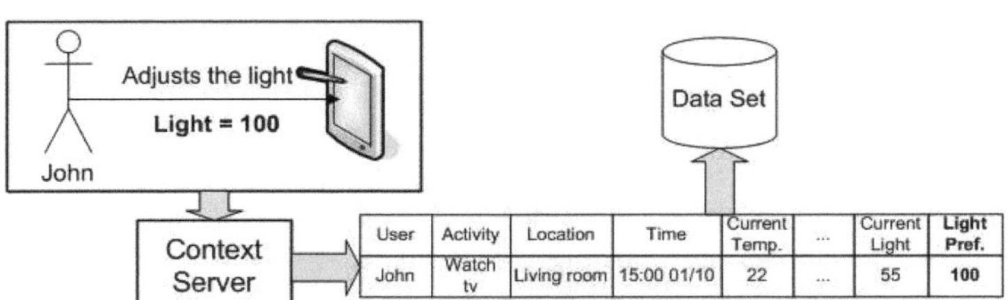

Figure 2. A parameter configured by the user is stored as a preference with the current user context.

Machine learning algorithms usually need large sets of training data to obtain sufficiently precise results. However, some algorithms like KNN are able to offer accurate results if new examples are similar to the training examples. Filtering examples from the dataset according to the current context and using the KNN algorithm is possible to obtain the user preferences for all parameters (see Figure 3). In the example the learning process is launched for *light*.

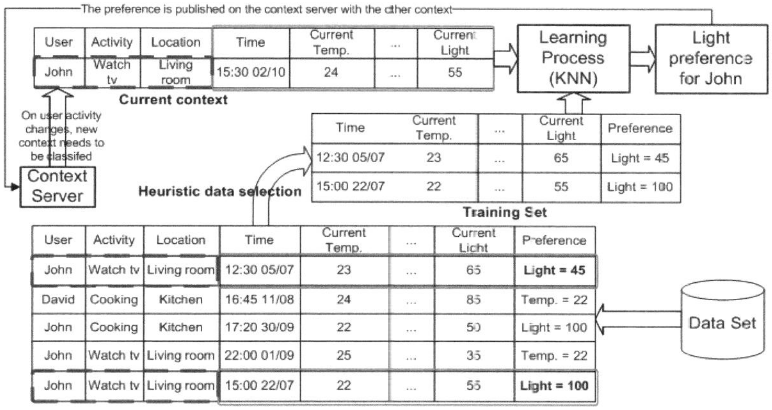

Figure 3. Example of iteration in the machine learning process (one iteration per preference).

Example filtering for the construction of the training set is carried out by observing the current situation after a user activity change, retrieving only those examples with the same user, activity and location as the current context. This is possible in the case of a single user or a group of users. Thus, new situations are classified taking into account only past situations with a high degree of similarity, reducing the number of examples needed to obtain an adequate accuracy.

Concept drift [15] is a well-known problem in machine learning, produced by changes in the target concept over time, so static models become ineffective in the classification of new examples. This is the case of human behaviour: new tastes, preferences evolution, etc. To solve the problem of concept drift it is possible to use a temporal window [16] limiting the examples which are used as training set as in our proposal, that is, implemented in the example filter. The right size of this window can be determined after an experimentation process.

In a smart environment, users expect automatic adaptation to take place immediately according to their needs. To meet this expectation, system response time and more specifically, the learning module preferences response time, must be acceptable enough for each user in each situation. In addition to response time, the accuracy of the learning process is another key factor to be considered.

The proposed machine learning process uses several types of information as a training set: user information; sensor information; and preference information. Both, the sensor information and the preference information, are obtained directly from the elements in the system (sensors and user interfaces respectively), as well as user identification and location. However, knowing the activity performed by the user is not a trivial task. In this research field there are several works that infer users' activity depending on their interaction with the environment, such as triggered sensors [13] or used objects [17].

4. Implementation

Implementation is based on a component architecture based on Java and the OSGi technology (http://www.osgi.org/). Internally, the context server uses the Virtuoso database (http://virtuoso.openlinksw.com/wiki/main/), as a repository of all the context information in RDF format (underlying OWL). The Virtuoso database is an object-relational SQL database which supports SPARQL embedded into SQL for querying RDF data stored. The ontology used to model and store the information is not reasoned, as this would be too expensive computationally [8][10].

Each context source is a component that produces a context fragment (in RDF/XML format according to the ontology in OWL) which is sent to the context server to be combined with the other context information. When a client needs to retrieve information, it will use a service from the context server that can execute a SPARQL query on context data and get a result. For receiving events of context changes, sources need to be registered providing a similar SPARQL and the change conditions. The server will only notify registered clients when the result of the query changes.

The learning system implementation follows the same modular guidelines as the rest of the system. The KNN algorithm implementation is given by Weka (http://www.cs.waikato.ac.nz/~ml/), whereas the collected data is stored on a MySQL database.

5. Evaluation and results

To evaluate the real applicability of our approach, we have measured the system response time simulating two processes with synthetic data: subscription response of the context server and preference learning. The complete response time to infer one user preference is calculated by adding the context server response time and the learning time.

The response time of the context server depends on the number of existing context processors and on the complexity of the subscriptions. The response time of the learning subsystem for each preference is given by the time of retrieving data from data base and the time of the KNN classifier.

In tests carried out, the context server was initialized with 100 context sources (not all should be acquired), and 3 context processors were defined in order to abstract the user location, infer the user activity and infer the user preference. Data used in the learning process was generated automatically using a stochastic algorithm. 36.500 examples were created for one user with one preference (100 parameter adjustments per user per day), and the size of the temporal window was set as big as the entire data set, which is the worst possible window size.

Results have shown that the response time of the context server depends on the number of context sources relevant to the learning system (data to be included in the classification process) as shown in Figure 4a. Experiments have shown a linear response time (see Figure 4b) on the number of examples stored in the database and the number of preferences, regardless of the nature of the stored data. The time consumption is caused by the lazy learning approach, as it must build a different training set for each preference according to the current context. Although an eager approach could solve this performance problem, it was initially discarded due to constraints such as concept drift [18] and the difficulty for using one model to approximate all context states with appropriate accuracy (complexity of the target function [19]).

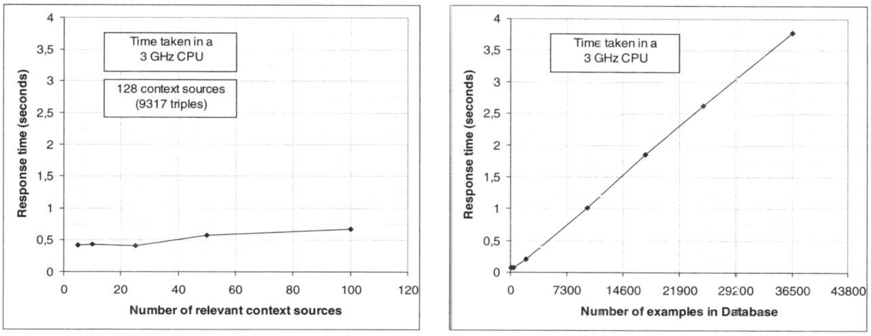

Figure 4. a) Context server response time; b) Learning process response time.

As yet, the response time of this proposal cannot be acceptable enough in some situations (i.e. setting light level), although it has a O(n) time complexity as the empirical models shown. In any case, it is important to take into account that less restrictive applications such as temperature setting, humidity control or multimedia suggestions are perfectly reasonable with these times.

Pending real information concerning the volume of data, the response times of the simulations for high level context generation are similar to the ones based on ontology reasoning presented in [8][10]. Nevertheless, more detailed information about those simulation conditions would be necessary in order to determine the impact of relevant differences between both approaches, if indeed such differences exist.

6. Conclusions and future work

The work presented is intended to serve as the basis for the development of context-aware applications in home environments using automatically learned user preferences. The approach presented here is based on a combination of ontologies and automatic learning algorithms, and shows great potential in the search for applications independent of infrastructure hardware. The approach uses a data-centric architecture combined with abstract models which function autonomously.

The proposed user preference learning allows the dynamic inclusion of new types of contextual information in the learning process. As new user interface devices appear in the system and are used to configure new parameters, these parameters are considered as new preferences. The presented solution using the KNN algorithm can operate with a small dataset of examples and solves the concept drift problem using instance selection and online learning.

The learned preferences can be use in context-aware applications built on top of the provided infrastructure, in order to provide a proactive environmental adaptation to user preferences. By now, the available implementation results show that only some kinds of preferences can be learnt in times immediate enough. In any case, remark that user perceptions will be always dependent on each user and each particular situation.

The performance of the approach and the real applicability of the system have been determined. Future work will include tests to determine the accuracy of the learning approach and the consistency of the new context information aggregated, as well as ways of dealing with the uncertainly regarding their quality.

Acknowledgments

To the companies involved in the CETICA project, especially to ArcelorMittal, Satec and Getlab for their support. The project CETICA is a Spanish R&D initiative funded by CDTI.

References

[1] M. Weiser, The Computer for the 21st Century. *Scientific American* Vol. 265 No. 3 (1991), 94-104.

[2] A.K. Dey, G.D. Abowd, D. Salber, A Conceptual Framework and a Toolkit for Supporting the Rapid Prototyping of Context-Aware Applications *Human Computer Interaction* Vol.16, No2-4(2001),97-166

[3] D.J. Cook and S.K. Das, How smart are our environments? An updated look at the state of the art. *Pervasive and Mobile Computing* Vol. 3 No. 3 (2007), 53-73.

[4] C. Magerkurth, R. Etter, M. Janse, J. Kela, O. Kocsis, F. Ramparany, An intelligent user service architecture for networked home environments, *2nd IET International Conference on Intelligent Environments* (2006).

[5] G.M. Youngblood, Automating inhabitant interactions in home and workplace environments through data-driven generation of hierarchical partially-observable Markov decision processes, University of Texas at Arlington, Arlington, TX, USA, 2005.

[6] H. Hagras, V Callaghan, M Colley, G Clarke, A. Pounds-Cornish, H. Duman, Creating an ambient-intelligence environment using embedded agents, *Intelligent Systems*, IEEE, Vol. 19 (2004), 12-20.

[7] M. Baldauf, S. Dustdar, F. Rosenberg, A survey on context-aware systems. *International Journal of Ad Hoc and Ubiquitous Computing*. Vol. 2, No. 4 (2007), 263-277.

[8] X.H. Wang, D.Q. Zhang, T. Gu, H.K. Pung, Ontology based context modeling and reasoning using OWL. *Pervasive Computing and Communications Workshops, 2004.*

[9] T. Strang, C. Linnhoff-Popien, A context modeling survey. Workshop on Advanced Context Modelling, Reasoning and Management, *The Sixth International Conference on Ubiquitous Computing* (2004).

[10] D. López-de-Ipiña, A. Almeida, U. Aguilera, I. Larizgoitia, X. Laiseca, P.Orduña, A. Barbier, J.I. Vazquez, Dynamic Discovery and Semantic Reasoning for Next Generation Intelligent Environments, *Proceedings of The 4th IET international conference on Intelligent Environments IE08* (2008).

[11] R. L. de Mántaras and L. Saitta, editors. The use of temporal reasoning and management of complex events in smart homes. *IOS Press* (2004).

[12] M. Muehlenbrock, O. Brdiczka, D. Snowdon, J. Meunier, Learning to detect user activity and availability from a variety of sensor data, *In Proceedings of the IEEE International Conference on Pervasive Computing and Communications* (2004).

[13] E. M. Tapia, S. S. Intille, K. Larson, Activity recognition in the home using simple and ubiquitous sensors. *In Proceedings of Pervasive* (2004), 158–175.

[14] G.I. Webb, M.J. Pazzani, D. Billsus, Machine Learning for User Modeling, *User Modeling and User-Adapted Interaction*, vol. 11 (2001), 19-29.

[15] G. Widmer, M. Kubat, Learning in the presence of concept drift and hidden contexts. *Machine Learning* 23 (1996), 69-101.

[16] R. Klinkenberg, I. Renz, Adaptive information filtering: learning in the presence of concept drift. *Workshop on Learning for Text Categorization* (1998).

[17] M. Philipose, K.P. Fishkin, M. Perkowitz, D.J. Patterson, D. Fox, H. Kautz, D. Hähnel, Inferring Activities from Interactions with Objects, *IEEE PERVASIVE COMPUTING* (2004), 50-57.

[18] A. Tsymbal, The problem of concept drift: definitions and related work, Department of Computer Science, Trinity College, 2004.

[19] T.M. Mitchell, *Machine Learning*, McGraw-Hill International Editions, USA, 1997.

Intelligent Environments 2009
V. Callaghan et al. (Eds.)
IOS Press, 2009

doi:10.3233/978-1-60750-034-6-185

Transferring Learned Activities in Smart Environments

Parisa RASHIDI [a,1], Diane J. COOK [a]
[a] *Washington State University, Pullman, WA, USA, 99163*

Abstract. Most commonly-used techniques in smart environments such as ADL recognition are designed and tested for a specific space and a specific person; therefore learning in each environmental situation is treated as a separate context. In this paper, we try to develop a method for recognizing and transferring learned knowledge of activities between different residents. Our method is able to map activities despite intra-subject variability and inter-subject variability, by using a discontinuous mining method and a similarity measurement method. At the end, we will provide the results of our experiments on real data obtained from a smart apartment.

Keywords. Smart Environments, Data Mining, Transfer Learning, Activity Mapping

Introduction

Smart environments provide many benefits such as comfort, security, energy efficiency, and health monitoring of elderly or people with disabilities [13], by using machine learning techniques to process data from various sensors in order to predict upcoming events [6], recognize activities [9], and automate interactions with the environment [5].

Activity recognition can be used to monitor the well being of the residents and also to respond in a context-aware way to their needs. For example, if people with memory deficits are provided with appropriate activity cues, they will be able to complete the Activities of Daily Living (ADL) [13] more easily, and as a result to live independently. There have been a number of methods for recognizing activities, such as Naïve Bayes [2], decision trees [12], Markov models, dynamic Bayes networks, and conditional random fields [7,16]. None of these approaches address the issue of transferring learned knowledge to new contexts to make the systems more scalable. All of the approaches make the assumption that a sufficient amount of data is available, and as supervised models they assume that the activity is predefined in a consistent manner without missing steps. A challenge that researchers face in modeling resident activities in real world is the variability that occurs from one individual to another (inter-subject variability) as well as across multiple executions of an activity by the same individual (intra-subject variability) [22]. We anticipate that different individuals might perform an activity in such vastly different ways that one model cannot perform well for many different users. In this paper, we introduce an unsupervised method to recognize and transfer learned activities across differ-

[1]Corresponding Author: Parisa Rashidi, Washington State University, Pullman, WA, USA, 99163; E-mail: prashidi@eecs.wsu.edu.

ent residents. We have developed a discontinuous misplaced sequential mining method (DMSM) to discover interesting patterns in data in order to capture intra-subject variability. More importantly, we also have developed an activity mapping method (AMM) to map activities from a source space to a target space to address inter-subject variability and to provide a degree of similarity between two sets of activities.

In a preliminary work, Kasteren et. al [21] describe a simple transfer learning method to recognize activities across different physical spaces, by simply transferring the transition probabilities for the two Markov models. It does not address how activities in a target context can be found using knowledge from the source space; and many important features of activities are ignored, such as mapping of the states, duration of the states, or order of the states. Our model is able to find relevant activities using our DMSM mining method by detecting variations of interesting patterns that might even be discontinuous or misplaced. In addition, we consider each state of the activity to have arbitrary attributes, such as duration or frequency which contribute to finding an appropriate mapping. Also, we do not require target activities to have the same structure as the source activities, e.g. equal number of states. Considering such general aspects, we will define a flexible method to map and measure similarity between source and target activities. In addition to reducing the required amount of data, finding a mapping between activities allows us to exploit gained knowledge in the source context, for example if we have discovered that certain types of cue detail and cue timing work best for a specific source activity, that can be used for the mapped target activity too, depending on the similarity degree.

In following sections, we first explain the general model, and then we describe each of the components in more detail. Finally we will present the results of our experiments.

1. Model Description

In our model, we hypothesize that the data collected for one resident in the source space Φ_s can be used to recognize activities for that resident, and more importantly can be transferred to a target space Φ_t to learn activities for a different resident. The obtained mapping and similarity measure will allow us to transfer source activity's related knowledge later, such as cues, details of cues and timings, etc. In current work, as a first step, we consider transferring between different residents, however a similar method can be used for transferring knowledge between different physical spaces, or between spaces with different sets of sensors. In our model, the input consists of activities $\mathcal{A}$ from Φ_s, and a small dataset $\mathcal{D}$ from Φ_t. Using DMSM, we first identify interesting patterns $\mathcal{P}$ as sensor sequences that usually appear together in $\mathcal{D}$. Next, we cluster $\mathcal{P}$ into $|\mathcal{A}|$ clusters where $|\mathcal{A}|$ is the number of activities in $\mathcal{A}$. By comparing each cluster k's representative, c_k, to each activity in $\mathcal{A}$, and finding a similarity measure between them, we are able to generate a mapping from Φ_s to Φ_t (see Figure. 1). Note that an activity can be mapped to another activity with more or less states, and with different state attributes. In addition, during a mapping the order of states need not be preserved.

In the following sections, we will describe each one of the mining, clustering, and similarity measurement components in more detail.

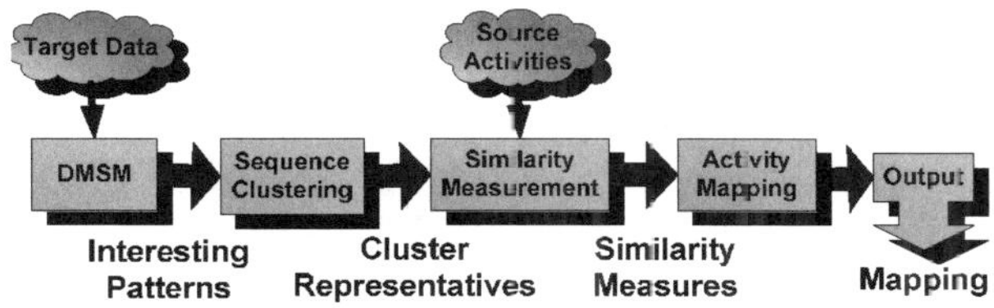

Figure 1. System's architecture and its main components.

2. Finding Interesting Patterns in Data

Many methods have been proposed for mining sequential data, such as frequent itemset mining [1], frequent pattern mining using regular expressions [4], constraint based mining [15], and simultaneous frequent-periodic pattern mining [17]. Those approach do not discover discontinuous misplaced patterns, which can appear in the daily activity data due to the erratic nature of human activities. For example, in meal preparation activity the steps do not always follow the same strict sequence; rather their order is changed and is interleaved with random actions. In smart environments it's important to be able to discover such discontinuous misplaced patterns to deal with intra-subject variability. Ruotsalainen et al. [10] introduce GAIS for detecting interleaved patterns using genetic algorithms, but it is a supervised solution that looks for matches of specified patterns. Other works proposed for mining discontinuous patterns cannot find certain continuous patterns [14,23], and the work by Chen et al. [3] to mine hybrid patterns is not able to find misplaced patterns such as $\langle x, y, z \rangle$ as a variation of for example $\langle y, x, z \rangle$. We propose a model to find a general hybrid pattern from discontinuous misplaced instances, e.g. the general pattern $\langle x, y \rangle$ from instances $\{y, t, c, x\}$, $\{x, y, q\}$, and $\{x, u, y\}$. Our approach is different from frequent itemsets mining, as we are taking into account the order of events, and for each general pattern we report a prevalent pattern and a number of variations that differ in the order of their events. We denote the ith individual variation of a general pattern a as variation a_i, and the most frequent variation as a prevalent variation. We also refer to each single component of a pattern as an event.

First we identify all events in $\mathcal{D}$ with a frequency above the minimum frequency f_{min}, and place them in a reduced dataset $\mathcal{D}_r$. We should keep f_{min} small, as an activity might not appear very frequently in a small dataset. Next we find increasing length patterns by sliding a window across $\mathcal{D}_r$. The window size initially is set to 2, and increased in each iteration. While sliding window across $\mathcal{D}_r$, all patterns that can be permutated into one another, are saved as variations of the same general pattern in a hash-table. For general pattern a, we define its frequency f_a as the sum of its variations' frequencies (the variations with frequency below a certain fraction of f_a are eliminated). We identify interesting general patterns as patterns satisfying Eq. 1, where C is the compression threshold according to minimum description length principle [18], L represents the input data length, and $\Gamma_g(a)$ represents continuity of general pattern a.

$$\frac{|a| * f_a * \Gamma_g(a)}{L} > C \tag{1}$$

To understand what the continuity factor means, consider general pattern $\langle x, y, z \rangle$ in Figure. 2, and instance "xygeqydz" with irrelevant events "geqyd" separating xy from z.

Though we still might consider this instance as a variation of the general pattern $\langle x, y, z \rangle$, at the same time we should take into account the continuity between xy and z.

Figure 2. A small dataset containing prevalent pattern $\langle x, y, z \rangle$.

The general pattern's continuity, Γ_g, is defined as the weighted average continuity of its variations. The continuity of a variation, Γ_v, is then defined as the average continuity of its instances; and the instance continuity Γ_i shows how continuous its component events are. The continuity between component events, Γ_e, is defined for each two consecutive events in an instance. For each frequent event x, we record how far apart (s_x) it is from a preceding frequent event in terms of number of events separating them in $\mathcal{D}$ (in above example, $s_x = 5$). Then $\Gamma_e(x)$, the event continuity for x is defined as $\frac{1}{s_x}$; the more the separation between two frequent event, the less will be the event continuity. If s_x is zero, we define $\Gamma_e(x) = 1$ (perfect continuity). Based on this, $\Gamma_i(a_i^j)$, for an instance j of a variation a_i will be defined as in Eq. 2 where $|a_i^j|$ shows the length of a_i^j. $\Gamma_v(a_i)$ is defined as in Eq. .3, where n_{a_i} shows the total number of instances for variation a_i. Γ_g is defined according to Eq. 4, where the continuity for each a_i is weighted by its frequency f_{a_i} and n_a shows the total number of variations for general pattern a. If continuity happens to be less than a minimum threshold γ_{min}, we discard that instance (or variation or general pattern).

$$\Gamma_i(a_i^j) = \frac{1}{|a_i^j|} \sum_{k=1}^{|a_i^j|} \Gamma_e(k) \tag{2}$$

$$\Gamma_v(a_i) = \frac{1}{n_{a_i}} \sum_{j=1}^{n_{a_i}} \Gamma_i(a_i^j) \tag{3}$$

$$\Gamma_g(a_i) = \frac{\sum_{i=1}^{n_a} \Gamma_v(a_i) * f_{a_i}}{\sum_{i=1}^{n_a} f_{a_i}} \tag{4}$$

After calculating Γ_g, we can decide which general patterns are interesting according to Eq. 1. We find patterns of increasing length by increasing the sliding window's size at each iteration. We will stop increasing the window size until a certain number of user defined iterations has been reached, or if no more interesting patterns are found. A postprocessing step records attributes such as durations of events, and prunes non-maximal patterns, i.e. those patterns that are totally contained in another larger pattern.

3. Activity Mapping Method (AMM)

Next, we will cluster discovered patterns $\mathcal{P}$ into $|\mathcal{A}|$ clusters, the number of activities in Φ_s. Clustering $\mathcal{P}$ into $|\mathcal{A}|$ clusters allows us to find a 1-1 mapping between source and target activities better, as we will compare each cluster's representative c with each activity $a \in \mathcal{A}$, instead of comparing every $p \in \mathcal{P}$ with each $a \in \mathcal{A}$. The clustering method we are using is a standard k-means clustering [11], however we need a method for comparing activities in order to form clusters.

Two methods for comparing similarity of sequences are "edit distance" [8] and "LCS" [20] for simple sequence of symbols. Saneifar et al. [19] have proposed a similarity measure for more complex itemset sequences based on the number of common items. Those methods do not satisfy our complex definition of an activity as a sequence of events with arbitrary state attributes, and do not deal with general aspects of sequences such as temporal information, order of states, etc. Besides, in our model it's possible to map combination of two states to one state, e.g. if two states' total duration in the source context is close to duration of a single state in the target context.

Here the pattern component is a "state" as an event in DMSM, but it is enhanced to include additional information such as the type and duration of the sensor events. To calculate similarity between two activities a and b, we need to determine similarity between their set of states $\mathcal{S}_a$ and $\mathcal{S}_b$, in addition to the order similarity. It's possible to combine several states during mapping, in case one state immediately follows another state with a sensor of the same type that provides the same functionality. To find possible combinations of states, we define $Ext(\mathcal{S})$, the extension of a state set $\mathcal{S}$, by considering possible combinations between consecutive states with sensors of the same type to form a new state. For example, for three consecutive sensors of the same type (x, y, z), it's possible to consider three new extended states, $x' = \{x, y\}$, $y' = \{y, z\}$ and $z' = \{x, y, z\}$. Note that additive attributes such as duration will be added together. We denote the union of actual and extended states for an activity a as $\Pi_a = \{\mathcal{S}_a \cup Ext(\mathcal{S}_a)\}$.

We also need to define order similarity, to see if activities a and b have the same relative order. We define the order similarity, $s_o(i, j)$, between state $i \in \mathcal{S}_a$ and state $j \in \mathcal{S}_b$ as in Eq. 5 where $pos(s)$ shows position of state s in its corresponding activity (for extended states, total number of states will not be equal to $|\mathcal{S}|$, therefore it is replaced by corresponding new size).

$$s_o(i, j) = 1 - |\frac{pos(i)}{|\mathcal{S}_a|} - \frac{pos(j)}{|\mathcal{S}_b|}| \tag{5}$$

To measure similarity between two activities a and b, we need to find the best possible mappings between their states. We start with an initial mapping and then will resolve any possible conflicts, e.g. if two separate actual or extended states are mapped to the same state. For each state $i \in \Pi_a$, we find the best possible mapping state $j \in \Pi_b$. The state similarity, $s_s(i, j)$, between two states i and j is defined as in Eq. 6. Here attribute k found in both states i and j is denoted by k_i and k_j; w_k is a weight applied to attribute k to indicate the importance of k in calculating similarity (e.g. we might consider duration more important than frequency); and m denotes the total number of attributes. In our model, we only map sensors of the same type (e.g. motion sensors to motion sensors).

$$s_s(i, j) = 1 - (\sum_{k=1}^{m} w_k * (\frac{k_i}{max(k_i)} - \frac{k_j}{max(k_j)}) * s_o(i, j)) \tag{6}$$

Then, the best possible mapping for state $i \in \Pi_a$ is defined as in Eq. 7.

$$map(i) = argmax_{j \in \Pi_b}\{s_s(i, j)\} \tag{7}$$

The cumulative similarity, $s_c(a,b)$ between a and b is defined as in Eq. 8, note that the subset of states selected from Π_a and Π_b for mapping will be denoted by Υ_a and Υ_b.

$$s_c(a,b) = \frac{1}{\Upsilon_a} \sum_{i=1}^{|\Upsilon_a|} s_s(i, map(i)) \tag{8}$$

To resolve any conflicts between a subset of states $\mathcal{S}_c \subset \Pi_a$ that map to a single state c, we will find a new mapping for each of the states $s \in \mathcal{S}_c$. The new mappings will be selected from $\Pi_b - \{c \cup \Upsilon_b\}$. The state with the least new similarity will be mapped to c, as such an assignment will cause the least amount of decrease in the cumulative similarity. The rest of the states will be assigned according to new mappings. If still there is any conflict, it will be resolved in an iterative manner. If no mappings can be found for a state, it will be mapped to a null state.

The cluster centroid for each cluster is defined as the activity that has the highest degree of similarity with all the other activities in the same cluster. After clustering is finished, we will compare each $a \in \mathcal{A}$ to each c_k, and by finding $argmax_k\{s_c(c_k, a)\}$, we are able to provide a mapping between activities in Φ_s and Φ_t. This mapping and similarity measure can act as a guideline for transferring activity's related knowledge.

4. Experiments

The testbed is a 3-bedroom smart apartment (Figure. 3), located on Washington State University campus. Sensor data was collected from 59 sensors inclusing motion, temperature, water, burner, phone usage, and the presence of key items; the values for convenience are all binary.

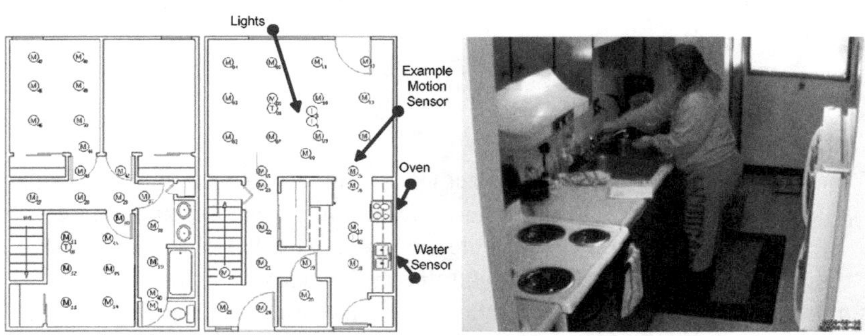

(a) Smart apartment's layout. (b) Participant performing "hand washing".

Figure 3. Smart apartment testbed.

We brought 23 participants into the smart apartment, one at a time. Each participant was asked to perform a script of five I/ADL, typically found in clinical questionnaires assessing everyday functional activities [13]; including (1) telephone usage, (2) hand washing, (3) meal preparation, (4) medication use, and (5) household cleaning. Our data sets consisted of sensor event data for the series of 5 ADLs, each repeated for about 3 times with random events injected between activities up to 50%.

Using a 10-fold cross validation approach, we assessed the ability of our algorithm to accurately recognize activities for new target participants based on models learned from a source participant. DMSM was able to find correct patterns for each participant, despite discontinuous misplaced steps with intra-subject variability of up to 20%. In these experiments, we set $C = 0.3$, $f_{min} = 2$, and $\gamma_{min} = 0.5$.

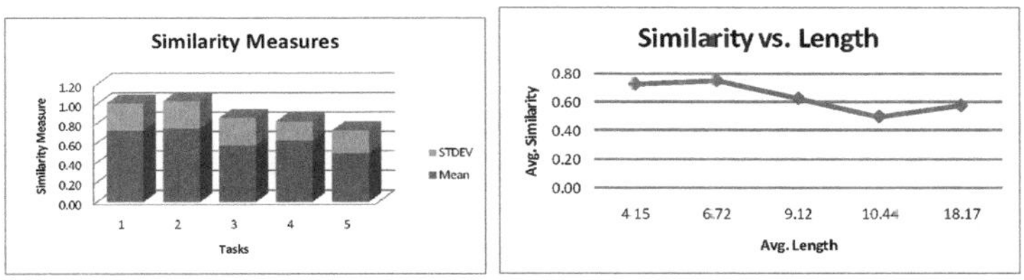

(a) Similarity measures for all 5 tasks. (b) Similarity vs. Length

Figure 4. Similarity measure results.

Our model was also able to map and measure similarity between activities correctly, despite the fact that the activities were performed in vastly different ways, with different sensor reading's order, different durations and different activities' length (see Figure. 4). It was interesting to note that longer patterns usually had a lower similarity measure.

Next we randomly changed the order of events in above datasets to simulate the effect of misplaced steps, one dataset containing shorter patterns of 1 to 14 events, and the other containing longer patterns of 14 to 47 events. Though for longer patterns the misplacement can generate much diverse patterns and therefore making it more difficult to detect patterns, still our algorithm was able to find patterns (see Fig. 5).

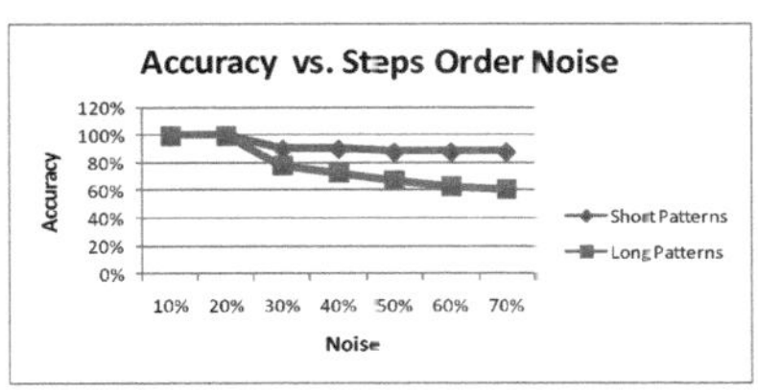

Figure 5. Accuracy vs. injected order noise for short and long patterns.

The above results confirm our hypothesis that our method is able to find patterns in data despite intra-subject variability, and to map activities despite inter-subject variability. The small datasets used for those experiments (each dataset containing an activity repeated three times with 50% random activities in between) also show how our method can use knowledge from source space to effectively recognize activities in target space.

5. Conclusions

In this paper, we introduced a model for transferring and measuring similarities between activities performed by different residents. Our DMSM method captures intra-subject variability, and AMM method provides mappings despite inter-subject variability. In the future, we intend to transfer activities for different spaces and different sensor types. We also want to relate similarity measurement with activity cues, to see how similarity can be used as a guideline for transferring various aspects of cues, such as timing, detail, etc.

References

[1] R. Agrawal and R. Srikant. Mining sequential patterns. In *international conference on data engineering*, pages 3–14, 1995.

[2] O. Brdiczka, J. Maisonnasse, and P. Reignier. Automatic detection of interaction groups. In *Proceedings of the 7th international conference on Multimodal interfaces*, pages 32–36, 2005.

[3] Y. L. Chen, S. S. Chen, and P. Y. Hsu. Mining hybrid sequential patterns and sequential rules. *Inf. Syst.*, 27(5):345–362, 2002.

[4] M. N. Garofalakis, R. Rastogi, and K. Shim. Spirit: Sequential pattern mining with regular expression constraints. In *International Conference on Very Large Data Bases*, pages 223–234, 1999.

[5] L.B. Holder G.M. Youngblood, D.J. Cook and E. Heierman. Automation intelligence for the smart environment. In *Proceedings of the International Joint Conference on Artificial Intelligence*, 2005.

[6] K. Gopalratnam and D. J. Cook. Online sequential prediction via incremental parsing: The active lezi algorithm. *Intelligent Systems, IEEE*, 22(1):52–58, Jan.-Feb. 2007.

[7] H. Kautz, D. Fox, Oren Etzioni, Gaetano Borriello, and Larry Arnstein. An overview of the assisted cognition project. In *In AAAI Workshop on Automation as Caregiver*, 2002.

[8] V. I. Levenshtein. Binary codes capable of correcting deletions, insertions, and reversals. Technical Report 8, 1966.

[9] L. Liao, D. Fox, and H. Kautz. Location-based activity recognition using relational markov networks. *In Advances in Neural Information Processing Systems (NIPS)*, 2005.

[10] A. Visa M. Ruotsalainen, T. Ala-Kleemola. Gais: A method for detecting discontinuous sequential patterns from imperfect data. In *ICDM*, pages 530–534, 2007.

[11] J. B. MacQueen. Some methods for classification and analysis of multivariate observations. In *Berkeley Symposium on Mathematical Statistics and Probability*, volume 1, pages 281–297, 1967.

[12] U. Maurer et al. Activity recognition and monitoring using multiple sensors on different body positions. *Workshop on Wearable and Implantable Body Sensor Networks*, page 116, April 2006.

[13] M.B. Patterson and J.L. Mack. The cleveland scale for activities of daily living (csadl): Its reliability and validity. *Journal of Clinical Gerontology*, 7:15–28, 2001.

[14] J. Pei et al. Prefixspan: Mining sequential patterns efficiently by prefix-projected pattern growth. In *In Proc. Int. Conf. Data Engineering*, pages 215–224, 2001.

[15] J. Pei, J. Han, and W. Wang. Constraint-based sequential pattern mining: the pattern-growth methods. *J. Intell. Inf. Syst.*, 28(2):133–160, 2007.

[16] M. Philipose, K.P. Fishkin, M. Perkowitz, D.J. Patterson, D. Fox, H. Kautz, and D. Hahnel. Inferring activities from interactions with objects. *Pervasive Computing, IEEE*, 3(4):50–57, Oct.-Dec. 2004.

[17] P. Rashidi and D. J. Cook. An adaptive sensor mining model for pervasive computing applications. In *KDD Workshop on Knowledge Discovery from Sensor Data*, pages 41–50, 2008.

[18] J. Rissanen. Modeling by shortest data description. *Automatica*, 14:465–471, 1978.

[19] H. Saneifar, S. Bringay, A. Laurent, and M. Teisseire. S2mp: Similarity measure for sequential patterns. In *AusDM*, volume 87, pages 95–104, 2008.

[20] K. Sequeira and M. Zaki. Admit: anomaly-based data mining for intrusions. In *Proceedings of the international conference on Knowledge discovery and data mining*, pages 386–395, 2002.

[21] G. Englebienne T.L.M. van Kasteren and B.J.A. Krose. Recognizing activities in multiple contexts using transfer learning. In *AAAI AI in Eldercare Symposium*, 2008.

[22] Robert E. Wray and John E. Laird. Variability in human behavior modeling for military simulations. In *In Proceedings of Behavior Representation in Modeling and Simulation Conference*, 2003.

[23] M. J. Zaki, N. Lesh, and M. Ogihara. Planmine: Sequence mining for plan failures. In *In Intl. Conf. Knowledge Discovery and Data Mining*, pages 369–373, 1998.

Intelligent Environments 2009
V. Callaghan et al. (Eds.)
IOS Press, 2009

doi:10.3233/978-1-60750-034-6-193

An Approach to Achieve Context-aware Maps: Combining Semantic Web Technology with Sensor Data

Xiang SU*, Jukka RIEKKI* and Sasu TARKOMA†
*Intelligent Systems Group and Infotech Oulu, University of Oulu, Finland**
Helsinki Institute of Information Technology, Finland†
{Xiang.Su, Jukka.Riekki}@ee.oulu.fi, Sasu.Tarkoma@hiit.fi

Abstract. In this paper, we present our work towards achieving context-awareness in mobile devices by combining Semantic Web technology with sensory data. Our investigation shows that some context data pertaining to the user, such as location, time, and physical surroundings, is vital for the realization of intelligent maps. Hence, embedding context-awareness into intelligent maps may prompt the usability of mobile map applications. Aiming at this goal, we suggest Semantic Web technology-based solution. We present a data representation, Entity Notation, to connect sensors to Resource Description Framework (RDF), the basis of Semantic Web data, in the data interchange level. At the same time, our data representation is lightweight enough that any resource-constrained sensors can support and process it. Ontology and ontology-based inference engine are developed to reason on the sensory data. Finally, intelligent maps could utilize its inference output to achieve context-awareness. We demonstrate our methods with a simulator and discuss the future work.

Keywords. Location Sensor, Entity Notation, Context-aware Maps, Semantic Web Technology, Inference

Introduction

Context-awareness is useful for many applications in mobile and pervasive computing. Mobile map applications can be extended with context-awareness in order to make them provide more relevant information in a palatable format. Users may need various types of maps according to the real situation, or different purpose they have. It's ideal for the user to just have a right type of map on hand with suitable scale and symbology adapted for the specific usage situation. A context-awareness system, together with sensors embedded in mobile devices, would offer the opportunity to let the users have the ideal map they need. Some previous work, e.g. by Nivala et al [1] [2] examined the contexts relevant for the use of maps in mobile devices by the field test. Obviously, user's current location is the most important element for the context-awareness. Other elements worthy of attention include the feature of the mobile systems, the purpose of use, time, physical surroundings, navigation history, orientation of the map, users, culture and social factors.

Sensing technology has gained significant research attention in these years. Sensors can be deployed for capturing real-time measurements of the environment, from simple phenomena to complex situations. We consider what kind of valuable sensory data could be offered to context-aware map applications. By examining all the context elements mentioned above, location, time, physical surroundings and users are highlighted elements. Location sensors, like GPS receivers, could locate the user's position, which makes multiple context-aware functionalities for intelligent mobile maps possible. A real-time clock in the sensor could offer the time context: the time of day and the time of year. This is especially important information from the user's point of view. Maps of some areas, like national parks in Finland, could be totally different during summer and winter seasons, because users can ski on lakes and swamps during the winter time. Physical surroundings may include illumination, background noise, temperature and weather [3]. Ambient light sensors, noise sensors, thermometers, humidity sensors, and atmosphere pressure sensors could provide clues about these environmental factors. The user's characteristics, including user's physical abilities, cognitive and perceptual abilities, and personality differences, were thought to be the most difficult elements to be interpreted. We believe wearable sensors could detect some activities of user's and get some information about this.

On the other hand, Semantic Web technology presents a potential to implement multiple intelligent functionality for context-awareness. For example, Semantic Web reasoners could formally reason about the real-world situations. In practical applications, reasoner could reason on the data from the sensors, and adapts the system to the changing environment. Semantic Web technology can also be used to detect the emergency of relevant context from changing environment. Besides, it can be used at the server side to provide context-aware information to mobile devices [4]. The challenge here is that Semantic Web technology needs rich representations, which conflicts with the simple raw data format from sensors.

In this paper, we present our solution to achieve context-awareness by combining sensors with Semantic Web technology. We propose to utilize a lightweight data representation, Entity Notation (EN) [5], to transfer data from sensors to RDF statements, the basis of Semantic Web technology. Hence, ontology and ontology-based reasoner could straightforwardly deduce new knowledge based on the sensory data and other context elements predefined by the users or from the mobile system. Intelligent map applications could use the deduced knowledge to present a map suitable for the users.

Our contributions are threefold. Firstly, EN would make the simple raw data from the sensors having semantics, as the raw data can be transferred to Semantic Web representation in a straightforward and unambiguous fashion. This will tackle the gap between resource-limited sensors and Semantic Web at data interchange level. Secondly, sensors and Semantic Web reasoner would compose a simplest context-awareness system for mobile devices. Sensors detect the environment and inform the reasoner of the sensory data. Reasoner deduces the sensory data, and adapts the system to the changing environment. In this way, awareness system can "understand" the sensor data and provides maps suitable for the users' situation and environment. Finally, our solution is general and extensible. New sensors can be easily integrated into our system, if only they can handle our lightweight representation. What we only need is to add new rules in inference engine to interpret and reason on the new sensory data. We do not need any new code at all.

The rest of the article is organized as follows. Section 1 presents the communication architecture. Section 2 introduces data format of Entity Notation in brief. Ontology and ontology-based inference for context-aware map will be presented in section 3. Section 4 utilizes an EN location sensor simulator to demonstrate the intelligent map. Section 5 presents the related work; and section 6 discusses the future work and concludes the paper.

1. Communication Architecture

Figure 1 presents a general architecture from sensors to context-aware map, which includes sensors, an EN composer, an ontology, an inference engine, a context-aware map client, and an intelligent map as the main components. Sensors monitor the environment, and compose the lightweight EN packets to transfer the sensory data to the server side over HTTP protocol. The EN decomposer component decomposes the EN packets and transfers them to RDF statements. RDF statements, including the sensing information, will be added to an ontology and trigger the inference engine, which will deduce new statements. New statements could include the facts about the environment, suggestions for the mobile user or anything else. The context-aware map client parses these new RDF statements, and provides the intelligent map user interface to user's mobile client.

Currently, we focus on sensory data from location sensors, as it is the vital data to make the whole system work. More sensor data, including measurements from ambient light sensor, temperature sensor, humidity sensor, could be integrated into the context-aware system easily. When a new kind of sensors needs to be added into the system, they need a small composer to serialize data in EN packets. At the server side, we only add information about new sensors into ontology model and new rules into inference engine to interpret and reason on the new sensory data. We do not need any extra code at all. Then, the system is easy to maintain and extensible for many different kinds of sensors.

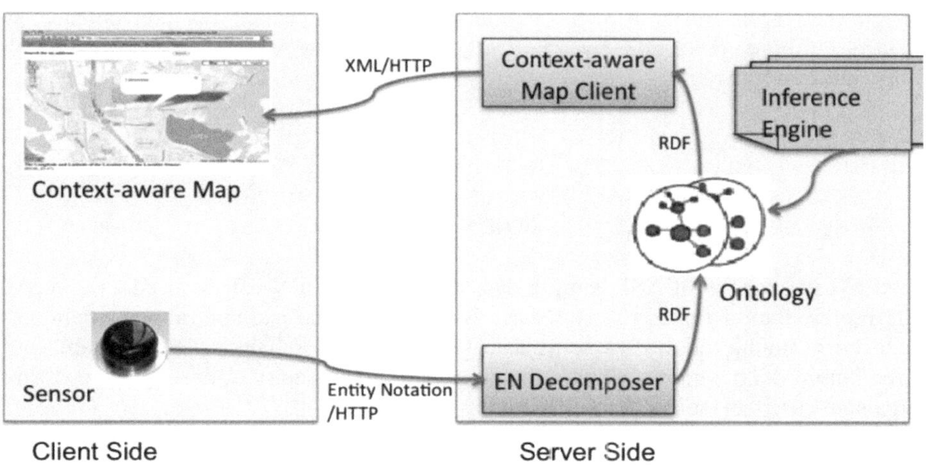

Figure 1. Data flow from Sensors to Context-aware Map.

2. Entity Notation in Brief

We present the Entity Notation briefly in this section, and more detailed description can be found in [5]. EN was designed as a lightweight representation for exchanging information between nodes of a distributed system, and still can support advanced Semantic Web technology. But now we are focusing on its utilization in context-aware applications in this paper. It can be used by resource-constrained sensors, and its packets can be transformed into RDF in an unambiguous fashion. To achieve these, EN offers complete packets and short packets. EN short packets in their simplest form can be less than 40 bytes long, while complete packets that can be transferred to RDF in a straightforward way. Complete packets and short packets can be transferred between each other easily. An EN packet is a kind of data serialization of the EN format. EN packets are assumed to be the payload of some underlayer protocols, like HTTP, TCP/IP, or some sensor network protocols.

The Entity Notation, as its name implies, describes entities. Any identifiable whole, like a sensor, a web page, a person, a map is an entity. The complete EN packet format closely follows the RDF format, which contains a sequence of (subject, predicate, object) triplets. It's a sequence of entity description with the form:

```
[EntityType EntityID
   PropertyName PropertyType PropertyValue
   ...
   PropertyName PropertyType PropertyValue
]
```

An entity description contains a set of triplets about a single entity, the EntityID specifies the subject, the PropertyName is a predicate, and the PropertyValue is an object. EntityType and PropertType specify the types of the corresponding subject and object. Here is an example of a location sensor's data packet. For convenience, we replace "http://ee.oulu.fi/o" by "EE" and "http://www.w3.org" by "W3" in the following examples.

```
[EE#LocaSensor EE#locaSensor767
 EE#ownerID W3/2001/XMLSchema#String "XiangSu"
 EE#longitude W3/2001/XMLSchema#float "25.47"
 EE#latitude W3/2001/XMLSchema#float "65.06"]
```

EN can support all XSD simple data types. Hence, EN can be used as a general data representation for any sensor data. As shown in the example above, literals are enclosed in double quotes, as some data types, like base64Binary, can contain white space but no double quotes. Binary data encoded in hexBinary or base64Binary format can also be used as the content of EN.

A complete packet can be transferred to a RDF description in a straightforward fashion because of their natural relationship. The entity type can be represented as a resource class (using the rdf:type property), while the entity identifier is the identifier of the resource. Property names and values can be mapped directly, and the property type can be represented by adding a rdf:type attribute to the property element. We use the shorthand for the resource classes, that is, we replace the rdf:Description with the resource type and omit the rdf:type property. We also use identifiers, i.e. the rdf:ID is used to instead the rdf:about. Here is the RDF graph of the example above:

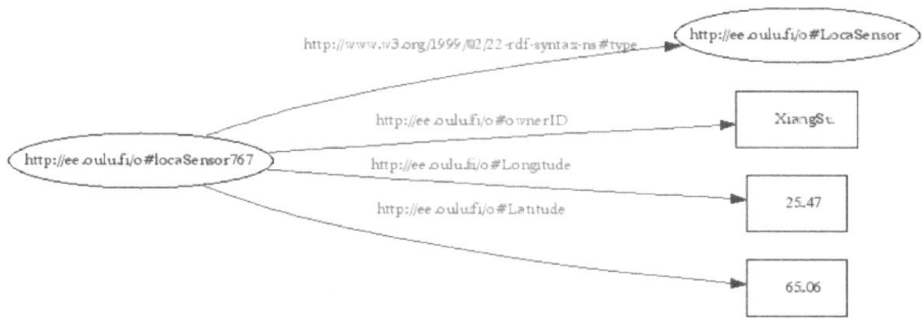

Figure 2. RDF Graph representing location sensor owner and sensing longitude, latitude

We utilize a technique based on templates and prefixes in order to reduce packet data sizes. The basic idea is that a template contains a description of the constant part of a packet and placeholders for the variable parts, which differ in each packet. The short packet needs to contain only the template identifier and the changing information. A complete packet can then be assembled by replacing the template's placeholders with the values contained in the short packet. Prefixes are used where the values are URIs. Universally Unique Identifier (UUID) can be used as an identifier that is guaranteed to be unique across space and time. UUIDs can be created independently in a distributed fashion, and still be unique at a very high probability at the same time. For the above example, we can have the template for the packet:

```
[EE#LocaSensor EE#locaSensor767
   EE#ownerID W3/2001/XMLSchema#String ?1
   EE#longitude W3/2001/XMLSchema#float ?2
   EE#latitude W3/2001/XMLSchema#float ?3]
```

And the template has an identifier urn:uuid:7bcf39. One short packet, as small as 49 bytes, is presented below.

```
[urn:uuid:7bcf39 "XiangSu" "25.47" "65.06"]
```

3. Ontology and Ontology-based Inference

An ontology-based approach lets us describe the environmental information in a formal, explicit way. We developed a context-aware map ontology to describe the common understanding of the context related to intelligent map applications. Important concepts in the map application scenario, including sensors, users, time, and physical surroundings are described in this ontology. It will benefit the inference and other formal analysis of intelligent map context information. Web Ontology Language (OWL) [6] is utilized as the description syntax, which is standard W3C ontology language that facilitates context sharing and context reasoning.

Figure 3 illustrates the relationship between context sensing and ontology from the viewpoint of knowledge representation. Ontology is composed of T-Box and A-Box, which include assertions on concepts and assertions on individuals respectively [7]. EN packets include the information from context sensing from the environment, and they can map to RDF statements in A-Box directly. Statements in the A-Box can then be mapped to the formal definition of concepts in the T-Box. Therefore, the description logic inference over real world sensing context is possible.

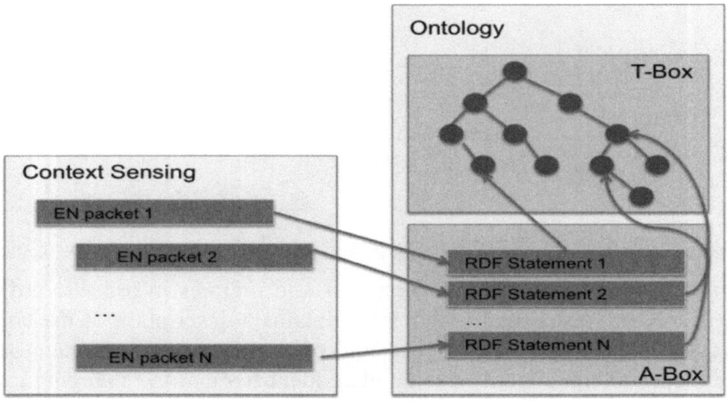

Figure 3. From Context Sensing to Ontology

In our application, the inference will be triggered when the RDF statements with the sensing information are added into the context-aware map ontology. New RDF statements can be produced by reasoner, and then be delivered to the map client. Currently, our inference mechanism supports an OWL Lite reasoner and a rule-based reasoner. The rule-based reasoner could provide rule-based inference over RDF. In table 1, we list a set of rule examples implemented in Jena [8]. The first rule is the most essential functionality for the EN packets from a location sensor, it can judge whether one person is inside an area, like Linnanmaa campus, according sensory latitude and longitude value from user's location sensor. The following rules pertain to the points of interests that can be marked by the users in advance, which is a very useful clue for social web applications. According to previous experience, we marked the position (65.053, 25.468) and nearby area is an excellent place for collecting blueberries in August and September. Then, when we pass by this area, namely the distance between the current location and the marked location is small than 0.008 in longitude or latitude, at good blueberry collecting time, the intelligent map could highlight this place and suggest to collect some blueberries from there. The last rule is based on the fact that in northern Finland, lakes are frozen during winter season, especially December, January, and February. The lake kuivasjärvi would become the tracks of skiing and walking. Then, in case the user want to visit a friend live at the other side of the lake, the map could indicate that he or she can walk through the lake, rather than choose longer path. This rule can deduce the fact that one person can ski or walk at winter season on this lake. Map navigation software could use this knowledge, when choosing paths for the users. We roughly define the lake at December, January, and February is safe for walking, but ice thickness could be considered as a more accurate factor in the future.

Table 1. Rules examples for context-aware map.

```
(EE#locaSensor767 EE#ownerID ?person), (EE#locaSensor767 EE#latitude
?la), (EE#locaSensor767 http://ee.oulu.fi/o#longitude ?lo),
greaterThan(?la,65.055), lessThan(?la,65.063), greaterThan(?lo,25.46),
lessThan(?lo,25.475) -> (EE#Linnanmaa EE#hasPersoninside ?person)
```

```
(EE#locaSensor767 EE#ownerID ?person),(EE#locaSensor767 EE#latitude ?la),
(EE#locaSensor767 EE#longitude ?lo), difference(?la,65.053, ?ladistance),
difference(?lo, 25.468, ?lodistance),
lessThan(?ladistance,0.008),lessThan(?lodistance,0.008),
now(?currentTime) greaterThan(?currentTime,"2009-08-
01T00:00:01"^^xsd:dateTime),lessThan(?currentTime, "2009-09-
30T23:59:59"^^xsd:dateTime) -> (?person EE#gotoCollectBerries
EE#POIBlueBerries_Syynimaa)
```

```
(EE#locaSensor767 EE#ownerID ?person), now(?currentTime)
greaterThan(?currentTime,"2008-12-
01T00:00:01"^^xsd:dateTime),lessThan(?currentTime, "2009-02-
28T23:59:59"^^xsd:dateTime) - >(?person EE#ski EE#kuivasjärvi)
```

4. SIMULATOR AND CONTEXT-AWARE MAP

A sensor simulator was developed to simulate the composition and decomposition of EN packets from different sensors and a server. We focus on the location sensor panel only among different sensors. Users can specify the packets content from this location sensor panel, assemble short packets into complete packets and transform packets into RDF statements. The dialog box in figure 4 shows the situation in which the location sensor has sent a short packet. This short packet has been explained as an example in section 2.

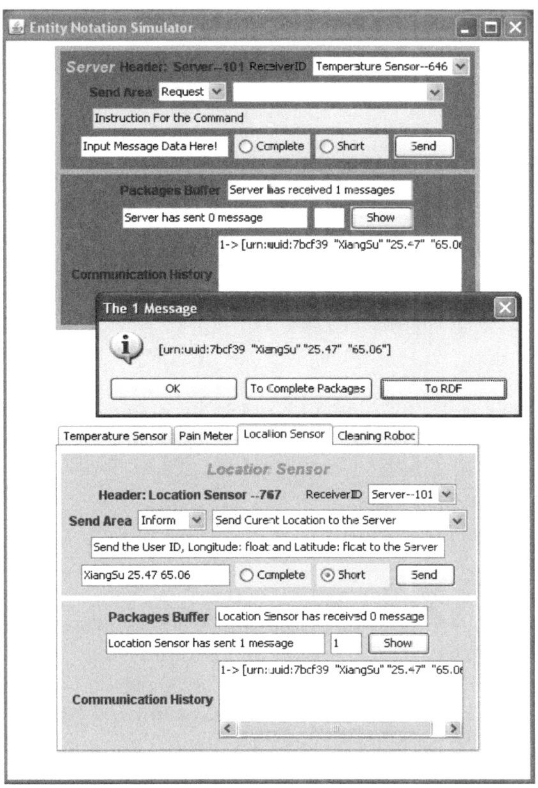

Figure 4. EN Simulator

The short packet of location sensor only contains 12.87% of the characters, comparing with the characters of corresponding complete packet and 9.45% of the characters, comparing with the characters of corresponding RDF format. At the same time, short packet includes the same semantics of complete format and RDF format. Our simulator can simulate 5 devices, including a location sensor, a temperature sensor, a pain meter, a cleaning robot and a server, which can deliver 12 different packets. When we consider all these packets, EN short packets contain only about 11.50% of the characters that complete packets contain, and about 7.30% of the characters that the corresponding RDF format contains.

As explained in section 3, inference engine will be triggered by new statements from the EN packets of the location sensor; and deduces based on sensory data and other context elements predefined in the system. Figure 5 presents the map user interfaces applying rules introduced in section 3. We use Google map API [9] to locate the positions, persons, etc. In A), the user inference shows the current position of the sensor owner is in the Linnanmaa campus. In B), the user interface shows the current location of the sensor user is nearby the pre-marked blueberry collection place. Therefore, map highlights that place and reminds the user to collect blueberries if necessary. In C), the user interface shows the case when the user want to visit his or her friend at Norkkotie 1 from Tuulikintie 3 at February 10th, and the system would suggest he or she ski through the lake kuivasjärvi.

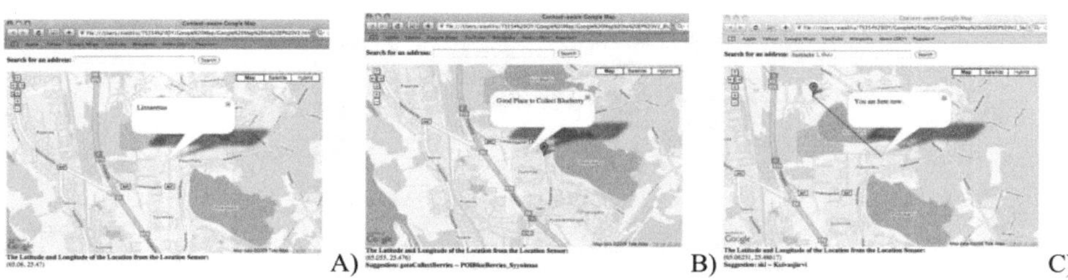

Figure 5. Google Map Use Cases Study

5. Related Work

We compare our approach with related work in different aspects, including other lightweight data representations and context-aware intelligent map applications in mobile devices.

5.1. Lightweight data representation

The EN is a lightweight data representation that can be transferred to Semantic Web representation straightforwardly. As using XML syntax can serialize RDF, XML compression technologies can be used for compressing RDF. Many XML file compression methods and tools have been suggested, like Gzip [10], XMill [11], and XMLPPM [12]. According to the survey and experiments by Wilfred Ng et al [13], XMLPPM achieved the best compression ratio, which can reach 8.25% of the original XML file size. Another alternative is binary XML formats, as they are also lightweight and easy to be serialized. In this area, there exist some competing formats, like Fast

Infoset[14], Efficient XML Interchange (EXI) [15], and Xebu [16]. They mainly use the token-based compression, and the schema-based optimization, in which each XML element, attribute, and so forth is encoded as a small integer value. According to the W3C's performance measurement at 2006 [17], EXI achieved the best compression rate among alternatives. The average compression ratio of EXI for 67 test cases can reach about 30%, by using all the optimization including the schema and the document analysis. Our simulator shows that EN can almost reach the compression ratio of XMLPPM, while presenting better performance than common XML binary methods. Furthermore, when compared to XML compression solutions, EN packets creation requires a minimal amount of computation, as a short packet can be created by concatenating a constant UUID and the produced values, rather than complex algorithms that cannot be handled by mobile devices. On the other hand, some lightweight markup/data serialization languages are also possible solutions for data exchange, like JavaScript Object Notation (JSON) [18], YAML [19], and SSDP [20]. But these serialization languages' design goals make them hard to be transformed into any knowledge representation straightforwardly. Besides that, they do not provide any method to shorten the message.

5.2. Context-aware Map in Mobile Devices

Many mobile maps [21] and navigation applications [22,23] have been reported, but rare applications provide solutions combining sensors with Semantic Web technology. In general, we provide Semantic Web capabilities for the mobile applications by using ontology and reasoning over pure sensor data. Users would have the possibility to get a map suitable for his or her real situation and purpose. Some notables previous work use Semantic Web technology in context-awareness. myCampus [24] leverages Semantic Web services in support of mobile devices, but do not support any location-based service. iJADE FreeWalker [25], is an ontology agent-based tourist guiding system, which combines ontology with GPS sensors. But this system focuses on retrieving the relevant information from web sites based on user's locations, rather than inference over the sensory data. Besides that, Bratislav Predic et al [26] introduced a client-server framework for context-aware mobile maps. They use directed acyclic graph as the context representation. On the client side, separate software interfaces are developed to convert context information from different sensors' data to XML files. On the server side, context information is inserted into rules and facts database and analyzed by rule-based expert system – CLIPS. Compared with this work, our solution is more general and lightweight: our date representation is general format can be implemented on any sensor, while we have fewer components on both the server and the client side.

6. Discussion

In this paper, we proposed a novel solution to achieve the context-aware map service by combining the Semantic Web technology with sensor data. We presented a general communication architecture for context-aware map application by using sensory data. A lightweight data representation, Entity Notation, and an ontology-based inference to reason on sensory data are introduced. The EN makes the raw data from sensors have semantics. It allows very short packets to be sent over simple and unreliable communication links by resource-constrained sensors, and also can be delivered to Semantic Web applications in a straightforward fashion at the same time. The simulation shows the result is very promising. The average length of short packets is less than 10% of the corresponding RDF document's length. Furthermore, when short EN packets are used, only a composer and a decomposer are needed for the pre-processing.

The ontology-based inference would provide semantic support for multiple intelligent functionalities. We presented the utilization of the EN from the knowledge point of view. A set of rules illustrates its usability for several typical scenarios in intelligent maps. Compared with other solutions, our architecture is simple and still have the potentiality to utilize the power of the Semantic Web inference effectively.

However, this work has some limitations. Firstly, we expect a mobile device become a self-adaptive system without any support from server side. The resource limitation of mobile devices would be a barrier for processing an ontology and an ontology-based inference engine. One direction of solving this problem is to study lightweight ontology and inference engine, which can be handled by mobile devices. Another direction is to develop electronics and material technology, which will make mobile devices of tomorrow have stronger process capability with smaller size. Besides, how to make use of sensory data very effectively, like how to integrate data from different sensors and context elements, is still a challenging problem.

Our future work includes examining the capability of the EN by using as many complex data structures as possible, like array and graph. At practical aspect, we will implement context-aware functionality suggested in this paper to mobile devices, like PDA. More intelligent map functionality will be investigated and implemented if possible. Furthermore, we will study how to utilize lightweight EN to express OWL ontology. The blueprint is that mobile devices would handle a small ontology shared from a domain ontology at the server side, and have simple inference functionality. EN could transfer the ontology to the server when complex inference needed. This would be an important stage for the intelligent pervasive computing.

ACKNOWLEDGMENTS

This work was funded by Infotech Oulu and the MOTIVE research program of the Academy of Finland.

REFERENCES

[1] Annu-Maaria Nivala, and L. Tiina Sarjakoski, Need for Context-Aware Topographic Maps in Mobile Devices, Proceeding of the 9th Scandinavian Research Conference on Geographical Information Science (2003), 15-29.

[2] Annu-Maaria Nivala, and L. Tiina Sarjakoski, An Approach to Intelligent Maps: Context Awareness, Proceeding of workshop "HCI in mobile Guides"(2003).

[3] Eija Kaasinen, User needs for Location-Aware Mobile Services, Personal and Ubiquitous Computing, 7 (2003), 70-79.

[4] Fabian Abel, and Jan Brase, Using Semantic Web Technologies for context-aware Information Providing to Mobile Devices, http://www.kbs.uni-hannover.de/Arbeiten/Publikationen/2004/abel_brase_KBS_hannover.pdf.

[5] Jukka Riekki, Xiang Su, and Janne Haverinen, Connecting Resource-Constrained Robots to Knowledge-Based Systems. Proceeding of Internation Conference on Modelling, Identification, and Control (2008).
[6] OWL Web Ontology Language Guide. http://www.w3.org/TR/owl-guide/
[7] Gigseppe De Giacomo and Maurizio Lenzerini, TBox and ABox reasoning in expressive description logics, Proceeding of the Fifth International Conference on the Principles of Knowledge Representation and Reasoning (1996), 316-327.
[8] Jean – A Semantic Web Framework for Jave. http://jena.sourceforge.net/
[9] Google Map API. http://code.google.com /apis/maps/
[10] Gzip. http://www.gzip.org/
[11] Hartmut Liefke, and Dan Suciu, XMill: an efficient compressor for XML data. Proceeding of the ACM SIGMOD International Conference on Management of Data (2000), 153-164.
[12] James Cheney, Compressing XML with Multiplexed Hierarchical PPM Models, Proceeding of the IEEE Data Compression Conference (2000), 163-172.
[13] Wilfred Ng, Lam Wai Yeung, and James Cheng, Comparative Analysis of XML Compression Technologies, World Wide Web 9(1) (2006), 5-33.
[14] W3C. XML Information Set. http://www.w3.org/TR/xml-infoset/
[15] W3C. Efficient XML Interchange (EXI) format. http://www.w3.org/TR/2008/WD-exi-20080919/
[16] Jaakko Kangasharju, Sasu Tarkoma, and Tancred Lindholm, Xebu: A Binary Format with Schema-based Optimization for XML Data. Proceeding of Web Information Systems Engineering. (2005), 528-535.
[17] W3C. Analysis of the EXI Measurements. http://www.w3.org/XML/EXI/report.html
[18] RFC 4627, The application/json Media Type for JavaScript Object Notation (SSON), http://www.ietf.org/rfc/rfc4627.txt
[19] YAML Specification, http://yaml.org/spec/.
[20] Yaron Y. Goland, Ting Cai, Paul Leach, Ye Gu, Simple Service Discovery Protocol/1.0, http://quimby.gnus.org/internet-drafts/draft-cai-ssdp-v1-03.txt
[21] W. Schwinger, Chi. Gruen, B. Pröll, W. Retschitzegger, and A. Schauerhuber, Context-awareness in Mobile Tourism Guides – A Comprehensive Survey. Technical Report, Johannes Kepler University Linz, IFS/TK, July 2005.
[22] TomTom. http://www.tomtom.com/.
[23] Nokia Maps. http://europe.nokia.com/maps.
[24] Mithun Sheshagiri, Norman M. Sadeh, and Fabien Gandon, Using Semantic Web Services for Context-Aware Mobile Applications, Proceeding of the Second International Conference on Mobile Systems, Applications, and Services. 2004.
[25] Bratislav Predic, Dragan Stojanovic, Slobodanka Djordjevic-Kajan, Developing Context Aware Support in Mobile GIS Framework, Proceeding of 9th AGILE Conference on Geographic Information Science. (2006), 90-97.
[26] Toby H.W. Lam and Raymond S.T. Lee, iJADE FreeWalker – An Intelligent Ontology Agent-based Tourist Guiding System, Studies in Computational Intelligence, 72 (2007), 103-125.

Intelligent Environments 2009
V. Callaghan et al. (Eds.)
IOS Press, 2009

doi:10.3233/978-1-60750-034-6-204

A Semantic Framework for Adapting Interactive Systems in Intelligent Environments

Matthias BEZOLD [a,1]
[a] *University of Ulm, Institute for Information Technology, Ulm, Germany*

Abstract. Intelligent environments communicate with the user through user interfaces, which can be improved by means of adapting them to an individual user, based on an observation of the user-system interaction. The power of the adaptations depends on the expressiveness of the underlying data model that represents the interactive system, the user, and the user-system interaction. Ontologies present a powerful formalism for describing a certain domain. We present an adaptation framework that employs an ontology to create an explicit semantic knowledge representation, on top of which adaptations are implemented. These adaptations are either specified by a system designer or inferred automatically by an adaptation component. Special emphasis is put on the user-system interaction, which plays a crucial role in adaptive interactive systems. A prototype implementation demonstrates the feasibility of this approach.

Keywords. Adaptation framework, ontologies, semantic representation.

1. Introduction

One approach for improving the usability of interactive systems in intelligent environments, such as digital TV systems or media centers, is the ability to adapt the interface, which can be both a graphical and a speech interface, to the current user. Adaptations are modifications of the interactive system that ease the interaction of the current user with an interactive system. For this purpose, the system observes the user and derives adaptations based on the user-system interaction. In doing so, the interactive system can better reflect individual capabilities and requirements of an individual user [9].

However, adaptations require a comprehensive description of both the interactive system and the user-system interaction, because only information available to the adaptation component can be considered in the decision process which adaptation to apply. Triggered by derivations performed by a user modeling component, an appropriate interface element as well as an adaptation are selected and the adaptation is carried out.

In this paper, we present an adaptation architecture that employs an ontology to create a uniform representation of the interactive system, the user, and the user-system interaction that serves as a basis for an adaptation component. Fig. 1 gives an overview of this

[1]University of Ulm, Institute for Information Technology, Ulm, Germany
matthias.bezold@uni-ulm.de

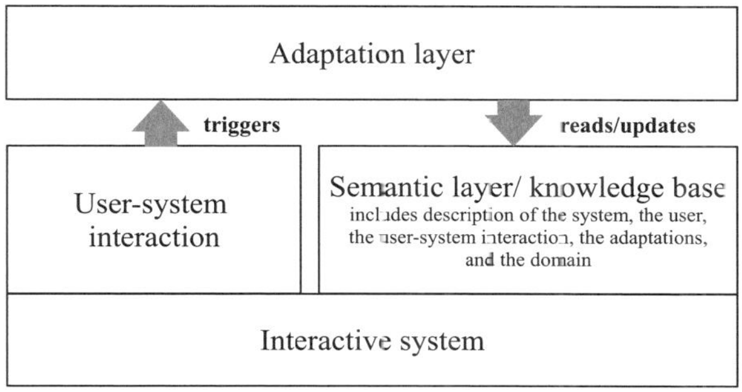

Figure 1. The architecture of the adaptation framework comprises a semantic layer and an adaptation component on top of it. Adaptations are triggered by the user-system interaction.

framework. On top of the interactive system, an ontology-based semantic representation layer provides an abstracted explicit semantic representation of the interactive system as well as other aspects of the user-system interaction to an adaptation layer, which is triggered by a user modeling component.

This paper is organized as follows. Section 2 introduces a semantic knowledge representation for the interactive system based on an ontology. Next, the definition of adaptations on top of this knowledge representation and how these adaptations are executed is introduced in Section 3. An overview of a prototype implementation is given in Section 4. Section 5 gives an overview of related work and Section 6 concludes this paper.

2. A Semantic Representation of Interactive Systems

An adaptation component decides when and which adaptations to apply to an interactive system. For this purpose, this component requires information about the user-system interaction that is provided by a user modeling component. On the other hand, the adaptation component requires information both about the system itself and the user to decide how and which parts of the system to adapt. Since the system can only consider available information, the representation of this information is crucial for an adaptive interface.

In addition to the amount of information, the formalism chosen for this representation is of great importance. Only by representing all aspects using a common formalism can the adaptation component access all this information in a uniform way. Ontologies provide such a formalism for defining a certain domain and are in this work applied to the domain of adaptive interactive systems. By describing all facets of the interactive system using this formalism, the adaptation component can include all information in the adaptation decision process.

In the following, we present how an ontology forms the basis of an abstraction layer on top of the interactive system that can be used by an adaptation component.

2.1. Ontologies

An ontology [6,10] is a formal representation of a certain domain, which it describes as a set of entities and the relationships between these entities. Each entity has properties, which are either primitive data types, such as string or numbers, or connections to other

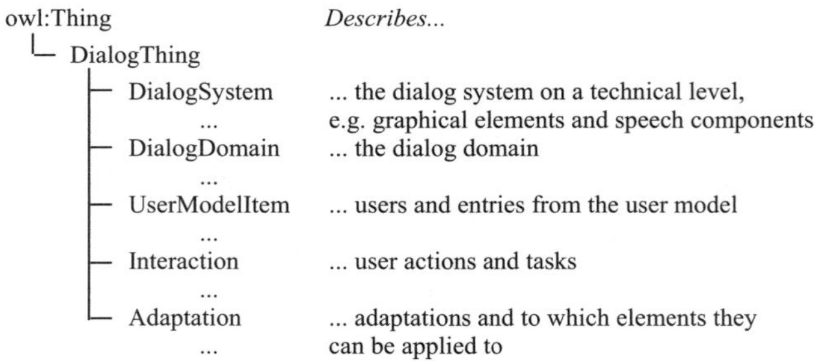

Figure 2. The hierarchical structure of the ontology with the five sub-models.

entities. Another important property of an ontology is the ability to inter new information from exsting information, e.g. by means of inference rules. These rules can encode general knowledge about the domain.

The Web Ontology Language (OWL) [13] is a formalism that allows to define classes of entities, which have a shared set of properties. Thus, items of the same kind are represented formally by a common class and share the same properties. Inheritance allows to create a hierarchy of classes that inherit properties from their parent class. Individuals are instantiated from a class, filling in all the properties defined by the respective class. Inference can also be performed on the OWL information, for instance on the inheritance information.

A set of OWL classes forms the basis of this framework. The ontology covers different parts of the adaptive interactive system, which are described by a set of OWL classes.

2.2. An Ontology for Interactive Adaptive Systems

This framework employs an ontology that covers different facets of adaptive interactive systems, such as the system itself, the user, the user-system interaction, and the adaptations. The ontology consists of a set of OWL classes, and each of these classes has a set of properties. For example, the name of a user represented by the "User" class is stored in a property called "hasName". The OWL classes form a hierarchy with a common base class called "DialogThing". Each part of the ontology, such as the description of the system or the user-system interaction, is again based on a common ontology class. For instance, all classes of the system description are derived from the "DialogSystem" class. Further knowledge can be encoded in the OWL representation, for instance as restrictions to properties or general knowledge about the system by means of inference rules.

An overview of the ontology structure is given in Fig. 2. The system description defines the structure of the interactive system and the interface elements, such as graphical buttons and lists or speech components, as well as their properties. Moreover, the dialog domain is described, such as the list of channels in an interactive TV system. User modeling information reflects data specific to the current user. In addition, the user system interaction is described by different user actions. Finally, adaptations are formalized as well. The ontology is restricted to a declarative description of the interactive system, i.e., it does describe the structure of the system, but not how it works.

2.3. Instantiating the Models

The previous section discussed how the structure of the dialog system is described by a set of OWL classes, i.e., how the structure of elements is and which properties they have. In order to describe one specific system, instances of these classes have to be created. For this purpose, the respective class is instantiated for each entity of the interactive system that the ontology covers to create an individual. A set of so-called ontology adapters carries out the work of creating individuals for a certain part of the system. For instance, a system ontology adapter creates an individual for each graphical or speech component of the system and interconnects them accordingly, whereas the user model adapter loads information about the user of the system. When the system starts, all adapters are executed and thus produce a common representation of different aspects of the system by means of a semantic representation. Therefore, these adapters bring together data from different information representations into a common ontology-based formalism.

Access to this semantic representation is provided by means of so-called queries, which return a set of ontology statements for a given input set, e.g. all individual for a certain class. The adaptation component performs such queries to determine which adaptations to apply. On the other hand, the adaptation component also updates the semantic representation to alter the interactive system. For this purpose, the adapters watch the respective entities, and if they are changed, they update the interactive system accordingly.

3. Performing Adaptations

Based on the semantic knowledge representation, adaptations are carried out. This section discusses how an adaptation component employs the semantic representation of the interactive system to apply adaptations to the system. Adaptations are triggered based on user behavior. For this purpose, a user modeling component, which is not discussed in detail in this paper, observes the user-system interaction and employs different algorithms to model user behavior. The results of the user modeling procedure are forwarded to the adaptation component as so-called adaptations triggers. These triggers can for instance be a prediction of the next user action or an update of a model that describes a favorite value, such as a TV channel or a cell phone number. After such a trigger was sent to the adaptation component, it selects an appropriate adaptation together with an interface element that should be adapted.

3.1. Representation of Adaptations in the Framework

The description of adaptations in this framework comprises two parts. First, an ontology class defines which elements of the interactive system an adaptation can be applied to and how the adaptation is triggered. For this purpose, the OWL class "Adaptation" has properties called "adapts" and "hasTrigger" that defines a list of adaptation subjects and adaptation triggers. For instance, an adaptation called "Emphasis" highlights a graphical button by increasing its size and selecting a more noticeable color. Since this adaptation works on graphical buttons, the OWL class "GraphicalButton" that describes these graphical buttons is listed as an "adapts" property of the "EmphasisAdaptation" individual. Similarly, the "hasTrigger" property contains the "User Action Prediction" trigger, which describes a prediction of the next user action by the user modeling component.

The second part of the adaptation description is information on how to execute the respective adaptation. For this purpose, the adaptation framework comprises a set of so-called adaptation executors. Each of these executors defines how to execute a certain adaptation on a specific interface element. An adaptation executor consists of a knowledge base update, i.e., it defines a set of properties and the new values of these properties that are applied to the individuals of the semantic representation. For instance, the previously mentioned “Emphasis” adaptation is executed for a graphical button by updating the “width” and “height” properties to increase the size of the button as well as by changing the color to a more noticeable one. An adaptation executor provides parameters, for instance the color of the button in the example.

In this way, the adaptation framework contains a description of where, when, and how to apply the adaptations. The following section discusses how the adaptation framework carries out adaptations based on the specification introduced in this section.

3.2. Execution of Adaptations

The framework provides two methods of executing adaptations: specification by the system designer and automatic execution by an adaptation component. Both methods follow a similar approach, but the adaptation component derives the decisions taken by the system designer from the semantic description of the adaptations automatically.

The execution of an adaptation comprises the selection of a combination of an adaptation and an interface element. This procedure is triggered by the user modeling component, for instance if this component detects a certain user action or predicts the next interaction step.

The first method for executing adaptations is to have the system designer define based on which trigger a certain adaptation is applied to an interface element. For this purpose, the designer selects interface elements and appropriate adaptations and connects these to an adaptation trigger that is raised by the user modeling component. Based on the information from the semantic representation, only matching elements are provided for selection, thus deriving intelligent tool support from the semantic representation. For instance, if the designer selects a graphical button, only adaptations that are applicable to graphical buttons are presented.

The second adaptation method employs an adaptation component to select an appropriate combination of interface element, adaptation, and adaptation trigger. For this purpose, the adaptation component has available a number of so-called adaptation selectors that each implement one specific strategy of selecting an interface element based on a user modeling event. Next, the information encoded in the semantic representation is used to derive appropriate adaptations, which are in turn executed on the selected interface element.

In the following, we demonstrate how the “Emphasis” adaptation introduced in Sect. 3.1 is executed in this framework. In a graphical system, each button executes a certain action. If the user modeling component predicts a user action, the “Emphasis” adaptation can highlight the respective button to propose it to the user. For this purpose, an adaptation selector reacts to action prediction from the user modeling component by selecting all interface elements that execute the suggested action, in this case a graphical button. Next, an adaptation is selected for each of the interface elements, for instance the “Emphasis” adaptation for the graphical button. Finally, the adaptation is executed, in this example by highlighting the graphical button by increasing the size and selecting more noticeable colors.

4. Implementation

In order to investigate the feasibility of this approach, we implemented a prototype of this adaptation framework. The adaptation framework was developed as an extension to a modeling tool called EB GUIDE Studio [5], which is used to specify multimodal interactive systems. The tool comprises a simulation component for executing the interactive system and thus serves as a dialog manager.

The framework extends the modeling tool with a semantic layer, which loads the ontology introduced in Sect. 2.2. A set of adapter classes instantiates the ontology classes to form the semantic layer as described in Sect. 2.3. This layer is available both at design time and at runtime of the system. The prototype provides both adaptation methods that were introduced in Sect. 3.2. The semantic layer is implemented based on the Jena framework[2], a Semantic Web library that supports OWL.

In addition to the semantic and the adaptation layers, the framework also comprises a user modeling component that describes the user-system interaction and provides information about user actions, such as detecting and predicting user actions, and preferred data of the user. The user modeling component is connected to the adaptations as triggers.

Based on this framework, an adaptive version of an interactive TV system was developed. This system provides an electronic program guide that lets the user browse the TV program. Different adaptations were implemented, such as providing adaptive help or emphasizing interface elements based on a prediction of the next user-system interaction.

5. Related Work

Since ontologies have a broad area of application, they have been used in multimodal systems for other purposes than adaptations, such as supporting semantic coherence checking [7] in the SmartKom project or domain reasoning in the dialog manager [3] in the Talk project. Moreover, ontologies have been used for modeling interactive systems. For instance, Obrenovic et al. [11] employ an ontology in addition to UML in the development process of multimodal interactive systems. Contrary to our work, the high-level model description is only available at design time to provide development support and for platform mapping, but not at runtime of the system as a knowledge representation for the interactive system itself.

Sophisticated adaptation architectures have been presented in the domain of adaptive hypertext systems. Dolog et al. present a formal definition of an adaptive hypermedia system [2]. The adaptation component consists of a set of rules expressed as first-order logic statements using a language called TRIPLE. The adaptations rely on a semantic annotation of the document space. The ODAS domain ontology presented by Tran et al. [14] is used in conjunction with adaptation rules in an adaptive hypertext portal. The authors reason that rules provide a better transparency and controllability for users than statistical adaptation methods. The ontology provides a knowledge foundation for the

[2]The Jena Framework: http://jena.sourceforge.net

adaptation rules and contains different models, such as a system model, a task model, and a resource model. All of these different frameworks employ logic-based reasoning or rules to express the adaptations, whereas our framework supports – in addition to adaptation rules – a more explicit representation of adaptations by embedding them in the knowledge base. Moreover, the focus of this framework is on interactive systems, rather than adaptive hypermedia, which are focused on the interface rather than documents and their interconnection.

Different approaches exist for the semantical description of certain aspects of interactive systems, such as user modeling or a system description. Razmerita et al. [12] present a general architecture for a user modeling server that is based on semantic technologies. Various ontologies were proposed specifically for user modeling. Golemati et al. [4] and Heckmann et al. [8] demonstrate sophisticated examples of such ontologies. The user model part of the ontology in our framework follows a similar approach, but keeps the user model concise. Dolog [1] introduces an OWL notation for statecharts, which is similar to a part of the system model in our framework. However, our framework extends the semantic description beyond statecharts to the whole system, but at the same time realizing a declarative rather than a functional description.

6. Conclusion and Future Work

In this work, we presented a semantic framework for adapting interactive systems to user behavior. An ontology forms the basis of an explicit semantic knowledge representation that covers the system, the user-system interaction, the user, and adaptations. In addition to the semantic representation, adaptation executors describe how a certain adaptation is applied to a specific interface element. Based on the knowledge representation, adaptations can be selected and executed, for which purpose two methods were presented. First, a system designer selects which adaptations are applied to which interface element, and the adaptation framework provides tool support accordingly. Second, an adaptation component performs the adaptation selection automatically. An overview of a prototype implementation and its application to an adaptive prototype was presented to show the feasibility of this approach.

As future work, we plan to further exploit the semantic representation, for instance for user modeling. Moreover, we plan to define a set of reusable adaptations that can be employed in different multimodal interactive systems.

References

[1] Peter Dolog. Model-Driven Navigation Design for Semantic Web Applications with the UML-Guide. In *ICWE Workshops 2004*, pages 75–86, 2004.

[2] Peter Dolog, Nicola Henze, Wolfgang Nejdl, and Michael Sintek. Towards the Adaptive Semantic Web. In François Bry, Nicola Henze, and Jan Maluszynski, editors, *PPSWR 2003*, volume 2901 of *LNCS*, pages 51–68. Springer, Heidelberg, Germany, 2003.

[3] Guillermo Perez Garcia, Jose Gabriel de Amores Carredano, Pilar Manchon Portillo, Fernando Gomez Marin, and Jesus Gonzalez Marti. Integrating Owl Ontologies With a Dialogue Manager. In *Procesamiento del Lenguaje*, pages 153–160, 2006.

[4] Maria Golemati, Akrivi Katifori, Costas Vassilakis, George Lepouras, and Constantin Halatsis. Creating an Ontology for the User Profile: Method and Applications. In *Conference on Research Challenges in Information Science (RCIS) 2007*, 2007.

[5] Silke Goronzy, Rachel Mochales, and Nicole Beringer. Developing Speech Dialogs for Multimodal HMIs Using Finite State Machines. In *9th International Conference on Spoken Language Processing (Interspeech), CD-ROM*, 2006.
[6] Thomas R. Gruber. Toward Principles for the Design of Ontologies Used for Knowledge Sharing. *International Journal Human-Computer Studies*, 43(5–6):907–928, 1995.
[7] Iryna Gurevych, Robert Porzel, and Rainer Malaka. Modeling Domain Knowledge: Know-How and Know-What. In Wolfgang Wahlster, editor, *SmartKom - Foundations of Multimodal Dialogue Systems*, pages 71–84. Springer, Heidelberg, Germany, 2006.
[8] Dominik Heckmann, Tim Schwartz, Boris Brandherm, Michael Schmitz, and Margeritta von Wilamowitz-Moellendorff. Gumo - The General User Model Ontology. In Liliana Ardissono, Paul Brna, and Antonija Mitrovic, editors, *User Modeling (UM) 2005*, volume 3538 of *LNCS*, pages 428–432. Springer, Heidelberg, Germany, 2005.
[9] Anthony Jameson. *Human-computer Interaction Handbook*, chapter Adaptive Interfaces and Agents, pages 305–330. Erlbaum, Mahwah, NJ, USA, first edition, 2003.
[10] Natalya F. Noy and Deborah L. McGuinness. Ontology Development 101: A Guide to Creating Your First Ontology. Technical Report KSL-01-05, Stanford Knowledge Systems Laboratory, March 2001.
[11] Zeljko Obrenovic, Dusan Starcevic, and Vladan Devedzic. Using Ontologies in Design of Multimodal User Interfaces. In Matthias Rauterberg, Marino Menozzi, and Janet Wesson, editors, *INTERACT 2003*. IOS Press, Amsterdam, Netherlands, 2003.
[12] Liana Razmerita, Albert A. Angehrn, and Alexander Maedche. Ontology-Based User Modeling for Knowledge Management Systems. In Peter Brusilovsky, Albert T. Corbett, and Fiorella de Rosis, editors, *User Modeling (UM) 2003*, volume 2702 of *LNCS*, pages 213–217. Springer, Heidelberg, Germany.
[13] Michael K. Smith, Chris Welty, and Deborah L. McGuinness. OWL Web Ontology Language Guide. Technical report, W3C, 2004.
[14] Thanh Tran, Philipp Cimiano, and Anupriya Ankolekar. A Rule-Based Adaption Model for Ontology-Based Personalization. In Manolis Wallace, Marios C. Angelides, and Phivos Mylonas, editors, *Advances in Semantic Media Adaptation and Personalization*, volume 93 of *SCI*, pages 117–135. Springer, Heidelberg, Germany, 2008.

Intelligent Environments 2009
V. Callaghan et al. (Eds.)
IOS Press, 2009

doi:10.3233/978-1-60750-034-6-212

Integrating Common Sense in Physically Embedded Intelligent Systems

Marios DAOUTIS [a,1], Silvia CORADESCHI [a] and Amy LOUTFI [a]
[a] *Applied Autonomous Sensor Systems Research Center, University of Örebro, Sweden*

Abstract. In this paper we describe an implemented framework that integrates knowledge representation and reasoning in a symbiotic system. In such systems a number of heterogeneous sensors pervasively embedded in the environment, mobile robots and humans co-exist and communicate. In this work, the integration is mediated through perceptual anchoring, which creates and maintains the correspondences between the symbol system and the perceptual data that refer to the same physical object. The overall framework is evaluated using ResearchCyc as the knowledge representation and reasoning system, within the context of a physical testbed, which consists of a small apartment-like home.

Keywords. Human-Computer Interaction, Knowledge Management, Ambient Intelligence, Symbol Grounding

Introduction

The symbiotic system paradigm where robotic devices, simple sensors pervasively embedded in everyday environments and humans cooperate in the performance of tasks are an increasing trend. Such paradigms includes ubiquitous robotic systems, intelligent spaces and robot ecologies and combine visions from autonomous robotics and ambient intelligence to integrate both simple and complex devices. In this paper a framework for using knowledge representation and reasoning (KR&R) within the symbiotic system is presented. A key feature of the system is the integration of KR&R together with information coming from physical perceptual data. This integration facilitates the mapping of non semantically structured perceptual information into pieces of knowledge that conform with a shared vocabulary (ontology). It allows for the information to be hierarchically structured, defining concepts at different levels of abstraction. Furthermore, information can be exchanged and queried between agents including humans.

The integration of KR&R with robotic systems has been an increasingly interesting topic for cognitive robotics. Examples are found in semantic mapping [1], improving planning and control aspects [2], and most notably HRI systems [3,4]. Typically, such systems have used small KR&R systems, tailored to the specific application at hand. We investigate the possibility to include a fully fledged KR&R system that has been developed independently of the intended application and has been maintained over an extended period of time. Furthermore, in this paper we concentrate on how the KR&R can

[1]Corresponding Author: Marios Daoutis, Applied Autonomous Sensor Systems Research Center – Mobile Robotics Lab, University of Örebro, SE-701 82 Örebro, Sweden; E-mail: marios.daoutis@oru.se.

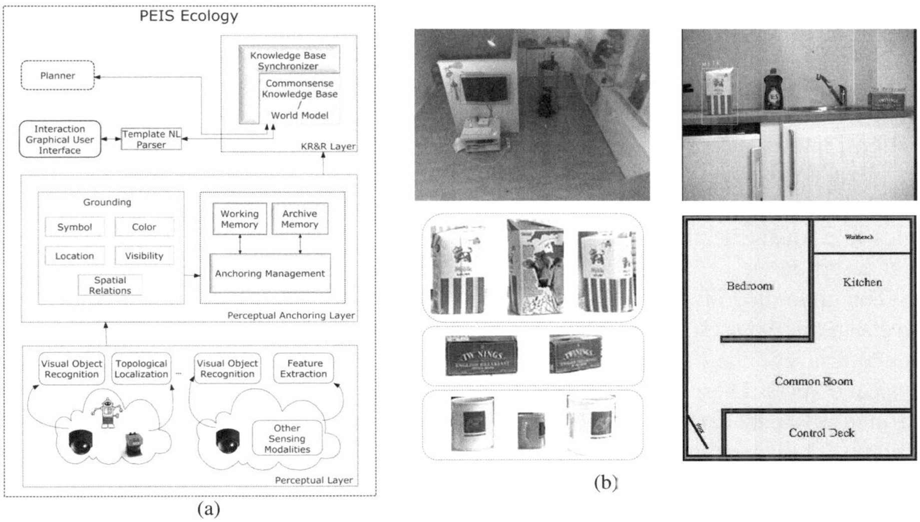

Figure 1. Architecture Overview 1(a), Object Recognition output 1(b)-Up, Training Images 1(b)-Bottom Left, PEIS-Home Topological Map 1(b)-Bottom Right

be integrated with the perceptual data that is available in the symbiotic system. To enable this integration an anchoring framework is used which creates and maintains the connection between the symbolic system and the perceptual data corresponding to physical objects. A further advantage exploited in this work is the use of common sense reasoning which is available in the KR&R components. In addition to enabling queries from the human users this common sense knowledge is used to reason about objects, their properties and functionalities. Finally, the overall system is evaluated in a testbed consisting of a number of sensors (cameras), a mobile robot and a human user. It should be emphasized that the presented work focuses on the system integration and is built upon a number of existing components which have been tested previously in isolation. Thus the key novelty is the integration of the components and the validation of the complete system in a real home-like environment.

1. System Overview

The implemented architecture is built upon a communication framework that allows the dynamic connection between different components. A component is any computerized system interacting with the environment through sensors and/or actuators and including some degree of "intelligence". Each component is called a PEIS or physically embedded intelligent system and can be as simple as a smart toaster and as complex as a humanoid robot. A PEIS-Ecology is the collection of all those components. In our realization of a PEIS-Ecology, the PEIS relies on a distributed middleware to communicate and cooperate. This PEIS-middleware implements a distributed tuple-space on a P2P network: PEIS exchange information by publishing tuples and subscribing to tuples, which are transparently distributed by the middleware. Each PEIS also provides a set of standard tuples, e.g., to announce its physical appearance or the functionalities that it can provide.

Figure 1(a), shows the interaction of the different components within the system. A central contribution in this work is the KR&R and the necessary components to interface with the anchoring/grounding processes. The KR&R system used is Cyc, which contains roughly 3 million assertions about 250,000 concepts. Operations (such as assertions, retractions, modifications and queries) are stated using Cyc's formal language, CycL. Essentially CycL is an extension to second order predicate calculus, which is unambiguous and enable mechanical reasoning. The extensions also include features of higher order logics (e.g. quantification over predicates, functions, and sentences) that allow higher order assertions.

The grounding of perceptual data presented in this work concern mainly household objects and in the presented system, it is the task of the anchoring modules to create and maintain in time the correspondence between symbols and percepts that refer to these physical objects. These modules consist of a grounding module, an anchor management, and memory management. The latter component is a novel addition which is used to facilitate the management of information to the knowledge base synchronizer that interfaces with the KR&R. More detail on the KR&R and anchoring module are given in the following Sections. The perceptual layers consist of a number of heteregenous sensors which publish perceptual information to the tuple space and are used for further processing. For visual processing, the experiments presented adopts a SIFT-based approach [5].The object recognizer is able to recognize multiple objects in real-time, and in each time cycle, the perceptual signatures from the recognized objects are published into the tuple space. This output is then available to the anchoring component. Figure 2 (Left) shows an example of the data contained in the perceptual system. For localization and navigation used by the robot system (shown on the left of the perceptual layer), a number of components are networked in the PEIS-Ecology. The detail on the implementation of these components are omitted.

2. Perceptual Anchoring

The task of anchoring is to create and maintain in time the correspondence between symbols and percepts that refer to the same physical object. This correspondence is reified in a data structure $\alpha(t)$, called an *anchor*. It is indexed by time as the perceptual system continuously generates new percepts; and the created links are dynamic, since the same symbol may be connected to new percepts every time a new observation of the corresponding object is acquired. So at each time instance t, $\alpha(t)$ contains a symbol identifying that object, a percept generated by the latest observation of the object, and a perceptual signature meant to provide the (best) estimate of the values of the observable properties of the object. For a full account refer to [8].

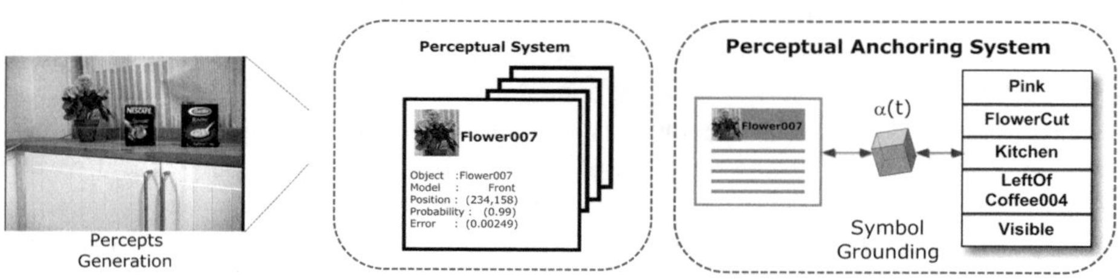

Figure 2. Percepts formulation in the Perceptual Layer (Left), Grounding of the perceptual signature to formulate an anchor in the perceptual anchoring layer (Right)

2.1. Grounding

To ground percepts from different sensing modalities an interface that allows to connect various grounding plugins is used where each plugin implements its own grounding relation. For the experiments of the current work, we address five different grounders that formulate a sufficient symbolic description from the perceptual signatures. Those are object category, color, location, spatial relations and visibility grounding. For color grounding we use a n-pixel random sampling algorithm applied to the segmented image of the recognized object, averaging the selected pixels, while the grounding relation maps the result between twelve classes of colors (1. Red, 2. Green, 3. Yellow, 4. Blue, 5. Black, 6. White, 7. Pink, 8. Cyan, 9. Gray, 10. Orange, 11. Brown, 12. Purple) that can be accurately differentiated by people with standard vision [6]. The location is derived by correlating the position of the robot or camera (using localization perceptual data) to the semantic map that is provided to the system. The object category is taken directly from the object recognition module as it is included in the unique identifier of the percept. An example of the anchoring system is illustrated in Figure 2 (Right).

Spatial relations constitute an important symbolic description, because they allow us to distinguish objects by their location with respect to other objects, possibly identical, and plays an important role when it comes to human-robot interaction. Two classes of binary spatial relations between a reference object and the located object are considered: the distance (topological) relations "at" and "near" and the directional (projective) relations "front of", "behind", "right" and "left". For reasons of simplicity we assume a deictic frame of reference with an egocentric origin coinciding with the robot platform. For the computation and evaluation of these spatial relations within the grounder plugin, we use the model presented in [7]. The computation of the spatial relations in the anchoring module have been validated previously in [8]. Lastly, visibility is grounded by default as true during grounding, since all the percepts generated by recognized objects are visible at the time. This attribute changes in the functionality of the anchoring management described below.

2.2. Management & Perceptual Memory

The Anchoring Manager, is responsible for distributing the recently grounded anchor candidates to the rest of the system. This is achieved by extending and modifying the anchoring's functional part originally proposed in [9]. The anchoring process concerns bottom up and top down information acquisition through the following functionalities: find, acquire track and reacquire. *Find* is used for searching through the anchoring space. It searches both the symbolic descriptions and perceptual signatures. It can be triggered by the grounding in order to search if there is already an anchor created for the specific grounded object, or similarly it can be invoked by a user command trying to identify an anchor against its symbolic description (e.g. "red" & "cup"). If we receive a candidate anchor which does not match any existing anchor, *acquire* is used to initiate a new anchor for this candidate. Else, if the candidate matches an existing anchor, *track* assures that the perceptual signature pointed to by the existing anchor is the most recent and adequate perceptual representation of the object, by updating the perceptual signature with the one from the candidate anchor.

The novel functions is the *perceptual memory management*. It consists of two memory structures, one for storing anchors currently perceived by an active perceptual agent (e.g. robot) (working memory) and another one which stores previously perceived anchors (archive memory). If, for example, the robot is not perceiving an object anymore, the anchor of the corresponding object is marked as not visible and then archived (archive function). While if we happen to identify an object that we have previously anchored, the *reacquire* function brings up the corresponding anchor from the archive memory.

3. Knowledge Representation and Reasoning Layer

The main challenge of integrating a large KR&R like Cyc is to be able to synchronize the information with the perceptual data coming from multiple sensors, which is inherently subject to incompleteness, glitches, and errors. The anchoring module provides a stable symbolic information despite fluctuating quantitative data through the grounding plugins. Nonetheless, instances of objects must be created in Cyc and as objects can be dynamic (e.g. in the case of changing properties) proper updating of information needs to be managed. Ultimately, to enable the synchronization of between the KRR and anchoring layers three aspects are considered, defining anchoring in the KRR, handling of assertions, and handling of ambiguities.

It is important to define the context of anchoring as Cyc is not consistent globally but rather tries to be consistent locally by exploiting the use of different contexts which are expressed as *MicroTheories*. Through the Anchoring *MicroTheory* it is possible to connect concepts about objects that are currently present in the anchoring module, to the structured hierarchical knowledge in Cyc and concurrently inherit the common sense reasoning about this knowledge. For instance, if the location of "cup" stored in the anchor, is the Kitchen, then this object and the kitchen are instantiated into Cyc, inheriting all the properties related to the generalized concepts of the "kitchen" and the "cup", such as *Man Made Thing* or *Humanly Occupied Spatial Object*. To enable the Anchoring Mt, we needed to assert common sense rule formulae about the agent's perceptions and knowledge about those perceptions, along with the definition of concepts like *anchor* and *Self* (e.g. the perceptual self, or robot).

3.1. Knowledge Synchronization

To synchronize the knowledge in Cyc with the perceptual data, instances of the anchored objects present in both working and archive memory are asserted. The knowledge synchronization's role keep the Cyc symbolic system coherent with the symbolic descriptions of each anchor. This is done by translating the symbolic description of each anchor into a set of logical formulae that state the agent's perception about the object. Figure 3, exemplifies how assertions are made. When a particular predicate of the symbolic de-

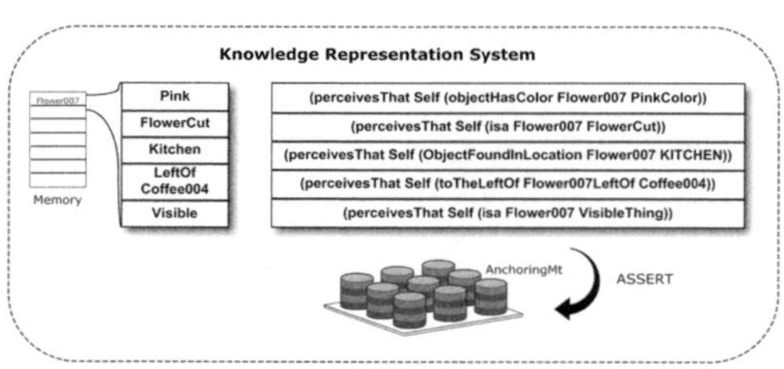

Figure 3. Transformation of the anchor's symbolic part, to logic formulae assertions about the agent's perception of the corresponding anchor (object).

Table 1. Sample translations from english to logical formulae using the NL parser.

Natural Language Question	Logical Query Translation
-What do you see ?	query:(sees AGENT ?OBJECT)
-Where is the red cup ?	query:(objectFoundInLocation (and (isa ?CUP Cup) (objectHasColor ?CUP RedColor)) ?WHERE)
-Do you know that the green flower is located in the kitchen?	query:(knows AGENT (and (isa ?FLOWER Flower) (objectHasColor ?FLOWER GreenColor) (objectFoundInLocation ?FLOWER KITCHEN)))

scription changes (e.g. when the location of an object is in another room), first an unassertion of the predicate is made, and a new assertion containing the updated information is performed.

Ambiguities may arise during the synchronization process and are resolved using the denotation tool interactively with the user. For example the anchoring of a "flower" triggers an ambiguity as Cyc contains multiple concepts denoting the term "Flower"; the possible options are: `CutFlower, Flower-BotanicalPart, FlowerDevelopmentEvent, FloweryPlant`.

Another aspect to synchronize is the information about the visibility of the object. This is important as the physically embedded agents still needs to maintain knowledge about an object, despite that the corresponding perceptual information is not currently available to the agent. For example the robot still needs to know that a cup is present in the kitchen, despite that the "cup" is outside its current field of view. This is achieved by 2nd order rule assertions as stated in Section 3 and an example how those are used is shown in the experiments in Table 2 .

3.2. NL Communication

To combine Cyc's natural language capabilities and enhance the communication with the user we allow Cyc to translate the results of queries or inferences, into natural language. In addition a console based graphical user interface is created allowing the user to type in questions or complementary assertions in natural language which are parsed by a template based NL parser, and in turn accesses Cyc to perform the required operations. All the occurances of the the word 'you' are reformulated to the agent's name. The NL parser is able to capture 15 categories of *what* questions, 19 categories of *who* questions, 7 categories of *is* questions and 18 other categories. In addition there are 11 other possible commands which include assertion types (set, *is*-A, generalization, assert, make), informational types (get, complete, explain, translate, guess-denote), retraction types (retract, delete). Some examples of how this translation are given in Table 1 .

4. Case Study

As part of the testbed, we use a physical facility, called the PEIS-home, which looks like a typical bachelor apartment of about $25m^2$. It consists of a living room, a bedroom and a small kitchen as shown in the Figure 1(b) (bottom right). The PEIS-Home is equipped with communication and computation infrastructure along with a number of sensors like camera's and localization components. In our ecology there is an interactive robotic system based on an ActiveMedia PeopleBot platform for indoor research. In addition to the usual sensors, the robot is equipped with a SICK LMS200 laser range finder and with

Table 2. Excerpt from the dialogue between the human and the Anchoring Robot.

User > What do you see?	Self > I perceive a Milk Box, a Washing Liquid and a Tea.
User > Where are you?	Self > I am located in the Kitchen.
User > Where is the Pink Flower?	Self > The Pink Flower is located in the Kitchen, to the left of Coffee, to the Left of Soup, (...) and to the right of Me.
User > What color is the Washing Liquid?	Self > Green.
User > What Things are capable of flying?	Self > Bird, Airoplane, (...) are capable of flying.
User > Is the Flower capable of flying?	Self > I cannot prove that.
User > Do you know that the yellow cup is located in the kitchen?	Self > Yes.
User > Do you perceive that the yellow cup is in the kitchen?	Self > No.
User > What is a Flower?	Self > Flower007 is a Flower. Flower is an Organism Part, a Finite Spatial Thing, a Biological Living Object, a Partially Tangible Thing, a Three Dimensional Thing, (...).
User > Is the Flower in the Kitchen, a Bird?	Self > I cannot prove that.
User > Where is the Television Set?	Self > The Television Set is located in the Living Room.
User > What Color is the Television Set?	Self > Black.

a Sony PTZ color camera. While from a technical point of view, communication occurs between the human user and the PEIS-Ecology, it is presented to the user as an interaction between the user and the robot, as this interaction has shown to facilitate a better HRI.

We initially presented the robot with 15 objects while capturing 2 to 5 training images per object from different viewpoints. Some training images samples are shown in Figure 1(b) (bottom left). It is important to mention that the robot recognizes instances of objects and not object categories. We placed those objects around the PEIS-home in a random manner, either close or far, covering a great amount of different combinations of spatial relations. We then allowed the robot to navigate around the environment so as to recognize and anchor those objects. Since the anchoring process is mainly an internal, with respect to the robot, process it is difficult to present what is been done inside anchoring throughout the test run but some indications are shown in Figures 2 and 3. One clear indication that the whole process is successful is through a dialogue between the user and the robot in order to verify that the robot's perception about the environment reflects the reality. We found that the robot correctly recognized and anchored all the trained objects. Also we verified that the anchors were correctly placed in the corresponding memory, according to the objects visibility, throughout the test run.

We then allowed the human to communicate with the robot, by typing into the console based graphical user interface, questions (related to robot's perceptions, or commonsense), or communication commands in natural language according to the NL part described in Section 3.2. An excerpt of the dialogue that took place is presented in Table 2. At the point where this dialogue took place, the robot was located in the kitchen looking at a milk box, a washing liquid and some tea, as indicated in Figure 1(b) (Up) which is the output of the object recognition component. We should mention here that in the robot does know about past percepts (e.g. things seen in the kitchen previously) while it does not perceive them anymore. Also with the commonsense representations we were able through rule assertions, as described in Section 3, to let the robot *know* about its perceptions as the commonsense fact that *seeing* is a subset of *perceiving* is present in Cyc. The length of the dialogue (60 questions, all handled correctly) was found satisfactory with respect to the quality of communication between the human user and the robot validating that the system behaves as proposed.

We are also able to use the visual sensors which are located in the ceiling and can observe things that the robot would not be able to observe because they are too large[2] or occluded. Another instance of the object recognizer was trained on the large objects from the PEIS-home (e.g. television set, couch, table, sink, etc). Through the knowledge base assertions which pertained a larger collection of objects of the environment, the robot is able to compensate for its limited ability of perception.

5. Conclusion & Future Work

In this work we have investigated the integration of Cyc with a perceptual system consisting of networked sensors. The common sense functionality in Cyc was exploited to reason about objects and their properties. Focus was concentrated on the perceptual anchoring and the necessary processes to synchronize the symbolic system with the perceptual data. The HRI has been used to validate the system. A number of issues will be considered for future validation. These include a consideration of a wider scope of sensors currently residing in the ecology and improvement of the NL parser by a more sophisticated method using the full spectrum of Cyc's natural language knowledge and capabilities.

References

[1] C. Galindo, J. Fernandez-Madrigal, J. Gonzalez, and A. Saffiotti, "Robot task planning using semantic maps," *Robotics and Autonomous Systems*, vol. 56, no. 11, pp. 955–966, 2008.

[2] O. Mozos, P. Jensfelt, H. Zender, G.-J. M. Kruijff, and W. Burgard, "An integrated system for conceptual spatial representations of indoor environments for mobile robots," in *Proceedings of the IROS 2007 Workshop: From Sensors to Human Spatial Concepts (FS2HSC)*, San Diego, CA, USA, November 2007, pp. 25–32.

[3] G.-J. M. Kruijff, P. Lison, T. Benjamin, H. Jacobsson, and N. Hawes, "Incremental, multi-level processing for comprehending situated dialogue in human-robot interaction," in *Symposium on Language and Robots*, Aveiro, Portugal, 2007.

[4] H. Holzapfel, D. Neubig, and A. Waibel, "A dialogue approach to learning object descriptions and semantic categories," *Robot. Auton. Syst.*, vol. 56, no. 11, pp. 1004–1013, 2008.

[5] D. Lowe, "Distinctive image features from scale-invariant keypoints," *International Journal of Computer Vision*, vol. 60, pp. 91–110, 2004.

[6] B. Berlin and P. Kay, *Basic Color Terms: Their Universality and Evolution.* Center for the Study of Language and Inf., March 1999.

[7] K. Gapp, "An empirically validated model for computing spatial relations," in *KI '95: Proceedings of the 19th Annual German Conference on Artificial Intelligence.* London, UK: Springer-Verlag, 1995, pp. 245–256.

[8] A. Loutfi, S. Coradeschi, M. Daoutis, and J. Melchert, "Using knowledge representation for perceptual anchoring in a robotic system," *"Int. Journal on Artificial Intelligence Tools"*, vol. 17, pp. 925–944, 2008.

[9] A. Loutfi, S. Coradeschi, and A. Saffiotti, "Maintaining coherent perceptual information using anchoring," in *The Nineteenth International Joint Conference on Artificial Intelligence (IJCAI '05)*, Edinburgh, Scotland, 2005, pp. 1477–1482.

[2] Due to PEIS-home space restrictions the robot is not able to position it self far enough in order to observe the whole couch or the whole television set

Special Session on Novel and Emerging Technologies

Intelligent Environments 2009
V. Callaghan et al. (Eds.)
IOS Press, 2009

doi:10.3233/978-1-60750-034-6-223

WADS: A Web Anomaly Detection System

Manuel García-Cervigón, Juan Vázquez
Technical University of Catalonia

Abstract. Nowadays, the Web has evolved into a mandatory business channel. Online banking is a good example of how millions of costumers rely on virtual channels for business transactions . Nevertheless due to multiple scandals regarding security flaws, it becomes complicated moving a business from a physical scenario to the digital world. Therefore, security applications become highly necessary. Monitoring systems like HIDS intend to create a more reliable scenario for companies but because number of sessions linked to e-banking Web servers it is barely impossible to detect fraud in real time. We propose a novel method for detecting anomalies in e-banking services by integrating efficient clustering systems based in sequence alignment and graph mining.

Keywords. Anomaly detection systems, Web mining

1. Introduction

Online-banking has become increasingly popular in the recent years. Although the first online services appeared in the early 80's, people's fear to fraud delayed the growth of these kind of services. Nowadays, millions of users make their transactions through the Internet trusting to the alleged security provided by antispyware and antivirus and the confidence on the bank detections systems.

The truth is that unfortunately antivirus regular updating is still a pending job for most of users and few solutions have emerged in order to detect and react against many attacks that can easily be obfuscated to both client and server security applications.UK payments association APACS estimates that online fraud increased from £22.6m in 2007 to £52.5m in 2008.

Although authentication systems have been improved from the old user/password to two factor authentication, they may become useless in many fraud scenarios.

On the bank side, incident detection systems (IDS) have been historically installed, but again, the poor effectiveness show that new focuses are needed. Signature detection systems are based on the comparison of certain information, normally URLs, with a data base of signatures representing known attacks. On the other hand anomaly detection systems (ADS) are able to detect known and unknown attacks by analyzing deviations from normal usage. In an e-banking environment, such deviations may be found in the clickstream and the operations made by users. As focused by many experiences three main problems can be found in anomaly detection: high percentage of false positives, high computational costs due to the data mining algorithms, and the dependence on the training data.

2. Click stream anomalies and trojan clusters

Web mining techniques have been normally used for e-commerce purposes such classifying users and implement different kinds of advertisements based on the different user patterns.

It may be of importance to know how a user session differs from a normal behavior in order to find new forms of trojans or a session performed by a hacker. Although it could be possible to find a navigation profile per user, it seems more efficient to compare new sessions with general profiles and therefore clustering seems to fit in that environment.

It is expected to prove that most sessions of a user will be found in the same cluster or general profile.

As an example, a novel user will spend some sessions surfing the portal while some experienced users may only make loan payments.

In order to perform a live detection, it is necessary to compare each new session with the user regular profile/cluster, that is a sequence of visited pages.

Some problems must be faced in this scenario:

- Clustering algorithms have been developed for continuous data [1][2][3][4] and in this case categorical variables must be compared and a similarity ratio must be found.
- Click stream behaviors may vary. Although each user will be assigned a general profile based in his first analyzed sessions, navigation behaviours can change so tt will be mandatory to periodically study user profile changes. General profiles will be compared to each session and an anomaly scoring will be applied depending on the distance between de user's normal profile and the one fitting the studied session.
- Other variables such the order of pages visited and time spent in each page should also be taken into account.

Sequence alignment has been widely used in genomics in order to find similarities among and sequences.

Although some interesting approaches have been investigated regarding the use of categorical variables with continuous based algorithms, sequences alignment distances seems to be an interesting way to solver the order problem [2].

Some investigations [6][7][8] have already taken use of sequence alignment for session clustering but there is a lack of analysis regarding the upper layer information of a session, that is, what is the user actually doing, what operations are been executed.

K-order Markov models will be extracted out of each cluster to better extract normality models for each general profile. K-order Markov techniques are useful to predict the next page to be visited from the information regarding the last k pages visited before.

Although it has been found that some trojans are capable of learning behaviors of an infected user, this technique is not widely spread and the same fraudulent patterns are expected to be found as far as clickstream and the time between clicks is concerned in most of the sessions belonging to an specific trojan. If the similarity distances to the regular clusters are far enough new clusters will show up.

When can then expect two types of clusters: the first related to regular user navigation patterns and the second one that hopefully will include sessions grouped by type of trojan.

3. Graph mining and anti-fraud heuristics

The increasing use of semi-structured data such as, XML, texts or trees benefited the use of data mining, but the amount of information grows exponentially and new ways of structuring data such as topological structures have emerged in order to better understand some environments [9]. Nowadays, the results expected from a query tend to be some relationships more than a list of entities.

As stated before, the amount of information to study and the need to have analyzed within milliseconds is an important issue in online-banking. Information regarding the money transactions made within a session is also a valuable source of information that must be correlated with the results extracted from the clickstream anomaly detection system.

In order to rapidly analyze each transaction the information is copied to Graphs Based Systems, where different types of nodes, new efficient relationships and levels of abstraction can be made in order to reduce the time to perform a query and manage different heuristics.

DEX [10] has been chosen as the graph storing system due to the high performance and the possibility of integrating different types of information sources. The query system facilitates the insertion of heuristics.

Moving data to nodes and edges involve some issues when e-banking transactions are handled. Information must be simplified into nodes, edges and attributes. For instance, different types of account identifiers must be merged into one type of node. Moreover, new information can be extracted: we can establish relation from account nodes to the countries nodes they pertain.

The graph system should be capable of creating new rules based on the analysis of click stream anomalies, that is, every time a anomalous clickstream is detected, the operations made during that session are compared to ones from other anomalous clickstreams with certain similitude.

Operations made during regular sessions are also important to update the different edges (transactions) among nodes (accounts) and the thresholds.

After analyzing different fraud techniques some basic heuristics have been included in order to study transaction validity in real time:

- Direct relationship. If the source and destination have been involved in previous transactions, no input will be added to the anomaly score.

- Family nodes relationship. Having a graph based forest it becomes in easy routine to find the number of account edges between source and destination. Depending on the distance between accounts, an anomaly scoring will be added.

- Transaction amount. Each account should have a transaction mount associated. The amount involved in a transaction should be within a threshold automatically updated and based in last non-anomalous transactions from the source account. The amount of transactions are studied by searching all the edges of a node.

- Money Mule's presence. The money mule's technique consists in convincing someone (the mule) to sign up for a new bank account and withdraw an amount of money after some transactions are made from hacked accounts to the mule's new account. Normally there is little time between the transactions and the moment the mule gets a phone call in order to withdraw the money. The automatic analysis of the number of account nodes that just generated edges to the mules account node as well as the period of time between the transaction and the withdraw can give a rapid idea of the presence of mules, that is, accounts from the same country as the source used to transfer money that will afterwards be again transferred from the mule account to a foreign country in a few amount of transactions.

- Level of suspiciousness. A Page Rank like algorithm has been developed in order to manage a level of suspiciousness per account node. If a node has been involved in an anomalous click stream session, a suspiciousness score is assigned. The level of suspiciousness can increase if the account is targeted by other suspicious accounts, that is, a virus like spreading is made.

Each heuristic has its own anomaly weight will be set to one if the heuristic threshold came over is and a final score will show the level of normality of the operations of a session.

We can define the final score as the sum of all weighted partial scores.

Equally, the operation normality scoring must be merged with the clickstream normality scoring in order to define decisions.

4. Future Work

Although partial experimentation has been done with synthetic data , real information is being anonymized in order to perform final experiments. The design of the system is completely finished, but test data is needed in order to establish the thresholds more accurately.

Neural Networks should be used in order to evaluate new costumer variables regarding the configuration of heuristics but data protection and privacy must be taken into account in order formulate investigations in an environment where mostly all variables belong to personal information sets.

References

[1] Er Strehl, Joydeep Ghosh, Raymond Mooney, *Impact of Similarity Measures on Web-page Clustering*, Workshop on Artificial Intelligence for Web Search, 2000

[2] Yue Xu, Li-Tung Weng, *Improvement of web data clustering using web page contents*, Intelligent information processing, 2004

[3] Xuanhui Wang, Dou Shen, Hua-Jun Zeng, Zheng Chen, Wei-Ying Ma , *Web Page Clustering Enhanced by Summarization*, Conference on Information and Knowledge Management , Proceedings of the thirteenth ACM international conference on Information and knowledge management , 2004

[4] Morteza Haghir Chehreghani, Hassan Abolhassani, Mostafa Haghir Chehreghani, *Improving density-based methods for hierarchical clustering of web pages*, Data & Knowledge Engineering, 2008

[5] Alberto P. García-Plaza, Víctor Fresno, Raquel Martínez, *Web Page Clustering Using a Fuzzy Logic Based Representation and Self-Organizing Maps,* Proceedings of the 2008 IEEE/WIC/ACM International Conference on Web Intelligence and Intelligent Agent Technology - Volume 01 , 2008

[6] Weien Wang, Osmar R. Zaïane, Clustering Web sessions by Sequence Alignment, Proceedings of the 13th international workshop on DEXA, 2002.

[7] Arindam Banerjee, Joydeep Ghosh, *Clickstream Clustering Using Weighted Longest Common Subsequence,* Proceedings of the Web Mining Workshop at the 1st SIAM Conference on Data Mining, 2001

[8] Chaofeng Li , Yansheng Lu, *Similarity Measurement of Web Sessions by Sequence Alignment,* 2007 IFIP International Conference on Network and Parallel Computing Workshops, 2007

[9] R. Angles and C. Gutiérrez, *Survey of graph database models*. Technical Report TR/DCC-2005-10, Computer Science Department, Universidad de Chile, 2008

[10] N. Martínez-Bazán, V. Muntés-Mulero, S. Gómez-Villamor, J. Nin, M. Sánchez-Martínez and J. Larriba-Pey, *DEX*: High-Performance Exploration on Large *Graphs* for Information Retrieval, Proceedings of 16th ACM Conference on Information and Knowledge Management, 2007

Intelligent Environments 2009
V. Callaghan et al. (Eds.)
IOS Press, 2009

doi:10.3233/978-1-60750-034-6-228

A Service Oriented Architecture Combining Agents and Ontologies Towards Pervasive Adaptation

Christos GOUMOPOULOS[a,1] and Achilles Kameas[a, b]
[a] *Research Academic Computer Technology Institute, DAISy group, 26500 Rion, Patras, Hellas*
[b] *Hellenic Open University, 23 Sahtouri Str., 26222, Patras, Hellas*

Abstract. Contemporary software technologies complying with the Service-Oriented Architectural (SOA) paradigm, such as OSGi, UPnP, and the Web services do not meet on their own the adaptability and interoperability challenges of the Ambient Intelligence (AmI) environments. In this paper we present a solution based on the combination of the SOA model with Agents and Ontologies. The agent approach complements the SOA infrastructure by providing high level adaptation to user's tasks, as an intelligent control layer above SOA. Ontologies are used to tackle the semantic heterogeneity that arises in AmI spaces and provide to agents a common repository of system knowledge, policies and state.

Keywords. ambient ecology, agents, SOA, adaptation, ontology

1. Introduction

Ambient Intelligence (AmI) is a paradigm that puts forward the criteria for the design of the next generation of UbiComp environments [11]. In this context we have introduced the *Ambient Ecology* (*AE*) metaphor to conceptualize a space populated by connected devices and services that are interrelated with each other, the environment and the people, supporting the users' everyday activities in a meaningful way [5].

In the context of the EU funded R&D project ATRACO [6] we aim to extend the AE concept by developing a conceptual framework and a system architecture that will support the realization of adaptive and trusted AEs which are assembled to support user goals in the form of *Activity Spheres* (*ASs*). Our approach is based on a number of well established engineering principles, such as the distribution of control and the separation of service interfaces from the service implementation, adopting a SOA model combined with intelligent agents and ontologies. Agents support adaptive planning, task realization and enhanced human-machine interaction while ontologies provide knowledge representation, management of heterogeneity, semantically rich resource discovery and adaptation. ATRACO ASs are dynamic compositions of distributed, loosely-coupled and highly cohesive components that operate in dynamic environments.

Therefore the architecture and the system we propose operate in an AmI environment, which is populated with people and an AE of devices and services. Our

[1] Corresponding Author.

basic assumption is that the AE components are all autonomous, in the sense that (a) they have internal models of their properties, capabilities, goals and functions, and (b) these models are proprietary and "closed", that is, (i) they are not expressed in some standard format and (ii) they can only be changed by the owner components. However, each component can be queried and will respond using a standardized protocol.

Previous research projects have applied the SOA paradigm to support dynamic service composition [1] or have combined SOA with ontologies to form a conceptual framework [9]. Most research efforts that have contributed to adaptation of ubiquitous applications during migration across different pervasive computing environments [10] provided little or no support for adaptation based on context information. Other research provided support for adaptation based on context information [1]. In other research efforts, ontology techniques, such as merging and mapping have been adopted, but they all use ontologies as static objects. ATRACO architecture builds upon previous research by supporting a multi-dimensional pervasive adaptation functionality into AmI spaces. Besides SOA a novel mechanism is proposed to achieve the different kinds of adaptation centered upon the management of knowledge, which is encoded in multi-layered ontologies, which are used by intelligent agents.

In the next section we will present the main concepts underlying our approach. In Section 3 we discuss the research and design challenges that the proposed architecture should tackle. In Section 4 we outline the architecture in the form of basic components and describe their role towards meeting the adaptability and interoperability requirements previously established. Finally our conclusions are given.

2. ATRACO World Model

The concepts discussed below constitute a critical subset of the ATRACO conceptual framework defined for building AmI applications.

Concept	Description
Ambient Ecology (AE)	The set of heterogeneous artefacts with different capabilities and provided services that reside within an Intelligent Environment (IE).
Activity Sphere (AS)	It is formed to support an actors' specific goal. An AS represents both the model and the realization of the set of information, knowledge, services and other resources required to achieve an individual goal within an IE. The concept of AS is a "digitization" of the concept of "bubble" used by the psychologist Robert Sommer [12] to describe a temporary defined space that can limit the information coming into and leaving it.
Intelligent Environment (IE)	A territory that has both physical properties and offers digital services. It is the container of AE. ASs are instantiated in an IE using the resources provided by its AE.
Artefact	A tangible object which bears digitally expressed properties; usually it is an object or device augmented with sensors, actuators, processing, networking unit etc. or a computational device that already has embedded some of the required hardware components.
Actor	Any member of AE capable of setting and attaining goals by realizing activities. Within the AE actors are users or agents.
Goal	Each actor may have its own set of goals and plans to achieve them. A goal is described as a set of abstract tasks, which is described with a task model.
Task Model	It may be *abstract* or *concrete*. An abstract task model describes what should

Concept	Description
	be done, without details of how it should be done or by the use of what kind of modality; these are described in the corresponding concrete model. The abstract task model may also contain several decomposition rules modelled as a set of subtasks.
Local Ontology(LO)	Each member of the AE stores locally descriptions of its properties, services and capabilities. It is a sub-class of the class Ontology
Sphere Ontology (SO)	The SO results from the LO of those AE members that are required to achieve the AS's goal based on the resolution of its task model. Apart from device and service ontologies, it may contain user profiles, agent rule bases and policies. It is another sub-class of the class Ontology.
Agent	A software module (is a kind of actor) capable of pursuing and realizing plans in order to achieve specific goals based on tasks. It includes three types of agents: *Task Agent* (e.g., *Fuzzy systems based Task Agent* or *FTA*), who manipulates sensors and actuators in order to realize specific tasks; *Planning Agent* (*PA*), who resolves an abstract task hierarchy into concrete tasks using the resources of the AE; and *Interaction Agent* (*IA*), who manages user-system interaction using a mixed-initiative dialogue model.
User	The actor that uses the available services and devices in order to perform a task. When a user performs a task, this can be subdivided into different activities. Users use devices, which provide them with services. Devices run these services in a physical environment (context). Users use these services according to personal conditions (user profile) and within a physical context.
Aim	It is attributed to a user; it is decomposed into a set of interrelated goals, which are distributed to the components of the AS.
Policy	Actors specify high-level rules for granting and revoking the access rights to and from different services. Examples of policy ontologies are privacy policy ontology, interaction ontology and conflict resolution policy ontology
Service	The entity which describes the service offered by a device.
Device	The entity that has physical/digital properties and offers a specific service.
Resource	A resource can be the *space*, an *entity*, or a *component*, such as managers (e.g. Ontology Manager, Sphere Manager) or other basic components.

The basic terms and concepts of the ATRACO world model are encoded in the ATRACO Upper Level Ontology (ULO). In general, ontology is used as the means to share information among heterogeneous parties in a way that is commonly understood [7]. An ontology is a network of concepts and entities, which can be associated with different types of relations (the most common being the hierarchical association, or is-a relation). More concrete (or domain) ontologies contain also instances of these entities with specific properties and values. More powerful ontologies contain constraints and rules that cause inferences for the entities. Figure 1 illustrates in UML representation the AS domain model which is also encoded as ontology in the ATRACO ULO.

3. Research and Design Challenges

Initial requirements, captured with applications scenarios, were used as input for a process of abstraction which allowed the identification of a set of challenges that must be addressed, in order to design adaptive pervasive systems. These challenges are listed in the following, together with the approach we have adopted in ATRACO in order to deal with them.

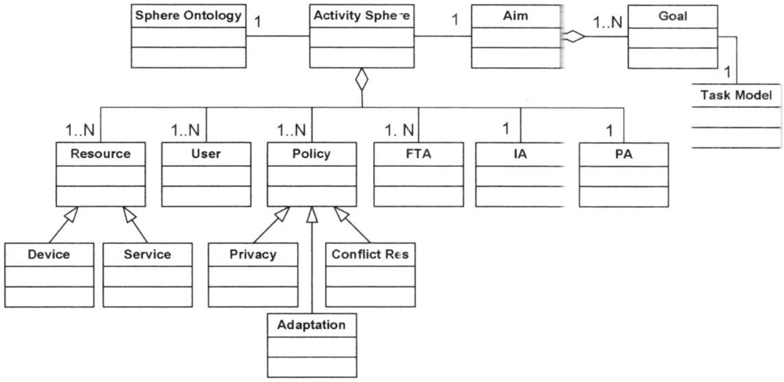

Figure 1. Activity Sphere domain model (part of ATRACO ULO)

3.1. Assemble/Dissolve Applications

Actors must be able to assemble and dissolve pervasive computing applications in the form of collections of resources, in order to achieve their goals. Such an action should be possible for both users or and software agents.

In the ATRACO system level, a service agent, called *Sphere Manager*, is defined that generates service compositions based on a detailed task model that is generated for the given goal. Other agents (*Planning Agent* and *Interaction Agent*) are involved when a human actor participates in the composition process guiding the composition to enable the user to perform activities in the way she wishes to do. A *Sphere Ontology* is defined by aligning the local resource ontologies using the ATRACO ULO (ULO will be explained in the next subsection). An *Ontology Manager* is defined as a separate component to provide access to the Sphere Ontology.

3.2. Adaptability

In ATRACO, at the AE level, the system supports the realization of the same AS in different IEs. At the same time, the system adapts to changes in the configuration of the AE (i.e., a new device joining, a device going out of service, etc.). At the task level, the system realizes the tasks that lead to the achievement of user goals using the resources of the AS. The artefacts also adapt to the uncertainties associated with the changes in the artefacts characteristics, context as well as changes in the user(s) preferences regarding these artefacts and their operation. Another dimension of adaptation concerns the interaction between the system and the user, in order to tailor the degree of system transparency to each specific user. A further dimension of adaptation is related to the network adaptation to allow devices and services to be used seamlessly by the ATRACO system and to simplify the discovery, management and access of networks in the home as well as in corporate environments.

We argue that in order to achieve complete pervasive adaptation in IEs, any infrastructure should provide adaptation in several forms: *functional adaptation* (the realization of the same AS in different AmI environments); *structural adaptation* (the persistent achievement of the goal when changes on the type of the available resources occur); *semantic adaptation* (changes in semantic models in order to deal with any disturbance that would affect meaning); *behavioral adaptation*, where the application logic is changed as a result of learning - specialized as artefact and user behavior model adaptation); *user interaction adaptation* and *network adaptation*.

3.3. Semantic Heterogeneity

As mentioned above, the deployment of any pervasive application over an IE requires the orchestration of available services in the IE. In the general case, we expect that these will be heterogeneous and that they would not adhere to a specific protocol. However, the system must ensure the interoperability and the user centric operation of the pervasive application. In order to achieve these we use ontologies to encode local resource information and user preferences. Then, to ensure the user centric operation of the sphere, we compose a SO by matching the LOs of the sphere resources, so as to ensure interoperability between the various services and devices. Moreover, the pertinent policy ontologies are matched to ensure correct sphere operation. Finally, the user profile ontology is matched to ensure that the sphere will serve a specific user goal (and its associated tasks) and take into account the user preferences and experience. The SO encodes the information and knowledge necessary for sphere operation; it also provides context representation for the components of the sphere.

Ontology matching is the process of finding relationships or correspondences between entities of two different ontologies. Its output is a set of correspondences between two ontologies, that is, relations holding, or supposed to hold, between entities of different ontologies, according to a particular algorithm, or individual. Current techniques for ontology matching require access to the internal structure of constituent ontologies, which must be verified for consistency, and result in static solutions (a set of mappings or a new ontology), which in addition have to be stored somewhere. But an AS is a transitory, dynamically evolving entity, composed of heterogeneous, independent, usually third-party components. That is why we choose to apply the ontology alignment technique [4].

3.4. Trustworthiness

Privacy and trust are two important properties of the design space of any pervasive application. Several approaches use centralized components or third party control; these approaches do not scale and imply loss of privacy and autonomy.

In ATRACO, we chose to control our resources through policies rather than fabricate new mechanisms. We follow a distributed scheme where each resource has its own polices encoded as ontologies using a declarative approach. This approach decouples the declarative policy expression from the mechanism that ensures the desired behavior. Identity Management and privacy policies encoded in a privacy policy ontology constitute the main mechanisms to address privacy and trust. Polices expressed as a set of factual and behavioral specifications that are binding on every computing element and resource within an AmI space can be specified independently, leaving dependencies and conflict management to a reasoning framework.

3.5. Sharing of Resources

Sharing of resources may lead to conflicts between pervasive applications. For handling such conflicts, it is necessary to apply specific policies. In ATRACO, an extension of the scheme discussed in the previous section is applied. A policy-based resource management scheme is defined and conflict resolution policies are encoded as ontologies. Such policies are used to describe and restrict the way each one resource is used, and to perform resource allocation when multiple applications have similar requests. Another use is to describe how the usage of one resource is dependent on (or constrained by) another.

4. Architecture

The ATRACO approach uses a Service-Oriented Architecture (SOA) that enforces a clear distinction between service interfaces and implementation. SOA has been envisioned as an evolution of the component-based architectures centred on the concept of service [1]. The SOA approach appears to be a convenient architectural style for realizing adaptable and reconfigurable systems.

In ATRACO we propose a combination of the SOA model with Agents and Ontologies. The agent approach complements the SOA infrastructure by providing high level adaptation to user's tasks, as an intelligent control layer above SOA. Agents have a local knowledge base that contains rules about the control of their behaviour and they may communicate and exchange messages which contain a high degree of semantics because of internal processing. In ATRACO, agents support adaptive planning, task realization and enhanced human-system interaction. Ontologies are used to tackle the semantic heterogeneity that arises in AmI spaces and provide to agents a common repository of system knowledge, policies and state.

On a system level ATRACO services will be provided by a set of system components. The role of each component has been specified so that their interaction can provide the adaptability and trust we envision as part of the realization of ASs. The architecture that supports the realization of ASs is shown in Figure 2. General functional blocks were defined, and the illustrated component diagram shows the overall functional blocks that were identified.

The Sphere Manager (SM) forms or dissolves an AS for a specific user goal. The SM is responsible for initializing the other system components and operates as an event service to them. SM implements a semantic-based discovery mechanism based on Sphere Ontology (SO) to resolve the services in the concrete plan provided by the Planning Agent (PA) to actual executable services provided in the AmI space. The SM composes an executable service workflow and implements an Execution Management and Control mechanism which is responsible for the execution of services on top of the SOA layer. An important role of the SM is to support the structural adaptation of ASs providing for the persistent achievement of the goal when changes on the type of the available resources occur. To achieve this, it monitors the state of execution of the task workflow and might change the composition of services in case of any problem.

The Ontology Manager (OM) matches local (i.e. device, agent, policy and user profile) ontologies according to the task model that fulfils the sphere goal. The OM is responsible for creating, dissolving and generally managing the SO and responding to queries regarding the SO. To that end, the OM maintains rules and provides inference services. The OM interacts with all system components.

One or more (depending on the goal complexity) Fuzzy Task Agents (FTAs) oversee the realization of given tasks within a given AmI space. These agents are able to learn the user behavior and model it by monitoring the user actions. The agents then create fuzzy based linguistic models which could be evolved and adapted online in a life learning mode [8]. The FTA maintains its own local knowledge base, which is initially formed by the SM, based on the task model and the SO.

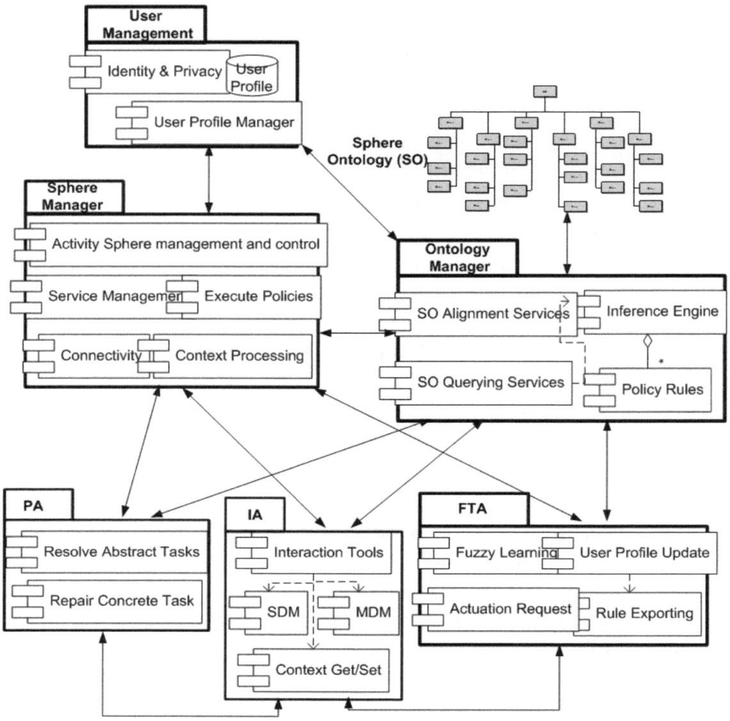

Figure 2. ATRACO component architecture

The Interaction Agent (IA) provides a multimodal front end to the user. Depending on the SO it optimizes task-related dialogue for the specific situation and user. The IA may be triggered both by the FTA and the PA to retrieve further context information needed to realize and plan tasks by interacting with the user. The IA uses two managers: Speech Dialogue Manager and Multimodal Dialogue Manager.

User Management (UM) contains the necessary functionality to provide, validate, and manage the information that forms the individual user's identity (user data) within the supported computing environment. More specifically, as a system component UM will include functionality for the provisioning, management and storage of multiple user identities, user specific preferences, and profiles.

The proposed approach has been validated in a real environment (iSpace facility). A prototype system has been developed based on the main components specified in the architecture and several basic components for controlling the environment (e.g., control of lights, HVAC, music player) and a sample AS was realized as outlined in Figure 3.

5. Conclusion

In this paper we have outlined an approach towards pervasive adaptation based on the combination of the SOA model with agents and ontologies. The mechanism we propose to achieve the different kinds of adaptation implied by this approach is centred round the management of knowledge, which is encoded in multi-layered ontologies, which are used by intelligent agents. The ongoing and future work will report on the full evaluations of the ATRACO system with multiple users and in various testbeds.

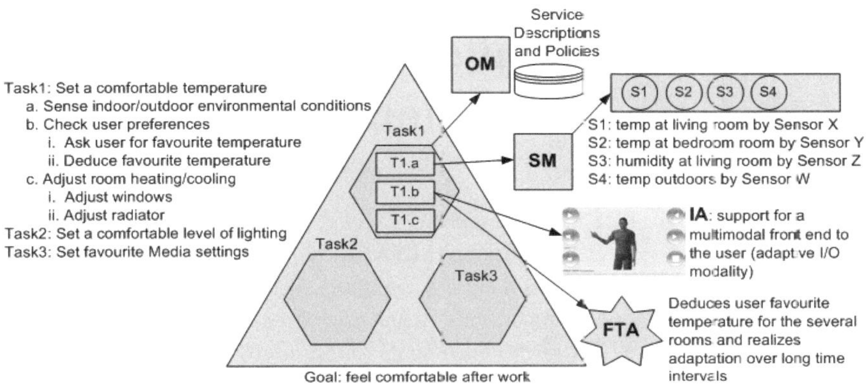

Figure 3. ATRACO AS for the user goal "Feel comfortable after work"

Acknowledgement

The research described is partly supported by the ATRACO (ICT-216837) project.

References

[1] Ambient Intelligence for the Networked Home Environment project, website: http://www.hitech-projects.com/euprojects/amigo/

[2] H. Chen, T. Finin, and A. Joshi, A context broker for building smart meeting rooms. In Proc. AAAI 2004, pp. 53–60.

[3] T. Erl, *Service-Oriented Architecture : Concepts, Technology, and Design*, Prentice Hall PTR, 2005.

[4] J. Euzenat, A. Mocan, F. Scharffe, Ontology alignments: an ontology management perspective, in: Ontology Management: Semantic Web, Semantic Web Services, and Business Applications, Springer, New-York (NY US), pp. 177-206, 2008.

[5] C. Goumopoulos and A. Kameas, Ambient ecologies in smart homes, *The Computer Journal*, doi: 10.1093/comjnl/bxn042, 2008.

[6] C. Goumopoulos, A. Kameas, H. Hagras, V. Callagan, M. Gardner, W. Minker, M. Weber, Y. Bellik, and A. Meliones, ATRACO: Adaptive and Trusted Ambient Ecologies, Self-Adaptive and Self-Organizing Systems, Workshop on Pervasive Adaptation (PERADA), IEEE CS, pp. 96-101, 2008.

[7] T.R. Gruber, Towards Principles for the Design of Ontologies Used for Knowledge Sharing, *International Journal of Human-Computer Studies*, 43(5/6), pp. 907–928, 1995.

[8] H. Hagras, F. Doctor, V. Callaghan, and A. Lopez, An incremental adaptive life long learning approach for type-2 fuzzy embedded agents in ambient intelligent environments, IEEE Transactions on Fuzzy Systems, 15(1), pp. 41–55, 2007.

[9] PalCom project, website: www.ist-palcom.org

[10] A. Ranganathan, C. Shankar, and R. Campbell, Application polymorphism for autonomic ubiquitous computing, *Multiagent Grid Systems*, 1(2), pp. 109-129, 2005.

[11] P. Remagnino and G. L. Foresti, Ambient Intelligence: A New Multidisciplinary Paradigm, *IEEE Transactions on Systems, Man, and Cybernetics*, 35(1), pp. 1- 6, 2005.

[12] R. Sommer, Personal Space: The Behavioral Basis of Design, Prentice Hall Trade, Englewood Cliffs, N. J., 1969.

Intelligent Environments 2009
V. Callaghan et al. (Eds.)
IOS Press, 2009

doi:10.3233/978-1-60750-034-6-236

Creating an Ambient Intelligent Environment with an Emotion-Aware System

Sherief MOWAFEY [a], Alexander SCHMITT [b], Hani HAGRAS [a] and Wolfgang MINKER [b]
[a] *The Ambient Intelligence Center, Faculty of Media Engineering and Technology, German University in Cairo, Egypt*
sherief.mowafey@student.guc.edu.eg & hani.hagras@guc.edu.eg
[b] *Institute for Information Technology, University of Ulm, Germany*
alexander.schmitt@uni-ulm.de & wolfgang.minker@uni-ulm.de

Abstract.
In this paper, we describe a novel approach of combining an emotion voice aware system with a fuzzy logic system to develop embedded agents aimed at creating an Ambient Intelligent Environment (AIE). This combined approach was evaluated in the GUC intelligent Classroom (iClass) which a is real world AIE testbed. The developed system aims to control the user environment on his behalf while taking into account the user's emotions. The agent learns online the fuzzy membership functions and rules from the user monitored actions to generate an agent that models the user behavior in an educational AIE like the iClass. The agent then operates in a life long learning mode where the agent can be adapted over long time intervals to the user's changing desires and preferences.

Keywords. Embedded Agents, Emotion Recognition, Fuzzy Logic Systems, Ambient Intelligent Environments.

1. Introduction

With the ever-increasing number of miniaturised and computerised artefacts and devices, information about state, location, roles and much more becomes transparent and with the pervasiveness of networks this information is made available to anyone, anywhere and at any time. These efforts of advancing technology to pervade everyday life and to foster wide availability and acceptance yielded in 1991 when Mark Weiser introduced his vision of ubiquitous computing in his famous seminal article "The Computer for the 21st Century" [14]. Ubiquitous computing eliminates the notion of a personal computer as an isolated computational identity [8]. The vision is that many heterogeneous computerised artefacts and devices will complement each other and through interconnections seamlessly work together to support efficient assistance for the user.

Ambient Intelligence (AmI) is a new paradigm that puts forward the criteria for the design of the next generation of ubiquitous computing environments [12]. In the AmI paradigm, intelligent computation will be invisibly embedded into our everyday environments through a pervasive transparent infrastructure (consisting of a multitude of sensors, actuators, processors and networks) which is capable of recognizing, responding and adapting to individuals in a seamless and unobtrusive way [6]. AmI offers great opportunities for an enormous number of applications such as health care, the efficient use of energy resources, public buildings, leisure and entertainment, education, etc.

Detecting emotions plays an important role in the control of AIEs. Various work has been done in the field of emotion detections, In Germany, Burkhardt et al. [2] have developed a voice portal prototype that integrate the recognition of anger in the caller's voice during a voice call with a machine agent and as a result the caller is transferred to a human agent. In USA, D' Mello et al. [4] developed an agile learning environment approach that is sensitive to a learner's affective state integrating a state-of-the-art, non-intrusive, affect-sensing technology with the AutoTutor system. Work at University of Illinois developed an intelligent tutorial system (ITS) to provide a computer-based environment for education in science and technology, including emotion recognition of children [16]. Pittermann et al. [11] have developed a spoken dialogue system which is capable of recognizing emotions from speech signals.

In this paper, we aim to embed intelligent agents in the user AIEs in order to control the user environments on their behalf. We will present a novel emotion detection system combined with fuzzy logic based learning and adaptation technique for agents that could be embedded in AIEs. This proposed agent learns and models the user behavior in controlling the environment. In addition, the agent adapts in a life-long mode over long time durations to the user changing desires and preferences to realize one of the main requirements of ambient intelligent systems [5]. We have performed experiments in which our intelligent agent has learned the user actions and his emotion during an extended experiment of three consecutive days in the intelligent Classroom (iClass) in the German University in Cairo (GUC) which serves as real world AIE test bed.

The rest of this paper is structured as follows. In Section II, we will introduce our test bed for AIEs which is the iClass. Section III presents a description of the life-long learning and adaptation technique AOEFA employed with the developed agent. Section IV presents the emotion recognition component of the agent. Section V presents the experiments and results. Finally Section VI provides the conclusion.

2. The GUC iClass

The iClass is one of the real world AIE testbeds located in the Ambient Intelligence Center (AMIC) at the German University in Cairo. The iClass is aimed at educational AIEs. The other testbed is the intelligent Studio (iStudio) which is an intelligent radio broadcasting station aimed at realizing AIEs for entertainment and media. The iClass as shown in Figure 1(a) is a test bed for AIEs. The iClass looks like any other class room containing normal furniture as in a usual room, including the desks, chairs and a white smart board. However, the iClass consists of a large number of embedded sensors, actuators, processors and a heterogeneous network [7]. The iClass is a multiuser space that can be used through different teaching activities.

As shown in Figure 1(a), there is a standard multimedia PC that combines a projector with a flat-screen monitor and another digital monitor, which is placed outside the class to inform students with the starting and ending time, name of the lecture topic and any

(a) (b)

Figure 1. (a) The iClass, (b) The external digital monitor of the iClass.

other announcements related to the given course as shown in Figure 1(b). The iClass can also take the automatic attendance of students where there is a long range RFID reader which can read the IDs of the students without the need to swipe these IDs. The RFID can also detect the lecturer once he enters the classroom and then the system checks with the automatic timetable to upload the slides and lecture material for the given lecture. The system also opens an empty notepad in the smart board which the lecturer can use and edit during his lecture. At the end of the lecture, this notepad file is saved together with the lecture notes in the course intranet so that the students can access these materials afterwards. This will save the students writing after the tutor and will enable them to have full concentration during the lecture.

Figure 2 shows the iClass network infrastructure. The iClass is equipped with a weather station. The iClass has also various sensors and actuators which consists of the following: time of the day and date, internal light level sensor, external light level sensor, internal temperature sensor, external temperature sensor, humidity sensor and a presence sensor. The effectors can control the following in the class: six dimmable spot lights, two window blinds and heater/cooler air conditioning. These sensors and actuators are obscured in the class with the intention that the user should be completely unaware of the intelligent infrastructure of the class, which is required to reach the aim of AIE [5].

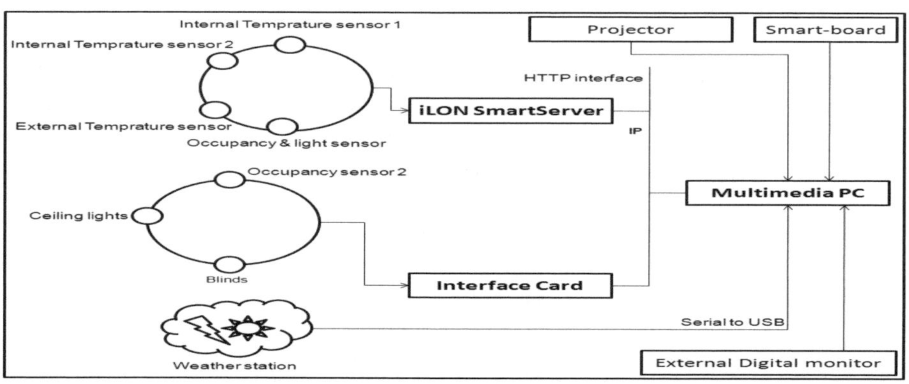

Figure 2. The logical network infrastructure of the iClass.

Figure 3 shows photos of the various sensors and weather station located with the iClass. The weather station is installed outside the iClass to measure the outdoor humidity, cloud cover, wind direction, wind speed, rain fall, solar radiation and the outdoor temperatures.

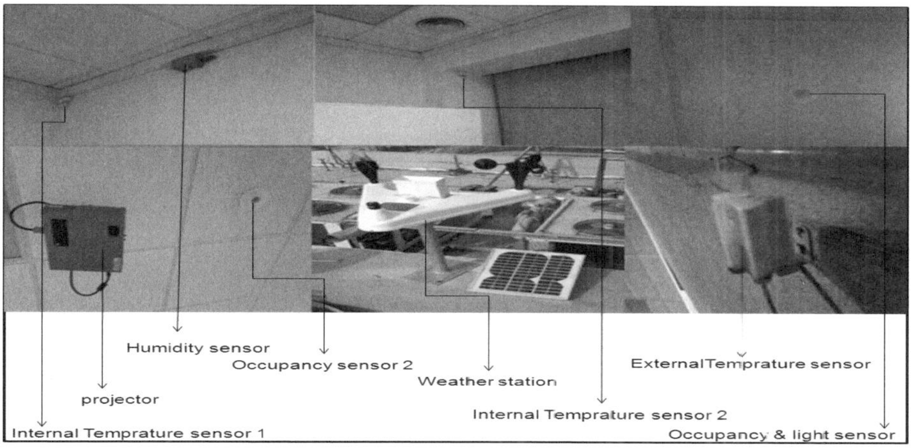

Figure 3. The iClass sensors, weather station and multimedia video projector.

Any networked computer that can run as standard Java process can access the iClass, thus, this multimedia PC can also act as an interface controlling the devices inside the class room as shown in Figure 4(a). Equally, the interface can be accessed from wireless devices such as the mobile phone shown in Figure 4(b) using a 3G interface, which is a simple extension of the web interface, which can monitor and control the iClass directly. Currently our fuzzy agent learning mechanism and interface operates from the standard multimedia PC in the iClass.

3. Adaptive Online Emotion Fuzzy Agent (AOEFA)

Fuzzy Logic Controllers (FLCs) are credited with being adequate methodologies for designing robust systems that are able to deliver a satisfactory performance when contending with the uncertainty, noise and imprecision attributed to real world settings [5]. In addition, a FLC provides a method to construct controller algorithms in a user-friendly way closer to human thinking and perception by using linguistic labels and linguistically interpretable rules. Thus FLCs can satisfy one of the important requirements in AIEs by generating transparent models that can be easily interpreted and analyzed by the end users. Moreover, FLCs provide flexible representations which can be easily adapted due to the ability of fuzzy rules to approximate independent local models for mapping a set of inputs to a set of outputs. As a result, FLCs have been used in AmI spaces as in [5], [13] and [12].

Our proposed technique, which is entitled Adaptive Online Emotion Fuzzy Agent (AOEFA), is an unsupervised data driven method for extracting fuzzy membership functions and fuzzy rules from data, in order to achieve a fuzzy controller that will learn and model the user's behavior. The data is collected by monitoring the user in the environ-

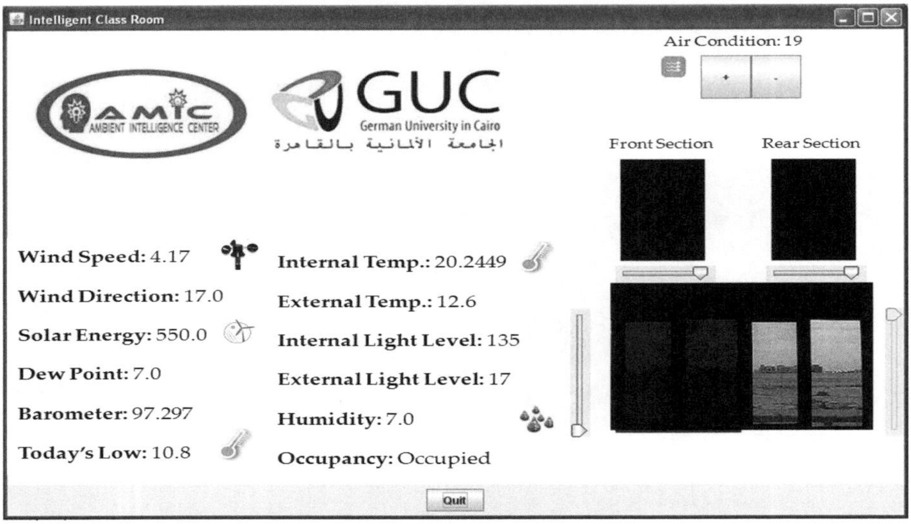

(a)

(b)

Figure 4. (a) PC interface, (b) Mobile phone interface.

ment for a certain period of time. The learned FLC allows for an interface mechanism that produces output control actions based on the present state of inputs. In addition, our adaptive FLC will manage and control the environment on behalf of the user and will also allow the rules to be adapted and extended online, assisting a life-long learning technique as the environmental conditions changes and the user behavior adjust with it. AOEFA consist of five phases:

1) Monitoring the user's behavior and capturing the input/output data with addition of the emotions that are associated with their actions.
2) Extraction of fuzzy membership functions from the data.
3) Extraction of the fuzzy rules from the captured data.
4) Controlling the environment by the agent.
5) Life-long learning and adaptation mechanism.

In this algorithm, the last two phases are control loops that once started, receive inputs as either monitored sensor changes. They produce the right control response based on the set of learned rules or user action requests that cause the membership functions and the learned rules to be adapted before an appropriate output control response take place. Figure 5 shows a flow diagram of the five phases.

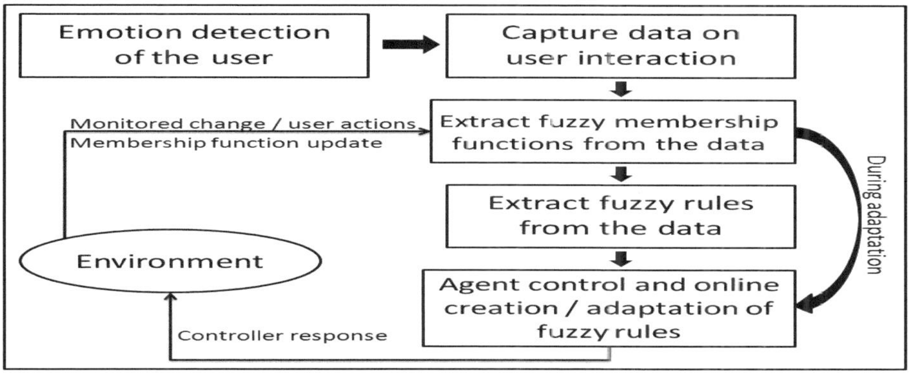

Figure 5. Flow diagram showing the five phases of AOEFA.

3.1. Capturing Input/Output Data

The agent initially observes the user actions in the environment. Every five minutes the agent records a "snapshot" of the current inputs (sensor states) in addition to recording a seven seconds audio file and also the outputs (actuator states with the new values of whichever actuators were modified by the user). All the recorded "snapshots" are gathered together over a certain period of time so that the agent learns as much as it can from the user behavior within the environment.

3.2. Fuzzy Membership Function Extraction

In order to start the FLC, it is important to be capable of categorizing the input/output data into fuzzy membership functions which enumerate the raw crisp values of the actuators and sensors into linguistic labels, such as normal, low, or high [5]. AOEFA is based on learning the individual behavior of the user, so as a result it requires these membership functions to be initiated from the user's input/output data saved by the agent.

A fuzzy-C-means (FCM) approach is used for extracting fuzzy membership function from the user's data. This algorithm is a data clustering algorithm in which each data point belongs to a cluster or a class to a degree specified by a membership degree [15]. We classify various dataset of instances (such as Internal light level, external light level, etc.) into five classes. Figure 6(b) shows a classification graph of the internal light level extracted after the agent finished the learning process in the iClass. The following function shows the calculation of each cluster center of the five clusters:

$$V_{ij} = \frac{\sum_{k=1}^{n} \mu_{ik}^{m'} \cdot x_{kj}}{\sum_{k=1}^{n} \mu_{ik}^{m'}} \qquad (1)$$

where V_i is the ith cluster, which is described by m coordinates and can be arranged in vector form, $V_i = \{V_{i1}, V_{i2}, ..., V_{im}\}$. μ_{ik} is the membership function of the kth data point in the ith class, $m' \epsilon$ is the weighted parameter which has a range $m' \epsilon$ [1,∞) and j is a variable on the coordinate space, i.e., $j = 1, 2, ..., m$ [15].

3.3. *Fuzzy Rule Extraction*

In order to extract our fuzzy rules, we combine the set of membership functions with the input/output data so we can model the behavior of the user. This fuzzy rule extraction approach used by the AOEFA is based on the version of AOFIS reported in [5]. This is a multi-input multi-output technique for extracting fuzzy rules from the recorded data. Fuzzy regions are constructed from the antecedents and consequents of the rules of the fuzzy sets [5].

3.4. *Agent Controller*

As soon as the agent extracted the membership functions and the set of rules from the user multi input/output data. The FLC now has learned the human behavior using the intelligent environment. Therefore, the FLC can start controlling the environment on behalf of the user with respect to his needs and emotions. The FLC starts to monitor the inputs of the environment (e.g., sensors, human emotion and weather station) and as a result it controls the actuators based on the rule model built before from the user interactions that has been made during the learning process in the intelligent environment. Figure 6(a) shows a block diagram of FLC, which consists of four major parts fuzzification interface, Fuzzy rule base, Fuzzy inference engine and deffuzification interface. In our agent, we will use singleton fuzzification, max-product composition, product implication and height defuzzification.

3.5. *Online Adaptation and Life-Long Learning*

In the above subsection, we have explained how the agent can learn the user behaviors. Nevertheless, the user may need to make some alteration to tune the system or their behavior might change as the user's desires changes over time. Consequently, our agent needs to adapt to the user new desires in a small amount of time and in a non-instrusivective way [5]. Whenever the user is not pleased with the agent's control actions, he can easily override the agent's control by altering the manual control of the system. When such a process acquires occurs the agent starts adapting the rule model online, either by adding new rules to the rule base if they did not occur before or the agent replaces the old rules with new ones. When such a process acquires the agent starts adapting the rule model online, either by adding new rules to the rule base if they did not occur before or replaces the old rules with new ones. Hence, the FLC takes a "snapshot" of the current situation and passes the sensors and the actuators parameters to the system, so it calculates the rule weight in order to determine if the product of the membership functions of the antecedents is greater than zero. If yes, it either adds to it the rule base with the consequent part as it did not exist before, or this means that the rule is fired and the agent needs to change the consequent part of such a rule found in the rule base to the new action taken from the user. In addition, the system also updates the fuzzy membership functions by introducing the adaption parameters of the user controls to the agent. For instance, if the user is not satisfied with the agent control over the environment and as a result the user adapts the environment according to his desires. Consequently, the agent takes a "snapshot" of the current situation of the environment and repeats the FCM algorithm process to achieve better clusters. This process is finished before updating the rule base

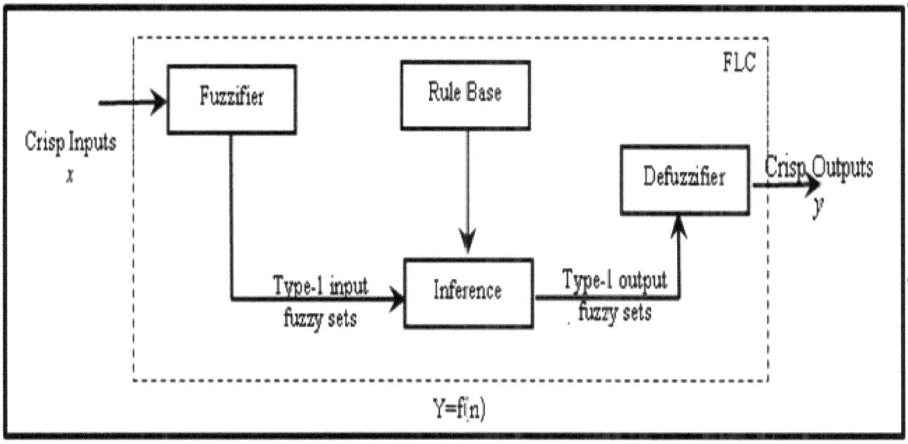

(a)

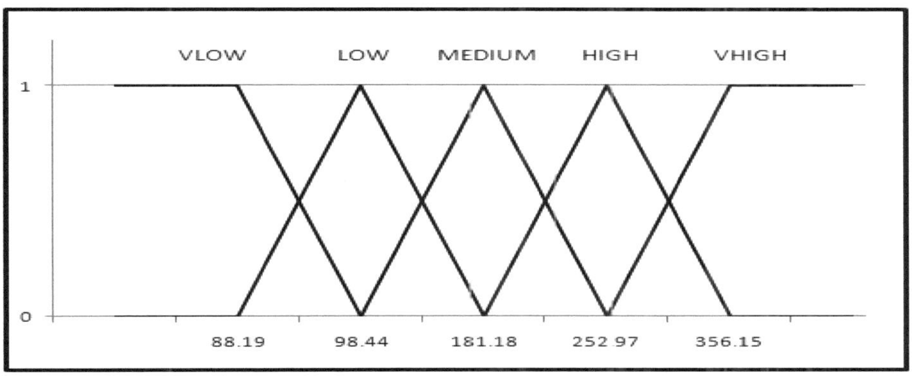

(b)

Figure 6. (a) Block diagram of the FLC, (b) Membership function for internal light level of the iClass.

as revealed in Figure 5, in order to achieve the best model for the user behavior. Figure 7(b) shows a graph that had occurred after the user has adapted the system parameters to his new behavior.

4. Emotion Recognition

The behavior of the Intelligent Classroom is not only limited to weather conditions, time etc. but incorporates also the emotional state of the Lecturer. In discrete time intervalls, the agent captures a snapshot of seven seconds of the current conversation and estimates the emotional state. Prior to classification, the speech signal is subject to an acoustic and prosodic feature extraction with the phonetic software Praat [1]. Currently, only "angry" and "neutral" as emotions are considered since a more differentiated emotion recognition would lead to lower accuracies [9]. In multi-speaker environments where potentially not only the teacher is speaking, a distinction of more than 2-3 emotions is hardly performable.

From the seven seconds snapshot we extract mean value, power, harmonicity, voiced pitch, pitch, intensity as well as their statistical derivatives like deviation, mean, minimum, maximum and the range. Further we extract prosodic features like jitter points, Mel frequency cepstral coefficients and formants. When Praat returns undefined values for pitch, we assume that the captured audio file does not contain speech. and no emotion recognition is performed. For building the emotion model that is employed for the classification we utilized the Berlin Database of Emotional Speech [3] comprising 15 speakers and a Rule Learner from the data mining framework RapidMiner [10]. Training has been performed with angry and neutral utterances.

5. Experiments and Results

In this section two kinds of experiments will be discussed. Firstly, we introduce the FLC experiment, where the agent has learned the user behavior and desires through a certain period of time. Secondly, we present the emotion recognition experiment that distinguished between two different emotions without a profound definition or a clear description of those emotions.

5.1. FLC

A user occupied the iClass for three consecutive days. The agent identifies the user using the iClass by typing his user name to the system. The user used the multimedia PC to monitor and control the iClass whenever he was unpleased with the environment current status. We recorded the history of the user decisions in a journal and we wrote a small parsing tool to convert the text file containing the fuzzy rules sets into a readable format. At the end of the experiment, the agent learned 7487 rules that model the user behavior in the duration of 3 consecutive days (72 hours) as shown in Figure 7(a) and we examined the rules by comparing the readable format rules with user's journal parameters to guarantee that the agent has successfully learned the behavior the user was anticipating.

5.2. Emotion recognition

To provide a rough benchmark for emotion recognition, we evaluated the emotion recognizer with 9 different speakers. Each proband was told to record three random utterances in an angry and neural manner respectively, leading to 27 neutral and 27 angry utterances. Only 11 utterances of the system were correctly classified as "angry", the remaining 43 utterances were categorized as "neutral". Presumably, the model was not appropriate so we trained the emotion recognizer again, this time with a subset of 10 speakers from the Berlin Corpus. Testing has been performed with the remaining 5 speakers (72 neutral and 74 angry utterances) resulting in a very high classification accuracy of 95,21%. Merely 7 neutral utterances have been falsely classified as angry. A closer look to the generated rule model in Listing 1 that is responsible for classification and which is generated during training explains this behavior.

```
if voiced_pitch_mean > 222.025 then anger
if intensity_minimum > 33.827 then neutral
```

```
else anger
```

Listing 1: Rule Model for Anger Recognition based on the Berlin Database of Emotional Speech generated with RapidMiner

The model turns out to be amazingly simple and explains the failure of the field tests: All falsely classified user utterances contained a larger intensitiy_minumum value than 34. This might be explainable due to a different microphone or noise which does not meet the conditions in the clean studio environment of the Berlin Corpus. We thus envision the creation of a real-life, non-acted corpus, that will be captured under real conditions in the intelligent class room to allow for a more robust emotion recognition.

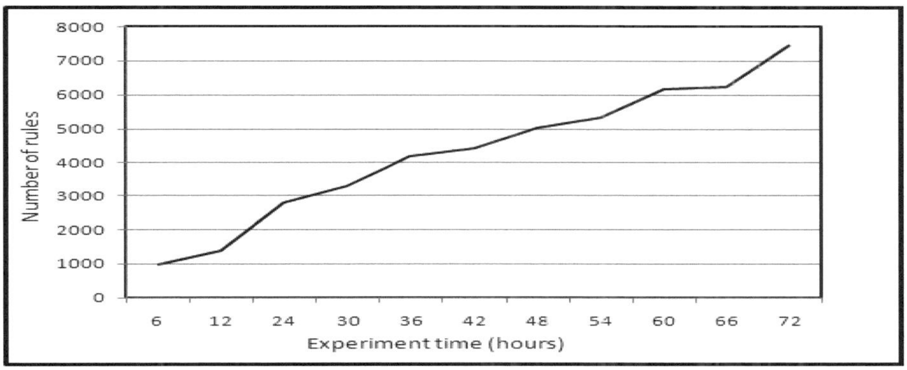

(a)

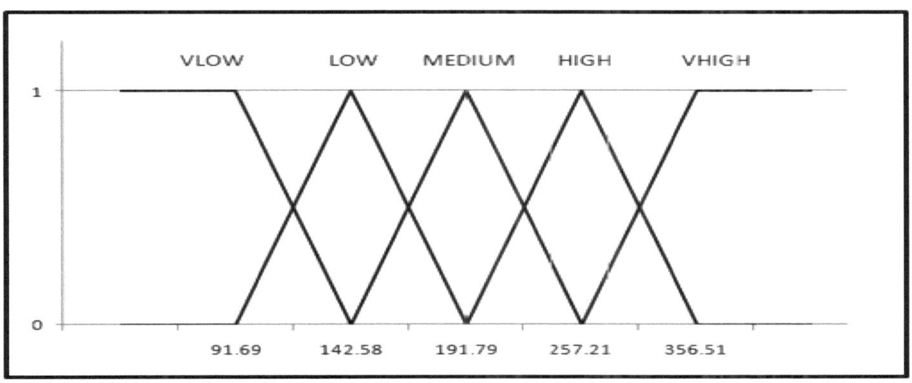

(b)

Figure 7. (a) The rules learned plotted against experiment time, (b) Updated membership function for internal light level of the iClass.

6. Conclusion

In this paper, we introduced a novel technique combining emotion recognition with fuzzy learning and adaptation controller for agents that can be embedded in AIEs. We hope that this will be a step forward in the realization of the ambient intelligence vision.

Our agent built a FLC that learned the user behavior and emotions and it was adaptive as it allowed the learning behavior of the user to be adapted online easily for life-long mode. The agent was responsive to the user's commands. The iClass environment infrastructure was built in transparent embedded devices that achieve the ambient intelligence vision. Therefore the user was surrounded by invisible responsive ambience intelligence that control the environment on his behalf according to his behavior and emotions.

In the future we intend to do more experiments in order to enhance the emotion model and add more emotions to the agent. We also intend to build the learning part of the emotion model using artificial neural networks (ANN).

References

[1] P. Boersma, "Praat, a System for Doing Phonetics by Computer", *Glot International*, Vol. 5, no. (9/10), pp. 341-345, 2001.

[2] F. Burkhardt, M. van Ballegooy, R. Englert, and R. Huber, "An Emotion-Aware Voice Portal", in *Electronic Speech Signal Processing ESSP,* 2005.

[3] F. Burkhardt, A. Paeschke, M. Rolfes, W. F. Sendlmeier, and B. Weiss, "A Database of German Emotional Speech", in *Proceeding European Conference on Speech and Language Processing (EUROSPEECH)*, pp. 1517-1520, September 2005.

[4] S. K. D'Mello, S. D. Craig, B. Gholson, S. Franklin, R. Picard, and A. C. Graesser, "Integrating Affect Sensors in an Intelligent Tutoring System", In *Affective Interactions: The Computer in the Affective Loop Workshop at 2005 International conference on Intelligent User Interfaces* , (pp. 7-13) New York: AMC Press.

[5] F. Doctor, H. Hagras, and V. Callaghan, "A Fuzzy Embedded Agent-Based Approach for Realizing Ambient intelligence in Intelligent Environments", *IEEE Transaction on Systems, Man and Cybernetics, Part A: Systems and Humans* Vol. 35, no. 1, pp. 55-65, January 2005.

[6] K. Ducatel, M. Bogdanowicz, F. Scapolo, J. Leijten, and J. Burgelman, "Scenarios for Ambient Intelligence in 2010", *IST Advisory Group Final Report,* European Commission, February 2001.

[7] H. Hagras, V. Callaghan, M. Colley, G. Clarke, A. P. Cornish, and H. Duman, "Creating an Intelligent Environment using embedded agents", *IEEE Intelligent Systems,* pp. 12-19, November/December 2004.

[8] R. Mayrhofer, "An Architecture for Context Prediction," *PhD Thesis*, October 2004.

[9] H. Meng, J. Pittermann, A. Pittermann, and W. Minker, "Combined speech-emotion recognition for spoken human-computer interfaces", *IEEE International Conference on Signal Processing and Communications,*pp. 1179-1182, November 2007.

[10] I. Mierswa, M. Wurst, R. Klinkenberg, M. Scholz, and T. Euler, Yale: Rapid prototyping for complex data mining tasks. In L. Ungar, M. Craven, D. Gunopulos, and T. Eliassi-Rad, editors, *KDD '06: Proceedings of the 12th ACM SIGKDD international conference on Knowledge discovery and data mining*, pp. 935-940, New York, NY, USA, August 2006.

[11] J. Pittermann and A. Pittermann, "Integrating emotion recognition into an adaptive spoken language dialogue system", in *Proceeding 2nd IET International Conference on Intelligent Environments,* Vol. 1, Athens, Greece, pp. 197-202, July 2006.

[12] U. Rutishauser, J. Joller, and R. Douglas, "Control and Learning of Ambience by an Intelligent Building", *IEEE Transaction on Systems, Man and Cybernetics, Part A: Systems and Humans*, Vol. 35, no. 1, pp. 121-132, January 2005.

[13] A. Sherwin, "Internet home offers a life of virtual luxury", *The Times,* pp. 10, November 1999.

[14] M. Weiser, "The Computer for the 21st Century", *Scientific American,* 1991.

[15] C. Wichasilp,W. Wiriyasuttiwong, and K. Kantapanit, "Design of Fuzzy Logic Controllers by Fuzzy c-Means Clustering", *Thammasat International Journal of Science and Technology,*Vol. 8, no.2, pp. 12-16, April-June 2003.

[16] T. Zhang, M. Hasegaw-Johnson, and S. E. Levinson "Children's Emotion Recognition in an Intelligent Tutoring Scenario", Interspeech 2004.

Intelligent Environments 2009
V. Callaghan et al. (Eds.)
IOS Press, 2009

doi:10.3233/978-1-60750-034-6-247

A Speech Recognizer Based Intelligent Agent For Ambient Intelligent Environments

Amr Elfaham, Hani Hagras
The Ambient Intelligence Center, Faculty of Media Engineering and Technology, German University in Cairo, Egypt

Abstract.
In this paper, we will present a new approach for agents embedded in Ambient Intelligent Environments (AIEs). The new approach is based on integrating a speech recognizer with an adaptable intelligent agent for controlling the AIE on the user behalf. The intelligent agent is based on fuzzy systems which is able to learn the user(s) behavior and adapt in a lifelong learning mode to the user changing desires and preferences. The speech recognizer based agent was tested in the German University in Cairo intelligent Classroom (iClass) which is a real world AIE testbed. The results have validated the proposed approach with real experiments involving real users in the iClass.

Keywords. Fuzzy Systems, Embedded Agents., Ambient Intelligence, speaker recognizer

1. Introduction

Recent years showed an accelerated growth in the usage of different microprocessors in the various daily tasks. This evolution has fueled the research in the Ambient Intelligence (AmI) field [1], [2]. In the AmI vision, instead of controlling a surrounding environment manually by adjusting different conditions to match the desired personal needs; a new approach is tackled by automating the surrounding by relating an action to a reaction. AmI involve combining the manual control of the user(s) environment with learning the user behavior through a digital environment that is aware of the user actions and context and that is able to control the environment on the user(s) behalf. [2].

In order to achieve a highly intelligent environment to improve quality of life, the AmI system has to be aware and responsive to the user(s) actions and needs [3], [4]. It is a necessity to have the system invisible in nature which will assist in achieving a natural and desired environment [4]. The AmI system has to program itself to adjust desired conditions without any interference from the user on the running system when configuring the surrounding environment to satisfy their personal needs [5]. These AmI requirements could be achieved by learning the user behavior through embedding intelligent agents in the user(s) environment [4]. The embedded intelligent agents keep track of the surrounding user(s) conditions/context and monitor the user(s) actions given the surrounding conditions/contexts. The agents learn then the user(s) behavior and control the AIE on the user behalf. Such agents should also adapt the learnt user(s) behavior in a lifelong learning mode (over long time intervals) to the changes in the environments and the user desires and preferences.

A natural human interface for controlling AIEs is through speech commands [6]. Speech commands appear as more natural human interfaces which can substitute the keyboard and mouse interfaces to adjust the preferred user needs on the surrounding environment [6], [7]. In this speech based approach, the AIE is controlled by originally relating each predefined voice command to a specific action in the system. Simple replacement to the keyboard or mouse by selecting among different utterances was not the main target in the implementation process for this approach. Involving the user into a dialogue to gather information, correct misunderstandings, enhance speech recognition was the main target for this approach [6].

In [6] an approach was reported where the user in an AIE wears wireless lapel microphone connected to a speech recognizer that picks the input speech signal [6]. To get the computer attention, user pauses input speech for a moment and then says "computer" in a high voice. After calling for the computer attention, the computer will move from the sleep state to pay attention for any incoming speech from the user. The user starts to get involved into a dialogue with the room. If the utterance is recognized by the room, an audible click which indicates that statement was understood is provided [6]. The room is capable of realizing utterances that will provide the user with predefined services. Utterances like "What appointments do I have today" and "what's the weather forecast for New York City" should be understood and answered by the computer. The Intelligent Room project in [8] was capable of addressing users via the Festival Speech Synthesis [8]. Utterances that are given by the system are shown on a scrollable LCD to make sure that the user gets the spoken utterance if the synthesized utterance were not understood by the user.

Another approach was reported in [9] for multiuser spoken language systems. In this approach, two human users are sitting in front of a computer and there are three cameras placed around the users. The first camera is located directly in front of the first user's (A1) face. The second camera is capturing what the first cannot see. The third camera is used to capture the whole scene. The camera placed in front of A1 is used to detect the direction of the eye gaze to know if the user is looking to the computer or the dialogue partner while speaking. As the project was not completely integrated, it was simulated as closely as possible to the true function therefore the system used the "Wizard of OZ" technique [9] to simulate the project main phases: speech recognition, natural language understanding and dialogue managing. An avatar was integrated and displayed on the screen all the time during the dialogue to represent the system's face. It acts as a third partner interacting with the users. It was added to test the users behavior about accepting the system as a third dialogue partner [10].

In [11], Cesta et al. have presented Lucia which is a cognitive Robot that contains software and sensors to predict and prevent hazardous behavior as well as monitoring the adherence to behavior constraints and the provision of a basic service for user interaction. This human – robot interaction requires speech recognition and synthesis. Lucia is capable of verbal skills, speech recognition which was achieved with the Sonic Speech Recognition System while speech synthesis occurs through the talking head made of a laptop consisting of sensors, laser range finder, stereo camera, directional camera and computational resources [11].

These abovementioned approaches were only embedding a speech recognizer inside an intelligent environment. However, using a speech utterance in the learning procedure for the controlling system was not implemented.

In this paper, we will present a new approach for agents embedded in Ambient Intelligent Environments (AIEs). The new approach is based on integrating a speech recognizer with an adaptable intelligent agent for controlling the AIE on the user behalf. In the proposed approach, the user will give voice commands which will be passed the fuzzy logic based engine which will allow the system to learn the user behavior through speech. When the user applies a certain adjustments and gives a voice command. The voice command is translated into text by an imported java speech recognition library (SPHINX) [12]. The sphinx library exports the input voice command to the system. It divides the input voice commands into two parts. The first part is concerned with the action that should be taken regarding a certain device. The second part is the device which the computer will apply the action defined in the first part on. Actions can be defined as open, close, increase and decrease. The device that can be controlled are the front/rear lights, front/rear curtains and the air conditioning. The system automatically relates the adjustments to the voice command to pass it to the fuzzy engine to learn the new rule and save it on the system. The proposed agent is able to learn the user behavior and adapt in a life long learning mode to the user changing desires and preferences. The speech recognizer based agent was tested in the German University in Cairo (GUC) intelligent Classroom (iClass) which is a real world AIE testbed. The results have validated the proposed approach with real experiments involving real users in the iClass.

The next section will introduce the GUC iClass and describe its layout. Section 3 will present the user identification by speech. Section 4 will present the integration of the fuzzy agent with the speech recognizer. Section 5 will presents the experimental results. Finally Section 6 presents the conclusions and future work.

2. The Intelligent Classroom

In the Ambient Intelligent Center located at the German University in Cairo we have two testbeds. The first testbed is an intelligent Classroom (iClass) used for experimenting with Ambient Intelligence (AmI) educational applications. The second testbed is an intelligent Radio Studio (iStudio) located at the campus for experimenting with Ambient Intelligence (AmI) media and entertainment applications. The iStudio uses digital broadcasting to transmit radio signals all over the campus.

The iClass is the testbed where all our experiments took place. All the sensors and display devices are connected to the multimedia PC that is present inside the iClass. There is a single LCD monitor located outside the classroom to display information about the session that is currently taking place inside the classroom. Information like the course name, lecturer name and announcements concerning the course are displayed at the LCD monitor during the session. The iClass is capable of taking the student attendance using long range RFID that identifies the students present inside the classroom without the need of passing the IDs individually for each student who enters the session. Once the lecturer enters the room, the system detects the lecturer information through the personal RFID and automatically updates the session information in the multimedia PC to update the outside LCD with the current session information and loads the lecturer rules file to adjust the classroom according the favorite adaptations that were previously adjusted by the lecturer.

The multimedia PC is also connected to:

1- LCD monitor located inside the classroom Figure 1(a).
2- A projector and a Smart Board to display the course content.
3- iLON smart server (as shown in Figure 1(b)) to get the output values for the different sensors embedded all over the room (connected to a Lonworks network).
4- Interface Card (as shown in Figure 1(c)) that is connected to control the different actuators in the iClass (ceiling light level, blinds level and AC adjustments).

(a) (b) (c)

Figure 1(a) Smart board and internal LCD (b)ILON smart server (c) Actuators interface card

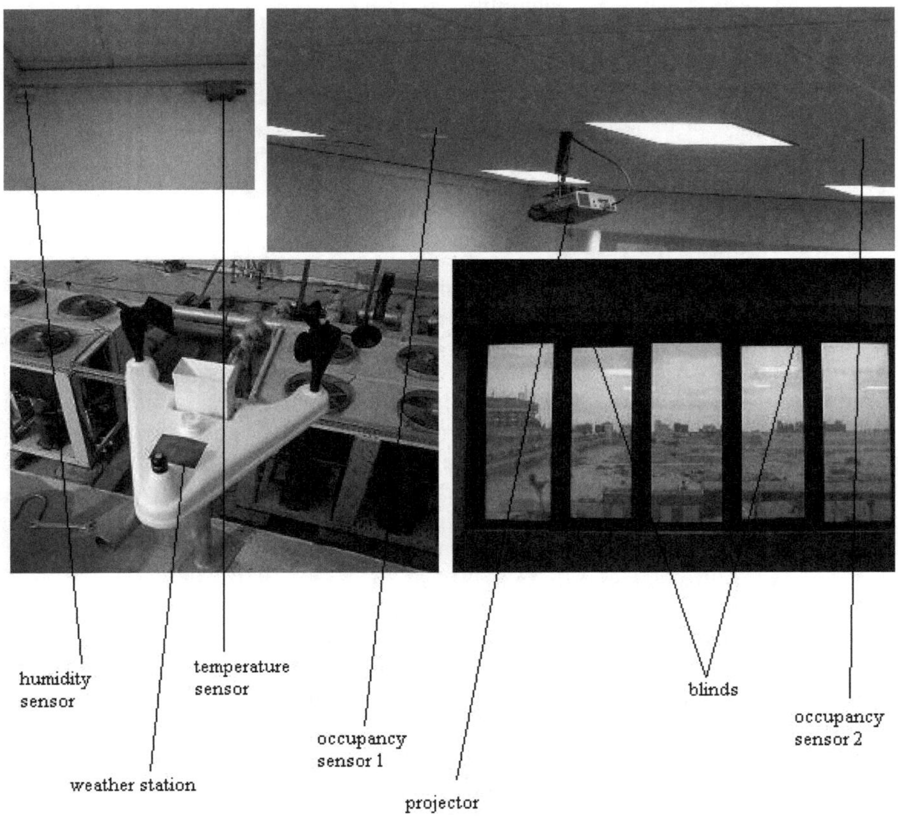

Figure 2. Sensors embedded all over the room + weather station

There are different sensors that are embeded all over the IClass. Sensors are divided into two sections. The first section is concerned with the sensors present inside the class room which includes internal temperature sensor, occupancy sensor, humidity sensor, light level sensor which are embedded all over the walls inside the Intelligent Classroom (as shown in Figure 2). The second section of the sensors is represented by the weather station located on the roof of the building. The weather stations updates the multimedia PC with the latest values for the Wind speed, Wind direction, Outside temperature value, Humidity, Pressure, Dew point, Solar radiation.

3. User Identification by speech

Each user has a unique behavior and attitude when using the surrounding environment facilities. Thus we can say that for each user there is a unique set of rules in order to achieve the user needs by adjusting the preferable setting on the surrounding environment. For each user there are previously recorded wave files saved on the system as a sample to be used later when differentiating between the users. When a user enters the room, a short sentence should be given to the system in order to identify the speaker.

Different combinations are included in the MARF library [13]. The following combination of functions was applied on the saved speech samples in the process of training because it produced high matching points when applied on the input speech:

1- A low pass filter is applied on the input signal to filter the frequency in the range of 0 to 2835 Hz [13].
2- Linear Predictive Coding (LPC) to appraise the windowed section of input speech and to retrieve set of coefficients to approximate the amplitude against the frequency function. That approximation is performed to store a small amount of information containing the replicate results of the Fast Fourier Transform. Information that is strongly required in analysis of speech [13].
3- Euclidean Distance classifier that uses the Euclidean distance equation to find the distance between a two feature vectors. A cluster is finally chosen according to the smallest distance calculated on the given feature vector [13].

When a user enters the classroom, a short sentence should be spoken through the microphone. After saving the sentence as a wave file, the system starts to process the input speech through an imported java library (MARF). The system recognizes now the speaker and is aware of the person who will be using the classroom. The previously saved rules are loaded from the database of rules on the system. The preferred settings will be adjusted automatically according to the surrounding environment conditions that are currently detected through the embedded agents all over the classroom.

An interface is implemented to use the imported speaker recognizer java library (MARF) as shown in Figure 3(a). This is the first screen that will appear for a user once he starts the system. The user starts to record a file. The file is then chosen to be saved as a wave file in the following properties [11]: • Audio Format: PCM signed (WAV); • Sample Rate: 8000 Hz; Audio Sample Size: 16 bit; Channels: 1 (mono); Duration: from about 7 to 20 seconds

The user clicks on the “Recognize” button to pass the saved file to the library to recognize the current speaker. After recognizing the speaker the system starts to load the set of rules that were generated during previous sessions that the user was using the classroom before.

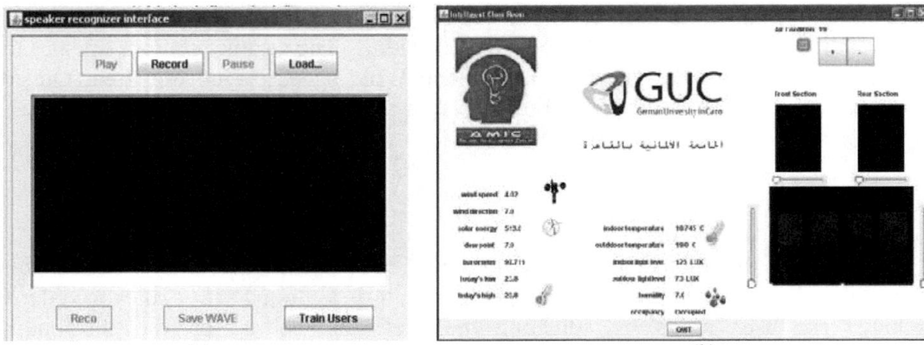

(a) (b)

Figure 3. (a)speaker recognizer interface (b) Graphical user interface that controls the intelligent classroom.

As shown in Figure 3(b), an interface appears immediately after successfully detecting the speaker by processing the speech through the library. The interface shows the different controls that are available to the user to adjust different setting on the intelligent classroom. The user can control the air condition temperature, front and rear lights intensity (from 0 to 100 %), front and rear curtains (from 0 to 100 % open). On the other hand the user is able to monitor the surrounding environmental conditions through the available data shown at the user interface. The user is able to monitor wind speed, wind direction, solar energy, dew point, pressure, indoor temperature, outdoor temperature, indoor light level, outdoor light level, humidity and room occupancy.

4. Integration of the Speech Recognizer with the Fuzzy Agent

There are many sensors that are embedded all over the room. For each sensor there should be a varying range of output values. Three states are applied on the varying output values: low, medium and high. Identifying the range for the output values is a process that is done through the user. After the system recognizes the room user, a short dialogue takes place between the system and the users to get the range of the sensor output values and generates the preferred fuzzy graph; an example for this dialogue will be as follows:

System: Hello.
User: Hello.
System: Please identify the temperature threshold in which you think it's cold.
User: 17
System: Please identify the range of temperature in which you think its medium.
User: 22 – 25
System: Please identify the temperature threshold in which you think it's hot.
User: 30

The system afterward generates the according temperature fuzzy membership graph as shown in Figure 4 that meets the user identified ranges.

The system is aware of any speech given by the user as long as the user is using the room. As many sensors are connected to the system, the microphone is considered one of the inputs to the fuzzy engine. To allow for the speech recognizer calibration, a period of 3 second is given to correct and adjust all the inputs applied to the system. If the speech recognizer detected a wrong voice command, the user will notice that by reading the detected speech on the interface. The user has to give another voice command to remove the old recognized speech in order to save the rule attributes correctly. The user adjusts the room manually and gives a voice command to the system. The system detects the new preferred adjustments and relates them to the voice command. The new rule is created and added to the previously saved set of rules on the fuzzy engine. When the surrounding environment conditions occurs again, the user should give out the same voice command given to train the system to adjust the room automatically to the preferred setting that was previously adjusted manually by the user last time.

In future work, the speaker should speak normally when giving the voice command. It should not be in certain format to make the system able to recognize the given voice command. The parser should be able to process and translate the speech to be able to put it on the right direction when relating the voice command by the manually adjusted settings. The grammar defined in the system should be expanded in order to reach the point that user is talking to the system through a normal human conversation.

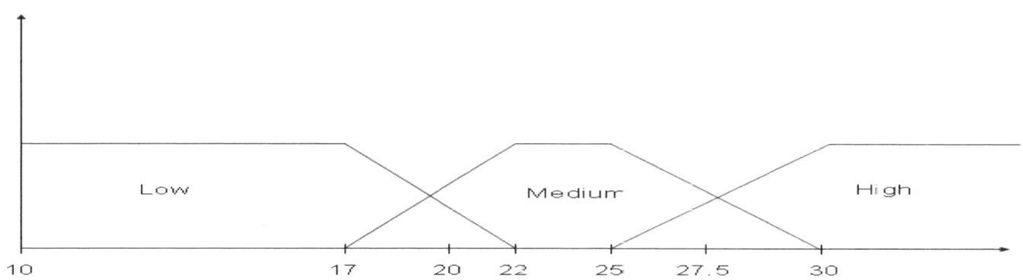

Figure 4. graph generated after the conversation

The fuzzy engine continuously detects the embedded sensor values and generates the fuzzy rules that match the current values that is detected by the sensors. The system then compares the generated rules by the previously recorded ones to apply the new rule if any is detected.

As considering the speech as one of the input sensors, the speech input is converted to the number that is equivalent to the predefined voice commands. Not like other sensors that have low, medium and high regions over the generated output values. Once the voice command number is generated, it will only have one range which is represented in our case as a number. The fuzzy engine gets the matching rules according the surrounding environmental conditions and the given speech command. Membership values are calculated to be able to pass it to the defuzzifier in order to get the fired the rules to meet the user preferred needs. In our agent, we will use singleton fuzzification, max-product composition, product implication and height defuzzification, this formula maps a crisp input n into a crisp output y = f(x) is written as follows:

$$y(x) = f_s(x) = \frac{\sum_{l=1}^{M} y^{-l} \prod_{i=1}^{n} \mu_{F_i^l}(x_i)}{\sum_{l=1}^{M} \prod_{i=1}^{n} \mu_{F_i^l}(x_i)} \quad (1)$$

where M is the total number of rules in the rule base, y^{-l} is the point having the maximum membership in the *l*th rule output fuzzy B^l, $\prod_{i=1}^{n} \mu_{F_i^l}(x_i)$ set is the product of the membership values of each rule's input fuzzy sets, and n is the number of inputs [4]. For multiple outputs, is repeated for each output parameter. The set of membership functions are combined with the input and output data in the process of extracting the fuzzy rules to model user behavior. The membership value for the input speech parameter is equal to one. This fuzzy rule extraction approach is based on the version AOFIS reported in [4]. This is a multi input multi-output technique for extracting fuzzy rules from the recorded data. Fuzzy regions are constructed from the antecedents and consequents of the rules of the fuzzy sets [4].

5. Experimental Results

In our experiments, the user used the intelligent classroom for 15 hours over three consecutive days. The system identified the user through the speaker recognizer who created a new rules profile for the user automatically as it was the first time to use the classroom. During the monitoring phase, the agent recorded different user interaction to adjust the intelligent classroom.

The user had the option to adjust the room in two ways, either by relating a voice command to a rule that will be learned to the system or giving the system a manual command that will be learned by the fuzzy engine to be fired if needed.

The system learned a total of 52 rules over the three days as shown in Figure 5. At the beginning of the experiment, the system had 0 rules saved in the user profile. The rate of learning rules was increasing rapidly at the beginning of the experiment. The system learned 38 rules after first 4 hours from the start of the experiment. The user started to adapt surrounding environment according to own preferences and relating a voice command to these conditions.

On the second day the system kept learning and adding more rules to the user profile. The rate of learning rules was different than the first day. The system learned about 11% of the rules on the second day while it learned 77% on the first day.

On the third day the user was using the system by the rules he applied on previous two days of the experiment. The user was satisfied with the system outputs on the surrounding environment during the experiment. The user almost didn't use the graphical user interface implemented to change any outputs on the intelligent class room.

User had the option to create different outputs at the same conditions by giving different voice commands to the system. This means that the system should apply different output settings on the same surrounding conditions. That can be only done by referring to the user who should give a voice command to decide which set of rules should be fired at that condition.

The user had the option to use the surrounding environment without speech. When the system learned this type of rules, it automatically adjusts the surrounding environments without waiting for a voice command that will be given from the user.

This kind of rules was used in actions that the user will decide the same output every time the surrounding conditions occurs. Using a voice command based rules gave the option to apply different output on the same surrounding environment conditions. When the user wanted to increase the classroom light level he had the option to open the room lights or to open the room curtains.

The speech recognizer accuracy was calculated on two phases. The first phase was done by testing the speech recognizer separately without being connected to the system. The speech recognizer showed an accuracy of 90%. When the speech recognizer was connected to the system, the missing voice commands were calculated during the period of the experiment. The accuracy obtained during the experiment was the same as when the speech recognizer was used without being connected to the system.

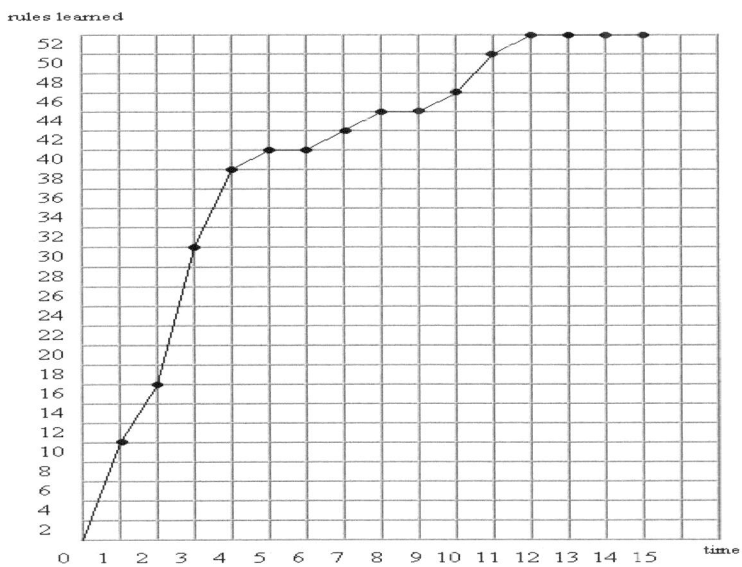

Figure 5. rules learned over time

6. Conclusions

In this paper, we presented a new approach for agents embedded in AIEs. The proposed approach is based on integrating a speech recognizer with an adaptable intelligent agent for controlling the AIE on the user behalf. The intelligent agent is based on fuzzy systems which are able to learn the user behavior and adapt in a lifelong learning mode to the user changing desires and preferences. The speech recognizer based agent was tested in the GUC iClass which is a real world AIE testbed. The results have validated the proposed approach with real experiments involving real users in the iClass.

Experimental results show that adding speech to intelligent systems will decrease the user manual interaction with the graphical user interface. Speech recognition system depends on that test bed as an accuracy of 90% was obtained.

The experiment obtained results show a great decrease on the rate of interaction between the user and the system manually. Rules related to speech and normal rules that was learned by the system was able to create a suitable environment to the user by applying the surrounding environment conditions according to user preferences.

The system should contain both rules, speech based rules and normal rules to give the option to the user to adjust the classroom automatically using the learned rules or by giving a voice command to choose which set of rules should be defuzzified and fired on the surrounding environment.

In the future work, we will be working on increasing the grammar learned in the speech recognizer. It should be a free grammar context in which user can give a speech commands in any format. We will be also working in increasing the speaker recognition accuracy to increase the reliability of the system.

References

[1] V. Callaghan, M. Colley, G. Clarke, and H. Hagras, "Embedding intelligence: Research issues for ubiquitous computing," in *Proceedings of the 1st Equator IRC Workshop on Ubiquitous Computing Environments*, Nottingham, U.K., Sep. 2001, pp. 110–130, September 2001.

[2] H. Hagras, "Embedding Computational Intelligence in Pervasive Spaces," *IEEE Pervasive Computing*, vol. 6, no. 3, pp. 85-89, July-Sept. 2007.

[3] K. Ducatel, M. Bogdanowicz, F. Scapolo, and J. Burgelman, "Scenarios for Ambient Intelligence in 2010, Tech. Rep.," Information Society Technology Advisory Group (ISTAG), Inst. Prospective Technol. Studies (IPTS), Seville, Feb. 2001.

[4] F. Doctor, H. Hagras and V. Callaghan, "A fuzzy embedded agent-based approach for realizing ambient intelligence in intelligent inhabited environments". *IEEE Transactions on Systems, Man, and Cybernetics, Part A*, Vol. 35, no. 1, pp. 55-65, 2005.

[5] H. Hagras, V. Callaghan, M. Colley, G. Clarke, A. Pounds-Cornish and H. Duman, "Creating an Ambient-Intelligence Environment Using Embedded Agents," *IEEE Intelligent Systems*, Vol. 19, No. 6, pp. 12-20, Nov./Dec. 2004.

[6] M. H. Coen, "Design principles for intelligent environments", *Proceedings of the fifteenth national/tenth conference on Artificial intelligence/Innovative applications of artificial intelligence*, pp.547-554, July 1998, Madison, Wisconsin, United States

[7] J. Krumm, S. Shafer and A. Wilson, "How a Smart Environment Can Use Perception", Ubiquitous Computing Group, Microsoft Research, Microsoft Corporation.

[8]A. Black and P. Taylor, "Festival Speech Synthesis System: system documentation (1.1.1)", Human Communication Research Centre Technical Report HCRC/TR-83U. University of Edinburgh. 1997.

[9] P. Strauss, H. Hoffmann, H. Neumann, W. Minker, G. Palm, S. Scherer, F. Schwenker, H. Traue, and U. Weidenbacher, "Wizard-of-Oz Data Collection for Perception and Interaction in Multi-User Environments". *Proceedings of the International Conference on Language Resources and Evaluation* (LREC), Genova, Italy, 2006.

[10] P. Strauss, H. Hoffmann, and S. Scherer. "Evaluation and user acceptance of a dialogue system using wizard-of-oz recordings". *In Proceedings of the third international conference in Intelligent Environments,* Ulm, Germany, 2007.

[11] Cesta, A., Pecora, F., Rasconi, R., Iocchi, L., Leone, R., and Nardi, D., "Lucia: a Cognitive Robot in an Intelligent Environment", *Proceedings of the Workshop on Socially Assistive Robotics*, Philadelphia, PA, USA,2006.

[12] W. Walker, P. Lamere, P. Kwok, B. Raj, R. Singh, E. Gouvea, P. Wolf and J. Woelfel,"Sphinx-4: A Flexible Open Source Framework for Speech Recognition", http://cmusphinx.sourceforge.net/sphinx4/.

[13] I. Clement, S. A. Mokhov, D. Nicolacopoulos and S. Sinclair, "Modular Audio Recognition Framework and Text-Independent Speaker Identification", The MARF Development Group, Montreal,, Quebec, Canada, 2003.

Intelligent Environments 2009
V. Callaghan et al. (Eds.)
IOS Press, 2009

doi:10.3233/978-1-60750-034-6-257

An Adaptive Type-2 Fuzzy Logic Based Agent for Multi-Occupant Ambient Intelligent Environments

Bahaa El-Desouky and Hani Hagras
The Ambient Intelligent Centre, Faculty of Media Engineering and Technology
The German University in Cairo, Egypt

Abstract. This paper presents an enhanced type-2 fuzzy logic based agent that can be embedded in multi-occupant Ambient Intelligent Environments (AIEs). The agent utilizes the power of type-2 fuzzy logic in modeling various types of uncertainties (especially inter-user uncertainties) and the agent non-intrusively learns the collective behavior of the occupants from their individual type-1 profiles. Knowledge about the users' behavior and preferences is encoded in the form of type-2 rules and membership functions. The agent then uses the captured behavior to control the environment on behalf of the users and adapt in the short term as well as to long term changes in the environment or the users' habits. Multiple real world experiments were carried out in the Intelligent Classroom (iClass), (which is based in the Ambient Intelligence Centre "AMIC" at the German University in Cairo (GUC) to evaluate the performance of the agent.

Keywords. Ambient intelligence, type-2 fuzzy systems, learning, agents

1. Introduction

The last few decades have seen a rapid decrease in the cost and size of computing devices going side by side with a reasonable improvement in their computational power. This, along with other factors, made it possible for huge numbers of embedded-processors to find their way into everyday objects like furniture, clothing, electric appliances, even the human body.

Trying to utilize the abundant computing power available around us, the EU IST advisory group proposed the concept of Ambient Intelligence (AmI) [1]; a vision where the emphasis is on greater user-friendliness, more efficient services support, user-empowerment, and support for human interactions. In the AmI vision, people are surrounded by intelligent intuitive interfaces that are embedded in all kinds of objects and an environment that is capable of recognizing and responding to the presence of different individuals in a seamless and unobtrusive way.

According to [2] an Ambient Intelligent Environment (AIE) is a living or a working space that interacts in a natural way and adapts to the user. By natural it's meant in a manner that is natural to the occupant while adaptation refers to the fact that it learns to recognize and adapt itself according to the identity and activity undertaken by the occupant with minimal intervention from the occupant.

Research has been actively going on in the field of AIEs lately. Several initiatives have been done in realizing AIEs including the University of Essex intelligent dormitory (iDorm) [3]. The iSpace is an extension of the iDorm research project where a two bedroom flat is equipped with pervasive computing capabilities and used for the study of intelligent buildings, ubiquitous computing and ambient computing. At MIT, (aire); a core component of the pervasive computing research project oxygen, is dedicated to examining how to design pervasive computing systems and applications for people. In the intelligent room [4] – one of the airespaces, research in device, network and perceptual technologies is carried out to realize the concept of human centric computing. The Georgia Institute of Technology Aware Home Research Initiative [5] is an interdisciplinary research endeavor that addresses challenges facing the future of domestic technologies. It focuses on three application areas namely: Chronic Care Management in the Home, Future Tools for the Home and Digital Entertainment and Media. The MavHome Smart Home [6] project is a multi-disciplinary research project at Washington State University and the University of Texas at Arlington focused on the creation of an intelligent home environment.

A classroom is a good example of a highly dynamic, highly interactive, multi occupant AIE. Examples of activities that take place in a typical classroom can range from lectures where a person lectures a number of attendees aided by the classroom PC(s), a projection device and/or a smart board. The lecturer takes control of the classroom nearly all the time. Another scenario is a group tutorial where the tutor leads a guided discussion about the class topic, frequently polling students for their response and opinions. Students can initiate discussions or lead the classroom for a while too. A third scenario could be a practical session where students work in groups on some assignment collaborating in a peer fashion forming autonomous workgroups that interact from time to time with their tutor. Other scenarios take place that vary in the degree of interaction among students and between students and the tutor. Managing different aspects of the classroom environment like the air conditioning, the light level and operating the classroom facilities (projectors, boards, displays, etc) represents a cognitive load for users and a waste of the class time on tasks irrelevant to the educational activity taking place. Thus, a classroom can greatly benefit from any assistance intelligently managing the environment conditions or coordinating work in the class. That would let the classroom inhabitants focus on more important tasks and increase their in-class productivity. Previous work has been done on realizing intelligent classrooms. Work was reported at the intelligent classroom at InfoLab, Northwestern University [7]. At California State University [8], an intelligent classroom was established where advanced educational facilities allow teachers better control and easier management of the class. Research done at the University Of Reading, UK focused on the evaluation of the effect of intelligent classroom use on the interactive behavior of students [9]. The McGill Intelligent Classroom [10] aims to reduce the complexity of operating electronic classroom presentation technology, automatically generating a multimedia (web-based) version of the class and providing the means for real-time audience response systems especially in large classes. Researchers at the Tsinghua University [11], developed The smart classroom which integrates voice-recognition, computer-vision, and other technologies to provide a tele-education experience similar to a real classroom.

The abovementioned research efforts in the field of intelligent classrooms focus on automating educational tasks or enhancing ease of access to the classroom by means of advanced multimedia technologies. However, to the knowledge of the authors, none of the previous projects tackled the problem of personalizing the classroom to the preferences of its multiple occupants by non-intrusively learning their behavior and applying it to control the environment on their behalf which will be the aim of this paper.

The following section presents the iClass; a unique testbed for AIE research for educational purposes. Section 3, explains our proposed intelligent agent approach. Section 4 will present results acquired from a series of real world experiments that assess the performance of the proposed approach. Finally Section 5 will present the conclusions and future work.

2. The iClass

The intelligent classroom (iClass) is based in the Ambient Intelligence Centre at the German University in Cairo (GUC). The iClass is a real world testbed for AIEs research in the context of educational AIEs. The iClass converts a typical classroom into a context aware, pervasive computing, smart environment. The iClass is richly and invisibly interwoven with a hybrid network of sensors and actuators that provide the ambient user interfaces for its inhabitants. Sensors are fitted in the surroundings of the iClass for acquiring environmental state parameters. The classroom contains a LonWorks based smart sensor network comprised of sensors for a acquiring (inside temperature, outside temperature, humidity, inside light level, outside light level, and occupancy) values.

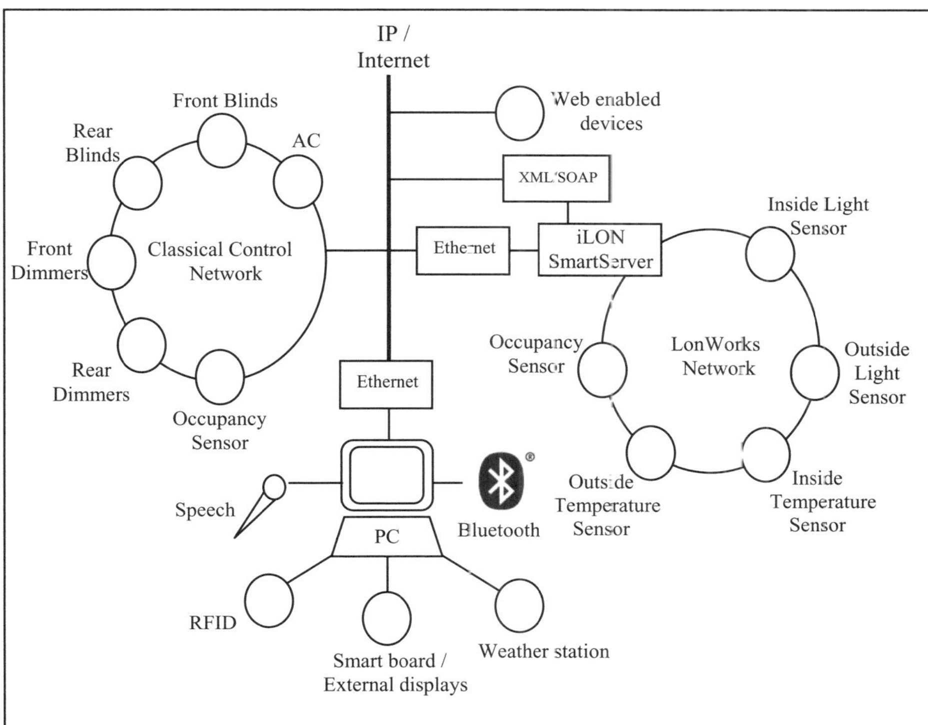

Figure (1): The intelligent classroom infrastructure

The LonWorks based network is connected to the iLON1000 smart server that acts as a gateway between the LonWorks based sensors/actuators and the IP-based Ethernet network as well as a classical control network containing other sensors and actuators. The iLON smart sever hosts an HTTP web server software that allows transparent access to the iClass infrastructure through any internet capable device. The embedded web server makes possible extracting information and controlling the various classroom sensors and actuators using a simple graphical user interface. Also, it provides a web-service based interface that enables secure real time programmatic access to the network. External weather conditions like solar energy level, wind speed/direction, humidity, etc are acquired using a weather station connected to the classroom PC. The iClass infrastructure controls multiple actuators such as dimmable lights for different sections of the class, air-condition controls (temperature, fan speed, heating/cooling, on/off), front/rear window blinds, a smart board as well as multiple digital displays. The smart board display inside the classroom is used for presenting the session content. Also, it is used as a touch user interface for interacting with the iClass system (as shown in Figure 2.a). An external display is used to publish announcements, schedule of the classroom and any information of interest about the current session (as shown in Figure 2.b). The iClass supports user identification through RFID technology. All of the computational artifacts as well as the sensors and actuators are accessible through many interfaces such as:

- Software installed on the classroom PC
- A speech based interface through microphones attached to the classroom PC or using handheld devices
- Bluetooth connectivity allowing programmatic access from any software agent hosted on a Bluetooth enabled device.
- Manual interfaces

(a) (b)

Figure 2: (a) The smart board in the iClass. (b) The external display in the iClass.

3. The proposed Intelligent Agent

Building an intelligent agent to track the state of the environment, control its actuators and adapt it to the users' preferences involves dealing with many uncertainties in the environment. Different sources of uncertainty exist in the intelligent classroom such as:

- Uncertainties in sensor inputs.

- Uncertainties in control outputs caused by imprecision of the actuators response and changes in the actuator characteristics due to wear, tear and environmental changes.
- Linguistic uncertainties as the meaning of words used in expressing the agent knowledge can be uncertain, since words mean different things to different people [12].
- Uncertainties associated with the change in the operating conditions of the agent controller.

Fuzzy logic is proved to provide a good framework for modeling various types of uncertainties in information. Fuzzy Logic Controllers (FLCs), the most popular application of fuzzy logic, provide an adequate methodology for designing robust controllers that are able to deliver satisfactory performance when contending with the uncertainty, noise and imprecision attributed to real world environments.

However, the linguistic and numerical uncertainties associated with dynamic unstructured environments cause problems in determining the exact and precise antecedents' and consequents' membership functions during the FLC design [13]. Type-2 fuzzy logic is an extension of ordinary type-1 fuzzy logic where the membership function is fuzzy rather than crisp. The membership functions of type-2 fuzzy sets are three dimensional and include a footprint of uncertainty; it is the new third dimension of type-2 fuzzy sets and the footprint of uncertainty that provide additional degrees of freedom that make it possible to directly model and handle uncertainties [13].

The interval type-2 FLC is a special case of the type-2 FLC. Interval type-2 FLCs use interval type-2 fuzzy sets to represent the inputs and/or outputs of the FLC. Our agent operation is divided into the following phases (as shown in Figure 3.a):

1- Building individual type-1 fuzzy profiles for input/output variables.
2- Building the type-2 model for input/output variables
3- Monitoring users' behavior
4- Generating the type-2 FLC
5- Agent control and adaptation

The following subsections will explain each of the steps needed by the agent

3.1. Building individual type-1 fuzzy profiles for input/output variables.

The agent starts by modeling individual type-1 fuzzy profiles for each user in the class room. The shape of the type-1 fuzzy sets is arbitrarily chosen (e.g. triangular, gaussian, trapezoidal, etc). The individual user values are acquired by one of two methods:

a) Monitoring: Users are monitored individually for a certain period of time and environmental parameters data is gathered. Fuzzy membership functions representing the input/output variables are then automatically extracted from data using some techniques such as FCM clustering technique [14]. This unobtrusively builds the model with minimal user intervention and with the least technical knowledge.
b) Surveys: This approach is used when monitoring is not feasible for any reason (e.g. insufficient stay time). Users are asked to express their individual linguistic labels (e.g. low, medium, high) for fuzzy sets of the various

input/output variables by filling in few values for each variable using software accessible via any of the following ways:

- Compact mobile applications on users' cellphones/PDAs.
- The classroom PC.
- Web served software over the internet or the campus LAN

It is important to note though that this approach requires more knowledge from the users' side and is less obtrusive as opposed to the monitoring approach.

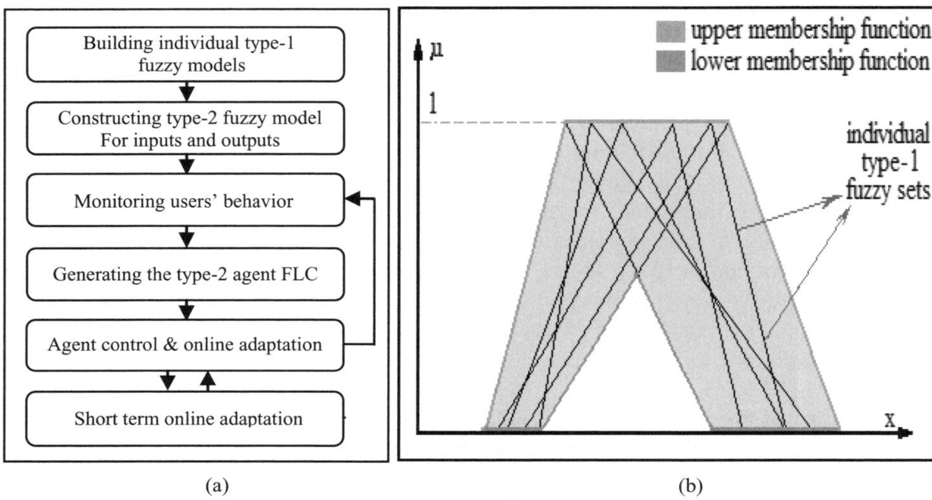

Figure 3: (a) Phases of operation of the proposed agent (b) Union of triangular type-1 fuzzy sets to create a type-2 set. The upper and lower membership functions are marked in orange and light blue respectively.

3.2. Building the type-2 model for input/output variables

In this phase the agent operates on the type-1 profiles acquired in the previous stage by aggregating them to produce the type-2 fuzzy model for the input/output variables. The type-1 membership functions acquired earlier characterize the particular users' behavior while the aggregated type-2 model characterizes the collective behavior of the class occupants. It effectively models the uncertainties present in the environment especially the inter-user uncertainties about the meanings of input/output variables.

Based on [15], our agent computes interval type-2 fuzzy sets from type-1 sets using union. Figure 3.b shows an example of such process.

3.3. Monitoring users' behavior

After obtaining the type-2 model for the input/output variables the agent then starts to monitor users' actions in the environment. Based on the IAOFIS approach [14], whenever a user changes actuator settings, the agent records a "snapshot" of the current inputs (sensor states) and the outputs (actuator states with the new altered values of whichever actuators were adjusted by that user). These "snapshots" are accumulated over a period of time so that the agent observes as much of the user's interactions within the environment as possible. The set of accumulated multi-input multi-output data pairs are then used to construct the rule base of the agent type-2 FLC.

3.4. Generating the type-2 FLC

The set of interval type-2 membership functions generated from phase 2 is combined with the accumulated user input/output data to extract fuzzy rules defining users' behaviors. We follow the IAOFIS approach reported in [14] for the rule extraction needed by the agent. After generating the interval type-2 membership functions in the previous stage and generating the fuzzy rules from the user data in the current phase we have a type-2 FLC that models the users' behavior in the environment, which makes the agent FLC ready to operate the iClass on behalf of its occupants.

3.5Agent control and adaptation

Once the agent FLC rule base is ready, the agent can take control of the environment. The agent FLC regularly reads sensory values and fuzzifies them into type-2 fuzzy sets. It then uses the rule base to do inference on the input sets and produce the type-2 output fuzzy sets representing the decision taken on behalf of the users. These type-2 sets are then type reduced using the center of sets type reduction technique to produce type-1 fuzzy sets which are then defuzzified into crisp values used to drive the different actuators in the classroom.

There are two modes of adaptation: (short term adaptation) and long term adaptation. In the short term adaptation, having built an approximation of the users' behavior, the agent starts to control the environment making decisions on behalf of the user. However, users might feel uncomfortable with the agent decisions at any time. Following are some possible reasons:

- Slight variations in the operation conditions due to time passage.
- Subtle changes in the user behavior.
- Encountering an uncovered point in the control surface that the agent hasn't learnt during the monitoring phase.

Users then can manually override the agent actions by adjusting the actuators the way they like. Then, the agent will record this intervention and update the rule base accordingly online. Thus, it non-intrusively adapts to the user behavior as well as environmental changes.

The details of how this takes place are as follows, based on [14]. Whenever a user intervenes by actuating one or more of the classroom actuators to override a control action taken by the agent FLC, the agent records a snapshot of the environment consisting of the values of the inputs along with the new altered values (i.e. the user desired values). The membership value of each of the crisp inputs to the corresponding antecedent fuzzy sets for every rule. The weights of the rules are calculated to find fired ones (i.e. ones with $wi^{(l)} > 0$). The consequent fuzzy set(s) that give the highest membership to the user altered actuator value(s) are selected to replace the consequent set(s) for the corresponding output(s) of all fired rules.

Using the above technique the agent can adaptively tune its performance as the users' behavior changes or as new uncovered points of the control surface are encountered.

On the long term, as the changes in users' behavior or in the operation conditions accumulate the amount of uncertainty that the agent has to model becomes big enough to degrade the system performance. It's then when the system has to transition to the long term adaptation. In the long term adaptation, when the agent becomes unable to appropriately model the users' behavior because of the increasing uncertainty levels, it jumps back to phase 3 where users are monitored again to rebuild the FLC rule base to more accurately reflect their preferences.

4. Experimental Work and Results

We've carried out a series of experiments to assess the performance of our proposed agent in the different stages of its operation. For these experiments, our agent starts by acquiring the type-1 models for users which are used to build the agent type-2 FLC that will represents the uncertainty associated with the current occupants of the classroom. The agent then extracts the collective preferences of the users and starts to control the classroom parameters on their behalf. The agent handles 7 inputs coming from different sensors (internal light level, external light level, internal temperature, external temperature, humidity, time and occupancy). The following actuators are controlled by the agent: front window blinds, rear window blinds, front dimmable lights, rear dimmable lights, air conditioning. The following phases were experimented with during experiments.

a) Phase 1 (Building individual type-1 profiles for input/output variables):
   Type-1 fuzzy profiles were built using both ways discussed in section 3.1:
   1- Monitoring: Two of our experiments used pre-learnt type-1 profiles acquired from five different users. The users were monitored alone in the classroom at different times. Their learnt type-1 membership functions which are stored on their cell phones were then downloaded using Bluetooth to the class room PC where they could be used in subsequent stages.
   2- Surveys: We've done surveys on six different student groups in the 3rd year at the MET faculty. Each group consisted of around 25 students. Students were asked to fill a form with few numeric values that precisely characterize the shape of their individual type-1 membership functions. Boundary membership functions were chosen to be trapezoidal, while non-boundary sets were triangular.

b) Phase 2 (Building the type-2 model for input/output variables):
   Experiments performed involved building type-2 models by combining a number of type-1 profiles that varied from 5 to 150 users. The resulting type-2 profiles were tested for acceptable footprint of uncertainty and unacceptable cases were corrected as in [16].

c) Phase 3 and 4 (Monitoring users and generating the type-2 FLC):
   In this phase we carried out monitoring experiments for 5 users for different periods up to 3 days. Figure 4.a shows the effect of the monitoring period on the size of the type-2 FLC rule base. Monitoring has been carried out for periods that are multiples of 5 hours:

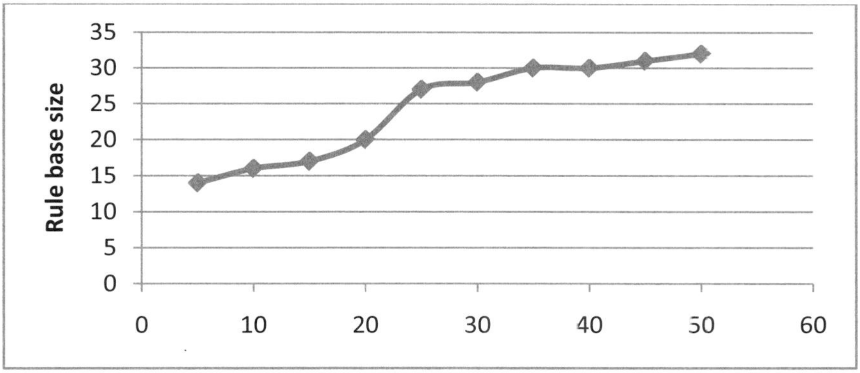

(a)

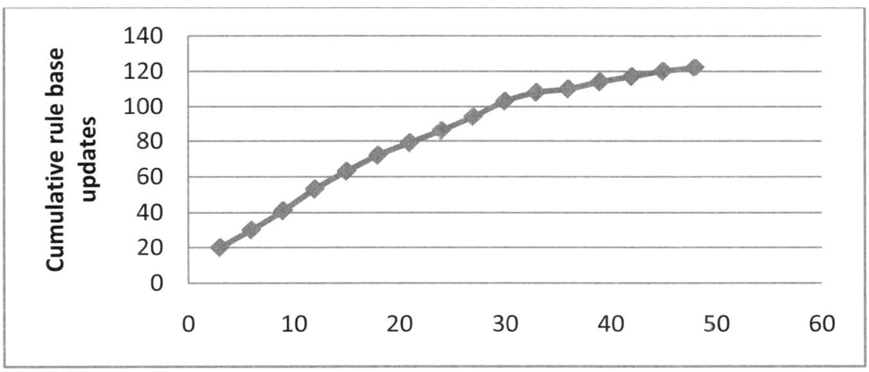

(b)

Figure 4: (a) The effect of the monitoring period in hours on the size of the initial agent rule base. (b) The cumulative number of rule base updates (adds or modifications) vs the operation time.

d) Agent control and adaptation:
To evaluate our agent's capability to adapt to changes in users' behavior and its effectiveness in modeling the inter-user uncertainties, we ran the agent controlling the environment for 48 hours and recorded the rule base updates; (rule base modifications due to user overrides or rule additions due to unseen environmental conditions). An important measure of the performance of our agent is users' satisfaction which is reflected in the number of rule base updates. As seen from Figure 4.b the number of rule base updates drops as time passes reflecting growing users' satisfaction with the agent FLC controller actions.

5. Conclusions

In this paper, we discussed the importance of achieving AmI in multi-occupant environments. We presented the application of AmI in classroom environments by developing a type-2 fuzzy logic based agent approach that efficiently models the numerous uncertainties encountered in the environment. The agent then learns in a nonintrusive manner the behavior of the class occupants and represents them as fuzzy rules. The agent can take control of the environment and take actions that reflect the users' preferences about the various environmental parameters. Also, it can adapt to changes in the users' behavior as well as changes in the operation conditions. Through a series of real world experiments, the agent proved capable of capturing the collective preferences of multiple occupants in the intelligent classroom. It could non-intrusively adapt to the short term and long term changes in the users' habits and the environment. Experimental results were shown that reflect how satisfied the users' were with the agent actions.

Our future work will continue enhancing the performance of the proposed agent by dynamically modifying the type-2 fuzzy logic model to reflect the preferences of only the current occupants at any instance in a real-time fashion. Also, we intend to work on developing a rule base reduction technique to increase the speed of operation of the agent in the face of the growing rule base. We intend to integrate environment specific considerations into the agent learning mechanism like assigning priorities for certain learnt profiles based on their role in the currently running educational scenario in the iClass.

6. References

[1] K. Ducatel, M. Bogdanowicz, F. Scapolo, J. Leijten and J-C. Burgelman, "Scenarios for Ambient Intelligence in 2010", tech. report, Information Society Technologies Advisory Group (ISTAG), Inst. of Prospective Technological Studies (IPTS), 2001.

[2] D. Monekosso, P. Remagnino, and Y. Kuno, "Intelligent Environments: Methods, Algorithms and Applications", Springer-Verlag, 2008.

[3] F. Doctor, H. Hagras, "A Fuzzy Embedded Agent-Based Approach for Realizing Ambient Intelligence in Intelligent Inhabited Environments", *IEEE Transactions on Systems, Man, And Cybernetics*, pp.55-65 Vol. 35, No. 1, 2005.

[4] R. Brooks, "The Intelligent Room Project", Proceedings of the 2nd International Cognitive Technology Conference (CT'97). Aizu, Japan, 1997.

[5] G. Abowd, D. Gregory, C. Atkeson, A. Bobick, I. Essa, B. MacIntyre, E. Mynatt, and T. Starner, "Living laboratories: The future computing environments group at the Georgia Institute of Technology", *Extended Abstracts of the ACM Conference on Human Factors in Computing Systems*, 2000.

[6] D. Cook, M. Youngblood, E. Heierman, K. Gopalratnam, S. Rao, A. Litvin, and F. Khawaja, "MavHome: An Agent-Based Smart Home", *Proceedings of the IEEE International Conference on Pervasive Computing and Communications*, pp 521-524, 2003.

[7] J. Flachsbart, "Gargoyle: Vision in the Intelligent Classroom", Master's thesis, University of Chicago, 1997.

[8] R. Freeman, "Cost-Effectiveness Of The Intelligent Classroom For Information Systems Instruction", *Journal of Information Technology Management*, Vol. 15, No1-2, pp. 39-43, 2004.

[9] Túlio Tibúrcio and Edward F. Finch, "The impact of an intelligent classroom on pupils' interactive behaviour", *Facilities Journal*, Vol. 23 Issue 5, pp. 262-278, Emerald Tech Publishing, 2005.

[10] L. Winer, and J. Cooperstock, "The Intelligent Classroom: Changing Teaching and learning with an Evolving Technological Environment", *Journal of Computers and Education*, (pp. 253-266), 2002.

[11] Y. Shi, W. Xie, G. Xu, R. Shi, E. Chen, Y. Mao and F. Liu, *IEEE Pervasive Computing*, Vol. 2, Issue 2, pp.47-50, 2003.

[12] J. Mendel, *"Uncertain Rule-Based Fuzzy Logic Systems: Introduction and New directions"*, Upper Saddle River, NJ: Prentice-Hall, 2001.

[13] Hani Hagras, "Type-2 FLCs: A new generation of fuzzy controllers", *IEEE Computational Intelligence Magazine*, Vol. 2, Issue 1, pp. 30-43, 2007.

[14] Hani Hagras, Faiyaz Doctor, Victor Callaghan and Antonio Lopez, "An Incremental Adaptive Life Long Learning Approach for Type-2 Fuzzy Embedded Agents in Ambient Intelligent Environments", *IEEE Transactions On Fuzzy Systems*, Vol. 15, No. 1, pp. 41-55, 2007.

[15] F. Liu, J. Mendel, "An Interval Approach to Fuzzistics for Interval Type-2 Fuzzy Sets", *Proceedings of the 2007 IEEE International Conference on Fuzzy Systems,* pp. 1-6, London, 2007.

Intelligent Environments 2009
V. Callaghan et al. (Eds.)
IOS Press, 2009

doi:10.3233/978-1-60750-034-6-267

An Intelligent System for Extracting Intro and Outré Times in Songs Using Artificial Neural Networks

Sarah Elkasrawy [a] Hani Hagras [a] and Moustafa Nawito [a,b]
[a] *The Ambient Intelligence Center*
[b] *Digital Media Campus*
The German University in Cairo, Egypt
sarah.el-kasrawy@guc.edu.eg; hani.hagras@guc.edu.eg; moustafa.nawito@guc.edu.eg

Abstract. In this paper, we will present a neural network based approach to extract intro and outré times of songs within an intelligent radio broadcasting studio (iStudio). The iStudio is located in the German University in Cairo (GUC) and it is a testbed for Ambient Intelligent Environments (AIEs) that are related to media and entertainment. The paper targets the challenging problem of producing a system that can predict the music intro and outré times of songs thus avoiding the need to manually measure these times for the huge number of songs that exist in any radio station library. The importance of predicting the music intro and outré times is crucial for realizing Ambient Intelligence (AmI) in radio studios as knowing these times will be essential for controlling the previous and following events of the given songs, especially in talk shows and DJ shows. The paper will explain the employed technique and we will present experiments to justify the success of the employed approach.

Keywords. Ambient Intelligence, Digital Studio, Neural Network

1. Introduction

Ambient Intelligence (AmI) is a new information paradigm aiming at enhancing people's life. Key features of Ambient Intelligent Environments (AIEs) are that they are embedded, context-aware, personalized, adaptive and anticipatory [1]. Embedded refers to embedding devices into the environment that can capture data from the user and surroundings to recognize the context of the user's situation. A system capturing information of the surroundings becomes context-aware, which it uses later on to personalize the service offered to the user [1]. Personalization is adapting to the user's preferences in a short term while adaptation involves adjustment to user behavior by monitoring the user over a longer time in order to anticipate the needs of the user [1].

AmI goal is to improve the quality of living for a user by creating an environment offering personalized, intelligent services [4]. Users should not be conscious to the computational elements in the environment, e.g. it's a transparent environment [4] where all computational systems are invisible to the user [9]. Intelligent means that the underlying technology can recognize the users living in this environment and adjust itself to their needs through monitoring and learning from their behavior over time [1], [4]. Furthermore, the system can adapt to the changes in user's behavior as well as the surrounding environment [4]. An AmI surrounding can give users information, services and access to entertainment systems at any point of time and place they desire with minimum user interference [1].

As Music is becoming an important part of our daily lives and music databases grow dramatically, it is becoming essential to organize music efficiently and hence AmI is envisaged to bring many benefits to this. However, music perception is a subjective issue therefore different people develop different emotions when listening to the same music which renders the design of a deterministic classification agent for music impractical. In [10], fuzzy systems were applied for music emotion classification where this system can measure relative strength of emotions that music produces. In addition, this approach also included a facility to measure music emotion variation during a song. In University of Westminister [5], UK, an intelligent system iHiFi, or intelligent HiFi, was proposed, which is an intelligent system to customize music according to user's preferences. iHiFi consists of embedded intelligent agents that learn and adapt to the user's taste to modify music pieces by changing tempo, tonality, add or remove instruments or vocals, re-harmonize the user's favorite pieces and keep the user library updated to create optimized music [5]. Another work in this field is the Smart Media Player, is a demonstration intended to verify a proposed design of a context-aware middleware which can gather and process information and context from the surrounding environment to choose the proper music according to user's desire [3]. In the realization of AmI work on the field of ubiquitous radio, research reported in [2] proposed a network of devices that operate in harmony to facilitate tasks for the environment users [2].

In this paper we present an approach to give a personalized evaluation of intro and outré times of a song given information of genre, artist and song length. In the following section we give an overview of the iStudio. In Section 3, we will introduce the importance of predicting the intro and outré times for iStudios. Section 4 will present an overview of the proposed system. Section 5 will highlight the employed neural network approach. Section 6 will present the experiments and results. Section 7 will present the conclusions and future work.

2. The Intelligent Studio Test-bed

The intelligent Studio (iStudio) is located in the Ambient Intelligence Center and the Digital Media Campus in the German University in Cairo (GUC). The iStudio is an AIE test-bed for media and entertainment. The iStudio is based around a Digital radio broadcasting station where the station studio can be personalized and controlled in an intelligent way. When introducing the concept of AmI to digital studios our focus was to create an environment for the radio show presenter and producer that would facilitate their tasks. Radio studio equipments, including mixers, microphones, faders, buttons and the different controllers are complex systems that only trained persons can operate.

The role of an AmI system is to train itself to understand the user's behavior and preferences while the user is learning the different facilities. After the system has sufficiently trained itself the iStudio can autonomously adjust itself to user's requirements. However, the system should be always controllable by the user.

The iStudio is based within the Digital Media Campus (DMC) at the German University in Cairo (GUC) which was established in September 2007. It is the result of cooperative effort of the GUC, the Fraunhofer Institute for Integrated Circuits IIS and Deutsche Welle (the German Broadcasting Corporation). The DMC is a radio and television station. The stations are based on Digital Radio Mondiale (DRM) and Digital Video Broadcasting for Handhelds (DVB-H) standards respectively [8]. The iStudio and the digital radio station within the DMC are shown in Figure (1).

The main goal of establishing the DMC is to allow advanced scientific research in the area of digital broadcasting, specifically DRM and DVB-H to be conducted [8]. Furthermore, the DMC and iStudio is a test bed for AmI projects. In order to fulfill this goal the DMC has to function as an industrial broadcasting station and at the same time allow experiments and research to be conducted on campus. The structure of the DMC is based on "three pillars" [8] giving it the industrial function as well as the experimental purpose. Those three pillars are:

- Open interface structure: this indicates that the system is flexible to have components added or removed without affecting the flow of the transmission. This property is especially useful for conducting lab experiments. The ability to remove and add components gives the researcher more control over adjusting the whole system to serve the experiment [8]. More specifically it adds flexibility into developing the DMC to an ambient intelligent test bed by adding the different sensors and actuators to the system.
- (Industrial) Reliability: the DMC functions not only as a test bed but also as a running digital broadcast station that can provide service continuously thus giving it a commercial aspect as well.
- Scalability: Due to the evolving technologies used in the DMC such as DRM and DVB-H they offer numerous research points. Our interaction with the DMC is through the digital radio station. Our main interest is the stored song database in the DMC, and how to integrate our methods of finding intro and outré into the radio station database.

The iStudio allows logging all the radio station knobs adjustments. Also, it supports controlling of all the radio station controls thus making possible monitoring the studio context and controlling the studio on the user behalf according to the presented program or context.

3. The Importance of Predicting the Intro and Outré Times for iStudios

For radio Disk Jockeys (DJs), the task of broadcasting interesting shows needs, nowadays, more than just a solid command of language and strong presence. Dealing with the myriad of technologies available in modern studios could sometimes become overwhelming, especially for new and upcoming radio broadcasters. This is an ironic situation, since these technologies are made available to make things easier for DJs, and not confuse them.

One way to solve this issue, is to attempt to make the interface between the DJ and the studio equipment more friendly, or precisely, more intelligent. All Modern digital studios are equipped with computers and microprocessor based devices, a fact which

Figure 1. Digital Radio Station at the DMC

presents numerous opportunities for alleviating unnecessary delays or obstruction in the workflow.

An important issue that concerns all radio broadcasters is the availability of certain descriptive data about the music they use on the shows. Specifically, knowing the lengths of a song's intro and outré is an invaluable piece of information. Introducing the song, adding a few text lines between music pieces, commenting or giving the listeners relevant information about the tunes being played, are examples of the standard techniques that all DJs use, and for which the knowledge of the intro and outré lengths is imperative. The problem is that retrieving this data about a song is a tedious task to say the least. A person would have to listen to the music from beginning to end, an approach that becomes increasingly cumbersome or even prohibitive if applied to the massive number of songs a radio station has stored in its library. To add to the complexity, most record production companies don't provide this data upon purchase of the tune which makes this a very difficult dilemma.

In this paper we approach a solution to extract the data that is not provided by the record company. To achieve this we make use of the given data, which is total length, genre and artist name and feed it to the intelligent system, which will output the missing data, e.g. intro and outré.

The intelligent system could, as an example, queue the DJs by means of countdown visible on a studio monitor, how many seconds of the intro and outré times are remaining. In the next section we present the envisaged intelligent system to retrieve the intro and outré information.

4. iGIO - An Intelligent System to Get Intro and Outré Times

iGIO (intelligent system to Get Intro and Outré times) is an intelligent system, which utilizes different computational intelligent techniques, to infer intro and outré time information given some data about the song. The system has different levels of processing the information to produce the personalized output, it starts by operating a neural network, that was trained on a set of input data which consisting of song genre, artist name and duration to infer the intro and outré time. After obtaining an estimation of intro and outré times from the neural network, this data is presented to several users through an interactive graphical user interface (interactive GUI) which is envisaged in Figure (2).

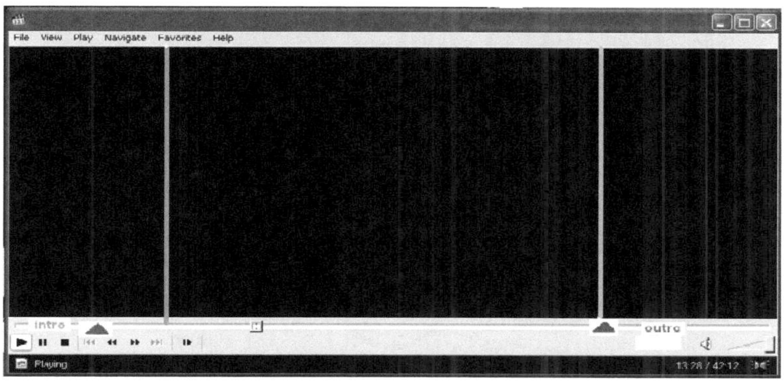

Figure 2. The envisaged interactive GUI

The interactive GUI is similar to any media player, except that it graphically depicts where the intro and outré occur by shading this area in the display with corresponding colors for intro and outré. Afterwards, users can adjust these outputs according to their personal evaluation of the song sections. Intro and outré times don't have a standard; therefore, different DJs will have different views on what an intro and what an outré of some song is. The subjective nature of the song sections evaluation emboses uncertainty on defining intro and outré time for songs which a deterministic evaluation system perform poorly. Fuzzy logic is a computational intelligence technique capable of modeling different types of uncertainties. This collection of individual different estimates will be translated to type-2 fuzzy sets which represents intro and outré as a part of a fuzzy logic system (FLS) to achieve better performance at intro and outré evaluation. The inputs to the system are genre, length and artist and its outputs are the intro and outré times.

In this paper we will focus on one component of the system which is the neural network component to retrieve the information on intro and outré.

5. A Neural Networks Based Approach for Predicting the Intro and Outré Times for iStudios

The first task of iGIO is to predict intro and outré times. Our approach is to realize this using neural network that takes certain input and outputs intro and outré time. The neural network inputs are genre, song length and artist name. We made the following assumptions concerning input and output data.

- Well-known data such as song length, song artist name and song genre are provided by the record company
- Each artist or band is known for playing a certain genre
- There exists a relation between song time divisions and the genre as well as the artist of a song, e.g. artists usually have a pattern for their songs, as well as genres have similar patterns. For instance, rock songs usually have guitar solos towards the end of a song, while pop songs don't have long intros like rock or metal songs.

In this section we explain details about how neural networks function, the architecture of the neural network used and the representation of the input data. Artificial Neural

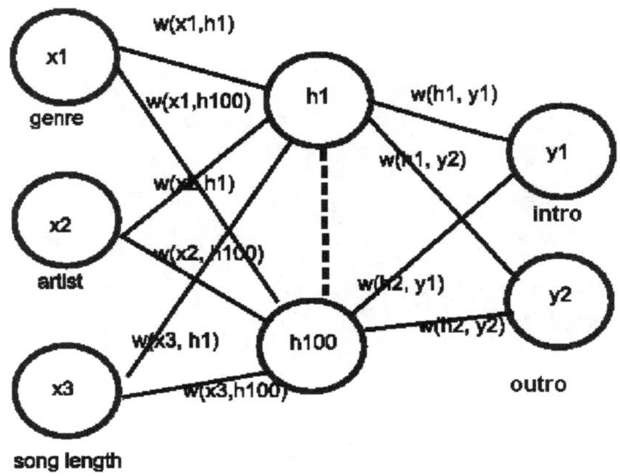

Figure 3. Neural Network Structure.

Network (ANN) is a computational intelligence paradigm [6] utilized to solve complex problems such as pattern recognition, classification, function approximation and modeling of biological neural networks [7]. When provided with example data and procedures for learning, ANN can generalize the given knowledge to solve problems for which no algorithm exists [6], [7].

The network architecture that we used is the feedforward backpropagation network. The designed neural network takes 3 inputs, namely song length, song genre and artist name of the song. Representing song length as a numerical value isn't a difficulty. The song time is converted to seconds forming a single numerical input for the neural network. As for the song genre, each existing genre has a randomly assigned value that is stored in a database. In order to add meaning to the value assigned to genre or artist, genres and artists were divided into groups, and according to the group, a number range was assigned to it. For instance, the genres rock, progressive rock, punk rock, alternative rock can all fall into the category of rock. Therefore numbers in the same range were assigned to them. Metal music is developed from rock. Metal genres were assigned to numbers in the next number range after rock.

Certain artists or bands in most cases play a certain genre. Artists were classified similarly like genre, e.g. if two artists play the same or similar genre, numbers from the same range are assigned to them.

Outputs of the neural network are the time when the intro and the time when the outré occur. The output number is the representation of the intro/outré time in seconds.

This value is then transformed to time in hour, minutes and seconds and outputted to the user.

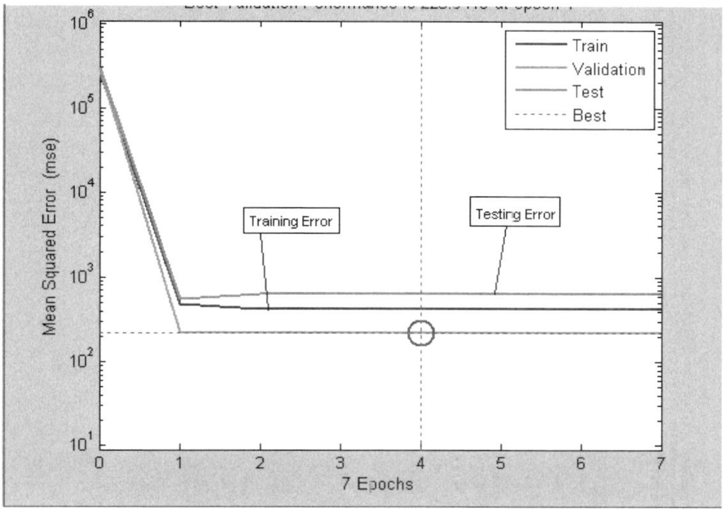

Figure 4. error graph for training and testing phases.

We constructed a training set of 48 song data entries; each entry consists of genre, artist and song length as input and intro and outré as output. The input is constructed from different genres and different artists and the estimated output is based on a subjective evaluation of the data provider. This training set was used to train different neural networks. After training the networks they were tested against another data set of 62 different songs that the network wasn't exposed to before. In this paper we present the best results of the tested networks.

The used network architecture consists of three layers; input, hidden and output as shown in Figure (3), a linear activation function was used for the hidden and output layer and a feedforward backpropagation algorithm was used for learning.

The training of the neural network was done using cross-validation as a method for obtaining optimized generalization ability. Cross-validation is a technique that divides the training set into training and testing sets where the training set is used to train the network and the testing set to enhance the generalization abilities of the network. The training set is further divided into estimation and validation set, where epoch by epoch the neural network is trained using the estimation set and immediately validated (tested) for performance using the validation set. The efficiency of training is improved through the early stopping method, which stops training when the validation error increases despite the fact that the estimation error is improving. The early stopping technique avoids the network to become overfitting which is a property of a neural network when its model is too complex and its generalization ability is larger than desired.

6. Experimental Results

The testing and training errors revealed by this network are relatively less than the other tested networks. Figure (4) plots the error curve for training and testing error. The results

Table 1. songs for further testing

Artist	Genre	length	intro	outré
Rima Kcheich	jazz	05 : 17	01 : 20	05 : 10
Iron Maiden	metal	07 : 10	01 : 02	06 : 55
Dire straights	rock	06 : 59	01 : 06	04 : 48
Linkin Park	Nu Metal	03 : 34	00 : 39	03 : 30
Scorpions	Hard rock	05 : 05	00 : 21	04 : 42
Eric Clapton	blues-rock	04 : 10	00 : 16	03 : 57
Red Hot Chili Peppers	Alternative rock	05 : 34	00 : 20	05 : 09

Table 2. Results from the employed neural networks

Artist	Genre	length	intro	outré
Rima Kcheich	jazz	05 : 17	01 : 14	05 : 11
Iron Maiden	metal	07 : 10	00 : 59	05 : 46
Dire straights	rock	06 : 59	00 : 42	05 : 25
Linkin Park	Nu Metal	03 : 34	00 : 32	05 : 11
Scorpions	Hard rock	05 : 05	00 : 33	04 : 27
Eric Clapton	blues-rock	04 : 10	00 : 19	04 : 09
Red Hot Chili Peppers	Alternative rock	05 : 34	00 : 22	03 : 54

Table 3. Error calculations for intro for the utilized network

song	error	squared error
1	6	36
2	3	9
3	24	576
4	−7	49
5	−11	121
6	−1	1
7	−2	4

of testing with other new data (which consisted of the 62 unseen data entries during the training phase) showed a mean square error (MSE) of **623.11** for intro and **8976.9** for outré. Table 1 shows the originally desired data while Table 2 shows some results of the tested data on the network.

The testing results for the network with linear functions in both hidden and output layer resulted close results to the desired output.

The testing with the new data set (62 songs) was performed on the network to produce the previously mentioned average MSE for intro and outré times. Furthermore, we presented some of the individual testing of the songs in Table 3 and Table 4, where Table 3 shows error and squared error for intro calculations and Table 4 shows the same for outré calculations.

Table 4. Error calculations for outré for the utilized network

song	error	squared error
1	−1	1
2	69	4761
3	−37	1369
4	−101	10201
5	15	225
6	−12	144
7	75	5625

7. Conclusions

In this paper we presented part of the iGIO system, a project held at the iStudio which aims at extracting intro end time and outré start time of a song given certain information of the songs. Such information as genre, artist and song length are in most cases provided by the record company. The presented component of the iGIO is the component that can make evaluation on intro and outré times by using a neural network to estimate this information. We implemented a feedforward neural network using linear activation function and applied backpropagation as a learning algorithm, where inputs to the network were the known data of a song and outputs are intro and outré time. To represent data of input to the network in a numerical form we assigned to each genre and artist a random number, where related genres or artists were assigned numbers from the same range. Song times (intro, outré, total length) is represented in seconds. The output from the network is also a number in seconds that is then converted to time in hours, minutes and seconds. The results of our experiments is a constructed neural network that can make a close estimation of intro and outré times using the provided song data of genre, artist and duration, which forms the first milestone of the iGIO.

Future work encompasses building an interactive GUI that acquires inputs from the user which will be translated as type-2 fuzzy sets in a type-2 fuzzy logic system to personalize the output of iGIO according to the operating user.

References

[1] E. Aarts, Philips Research, "Ambient Intelligence: A Multimedia Perspective", *Visions and Views*,pp. 12-19, January - March, 2004.

[2] F. Boekhorst, "Ambient Intelligence: the next paradigm for consumer electronics: how will it affect silicon?", *IEEE Solid-State Circuits Conference*,Vol. 1, pp. 28-31, 2002.

[3] C.-H. Cha, J.-H. Kim, and Y.-B. Ko, "Smart Media Player: The Intelligent Media Player based on Context-Aware Middleware and UBI-Sensor", *Internet & Multimedia Systems & Applications (IMSA2005)*,pp. 383-388, Honululu, Hawaii, August 2005.

[4] F. Doctor, H. Hagras and V. Callaghan, "A Fuzzy Embedded Agent-Based Approach for Realizing Ambient Intelligence in Intelligent Inhabited Environments", *IEEE Transactions On Systems and Humans*, Vol. 35, No. 1, pp. 55-65, January 2005.

[5] J. Eacott and M. d'Invemo, "Embedded Intelligent Music - or iHiFi the intelligent HiFi", University of Westminister, UK,*Digital Creativity, Swets & Zeitlinger*, Vol. 14, pp, 67-73, 2003.

[6] H.Hagras, "Embedding Computational Intelligence in Pervasive Spaces", *IEEE Pervasive Computing*, pp. 85-89, 2007.

[7] W. H. Joerding, Ying Li, and D. L. Young, "Feedforward Neural Network Estimation of a Ccrop Yield Response Function", *Journal of Agriculture and Applied Economics*, Vol. 26 No. I, pp. 252-263, July, 1994.

[8] M. Nawito, S. Nader, A. Heuberger, J. Oscheck and C. Forster, "The Digital Media Campus of the German University in Cairo", *9th Workshop on Digital Broadcasting*, pp. 18-19, Erlangen, September 2008.

[9] J.Pan, C.Tan and W. Lee, "Context-aware Service Protocol", *Wireless Communication and Networking IEEE*, Vol. 3, pp. 2058-2063, 2003.

[10] Y. Yang, C. Liu an H.H.Chen, "Music Emotion Classification: a Fuzzy Approach", National Taiwan University, *Proceedings of ACM Multimedia (ACM MM'-06)*, pp. 81-84, 2006.

Intelligent Environments 2009
V. Callaghan et al. (Eds.)
IOS Press, 2009

doi:10.3233/978-1-60750-034-6-277

Decision Support System for Hot Spot Detection

Esther SALAMÍ[a,1], Sol PEDRE[b], Patricia BORENZSTEJN[b], Cristina BARRADO[a], Andres STOLIAR[b] and Enric PASTOR[b]
[a] *Technical University of Catalonia*
[b] *Buenos Aires University*

Abstract. Forest fires are an important problem for many countries. Prevention, surveillance and extinguishing tasks are costly and sometimes risky. This paper focuses on the surveillance of the fire embers once the fire is extinguished. This is a post-fire task which requires an important amount of terrestrial resources, especially if the weather conditions may provoke the re-ignition of the fire. We propose the use of an Unmanned Aerial System to support fire fighters' decisions. Our proposal is to develop an intelligent system which can make or suggest tactical decisions to firemen on hot-spot surveillance. The Unmanned Aerial System consists of a small unmanned aircraft, a ground control station and several personal devices for the firemen on ground. All system elements are wirelessly connected. On board data acquisition and fast processing, together with an intelligent transmission and interpretation are the targets of the system.

Keywords. Unmanned Aerial System, Real-Time, Image Processing, Fire Fighting

Introduction

Forest fires are an important problem for many countries. The economic lost is the most visible impact in the short term. The ecological damage and the impact on the wild life diversity and on climate change are the most important lost in the long term [1]. In some dramatic cases, we should add the lost of human lives.

Prevention tasks are the first way to fight against forest fire. Although all important prevention efforts done at many levels, forest fire cannot be completely avoided in some extreme climatic circumstances. Fire extinguish tasks are the second resource for fire fighting. Previous experiences on the use of UAV in fire fighting mission have been done, especially in the monitoring of currently burning fires [2][3][4]. This paper does not target to use UAS in these tasks (detection or watering) because the current aerial means in charge of them do not want interferences of another aerial mean with autonomous behavior.

A third forest fire fighting task is also needed for fire embers surveillance once the fire is extinguished. At this time, an important amount of terrestrial resources is still devoted to post-fire tasks. Ground crew has to stay watering the smoking spots and many times this is done blindly. In this scenario, we propose the use of UAS to introduce intelligence to the fire fighting tasks.

[1] Corresponding Author: Esther Salamí, Computer Architecture Department, UPC; EPSC, C/Esteve Terradas 7, C4-004, 08860 Castelldefels (Barcelona), Spain; E-mail: esalami@ac.upc.edu

The rest of this document is organized as follows: The proposed system is presented in Section 1. Section 2 describes the framing models. Details of the real time image processing are given in Section 3. Section 4 shows the data fusion algorithm. Finally, main conclusions are summarized in the last Section of the document.

1. The UAS Based Intelligent System

The Unmanned Aerial System (UAS) is an intelligent system composed of the following parts (see Figure 1): The Unmanned Aerial Vehicle (UAV), the Ground Control Station (GCS), the Communication Channels (CC) and the Squad Information Terminals (SIT). UAV is the airframe and all the devices on-board it that compose the payload; GCS is a mobile device (i.e. laptop) which is used to control the UAS flight and mission; CC are the radio connections and their related electronics and antennas; SIT are very light devices used to inform the ground crew of the current fire state.

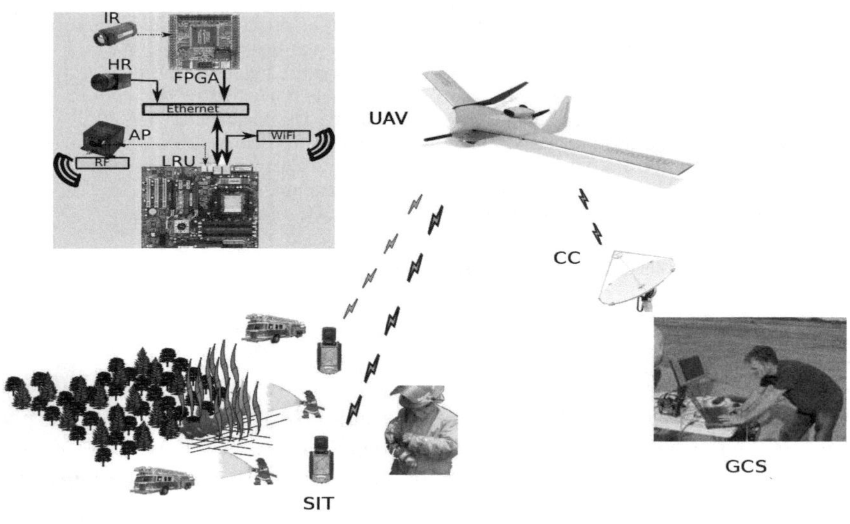

Figure 1. System components

The UAV should flight at low altitude (from 300 to 500 m) in a range of 2 hours. The command&control requires a real time CC to have direct control of the UAV flight from the ground in case of emergency. But this is not the case for the communications related to mission. As in previous work [5], images are processed on board for an intelligent interpretation. In this paper, we propose to improve the firemen decision making with the immediate communication of hot spots to the ground teams.

1.1. UAV Architecture

The payload on board the UAS is composed by two video cameras, a High Resolution (HR) camera and an Infra Red (IR) thermal one. Note that hyper-spectral cameras or scanners are not needed because the altitude is low enough to obtain good images with

COTS cameras [6]. We do not consider including a gimbaled payload because it would make the system too much expensive. The aircraft has inertial and positioning sensors incorporated inside the Auto Pilot (AP). Additionally, the AP has a Radio Frequency (RF) modem which creates a CC between the UAV and the GCS. The range of the radio link is 100 Km. Finally, a Wi-Fi Ethernet connector is used as CC between the UAV and the near by SIT of the ground teams. The Wi-Fi channel is also used as a backup CC for connecting the UAV and the GCS. Figure 1 shows the sensors of the UAV and their connections to the on board avionics. Our architecture is network centric with one or more Line Replaceable Units (LRU) to execute other avionic functions. For this specific problem, the proposal incorporates a Field Programmable Gate Array (FPGA) to execute the IR image processing in real time.

1.2. Flight Plan Definition

The flight of the UAV may need the repetition of flight patterns. It also may need modifications in case the burned area or the environmental conditions change. Thus a flexible and intelligent flight plan is needed to accomplish with the mission requirements. We define flight plan formalism as a set of stages directly related to the mission evolution. Figure 2 shows the Flight Plan stages: take-off, departure, en route, mission, arrival, approach and landing. The most relevant stage in this document is the mission stage, where the surveillance of the area to look for hot spots is done.

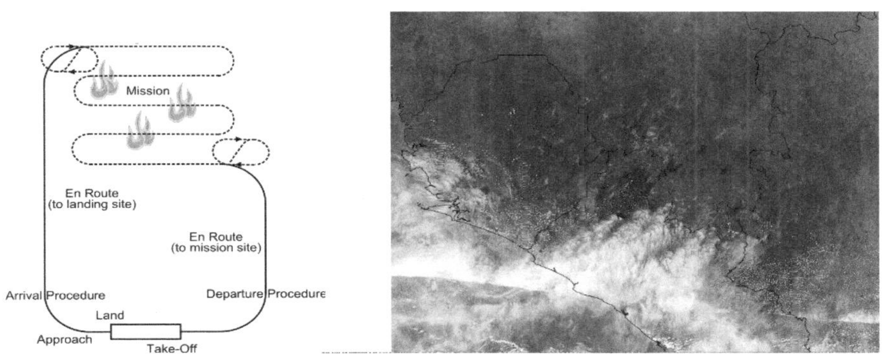

Figure 2. Flight Plan for fire surveillance

A Flight Plan consists of a list of RNAV based legs. We require two types of scans in a hot spot mission: an area scan and a point scan. An area scan leg is a flight pattern used to cover a whole area. This is used to locate hot spots if no previous information is given. The point scan leg is a repetitive eight turn over a fix point if the aircraft is fixed wing or a hold if the aircraft is a helicopter. It is used for a more detailed study of a possible hot spot in order to confirm or discard it. We also define parametric legs. They have dynamic behavior and allow adapting the flight to the mission evolution.

1.3 Hot Spot Mission

The mission is implemented as a set of software services that orchestrate the whole operation of the UAS. This operation is greatly dependent on the flight plan evolution and payload activation and deactivation is linked to the given UAV position. The

Mission Operator may introduce at any time of the mission the updates of the parametric values of a scan and the UAS will adapt the flight to the new coordinates automatically. Furthermore, the avionic services on board might also decide new parameters for the scan legs, for example if a hot spot is found.

The hot spot mission defines an initial scan area leg (like in Figure 2) with a flight altitude of 500 m. Thermal images are processed in real time to detect the hot areas. When the image processing algorithm of the FPGA detects a possible hot spot, the Mission Operator and the closest ground crew SIT will receive a notification with the fused image. The visual images, which contain the surroundings of the fire and can help experts to discard false positives, are annotated with the detected hot spots. In case of doubt the Mission Operator can start a scan point leg, with an altitude of 300 m, for a more precise image. Figure 3 shows the process and the results for a given input.

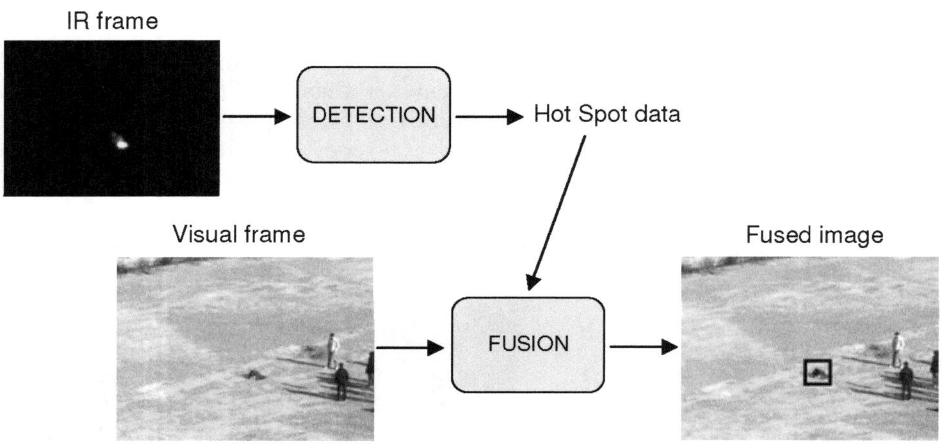

Figure 3. Software architecture for image fusion

2. Framing Systems Model

Because of price and performance trade-offs, we chose the FLIR A320 camera, a radiometric thermal camera working in the wavelength range from 7.5 to 13.0 μm and in the thermal range from 0 to 350ºC. It provides 320 x 240 pixel images of 32 bit floating point absolute temperature values. The visual camera is the Lumenera Le11059c 11 Megapixel network camera with Tamron A09 zoom lens. The relevant characteristics of these cameras are summarized in Table 1.

Table 1. Specifications of the cameras

ThermoVision A320		**Lumenera Le11059c + Tamron A09**	
Spectral range:	7.5 to 13 μm	Field of view:	75º-32º (diagonal)
Temperature. range:	0 to 350ºC (±2ºC)	Focal length:	28-75 mm
Field of view:	25.0º x 18.8º	F-number:	1-2.8
Focal length:	18 mm	Resolution:	4000 x 2656 pixel
F-number:	1.3	Frame rate:	3 fps
Resolution:	320 x 240 pixel		
Frame rate:	9 fps		

In our system, the thermal and the visual cameras are tied together in an upright position, as shown in Figure 4. We consider a simple projection model with the coordinate system centered in the focus lens. The focus distance (in our case the flight altitude) is large enough to assume that both cameras are positioned at the same point, thus the center of the thermal and visual pictures coincide; but as each camera has its own Field Of View (FOV), the captured areas are different in size. For the A320, when flying at an AGL of 300 m one thermal picture covers an area of 133 x 100 m^2, which represents a precision of 0.4 m per pixel. As the thermal camera has lower resolution, one pixel in the thermal image will match several pixels in the visual one.

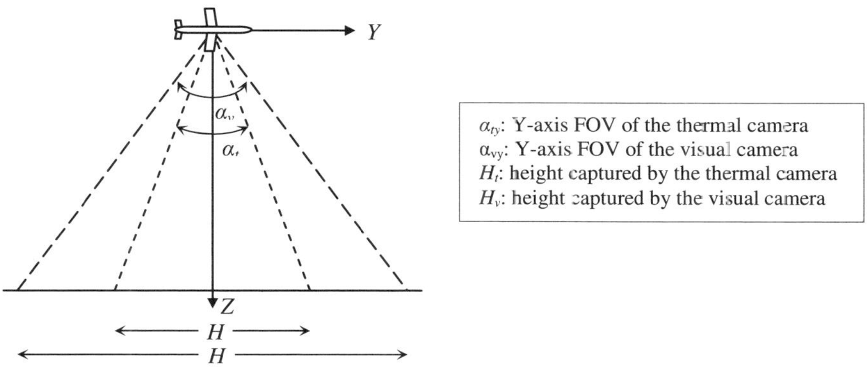

Figure 4. Cameras model (*Y* axis view)

3. Real Time Algorithm

The real time part of the algorithm processes video from the IR Camera and detects hot spots. The architecture (Figure 5) consists of an analog to digital converter for the cameras analogical output, an FPGA that performs the hot spot detection, and an Ethernet driver that transmits the resulting output in an UDP frame with the detected hot spot data: (a) the time stamp when the image was captured, (b) the rectangle containing the hot spot, and (c) the coordinates of the hot spot center of mass.

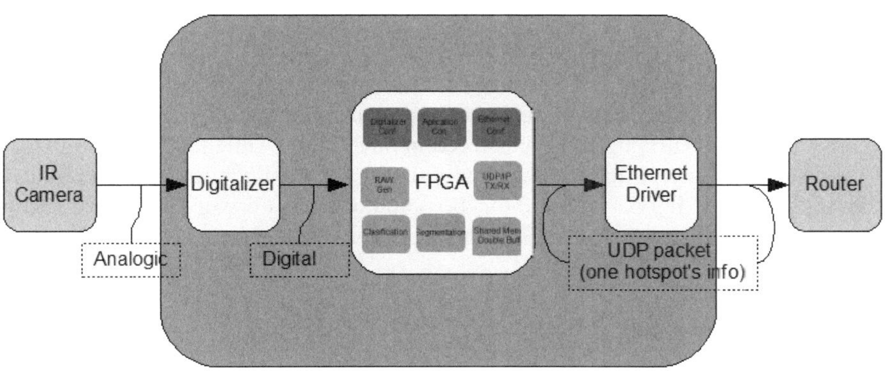

Figure 5. IR board architecture

The FPGA algorithm consists of five code modules and three input/output configuration modules. The first code module generates the RAW stream by extracting the temperature pixels from the digitalized video. The following module classifies each pixel as a hot spot depending on its IR radiation. A third module, the segmentation module, is the core of the detection algorithm. It groups the pixels belonging to the same hot spot. In image processing, segmentation is the process that divides an image in homogeneous regions. Its complexity lies in grouping the pixels in hot spots as the image is being captured. The developed algorithm (Listing 1) performs the segmentation of the image using only the current pixel and the previous line of pixels.

Listing 1. Segmentation algorithm

```
input: pixel(m,n) and previous line of pixels L
receive pixel(m,n)
    if (pixel(m,n) does not belong to a hot spot)
        mark in the line L that pixel(m,n) does not belong to a hot spot.
    if (pixel(m,n) belongs to a hot spot)
        if (pixel(m-1,n) and pixel(m,n-1) do not belong to hot spots)
            create a new hot spot for pixel(m,n)
            mark pixel(m,n) in the line L as belonging to the new hot spot
        if (pixel(m-1,n) belongs to hot_spot_x and pixel(m,n-1) does not belong to any hot spot)
           or (pixel(m-1,n) does not belong to any hot spot and pixel(m,n-1) belongs to hot_spot_x)
           or (pixel(m-1,n) and pixel(m,n-1) belong to hot_spot_x))
            add pixel(m,n) to hot_spot_x in the memory
            mark pixel(m,n) in line L as belonging to hot_spot_x
        if (pixel(m-1,n) belongs to hot_spot_x and pixel(m,n-1) belongs to hot_spot_y)
            add hot_spot_y data to hot_spot_x in the memory
            add pixel(m,n) to hot_spot_x in the memory
            mark pixel(m,n) in line L as belonging to hot_spot_x
            for each pixel in line L
                if (pixel belongs to hot_spot_y)
                    mark pixel as belonging to hot_spot_x
```

The 4th module is a shared memory double buffer. It is organized as a vector of records, with one record for each hot spot. Each record stores the coordinates of the rectangle containing the hot spot and the necessary data to calculate the hot spots center of mass. The segmentation module recalculates this data every time a new pixel is added to a hot spot or when two hot spots, say *hot_spot_x* and *hot_spot_y*, are unified. When *pixel(m, n)* is added to line *L*, *pixel(m, n-1)* is discarded. In this way, the line always contains the same number of pixels.

The last code module implemented in the FPGA generates UDP packages with the data in the shared memory. The memory module has been designed to have a double buffer such that the UDP module can execute in parallel with the segmentation. The partial results of the current image are stored in one buffer, while the final results of the previous image are stored in the other one. Finally, the data configuration modules are for the input digitalizing parameters, for the output Ethernet driver (IP address and port number) and for the threshold values of the classifier module.

4. Data Fusion Algorithm

Visual processing is the most time consuming part of the algorithm due to the high resolution of the image and to the JPEG coding and decoding process. Nevertheless, the proposed fusion of the two pictures takes less than 1.2 seconds to execute in a conventional computer, including the image file access. This time is acceptable for this part of the application, as thermal and visual fusion will be provided only for critical frames on which a hot spot is detected.

The fusion of the thermal and visual images is the result of two steps: First, mapping of the thermal and visual pixel coordinates, and second, acting on the visual pixel value.

Being $p_t[m_t,n_t]$ a pixel on the thermal image, there is a matrix of pixels $p_{vkl}[m_{vk}, n_{vl}]$ that correspond to the same physical area in the visual image:

$$p_t[m_t, n_t] \leftrightarrow \begin{pmatrix} p_{V11}[m_{V1}, n_{V1}] & \cdots & p_{V1L}[m_{V1}, n_{VL}] \\ \vdots & \ddots & \vdots \\ p_{VK1}[m_{VK}, n_{V1}] & \cdots & p_{VKL}[m_{VK}, n_{VL}] \end{pmatrix} \quad (1)$$

The relation between those thermal and visual pixel coordinates can be computed as the composition of scaling and translation functions:

$$\begin{aligned} m_{V1} &= \lfloor (m_t - T_{tm}) \cdot S_m \rfloor + T_{vm} \\ n_{V1} &= \lfloor (n_t - T_{tn}) \cdot S_n \rfloor + T_{vn} \\ m_{VK} &= \lfloor (m_t + 1 - T_{tm}) \cdot S_m \rfloor + T_{vm} - 1 \\ n_{VL} &= \lfloor (n_t + 1 - T_{tn}) \cdot S_n \rfloor + T_{vn} - 1 \end{aligned} \quad (2)$$

The translation and scale factors depend only on the angle of view and the resolution of the cameras, and can be inferred from Figure 4 applying simple geometry:

$$\begin{aligned} &T_{tm} = \frac{M_t}{2} \; ; \; T_{vm} = \frac{M_v}{2} \; ; \qquad T_{tn} = \frac{N_t}{2} \; ; \; T_{vn} = \frac{N_v}{2} \\ &S_m = \frac{M_v}{M_t} \cdot \frac{\tan(\alpha_{ty}/2)}{\tan(\alpha_{vy}/2)} \; ; \qquad S_n = \frac{N_v}{N_t} \cdot \frac{\tan(\alpha_{tx}/2)}{\tan(\alpha_{vx}/2)} \end{aligned} \quad (3)$$

Where

M: image width in pixels	N: image height in pixels
W: captured width in meters	H: captured height in meters
α_x: X-axis angle of view	α_y: Y-axis angle of view

Subscript *t* is used for the thermal camera parameters and subscript *v* for the visual ones. Usually both cameras have square pixels, and S_m and S_n are the same value.

The thermal coordinates of the rectangle and the center of mass provided by the FPGA are translated into visual coordinates using Eqs. (2). The rectangle coordinates are used to draw a black rectangle, by just zeroing the three color channels of the related visual pixels. The visual pixels corresponding to the center of mass, together with their neighbors in a radius of 8 visual pixels, are emphasized in red as follows: The red channel is enhanced ($p_v(r) = 127+0.5 \cdot p_v(r)$), the green component is removed ($p_v(g) = 0$), and the blue channel is softened ($p_v(b) = 0.5 \cdot p_v(b)$). An example of a resulting image is given in Figure 3.

5. Conclusions

In this document we present an aerial intelligent system designed to aid in the Catalonia local fires fighting. The mission objective is to provide the locations of the hot spots of a post-fire, using one UAS equipped with IR and visual cameras. The selection of this mission was done because: a) the closed air space limits the safety considerations, b) the current alternative solution has a high cost, c) the user learning process is fast, and d) the complexity of the solution can progressively be incremented.

The intelligent UAS is composed by a UAV, a GCS and several personal SIT. The UAS will evaluate an area and automatically inform to the closest ground firemen about the hot spots. The system is oriented to tactical response and it is supervised at any time by the operator in command. This is a new approach for the hot spot mission that takes advantage of an on board FPGA which executes a real time hot spot detection algorithm.

Since not all geographical scenarios are equivalent, countries with large unpopulated areas may require more emphasis on fire detection. On large countries like Australia, it may be interesting to work on fire perimeter detection. Crop monitoring, search and rescue, or any other missions may require more attention to ATM integration. Large endurance airframes are also of interest for future civil missions, once we can provide a successful story.

Acknowledgments

This work has been partially funded by AGAUR under contract 2007ITT-0014 and by Ministry of Education of Spain under contract TIN2007-63927.

References

[1] X. Ubeda et al, *Effects of prescribed fire on soil quality in Mediterranean grassland (Prades Mountains, north-east Spain),* International Journal of Wildland Fire, International Association of Wildland Fire, 2005.

[2] Ágoston Réstas. "Research and development of the aerial reconnaissance and extinguishing of forest fires". PhD dissertation at the National Defence University, Budapest, Hungary, Oct 2008.

[3] WRAP team, *WRAP project,* http.//geo.arc.nasa.gov/sge/WRAP/

[4] T.H. Cox, I. Somers, D.J. Fratello, *Earth Observation and the Role of UAVs: A Capability Assessment. Version 1.1,* NASA Report www.nasa.gov/centers/dryden/research/civuav, 2006.

[5] Enric Pastor, Cristina Barrado, Pablo Royo, Juan Lopez, Eduard Santamaria, Xavier Prats, and Josep M Batlle, *Red-Eye: A Helicopter-Based Architecture for Tactical Wildfire Monitoring Strategies.* AIAA Aerospace Conference, Big Sky, MT, 2009.

[6] S.E. Dunagan et al, *A Multi-Sensor Imaging Payload for Mission-Adaptive Remote Sensing Applications,* AIAA Infotech@Aerospace, Arlington, VI, 2005.

Intelligent Environments 2009
V. Callaghan et al. (Eds.)
IOS Press, 2009

doi:10.3233/978-1-60750-034-6-285

An Intelligent Scenario For New Unmanned Aerial Systems

Joshua TRISTANCHO[a,1] and Sonia P. MANSILLA[a,2]
[a] *Technical University of Catalonia (UPC). Technical School of Castelldefels, 08860 Castelldefels, Barcelona, Spain*

Abstract. Many Civil Unmanned Applications require the development of an Unmanned Aerial System (UAS) able to flight a mission. In the present paper an Intelligent Scenario is proposed in order to develop a new Unmanned Aerial Vehicle (UAV) easily and in short time. This Integrated Scenario consists of a wind tunnel, an open source flight model and a real simulator cabin. With these three components it is possible to validate, from the scratch, a low cost UAV using fast prototyping techniques. A brief introduction to the actual integration of UAS in the airspace is presented as well as the development process of a new aircraft in the intelligent scenario. The two facilities, the real cabin simulator and the wind tunnel are explained. These facilities were constructed by students in their final bachelor thesis in collaboration with the authors and members of the ICARUS research group.

Keywords. Unmanned Aerial Vehicle, Wind Tunnel, Flight Model, Cabin Simulator, UAS

Introduction

In 2004, the *Escola Politècnica Superior de Castelldefels* of the *Universitat Politècnica de Catalunya* (EPSC) got a Cessna 150 chassis. The chassis was transformed in a flight simulator cabin with 120° of view and a panel equipped with several instruments including a TFT screen.
In 2006, the Department of Applied Physics of the EPSC built a 3.5 meters large wind tunnel with 40 centimeters of test chamber span.
In 2007, ICARUS, a research group of the EPSC, brought the UAS Shadow MK-1 (Figure 1), which is able to fly like a radio controlled aircraft model. It was installed an autopilot in the model and hence, became an unmanned aerial vehicle (UAV). The autopilot, though, requires a flight model of the new Unmanned Aerial System (UAS).
Consequently, the EPSC decided, as a strategic project of the University, to create an intelligent scenario for developing this UAS and others. This Integrated Scenario consists of a wind tunnel, an open source flight model and a real simulator cabin. With these three components it is possible to validate, from the scratch, a low cost UAV using fast prototyping techniques.

---

[1] Department of Computer Architecture. Corresponding author: jtristancho@ac.upc.edu
[2] Department of Applied Mathematics IV. Supported by the project MTM2008-C6620-C03-01/MTM of the Spanish Ministry of Science and Education and the project 2005SGR00256 of the Catalan Research Council.

Figure 1. The UAS model Shadow MK-1.

1. The integration of UAS in the airspace

An Unmanned Aerial System (UAS) is an airplane able to fly autonomously all the phases of a mission. These vehicles used to be typically military, but nowadays are suitable for civil applications whenever they are low cost. Military UAS are still '*User Specific*', this is to say, they require high development costs and have a low volume production produce and consequently, a high acquisition cost and a high ownership cost. In addition to that, there are no standards, no airworthiness norm and no certification norms. Moreover, there are no air-traffic management regulations. As a result, the market of non-military, scientific and commercial applications can not emerge.

1.1. UAS Study Group

Many efforts have to be done [1] in order to solve the critical issues: UAS has to '*Sense and Avoid*' autonomously, the spectrum and bandwidth have to be assigned to the UAS and there is insufficient research and development funding. Coordination and cooperation are required on both sides of the Atlantic and between military and civil organizations. Efforts have to be coordinated internationally beyond Europe and USA with Australia, Canada, China, India, Japan, New Zealand, Russia, South Africa, Singapore, etc. Standards have to be defined consensually and a common terminology in English should be agreed. In the near future, the International Civil Airworthiness Organization (ICAO) is expected to create a UAS Study Group which we will be able to propose international civil rules to be followed by the member nations.

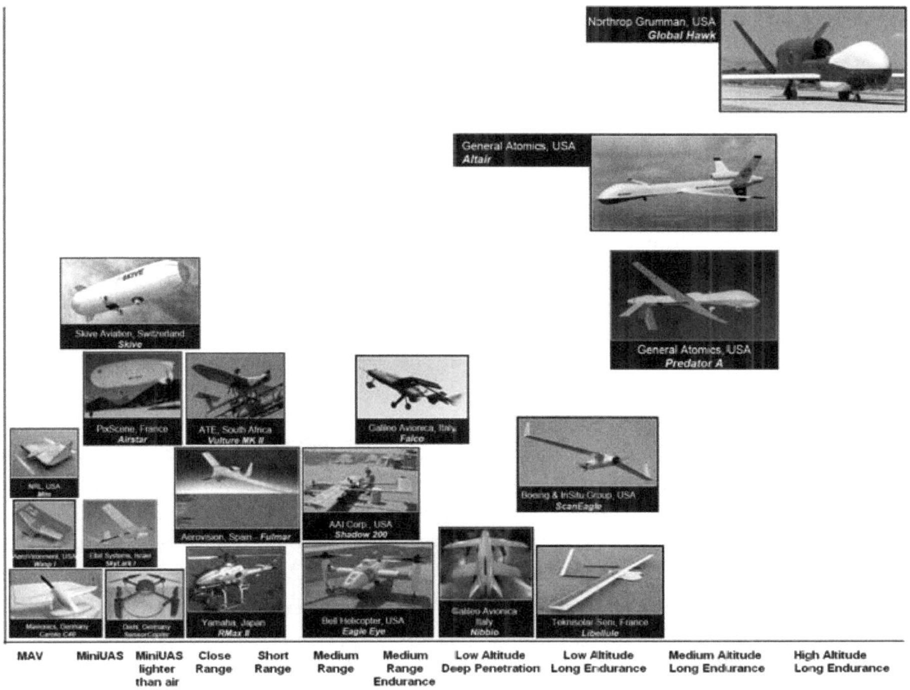

Figure 2. UAS classified by range, endurance and altitude.

1.2. UAS classification

Following the Unmanned Vehicle Systems International [http://www.uvs-international.org/] recommendations, in 2008 there were 262 producers of UAS technologies. In the world there were 45 countries having UAS, from which 16 were European.

A model aircraft is not considered an UAS because of its recreational purposes. These aircrafts are classified in toys lighter than 25 kg (MAVs), lighter than 150 kg and heavier than 150 kg (UAVs). Many of these model aircrafts are radio controlled by a person on ground and they do not exhibit an autonomous flight. In Figure 2, UAS are presented classified by range, endurance and altitude as follows:

- **MicroUAS:** Mite (NRL, USA), Carolo C40 (Mavionics, Germany), Wasp I (AeroVironment, USA), etc.
- **MiniUAS:** SensorCopter (Diehl, Germany), SkyLark I (Elbit Systems, Israel), etc.
- **MiniUAS lighter than the air:** Airstar (PixScene, France), Skive (Skive Aviation, Switzerland), etc.
- **Close Range (CR):** RMax II (Yamaha, Japan), Silver Fox (Adv. Ceramics Research, USA), etc.
- **Short Range (SR):** Vulture MK II (ATE, South Africa), Fulmar, (Aerovision, Spain), etc.
- **Medium Range (MR):** Shadow 200 (AAI Corp., USA), Eagle Eye (Bell Helicopter, USA), etc.

- **Medium Range Endurance (MRE):** Falco (Galileo Avionica, Italy), etc.
- **Low Altitude Deep Penetration (LADP):** Nibbio (Galileo Avionica, Italy), etc.
- **Low Altitude Long Endurance (LALE):** Scan Eagle (Boeing & InSitu Group, USA), Libellule, (Teknisolar-Seni, France), etc.
- **Medium Altitude Long Endurance (MALE):** Predator A (General Atomics, USA), Altair (General Atomics, USA), etc.
- **Hight Altitude Long Endurance (HALE):** Global Hawk (Northrop Grumman, USA), etc.

2. The intelligent scenario

The intelligent scenario is able to interact with people and with simulated aircrafts through a working net. As mentioned before, the Integrated Scenario consists of a wind tunnel, an open source flight model and a real simulator cabin. With them, a low cost Unmanned Aerial Vehicle (UAV) can be validated using fast prototyping techniques. The iteration process is reduced to the minimum as it can be observed in the case of the UAV Shadow MK-1. From a given model of aircraft, a 3D digital model is created in a Computed-Aided Design (CAD). This 3D digital model is suitable for writing documentation such as the Flight Manual (FM), the Illustrated Part Catalog (IPC) and the Maintenance Manual (MM). Moreover, this 3D model is threefold: simulated, using GAMBIT and FLUENT, arithmetic, using the DATCOM and experimental, using the wind tunnel. The model gives the Performances of the new aircraft before flying. The next step consists of giving these parameters to the autopilot and to the ground operator so that the operator can train in the real simulator cabin. The UAS is tested and virtually flown before building the real UAS. The interaction produced in different moments of the development process of a new aircraft is shown in Figure 3. A real example of development process is presented. Related to UAV design, drawings were made by Jordi Tudela Ramos [2] in 2008 using CATIA V5; the Illustrated Part Catalog was done by Carlos Pérez Oliva [6]; arithmetic approximations using DATCOM as well as CFD simulations using GAMBIT and FLUENT were done by Carlos Pérez Arroyo and Pol Sintes Arroyo [3]; performances were modeled using JSBSim by María Teresa Marín Hermosilla and Mar Noguera [4] and later modeled in Flight Gear and tested by Joshua Tristancho and others.

The two facilities, the **real cabin simulator** and the **wind tunnel,** were made by students in final bachelor thesis in collaboration with the authors and some others members of the faculty of the *Escola Politècnica Superior de Castelldefels* (EPSC). Now, these two facilities are available for anyone who needs them at the EPSC in Barcelona. The cabin simulator was constructed by many students such as Fran Campón Lara, who made the structure; Osvaldo Betancourt Castellanos [5] made the flight instruments panel; Sergio Ros Salvador [8] made the joystick integration with the flight controls; Albert Fajula Catllà [7] designed the dynamic platform; Pablo Quirós Álvarez and Carlos Zurita Sierco [9] made the dynamic actuation system. Finally, the wind tunnel was designed by Sergio García Horcas [10] and the detectors were installed and tested by Alba Romero Ponce and Anna Vallespí Antolí [11]. Refer to EPSC aeronautical facilities web for details [12].

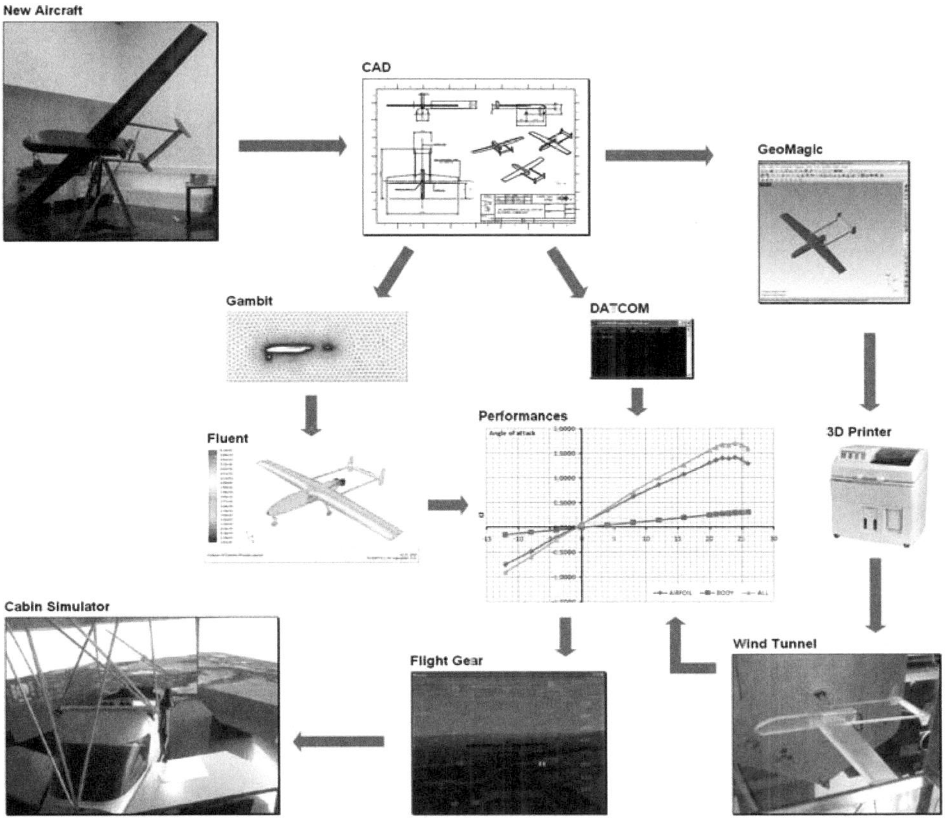

Figure 3. Development process of a new unmanned aerial vehicle in the intelligent scenario.

2.1. The real simulator cabin

In 2004 the UPC University got for the *Escola Politècnica Superior de Castelldefels* (EPSC) a Cessna 150 chassis. The chassis was transformed in a flight simulator cabin with 120º of view and a panel equipped with several flight instruments including a TFT screen dedicated to new digital instruments.

The distributed simulator consists of at least two computers inside a net. The main computer, called Simulator, is devoted to the human interface: the simulation of the UAV, the visualization in the three screens a synthetic view of the flight scenario, the instrument panel control and the dynamic of the cabin. The other computer, called Co-simulator, gives the information to the main computer about virtual vehicles through the net. Additional computers can be connected to the net. All these computers implement AI (Artificial Intelligence) algorithms interacting with the simulated UAV and the ground operator. Furthermore, it is possible to visualize the scenario information inside an external monitor and show a different point of view in order to manage the air-traffic of the virtual scenario and to speak to the person acting as ground operator.

Figure 4. The real simulator cabin with 120º of view.

This integrated scenario is twofold:

- It allows an easy way to test new vehicles.
- It provides training to the new ground operators before flying.

In addition to that, it is possible to test a mission inside the simulator where more than one person are involved and more than one virtual vehicle interact, not only another airplane, but also a boat or a car. That way, safety is significantly increased and the cost of a new operator development significantly reduced. Moreover, the cost of the missions which can be tested inside the simulated scenario before the real mission takes place can be reduced.

Some virtual test flights were flown by real pilots and other users in order to test the performances of the simulated model. In the following, a list of advantages of simulating the complete UAS scenario is presented:

- We are able to test our future UAS inside a real mission design, thanks to this intelligent environment.
- We can test some ergonomics aspects of the mission and prepare the operator's procedure before building the real UAS.
- We can choose the final aerodrome from a selected number of candidates and evaluate pros and cons before having the airworthiness authorization, since there is no clear framework of regulations regarding UAS.

2.2. The wind tunnel

In 2006, the researchers of the Department of Applied Physics at the EPSC built a 3.5 meters large wind tunnel with 40 centimeters of test chamber span inside the test chamber. The so called *Wind Tunnel* is designed to generate a laminated and constant air flow of 40,500 m^3/h (cubic meters per hour) with a turbulence lower than 0.52% for a Reynolds numbers of $1.38{\bullet}10^6$ in the flow direction, which means that for a turbulent flow only 0.52% of the flow is disturbed. At 1,450 rpm (revolutions per minute) the fan generates a pressure drop of 369 Pa Pascals and an average speed of 42.4 m/s (meters per second). This speed is equivalent to a Mach number 0.11, which means that this wind tunnel is focused in subsonic incompressible flows, lower than 150 km/h (kilometers per hour). The aim of this wind tunnel is to validate experimentally the results provided by simulation, using GAMBIT and FLUENT, or arithmetically, using the DATCOM program. In the wind tunnel, the results are very accurate due to the fast prototyping technique based on 3D printers with resolutions lower than 0.01 millimeters in the scaled aircraft model.

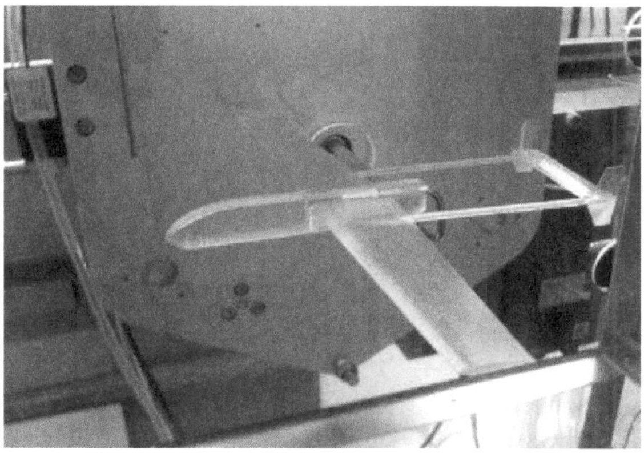

Figure 4. The wind tunnel with 40 centimeters of test chamber span.

We tested the UAS Shadow MK-1 model inside the wind tunnel in order to obtain the basic values of lift, drag and moment. Having this values, we can calibrate simulations in FLUENT. When same results are obtained, the simulator model is validated and we can modify the design in GAMBIT in order to test the impact of each fuselage component without the need to build a new model. In this sense, iteration process is reduced.

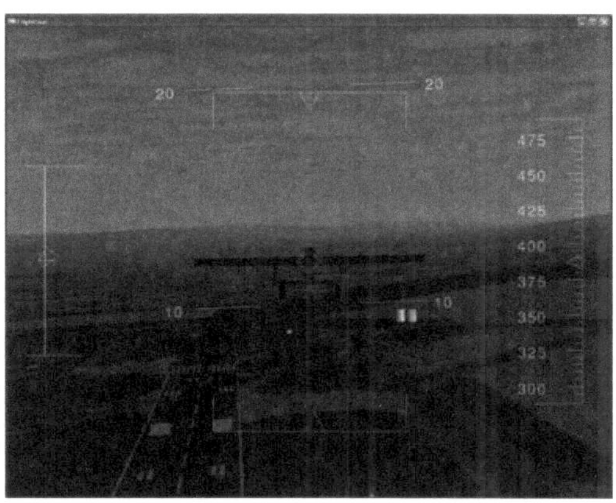

Figure **5.** A view of the open source Flight Gear with the flight model of the tested UAS.

2.3. The open source flight model

The UAS Shadow MK-1 is able to fly like a radio controlled aircraft model. An autopilot was installed in order to be an autonomous unmanned aerial vehicle. This autopilot requires a new UAS flight model generated from the DATCOM program and tested by means of Computation Fluid Dynamics (CFD) and by experimental means inside the wind tunnel. In Figure 5, the result is presented after composing some XML filer configurations for the JSBSim engine simulator of the open source Flight Gear simulator. An extra AC file was extracted from the GAMBIT model for the Graphical model. Finally, a very realistic result is achieved inside this intelligent environment.

3. Future lines

Shadow MK-1 aircraft model was transformed in an UAS contributing to the actual UAS industry. The UPC University, and in particular, the *Escola Politècnica Superior de Castelldefels,* offers to anybody interested the opportunity to test new UAS technologies in the intelligent scenario: testing new systems inside the Cessna 150 cabin, giving training for ground operators, providing new open source flight models and testing them inside the wind tunnel.

4. Acknowledgement

The first author acknowledges the support of the ICARUS research group of the Technical University of Catalonia (UPC).

5. References

[1] Blyenburgh. Peter Van, UNMANNED AIRCRAFT SYSTEMS The current situation, *UAS ATM Integration Workshop* (2008), Brussels, BELGIUM.
[2] Tudela Ramos. Jordi, DISEÑO DE UN PAYLOAD BAY PARA UN UAV DE APLICACIÓN CIVIL (Submitted), UPCOMMONS (2009), Barcelona, SPAIN
[3] Pérez Arroyo. Carlos, Sintes Arroyo. Pol, AERODYNAMICS, STABILITY AND CONTROL COMPUTATIONAL ANALYSIS FOR UAVs, UPCOMMONDS, http://hdl.handle.net/2099.1/4244 (Jul, 2007), Barcelona, SPAIN
[4] Marin Hermosilla. María Teresa, Noguera. Mar, MODELADO DE AERONAVES USANDO LIBRERÍAS JSBSim, UPCOMMONDS, http://hdl.handle.net/2099.1/6027 (Oct, 2008) , Barcelona, SPAIN
[5] Betancourt Castellanos. Osvaldo, POSTA EN MARXA DE UN SIMULADOR DE VOL DE LA EPSC, UPCOMMONDS, http://hdl.handle.net/2099.1/4206 (Jun, 2007), Barcelona, SPAIN
[6] Pérez Oliva. Carlos, CREACIÓ DEL ILUSTRATED PART CATALOG DEL UAV MODEL SHADOW, UPCOMMONDS, (Gen, 2008) , Barcelona, SPAIN
[7] Fajula Catllà. Albert, ESTUDI DE VIABILITAT D'UNA PLATAFORMA DINÀMICA PER A UN SIMULADOR DE VOL, UPCOMMONDS, http://hdl.handle.net/2099.1/3825 (Feb, 2006), Barcelona, SPAIN
[8] Ros Salvador. Sergio, IMPLEMENTACIÓN DE SISTEMA DE MANDO DEL SIMULADOR CESNA (Submitted), UPCOMMONDS, (2009), Barcelona, SPAIN
[9] Quirós Álvarez. Pablo, Zurita Sierco. Carlos, IMPLEMENTACIÓN DE SISTEMA DE ACTUACIÓN DEL SIMULADOR CESNA (Submitted), UPCOMMONS, (2009), Barcelona, SPAIN
[10] García Horcas. Sergio, CONSTRUCCIÓ D'UN TÚNEL DE VENT SUBSÒNIC, UPCOMMONS, (2006), Barcelona, SPAIN
[11] Romero Ponce. Alba, Vallespí Antolí. Anna, INTEGRACIÓ D'INSTRUMENTS DE MESURA EN UN TÚNEL DE VENT DE LABORATORI, UPCOMMONS, http://hdl.handle.net/2099.1/4177 (Jul 2007), Barcelona, SPAIN
[12] Laboratoris d'Aeronàutica de l'EPSC. https://epsc.upc.edu/ca/?q=node/616 (Updated May 2009)

Special Session on Pervasive Computing

Intelligent Environments 2009
V. Callaghan et al. (Eds.)
IOS Press, 2009

doi:10.3233/978-1-60750-034-6-295

Plan Recognition in Instrumented Environments

Michael SCHNEIDER [1]
German Research Center for Artificial Intelligence (DFKI), Germany

Abstract. Plan recognition is the process of inferring a user's plans and goals by observing her behavior. With their sensors, instrumented environments provide a good infrastructure for the application of plan recognition, and in return can benefit from plan recognition knowledge by better supporting their users. This article addresses specific issues that arise if plan recognition is applied in physical environments. A plan recognition model based on dynamic Bayesian networks is presented and practically applied in an instrumented kitchen scenario. Furthermore, a utility function for sensor information is derived from this model, which can be used to solve the problem of sensor selection in real-world plan recognition applications.

Keywords. Instrumented Environments, Plan Recognition, Sensor Selection

Introduction

Knowledge about a user's goals and future actions is important for intelligent environments in order to proactively support the user, to anticipate her needs, and to adapt themselves according to her upcoming tasks. A possible source for such information is *plan recognition*, which is the process of inferring a user's plans and goals by observing her behavior. With their multitude of sensors, intelligent environments provide a good infrastructure for the application of plan recognition techniques in real-world scenarios.

In contrast to virtual environments like operating systems or computer games, where user actions can be directly observed via software probes, plan recognition in real-world environments faces some specific challenges: On the one hand, most physical sensors measure (partial) state information instead of actions. Although it is often possible to infer actions from state changes, this approach is difficult and ambiguous in the general case. Plan recognition for instrumented environments thus should consider explicit state information in addition to "regular" user actions. Secondly, it might be impossible or unreasonable to run all sensors in an environment at all times due to physical or economical resource constraints. Thus, a plan recognition system should be able to support an eventually applied *sensor selection* process by providing it with an estimation of the usefulness of certain information items with respect to the plan recognition process.

In this article, we propose a state-aware plan recognition model and show how a utility function for sensor information can be derived from this model. The article concludes with first results of an empirical evaluation of the proposed utility function.

[1]Corresponding Author: Michael Schneider, German Research Center for Artificial Intelligence, Stuhlsatzenhausweg 3, 66123 Saarbruecken, Germany. E-mail: michael.schneider@dfki.de.

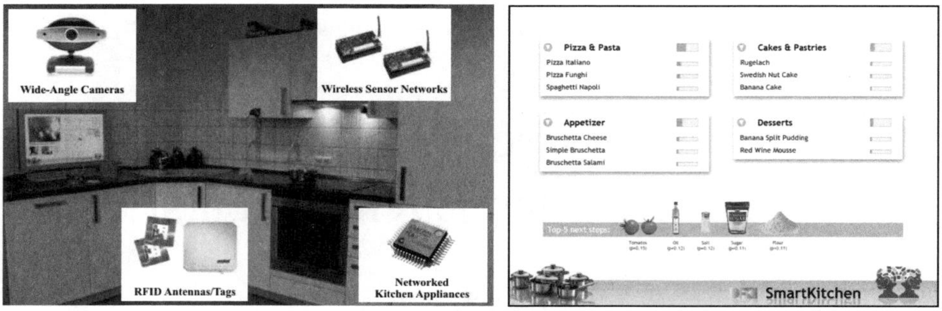

Figure 1. Smart Kitchen environment (left) and recipe prediction through plan recognition (right).

1. Example Scenario: Smart Kitchen Environment

A *Smart Kitchen* environment was chosen as a practical testbed for the presented research. The environment comprises a kitchen which was post-hoc instrumented with different sensors, including radio frequency identification (RFID) antennas in shelves and countertop, RFID-tagged ingredients and kitchen tools, "micaZ" wireless sensor network nodes attached to a variety of objects and locations, networked kitchen appliances like stove or oven, and multiple wide-angle video cameras (cf. Figure 1, left).

These sensors observe the user's cooking process and feed their information into the *Semantic Cookbook* application [13]. The application uses the provided information to create a digital collection of the user's personal recipes. These recordings include an audio/video stream as well as formally represented information about the user's interactions with ingredients, tools, and kitchen appliances. Recorded recipes can be shared over the internet with other users. Later, users can repeat recipes from their own or other users' collections. The cookbook application provides assistance in form of preparation instructions and issues warnings if the user deviates from the recorded process.

Plan recognition is used by the Smart Kitchen environment in two ways (cf. Figure 1, right): *Prediction of recipes:* If the user starts cooking without explicitly choosing a recipe, the system tries to infer the intended recipe. It calculates the likelihood of each recipe and presents to the user a sorted list of candidates. On new events, these probabilities are updated and the list is reordered. *Prediction of next actions:* The system tries to predict the user's most probable next actions. This information is used to remind the user of upcoming steps and to proactively provide additional instruction on how to use certain tools or ingredients. The kitchen environment is well suited for the application of plan recognition, as the set of possible actions is restricted, which facilitates the adoption of a closed world model. The plan library that is required by the plan recognition system is automatically generated from a statistical analysis of recorded and shared recipes.

2. Related Work

Plan recognition systems have been applied to a broad range of applications. The first system was developed for story understanding [17].Further applications included the recognition of plans in the military domain [12], and real-time strategy games [4]. One of the first general purpose plan recognition approaches used propositional logic to formulate plan recognition as a problem of theorem proving [10]. A drawback of such logic-based systems is their inability to deal with competing hypothesis. Thus the use of techniques for reasoning under uncertainty has been proposed, including Bayesian Networks [3], Dempster-Shafer Theory [1], and Abstract Hidden Markov Models [2].

The problem of sensor selection has been studied in application-specific and generalized variants. Areas of application include robotics [7], target tracking [15] and wireless sensor networks [19]. Generalized variants have been studied in the context of dynamic systems [6], hypothesis testing [5], and discrete-event systems [8]. The general complexity of the sensor selection problem depends on the number of sensor subsets that are considered. Given a set of n sensors, there exist 2^n subsets. Clearly, direct enumeration of all subsets is not practical unless n is very small. By using approaches like "branch and bound" the sensor selection problem can be exactly solved without evaluating all subsets in the average case [16]. Several heuristics have been proposed to approximately solve the sensor selection problem. These include application specific heuristics as well as generic methods like evolutionary algorithms [18] or randomized rounding [11].

3. State-Aware Plan Recognition in Instrumented Environments

Typical plan recognition approaches take as input a sequence of observed user actions. Most physical sensors in an instrumented environment however do not directly detect user actions, but instead observe partial aspects of the environment's physical state. RFID sensors for instance detect the position of objects. Although one might conclude from a relocation of an object the execution of a hypothetic "move object" action through the user, this conclusion is not always possible or valid. This especially holds if more complex actions than the moving of objects should be observed.

The idea of state-aware plan recognition is to ease this problem by explicitly representing and considering state information in the plan recognition's reasoning process. This has two advantages: It relieves the infrastructure from the burden of inferring user actions from state changes, and it makes the plan recognition more robust to missed observations (as the new state resulting from an action can in most cases still be observed even if the action itself has already terminated). The central concept of state-aware plan recognition is the so-called *plan execution state space*, which is a finite set of states. It contains an obligatory *idle* state and a set of goal states. Each goal state corresponds to the completion of a certain plan. The user executes actions from her finite *action repertoire* in order to move from the *idle* state towards a desired goal state. Intermediate states represent the progress of the user's plan execution process and correspond to partial "configurations" of the environment that occur as a result of the executed actions. We assume that these can (at least to some extend) be observed via sensors (cf. section 3.1). The new state that results from executing some action depends on the old state and the chosen action in a way that is described by a so-called *plan library*. For each state it defines the a-priori probabilities of certain actions, as well as the probabilities of the resulting transitions. The dependency of actions and state transitions can be visualized as a directed graph, where nodes correspond to states and edges correspond to transitions that result from single actions. Figure 2 (left) shows a sample plan library with the following three plans: $[\alpha_1, \alpha_2, \alpha_3]$, $[\alpha_1, \alpha_2, \alpha_2]$, and $[\alpha_2, \alpha_3, \alpha_1]$. Goal states are $goal_1$, and $goal_2$. Formally, state space and plan library together can be understood as a probabilistic automaton, which models the user's plan selection and execution process.

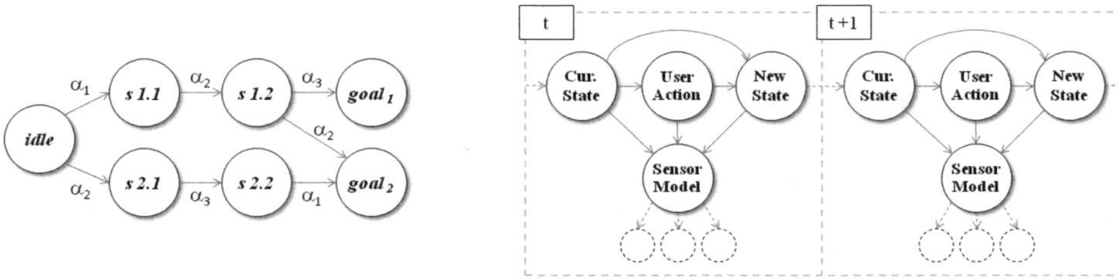

Figure 2. Example plan library graph (left) and dynamic Bayesian plan recognition network (right).

Given such a representation, the problem of plan recognition then is to estimate the user's current (hidden) plan execution state given a sequence of sensor observations. The resulting plan recognition hypothesis is represented as a probability distribution over the plan execution state space. From this information and the plan library, all other relevant information like a probabilistic prediction on possibly targeted goal states and planned future actions can be easily derived.

3.1. Plan Recognition Model

The actual plan execution and recognition process can be modeled as the dynamic Bayesian network (DBN) shown in Figure 2 (right). The upper three nodes *current state*, *user action*, and *new state* model the user's plan execution process. The domain of the state nodes equals the plan execution state space; the domain of the action node equals the user's action repertoire. The lower half of the network represents the environment's *sensor model*. It describes the probabilistic dependencies between plan execution state, user actions, and the resulting sensors readings. Although the sensor model is shown as a single node for reasons of clarity, it might be far more complex in practical applications. Its concrete structure depends on the environment's implementation and used sensors. One iteration of the actual plan recognition process then is a 3-step algorithm:

1. The *current state* node's a-priori distribution is set to the current plan recognition hypothesis (which initially is $p(idle) = 1$ and $p(s \neq idle) = 0$).
2. Observation data (if available) is assigned as evidence to the according nodes in the sensor model subnetwork.
3. After performing probabilistic inference on the resulting DBN, the updated plan recognition hypothesis can be queried from the *new state* node.

3.2. Sensor Selection for Plan Recognition

While from the plan recognition system's perspective it is desirable to acquire as much observation data as possible, it is often not reasonable or feasible to run all sensors in an environment at all times due to technical or economical reasons. Such reasons are generally related to resource restrictions of the used components: Mobile devices and sensor networks for instance usually have limited power supply, wireless communication bandwidth, and processing power. Thus one might want to deactivate certain sensors or devices when they are currently not required. The general problem of selecting the "most promising" subset S^* of all sensors S given limited resources $\hat{r}$ is known as *sensor selection problem*, and can be formulated as the following optimization problem:

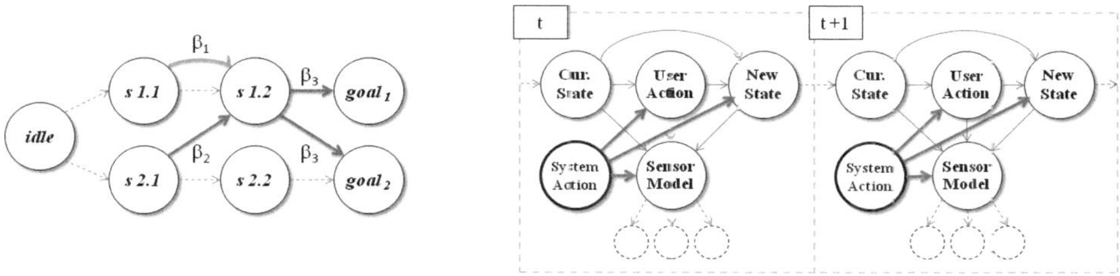

Figure 3. System support graph (left) and extended dynamic Bayesian plan recognition network (right).

$$S^* = \arg\max_{S' \subseteq S} EUS(S') \text{ subject to } \sum_{s \in S'} r(s) \leq \hat{r}$$

where $EUS(S')$ is a function that calculates the expected utility of running a set S' of sensors (defined below), $r(s)$ is the resource consumption of a single sensor $s \in S$, and $\hat{r}$ is the maximum amount of resources available. Let $\{r_1, \ldots, r_n\}$ be the set of limited resources, then $r(s)$ and $\hat{r}$ are vectors from $\mathcal{R}^n$, where the ith element corresponds to the cost/resource limit associated with r_i. The expected utility $EUS(S')$ of a set S' of sensors is calculated by summing up the individual expected utilities of each possibly observable set of sensor readings, weighted by the probability of its occurrence:

$$EUS(S') = \sum_{i \in I(S')} p_{\mathcal{H}}(i) EUI(i)$$

where $I(S')$ is the superset of all readings eventually observed by S', $p_{\mathcal{H}}(i)$ is the probability that a set i of readings is observed given the current plan execution hypothesis $\mathcal{H}$ (the values of $p_{\mathcal{H}}(i)$ can be directly computed from the DBN's sensor model part), and $EUI(i)$ is the *expected utility of information* of some set of sensor readings. The question now is how to define EUI in the plan recognition case.

3.3. Information Utility in Plan Recognition Applications

We propose a decision-theoretic utility measure for (sensor) information in plan recognition applications, which can be used to solve the sensor selection problem introduced in the previous section. According to decision theory [14], an information item's value can only be assessed indirectly by comparing the revenue of a certain decision situation with and without having the information in question available. In our case, this revenue is the added value that the user experiences as a result of the plan recognition process. A system might contribute to this added value in two ways: (1) By helping the user to reach "higher valued" goals, and (2) by helping the user to reach her goals more efficiently. In both cases, the system might either choose to actively influence the plan execution process (i.e. by automatically operating the kitchen's oven), or to passively influence the user by the provision of helpful information (i.e. by displaying preparation instructions).

We use the plan library graph introduced in section 3 to model these interventions. We assume that the plan recognition system possesses a set of *support actions*. These actions either directly lead to state changes, or indirectly influence the probability of certain user actions and/or state transitions. A special *none* action represents the case when the system currently provides no support. Figure 3 (left) shows our sample plan library with three exemplary system actions: β_1 executes an action on behalf of the user, β_2 intervenes the user's plan execution process, and β_3 passively changes the probabilities that certain user-caused transitions occur. The effects of all support actions are represented by a formal *support model*. For each possible system action and plan execution state it defines the probabilities that certain user actions and resulting transitions occur. Note that usually single support actions are only applicable in certain states. In all other states they have either none or negative effect. These relations also have to be represented in the support model. The (positive or negative) effects of the system's actions on the user's added value are defined in a separate *cost/reward model*. This model associates a positive reward or negative cost to each possible goal state, user action, and system action.

The desired utility function can now be derived from the plan recognition system's *support decision problem* (SDP), which is to choose the best support action given the current plan hypothesis. Decision theory introduces the notion of *expected utility* (EU), which is the utility that results for a decision maker from choosing a certain decision alternative. The *maximum expected utility* ($\overline{EU}$) is the utility of the best available alternative (which a rational decision maker is assumed to always take). We will later see how $\overline{EU}_{SDP}$ can be easily computed form the plan library, support model, and cost/reward model. Then the expected utility of some set i of information items can be defined as

$$EUI(i) = \overline{EU}_{SDP}(PR(i, \mathcal{H})) - \overline{EU}_{SDP}(PR(\emptyset, \mathcal{H}))$$

where $\overline{EU}_{SDP}(\mathcal{H}')$ is the maximum expected utility of SDP given a plan hypothesis $\mathcal{H}'$, and $PR(i, \mathcal{H})$ is a function which represents one iteration of the plan recognition process and returns an updated plan execution hypothesis based on a current hypothesis $\mathcal{H}$ and a set of sensor observations i (a modified version of the plan recognition DBN has to be used here, cf. Figure 3, right). $\overline{EU}_{SDP}$ can be easily computed by representing SDP as a Partially Observable Markov Decision Process (POMDP).

Formally, a POMDP is a tuple (S, A, O, P, R), where S is a finite set of states, A is a finite set of actions, P is a finite set of probabilities, O is a finite set of observations, and $R : A, S \mapsto \mathbb{R}$ is the reward function. Each time period, the environment is in some state $s \in S$, the agent takes an action $a \in A$. Taking action a makes the environment transition to state s' with probability $P(s' \mid s, a)$ and the agent receives a reward for it, with expected value $r(s, a, s')$. In the case of SDP, the state space S equals the plan execution state space, A equals the set of system actions, O equals the set of user actions, function P can be derived from the plan library and support model, and function R can be derived from the cost/reward model. The concrete definitions for P and R have to be omitted due to space restrictions, but can be easily derived by the interested reader. The resulting $POMDP_{SDP}$ can now be solved offline using methods like presented in [9]. The resulting policy can then be used to efficiently calculate $\overline{EU}_{SDP}$ and thus EUI.

3.4. Evaluation

In order to test the performance of the utility function proposed in section 3.3 we performed a randomized evaluation study. The study was conducted with a plan library/support model containing a total of 1000 states and 30 user and support actions each. Support actions were only effective at some randomly chosen states, but ineffective otherwise. All models were randomly created within the given bounds in order to minimize the danger of accidentally choosing models which prefer the proposed utility measure. Then, 1000 individual, randomly chosen plans from this library were executed by a simulated user in a simulated environment. After each user action, a new set of

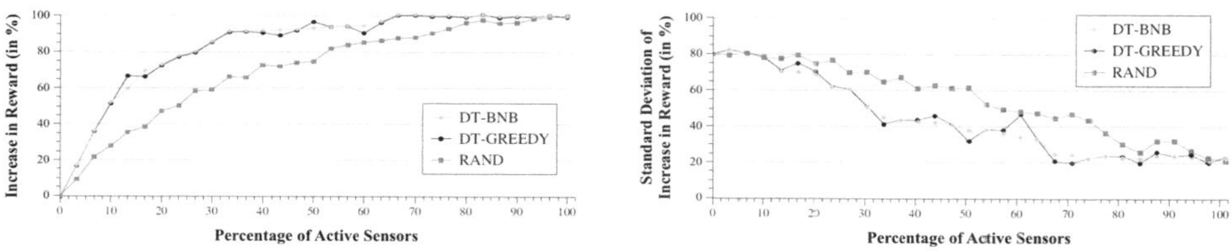

Figure 4. Increase in reward value (left) and standard deviation (right) of evaluated algorithms.

sensors was select and activate. Simulated observation data was only forwarded to active sensors. In each run, the simulation framework recorded the true costs and rewards.

A simulation setup was chosen for two reasons: Due to the probabilistic nature of our approach, a huge number of samples need to be taken in order to get reliable results about the average performance, which is hard to achieve with human users. On the other side, our approach requires a true interaction between the user and the system to take place at run time, so that pre-recorded sensor data could not be used in this case.

Each experiment was repeated multiple times while choosing $\hat{r}$ such that a varying percentage of sensors were selected in each iteration (for reasons of simplicity we assumed that all sensors have the same, fixed cost). We repeated each run with three different sensor selection algorithms: *DT-GREEDY* founds an approximation solution by iteratively adding the highest-rated unselected sensor to the set of chosen sensors, *DT-BNB* uses a branch and bound approach to find an optimal set of sensors, and *RAND* randomly selects sensors[2]. Figure 4 (left) shows the average results of each algorithm at different ratios of selected sensors. The y-axis gives the percental increase in absolute reward, where 0% corresponds to the value reached with no sensors selected, and 100% corresponds to the value reached with all sensors selected.

The results show that on average the sensor selection algorithms that used the proposed decision theoretic utility measure achieved a higher increase in reward than a random selector. At the same time, the standard deviation of reward of the decision theoretic approaches were lower than for the random selection (cf. Figure 4, right). This indicates, that *DT-BNB* and *DT-GREEDY* achieve more "stable" results in the general case, while *RAND* sometimes is lucky guessing the correct sensors and sometimes not.

4. Conclusion and Outlook

In this article we discussed selected aspects related to plan recognition in instrumented environments. We emphasized the need for state-aware plan recognition approaches and proposed a general DBN model for plan recognition in instrumented environments. We further addressed the problem of sensor selection in plan recognition applications and proposed a decision-theoretic utility model that allows to estimate the utility of sensor information in plan recognition applications. First results of an empirical evaluation study suggest the validity of the proposed utility model.

Future research will have to focus on a more detailed evaluation of the proposed utility model. Open questions include the influence of certain properties of the plan li-

---

[2] *RAND* was introduced as a simple crosscheck. To the best of our knowledge there exists no other measure for information utility in plan recognition applications which could be used to compare our approach to.

brary's structure and support/cost/reward model on the information utility model's performance, as well as on the robustness of the proposed model towards deviations of the user's behavior from the underlying plan selection and execution model.

Acknowledgements

The research presented in this article was conducted within the project SharedLife. SharedLife was sponsored by the German Federal Ministry for Education and Research (BMBF) under contract 01 IW F03 from January 2006 through December 2008.

References

[1] M. Bauer. Integrating probabilistic reasoning into plan recognition. In *Proceedings of the 10th European Conference on Artificial Intelligence*, pages 620–624, Amsterdam, Netherlands, 1994.
[2] H. H. Bui. A general model for online probabilistic plan recognition. In *Proceedings of the International Joint Conference on Artificial Intelligence*, pages 1309–1318, Acapulco, Mexico, 2003.
[3] E. Charniak and R. P. Goldman. A bayesian model of plan recognition. *Artificial Intelligence*, 64(1):53–79, 1993.
[4] D. Cheng and R. Thawonmas. Case-based plan recognition for real-time strategy games. In *Proceedings of the 5th International Conference on Intelligent Games and Simulation*, pages 36–40, Gent, Belgien, 2004.
[5] R. Debouk, S. Lafortune, and D. Teneketzis. On an optimization problem in sensor selection. *Discrete Event Dynamic Systems*, 12(4):417–445, 2002.
[6] V. Gupta, T. Chung, B. Hassibi, and R. Murray. On a stochastic sensor selection algorithm with applications in sensor scheduling and sensor coverage. *Automatica*, 42(2):251–260, 2006.
[7] G. Hovland and B. McCarragher. Dynamic sensor selection for robotic systems. In *Proceedings of the IEEE International Conference on Robotics and Automation*, pages 272–277, Albuquerque, NM, USA, 1997.
[8] S. Jiang, R. Kumar, and G. Garcia. Optimal sensor selection for discrete-event systems with partial observation. *IEEE Transactions on Automatic Control*, 48(3):369–381, 2003.
[9] L. P. Kaelbling, M. L. Littman, and A. R. Cassandra. Planning and acting in partially observable stochastic domains. *Artificial Intelligence*, 101:99–134, 1998.
[10] H. Kautz and J. Allen. Generalized plan recognition. In *Proceedings of the 5th National Conference on Artificial Intelligence*, pages 32–37, Philadelphia, PA, USA, 1986.
[11] R. Motwani and P. Raghavan. *Randomized Algorithms*. Cambridge University Press, 1995.
[12] F. Mulder and F. Voorbraak. A formal description of tactical plan recognition. *Information Fusion*, 4(1):47–61, 2003.
[13] M. Schneider. The semantic cookbook: Sharing cooking experiences in the smart kitchen. In *Proceedings of the 3rd International Conference on Intelligent Environments (IE)*, pages 416–423, Ulm, Germany, 2007.
[14] G. Shafer and J. Pearl. *Readings in uncertain reasoning*. Morgan Kaufmann, San Mateo, CA, USA, 1990.
[15] H. Wang, K. Yao, G. Pottie, and D. Estrin. Entropy-based sensor selection heuristic for target localization. In *Proccedings of the 3rd International Symposium on Information Processing in Sensor Networks*, pages 36–45, Berkeley, CA, USA, 2004.
[16] W. Welch. Branch-and-bound search for experimental designs based on d-optimality and other criteria. *Technometrics*, 24(1):41–48, 1982.
[17] R. Wilensky. Why john married mary: Understanding stories involving recurring goals. *Cognitive Science*, 2:235–266, 1978.
[18] L. Yao, W. Sethares, and D. Kammer. Sensor placement for on-orbit modal identification via a genetic algorithm. *American Institute of Aeronautics and Astronautics Journal*, 31(10):1922–1928, 1993.
[19] F. Zhao and L. Guibas. *Wireless Sensor Networks: An Information Processing Approach*. Morgan Kaufmann, 2004.

Intelligent Environments 2009
V. Callaghan et al. (Eds.)
IOS Press, 2009

doi:10.3233/978-1-60750-034-6-303

Synthesizing Datasets for Pervasive Spaces

Andres Mendez-Vazquez[a,1], Abdelsalam (Sumi) Helal[a] and Diane Joyce Cook[b]
[a] *Mobile and Pervasive Computing Lab, University of Florida*
[b] *School of Engineering and Computer Science, Washington State University*

Abstract. Persistent problems in obtaining test data while developing technologies for pervasive spaces include the lack of data generation and representation standards, limited amount of available test data, incompleteness of existing data sets, and high cost of implementing a given pervasive space. This not only hinders the development and design of pervasive spaces, but also decreases the ability of researchers to compare results with those of other areas in computer science. For example, in the interaction between sensors and actuators, testing the robustness of new algorithms and evaluating risk requires large datasets that portray different scenarios. However, associated costs can be prohibitive as the data burden increases. In response to this situation, we propose a *Pervasive Space Simulation Technique* (PSST) that uses Markov chains, non-homogenous Poisson processes, and distribution fitting for generation of synthetic test data. PSST provides a realistic simulation of events in the pervasive space.

Keywords. Pervasive spaces, simulation, event generation, probabilistic models

Introduction

The increasing cost of building pervasive spaces makes the initiation and progress of research in this area extremely challenging [1]. In particular, many research groups lack the large budgets required to build a pervasive space for testing new algorithms and ideas. Even if budgetary issues are not crucial, it is usually very time consuming to generate enough data to adequately capture a realistic collection of patterns or events.

In response to this situation, we have developed alternative technique, PSST, to create realistic simulations of events. An immediate benefit of PSST is the degree of control that can be exercised on the type of generated data.

PSST employs a combination of Markov chains [2][10], non-homogenous Poisson processes [3][11] and probability distribution fitting [4] for event simulation. Furthermore, we consider the case when some real data exists about the ADLs. An immediate problem with learning ADLs is the huge complexity of an ADL. To solve this problem, we propose the use of the Baum-Welch algorithm [8][9] to learn the state machine for simulation, a histogram technique [14][15] to learn time rate function of each sensor, and the use of distribution fitting tools [4][13] to learn the probabilities of each sensor output.

This paper is organized as follows. Section 1 is an overview of basic concepts. In Section 2, we explain the generation of synthetic data through the use of Markov chains, Poisson time generators, and probability distributions. Section 3 presents pseudo-code

[1] Corresponding Author.

for the simulation algorithm. Section 4 gives the basic methods for learning the parameters for the simulation model. Pseudo-code for this learning algorithm is presented in Section 5. Section 6 analyzes the validation of the proposed algorithms using two realistic data sets.

1. Basic Concepts

1.1. Markov Chains

A discrete Markov chain [2][10] is generated by a state machine where each node represent the present state of the chain at time *t*, and the collection of outward edges from a node to the other nodes has the following multinomial distribution [4]:

$$f\left(n_1,\ldots,n_k \middle| n,p_1,\ldots,p_k\right)=\frac{n}{n_1!\cdots n_k!}p_1^{x_1},\ldots,p_k^{x_k}, \text{ with } \sum_{i=1}^{k} x_i = n, \quad (1)$$

1.2. Poisson Time Generator

A Poisson time generator is a non-homogeneous Poisson process [5]. Given an interval $(0,T)$, the probability of *n* occurrences in a sub-interval $(t_1,t_2)\subseteq(0,T)$ is

$$P\{n \text{ occurrences in } (t_1,t_2)\} = e^{-\langle n\rangle}\frac{(\langle n\rangle)^n}{n!} \text{ with } \langle n\rangle = \int_{t_1}^{t_2} r(t)dt. \quad (2)$$

1.3. Baum-Welch Algorithm

The Baum-Welch algorithm [8][9] is an Expectation Maximization (EM) algorithm that finds transition probabilities of the hidden states in Hidden Markov Models (HMM). Given a sequence of observations $x_1,x_2,\cdots,x_m$ and a sequence of hidden states $\omega_1,\omega_2,\cdots,\omega_k$, Baum-Welch finds the transition and emission matrices.

2. Synthetic Data Generation Algorithm

In the analysis of behaviors within pervasive spaces, one of the most important tasks is the learning of activity patterns. Such learning can help to create more "intelligent" environments.

Thus, given an activity, PSST must learn how to simulate it. As a result, we need to simulate the order in which each sensor is activated by a given human activity.

2.1. Transition State Simulation

Observe that a succession (or chain) of events comprising an activity can be viewed as a sequence of events over time. Then, a natural map exists between the chain of events and a state machine. We can use this state machine to represent specific behaviors by assigning to each state (or sensor) *s* a multinomial distribution (Eq. 1) where each probability p_{si} represents the arrow going from *s* to *i*. Then we can simulate the chain of events in the following way:

i. Given $N = 1$, K the size of simulated chain, and a state s with probabilities $p_{s1}, p_{s2}, \ldots, p_{sN}$;
ii. Generate a random transition to a state r, via the multinomial distribution (Eq. 1).
iii. Assign $s = r$ and $N = N+1$ and if $N<K+1$, go to Step ii.

2.2. Poisson Time Generator

In order to solve the problem of timestamp generation for each sensor, we assume that each sensor has a time density function $r(t)$ restricted to a time interval $(0,T)$. Then, we can generate the time stamps from the non-homogenous Poisson process (Section 1.2).

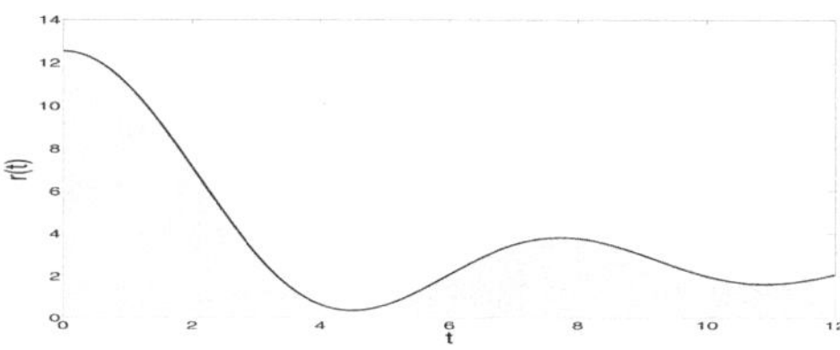

Fig. 1 Example of density function.

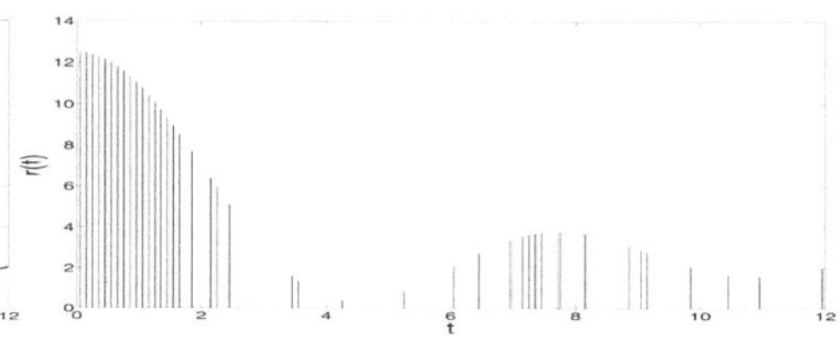

Fig. 2 Time stamps represented by bars with the height given by the value of the rate function $r(t)$ at time t.

Given the rate function in (Fig. 1) as $r(t)$, we obtain the time stamps shown in (Fig. 2). Observe that, as the rate decreases, the number of time stamps also decreases. This supports the learning of an approximation to the function $r(t)$, as discussed in Section 2.2. We need only ensure that the correct initial time t_0 is input to the Poisson model, resulting in generation of time stamps in the interval (t_0,T).

2.3. Using Probability Distribution for the Generation of the Sensor Value Parameters

For simplicity, we use two distributions for range-dependent simulation of sensor output. First, the multinomial distribution (Eq. 1) is used when a sensor produces a finite number of values. This choice is natural for the generation of finite discrete random values. Second, if a sensor has continuous output, we assume normality and lower limit constraints on the output i.e. the left-truncated Gaussian distribution [4][13].

3. Proposed Algorithm For Simulation

Given the preceding models, we next describe the synthetic data generation algorithm.

Synthetic Data Generation Algorithm

i. Given the following input information:
   a. A state machine Tr representing the relations between all sensors.
   b. A probability distribution $p(s|\theta)$ output generator for each sensor.
   c. A time density function $r_s(t)$ for each sensor s.
ii. Set *TimeStamp* = 0. An initial time reference.

iii. Set EVENT = initial event.
iv. Set N = Total number of sensors.
v. Set storage for the chain of actions $CHAIN = \varnothing$.
vi. For i = 1 to N
   a. Generate an output value O using the probability $p(EVENT|\theta)$.
   b. Generate a time stamp t by using the time generator and *TimeStamp*.
   c. Update *TimeStamp* = *t*.
   d. $Chain = Chain \bigcup \{EVENT_{ID}, t, O\}$.
   e. Get a transition RT from the distribution $p(\text{EVENT}|p_1,\ldots,p_k)$.
   f. Change EVENT = *RT*.
vii. End For

Although this algorithm is simple, it can be difficult to find the correct transition probabilities. This can be problematic if the events to be simulated are complex or correlated. Second, it can be difficult to obtain *a priori* knowledge of each sensor's output distribution. Finally, each time rate $r(t)$ depends on the activity to be simulated as well as on sensor response.

A possible solution to all these problems is oversampling the output data. Then, we can use learning methods to obtain the inputs for the simulation.

4. Learning the Simulation Model

In this section, we describe the learning of the parameters for the simulation algorithm.

4.1. Learning of the State Machine

A state machine, representing the transition probabilities of a Markov chain, can be seen as a special case of HMMs where each hidden state has only one possible output. The Baum-Welch algorithm enforces the constraint of one emission per hidden state by using an initial emission matrix [8][9] equal to the identity matrix. This initial constraint reduces the learning of the HMM to an estimation of the transition probabilities.

4.2. Fitting the Correct Distribution

Given the chain of values $v_{i_1}, v_{i_2}, \ldots, v_{i_l}$ for each sensor, we need to select between two possible probability distributions, the multinomial and the truncated Gaussian. This selection depends on the type and number of values: if the values are non-numerical, we use the multinomial distribution otherwise we use the truncated Gaussian. However, this rule can change depending on sensor type, and output value range. Once the distribution is selected, we use available tools [4][6][13] to find its parameters.

4.3. Learning the Rate Function $r(t)$

It is possible to use histograms [14][15] to calculate the time rate function. For example, if we use the time stamps from (Fig. 1), we obtain the histogram (Fig. 3).

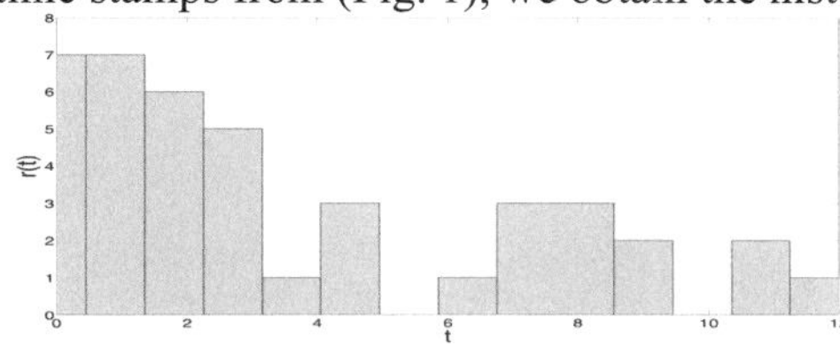

Fig. 3 Histogram of time stamps.

Then, by adjusting a continuous function to the centroids of each bin, and the bin height, we can obtain a continuous approximation to the rate $r(t)$. It is clear that the approximation depends on the density of the temporal information. The larger the set of time stamps for a specific sensor, the better the approximation.

5. Learning Algorithm

We next describe PSST's learning algorithm.

Learning Algorithm

i. Given the following data:
   a. Chain of sensor events $s_1, s_2, \ldots, s_k$.
   b. A corresponding chain of values for each chain of sensor events $v_1, v_2, \ldots, v_k$.
   c. A corresponding chain of time stamps for each event $t(s_1), t(s_2), \ldots, t(s_k)$.

ii. Use the chain $s_1, s_2, \ldots, s_k$ as an input for the Baum-Welch algorithm to obtain the simulation's state machine, initializing an identity *emission* matrix of size $N \times N$, where N denotes the number of different sensors.

iii. Use the values of each sensor $v_{i_1}, v_{i_2}, \ldots, v_{i_l}$ to fit the distributions:
   a. A Multinomial Distribution, if the sensor has a non-numeric range.
   b. A left truncated normal, if the sensor has a numeric range.

iv. Use the time stamps of each sensor in a histogram, with function fitting to obtain the rate function $r(t)$.

These two methods allow us to obtain a map between real data and simulated data.

6. Validation Against Real Data

In this section, we test the learning and generation algorithms against two different data sets. The first data set was obtained by a single actigraph sensor [12], and the second data set was obtained during a data gathering in the CASAS smart space [6].

6.1. Actigraph Simulation

Consider data gathered using an actigraph unit [12] whose output represents subject activity. Each entry in the data set contains the following four fields:

- *Label* - sleep, walk, sit, read, exercise, house working.
- *Time* – in hours.
- *Outdoor temperature* – in Fahrenheit.
- *Energy expenditure* – in calories.

We use these labels as node names in the Markov state machine. In this particular case we did not use the Poisson time generator because the time labels in the original data set are expressed in calories per hour. Therefore, it is not necessary to have a randomized time generator.

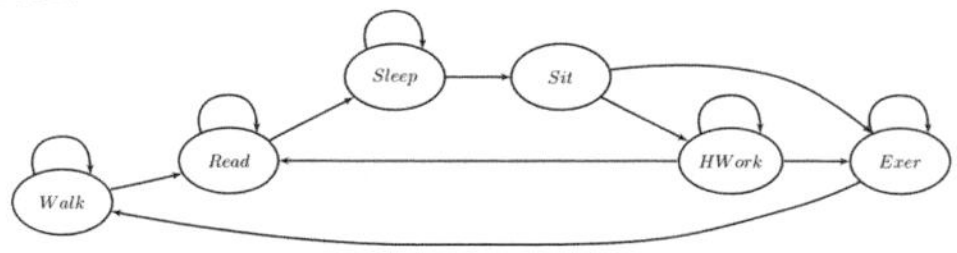

Fig. 4 State Machine for the simulation of the actigraph sensor.

The edge probabilities and sensor range activities in the Markov model (Fig. 4) were assigned to represent the activity graph illustrated in Fig. 5. Here, the *X*-axis represents time (hours), and the *Y*-axis represents energy consumed (kilocalories). Normal Gaussians with manually adjusted parameters were used instead the truncated Gaussian because the scarce number of values for each event.

We can see that the simulated activity graph (Fig. 6) resembles the real activity graph in the succession of patterns of activity. For example, it is possible to see from $t = 28$ to $t = 45$ in Fig. 6, that the person transitions from walking to reading, then to sleeping. These patterns are similar to the activities shown in Fig. 5 from $t = 20$ to $t = 32$. In order to quantify these similarities in the patterns, we use dynamic time warping [8]. Given, two chains of events $Q = q_1,...,q_n$ and $C = c_1,...,c_n$. We sought to minimize the metric cost function

$$D(Q,C) = \sqrt{\sum_{i=1}^{L} w_i} \Big/ K , \tag{3}$$

via dynamic programming [6]. The sum term $\sum_{i=1}^{L} w_i$ in the numerator represents the total number of changes made to convert between chain of events, and the denominator K is the length of the warping path. The dynamic time warping converts one chain of events into another by inserting and deleting elements in the chain. The cost of these changes is recorded in $w_1,...,w_L$.

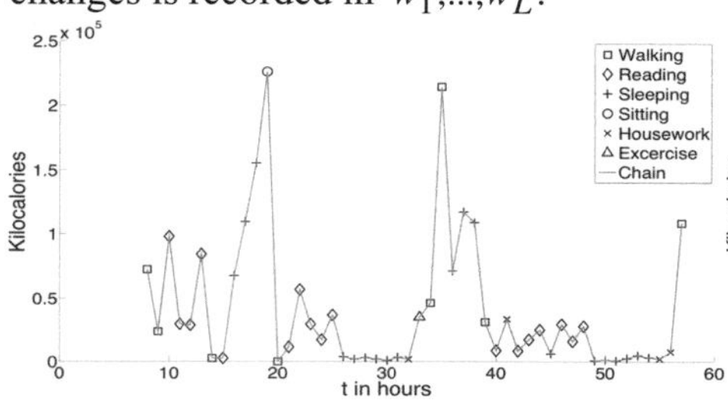

Fig. 5 The activity graph to be simulated.

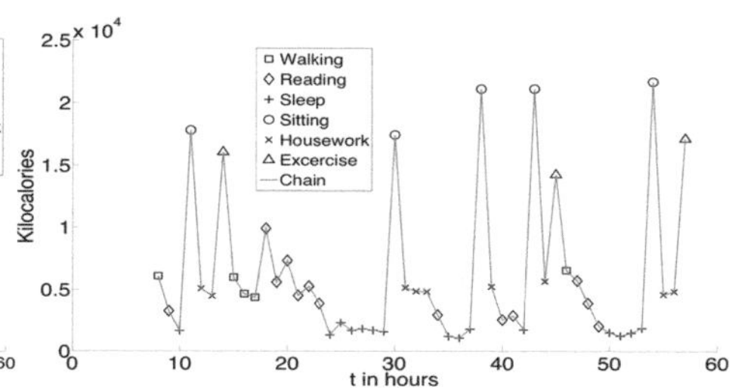

Fig. 6 The simulated activity graph.

Fig. 7 shows the different values for the defined metric, starting with a constant chain of events. This chain of events can be simulated with a state machine of one node and one edge. We will call this machine a Constant State Machine (CSM). Then, we introduce one node and the necessary edges. At each step, we simulate a chain of events of size equal to the activity graph, and then compare the simulated graph with the actual activity. The CSM produces the worst error with $D(Q,C) = 8.68$. The PSM produces the pattern with significantly improved error $D(Q,C) = 0.5714$.

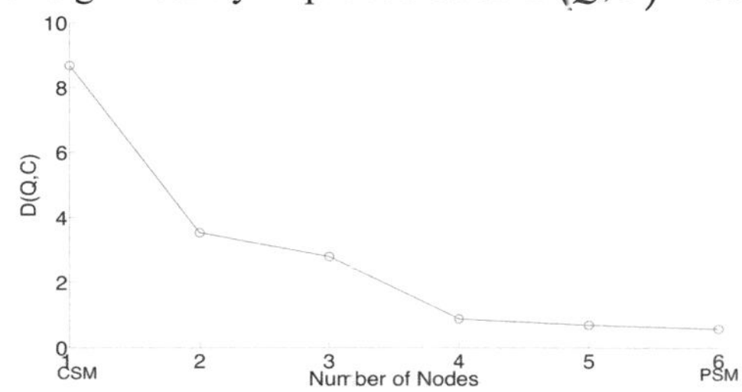

Fig. 7 Values produced by the metric going from the constant state machine to the proposed state machine.

Application of the Baum-Welch algorithm produces a value for $D(Q,C)$ metric of 0.3210. This is less than the value 0.5714 obtained from the simulation of the PSM (Fig. 7). This means that the Baum-Welch state machine is as good or better as the PSM.

6.2. Testing the Realism of Synthetic Data

We hypothesize that our synthetic data generator can create data reflective of sensor event that would occur in a real pervasive space. If the data is realistic, then it can fill the role of real data sets, allowing a greater breadth of situations to be explored and facilitating greater depth of analysis and comparison. We are interested in determining how well the simulator can emulate real data. To assess this feature, we gather data from a real pervasive space and use the parameters from the data to constrain the synthetic data generator, which in turn generates simulation data consistent with the real data.

For our experiments, we utilized sensor data collected in the CASAS smart apartment. For this experiment, we brought 20 volunteer participants into the apartment and asked them to perform a series of five activities: 1) look up and dial a phone number, 2) wash their hands in the kitchen sink, 3) cook according to the written directions, 4) eat the oatmeal together with medicine, and 5) clean up the dishes and the kitchen.

Table 1 Results over real and synthetic data.

Train	Test	Accuracy
Real	Real	85%
Synthetic	Synthetic	79%
Real	Synthetic	91%
Synthetic	Real	70%
Real+Synthetic	Real+Synthetic	97%

To learn the activity models we construct a Markov chain for each activity. The accuracy of the Markov-based classifier for different combinations of real and synthetic data is summarized in Table 1. As the results show, the algorithms perform better with real data than synthetic data, indicating that there may be more variation in the synthetic data than in the real data. However, the synthetic data shows a remarkable consistency with the real data. For example, the accuracy is improved when the algorithms are trained on real data but tested on synthetic data.

The consistency of the real and synthetic data provides opportunities for learning even in data-poor environments. In these situations the addition of synthetic data can "boost" the performance of the learning algorithm by providing the additional data it needs to learn the concept with satisfactory accuracy.

7. Conclusion

In this paper, we propose novel and simple learning and simulation algorithms for the synthesis of activities in pervasive spaces. These algorithms employ established techniques to learn and simulate probabilistic models. In particular, the learning algorithm is applied to real data, and its results are input to the simulation algorithm to extend datasets that represent pervasive space. This helps to improve the training of algorithms for the recognition of ADLs. This approach also opens the door for the generation of totally new data sets by the modification of the learned model.

In order to do this, we envision that the eventual generation of new data will require inclusion of a physical description of the pervasive space into the simulation model. Additionally, in our research, we are investigating the use of spatial locality functions to modify the probabilistic-causal relations between sensors. This will facilitate the optimization design of new pervasive spaces.

References

[1] I. Armac and D. Retkowitz, "Simulation of Smart Environments," *IEEE International Conference on Pervasive Services*, pp.257-266, 15-20 July 2007.

[2] P. Bremaud, Markov chains. Gibbs fields, Monte Carlo simulation and queues, 3ed ed., New York:Springer, 2008.

[3] D.R. Cox and V.I. Isham, *Point Processes,* Chapman & Hall, 1980.

[4] G. Casella and R. L. Berger, *Statistical Inference*, 2nd ed. Pacific Grove: Duxbury Press, 2002.

[5] D. Heeger, "Poisson Model of Spike Generation," handout, Sept. 2000.

[6] L. R. Rabiner and B. Juang, *Fundamentals of speech recognition*, Prentice-Hall, Inc., 1993.

[7] D. Cook and M. Schmitter-Edgecombe, "Activity profiling using pervasive sensing in smart homes," *in Methods of Information in Medicine, 2009.*

[8] L. E. Baum, T. Petrie, G. Soules, and N. Weiss,"A maximization technique occurring in the statistical analysis of probabilistic functions of Markov chains," *in Ann. Math. Statist.*,vol.41,no.1,pp.164-171, 1970.

[9] R. O. Duda, P. E. Hart and D. G. Stork, *Pattern Classification (2nd ed.)*, John Wiley and Sons, 2001.

[10] C. P. Robert and G. Casella, *Monte Carlo Statistical Methods (Springer Texts in Statistics)*. Secaucus, NJ, USA: Springer-Verlag New York, Inc., 2005.

[11] D.L. Snyder and M.I. Miller, *Random Point Processes in Time and Space,* Springer-Verlag. 1991.

[12] H. Pigot, B. Lefebvre, J.G. Meunier, B. Kerhervé, A. Mayers and S. Giroux, "The role of intelligent habitats in upholding elders in residence," *5th international conference on Simulations in Biomedicine*, April 2003, Slovenia.

[13] W. H. Greene, *Econometric Analysis*, 5th ed, Prentice Hall Inc, 2003.

[14] D. W. Scott,"On optimal and data-based histograms," *Biometrika*,vol.66,no.3,pp.605-610, 1979.

[15] D. Freedman and P. Diaconis, "On the histogram as a density estimator:l2 theory," *Probability Theory and Related Fields*, vol. 57, no. 4, pp. 453-476, December 1981.

Intelligent Environments 2009
V. Callaghan et al. (Eds.)
IOS Press, 2009

doi:10.3233/978-1-60750-034-6-311

Universal Device Access with FreeMote

Markus HIPP, Thorsten MAHLER, Christian SPIKA, Michael WEBER
Institute of Media Informatics, University of Ulm, Ulm, Germany

Abstract. With the FreeMote system, we present a solution for easy and intuitive universal device control. Based on the Wii Remote Controller real world device functions can be accessed and controlled via gestures. Gestures include predefined sets apt for standard functions present in many devices as well as user definable gestures. Offering both possibilities, the users are free to choose and adapt the gestures to their needs while reducing the mental load. Along with the gesture interface, FreeMote offers a simple way of enabling everyday devices for FreeMote controlling. FreeMote makes use of the spatial nature of real world environments in device selection and in function controlling via gestures. Thus, FreeMote system supports the user in finding enabled devices, makes selecting devices easy and provides an intuitive way of controlling devices via gestures.

Keywords. Wii Remote Controller. Gesture Control. Universal Remote. Tangible User Interfaces. Spatial Interaction.

Introduction

Mark Weiser predicted a new computer era based on miniaturization and the rise of implicit computer interaction in his visionary article "The Computer for the 21st Century" [16]. He had an environment in mind where computers react to human actions in the real world. Making the computer disappear, he envisioned a world where computers are supportive and ever present with all information in every place. Clearly, we do not live in such a world yet, but the miniaturization and computerization of everyday objects goes on and can be witnessed in our daily surrounding.

The ever increasing number of devices that are computerized and can be controlled electronically also dramatically increase the interaction possibilities. A once simple device nowadays provides an increasing number of very special functionality, sometimes even clouding the basic devices purpose [12]. The vast number of functions is by no means the only problem: the diversity of the devices and the very different interaction realizations make the interfaces ever more confusing; it complicates the handling and makes accessing functions difficult. The sheer number of different interfaces means high mental load and asks for highly experienced users or induces restraints to few basic functions.

1. Universal Remote Challenges

Controlling a multitude of different devices, possibly every single device equipped with its unique remote control, is getting more and more complex. A solution offered is the use of a single standard universal remote control to handle every remotely operated device.

However, this solution often results in even more chaos for the user. Crammed with buttons and different interaction opportunities, the use of a standard universal remote control is rather complicating than relaxing the interaction.

To achieve a practical and comfortable solution that will master this situation, a system has to solve the following problems:

Universal Remote: Because of the high amount of devices controllable remotely, the offered system must be powerful enough to handle every available device.

High Expressivity: In order to handle a high number of device specific functions the system has to offer many degrees of freedom to support the identification and execution of every function needed.

Mental Load: The device control must not overstrain the user but reduce the cognitive load.

Simplicity of Use: As proposed by Chang et al. in [2], the addition of buttons to a remote control does not help usability, as it does not reduce mental load for the user. Instead, an interface must provide an interaction realization that is simple in design and pleases the user [9].

Non Invasive: To increase the simplicity of use, the system needs to be usable fast and without preparation. A system that is non invasive but easy graspable and known increases the comfort of the user.

Device Selection: The system has to provide a way to transparently inform the user of which devices can be controlled in an environment, how they can be selected and which device is activated at a time.

Personalization: The users should be able to define their personal, easy to remember interaction sequences. These personal ways of interaction should be easily transferable to other devices or even environments.

2. The FreeMote Solution

To tackle the challenges mentioned above we devised an interface which easily integrates into everyday life, the FreeMote. It provides the user with a new intuitive but at the same time facile option to interact with everyday devices. The FreeMote consists of two pieces of hardware: Firstly, the FreeMote controller used as a remote control replacement as well as for transmitting the identification data and secondly the FreeMote sensorbar equipped with three LED lights, working as the device identifier.

2.1. Hardware for Gesture Recognition

In 2006 Nintendo released his latest game console, the Nintendo Wii. The most innovative feature is its new game pad, the Wii Remote Control (see figure 1). With its acceleration sensor it is able to detect movements in all three dimensions. Also, it is equipped with an IR camera, which is able to recognize up to four light sources. Due to this fact we are able to use different FreeMote sensorbars for different devices. For the wireless connection the Wii Remote Controller uses bluetooth, which makes it easily accessible by every bluetooth enabled PC [10].

Another important reason is the growing profile of the Nintendo Wii and its remote controller: With its few buttons and its clean design it is a non-invasive and very easy

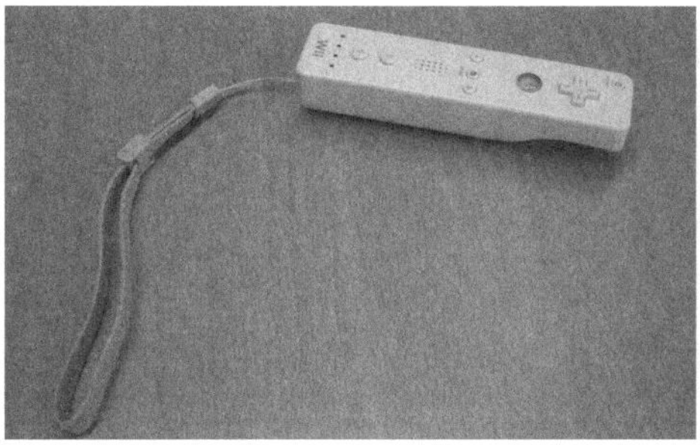

Figure 1. The Wii Remote Controller is used as universal gesture input device.

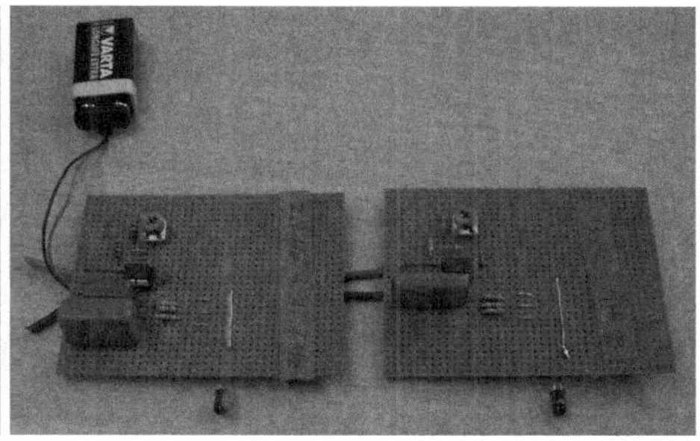

Figure 2. Early Prototype of the identification systems. 2LEDs are enabled for frequency coding.

to handle remote control understandable for everyone. In addition, the Wii Remote Controller is highly available compared to other, often prototypical comparative products. From a application development point of view, the Wii Remote Controller is a good choice because it can easily be integrated into a software system with the help of many already existing frameworks in different computer languages. Considering these facts, we decided against assembling another accelerator enabled nicely designed artefact but to use the standard Wii Remote Controller to be our universal remote hand set.

2.2. *Hardware for Device Identification*

In order to identify the Wii Remote Controller's position, Nintendo uses a sensorbar usually located on top of the display to be controlled. The sensorbar consists of two infrared LED light sources placed at the right and left end of the roughly ten inch wide bar. Combined with the IR camera of the Wii Remote Controller it is possible to compute its position, usually used to control the mouse pointer on the screen.

FreeMote utilizes the capability of the Wii Remote Controller to even recognize up to four light sources. Thus it is possible to expand the sensorbar with one more LED light source: Basically, the FreeMote sensorbar is composed of three equispaced light sources lined up in a row. While two LEDs are needed for defining the gesture‘s shape recognized by the FreeMote system, the third light is blinking in a defined frequency. Having a FreeMote sensorbar on every controllable device it is possible to identify the devices due to the individual blinking frequency of their sensor bar. Figure 2 shows an early prototype of this identification system.

3. Implementation

The FreeMote system front end consists of the FreeMote Controller and the three LED FreeMote sensorbar for creating input data. The software application on the back end handling the input data is implemented in JAVA. It extends the WiiGee library [15] and runs on a standard PC platform. The only further requirement is a bluetooth stack (we tested the system with the WIDCOMM and Avetana stack) to connect to the FreeMote Controller.

3.1. Gesture Recognition

Due to the unhandiness of most common universal remote controls we decided to create a new innovative interface to handle every device. Based on the Nintendo Wii Remote Controller our system uses only three buttons in combination with gesture recognition for controlling devices. The FreeMote controller has a built-in accelerometer with the ability to sense acceleration along three axes. Connected over bluetooth, the accelerometer provides the input system with data consisting of vectors representing the acceleration of the controller in all three dimensions. We decided to base the input system on the WiiGee library [15]. This implementation is freely available and allows a stable gesture recognition which could be proven in user studies where Schlömer et al. reached an average of 90% correctly recognized gestures. The Freemote system offers to interact with a device by gesture control. To reduce the mental effort but at the same time preserve the freedom of use for the user, we divide gesture control into two different types of gestures:

Standard Gestures: In order to reduce the cognitive load for the user, we equipped FreeMote with a variety of standard gestures used for the most common options of nowadays devices, e.g. on and off, louder and softer, darker and lighter. By using a set of standard gestures for every device the user is only forced to learn these once and thereby the mental load of common universal remotes (e.g. searching the right button for a specific device) is prevented. For instance a fast left to right movement is used to switch to the next channel for a TV set or the next song for the hifi set.

User Defined Gestures: Besides the advantages of standard gestures we still give the user the freedom of choice to create and use his own set of gestures for one or even all devices and functions. The user is free to create any gesture that is possible in 3D space and bind it to a function of a specific device. This enables him to form a personal controlling of his devices and as a result, confers FreeMote individuality. For instance, in preliminary tests one user defined a cross movement to stop the hifi playback.

3.2. Use of Gestures

In order to start the gesture recognition, a button on the FreeMote controller is need to be held down. This marks the beginning of the now following motion sequence that describes a gesture. It is now possible to execute one of the provided standard gestures or one of gestures that were created by the user. To end the gesture recognition the button is released. At that point, the FreeMote system automatically analyzes the performed gesture, compares it with the stored gestures and, if a match has been detected, executes the associated function of the device.

To activate the training mode for creating new gestures the user needs to press and hold down a different button on the controller and is now able to create a motion sequence which will be saved as a new gesture. By releasing the key followed by a quick press of a button that marks the end of the whole gesture training, the gesture will be stored together with the related function of this device. In order to improve recognition rate and smoothness of a gesture it is advised to iterate the training sequence three four times.

As a result of only one device being activated at a time, FreeMote does not need miscellaneous gestures for several devices. Instead, every device can be controlled by the same set of gestures. This again reduces the cognitive load for the user and simplifies the use and control of every device. See figure 3 for a typical gesture. For storing and retrieving of gestures we use an XML structure, since it is easy to integrate and nowadays used as the standard for modelling hierarchically structured data. It also allows the device associated gestures to be portable on every FreeMote interface available.

3.3. Device Identification

Virtually, making the PC disappear, the interaction takes place between the user and the specific device or artefact. The user has the feeling of interacting with a controllable device instead of a PC, while technically a PC in the background translates the users actions into device functions.

The process of detecting controllable devices is divided in two steps: The first step is to detect the shape of a FreeMote sensorbar. Therefore we implemented a detection algorithm, which analyzes the light sources seen by the IR camera in order to detect the shape of the FreeMote sensorbar on the one hand and to filter lightsources caused by reflection or insolation on the other hand. On the basis of a probability function the software decides if a FreeMote sensorbar is detected or not.

If a FreeMote sensorbar is detected, the software proceeds with the analysis of the frequency of the third light. Computer vision algorithms are used to steady the detected image. This image is analyzed to identify the frequency, which can be determined even if the user is moving the FreeMote controller. With this simple approach the whole process of device detection and identification takes about one second and is confirmed to the user by vibration in case of success.

We also take advantage of the detection algorithm in another context. Without knowing which devices in a room are actually controllable by FreeMote the user can move the Freemote controller around in the room resulting in a short vibration whenever the system is detecting a FreeMote sensorbar. This very helpful feature of FreeMote makes it easy for the user to find out which devices are controllable in general.

To add a new device to the system, the user starts the hardware wizard. The FreeMote core thereupon checks the XML device description for available free frequencies and prompts the user to manually adjust the FreeMote sensorbar frequency. Depending on the chosen hardware template, the new device is added to the XML device file and therefor available, providing a standard set of gestures.

4. System Walk Through

In a typical scenario a user wants to activate one of many devices present in his living room, for instance. First of all, the corresponding device needs to be focused with the FreeMote controller in order to identify and thereby activate the device. Hereby, the device can be a complex device like a TV set or a hi-fi system as well as such devices as speakers or lights. The only necessary requirement is its tagging by a FreeMote sensorbar (see figure 4). After identification the user has full control over the functions offered by the device. In our particular scenario the set of controllable devices consisted of a computer controlled TV, a computer controlled hi-fi system and an ethernet accessible lamp with dimming function. We used the same gestures for similar functions on different devices, for example 'next channel' on the tv and 'next track' on the hi-fi system. Nevertheless, the user is free to define gestures to control the functions himself. We are also able to switch between devices by identifying them with aid of the combination of

Figure 3. Executing a user defined gesture controlling a device (stopping music playback in this case).

Figure 4. One of the speakers connected to the hi-fi-system which has been enabled for identification via the portable Freemote sensorbar.

the IR camera of the Wii Remote Controller and the FreeMote sensorbars due to the different frequencies of the pulsing LED.

In summary, we created a powerful software tool to support the user in his familiar device-handling. Above all, the Wii Remote Controller with its intuitive handling and its simplicity turned out to be a very good alternative to all existing universal remote controls.

5. Related Work

Considerable research has been done regarding spatial interaction and remote control, ranging from gesture recognition to systems for free device controlling. Freeman et al. for instance set up a system to control a TV set via free hand interaction. A camera tracks the hand position which is used as pointing into a graphical interface display on the TV. This way, they are able to attain a large number of functions while keeping the interaction simple and comprehensive [4]. While this approach clearly solves the controlling of home devices in a non invasive way, it heavily depends on a well equipped environment especially when it comes to controlling multiple devices.

While still using hand recognition, a different approach is taken by Kölsch et al. They use a more sophisticated way to track hands in order to recognize even hand poses which increases the gesture interaction possibilities dramatically [6]. Still using a camera to track the hand movement, they offer new possibilities by implementing the camera together with the tracking into a Head Mounted Unit (HMU). This way they are not bound to a specially equipped room, but are free to move [7]. Kölsch et al. also propose to use a graphical interface superimposed on a camera image via a HMU. Nevertheless, the system itself is very invasive contradicting one of the basic ideas of ubiquitous computing.

A system that is not dependent on cameras but uses a special glove to track hand movements is the Glove-TalkII system by [3] et al.. They implemented a gesture driven interface to translate hand movements into speech. By using the highly developed glove they can rely on high expressivity but they also stated that the interface itself needs training and experienced users to be used. In our opinion [3] et al. presented an approach that would be feasible for the gesture part of our system but itself is highly invasive.

A system that tackles the simplicity of use and focuses on the joy of use is the WorldBeat system presented by Borchers et al. [1]. Here, batons are used as devices for music creation. The batons were simply equipped with infrared lights enabling them to act as pointing devices. This simple but highly appreciated interface enabled the user for 3D interaction. While this exhibit is clearly a no gesture device, it impresses by it's simple usage and non invasiveness.

Ouchi et al. translated this approach to home appliances. In their MagicWand system, they already combine simple gestures with baton interaction [13]. However, this system lacks a proper way to identify devices. They use only a very simple and fixed gesture set, neither allowing for a high number of functions nor for user defined gestures.

The importance of both standard gesture sets and user defined interaction gestures are verified by Kela et al.. In [5] they present an evaluation and comparative study of accelerometer-based gesture controls in mobile interaction and different application scenarios. Users responded very well to the naturalness of such interaction.

Other studies indicate the feasibility of gesture recognition for application input. For a stereo camera environment Lichtenauer et al. validated a 3D hand-recognition system in a user study with 70 persons using a set of 120 3D-signs and could show very promising results for gesture recognition [8]. Similar systems are proposed based on a 3D-accelerometer and on the same algorithms by Pylvänäinen in [14].

In recent research papers, these findings are implemented in libraries for instance the freely available WiiGee library [15]. Schlömer et al. present a accelerator based gesture library that is capable to recognize trained gestures. It works with the widely available Wii Remote Controller, the device we also favor for our system. With its initial user evaluation and its promising results it builds a fast and solid foundation for our FreeMote gesture subsytem.

6. Conclusion and Future Work

With FreeMote we presented a universal remote control system. Based on the Wii Remote Controller we offer an interface that is both easy to use and well accepted by the users. Using the capabilities of the Wii Remote Controller integrated device we are able to recognize real world devices and to control them via 3D-gestures. While the identification of different devices can focus the number of possible interaction down on the device, the degrees of freedom of the integrated accelerometers make way for controlling a huge number of different functions.

By pointing the FreeMote on an enabled device like a lamp, a TV set, a hifi-system or even only a speaker, the respective device can be controlled. Thus the interaction is virtually reduced to an interaction between the actual device and the user. Therefore the set of functions can be further reduced making the interface easier to be handled. Furthermore, the interaction is dissolved from one single appliance like, for instance, the light switch for all lamps in the room. Instead the spatial awareness enables the targeting of exactly one lamp. It makes way for higher granularity while concurrently easing the identification and reducing function clutter. The use of one device makes it easy to use the same interaction pattern for similar functions on different devices, thus reducing mental load rendering the multitude of different remotes with different interfaces obsolete.

The FreeMote turns an equipped room itself together with the devices in it to an interface making use of its spatial nature. The interaction virtually takes place between the user and the devices themselves being controlled directly.

The gestures used to control functions of devices can be freely defined by the user. Nevertheless, we found it useful to provide a set of standard gestures that represent often needed functionality. These standard gestures simplify interaction by reducing the number of overall gestures with the goal to lower the mental load.

In the future we plan to work on making the standard gesture set even more comprehensible for the users. This includes to implement the system in an intelligent living or meeting room where the system can be tested and evaluated over a long time under real life conditions. Furthermore, in the current form the identification of the devices is limited to a relatively small number of devices. To be used in large rooms or buildings their number can be quite high however. Here, coding information is a suitable way to reach this goal.

All in all, we could present a universal interface suitable as alternative for the everyday collection of remote controls that is easy to use and comprehensible.

Acknowledgements

The authors are thankful to the students taking part in programming and completing the FreeMote system, Frank Wahnschaffe and Kevin O'Brien.

References

[1] Borchers, Jan O., WorldBeat: designing a baton-based interface for an interactive music exhibit, *Proceedings of the SIGCHI conference on Human factors in computing systems*, (1997), 131–138.

[2] Chang, Angela and Gouldstone, James and Zigelbaum, Jamie and Ishii, Hiroshi, Simplicity in interaction design, *TEI '07: Proceedings of the 1st international conference on Tangible and embedded interaction*, (2007),135–138.

[3] Fels, Sidney and Hinton, Geoffrey,Glove-TalkII: an adaptive gesture-to-formant interface, *Proceedings of the SIGCHI conference on Human factors in computing systems*, (1995), 456–463.

[4] Freeman, W. T. and C. Weissman, Television control by hand gestures, *Intl. Workshop on automatic face- and gesture-recognition*, (1995), 179–183.

[5] Kela, J., Korpipää, P., Mäntyjärvi, J., Kallio, S., Savino, G., Jozzo, L., and Marca, D., Accelerometer-based gesture control for a design environment, *Personal Ubiquitous Computing* **10, 5**, (2006), 285–299.

[6] Kölsch, M. and Turk, M. and Hollerer, T., Fast 2D Hand Tracking with Flocks of Features and Multi-Cue Integration, *Conference on Computer Vision and Pattern Recognition Workshop*, (2004), 158–158.

[7] Kölsch, M. and Turk, M. and Hollerer, T., Vision-based interfaces for mobility, *International Conference on Mobile and Ubiquitous Systems: Networking and Services*, (2004), 86–94.

[8] Lichtenauer, J.F. and ten Holt, G.A. and Hendriks, E.A. and Reinders, M.J.T., Sign language detection using 3D visual cues, *IEEE Conference on Advanced Video and Signal Based Surveillance*, (2007), 435–440.

[9] Maeda, John, *The Laws of Simplicity (Simplicity: Design, Technology, Business, Life)*, The MIT Press, Cambridge, MA, 2006.

[10] Wii at Nintendo, Nintendo, *http://www.nintendo.com/wii*, March, 2009.

[11] Norman, Donald A., *The Psychology of Everyday Things*, Basic Books, New York, NY, 1988.

[12] Norman, Donald A., Simplicity is highly overrated, *interactions*, **14, 2**, (2007), 40–41.

[13] Ouchi, K. and Esaka, N. and Tamura, Y. and Hirahara, M. and Doi, M., Magic Wand: an intuitive gesture remote control for home appliances, *Proceedings of the 2005 International Conference on Active Media Technology*, (2005), 274.

[14] Timo Pylvänäinen, Accelerometer Based Gesture Recognition Using Continuous HMMs, *Pattern Recognition and Image Analysis*, (2005), 639–646.

[15] Schlömer, Thomas and Poppinga, Benjamin and Henze, Niels and Boll, Susanne, Gesture recognition with a Wii controller, *TEI '08: Proceedings of the 2nd international conference on Tangible and embedded interaction*, (2008), 11–14.

[16] Mark Weiser, The Computer for the 21st Century, *Scientific American*, **265**, (1991).

Intelligent Environments 2009
V. Callaghan et al. (Eds.)
IOS Press, 2009

doi:10.3233/978-1-60750-034-6-319

User Modeling from Basic Events in Interactive Systems for Intelligent Environments

Matthias BEZOLD [a,b]
[a] *University of Ulm, Institute for Information Technology, Ulm, Germany*
[b] *Elektrobit Automotive Software, Erlangen, Germany*
matthias.bezold@uni-ulm.de

Abstract. One advanced feature of interactive systems in intelligent environments is adaptation: The interface improves itself based on observed user behavior. Therefore, the description of user behavior from observations that the interactive system makes plays a crucial role in adaptive interfaces. This paper presents an architecture for modeling user behavior from these basic events. Different components, such as an interaction and task model, use a common bus system to exchange information through these events. A user modeling component extracts information from events and performs further derivations from existing knowledge, e.g. by means of Markov chains, thus facilitating a comprehensive description of user behavior. A prototype implementation of this architecture, which is applied to an adaptive multimodal digital TV system, demonstrates the feasibility of this approach.

Keywords. User modeling framework, user behavior as basic events, adaptive digital TV.

1. Introduction

An adaptation of the interface to the current user is one approach for intelligent environments to improve the user-system interaction. These adaptive interfaces observe a user's behavior, draw conclusions, and adapt themselves accordingly based on these observations to better reflect the requirements of an individual user. The process of observing a user and drawing new conclusions, which is crucial for adaptive systems, is called user modeling. In order to enable adaptivity for different interactive systems, a general architecture for user modeling is required. Such an architecture comprises two phases: extracting information from basic observations and drawing further derivations using different user modeling algorithms. Extensibility and a generic structure are prerequisites for supporting the algorithmic requirements of different adaptive interfaces.

Assume that the interactive system generates a sequence of low-level events for each user-system interaction, which can therefore be described as a sequence of these events. User behavior is modeled by extracting information from this sequence, such as what action the user is performing or which values are selected most frequently. Based on this information, further derivations are computed, such as predicting user actions or most likely values.

```
1 [1181741700770] utterance text="select channel CNN"
2 [1181741700770] event name=e.ChannelChange
3 [1181741700771] state name=ChangeChannel
  ...
4 [1181741702780] interaction name=ChangeChannel channel=CNN
5 [1181741702784] taskprediction name=ChannelSelection
```

Figure 1. Exemplary log lines, showing a speech utterance that changes the current channel (line 1), reactions of the system (lines 2–3), and further derivations from other components (lines 4–5).

In this paper, we present a reusable and generic user modeling architecture for interactive systems. Higher-level models create new events from these basic events, which are eventually fed into a user model with the ability to infer new information from existing information. The architecture supports complex data types by means of an extension facility, which are needed to handle non-simple data for arbitrary algorithms efficiently. A prototype implementation as well as its application to an adaptive digital TV system are presented to attest the feasibility of this approach.

This paper is organized as follows. First, an architecture for describing user behavior from a sequence of basic events is introduced. Next, a user modeling component is introduced, followed by a brief overview of an implementation as well as its application to an adaptive interactive TV system. After a review of related work, conclusions and future work conclude the paper.

2. User Interactions as a Sequence of Events

Imagine a user working with an interactive system, such as a digital TV system, and the user wants to change the channel using speech interaction. The interactive system observes a speech utterance as well as system reactions to this input, for instance internal state changes or property changes. Each of these observations is represented by a basic event. Further interactions by the user thus create a longer sequence of events.

The view of the system is limited to these events, i.e., only what can be observed (possibly also by additional external sensors) and represented as an event can become part of the user modeling process. Therefore, the user-system interaction can be regarded as a sequence of events [3]. An event is the basic element of the user-system interaction and consists of a time stamp, a type, and a type-specific set of properties. These events are caused by different modalities, such as speech and haptic input. An example is given in line 1 of Fig. 1: an event of the type "utterance" has a property "text" that describes what the user said, in this case "select channel CNN".

In the following, we present a user modeling component that uses a generic communication bus to connect different components, which contribute to the user modeling process. While the component is generic, we present sample techniques to illustrate the architecture. An overview of the user modeling component and how it is connected to an interactive system is shown in Fig. 2. The user modeling component is tightly coupled with the interactive system, but it is a reusable component that can be employed in different interactive systems.

Different components of the system exchange events through an event bus, which is conceptually similar to blackboard architectures (cf. Corkill [2]). Producers submit

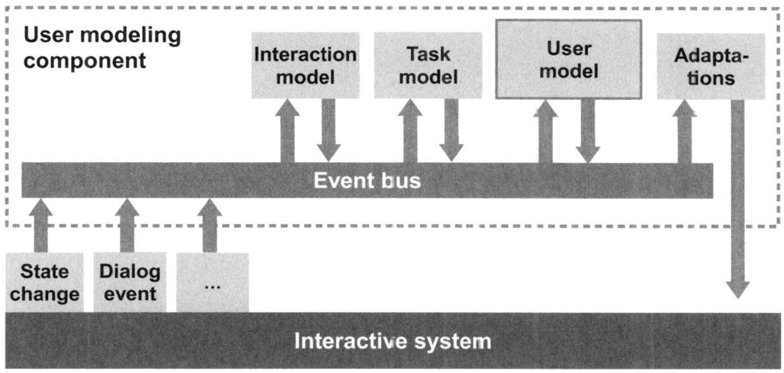

Figure 2. The event architecture transmits events from different sources, such as the interactive system or higher-level components.

events to the bus, e.g. the interactive system submits events when it observes a button press, a speech utterance, or a state change. Other components subscribe to the event bus, either to all events or certain event types with specific parameter values, and are notified when matching events have been submitted. Therefore, the event is a common and generic interchange format between different components.

Higher-level models observe the sequence of events and submit new events to the event bus. For instance, an interaction model may subscribe to specific events and submit a new interaction event when a certain interaction pattern was observed. For this purpose, machine learning techniques are used to extract a certain event sequence from the event bus that represents a certain action. In our framework, probabilistic automata [11] are trained from annotated data to recognize certain event sequences. The interaction model not only detects user actions, but also extracts parameters of these actions, such as the name of the channel in a channel change action. A task model component observes the events created by the interaction model and creates a new event when a task was finished. The task model uses a description similar to ConcurTaskTrees [8] to define possible user interactions, with the individual interaction steps being defined by the interaction model. In Fig. 1, the interaction model observes different events (lines 1–3) and emits a new "interacton" event for a "ChannelChange" user action (line 4), with the "channel" parameter being set to the respective value. The task model observes this action and concludes that the "ChannelSelection" task was finished, thus emitting a respective "task" event (line 5).

Another component, the user model, which models the user based on events and additional derivations, is discussed in detail in the following section. Finally, an adaptation component is subscribed to the event notifications and adaptations are invoked by certain event triggers. This lineup of components provides a comprehensive description of user behavior, but additional components can be connected to the event bus if the need should arise for different applications. Therefore, a generic event bus connecting different components that build on each other provides a foundation for describing user behavior from low-level events.

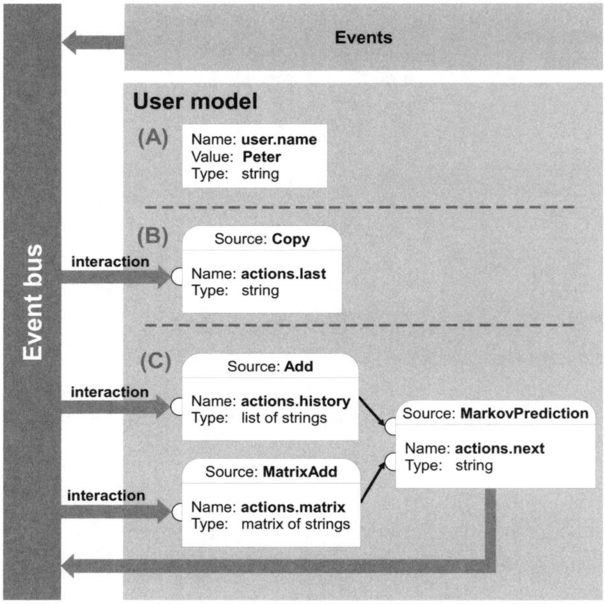

Figure 3. An example user model with derivations.

3. The User Model

This section describes the user modeling component that serves two purposes: extracting information from events and deriving new information from existing information.

3.1. Architecture

The user model is a store of entries consisting of typed name-value pairs. It supports basic data types, such as strings or numbers, but also more complex types by means of an extension facility. Complex data types are needed to represent data that is used by user modeling algorithms, which simple data types do not fulfill. These types can be compound types of simple types, such as list, map, or matrix, but also arbitrary other types. In section (A) of the example user model given in Fig. 3, an entry "user.name" of the type `string` stores the name of the user "Peter". Each entry is stored separately for each individual user and default values can be defined by means of a template role assigned to the user. For instance, the "beginner" role provides values of users who are not experienced with the interactive system.

Since the system is implemented in the Java programming language, user-defined data types can be integrated by means of additional Java classes, allowing for very specific data types if the need should arise.

3.2. Derivations

One application of the user model is to provide a store for reading and writing user-dependent data to the interactive system. But the user model also loads values directly from events and updates them from the values of other user model entries, called derivation. For this purpose, every user model entry can have a source that defines how the data is loaded or updated. A source consists of data elements, which can either be events or other user model entries, and an operator that defines how new information is derived. Based on the values of the data sources, new values can be computed. The simplest operation is copying the value from the source to the entry. An example is shown in section (B) of Fig. 3: the source `Copy` copies the name of the last user action from the respective "interaction" event into the "actions.last" entry.

The architecture also allows to define more complex operations. Moreover, the outcomes of computations, which are stored in user model entries, can again serve as sources for computations of other entries. In example (C) in Fig. 3, user action prediction illustrates the use of complex data types and derivations in the user model. Sarukkai [10] presents an algorithms for link prediction in websites that is based on first-order Markov chains, a tool for modeling sequential processes. We apply this approach to user actions. After a brief introduction to the algorithm, its implementation in this framework is presented.

First, an numerical value is assigned to each possible action to be able to store actions in vectors and matrices. The last N=5 interactions are stored in a vector h and each of these interactions is again represented by a vector. The size of such a vector is equal to the number of possible interactions. In each vector, all indices are set to 0, except for the index of the index of the corresponding interaction, which is set to 1. A matrix A stores the probabilities a_{ij} that action j follows action i. A prediction for the next interaction can be computed using formula (1).

$$s(t) = \sum_{j=1}^{N} d(j)h(t-j)A^j \tag{1}$$

$s(t)$ represents the next step and d is a dampening factor that decreases the weight of older elements. The transition matrix T can be trained as follows. If the last action was i and an action j occurs, the value t_{ij} of T is incremented by 1. The probability transition matrix A is computed directly from T by dividing each value by the sum of the respective row.

This algorithm is implemented as follows in this framework (see Fig. 3.C). The list of past interactions is stored in the user model entry "actions.list" and updated by the `Add` source that appends a new interaction to the end of the list. Moreover, the matrix "actions.matrix", which corresponds to T, stores the number of transitions between two interactions, and the `MatrixAdd` operator updates the matrix when a new "interaction" event is observed. These two entries are used by the "MarkovPrediction" source of the "actions.next" entry to compute the most likely next interaction using the prediction algorithm, which converts the matrix "actions.matrix" into a probability matrix and combines it with the interaction history stored in "actions.list" to compute the prediction.

Thus, arbitrary derivations, such as modeling the user's favorite channel from the respective event parameters or predicting the most likely entry in a list, can be performed with values extracted from events by combining (and possibly creating new) operations. Other algorithms, such as the algorithms presented in [12], can be implemented similarly within this framework, deriving information directly from observed user behavior. An extension mechanism allows for the definition of custom operators as well as specific data types for these operators.

4. Implementation and Example Scenario

To investigate the feasiblity of this framework, we realized a full implementation of the presented architecture. This section gives a brief overview of the implementation and the application of the framework in an adaptive prototype system.

4.1. Implementation

A prototype of the architecture was implemented as an extension for a modeling tool called EB GUIDE Studio [4]. The tool comprises a simulation component that is used to execute the application. When the application is running, all observed events are submitted to the user modeling component, which distributes the events to the components subscribed to the event bus. One of these components is the user model, which loads information from the events and performs further derivations.

The type system employed in the user model is based on the type system of XML Schema (XSD)[1] to ensure interchangeability. However, only simple data types, such as strings and numbers, can be represented by this type system. Complex data types, such as lists and matrices, are not represented by XSD to allow algorithms to access data in an efficient way. However, the data contained in the complex types, such as numbers in a list, is defined by XSD.

Since the prototype system is implemented in Java, it provides comprehensive extension facilities. First, custom components can be registered at the event bus to process basic events. With regard to the user model, custom user modeling algorithms can be provided as derivation operators as well as custom (complex) data types needed for these algorithms.

4.2. Example Scenario: A Digital TV System

In this section, we present the application of the user modeling architecture to a prototype of an interactive TV system. For this purpose, an adaptive version of a prototype of the DICIT [6] system was created, which is a speech-enabled digital TV system. In the following, we present how the user modeling was performed. The resulting adaptations are only discussed briefly.

All events from the user-system interaction are submitted to the event bus, such as key presses or speech utterances by the user or system reactions to this user input. When the user requests a channel change by voice, e.g. using the phrase "please change channel to CNN", a number of events are created as a result (see Fig. 1). The recognition is the first event, followed by a number of system reactions. The interaction modeling component then detects the "channel change" action, with the channel parameter being set to "CNN".

Based on this interaction event, different aspects about the user can be modeled in the user model. First, the favorite channel of the user is computed by storing how often

[1] http://www.w3.org/XML/Schema

each channel was selected. The favorite channel is then highlighted in a channel selection list. Moreover, a program guide could also reflect this information.

User action prediction, as introduced in Sect. 3.2, triggers different adaptations in the prototype application. First, if a certain graphical button is connected to a predicted action, the button is emphasized to focus the user on this button. Second, adaptive help supports the user by providing help about predicted actions.

4.3. Assessment

A performance assessment was carried out to investigate the applicability of the presented architecture and implementation. For this purpose, the average processing time of events generated by a short walk-through of the system was measured. On a standard PC, this average processing time, which includes the user model derivations, was 25 ms. For algorithms with a longer run time, the computation could however be performed in the background. Therefore, the feasibility of the presented approach was attested by applying it to a digital TV system.

5. Related Work

There are numerous approaches and systems for user modeling. In this section, we introduce a few of them and compare them to our approach with regard to how inference of new information is performed.

The Doppelgänger User Modeling System [7] is a generalized user modeling system. Learning is supported by means of different techniques, such as linear prediction and Markov models. However, custom learning techniques cannot be added and the data accumulation is left to the application. In systems with logic-based representations, inferences can be drawn by means of logical reasoning. In the BGP-MS system [5], the internal representation is converted to first-order logic to use a logic reasoner. Moreover, inferences about the user can be drawn by rules, e.g. from user interviews. However, more complex derivations (e.g. Markov chains) are not part of the user model. A user modeling framework for intelligent learning environments that implements both supervised and unsupervised learning is presented by Amershi and Conati [1].

Research on user modeling algorithms as well as machine learning provides a multitude of approaches, each suited for different conditions. An extensive overview of predictive models for user modeling is for instance given by Zukerman and Albrecht [12]. Depending on the requirements of the interactive system, these algorithms can be implemented within this framework in addition to the existing ones.

6. Conclusion and Future Work

We presented an architecture for user modeling from basic events. The main building blocks are events and an event distribution system, which different components can use to exchange events. A user modeling component was introduced that allows for modeling derivations from events and user model entries. The aim of this architecture is to provide a reusable user modeling component for different adaptive interactive systems, which can have very different requirements. The feasibility of this architecture was demonstrated by a prototype implementation that was applied to an adaptive digital TV system.

As future work, we plan to implement more user modeling algorithms within this framework. Moreover, we plan to explore how to combine a generic user modeling system with custom data types with the advantages of a semantic and ontology-based description of the user model. Ontology-based user modeling systems, such as the one presented by Razmerita et al. [9], provide a well-formalized representation of user data, but cannot easily integrate complex data types required by some user modeling algorithms, such as matrices.

References

[1] S. Amershi and C. Conati. Unsupervised and Supervised Machine Learning in User Modeling for Intelligent Learning Environments. In *Intelligent User Interfaces (IUI) 2007*, pages 72–81. ACM, New York, NY, USA, 2007.

[2] D. D. Corkill. Blackboard systems. *AI Expert*, 6(9):40–47, 1991.

[3] A. Dix, J. Finlay, and R. Beale. Analysis of User Behaviour as Time Series. In *Conference on People and Computers (HCI) 1992*, pages 429–444. Cambridge University Press, Cambridge, UK, 1993.

[4] S. Goronzy, R. Mochales, and N. Beringer. Developing Speech Dialogs for Multimodal HMIs Using Finite State Machines. In *9th International Conference on Spoken Language Processing (Interspeech), CD-ROM*, 2006.

[5] A. Kobsa and W. Pohl. The User Modeling Shell System BGP-MS. *User Modeling and User-Adapted Interaction (UMUAI)*, 4(2):59–106, 1994.

[6] M. Matassoni, M. Omologo, R. Manione, T. Sowa, R. Balchandran, M. E. Epstein, and L. Seredi. The DICIT Project: An Example of Distant-talking Based Spoken Dialogue Interactive System. In *IIS 2008*, pages 527–533. Academic Publishing House EXIT, Warsaw, Poland, 2008.

[7] J. Orwant. Heterogeneous Learning in the Doppelgänger User Modeling System. *User Modeling and User-Adapted Interaction (UMUAI)*, 4(2):107–130, 1994.

[8] F. Paternò, C. Mancini, and S. Meniconi. ConcurTaskTrees: A Diagrammatic Notation for Specifying Task Models. In *INTERACT 1997*, pages 362–369. Chapman & Hall, London, UK, 1997.

[9] L. Razmerita, A. A. Angehrn, and A. Maedche. Ontology-Based User Modeling for Knowledge Management Systems. In *User Modeling (UM) 2003*, volume 2702 of *LNCS*, pages 213–217. Springer, Heidelberg, Germany, 2003.

[10] R. Sarukkai. Link Prediction and Path Analysis Using Markov Chains. *Computer Networks*, 33(1-6):377–386, 2000.

[11] E. Vidal, F. Thollard, C. de la Higuera, F. Casacuberta, and R. C. Carrasco. Probabilistic Finite-State Machines-Part I. In *Pattern Analysis and Machine Intelligence*, volume 27, pages 1013–1025. IEEE Computer Society, Washington, DC, USA, 2005.

[12] I. Zukerman and D. W. Albrecht. Predictive statistical models for user modeling. *User Modeling and User-Adapted Interaction*, 11(1-2):5–18, 2001.

Intelligent Environments 2009
V. Callaghan et al. (Eds.)
IOS Press, 2009

doi:10.3233/978-1-60750-034-6-327

u-Photo Mobile: Interacting with Smart Environments via Clickable Photos on Mobile Phones

Soko AOKI [a,1], Masaki ITO [a] Junichi YURA [a] Jin NAKAZAWA [b]
Kazunori TAKASHIO [a,b] Hideyuki TOKUDA [a,b]
[a] *Graduate School of Media and Governance, Keio University, Japan*
[b] *Faculty of Environment and Information Studies, Keio University, Japan*

Abstract.
This paper presents u-Photo Mobile a clickable digital still image to visualize and operate ubiquitous services. U-Photo Mobile is designed and implemented to be executed on smart phones e.g. Apple's iPhone. Users shoot the ubiquitous services attached with a two-dimensional bar-code. The u-Photo Mobile system decodes the ID and finds functions of the service. The touch screen of u-Photo Mobile lets users check and control the service. The operation of ubiquitous services are realized by making a network connection between u-Photo Mobile and the services. With this intuitive method, the users can interact with ubiquitous service through the metaphor of "taking and tapping a photograph." The u-Photo provides users with an instinctive technique, which realizes a seamless interaction between user's mobile phones and intelligent environments.

Keywords. Visualization, Operation, Ubiquitous Service, Human-Computer Interaction

1. Introduction

With the advancement of ubiquitous computing technology, we have various kinds of intelligent environments in our daily lives. These intelligent environments contain networked services such as displays, speakers, and sensors. On the other hand, the users usually bring their moblie smart phone when they move from one place to another. The smart devices and services are placed on both human side and environment side.

The increase of these ubiquitous services requires a method to access to the public ubiquitous services with intuitive interaction. For the users who have smart phones with them, inputting a URL or taking a photo of two-dimensional bar-code are typical access method to the public information. This method works with such services that require no interaction between users and services e.g. information acquisition from an advertisement poster. However, public services which can be operated and personalized by users, need additional control sequences. For example, the users can not control the public display showing a digital signage from their mobile phone yet.

[1]Corresponding Author: Soko Aoki, Graduate School of Media and Governance, Keio University, 5322, Endoh Fujisawa Kanagawa, Japan; E-mail: soko@ht.sfc.keio.ac.jp.

Our approach uses clickable digital still image for intuitive service discovery and operation. U-photo Mobile is a lightweight implementation for generic smart devices of u-Photo [1] which is a digital still image with information of ubiquitous services. U-Photo uses the simple action of taking a photograph to discover services, and then uses image-based intuitive GUI to operate the services. A two-dimensional bar-code is attached to each ubiquitous service to let the u-Photo recognize the identification of services.

The rest of this paper is organized as follows. Section 2 describes the visualization and operation of ubiquitous services. Section 3 introduces the design and implementation of u-Photo Mobile which uses clickable digital still image to discover and operate the services. Section 4 discusses the evalution of u-Photo mobile. Section 5 introduces related work and section 6 conludes this paper with future work.

2. Visualization and Operation of Ubiquitous Services

In this section, we define ubiquitous services and describe the characterization of these services. We also classify the variation of user's access to ubiquitous services.

2.1. Definition of Ubiquitous Services

Various kinds of devices are embedded in our intelligent environment. These devices can be roughly classified into three categories: sensors, processors, and actuators. Sensors detect environmental information. Processors compute or process the data. Actuators output the data by means of displays, speakers, and physical movement. Ubiquitous services are provided by these three kinds of devices.

In this paper, we define a ubiquitous service as a service which can be controlled via a network connection. These services should not only be accessed by users to observe the data (such as observing the sensor data), but also controlled from the user (such as changing the displayed contents in digital signage) via network. Therefore we provide the mechanism not only to observe the services but to interact with services with user's mobile devices..

2.2. Users Access to Ubiquitous Services

The users' access to ubiquitous services can be classified into three stages below. Our research aims to provide intuitive method to improve these three users' interaction with services.

- Service Discovery
  An user first visually discovers the service.
- Information Acquisition and Visualization
  Then the user acquires the information of this service.
- Operation
  Finally the user controls the service.

If users only need to visualize the ubiquitous services such as viewing the sensor data of his environment, the communiation between the users and the services will be unidirectional. However if users need to operate the service, the communication needs to be bidirectional. For this device human interaction, we have designed and implemented an intuitive method using clickable digital still image.

Table 1. Implementation Environment

Hardware Platform	Apple iPhone
Operating System	iPhone OS 2.2.1
Programming Language	Objective-C 2.0 and C
Network Protocol	Bonjour
Two-dimensional Bar-code	ARToolkitPlus [2]

2.3. Previous Work: u-Photo

The concept of u-Photo is using a digital still image to visualize and operate ubiquitous services. Each service is attached with a two-dimensional bar-code. The users shoot these services by a camera and the camera executes the image recognition mechanism to identify what the service is. After recognition of services, the users can control the service through the screen of his camera.

This concept is first described in our previous work [1]. In the first prototype of u-Photo, we used a general notebook computer and USB camera connected to this computer. This previous u-Photo had mainly three problems: size, network connectivity, and service barcode mapping. Although the user interface and functions were very rich thanks to the computer's rich capability, the weight of total system was 600g and it was a little too heavy to carry in our daily life. Since the computers connect to the network only when there is a Wireless LAN, the previous u-Photo has limitation in network connectivity. Furthermore, to use the u-Photo system, we need to map a service and a bar-code ID. Conventionally we inputted this mapping information manually.

To overcome these problems in the previous work, we ported the similar concept into a mobile phone which weighs quater of original u-Photo. We call this new u-Photo ported on a smart phone as u-Photo Mobile.

3. u-Photo Mobile

U-Photo Mobile overcomes these three problems mentioned above. First, since we re-implemented the system on smart phones, we could reduce the size and weight of hardware devices. Second, we utilized the smart phone which has both wireless LAN connection and 3G phone connection to improve the network connectivity and ubiquity. Third, we implemented semi-automatic barcode-service mapping system on smart phones to improve the usability of generating barcodes. In this section, we describe the details of u-Photo Mobile.

3.1. Overview

We used a smart phone with a camera and a touch screen to realize the visualization and operation of ubiquitous services. Because the Apple's iPhone has a camera, a screen, and network connectivity, we adopted this device as our implementation environment.The details of implementation environment of u-Photo Mobile is listed in Table 1. The image of using u-Photo to control a display is shown in Figure 1.

u-Photo Mobile saves the shot image in a JPEG file format. The detail information of ubiquitous services such as a hostname and a list of functions are written in the EXIF

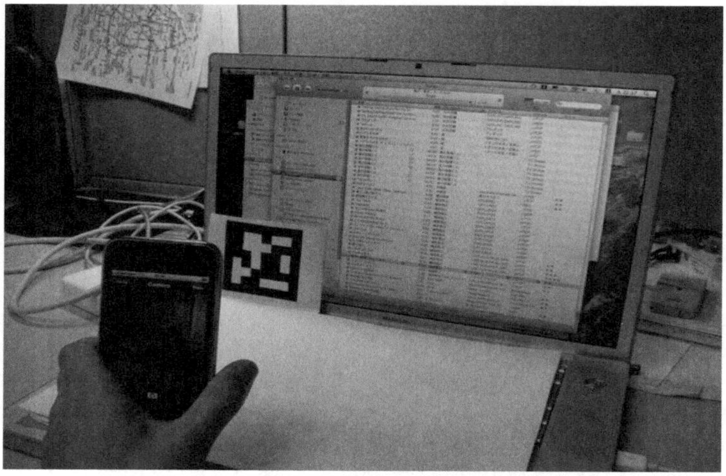

Figure 1. Interaction Image using u-Photo Mobile

area of JPEG. This EXIF area is a general purpose area especially for digital camera. By utilizing this EXIF space, we can share the u-Photo with other users only by sending the u-Photo (JPEG format.)

3.2. System Architecture

The system sequence of u-Photo Mobile is shown in Figure 2. The iPhone hosts the u-Photo controller. Each ubiquitous service has a mechanism to control its service via network connection. One bar-code server is placed in one network environment. As the Figure 2 shows, the initial connection between uPhoto Mobile, Barcode Server, and Service is done by using Bonjour protocol [3], a zero configuration service discovery protocol. The detail of operation sequence of these devices are described below.

1. Registration
   Each service registers its name and functions to the bar-code server. The bar-code server manages lists of services in its database.
2. Acquisition of Registered Data
   U-Photo controller acquire the lists of registered service from the bar-code server. This acquistion automatically happens once the u-photo connects to the network.
3. Configuration of Service by Mapping ID
   Users map the service and ID (bar-code) by using the u-Photo controller.
4. Shooting the Service
   Users shoot the service attached with bar-code.
5. Acquistion of Service ID
   U-Photo controller acquire the ID of service from the service. The u-Photo controller generates the list of function the service provides according to the data acquire in step 2.
6. Controling the Service
   Users control the service by tapping the touch screen of mobile phone. And service controls itself according to the command sent by u-Photo Mobile.

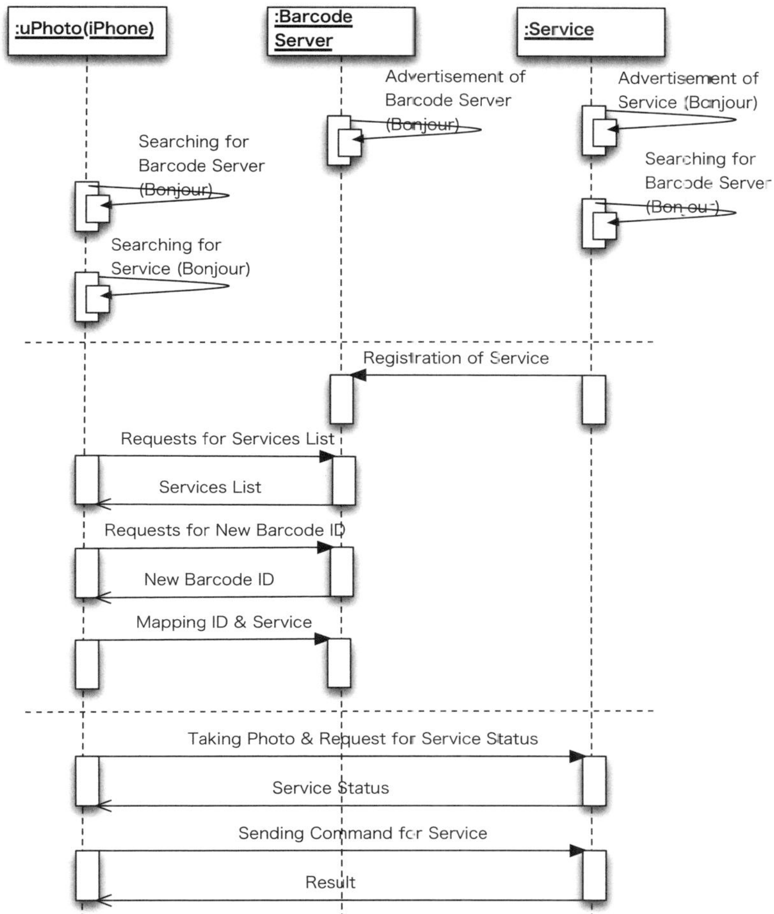

Figure 2. Sequence Chart of u-Photo Mobile

3.3. Three Modes of u-Photo Mobile

U-Photo Mobile has three modes to realize visualization and operation of ubiquitous services. These three modes are configuration mode, camera mode, and photo mode. The screen shots of these mode are shown in Figure 3 and detail descriptions are as follows.

3.3.1. Configuration Mode

Configuration mode let users add a new service which users want to control from u-Photo Mobile. The user selects the server which hosts the service and provide an ID and a two-dimensional bar-code for each service. The service will be controllable by printing out the bar-code and attaching it to the service.

Configuration Mode Camera Mode Photo Mode

Figure 3. Screen Shots of u-Photo Mobile

3.3.2. Camera Mode

Camera mode let users shoot the photos of services. The display of mobile phone shows the real entity of a service with an overlayed marker indicating the name of service. The photo shot by users will be saved in the phone and can be shared with other users by sending it via e-mail.

3.3.3. Photo Mode

Photo mode let users control the services by showing the graphical user interface of each services. This mode shows the list of commands and by choosing one of the command, the phone starts to communicate with service by using network socket communication. This mode also enable users to check the status of each service such as the name of the file or playing time of the display service. The users can upload and download the u-Photos taken by himself or others to share the controlling status of ubiquitous services.

3.4. Applications

We implemented two applications: a movie player and a music player. We wrote scripting programs for Quicktime player and iTunes music player so that we can utilize these applications as examples of ubiquitous services. We can start, stop, fast-forward, and rewind multimedia files using these programs. We used AppleScript for the implementation language.

4. Discussion

We evaluated the usability of u-Photo Mobile with some test users. The result shows that implementation on general mobile phone improved the portability and usability of services compared to old u-Photo which weighs about four times. But there is a problem

Table 2. Comparison Between Conventoinal u-Photo and New u-Photo Mobile

item	u-Photo	u-Photo Mobile
Model	Sony Vaio Type U (VGB-U70P)	Apple iPhone 3G
Size	167mm x 26.4mm x 108 mm	115.5mm x 12.3mm x 62.1mm
Weight	about 600g (with external camera)	133g
Display	800x600(5.0inch)	320x480(3.5inch)
Camera	PCGA-UVC11 0.37M Pixels (External)	2M Pixels
Two-Dimensional Bar-code	ARToolkit [4]	ARToolkitPlus [2]
Detection Frame Rate	30 frame/second	about 8 frame/second

in the display refresh speed which derives from camera's frame rate and u-Photo Mobile's program. Currently u-Photo Mobile detects two-dimensional bar-code at the rate of 12 frames per second where the conventional u-Photo detects at 30 frames per second.

Since u-Photo Mobile is basically a porting version of u-Photo, we compared these two versions of u-Photo. The comparison table is shown in Table 2. We could reduce the size and weight ot u-Photo Mobile hardware to one-quter of u-Photo original. In the original u-Photo, controling menu of a service is super-imposed on the photo, but since u-Photo Mobile's display is small, we need to realize the transition of GUI to change from photo view to controlling interface.

We focused on ubiquitous services such as sensors and actuators as controlled services in this research. However, same notion can be applied to other things which are not realized by hardware such as human and environment. For example, suppose each room has two-dimensional bar-code on its wall and by shooting that bar-code users can know past and current status of the room. Knowing the status of the room, users may control its setting to make the environment more confortable. If users shoot a human, they can know the human's profile or movement history. This kind of expansion is future work of our project.

5. Related Work

There are various methods to transfer the data from device to device. Passage [5] and mediaBlocks [6] use physical objects to transfer information between devices. In Passage, physical objects such as a watch and a key chain are called the "Passenger." When users want to transport digital objects, they only move the Passenger from the source device to the destination device. The media-Blocks, which are electronically tagged wooden blocks, serve as physical icons that transport online media. Using physical objects is useful for the immediate use of personalization service but unsuitable for long-term use of multiple objects. This method is not suitable to transfer multiple digital objects since there is not any mechanism to identify each objects. On the other hand, since u-Photo Mobile includes the still image, it would be easier to grasp the binding between files and information.

There is a wide variety of systems that visualize environment information. NaviCam [7] displays situation-sensitive information by superimposing messages on its video see-through displays using PDAs and head mounted displays. InfoScope [8] is an information augmentation system that uses a camera and a PDA's display without any tags on objects. When a user points his or her PDA to buildings or places, the system displays the name of them. DigiScope [9] annotates an image-using, visual, see-through tablet. A user can interact with embedded information related to a target object by pointing at the object. Although these researches are similar to u-Photo Mobile in terms of annotating an image, the researchers focused on real-time use where a user can interact with a target object in front of the user now. On the other hand, we concentrated on recording pervasive services information and reusing it.

6. Conclusion

This paper presented u-Photo Mobile, a visualization and operation mechanism of ubiquitous services using a clickable digital still image. U-Photo shoots a service with a two-dimensional bar-code, recognizes the ID of a service, and controls it via network. With this technique, users can intuitively visualize and operate ubiquitous services around them. Since the u-Photo Mobile is lightweight software and implemented on a generic smart phone, the burden for users to carry it in their daily life is quite low. With the method of using digital images as visualizaion and operation user interface, it let users easily share u-Photo among multiple people. The future work of this research includes extended implementaion of services to cope with visualization and operation of space and human.

Acknowledgement

This research is partially supported by the Ubiquitous Service Platform Research of Ministry of Internal Affairs and Communications, Japan.

References

[1] G. Suzuki, S. Aoki, T. Iwamoto, D. Maruyama, T. Koda, N. Kohtake, K. Takashio, and H. Tokuda, "u-photo: Interacting with pervasive services using digital still images", in *The Third International Conference on Pervasive Computing (PERVASIVE)*, 2005.

[2] Christian Doppler Laboratory, Graz University of Technology , "ARToolkitPlus", 2006, http://studierstube.icg.tu-graz.ac.at/handheld _ar/artoolkitplus.php.

[3] Apple Inc. , "Bonjour Protocol Specification", 2009, http://developer.apple.com/networking/bonjour/specs.html

[4] ARToolWorks Inc. , "ARToolkit", 2007, http://www.artoolworks.com/ARToolKit _Professional.html.

[5] N. A. Streitz and S. Konomi andC. Muller-Tomfelde, "Passage: Physical transportation of digital information in cooperative buildings", in *2nd International Workshop on Cooperative Building(CoBuild1999)*, 1999.

[6] H. Ishi, B. Ullmer, and D. Glas, "mediablocks: Physical containers, transports, and controls for online media", in *Computer Graphics Proceedings (SIGGRAPH'98)*, 1998.

[7] J. Rekimoto and K. Nagao, "The wolrd through the computer: Computer augmented interaction with real world", in *Symposium on User Interface Software and Technology*, 1995.

[8] I. Haritaoglu, "Infoscope: Link from real world to digital information space", in *3rd International Conference on Ubiquitous Computing (Ubicomp2001)*, 2001.

[9] A. Ferscha and M. Keller, "Digiscope: An invisible worlds window", in *Adjunct Proceedings of the 5th International Conference on Ubiquitous Computing (Ubicomp2003)*, 2003.

Special Session on the Art and Design of Intelligent, Hybrid Environments

Intelligent Environments 2009
V. Callaghan et al. (Eds.)
IOS Press, 2009

doi:10.3233/978-1-60750-034-6-337

Insights into the design of communicative location-based experiences

Charalampos RIZOPOULOS and Dimitris CHARITOS[1]
Department of Communication and Media Studies
National and Kapodistrian University of Athens

Abstract. This paper presents a study of the communicative experience of locative media users participating in a multi-user pervasive game in an attempt to provide insights on the design of such experiences. The study presented therein is a follow-up to earlier work outlining a theoretical model of locative media use for the purposes of communication and social interaction.

Keywords. Locative media, communication, design, group interaction.

1. Introduction

Locative Media (LM) are defined as communications media utilising location detection for the purpose of content delivery, which have the potential to become significantly more widespread as GPS-enabled mobile devices become more affordable. The introduction of physical location as a criterion for determining access to digital content has resulted in a strong correlation between the physical environment and purely digital information. The impact of such a connection on the users' everyday communicative practices may be significant.

Additionally, location awareness can be used for the purpose of communication. Designing communication-oriented location-aware applications necessitates new design practices and methodologies that will take into account the fundamentally hybrid spatial experience provided by LM, as well as the opportunities for socialisation and communication they can offer. In this paper we briefly present some related findings obtained through the use of a location-based system we designed and implemented as part of a related research project titled LOCUNET ("Location-Based Urban Network"). These findings are a follow-up to earlier work (e.g. [4], [12]) that outlines the theoretical framework of communication during LM use that supported the design and implementation of our system.

2. The experience of location awareness in mediated communication

Although location-awareness should not be considered particularly innovative from a technological standpoint, its impact on the users' everyday communicative practices can be significant and is not yet fully understood. In this section we briefly present

---

[1] Corresponding Author.

some of the ways in which computer-mediated communication (CMC) among users is transformed as a result of location-awareness.

LM contribute to the partial re-spatialisation of digital information and the social and communicative practices associated with it (Charitos, 2008) by making the user's actual location in a physical setting a condition for determining access and use of digital information. Green ([7], pp. 250-251) argues that individuals have been "dislocated" (or disconnected) from their common spatial and temporal context due to urban expansion and technologies that overcome the barriers of time and distance. Until now, lack of locality has been a defining characteristic of CMC. Internet-based and mobile communication is often seen as taking place in a placeless, indeterminate space always experienced as "elsewhere" [9]. On the Internet, bandwidth is more important than actual physical location, a phenomenon termed as "spaceless proximity" [1]. Online communication is fundamentally de-territorialized, occurring in the immaterial, boundless and ever-expanding matrix of Internet connections. For instance, computer-mediated communication (CMC) via the Internet has allowed physical meeting places to "immigrate" to a "virtual" spatial context, as in the case of various graphical online communities.

Conversely, de Souza e Silva [3] highlighted the social significance of mobile LM, which allowed virtual worlds to move from the Internet to the urban environment—from the digital realm back to the physical world. The Internet can be understood as a non-centralised network of communication. Through the combination of Internet access and mobility, the decentralised and 'bottom-up' nature of the Internet passes on to mobile telephony, which has so far been a centralised communication network. Location-awareness re-introduces the parameter of real location and corporeal presence in CMC, thus mapping the "virtual" mental space of communication to physical space inhabited by communicating participants. LM map the virtual spatial context of a communicative activity onto the physical world, thus producing a hybrid topography that encompasses elements from both real and virtual space.

The significance of utilising actual physical location in an ICT system lies in its naturalness; humans continuously use location-related information, even in the most mundane everyday activity. Context remains important even in aspects of CMC from where it has been seemingly left out. Although it can be argued that CMC renders it irrelevant by downplaying or entirely removing the physical environment, context still plays a prominent role in many forms of mediated interpersonal interaction, mainly through explicitly conveyed contextual information. In the case of LM, geography regains its importance. Consequently, modern cities become actual "technospaces", a novel type of spatial formation where technology meets human practice and the linkage between built environment and information is reaffirmed. Because of the process of re-spatialisation they bring about, LM also hold the potential of bringing forth not only the geographical, but also the cultural contextuality, expressed as the notion that spaces have a history and a material continuity. This facilitates the transformation of abstract and neutral spaces into meaningful places.

In addition to the key issue of locality, the seemingly paradoxical convergence of the physical and the digital environment may undermine other typical characteristics of Internet communication, such as the adoption of multiple identities, anonymity, and absence of visible social markers, such age or gender. In so doing, multi-user LM may invigorate collective identities, mainly by moderating the individualism that is typical of CMC. The role of non-verbal social cues is another distinguishing point. Internet communication inhibits the use of social cues [11], since the body and the nuances and social meaning inherent in non-verbal communication are absent. Although this does not necessarily eliminate the potential for personalized communication, CMC is significantly lower on "social presence" compared to face-to-face communication [10].

LM essentially combine both CMC and face-to-face interaction. The frequency and intensity of interpersonal interaction during LM use may be influenced by factors related to design choices or system specifications, as for example:

- **the degree of location awareness of communication via LM:** if one can communicate with everybody from anywhere, the need for proximity and interpersonal communication is somewhat diminished.
- **the limitations imposed by the device on the richness of communication:** a device that supports multimodal communication may be more successful in narrowing the gap between CMC and interpersonal communication; thus, the need for proximity and interpersonal communication may also diminish.
- **whether LM use is part of a purposeful and structured activity involving several users** (a location-based game for instance)**:** if users participate in a multiuser activity, they are expected to engage in CMC or interpersonal communication more frequently. On the other hand, a purely informative application of LM (e.g. advertisements), will probably remain focused on the individual.
- **the limitations resulting from the design of the application:** it is possible to regulate by means of location detection the user's ability to access stored information or communicate with one another. For instance, in the LOCUNET system a user must be a short distance away from a geo-tag in order to access it.

3. Researching the users' experience of using LM

For the purpose of evaluating part of the theoretical framework of locative media use presented elsewhere ([4], [12]), a location-based multiplayer activity took place at the city centre of Athens. Due to the complicated nature of LM use in urban space, this activity served as a means of evaluating only part of this framework. More specifically, the evaluation presented in this paper refers to the relationship between the individual user and the system (HCI aspect) and to the relationship among users who interact via the system (CMC in the context of groups).

3.1. The activity and the system

Two opposing "teams" (groups of users equipped with GPS-enabled cellphones) sought and captured a number of digital objects scattered throughout the play area. The activity took place in an area that was well-suited to pedestrian traffic and had numerous features that promoted playful behaviour (such as hiding places, bridges, footpaths, etc.). A map designed in a way that certain elements that are particularly useful to pedestrians (such as bridges, gardens, parks, etc.) would be visually enhanced was displayed on each mobile device.

As users walked around the play area, certain digital "objects" appeared on their screen depending on their actual geographic location. If the users were sufficiently close to an object, they could "collect" it, and the user's avatar changed accordingly, signifying that the user was carrying an object. Once collected, an object remained in a player's possession for two minutes unless intentionally dropped sooner. Once the two-minute time limit had been reached, the object was automatically dropped wherever the player happened to be at the time, and could not be immediately picked up by the same player again. Thus, players were required to collaborate in order to capture them. An object was captured when dropped on an area designated as "team headquarters". The team that captured most of the objects was declared the winner.

Apart from these movable objects, another type of digital element featured was named "info pack"—essentially containers of digital information (text, sound, images, or video) associated with a physical location and accessed depending on proximity. Users could create their own info packs by typing text or using the phone to take pictures and record sound or video. In addition to the info packs, the users could communicate via text messages.

3.2. The research procedure

Before the activity (which lasted for approx. one hour), participants attended a briefing session about the activity they would participate in and were asked to fill a demographics questionnaire. After the activity had taken place, participants filled questionnaires regarding the usability of the system, the communicative acts they engaged in, their attitudes towards LM, and their perception of the environment. They were also asked to produce sketches of the environment they had experienced during the activity for the purpose of investigating their spatial memory. Subsequently, they participated in two focus groups: one regarding the experience of using the system (which complemented the quantitative usability evaluation methods) and another one regarding group-based communication during the activity as well as an evaluation of the overall experience.

The questionnaires that dealt with the communicational aspect of the experience were subjected to both quantitative and qualitative analysis and the results are presented in the following section.

4. Evaluation

The number of participants was 17, with a mean age of 28 (S.D. $\approx$ 3.75). None of them had previous experience in using LM and their familiarity with online gaming varied.

4.1. Quantitative analysis

A composite questionnaire was constructed for the purposes of gathering data about the participants' experience of using the LOCUNET system and the attitudes formed as a result. The issues addressed by the questionnaire were:

- **Evaluation of the activity as an experience:** participants expressed their level of agreement to a set of four characterizations ("entertaining", "interesting", "pleasant" and "dangerous") on 1-5 Likert scales.
- **Establishment of group identity:** six criteria indicative of the establishment of group identity were provided. Participants were asked if they identified

each of these criteria during the activity. The criteria were: i) *team spirit*, ii) *sense of belonging*, iii) *sense of belonging induced by the other members' behaviour*, iv) *effectiveness of cooperation with other members*, v) *feeling of self-importance induced by other members' behaviour*, and vi) *possible retention of the team for other activities*.

- **Perception of the activity as public or private** (one question)
- **Perception of the activity taking place in physical or virtual space** (one question)
- **Sense of immersion in the hybrid environment:** a set of five questions, on a 1-5 Likert scale. The corresponding criteria were i) *loss of sense of presence in the physical environment of the city*, ii) *total immersion in the virtual space*, iii) *annoyance caused by passersby*, iv) *ease of navigating*, and v) *transformation of the perception of urban hotspots as a result of the activity*.
- **Attitudes towards LM use** (set of five questions): participants were asked whether they agree or disagree with the following statements: i) *desire to participate in the activity if it lasted longer*, ii) *willingness to participate again in such an activity*, iii) *willingness to participate in similar activities*, iv) *motivating friends to participate*, and v) *attitude towards the proliferation of LM activities in the commercial market*.

4.1.1. Results and discussion

Users were generally favourably disposed towards the system, as shown in table 1.

Table 1. Mean scores of characterizations attributed to the activity experience on a 1-5 Likert scale rating.

Characterization	Mean	Standard Deviation
Entertaining	4.24	0.66
Interesting	4.24	0.83
Pleasant	4.06	0.55
Dangerous	1.52	0.71

According to the participants, the criteria for group formation were adequately met during the activity. Out of a total of the six criteria, regarding the establishment of group identity, (maximum score=6), the mean was 4.36 (S.D.=0.63). The participants' general attitude towards LM was also very positive. The mean of the 1-5 Likert scale rating that was used in the five corresponding questions was very high (mean=4.60, S.D.=0.63).

When asked whether the activity took place in the physical or the virtual spatial context, 13 out of 17 users responded that "the activity took place equally in the urban (physical) space and the (virtual) space of the screen", while the options "mostly in the urban environment" and "mostly on the screen" were favoured by 2 users each. Additionally, 7 out of 17 users perceived the experience as taking place in a public space, 4 users considered the place private, while the remaining 6 perceived the place of the activity as both public and private.

At the set of questions addressing the issue of immersion into a hybrid (both virtual and physical) space, the mean score was 3.45 (S.D.=0.51). The score at the question about the "*loss of feeling of navigating in the city*" was moderately correlated to forming a positive attitude towards LM- the latter is derived from the abovementioned last set of evaluative questions (Spearman's rho=0.541, sig.=0.037). The same correlation exists among this attitude and the level of "*differentiation in the way participants view urban hotspots*" (Spearman's rho=0.533, sig.=0.027).

Another correlation was found between assessing the activity as "*dangerous*", the "*level of annoyance induced by passersby*" and (negatively) the degree of "*immersion into the hybrid environment*" (table 2).

Table 2. Spearman's rho: assessment of the experience as dangerous.

	Annoyance induced by passersby	Immersion in hybrid environment
Correlation Coefficient	.503(*)	-.564(*)
Sig. (2-tailed)	.040	.018
N	17	17

* *Correlation is significant at the 0.05 level (2-tailed)*

A difference was also observed in the "*level of annoyance induced by passersby*" between those who considered the place of the activity as public and those who expressed the attitude that it was a private one or both public and private. Participants that experienced the activity as public were less annoyed (mean=1.14, S.D.=0.38), compared to the other two categories (mean=2.20, S.D.=1, no differences between the two latter groups). This difference is statistically significant (Welch $statistic_{(1,12.108)}$=8.794, sig.=0.012). Finally, there was moderate correlation between frequency of Internet use and ease of navigation in the hybrid environment (Spearman's rho = 0.533, sig.= 0.027). In summary, it can be suggested that users were positive towards both the specific experience and LM applications in general. The participants' ability to immerse themselves into the hybrid environment is related to favourable attitudes (both constructs received high ratings), and considering the activity as public also enhances the quality of the experience, since it seems to lead to greater immersion.

Although it is not possible to identify the direction of the correlation, experiencing the activity as public may relate to greater immersion, less annoyance by passersby, while it minimizes possible feelings of danger; all of these result to a more pleasant experience and a more favourable attitude.

Specific aspects of the experience also seem to strengthen individuals' positive assessments:

- A sense of being present simultaneously in both the physical urban landscape and its digital representation within the "virtual" environmental context
- An enhancement of the participants' view urban hotspots as a result of using the particular LM.

In spite of the short duration of the activity, participants generally felt they had fulfilled a considerable number of group formation criteria.

The above findings are not conclusive but indicative of trends. The small number of participants does not allow extensive statistical analysis, and these results should be replicated in consequent experiments in terms of reliability.

4.2. Qualitative analysis

The qualitative analysis of the data obtained through questionnaires showed that the majority of the participants found the combination of physical and virtual elements during LM use very appealing and satisfying. Users who perceived urban space as primarily private and personal tended to experience a greater degree of immersion compared to users who perceived the same space as predominantly public. Although this may, at first glance, seem contradictory to the results of the quantitative analysis, it is not surprising when viewed through the lens of social psychology. Spaces that are perceived as private tend to "insulate" the individual from environmental characteristics that may act as distractions or impediments in the flow of communication. When in a public space, one tends to behave in a manner perceived as appropriate for the setting. In this way, one often feels compelled to control oneself and be careful not to fall short of the audience's expectations. In Goffman's words [6], one strives to preserve one's "foreground", i.e. one's "public face" (an approach known as Goffman's *dramaturgical model*). This constant self-regulation does not encourage a sense of immersion. In contrast, one is more likely to "be oneself" when in the relatively "protected" private space. It may be argued, therefore, that a user who manages to disregard passersby feels less pressure to conform to their social standards and thus does not experience an intrusion in his/her personal space.

In general, participants described the experience of LM use in an urban setting as highly satisfying. This suggestion is supported by the following results:

- Users reported that they liked a number of the activity's elements, such as the combination of physical and virtual space into a hybrid reality, the game-like nature of the activity and interacting with other users.
- The majority of the participants would be willing to take part in a similar activity with a longer duration. This tendency is indicative of the enjoyment they derived by participating.
- Participants characterised the affective impact of their experience positively, using adjectives such as "entertaining" and "pleasurable".
- The participants indicated their satisfaction about the originality of the activity by describing it as "interesting", "novel" and "original".
- Intra-group communication received an equally positive evaluation. The groups' atmosphere was reported as "friendly", "cooperative" and "pleasant" by nearly every participant.
- Participants would be willing to take part in the same activity again, even with the same users.
- The vast majority of participants would encourage their friends to participate in such an activity.

There are also a number of elements that users found rather problematic and which might have adversely affected the users' experience. More specifically:

- Users perceived the duration of the activity as short, and believed that it prevented them from engaging in communication as often or as well as they would like.

- Technical issues that disrupted the flow of the activity.
- The difficulty of using the text messaging function of the system and its and indirectness as a means of communication
- Issues related to the representation of users and objects on the screen of the mobile device.
- The relative lack of complexity regarding the activity's objectives. More complex and event-driven hierarchies of objectives could potentially solve this problem.

These difficulties notwithstanding, the participants found that LM use augmented intra-group, intergroup and interpersonal communication.

Despite its short duration, the activity was perceived as predominantly group-oriented. According to almost all participants, "team spirit" never faltered once established, as there was a collective sense of belonging to the group. Both "team spirit" and sense of belonging are indications that a group has been or is in the process of being formed. The sense of belonging experienced by the participants was reinforced by the other group members' behaviour, which was reported as friendly. Even the one participant who did not agree that a "team spirit" existed reported having felt "part of a group". These groups were not groups in the fullest sense of the word, since the duration of the activity was too short for 'true' groups to emerge. However, 'group' members were connected to one another, forming a network of "behavioural interdependencies", (e.g. fellow team members are expected to work together whereas members of opposing teams are expected to compete with one another). Therefore, the social formations in question were task or performance groups utilising a common definition of a situation (as per Goffman). Additionally, some form of bonding among the participants was observed. Nearly all of them said they would like to keep in touch with their fellow players, even outside the context of the activity undertaken—a clear indication of attraction which can be seen as a precursor to the formation of fully fledged relationships [8]. Thus, it is assumed that, had the activity lasted longer, more significant interpersonal and intra-group relationship patterns would have emerged.

4.3. Focus group

The main reason for conducting a focus group was the need to investigate the social aspect (and qualitative dimensions) of LM use so that the effectiveness of LM as a means of interpersonal and intra-group communication would be evaluated. The main parameters examined were: the groups' nature and organisation, interactions among team members, hierarchies and roles within the groups, and the sense of belonging to the group.

As a general note, notions such as "cooperation", "strategy", "competition", "interest", or "disappointment" were prevalent in the participants' description of the activity and the emotions they experienced as a result.

The adoption of a number of rules resulted in some kind of social organisation. Rules serve to define what Goffman [6] called a *situated activity system*. Group members implicitly agreed to focus their cognitive resources and visual attention on accomplishing the same collective goal. In so doing, they implicitly accepted and approved a number of specific rules on preventing and managing tension.

The interrelations observed during the activity indicate a process of group formation that is still at its initial stages, encouraged by the physical co-presence of the participants. A number of characteristics usually associated with group formation were present in the interaction among the participants[2]:

- **Focus of attention:** The participants maintained a common focus of attention. By doing so, they facilitated their experience of *spontaneous involvement*, a sense of being a vital component of the situation and a feeling of immersion in the activity and encounters taking place during its course.
- **Pursuit and fulfilment of goals:** The participants actively pursued their group's goals. More specifically, the group's goals were identical to those of its members. In addition, the groups' goals did not deviate from the goals of the activity as described in the application scenario.
- **Sense of belonging to a group:** The participants often used the first person plural when referring to what transpired during the activity (e.g. "*we* managed to attain *our* goals"). They explicitly stated that they had felt being part of a group and the desire to contribute to the group's effort. The members of the winning team reported having experienced feelings of joy as a result of their group's victory. Additionally, most participants were willing to keep in touch with other group members in the future.
- **Roles within groups:** Although the duration of the activity was short, it was found that the participants assumed certain functional roles in their groups. These roles included that of the "leader", the "coordinator", the "efficient person who pursues the group's goals", and even the person who offers encouragement to the other group members.

All participants engaged in interpersonal communication. They also tried to communicate via text messages, but they expressed their disappointment in the fact that this facility did not prove as practical or functional as they would have liked. It may therefore be suggested that the advantage of using LM as opposed to more conventional information and communication technologies lies in the possibility of immediate interpersonal communication, which helps users address some of the limitations of computer-mediated communication.

5. Conclusions and Future Work

From the results of the user research study, we have concluded that users of LM in the city are very likely to experience urban space as hybrid. LM use in public places can lead to a greater sense of immersion if passersby are not perceived as threatening to the user's private or personal space.

Users are favourably disposed toward the possibility of participating in such an activity, partly because of the relative novelty of multi-user LM in everyday life. The

[2] These findings are, to some extent, contrary to the data obtained through questionnaires. This discrepancy may be attributable to the research methods employed, given that the focus group investigated the participants' attitudes and beliefs to greater extent than the questionnaires. Therefore, it is possible that the focus group was able to yield more in-depth results regarding the way the participants interacted with one another both, within and outside their groups.

participants considered their experience of the use of the system as satisfying and pleasurable, and none of the perceived disadvantages of the activity was due to the behaviour of other group members or factors of group dynamics in general. This fact may suggest that group dynamics are an important factor in the participants' experience of the use of such media and the satisfaction they derive from it.

Even though the groups that were formed in the case of the LOCUNET system were task- or performance-oriented, our results indicate that, even when the users do not know one another or the duration of the multi-user activity they participate in is short, signs of an emerging group identity may still be observed, since the participants behaved in a manner that satisfied several criteria that are generally assumed to indicate the existence of a group. More specifically: the participants collaborated efficiently towards attaining their common goal, devoting their cognitive resources and attention to that end, thereby creating a *situated activity system*; they experienced a sense of spontaneous involvement, as well as a sense of belonging to the group; they took steps towards assuming discrete roles. In such cases, a multi-user LM activity may be the first step towards the formation of fully-fledged groups. The hybrid nature of LM use becomes evident in the participants' eagerness to engage in interpersonal communication. This eagerness may be (to an extent) attributable to the requirements of the activity that was implemented and the limitations of the communication functionality that was offered by the system. However, compared with interpersonal communication, computer-mediated communication has a number of well known limitations, and LM users are able to overcome them by acting in both the physical and the virtual space. Interpersonal communication during LM use may also help establish group identity by promoting interaction among group members in both aspects of the hybrid environment in which it occurs. Moreover, the fundamentally hybrid nature of LM use may increase a medium's overall appeal, as in the case of LOCUNET.

Social interaction can be encouraged or discouraged by game rules. In the case of LOCUNET, players were encouraged by the rules to cooperate with fellow team members in order to maximise their chances of winning, without having been explicitly told to. Interestingly, the players also reported that part of the 'magic' of the experience was the fact that they interacted with each other in a cooperative manner. This process also instigated interpersonal communication among users.

LOCUNET participants who felt inhibited or threatened by the presence and activity of passers-by were less able to immerse themselves in the game. Goffman's dramaturgical model (discussed earlier) may explain this finding. In accordance with Goffman's model, users who were negatively affected by passers-by reported having thought of the context where the game took place as private space. These users perceived passers-by as invading their personal territory and were forced to adapt their behaviour accordingly. When designing a LM-supported activity in urban space, it is important to take this fact into account.

Immersion is an important factor of the experience of LM use. In addition to the above, a clear connection between the users' sense of immersion and the satisfaction they derived from the game has been observed. Users suggested that they would have felt more immersed had the game lasted longer. The more able users are to filter out extraneous stimuli, the more immersed they feel and the more they enjoy the activity as a result. Thus, when designing a LM-supported activity, it is important to select the area carefully; when the game takes place in an area perceived as dangerous to pedestrians, users will probably not have enough cognitive resources to mind their own safety and, at the same time, immerse themselves in the game. Such an inability to feel immersed on the part of the players is clearly detrimental to the satisfaction they derive from the game and may also impair their performance. Finally, game rules maybe appropriately set for encouraging or discouraging social interaction. Kaplan (as quoted in [5], p. 280) has suggested two criteria of environmental preference: *coherence* (the organisation or degree to which a scene 'hangs together') and *moderate uncertainty* (provided by variety, moderate complexity, moderate spaciousness and occasional structural irregularities). Selecting a suitable area for a LM experience to take place in and incorporating all digital elements of the activity within this environment are significant aspects of the design process. In the case of LOCUNET, the area of the activity contained ramps, stairs, bridges, hiding places and other such environmental elements that induced a sense of moderate uncertainty and encouraged exploratory and playful behaviour during navigation. Info-packs and objects were appropriately positioned in relation to these physical elements so as to lead to an overall interesting and fulfilling navigation and search activity by maintaining a balance between legibility and ambiguity in the configuration of both physical and digital environmental elements.

LOCUNET participants confirmed that the experience of LM takes place within a hybrid environment and also reported that this characteristic was one of the most appealing elements of the entire activity. Therefore, neither the physical nor the digital aspect of the environment should be neglected when designing a LM experience. Ultimately, attention should be paid to digital and physical environmental elements – and the actions they afford. These elements should be seen as integral parts of the situation that unfolds during the activity. Elements that encourage exploratory behaviour (e.g. ramps, stairs, bridges, hiding places etc.) may improve the overall quality of the experience. In short, maintaining a certain balance between legibility and uncertainty in the environment is crucial when designing LM.

In the future, the LOCUNET system will be improved in terms of usability and expanded in terms of functionality. LM do not necessarily include only mobile media, but even conventional desktop systems that allow the user to interact with other users in spatial representations. Thus, a 3D environment modelled after the actual area in which the activity took place is being developed and integrated into the LOCUNET system so as to allow desktop and mobile users to navigate the same space (or its representation) simultaneously. Furthermore, the scenario of the activity will be enriched so that the activity will become more interesting to the users. A more complex scenario would increase the level of uncertainty of the experience as a whole, which is desirable, provided that it continues to conform to Kaplan's criterion of moderate uncertainty. Ideally, the level of uncertainty will be evenly distributed between the environment and the scenario of the activity. In addition to participant interest and satisfaction, a more complex – and less predictable – scenario may allow for more complex forms of social organisation and communicative practices to emerge, thus having a direct impact on the communicative potential of LM.

Acknowledgements

The research project titled "LOCUNET" is supported by the Greek General Secretariat of Research and Technology under the framework of the Operational Program PEP Attikis, Measure 1.2. The Programme is co-financed (70%) by the European Fund of

Regional Development (EFRD), which aims to facilitate the reduction of the inequalities within the European Union regions.

References

[1] Baym, N. "Interpersonal Life Online". In: Lievrouw, L.A. & Livingstone, S. (eds.). The Handbook of New Media (Updated Student Edition), pp. 35-54. London: Sage, 2006.
[2] Charitos, D. "Precedents for the design of Locative Media". In: Saariluoma, P. & Isomäki, H. (eds.) "Future Interaction Design II", London: Springer.
[3] De Souza e Silva, A. 'Mobile Networks and Public Spaces: Bringing Multi-user Environments into the Physical Space'. In R. Ascott (Ed.). Electronic Proceedings of the 2003 Consciousness Reframed International Conference. CaiiA STAR, University of Wales College, 2003.
[4] Diamantaki, K., Charitos, D., Tsianos, N., Lekkas, Z. Towards Investigating the Social Dimensions of Using LM Within the Urban Context, Proceedings of the 3rd International Conference on Intelligent Environments, Ulm, Germany, September 2007, pp. 53-60.
[5] Evans, G.W. 'Environmental Cognition'. *Psychological Bulletin*, 88 (2), 1980, pp. 259–287
[6] Goffman, E. The Presentation of Self in Everyday Life. Penguin, London, 1990.
[7] Green, N. "On the Move: Technology, Mobility, and the Mediation of Social Time and Space". In: Hassan, R. and Thomas, J. (eds.). The New Media Theory Reader, pp. 249-265. Open University Press, Maidenhead, UK, 2006.
[8] Hare, P., Blumberg, H.H., Davies, M.F. and Kent, M.V. (eds.). Handbook of Small Group Research. The Free Press, New York, 1976.
[9] Hemment, D.: The Mobile Effect. Convergence 11 (2), 32-39, 2005.
[10] Hine C.: Virtual Ethnographer, London: Sage Publications, 2000.
[11] Kiesler S., Siegel J., McGuire T.W. "Social psychological aspects of computer-mediated communication", American Psychologist, 39 (10): 1123-1134, 1984.
[12] Rizopoulos, C., Charitos, D., Koutsompolis, D., Kaimakamis, N. 'Towards a Theoretical Model of Communication Via Locative Media Use'. *Proceedings of the 4th IET International Conference on Intelligent Environments*, Seattle, WA, July 2008.

Intelligent Environments 2009
V. Callaghan et al. (Eds.)
IOS Press, 2009

doi:10.3233/978-1-60750-034-6-349

Information Places: Defining Settings for Locative Media

Katharine WILLIS[a]
[a] *Locating Media Project, University of Siegen, Germany*

Abstract. In our everyday life we are used to using physical settings as backgrounds for social encounters; we might agree to 'Meet on the corner' or 'See you at the café'. But information available and delivered on mobile devices enables a different relationship with our spatial world. Instead we may agree to catch up once the other person comes into Bluetooth range, or to meet on a Myspace page. These interactions still have a relationship with location; we still have to physically be somewhere even if it remote from the person we are communicating with, but it is more complex and layered. The situated nature of the interaction creates opportunities for behaviours that transcend existing concepts of space. This research proposes both to develop a theoretical approach and to undertake a series of empirical studies, which attempt to understand the particular role that the physical and social setting has on how and why people acquire and act on digital spatial information.

Keywords. Settings, locative media, location, space

Introduction

This research takes the standpoint that rather than seeing individuals, the environment and media as separate entities, the way we interact with the world means that our actions are situated. In its approach it draws on the concept of 'situated actions', a concept developed in 1980's by Lucy Suchman which attempts to find a way of understanding and responding to the relationship of humans with technology in real world situations. In her discussion of the concept of 'situated actions', human communication, instead of being structured by a set of predefined plans is instead considered as situated in the sense that '*knowledge remains under construction within the framework of each action'* (Suchman 1987). The concept of situated-ness has been explored by many researchers and theorists, and despite many similarities in ideas of what characterises situated-ness, these approaches also expose different perspectives. These viewpoints originate from an extraordinarily broad range of fields; sociology (Goffmann 1969, Meyrowitz 1986), HCI (Dey and Abowd 1999, Dourish 2001), anthropology or ethnography (Suchman 1987), cognitive psychology (Hutchins 1995, Wilson 2002), architecture (McCollough 2005) and geography (Batty 2000, Massey 2007). Despite varying perspectives, one common concept seems to persevere is that context is a relational property (Dourish 2004), which means that the various aspects of a situation cannot be seen as isolated, but are fundamentally interrelated. The urban planner Kevin Lynch underlined this as follows; *'nothing is experienced by itself, but always in relation to its surroundings, the sequence of events leading up to it, the memory of past experiences'* (Lynch 1960, p. 1). Consequently the situation of the action can be defined as the full range of resources that the actor has available to convey the significance of his or her own actions, and interpret the actions of others, which implies some form of common ground.

In this context, it is perhaps also necessary to reflect on the the word 'locative', which is becoming ubiquitous as a way of describing projects and research that look at the role location has on experience and behaviour. The current use of the term in relation to media is generally attributed to Kazys Varnelis (e.g. Tuters and Varnelis 2006), but a key definition of its usage can be found in the following book; John Lyons (Lyons 1977), in which he states '*how do we explain to someone where an object is? And how do we describe the spatial characteristics of particular objects - their extension in space and shape? Places are not entities though they may be ..treated as entities in particular languages. As places are not entities, so entities are not places; but in so far as they occupy space, entities may serve to identify the spaces they occupy'*.

This underlines the characteristic of 'locativeness' as a way of describing the nature of a relationship with a place. It is not a condition in itself, but a linking or associative factor. In the course of an interaction this relational quality provides a setting for the flow of information. In this sense space is enacted (Varela, 1991), which acknowledges the co-creation of observer and observed through the construction of their relation. It does not exist a priori in some form of contained and constrained structure, and is instead constructed dependent on a whole range of changeable circumstances, most of which are local in relation and effect. This provides the motivation for the proposal; to discover how this relation is constructed in everyday practices with media.

1. Approach: Situations

Interaction with locative media cannot be considered to be occurring in 'places' or sites in the way we have come to consider location. Instead such technologies take place in social settings, which have a loose but intense connection with the physical setting in which they occur. One of the main consequences of communications technologies in urban settings is the changing nature of the experience of place, with the consequence that multiple social realities can occur one place. The same physical space may be caught within the domain of two different social occasions. The social situations that occur in these overlapping behavior settings support gatherings that possess a special characteristic in that they exist on more than one social level. The possibility that the same physical space can come to be used as a setting for more than one social occasion is regularly recognized. Thus in the case of public streets, there is a tendency in western society to define these places as the scene of overriding social occasion to which other occasions should be subordinated (Goffman 1963, p. 20). For example, presence in public space and interaction has traditionally been equated with face-to-face contact. Yet, presence in public space as mediated by new technologies has a different type of aesthetic, no longer dominated by visual access but by informational access. The features and structure of the interaction is enabled by a connection, which is not necessarily achieved through physical movement from one location to another. As such, everyday actions and behaviors no longer belong to particular places, and are now multiplexed and overlaid; there now exists the possibility to switch rapidly from one activity to another while remaining in the same place, so we end up using the same place in many different ways. On one hand, this gives rise to confusion, and ambiguous and contested zones emerge (Mitchell 1995, p. 101), where the multiple and overlapping behaviors created create disparate, fragmented and discontinuous spatial references. On the other hand, we can consider space as a 'field of interaction, composed of intersections of mobile elements it is in a sense actuated by the ensemble of movements deployed within it' (de Certeau 1984, p. 117). In this case space is perceived as practiced place rather than a fixed and intransitive bounded entity, and as such emerging practices can only serve to enhance the richness of our spatial experience.

The experience of space as mediated by mobile and wireless technologies transcends these concepts of space. Space enacted through such technologies conforms to a different concept of bounded-ness(Willis, 2008). Instead of some form of definable extent, space is instead experienced more in terms of regions that are not only defined by spatial extents but also by patterns of informational or social access. Consequently, collectively defining boundaries becomes part of the pattern of communication; for example the common practice of asking for and reporting location at the beginning of a mobile phone call. Boundaries are still an omni-present characteristic of space, but moving in and out of bounded zones can occur much like the flicking of a switch, rather than involving some form of graduated change. Similarly displacement in layered media spaces is not confined to the physical properties of 'real world' objects, but also extends to include the specific ranges of technologies. For instance Bluetooth enables interaction within a radius of approximately ten metres, whereas WiFi nodes offer access within a range of up to one hundred meters. As such the definition of interaction in a space of communication flows is structured around spatial nodes of opportunity. But perhaps the key characteristic of such spaces is that the concept of linkage is intensified, and in many ways more subtle and differentiated levels of connectivity frame interaction. Mobile and wireless technologies typically operate in infrastructures where connections are characterised by a whole array of weak and strong links, rather than being defined by the nature of their direct physical proximity. As these networked infrastructures start to dominate over physical spaces, so the relational quality of people and space becomes less a case of physical presence and more a degree of how people considered themselves related to places and spaces; their attachment, or lack of, to the situation they are in.

In the practices's of locative media this manifests itself in daily interactions; for instance the phenomena of 'cara gattai' identified by the researcher Christian Licoppe in his sociological study of the use of a GPS based locative game in Japan. In this example the individual literally plays with the possibility for a situtaion where a physical space in the city and technological space are not simultaneous: *'Without intending it, the designers of Mogi have left open the possibility for players to "freeze" their positions in a given place, by getting there, connecting to the game, and not refreshing their radar screen after they have left the place. Players have been quick to discover and exploit this loop in the game software. They have used it to invent a new form of playful encounter based on the disjunction of their actual embodied location and the apparent onscreen location of their icon that such a "freezing" of the icon's position on the game map allows. The goal is for a player to position his icon at a given place so that later another player will move so that his own icon will appear onscreen close to the first one, or, better still, will touch it. This practice is called 'cara-gattai', cara standing as an abbreviation for character or icon, and 'gattai' referring to the concept of joining, or rejoining. The practice of doing 'cara-gattai' ostensibly relies on the disjunction between what happens in the screens and in the space of ordinary perception: 'cara-gattai' is meaningful in the way it actually disjoins co-proximity and co-presence.* '(Licoppe & Inada 2007).

This proposal seeks to explore the nature of situatedness as it is experienced through locative media. It will investigate what settings in the city become sites for the interaction with locative media. It will answer questions such as where does it feel right to receive a Bluetooth message, where do my GPS trails become physically present in the city, and how does the dynamic of my social network, as supported by locative media find its place in the everyday locations I visit or pass through? In a sense it seeks to rediscover the location or locality of media, to define the social and spatial glue that locate it in the shifting settings which structure everyday practices.

2. Aims

This proposal seeks to explore the nature of situatedness as it is experienced through locative media. It will investigate what settings in the city become sites for the interaction with locative media. It will answer questions such as where does it feel right to receive a Bluetooth message, where do my GPS trails become physically present in the city, and how does the dynamic of my social network, as supported by locative media find its place in the everyday locations I visit or pass through? In a sense it seeks to rediscover the location or locality of media, to define the social and spatial glue that locate it in the shifting settings which structure everyday practices. This proposal will seek to investigate exactly what it means for information to be 'locative'. It will seek to understand where the domains of media and those of space operate on similar terms, in the sense that they frame social encounters. The initial stage of the research will be as follows:

2.1. Stage 1:

This proposal seeks to undertake a detailed study of how social behaviour and the physical setting is related to the use of technology. This will be done both through developing a theoretical basis and also through complimentary empirical studies in real world conditions. In these studies, it is necessary to focus on a specific participant group to enable direct comparison across a section of users. In order to do this, a study would need to take place over a longer period of time, ideally three to six months, to enable a broad and comprehensive data set to be obtained and studied. Participants would agree to be part of the study for a specific period of time and record their behaviour on a daily basis. Typically they would be asked to keep a fairly accurate diary of their social interactions; such as where and when they meet people; their phonecalls etc. This data would be compared against tracking data that would show where these interactions took place. Once such a data set had been obtained it would also be able to build up a pattern of social connections, how people operated within social networks and how this might relate to the place in which they chose to enact social behaviour. This will establish how people view and at upon their interactions with technology in their everyday life not necessarily in a purely spatial sense, but more importantly how they are situated within their social networks.

This data would be collected through GPS trails and a weblog running on an iPhone. This record would include a description of when they accessed any form of mobile or wireless technology, how long and most importantly the location. Also critical would be to know what activity they undertook through the technology; checking email, looking up a place to eat, making a phone call to a friend etc.

3. Outcomes

A key outcome is to develop a series of project-based proposals for implementing the findings of the research, which will seek to support localized practices. These will integrate the technologies of locative media, with a particular focus on GPS and Bluetooth, to explore the conditions in real world settings with everyday participants. In conclusion the research will draw on the outcomes of the studies to establish how we might better embed and integrate information in place so that it enables a more relational and shared experience in the interaction between people and technologies.

References

[1] Brown, B., Laurier, E., (2004). Maps and Journeys: An Ethnomethodological Investigation. Cartographica 4,3, 17-33.
[2] De Certeau, M. (1984), The Practice of Everyday Life. London: University of California Press.
[3] Dix, A., Rodden, T,., Davies, N., Trevor., J, Friday, A., Palfreyman, K.. (2000). Exploiting Space and Location as a Design Framework for Interactive Mobile Systems. ACM Transactions on Computer-Human Interaction (TOCHI), v.7 n.3, 285-321, Sept. 2000.
[4] Dourish, P. (2001). Where the Action Is: The Foundations of Embodied Interaction. Cambridge, MA: MIT Press.
[5] Goffman, E. (1963), Behavior in Public Places; Notes on the Social Occasion of Gatherings (New York: The Free Press).
[6] Goffman, E. (1969). The Presentation of Self in Everyday Life. The Penguin Press, London
[7] Hollan, J., Hutchins, E., Kirsh, D. (2000). Distributed Cognition: Toward a New Foundation for Human-Computer Interaction Research. ACM Transactions on Computer-Human Interaction, 7(2), June 2000, pp. 174-196,.
[8] Hook, K, Benyon, D & Munro A.J. (Eds.) (2003). Designing Information Spaces: The Social Navigation Approach. UK: Springer-Verlag
[9] Hutchins, E. (1995). Cognition in the Wild. Cambridge, MA: MIT Press.
[10] Licoppe, C., Inada, Y (2007). Supporting the Emergence of Specific Forms of Encounters through Location Awareness : the Case of the Mogi Players. In Proceedings of Shared Encounters Workshop, CHI2007, USA
[11] Lyons, J.,(1977). Semantics (Volume 2), Cambridge University Press., pp. 690 ' Spatial expressions'
[12] Mackenzie, A. (2005). Untangling the unwired: Wi-Fi and the cultural inversion of infrastructure. Space and Culture 8: 3, 269-285
[13] Massey, D (2005) For Space. Sage Publications, London.
[14] McCollough, M. (2005). Digital Ground. Cambridge, MA: MIT Press.
[15] Meyrowitz, J. (1986). No Sense of Place: The Impact of the Electronic Media on Social Behaviour. (USA: Oxford University Press Inc.
[16] Milgram, S. (1977). The individual in a social world. Essays and experiments. Reading : Addison-Wesley
[17] Suchman, L. (1987). Plans and Situated Actions. Cambridge University Press, NY.
[18] Suchman, L. Blomberg, J. Orr, and R. Trigg. (1999) Reconstructing technologies as social practice. In Lehman, P. and N. Wakeford (eds.), Analyzing Virtual Societies: New Directions in Methodology. Special Issue of Applied Behavioral Sciences Journal: 43:3:.
[19] Tuters, M., Varnelis, K., Beyond Locative Media, retrieved 2 Jun 2007
[20] http://networkedpublics.org/locative_media/beyond_locative_media

[21] Varela, F., Thompson, E., Rosch, E. (1991). The Embodied Mind: Cognitive Science and Human Experience. Cambridge, MA: MIT Press.

[22] Willis, K. (2007). Situated Interactions: Spatial Setting and Mobile and Wireless technologies. Encyclopaedia of Mobile and Wireless Communications. Taylor and Page, US

Intelligent Environments 2009
V. Callaghan et al. (Eds.)
IOS Press, 2009

doi:10.3233/978-1-60750-034-6-355

Designing habitable interactive spaces: a smart home case study in Greece

Vassilis BOURDAKIS
University of Thessaly, Volos, Greece

Abstract: This paper discusses the design of habitable interactive spaces, drawing from the experience of designing, implementing, coding and monitoring a smart home over the last five years. The design loop is described, failure areas identified and discussed with particular focus on users' behaviour. A series of questions are set, addressing–from a design perspective–occupancy, data collection, processing and re-actions of an interactive environment.

Keywords: architectural design, designing interactions, smart home, sensors, actuators, users' perspective

Introduction

A field that is attracting considerable attention in construction is smart homes as defined by Aldrich (2003) "…residence equipped with computing and IT which anticipates and responds to the needs of the occupants, working to promote their comfort, convenience, security and entertainment through the management of technology within the home and connections to the world beyond" (p.17). Departing from this definition, a wealth of fields and routes to exploring relevant technologies but most importantly, ways of understanding and evaluating user needs, behaviours, etc emerge. This paper addresses the design of habitable interactive spaces through the analysis of a smart home case study in Volos, Greece.

Designing interactive/intelligent environments is a task demanding spatial design skills typically found in disciplines such as architecture or sculpture, as well as programming (database creation and maintenance, process control) and finally human computer interaction (HCI). An in depth lock into the construction industry reveals that designers are not involved in the interactive design process and most importantly are oblivious of the emerging potential and capabilities. Lacking specific knowledge that would help them comprehend the intrinsic problems and find solutions seems to be the main reason. Furthermore, to the uninitiated designer, modelling interactivity doesn't look a very "design" task with high architectural/artistic merit; it is just seen as a job for the electrical engineer or even worse for the electrician/cable installer.

Following an interview with the managing director of the only Greek company producing home automation and intelligent systems for buildings (ranging from a small 50sqm shop to a 1000sqm villa, or office buildings, hotels, factory production floor, etc) and whose clients are typically on the upper end of the market, not even one in 10 architects/interior designers comprehends the potential and implications of designing interactive spaces. He confirmed that designers are simply not interested, they only submit the construction drawings to his company and will not even suggest ways spaces need to work, nor have a "vision" for particular areas or occupancy patterns within the building. As he states, a smart home is, for the typical designer, a trend s/he simply must follow so that they fare better than the competition, sad but true nevertheless. This mentality is apparent and voiced on a series of informal surveys carried out by the author on a sample of relatively young, well trained and highly regarded architects. It seems that we will need the new generations of IT capable virtual architects or cybertects (Bourdakis et al 1999, de Kerckhove 2001) in order to alleviate this image.

To complicate things even further, marketing strategies of large electronic companies are pushing the individual intelligence of standalone or networked devices (be it a PA system, an audiovisual setup, a fridge, an alarm system an energy monitoring device, etc) rather than pushing for networking intelligence of the overall environment. Finally there is a general criticism on many attempts being a typical case of "technology push" rather than "consumer pull".

1. New design criteria

The creation of intelligent/interactive environments implies that all parties involved in the design and occupancy cycle have to reconsider the design process and re-evaluate their design criteria and preconceptions:

- Designers have to alter the way physical space is conceived and formulated. Architects/designers need to also understand, design for, implement and configure interactivity; something not yet addressed in architectural education curricula[1] and often considered outside the architectural design realm.
- Users must "adapt" to new and typically non-familiar setups, psychological issues involving confrontations with the unknown, or miss configured behaviours based on inapplicable conjectures. Systems are forced upon the users by designers/developers working independently without any formal users' feedback mechanisms in place. Hence objections and eventually denial are hindering development and research with post-occupancy evaluations lacking in depth analyses.

In the following, there will be an attempt to analyze design implications, discuss complications and identify failure areas with regards to interactive spaces from the author's personal experience in designing, coding and customizing such a system over the last five years. Furthermore, users' behaviours and opinions are presented based on the close monitoring of the abovementioned case study project.

[1] It should be noted that there are a series of courses on interactive game design and there is great potential in involving both architecture and game design courses in intelligent environment design. In the Department of Architecture at the University of Thessaly, the author has been teaching the course *Virtual reality: Designing Synthetic Spaces*. Next academic year, a new course is introduced, linking the experience gathered in virtuality back to real space. Sensors and actuators will be employed in real space and coding and testing will take place in the real environment of the school building.

2. Designing Interactions-Reinterpreting space using binary & 0-5V

2.1. Comprehending

Designing interactive habitable spaces does not end at the stage of sculpting or generating spatial formations with mortar, bricks, doors and windows alone. Designers must be able to utilize "softer" actions in order to shape seemingly inanimate constructs using suitably formulated behaviours that they have to design and comprehend their implications. In order to do so, designers have to use input-output devices broadly organized in two categories; *sensors*, collecting information from the environment and passing it on to the "spatial intelligence mechanism" and *actuators* that alter the space based on the input and the operational scenario/code programmed by the designer through the above mentioned "intelligence mechanics" *(Figure 1)*.

Sensing is typically carried out by binary devices (recording a yes/on or a no/off) such as motion sensors, magnetic contacts, humidity, gas, smoke fire sensors, radio frequency identification (RFID) tags (in this case yes is the actual ID number of the tag), or analogue subsystems (typically reporting 0-5Volt) including light meters, thermometers, anemometers, liquid level meters, etc. *Actuators* are linked to the real environment via relays and dimmers that handle electrical current in lighting fixtures, motors, motorised valves, etc, helping in controlling and altering environmental conditions as well as implementing security.

Concluding, the whole design process is going through a paradigm shift: ways of thinking are different, needs the designer caters for are increasing in breadth as well as focus, tools are different even (re)actions are different. The whole process is pushing towards a new set of rules and metaphors that must be understood, analysed, discussed and finally implemented.

2.2. Implementing

Habitation modes and flows of movement within the space must be comprehended using new codes. Hence the need for the development of logical flow diagrams vis-à-vis the traditional architectural sketches. Designers are generally aware that the qualities of space can be affected by temperature, lighting conditions (both artificial and natural), views, HVAC operation, introducing a few more variables into the typical architectural design scenarios of user/space interaction. However the passive approach to addressing such problems must be exchanged for an active methodology applicable in the design phase and with the flow diagrams converted in usable/downloadable code.

More specifically, in any intelligent habitable environment, “actions” or “events” trigger preset “re-actions”. For example relays may shut off the water supply when a leak is identified, shut off the gas supply when a gas leak is sensed, call the police or the owner or the private security company in case of a burglary, call the fire brigade in a fire alert and so on. This calls for an extra stage of filtering by assessing the severity and testing combinations of events that may indicate actual conditions different to what the initial trigger implies.

Similarly, passive energy housing occupancy demands can be eased out with relatively simple intelligence built in the system. Temperature sensors outside the space and others at floor and ceiling level within the space together with a light meter can automate blinds, windows opening and closing and lighting creating high comfort levels without the effort typically involved in manual systems and which is responsible for their failure.

Mapping flows of information can even be reversed as a process enabling the visualization of a particular timeline within a space by redefining, re-evaluating and re-rendering space using suitable metaphors. These may well include the absolute values (of temperature, light and wind speed), the Boolean values (on-off, in-out, activity-non activity) and the various configured loops and if-then-else conditions. Understanding the implications and complexities of such an approach, dictates the formulation of multidisciplinary teams of programmers, electrical and mechanical engineers. This may not be fully in line with the renaissance logic of the artist/architect master-builder, but more of the orchestrator of an ever increasing– in terms of both size and complexity– team of professionals related to the production of interactive space.

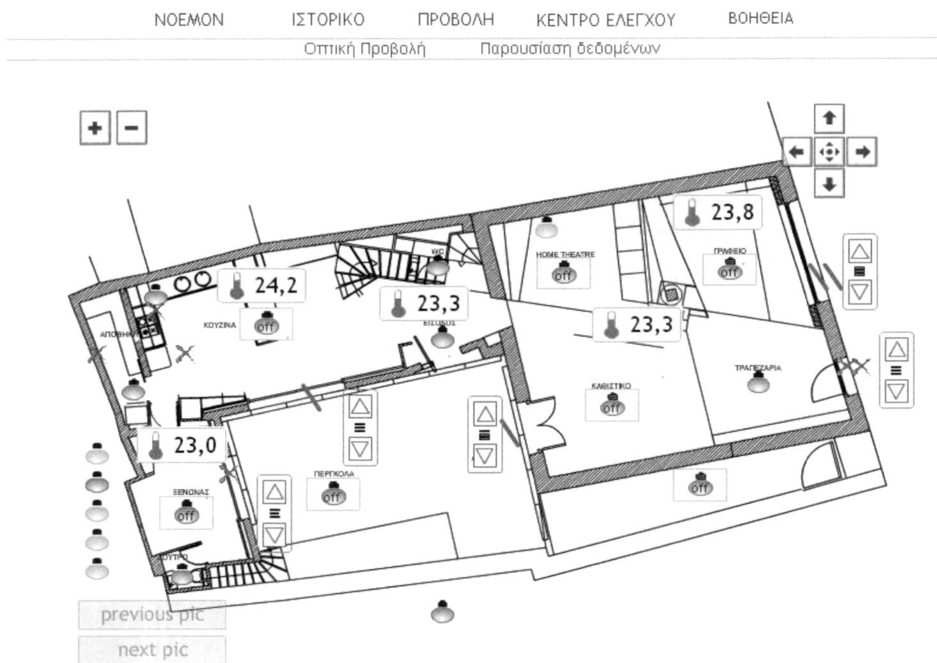

Figure 1. Ground floor plan with sensors and actuators as seen through the web interface

2.3. Feedback and Fine-Tuning

The final stage in a design implementation loop is introduced whereby the designer tests the interactivity and fine-tunes it to the particular building/space (tuning can be optimized and shortened as a process based on experience, common practices, particularities of the building envelope, prevailing concept of space, expected use, etc). There are preset scenarios that have a series of configurable settings such as delay for activation, extend of broadcasting events, duration of event, etc *(Figure 2)*. A simple example is the process of tuning lighting levels in particular spaces such as corridors, staircases, living room, etc. A light meter records overall exterior lighting conditions, whereas light meters in each space track interior lighting levels. When a condition is met, dimmers are activated at preset levels that differ in summer versus winter, since sun angles are different (not reflected on external light meter values) and natural shading due to spring/summer vegetation can drastically reduce interior lighting levels.

Further complications are often caused by occupants not informed (or rather introduced/trained) into understanding what is happening, nor briefed into what to expect. This is a common malpractice in emerging technological fields and bound to create problems and disputes. Designers must become aware of this issue and help users comprehend, negotiate with them alternatives and budget for revisions and alternations during the occupation running in period. Bearing in mind that even extensive alterations in an intelligent space are almost exclusively code oriented, no serious disruption occurs due to initial implementation problems.

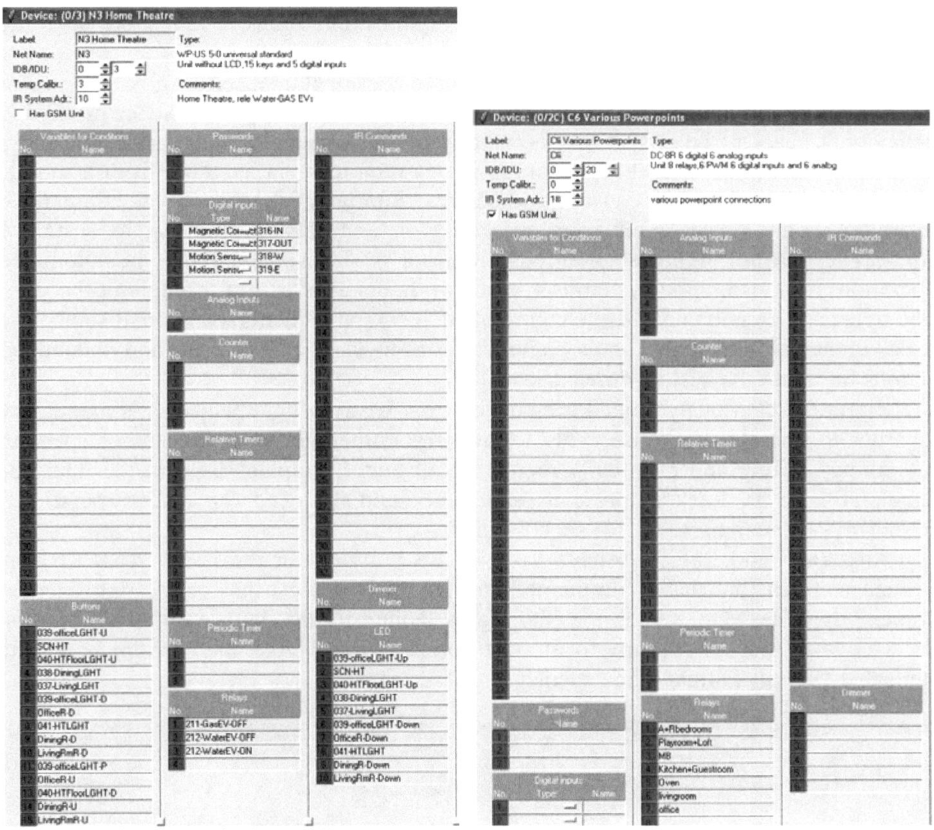

Figure 2. Coding Forms for Control Units

3. Users' Perspective

The ideal case scenario is the creation of intelligent environments that are well thought out, carefully designed and capable of collecting the necessary data on users' patterns of usage. A system that anticipates habitual patterns and reacts smoothly and in time, without ever making mistakes. It is however widely acknowledged that this is a much idealized scenario, a digital utopia rarely, if ever, attainable. There are many reasons for this failure, but it is mainly the intrinsic design criteria and operational methodology of the typical sensors used that is problematic; using bodily and action triggered sensing equipment often fails in identifying particular subjects, postures, attention and intention in order to successfully predict behaviours. Going a step further and properly embedding RFID antennas in construction elements, for example making all doors effective loggers for human movement, should help in reducing prediction failure rates to acceptable levels. At the moment implementing movement sensors works acceptably in single task spaces such as corridors, staircases and bathrooms, whereas there is an alarmingly high prediction failure rate that annoys users and increases confrontations, disbeliefs and ruins confidence in all other presence and activity prediction scenarios.

In order to better illustrate users' feelings and impressions, a few short cases are presented:

Anna 44, mother of Angelo 8 and Rafaela 6, is critical on a series of issues; size of interface panel buttons, failure of the system in "comprehending" and hence predicting behaviours, fears of what if it breaks, among a few. The automated shutdown, alarm arming and the general ability to handle issues remotely via an SMS from a mobile phone is a plain fact that causes no concerns. Similarly, she has never complained regarding lights in occupied areas switching on and slowly dimming to sustain a comfort level when lighting conditions alter, nor is she worried about the automated operation of the irrigation system triggered two hours after sunset throughout the year. The transparency and unobtrusive nature of such computed actions and the distance she feels, create an acceptable safety and comfort level, whereas bold and misjudged actions highlight the system drawbacks.

Maria 65, cautiously voiced her concern that wearing her spectacles is mandatory in order to operate the house. This follows the numerous hours the author spent in rethinking, editing and eventually recreating all button graphics used in the interface panels (Figure 3). Lack of previous experience and the need for a new operational framework is the main cause for such failures.

Angelos 8 and Rafaela 6 have lived in this building for the last 4 years. If feels strange to them (and have commented strongly on the fact) that on visiting friends' homes, they have to switch on the lights going to the bathroom, it's common knowledge to them that going to the restroom, running across the corridor or up the steps there simply ***is*** light when needed.

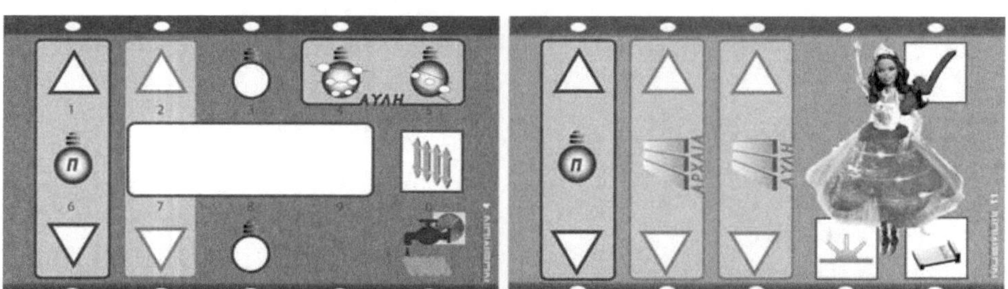

Figure 3. Interface panels (typical controller featuring a two line message area left, girls' bedroom right)

4. Conclusions

It is important to assess how the user perceives the intelligence of the space s/he occupies, to what extend s/he feels that has lost control of the space and the overall perceived benefits versus drawbacks. Where and how is intelligence acceptable and expected, where is it desirable, where is it a nuisance and why? In the eyes of the user, inanimate, "soul-less" objects such as the doors, windows, shutters, lights, AV systems, ovens, HVACs, that under typical circumstances the user has full control, "wake up" and demand attention, become semi-autonomous, voicing their designer's (and not necessarily their owner/user) opinion–this is often not seen favourably.

Concluding, it all comes down to integration, sense of security, privacy and understanding of the behavioural patterns of the overall hardware system: if the behaviour is apparent to the user, the system is a failure, the more transparent the better. Password sniffing, cracking and hacking is a cause of concern–grossly exaggerated by the media–strongly questioning *the security* of remotely operating one's home/office via a mobile phone, or a password protected web interface. *Privacy violation* must also be addressed as users are unaware of if, what, how and what for is data collected. As with all computing implementations, reliability concerns are often voiced. Last but not least, it's a HCI issue: simplicity of the interface is vital, as stressing the user typically results in confrontation and ultimately rejection.

References

F. Aldrich, Smart Homes: Past, Present and Future, In R. Harper, (ed) *Inside the Smart Home,* Springer, 2003

V. Bourdakis and D. Charitos, Virtual Environment Design - Defining a new direction for architectural education In *eCAADe99 Proceedings*, eCAADe publications, 1999, pp.400-410.

R. Harper, *Inside the Smart Home*, Springer, 2003

D. de Kerckhove, *The Architecture of Intelligence*, Birkhauser, 2001

B. Moggridge (ed) *Designing Interactions*, MIT Press, 2007

Intelligent Environments 2009
V. Callaghan et al. (Eds.)
IOS Press, 2009

doi:10.3233/978-1-60750-034-6-362

An Application of Swarm Robotics in Architectural Design

Socrates YIANNOUDES[1]
National Technical University of Athens

Abstract: This paper examines the potential of applying swarm intelligence concepts onto the design of architecture, and in particular transformable structures. Recently, swarm intelligence concepts have inspired research for the design and implementation of collective robotic systems as well as transformable flexible buildings. I argue that the latter exhibit limited capabilities for flexibility, both functional and physical, contrary to the architects' initial intentions, whereas swarm based robotics present a more promising future for technological swarm applications. Based on these arguments, a concept for a transformable environment, called *Swarm-Roof*, is proposed and described, drawing from swarm robotics technologies and ideas.

Keywords: swarm intelligence, swarm robotics, transformable architecture

Introduction

Swarm intelligence deals with both natural and artificial systems composed of many interacting individual entities that can self-organize and co-ordinate themselves using decentralized control. Swarm intelligence focuses on the collective behaviors that result from the local interactions of the individuals with each other and with their environment based on simple behavioral rules [1]. Examples of swarm intelligence systems include ant colonies, schools of fish, flocks of birds, herds of land animals as well as human artifacts like multi-robot systems (robot swarms), and also certain computer simulations and programs written to tackle optimization and data analysis problems [1].

Swarms have been used for the study and simulation of the collective behavior of interacting individuals (not only biological) but also in social (human crowds), economic (market), or traffic systems [2]. *Boids,* for instance, is a program designed by Craig Reynolds in 1987 [3] able to simulate apparent flocking behavior whereas the functioning of army ants has been used as a model for the American army [4].

Whether swarm intelligence can be applied to study the collective behavior of non-biological systems is a matter of debate which I will not attempt to examine here.[2] However swarm intelligence concepts have inspired the design of artificial technological artifacts, namely swarm-robotics and architectural projects. These applications are in no way bio-mimetic or replications of biological swarms.

[1] Socrates Yiannoudes: 42, Parnithos Str. 15234, Athens, Greece. E-mail: syiannoudes@hotmail.com.
[2] For a relevant discussion see: Thacker, E. (2004). *Networks, Swarms, Multitudes: part one.* (A. Kroker, & M. Kroker, Επιμ.) Retreived February 2, 2009, from ctheory.net: www.ctheory.net/articles.aspx?id=422.

Researchers in swarm robotics have argued that their work "is loosely bio-inspired, in the sense that many of our choices and techniques have as inspiration some natural process or biological observation". They explain that they "do not try to replicate faithfully any natural system" but rather take *inspiration* from natural processes and let these principles guide their engineering choices [5].

Yet swarm intelligence is by definition the study of both biological and technological systems [1]. With this in mind we can call the following technological applications as swarm intelligence systems.

Within architectural design there is a developing interest in the application of swarm systems for the design of transformable structures (in the work of Kas Oosterhuis in particular, which is examined below). Again, this application of swarms should not claim any bio-mimetic replication of biological swarms nor should this project be assessed in terms of its relevance to biological swarms.

1. Transformable Architecture and Swarm Intelligence

1.1. Kas Oosterhuis' Hyperbodies

Architect Kas Oosterhuis, professor at TUDelft and director of the *Hyperbody Research Group,* uses ideas from swarm intelligence to describe the kind of transformable architecture that he envisages. His proposals (called "Hyperbodies") are conceived as parts of a real time information exchange network, which involves external and internal factors, local users, other connected buildings or internet users. Both the nodes of the kinetic apparatuses and the users are conceived as different swarms the units of which communicate with each other and with the members of other swarms [6]. The swarm here is not a digital simulation (as in the Boids project) but a physical body – a system consisting of interacting units (actuators) as well as other subsystems (local users, and internet users) which influence the building [7].

The external structure of the projects consists of a mesh of individually controlled tensile contracting and relaxing industrial actuators acting together and able to modify the overall physical form. They are conceived as swarms, because, like Boids, the members are active calculating in real time their positions in relation to the rest developing local relations with their neighbors and interacting with each other without having a knowledge of the overall form of the structure. Calculations are limited and are based on these simple rules:

- Distance: "don't come too close to your neighbors"
- Speed: "adjust your speed to the neighbor's speed"
- Direction: "try to move towards the center"

These rules are completely local and refer to what each neighboring member can see and perform within its immediate territory [8].

1.2. Trans_PORTs 2001

One of these projects is the *Trans_PORTs 2001* (figure 1), a proposal for a series of connected active buildings able to respond to incoming information changing shape and content in real time [7]. According to Oosterhuis, data received from internet users, the actions of local visitors and the capacities of the buildings to process that information, activate their physical structure in unpredictable ways. As the visitor moves through the building the values of the positions of the nodes of the structure change. These nodes are the points of intersection of the actuators of the external mesh structure ("Fluidic Muscle" pneumatic cylinders without piston rod by Festo) which can modify their length depending on the air that is pumped into them. The shape of the building is wrapped in a mesh of these cylinders and each one is controlled individually thus changing the whole form of the building.

There are not only interactions among the nodes of the structure and the other interconnected buildings but also among the visitors and the data coming from internet users communicated to the visitors as information projected on the interior of the building [7].

Figure 1: Trans_PORTs 2001 and Muscle NSA

Oosterhuis argues that the building has many identities because in a few minutes it can transform into a totally different entity, while the interior can adapt to a variety of uses: "The Trans-ports pavilion passes through a multitude of identities –in only a few minutes the structure can transform completely into another entity... the structure effortlessly adapts to a variety of uses. Trans-ports can be tuned into different modes…" [8].

He proposes 8 such different modes - functional possibilities of the building. The building he argues can be used as information space, performance space, disco room, TV room, research room, reception, art gallery, or stay inert [8]. Practically, however, the potential for physical change of the building is rather limited because of structural and technical factors: The envelope has certain deformation limits (which are based on the extension and shrinkage limits of the pneumatic cylinders as well as on the elasticity limits of its external skin) while the basic form cannot transform drastically. Kari Jormakka explains that *Trans_PORTs* has a strong form which does not seem to change significantly. It cannot claim that it has identities other than the ones it already has, namely that of a sculptural object albeit kinetic [9]. Since the potential for physical transformation of these structures is limited their functional potential is also limited, despite Oosterhuis' claims and intentions.

The Hyperbody Research Group and Kas Oosterhuis have implemented a number of small scale prototypical kinetic architectural structures based on the above ideas: *Muscle NSA* (figure 1), *Muscle Tower I* and *Muscle Tower II*. Although they are based on swarm intelligence concepts, the results, (the actual implementations of the "hyperbodies") do not seem to have the formal dynamism and flexibility of biological or digital swarms. The structures exhibit limited potential for formal change (modifications of the external structure) and flexibility.

2. Swarm Robotics

The potential of technological swarms seems more promising in applications in the area of robotics called swarm robotics. Such systems consist of individual autonomous units able to develop swarm behavior as they interconnect. Their flexible interrelations and structure gives them the freedom to achieve a great number of physical reconfigurations and behaviors. Two examples of swarm robotics projects are examined below.

2.1. Swarm-bot

Swarm-bots is a research project funded by the European Union.[3] Its main scientific aim is to study a new approach to the design and application of self-organizing and self-assembling objects. The theoretical ground of this approach is based on swarm intelligence [10].

Swarm-bot is a robotic system composed of a number of simple robots, the *s-bots* which are combined through a swarm simulation control software. Their behavior is tested through the use of the simulation as well as through the implementation of the *Swarm-bot*. The result is a dynamic cooperative system able to reconfigure its form in order to effectively perform a series of tasks which cannot be achieved by a single robot.

Every unit in the Swarm-bot can be interconnected to the others either through an inflexible or a flexible link, articulated on its main body. Those two ways of connection have complementary roles in the operation of the Swarm-bot. The inflexible connection is used mostly to form inflexible chains (when for instance it needs to bridge a long gap) while the elastic connection allows each unit to maintain its mobility within the construction of the Swarm-bot. When those two ways of connection are combined the Swarm-bot can achieve more complex tasks.

S-bots have a wide range of sensory systems, used both for the perception of the surrounding environment and for proprioception (they can detect obstacles, other *s-bots*, holes, the terrain's roughness and lights). The s-bot includes 3-axes accelerometer, and incremental encoders on each degree of freedom. In order to be able to detect and communicate with other s-bots each s-bot is also equipped with an omni-directional camera, colored LEDs around the *s-bot's* turret, microphones and loudspeakers.

When the s-bots' task is to self-assemble then color detection is used (figure 2). An *s-bot* moves towards the nearest red object and avoids collisions with blue objects. If an *s-bot* manages to successfully connect to a red object, it changes its color ring from blue to red. In so doing, it becomes itself an object with which other *s-bots* seek to establish a connection [10].

The specific Swarm-bot project has been proposed for a specific scenario of activities: coordinated motion, avoidance of obstacles, passing over a hole, motion on a rough terrain, assembly, finding of an object target, and cooperative transport of object (figure 2) [11]. Future functional possibilities of the Swarm-bot, according to the researchers, could include tasks in areas where human access is limited or dangerous, or the

[3] Sixth Framework Programme, Retrieved March 2, 2008, from http://cordis.europa.eu/fp6/dc/index.cfm?fuseaction=UserSite.FP6HomePage.

formation of structures to permit access to human rescue teams in emergency events (e.g. a flood event), transport of objects or humans in rough terrains, etc [5].

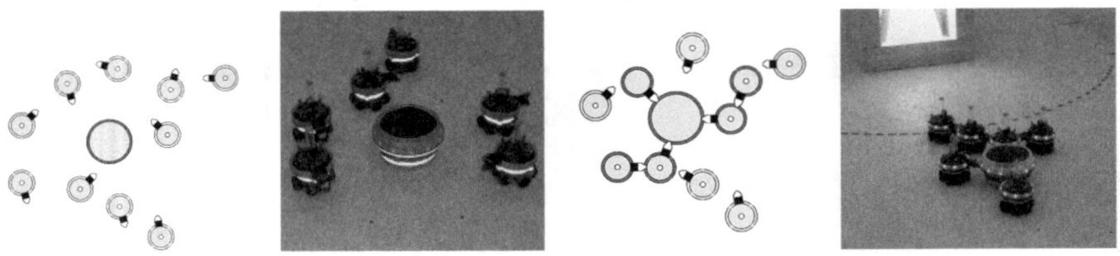

Figure 2: Swarm-bots (Self-Assembly and Cooperative Transport)

Similar swarm robotics application have been implemented by others (for instance see James McLurkin's work at MIT's CSAIL) with similar applications and functional possibilities [12].

2.2. Assessment of swarm robotics potential for architectural applications

Robotic swarms seem attractive for transformable architecture applications, because, their distributed form and the fact that they consist of autonomous independent units, accommodates various alterations of position, shape reconfigurations and multiple relations between the units. The specific system however, the *Swarm-bot,* and the way that it has been technically implemented – that is the apparatuses and the connections of the s-bots – limit its functional potential to the specific applications mentioned. Nevertheless, the researchers argue that for swarm robot units to be able to perform tasks with greater complexity it would be necessary to complement the functional and structural characteristics of their control system with memory and learning mechanisms. Those mechanisms can allow the s-bots to integrate over time sensorial cues and to exploit their perceptual data in order to make individual and collective choices [5]. Such systems could cooperate, make decisions, and act proposing continuously new adaptable configurations.

Swarm robotics are interesting in relation to transformable architectural design because they apply swarm behavior in real artifacts. Transformable architecture based on such systems could involve a flexible form unconstrained by the physical limits of its structure (namely the joints and links of its envelope apparent in Oosterhuis work) as well as by the need for structural support. We can therefore imagine architectural environments which consist of autonomous units (building blocks) able to transform according to swarm behavior and change configurations according to human need and desire, attributing limitless flexibility and indeterminate transformability to the system. Yet, such applications are only imaginary in the present time, although the researchers of the Swarm-bot project mention a more interesting for architects potential application: the design of self-organizing unfolding of structures without any human intervention, from space stations or satellites to scaffolds [5].

Having discussed the pros and cons of swarm robotics and the most important ideas and applications of swarm intelligence as well as the basic limitations and difficulties for potential architectural applications I will now proceed with proposing an architectural application which attempts to incorporate swarm robotics ideas and technologies.

3. The Swarm Roof: an architectural application

3.1. Description

Before I proceed I would like to remind the reader that this proposal and this paper is not about the specifics of swarm technology systems (the hardware or the computational system that supports swarm applications). Below, however, computational systems *will* be proposed in order to show ways of implementation of the *Swarm-Roof.* Yet, they are based on already existing systems and methods taken from the swarm robotics applications described in section 2.

The *Swarm-Roof* is a design proposal for a transformable roof, exhibiting variable density and shadow transparency based on swarming behavior. It can be applied to interior spaces (atrium areas) or outdoors areas. A group of interacting disks are located inside a Plexiglas box –the main roof layer. The swarm disks configuration can be variably changeable according to commands taken from users. Such commands could be: "distribute evenly across the surface of the box"; "assemble to a point"; "create several assembly points" (see figure 5). By changing configuration the swarm-roof can adjust its density and transparency (shadow casting) according to demand (functional aspect) and can create a very elegant shadow casting effect (aesthetic aspect).

Each disk comprising the swarm is composed of the following technical details (see figure 3):

- The main platform running LINUX and equipped with wireless LAN controlling sound and movement systems.
- 8 infrared sensors distributed around the main cylindrical body able to detect other robotic discs over no longer than 45 mm distance.
- 4 directional microphones and 1 loudspeaker. These allow the disks to detect each other over longer distances than the infrared sensors. The loudspeaker can be used to emit a sound signal varying its frequency and intensity. The sound signal is detected by the microphone and is processed by the in-built CPU to define the intensity and frequency of the sound emitted.
- Two motors on every disk controlling the speed of the two respective wheels and a simulated speaker.
- An omni-directional camera on the top which allow s-bots to grab panoramic views of their surroundings and can detect light color.
- Two rows of colored LEDs (blue and red) mounted around the cylindrical body.

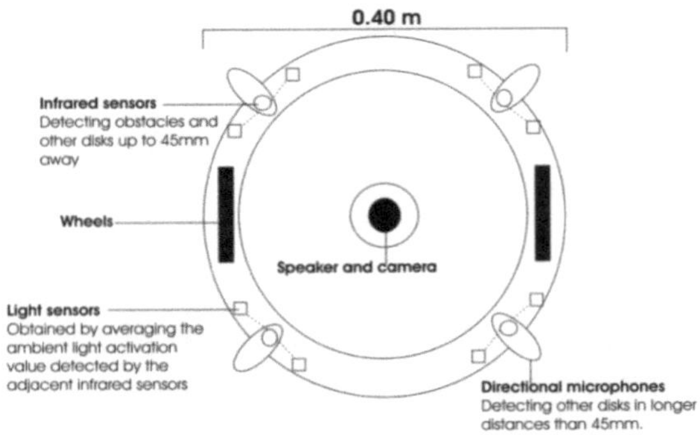

Figure 3: Diagram of disk configuration

3.2. Functional scenarios

3.2.1. Self-assembly of one group

While the disks are randomly dispersed across the surface of the roof users manually select one of them and assign it as the "leader" (through touchscreen monitors on the user level). The "leader" disk turns its blue light on. The disks start moving towards the "leader". When they arrive at the "leader" their blue light turns on. The simple rules that the disks have to follow are:

- Head towards blue light ("leader" disk) (captured by the camera)
- Turn blue light on when arrive at "leader"
- When blue light intensity is highest, then stop moving and turn blue light on

3.2.2. Self-assembly of two groups

In this case the users manually select two disks and assign them as "leaders". The first "leader" turns its blue light on and the second "leader" turns its red light on. The system gives to half of the disks the command to head to the blue light "leader" and the other half to head to the red light "leader". The disks start moving towards the "leaders". When they arrive at the "leaders" their blue or red light turns on, according to the light color of their "leader". The simple rules that the disks have to follow are:

- Head towards blue light or red light (according to the light color of their "leader") (captured by the camera)
- Turn blue or red light on when arrive at the respective "leader"
- When blue or red light intensity is highest, then stop moving and turn blue or red light on

3.2.3. Equidistribution

To achieve equidistribution of the disks across the roof surface the disks have to exhibit the following behaviors:

- Obstacle avoidance: When infrared sensors detect a neighbor disk in close distance (≤45mm) then the disk stops and heads away from the neighbor.

- Synchronization with the other disks: This is activated when the disk is not trying to avoid obstacles. The disk will change its velocity vector according to the other neighboring disks in order to achieve the desired distance from them.
- When the desired distance is achieved (e.g. 60cm) the disks stop moving.

The process can be described by the diagram shown in figure 4 and equation (1) which are based on a similar diagram and equation taken from swarm robots applications (The Swarm-bot project). *N* stands for the neighboring disks and *M* is the distance between the disk and its neighbors. The disk collects information regarding the distance n_i and direction for its *m* neighbors. Considering, the minimum desired distance (60cm) for equidistribution each disk calculates the center of mass *CoM* of its neighborhood as shown on Eq. (1). To calculate the change of its direction it uses the last value of its center of mass *CoMprev* thus assigning the proper speed to the left and right wheel. In this way it redirects itself properly correcting it position in relation to its neighbors.

$$CoM = \sum_{i=1}^{m} \left(\frac{\|n_i\| - 60cm}{N}, \widehat{n_1} \right) \quad (1)$$

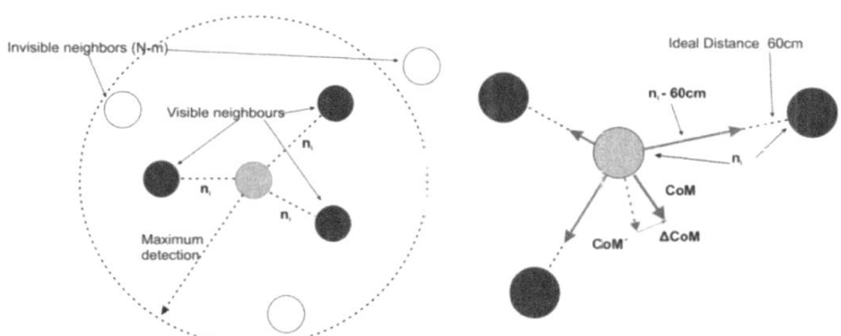

Figure 4: Equidistribution Diagram

Figure 5: Swarm-Roof: Equidistribution; Self-assembly of one group; Self-assembly of two groups

4. Conclusions – Discussion

This paper discussed the potential application of swarm intelligence and in particular swarm robotics concepts and technologies on the design of a transformable architectural environment - the *Swarm-Roof*. I believe that in order to apply effectively swarms in transformable architecture we need to understand the physical limitations before we proceed with implementing such fantasy structures like *Trans_PORTs 2001*. A weakness of the *Swarm-Roof* is that it is two-dimensional whereas Oosterhuis' work involves three-dimensional structures, a more difficult task to engineer. Furthermore, Oosterhuis' "hyperbodies" are self-supporting structures, an attribute which was not the case in the *Swarm-Roof.* Swarm architectural applications will need a separate support system, which, in the *Swarm-Roof,* was the Plexiglas box, enclosing the swarm disks. Although the project is theoretical, it could trigger a debate regarding the limits and the significance of using swarm robotics in architectural applications beyond the constraints imposed by the rigidity of kinetic structures like Oosterhuis' "hyperbodies".

References

[1] E. Bonabeau, M. Dorigo, & G. Theraulaz, *Swarm Intelligence: From Natural to Artificial Systems*, Oxford University Press, New York, 1999.
[2] R. Morris, *Artificial Worlds: Computers, Complexity, and the Riddle of Life*, Plenum Trade, London & New York, 1999.
[3] Boids, Retrieved November 18, 2007, from Reynolds Engineering and Design: http://www.red3d.com/cwr/boids.
[4] E. Thacker, Networks, Swarms, Multitudes: part two. (A. Kroker, & M. Kroker, Ed.) Retreived February 2, 2009, from ctheory.net: www.ctheory.net/articles.aspx?id=423.
[5] M. Dorigo et al., SWARM-BOT: Design and Implementation of Colonies of Self-assembling Robots. In G. Y. Yen, & D. B. Fogel (Eds.), *Computational Intelligence: Principles and Practice*. IEEE Computational Intelligence Society, New York, 2006, 130-131.
[6] K. Oosterhuis, *Hyperbodies: Towards an E-motive Architecture*, Birkhäuser, Basel, 2003.
[7] K. Oosterhuis, A new kind of Building. In G. Flachbart, P. Weibel (Eds), *Disappearing Architecture: From Real to Virtual to Quantum*, Birkhäuser, Basel, 2005, 90-115.
[8] K. Oosterhuis, *Architecture Goes Wild*, 010 Publishers, Rotterdam, 2002.
[9] K. Jormakka, *Flying Dutchmen: Motion in Architecture*, Birkhäuser, Basel, 2002.
[10] Swarm-bots, *Project summary,* Retrieved March 2, 2008, from http://www.swarm-bots.org/index.php?main=1.
[11] Swarm-bots, *Control,* Retrieved March 2, 2008, from http://www.swarm-bots.org/index.php?main=3&sub=35.
[12] James McLurkin, Retrieved March 2, 2008, from CSAIL MIT, http://people.csail.mit.edu/jamesm/swarm.php.

Intelligent Environments 2009
V. Callaghan et al. (Eds.)
IOS Press, 2009

doi:10.3233/978-1-60750-034-6-371

The Art of Mobility:

How transdisciplinary artists' projects are testing the boundaries of mobile media design

MARTIN RIESER
Professor of Digital Creativity,
Institute of Creative Technologies, De Montfort University, UK

"Locative media emerged over the last half decade as a response to the de-corporealized, screen-based experience of net art, claiming the world beyond either gallery or computer screen as its territory. Initially coined as a title for a workshop hosted by RIXC, an electronic art and media center in Latvia during 2002, the term is derived from the "locative" noun case in the Latvian language, which indicates location and vaguely corresponds to the English prepositions "in", "on", "at", and "by." "[1]

Abstract: This paper will examine and critically align a number of projects using mobile and pervasive technologies, which have challenged the design and delivery of mobile services from around the world, as documented on the author's weblog and forthcoming book *Mobile Audience*. The examined range of artist's work in locative media also raises key questions on the underlying conceptual frameworks necessary for an effective locative experience.

Keywords: Locative, Pervasive, Media , Art, Design

Space and Place

Screen cultures to date have been dominated both by narrative and by its modes of framing. Dispersed modes of interaction raise a series of questions about emergent new media art forms, particularly in relation to an audience's changing modes of participation and reception. The convergence of mobile technologies and pervasive computing methods are creating a world where information-rich layers can be mapped directly onto urban topologies. This opens up a series of interrogations around changing concepts of space and place and new perceptions of urban space for a wide range of traditional disciplines from art and architecture to cultural studies. The blurring of the boundaries between physical and virtual demands a new theory-base to explain our changing concepts of the "real", and, with the growth of hybrid environments, the concomitant changes in sociability and communication patterns.

The nature of audience interaction is responding to a socio-cultural dynamic that, although yet far from being quantified, demonstrates both a desire for a greater degree of 'participation' (evidenced in popular broadcast television e.g. Big Brother and its interactive outlets) and in the meteoric expansion of social networking on sites such as MySpace and Facebook. Where both these participatory and networking imperatives meet with pervasive media, an emergent art practice is developing, which is pushing at the boundaries of these technologies.

What therefore is the potential for the emergence new visual and auditory languages and strategies of narrative in the new paradigm of locative and pervasive media? Analysing and redefining the emergent visual and auditory languages required to enable the realisation of effective interactive narrative and art forms in urban and site-specific environments is a huge challenge. But only through such an understanding of the new and radical forms of experiment, can we attempt to map changes in sociability and communication patterns and new forms of collaboration.

How can this extension of interactive technology from fixed installation to real urban geographies radically alter the modes of audience participation and reception? If the physical space overlaps the space of diegesis, can this emergent space for art and performance create new perceptions of space and place in an audience? We appear to need a redefinition of the concept of physical space (including hybrid environments), since through such technologies a new perception of urban space is emerging which is not visual, but conceptual.

Much reflection on Locative media art has been premature, for as Drew Hemment observes

"It is too early to offer a topology of locative media arts, however, or to tie the field down with strict definitions or borders. While artists such as Masaki Fujihata (JP), Teri Rueb (CN) and Stefan Schemat (DE) have been producing work in this area for many years, more widely there have been only a handful of fully realised locative art works, with many projects remaining in the beta-stage, if not still on the drawing board. We have not yet reached the point at which the technology disappears - all too often the tendency is to focus on the technology and tools rather than the art or content."[2]

The waters have been further muddied by the convenient way in which artist's projects have often aligned with the consumer research interests of the mobile phone companies, where yesterday's locative project becomes tomorrow's "killer app"

"Mike Liebhold of the Institute for the Future (IFF) regards "geohackers, locative media artists, and psychogeographers" as key players in developing the "geospatial web," in where the web becomes tagged with geospatial information, a development that he sees as having "enormous unharvested business opportunities." and believes that this context-aware computing will emerge as the "third great wave of modern digital technology."[3]

Locative artworks, based on digital mobile technologies are a relatively new phenomenon. Yet art practice based on site-specific works and nomadic strategies is not just old, but ancient. Locative Art, by its very nature, trespasses into the realm of Public Art, but by its interaction with the public, transforms our notions of site-specific and ambulant practices, defined over the last three decades by artists such as Richard Long, Hamish Fulton, Vito Acconci and Sophie Calle. The history of located and nomadic art is a very long one indeed- stretching back beyond Robert Smithson and Richard Long to Aboriginal Songlines and spatialised religious rituals. I pose here the question whether, by similarly rooting locative practice in profound cultural and psychological structures, locative work can gain greater artistic resonance. Respect for place and space has long gone from our social uses of location-based technologies and may only be reclaimed by artists.

While the tagging of urban space is a process enabled by the commercial concerns of big sotware players such as Microsoft and Google, it will probably only be when that process meets the next generation of GPS enabled mobiles that the really interesting art works will begin to emerge, possibly on individual issues of sustainable lifestyles- as in Katherine Moriwaki's *Inside Outside* pollution-sensing handbag.[4] Social uses of technology are always beyond prediction. Christian Nold for example has definitely found a new way to exploit the personal context of the technology with his emotion mapping and bio-sensing in relation to location.[5] I am sure such hybridity combined with the collective construction and augmentation of site-specific knowledge through wiki-like interfaces is an evolving future for locative art.

Which bring me to a further question relating to the art itself. Much of what is named 'Locative Art' is not really art, but rather games-based work or spatial documentary or simply advanced toolsets that happen to use this technology. I think the potential is there, but art has a different function to these uses and when it is truly present you can smell and see it from afar. This brings us back to my earlier question about the pleasures and modes of user experience and how we can distinguish these from other media art forms or genres of work?

Figure 1: GPS Tracking of referee's movements in a match (Jeff Knight DMU)

In defining the pleasures of the medium the *Mobile Bristol* project made an attempt to identify these through a seminar series in 2005, where for example, it was discovered that the accidental overlapping of ambient environmental sound and augmented sound with in a locative work created delicious ambiguity and extra resonance for an audience.[6] What is needed most I think is to understand both the social context of these new artworks and the pleasures of their reception and use. These are dependent on haptic and spatial senses such as *proprioception*, which are little understood by artists.

A Gendered form

The political and economic shape of society ultimately forms contemporary modes of narrative. The contradictory pressures of neo-liberal economics, which drive the growth of personalised and peer-to-peer media and the interpenetration of workspace and private space, also seem to offer a unique opportunity to break Mulvey's determinist "male" control of narrative vision, which dominated narrative in the 19th and 20th centuries and to promote a more de-centered and subtle mapping.[7]

Feminist critics have often raised alternative strategies to break the negatives of a culture of male "control". Not surprisingly,[8] some interesting female locative practice explores precisely this area. Teri Rueb's *Drift*, for example, tied a sound landscape to the movements of the tide on a north European beach. The installation covered a 2 km x 2 km region on the Wadden sea that is filled with areas of interactive sound. The piece creates a space of flows consisting of sounds and words that travel like particles on simulated air and water currents loosely based on actual oceanographic and meteorological data. The audience had either give itself up to the primal cycles of nature or risk terminal confusion and data loss.

Performance or Game-play?

Mobile devices already appear performative in their nature, with public space interpenetrating our private concerns, so that any conversation has its willing or unwilling eavesdroppers. Add to this the potential for social interaction, crudely demonstrated by *Flashmobs* and in more sophisticated ways by mobile gaming you have a case of new technology creating adaptive social behaviours, which contain strong performative elements.

"The mobile games industry has long been the poor relation of the PC and console markets, but a combination of new technology, services and investment is fuelling optimism that mainstream adoption is not too far off. Ask anyone to name a mobile phone game and the most common response will be Snake or Tetris. And while the classic Russian puzzler is the world's most played and downloaded mobile game it is not an accurate reflection of the industry." [9]

Far more demanding games are already being played using mobile technologies such as *Catchbob* [10]and Blast Theory's *Uncle Roy All Around You,* which combine Internet and mobile technologies, where the city and the Internet were regarded as related stages on which we play, regardless of the specific context. Steve Benford of Nottingham University now talks of "seamful" media where players have learnt to exploit GPS "shadows" (where tall buildings block satellite triangulation) to their own advantage during game play, describing how such unforeseen effects of the technology encouraged new kinds of movement through the city.[11]

The failure of such works is often in terms of misapplied contextual practice: I once tested Valentina Niisi's *Media Portrait of the Liberties* in Dublin before the demise of MIT 's Eurolab.[12] We had gone about a block when the local youths began stoning us. The technology was certainly impressive, but this new form of public art was alien even to the children of the collective contributors to the artwork. When participating in Blast Theory's *Uncle Roy All Around You,* I reflected on how the game's format had reduced the richness of the city to a few textual clues and a dangerous process of frantic searching, with users crossing roads with even less awareness than the average iPod listener.

Spatial Annotation

Spatial annotation has emerged in the last three years as a major Internet phenomenon, particularly with the growth of Google Maps and social photosharing sites such as Flickr. In spatial annotation projects like *Yellow Arrow* [13] and *Neighbornode* [14] and in my own *Starshed* [15] (Fig 2) for Electric Pavilion, cities are increasingly being treated as surfaces on which individuals can inscribe annotation, and which will ultimately become repositories of collective memory. Such story-telling projects allow for new social and cultural readings of space, allowing private narratives to become public and subject to reinterpretation.

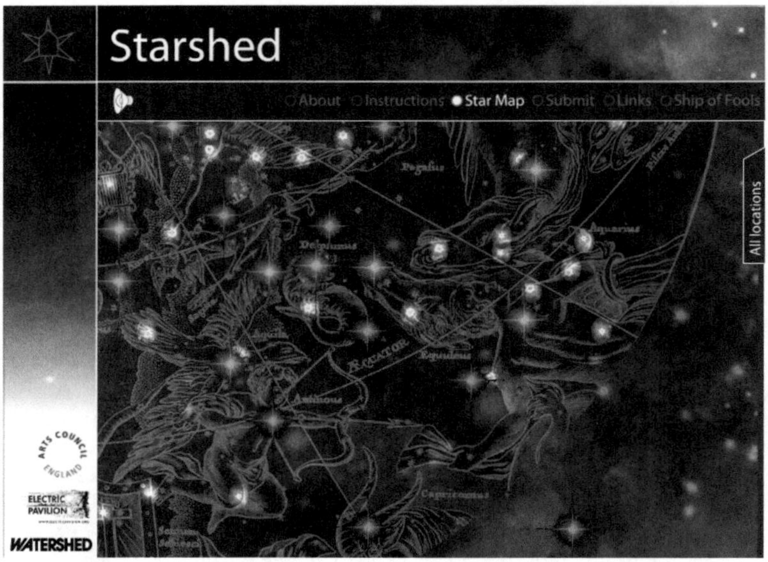

Figure 2: Starshed (Martin Rieser/SOF)

Satnav systems tend to reduce our world to roads between A and B. The specific tagging potential of the locative can certainly overlay this reductive idea of space with all the richness of personal experience, but that depends on the framework provided and the context set by the artist, and in many projects this is so loosely drawn that we simply achieve a kind of public palimpsest.

In their project *34n 118w*, Jeffrey Knowlton, Naomi Spellman, and Jeremy Hight had users take Tablet PCs with Global Positioning Devices and headphones onto a former railway yard in downtown Los Angeles. As participants walked around the site, they could hear fictional statements recounting the history of the place. To quote Hight:

> *"The story world becomes one of juxtaposition, of overlap, of layers appearing and falling away. Place becomes a multi-tiered and malleable concept"* [16]

There are other contemporary narratives resonant with the reinforcement of site and story. *Riot1831!* from Mobile Bristol depicted the Bristol Riots of 1831.[17] This first GPS-enabled locative drama was an immersive and powerful experience, engaging with the immediate spaces of history, mapped onto a Georgian square where the original events took place.

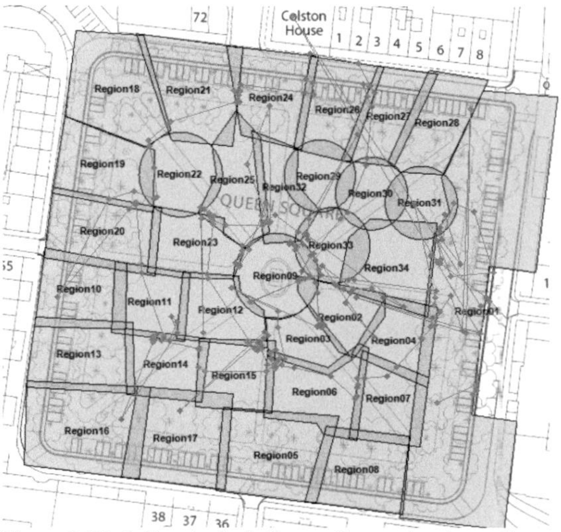

Figure 3: Riot!: User tracks in Queens Square showing audio zones

Figure 4:Riot! Users in Square

At first sight it seems contradictory that such engaging locative works tend to deal with an historical past rather than the lived present. After all Paul Virilio identified new media as promoting the change from considered diegesis to continuous and automatic present, the user creating the narratives both as subject and object; the visual subject becoming transferred to a technical effect, which forms a sort of 'pan-cinema', turning our most ordinary acts into movie action. However where these locative works succeed, they seem to overlap the user's enactment of a continuous present with the user's immediate perception of a contiguous past.

The ever increasing technologising and enclosure of urban and public spaces is a phenomenon associated with the growth of 'Herzian' Space and what Mark Augé[18] has termed to growth of "no place" (The anonymous motorway or mall). Stephen Graham points to how:

"places [are] becoming increasingly constructed through consumer decisions which, in turn, are influenced through the... surveillance, and sorting, of cities".[19]

Such cities, increasingly "sorted" through the software and networking, point up a related political question about the embedding of previous relations of power, class and ownership in the new infrastructures and whether this perpetuates ancient divisions or raises further questions related to the potential for community and individual empowerment.

Mapping as Critique

Apart from the arguments that the technology is intrusive and very commercial and is being "sold " to us via arts projects, there are those about the role of Situationist ideology in locative media (something about which I am personally deeply sceptical, mainly because so few artworks succeed in the 'Detournment' of the original movement). The GPS mapping practice of modern psychogeographers, (see http://www.gpsdrawing.com and http://socialfiction.org) are seemingly related to the writings of Guy Debord and his practice of the 'Dérive' [20], but in reality seldom appear to achieve anything identifiably subversive.

To quote one cultural critic:

"Locative media is: Psychogeography without the critique. Algorithmic psychogeography, the term used by http://socialfiction.org to describe their rule-based derives through the city, is not just a development, but actually a fundamental reversal of the critical use of this Situationist tool." [21]

The "Dérive" or 'drift' was a method for subversion, of remapping the world with 'uncontrolled' clarity, for identifying the secret flows of money and power below the surface of the city. However, one strategy Debord does cite: "the introduction of alterations such as more or less arbitrarily transposing maps of two different regions", has been successfully adapted in several locative works. Jen Southern and Jen Hamilton in *Distance Made Good* [22], used parallel mirrored journeys on two continents; in *Shadows from Another Place*, [23] Paula Levine creates a hybrid space between Baghdad and San Francisco composed of the superimposition of their city centres. A mapping of the initial US attack on Baghdad is superimposed upon downtown San Francisco. The longitude and latitude of each bombsite is marked in San Francisco using a GPS device. C5 in *The Other Path* [24] set out on a month long Great Wall trek, starting in the northwest desert of China and following the Wall eastward to where it runs to the edge of the Yellow Sea. GPS data collected during this trek was used to develop a pattern matching search procedure for locating the most similar data model in the most similar terrain in California.

Mark Tuters has perceptively identified how such annotation and tracing fits into the legacy of Situationism, which Locative Media has claimed as a philosophical base from its inception.

"Roughly, these two types of locative media, Annotative and Tracing, correspond to two archetypal poles winding their way through late 20th century art, critical art and phenomenology, perhaps otherwise figured as the twin Situationist practices of detournement and the derive."[25]

Situationism in Locative media resists easy definition, but may best be represented says Tuters, by one of Deleuze and Guattari's maps which distinguish between annotation and tracing:

"The map is open, connectable in all its dimensions, and capable of being dismantled; it is reversible, and susceptible to constant modification. It can be torn, reversed, adapted to montages of every kind, taken in hand by an individual, a group or a social formation. It can be drawn on a wall, conceived of as a work of art, constructed as a political action or as a meditation... Contrary to a tracing, which always returns to the 'same', a map has multiple entrances" [26]

Blast Theory, a locative media group composed of several London-based avant-garde theatre artists have gained renown for projects such as *Can You See Me Now* (2001), *Uncle Roy All Around You* (2003), and *I Like Frank* (2004), in which they used location-aware mobile mapping devices to coordinate interactions of audience and performers in both real and virtual space. *Uncle Roy All Around You* is one of the most lauded recent locative works, yet it appears an uneasy mix of performance and game, its full narrative only accessible to those who successfully complete their quest. The real and virtual sit in an uncomfortable relationship with the environment, which is only valued as a source of directional clues- and any casual bystander remains largely mystified and excluded. The charge levelled at Blast Theory at a conference was that of complacently and uncritically adapting new practice for the games industry, thus unwittingly acting as fashionable agents for intrusive and suspect technologies. For the flip side of ubiquitous communication and augmented location is the ability to track the audience: so a whiff of the totalitarian always haunts the liberating potential of the technologies. Matt Adams has rebutted this critique in interview, pointing to the collaborative co-dependency explored by the work.[27]

Their performances and installations have been supported through corporate sponsorship, public arts funding, and through a six-year collaboration with the Mixed Reality Laboratory at the University of Nottingham. The group's own web site claims:

"Blast Theory has a history of working with corporate clients to deliver innovative marketing strategies," thereby creating "commercial projects that draw global audiences to compelling, high adrenaline interactive experiences. The team of artists and scientists has

worked with blue chip clients in the television, apparel and telecoms sectors to launch products, build profile, inspire staff and engage customers."

An early locative project, which epitomized its emergent qualities was MILK, winner of a Golden Nica at Ars Electronica. With MILK, the artists, Esther Polak and Leva Auzina, used GPS to trace routes to create a form of landscape art for a network society. MILK was based in part on a project by Polak and the Waag Society, *Real Time Amsterdam*, in which GPS transponders mapped cyclists in Amsterdam on their traffic routes by the aggregation of their travel measured over a period of weeks. MILK suggested a god-like vision of locative technologies that allowed the tracking of freighted foodstuffs. In this case with heavy irony, since the dairy-rich Netherlands import their milk from Latvia making visible the contradictions and excess of a networked society.

The increasing importance of maps in defining space within these projects should not blind us to the fact that mapping is not a neutral process, but always has been a highly selective and subjective one, in which can be embedded various (invisible) ideological assumptions. Many gps mapping projects tend to forget this and even revel in the act of remapping without context.

Media artist Coco Fusco also launched a headlong attack on new media practices associated with networks and mapping, declaring:

"It is as if more than four decades of postmodern critique of the Cartesian subject had suddenly evaporated...In the name of a politics of global connectedness, artists and activists too often substitute an abstract 'connectedness' for any real engagement with people in other places or even in their own locale."[28]

Exploration of Tangible Objects

We are entering into a society based on ubiquitous networked objects or Bruce Sterling's *Spimes.*[29] Soon, objects will be the most frequent users of the Internet, as fridge talks to oven and RFID tags note the progress of stock to central computers. But what the ITU has termed the "Internet of Things" means far more than just tracked objects, as Tuters observes:

'Things' are controversial assemblages of entangled issues, and not simply objects sitting apart from our political passions. The entanglements of things and politics engage activists, artists, politicians, and intellectuals. To assemble this parliament, rhetoric is not enough and nor is eloquence; it requires the use of all the technologies, especially information technology, and the possibility for the arts to re-present anew what are the common stakes."

The pervasive and context aware object will partner a far more physical engagement with mobile devices. The Wii has fomented a revolution in indoor gaming. Devices such as the that of the US firm Gesturetek, which has developed software to use a phone's camera to interpret how the phone is being moved; translating gestures into action will promote the use of body actions in street level mobile gaming, but as John Vincent, president and founder of the firm, said:

"Being able to do natural movements, not just hand but also full body movement is the way forward."

The technology is embedded in phones released by NTT Docomo in Japan and allows gamers to move the phone, forward and backward, shake it, and roll the device to control action on the screen."[30]

Surveillance and Sousveillance[31]

In a C-Theory article entitled 'Operational Media'[32], Jordan Crandall spoke of the "resurgence of temporal and locational specificity witnessed in new surveillance and location-aware navigational technologies" and Stephen Graham has warned of the invisibility of such tools and the embedding of discriminatory and selective process in such things as network server logic. Steve Mann caught on to this process very early in 1998 and labelled its subversion as "Souveillance" or 'Surveilling the Surveillers'. Specifically he refers to Reflectionism as being especially related to "detournement": the tactic of appropriating tools of social controllers and resituating these tools in a disorienting manner.

Fears of surveillance are undoubtedly real and relate to the imperative of the State in an age of conter-terrorism, to quote Manovitch "to make the map equal the territory." Of course this technology is a double-edged sword, but then it is also made democratic by its distributive nature and is now in many hands. Artists who have questioned the vulnerability of the individual to tracking include Drew Hemment through his *Loca* project,[33] and Jonah Brucker Cohen with his *WiFi Hog*.[34] has challenged the enclosure of *Hertzian* space.

In the face of new enclosures of public electronic space, through surveillance and border control, biometrics and consumer tracking technologies, as Crandell puts it :

The challenge is not only to endeavor to understand this operational construct, but to understand the forms of opposition to it that are emerging in the globalized world. For the operational is only one "window" onto reality. There are other orientations that counter it, and for which, by its very nature, it is unable to account. It is powerless to envision terms of engagement that do not operate according to its logics. It can only assign them to the realm of the barbaric or irrational: that which lies outside of its license on reason. [35]

The compromised publics can choose to respond through collective action, violence or the through the "reflective" intelligence of these new forms of media art.

References

[1] Tuters, Marc and Varnelis, Kazys, Beyond Locative Media
http://networkedpublics.org/locative_media/beyond_locative_media accessed 12/03/08

[2] see http://www.drewhemment.com/2004/locative_arts.html

[3] Quoted in Beyond Locative Media by Marc Tuters and Kazys Varnelis. See also The Geospatial Web: A Call to Action- What We Still Need to Build for an Insanely Cool Open Geospatial Web
by Mike Liebhold, Senior Researcher, The Institute for the Future
< http://lists.burri.to/pipermail/geowanking/2005-May/001536.html> accessed 12/03/08

[4] http://www.kakirine.com/ accessed 12/03/08

[5] http://www.biomapping.net/ accessed 12/03/08

[6] http://www.mobilebristol.co.uk/NewSeminarsLanguage.html accessed 12/03/08

[7] Mulvey, Laura Visual and Other Pleasures (Theories of Representation and Difference)

[8] http://www.terirueb.net/drift/index.html accessed 12/03/08

[9] "How mobile got its game on" By Darren Waters
Technology editor, BBC News website, San Francisco
http://news.bbc.co.uk/1/hi/technology/7254123.stm accessed 12/03/08

[10] http://craftwww.epfl.ch/research/catchbob/

[11] Performing Space Arts and Humanities Research Council Seminar at Norttingham Trent University February 2008

[12] http://www.valentinanisi.com/liberties.html accessed 12/03/08

[13] http://yellowarrow.net/index2.php accessed 12/03/08

[14] http://www.neighbornode.net/ accessed 12/03/08

[15] http://www.electricpavilion.org/content/roots/starshed/index.html accessed 12/03/08

[16] http://34n118w.net/ accessed 12/03/08

[17] See: http://www.cs.bris.ac.uk/Publications/Papers/2000261.pdf.
[18] 3 Augé, Marc, Non-Places: Introduction to an anthropology of supermodernity, Verso, 1995

[19] S. Graham, "The Software-Sorted City: Rethinking the 'Digital Divide'", in S. Graham (ed.), *The Cybercities Reader*, London: Routledge (2004), pp. 324-331.

[20] "The Dérive (with its flow of acts, its gestures, its strolls, its encounters) was to the totality exactly what psychoanalysis (in the best sense) is to language. Let yourself go with the flow of words, says the psychoanalyst. He listens, until the moment when he rejects or modifies (one could say detourns) a word, an expression or a definition. The dérive is certainly a technique, almost a therapeutic one. But just as analysis unaccompanied with anything else is almost always contraindicated, so continual dériving is dangerous to the extent that the individual,

having gone too far (not without bases, but...) without defenses, is threatened with explosion, dissolution, dissociation, disintegration. And thence the relapse into what is termed 'ordinary life,' that is to say, in reality, into 'petrified life.' In this regard I now repudiate my Formulary's propaganda for a continuous dérive. It could be continuous like the poker game in Las Vegas, but only for a certain period, limited to a weekend for some people, to a week as a good average; a month is really pushing it. In1953-1954 we dérived for three or four months straight. That's the extreme limit. It's a miracle it didn't kill us" (Ivan Chtcheglov, excerpt from a 1963 letter to Michèle Bernstein and Guy Debord, reprinted in Internationale Situationniste #9, p. 38).

[21] Saul Albert <www.twenteenthcentury.com> (message dated Tue Apr 27 2004)

[22] Jen Southern and Jen Hamilton "Unfeasible Symmetry" Artists Newsletter Magazine (October 2003) article on Distance Made Good shown at The Gallery, Stratford-upon-Avon, UK. July 2002 http://www.theportable.tv/dmg/index.html accessed 12/03/08

[23] Paula Levine, Shadows from Another Place (2003)
Levine builds upon this link, creating Hybrid space between Baghdad and San Francisco composed of the transposition of Baghdad and San Francisco. A mapping of the first US attack on Baghdad is superimposed upon San Francisco. The longitude and latitude of each bombsite is marked in San Francisco using a GPS device.

[24] C5: The Other Path (April 2004) <http://www.c5corp.com/projects/otherpath/index.shtml>
In April of 2004, C5 set out on a month long Great Wall trek, starting in the northwest desert of China and following the Wall eastward to where it runs to the edge of the Yellow Sea. GPS data collected during this trek is being used to develop a pattern matching search procedure for locating the most similar data model in the most similar terrain in California.

[25] Beyond Locative Media by Marc Tuters and Kazys Varnelis

[26] G. Deleuze and F. Guattari, *On the Line*, New York: Semiotext(e), (1983) pp. 25-26.

[27] See Rieser, Martin The Mobile Audience, Rodopi 2009

[28] Coco Fusco, Questioning the Frame: Thoughts about maps and spatial logic in the global present < http://www.inthesetimes.com/article/1750/> accessed 12/03/08

[29] Ascendancies: The Best of Bruce Sterling by Bruce Sterling (Author), Jonathan Strahan (Editor) and also http://www.wordspy.com/words/spime.asp accessed 12/03/08

[30] How mobile got its game on By Darren Waters Technology editor, BBC News website, San Francisco <http://news.bbc.co.uk/1/hi/technology/7254123.stm>accessed 12/03/08

[31] Steve Mann, Jason Nolan and Barry Wellman, Sousveillance: Inventing and Using Wearable Computing Devices for Data Collection in Surveillance Environments in *Surveillance & Society* 1(3): 331-355 http://www.surveillance-and-society.org

[32] Crandall , Jacob 'Operational Media' CTheory Articles: a148 Date Published: 1/6/2005 <http://www.ctheory.net/articles.aspx?id=441>

[33] See http://leoalmanac.org/gallery/locative/loca/index.htm accessed 12/03/08

[34] See: http://www.coin-operated.com/projects/wifihog.html accessed 12/03/08

[35] Ibid CTheory

Intelligent Environments 2009
V. Callaghan et al. (Eds.)
IOS Press, 2009

doi:10.3233/978-1-60750-034-6-385

Power Relations in Mobile Connectivity

Miya Yoshida
Guest Researcher, InterArts, Freie Universität Berlin

Abstract. Mobile communications and mobile information spaces represent typical examples for the alleged "fluidity" of exchange in contemporary "networked" societies – a quality which allows change back and forth effortlessly between spaces separated by economic and/or socio-political boundaries. The commercial marketing discourse of "accessibility" suggests an even stronger form of empowerment – beyond contextual, special and geographic conditions. Visibility today seems to be something that is primarily organized around commodities and consumer goods. In societies of control, invisibility has become something that is organized as well. This means that, on the level of social communications, the division between the two has become increasingly difficult to explain – it has now been assigned to the psyche and intuition of user individuals to digest, to process, to understand what is actually "visible" and "invisible" in any given moment. Over recent decades, questions of visibility / invisibility have become a crucial topic, if not a paradigm in contemporary artistic practices. Accordingly, in my paper, I would like to introduce two art projects, which highlight one of the invisible geopolitical spaces shaped by mobile communication. Analyzing the kind of invisibility that is being represented by these works, I will attempt to discuss and to devise a new set of questions to reconsider visibility and invisibility in the context of power relations in the conditions of mobile connectivity.

Keywords geopolitical spaces, invisibility, mobile connectivity

Introduction

"Accessibility" is a term frequently used in the context of mobile telecommunications, mainly indicating two significations – one suggests that mobile telephony customers are enabled participation in a simultaneous network of global personalized access, the other points to that social/contextual accessibility which, potentially leveling social and hierarchical difference, always involves the negotiation of the individuals' temporal flexibility. Both senses of "accessibility" are expressed in the oft-used phrase of a "seamless connectivity" – which is emphasized both in media theory and in the advertising campaigns of major mobile phone companies.

The ideology of "seamlessness" that is applied to forms of communication that surpass geographical distance reminds us of other expressions developed for the discussion and promotion of media networking in the 1960s – expressions such as the "Global Village" used by Marshall McLuhan (1964), which set out to propose an existence beyond geographical boundaries.[1] Introducing the notion of a "nonplace community," Max Weber (1967) contested that the traditional concept of "communities" binding the individual should be replaced by a concept of "communities of accessibility".[2] In the present state of the diffusion of communication technologies, uneven though it still is, communities can actually exist regardless of their members' geographical locations. Since then, the notion of the "network" has become an increasingly popular model and a metaphor developed in order to imagine alternative organizational structures, not only with reference to community-related concerns, but also to other political, commercial, administrative, cultural, and other autonomous fields.[3]

More specifically, and looking at the larger dimension of communication technology, anthropologist Arjun Appadurai has pointed out that significant relational changes have happened with the installation of networks, arguing that this helped to bring about the emergence of what he calls "between-places", in communication technology.[4] Still following Appadurai's argument, the way in which the mobile phone is embodied and used to perform in society in order to gain "accessibility" reflects disjunctures between five different "scapes" – "technoscapes", "ethnoscapes", "media scapes", "economic scapes" and "political scapes"; however, notional frameworks like his, and terms like "Network Nation" and "between-places", are valid as suggestive constructions, but must remain painfully abstract. How can such notions help us more concretely to reconsider the complexity of spaces like these today?

As Andrew Barry has pointed out, it is important to distinguish between idealized images of global connectivity as imaginary concepts – and global "technoscapes", which include and connect only certain places and practices, whereas many others are excluded.[5] This becomes very clearly visible in the logistics industries that have been built to support global mobile communication. The race for raw materials such as Coltan, providing the technological possibility to keep the mentioned networks going – as one of the most striking examples of new global monopolist economies – has remained invisible, thus has to be a crucial part in the discussion about the topic of intelligent design today in order to understand the complexities within the topic[1]. What has been produced as a result of the capability of mobile communication? There are always complex global consequences, including the exploitation of material resources and labor; another space of economy is involved in the ideological space of mobile telephony. In the following paragraphs, I attempt to analyse more concretely power relations within mobile telephony starting from two different examples: one is Coltan, an essential component of the mobile telephone and some other portable electronic devices; the other is the specific mobile phone operation infrastructure in Kosovo, where I would like to re-think what sort of space tends to remain rather invisible in the midst of transnational technological and capitalistic expansion and imagining.

1. The Coltan Trading Industry: A Moving Shadow of Colonial Structures

Global advertising for mobile phones, with some remaining cultural specificities, frequently emphasizes an "almighty" connectivity, implying the promise to the user to reach to the other side of the globe at any given moment. However, the mobile phone is already part of a deep connection without any network – through some of the materials it is composed of. In order to build mobile phones, a variety of raw materials are required from different more or less dependent economies around the world, such as nickel from Chile for the battery, petroleum for plastic casting and for LCD (liquid crystal displays) from the Persian Gulf, Texas, Russia, or the North Sea, tantalum for

---

[1] I started to be interested in the issue of Coltan in 2002, and included the topic in the art project, The Invisible landscapes in Malmö 2003. In the three day symposium, there was a presentation about a research report based on the local investigations by Dr. Sofia Mikolo, a sociologist from Pole Institute, Institut Interculturel dans la Région des Grands Lacs, Democratic Republic of Congo. Please refer to the website: www.invisible-landscapes.net for further details.

capacitors from Australia or Africa, microprocessor chips from North America or Scandinavia, components from all around the world.[6] In a sense, the mobile phone can be seen as a condensed unit exemplifying the current structure of world trade.

1.1. Two Art Projects

Looking at practices and political circumstances around mobile telephony from such an angle, Alice Creischer and Andreas Siekmann, and a group of British artists, Graham Harwood, Richard Wright and Matsuko Yokokoji, (H.W.Y in short) have explored the seemingly simple question "Where does your mobile phone come from?" It is very important to understand and analyze how a geopolitical issue such as Coltan (the rare mineral required to miniaturize capacitors in mobile media that gives them relative energetic longevity) are presented and explored in a form of art, because art works always introduce a concrete approach and attitude to consider such issues. In the following paragraphs, I explain two art projects by the artists mentioned above, and will attempt to discuss the imaginary spaces they are opening up.

Figure 1. Coltan

Figure 2. Digging Coltan in North Kivu, DR Congo (provided by Pole Institute, 2002.)

The invisibility of those components, which are actually crucial for the functioning of mobile communication have a parallel in the character of most current systems of "info graphics". Departing from the historicity of this problem in the context of modern art in the West, Alice Creischer and Andreas Siekmann, artists and curators, have been working on a long-term project concerned with a re-evaluation of historic models of statistic representation. Their main goal, however, was to experiment with the possibility to put some such historical models into action related to present-day socio-political formations.

What is interesting in this context is that, as a part of their "Atlas" project, they have produced one special chapter on the issue of Coltan: "Monopolartige Produktionen / Der Fall Coltan" ["Monopoly-like Productions / The Coltan Case"] (2005) (Fig.3, 4) Among many other components, Coltan is maybe the best example to trigger an understanding of the power relations involved in the mobile communication industry, in international politics, in global economy. Coltan is the abbreviation and trade name of the mineral Colombite-Tantalite, from which the precious metals Tantalum (Ta), Colombium (Cb) and Niobium (Nb) are extracted. Each metal has a variety of industrial uses, but especially Tantalum, which is widely used in electronic components, chemical equipment, missile technology, and nuclear reactors.[2] However, the electronics industry consumes the majority (approx. 60%) of the worldwide Tantalum production for capacitors. When refined, tantalum can be used for the production of a heat-resistant powder that can hold a high electric charge and only slowly and gradually release the power. The main source of attraction of tantalum, the one market that has most relevantly formed the corresponding demand structure, has recently been its use in the construction of capacitors for mobile phones and all kinds of other IT products, laptops, pagers, gaming platforms, computer chips and many other electronics. Coltan-based capacitors extend the span of autonomous battery life of these products significantly. The UN says that companies trading minerals are the "engine of the conflict", and although many hi-tech manufacturers are trying to avoid "blood Coltan" it is nearly impossible to confirm the original source of the metal. As well as the human cost it has damaged the local ecosystem, endangering the guerrilla population.[7]

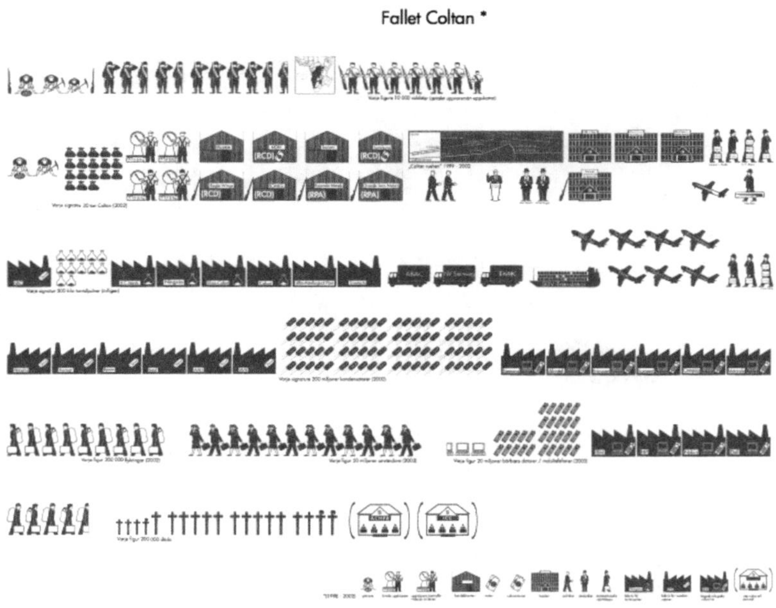

Figure 3. The Coltan Case" (2005) by Alice Creischer & Andreas Siekmann.

Here, based on their own research on the circulation of natural resources in capitalist economies, they created a visual interpretation of contemporary statistics, but on the basis of one specific historical model: The "Atlas Gesellschaft und Wirtschaft", a work that unfolds a pictorial method of applied sociology developed by social

[2] According to the Oxford Science dictionary, the 'other use of the metal is heat shields for rocket motors, radiation shielding, iron implanters in the manufacture of semiconductors. Tantalum parts are also used in surgery because of the un-reactive nature of the metal e.g. in pins to join bones.

researchers and artists Gerd Arntz and Otto Neurath in 1930s Vienna.[3] Adapting the pictorial graphics of Arntz and Neurath, Creischer and Siekmann made a contemporary version of their Atlas to visualize the complexity of disjunctures of different global "scapes", in a simple manner that gives the viewer a more "realistic" impression of the dimensions of people and things that are otherwise hidden in numbers.

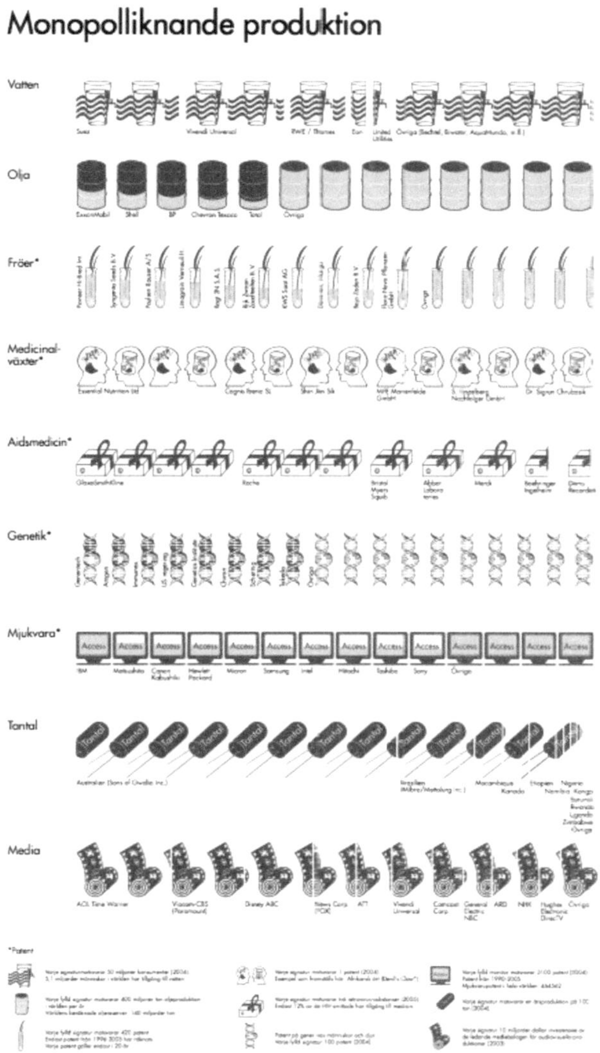

Figure 4." Monopoly-like Productions" (2005) by Alice Creischer & Andreas Siekmann.

---

[3] It was commissioned by the Bibliographisches Institut Leipzig. Sybilla Nikolow, "Gesellschaft und Wirtschaft. An Atlas in Pictorial Statistics produced by the Viennese Museum of Society and Economy in 1930", Institute for Science and Technology Studies, University of Bielefeld, Germany

In Europe, researchers like Arntz and Neurath, as well as other political artists' groups like, for instance, the "Cologne Progressives" (Franz Wilhelm Seiwert, Max Hoelz, among others), through the invention of "Atlas", tried to shift the interpretation of what "progress" was supposed to mean – compared to the standards of socialism and Marxism, seeing themselves rather as a continuation of the project of enlightenment within industrialization. To think of it in such a manner, the Coltan issue as represented in the Atlas really raises a set of precise questions for each viewer: How can we understand the interwoven elements of the political and economic world in all their complexity, when it comes to processes of mobile communication? Does it suffice to simply speak of a globalized "flow"? And would this also already imply a concept like "connectivity"? How should an imaginary of "progress" entangled with mobile connectivity be reconsidered?

H.W.Y. have presented a totally different approach and a method to think the issue of Coltan in a series of projects called "Tantalum Trottoire" and "Phone Wars" (2006). They focused on a result of the "Coltan Wars"[4] in Congo, and re-appropriated the social telephone networks in order to reveal and emphasize on a sociopolitical space caused by the mobile gadget. Previously, with a great interest in a vibrant Congolese culture based on music, spoken word and practices of communication with a rich historical significance, they collaborated with the London based radio programme, Nostalgie Ya Mboka, and launched a project called "Telephone Trottoire". "Telephone Trottoire" is an art project based on a telephone network system, which uses acts of gossiping to collect and to distribute information for Congolese participants. In the project, the Congolese both in the UK and around the world are asked to pass messages over their phones and record their own comments and new information. People randomly phone a set number and listen to some audio content – music, a story or topical news extract. Each listener is invited to join in by recording a comment, interacting in some other way and passing the call on to a friend by entering their phone number. This "contagious media" technique was referenced to the traditional Congolese practice of "radio trottoire" – the passing around of news and gossip on street corners to avoid state censorship. Based on the "Telephone Trottoire", H.W.Y. built "Tantalum Trottoire" (2006), a version developing audio content with the young people around the general theme of the Coltan wars and how their mobile phones are made. The phone system streamed the activities live during the course of the exhibition, with results being accessible on a project web site. As the final stage, under the title of "Phone Wars/Tantalum Memorial" (2006), the project presented the Strowger switchboard at the National Science Museum in London, which was reanimated for telephone access. (Fig. 5,6)

---

[4] Since August 1998 there have been 3.8 million deaths in the Congolese wars. Although the war officially ended in 2003 it has continued up to the present day. 361,720 refugees were created by 2001 and there are currently over 35,000 Congolese refugees in the UK alone. Much of this exodus is caused by political oppression and civil wars over control of the area's natural resources - the "Coltan Wars". Approximately 90% of Congolese people living in the UK are political refugees. The UK Congolese community suffers from social exclusion through distrust of official media and authority.

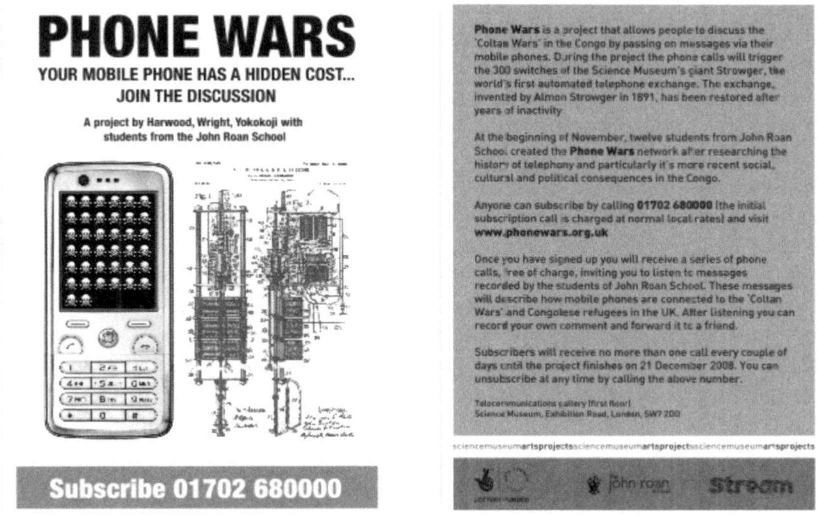

Figure 5. Post Card of "Phone Wars"

Figure 6. Installation of "Phone Wars/Tantalum Memorial" at the National Science Museum, London(2006) by Graham Harwood, Richard Wright and Matsuko Yokokoji

1.2. Visibility / Invisibility

Raising attention for the Coltan issue in and around Congo, "Phone Wars/ Tantalum Memorial" showed with a certain degree of self-reflexivity how it is possible to engage a public using telephone media. It explored the topic on three levels each of which mediated invisibility with visibility -1) the visibility of Congolese refugees in London, and the invisibility of their experiences and memories about war and suffering in Congo, 2) the visibility of a platform to discuss the issues with young people and invisibility of distributing the information through their social telephone network, 3) the visibility exemplified by the Strowger switchboard as a concrete material presence, the invisibility of the historical connection to technologies of mobile telephony today, as well as of the actual participants of "Tantalum Trottoire" and the African victims of the mobile phone wars. In the series of works, they shift a terrain between the invisibilities and the visibilities and navigate the public to be aware of possibilities to deal with invisibility within visibility. "Tantalum Torritore" appropriates the present condition of social relations and uses it positively to produce a flow of information based on the model and the power of gossip.

In other words, the project opened up a way to contribute a flow of personal networks to engage into the problem by "the" connectivity. H.W.Y. indicate the potentiality of "the" power of connectivity to be able to critically act not only on a global problem like the case of Coltan but also on other issues in general. "Tantalum Trottoire" accepts a stance of "instrumental action" and "communicative action" referring to the public sphere and critically used the linguistic communication for the process of production (for producing the potential to reconsider the problem). Relating to the power relations within mobile connectivity, in the next I would shortly like to introduce another example in Kosovo. The following example helps us to understand invisibility designed around commodified spaces of communication by effects of transnational capitalism.

2. Kosovo is in Monaco

In geopolitical areas where mobile telephony is a relatively new industry, connectivity is formulated as a result of negotiations on influence structures in local politics as well as in transnational enterprises. A representative example of a disjuncture of the location of power and its representation resulting from this novel situation is the case of Kosovo.[5]

While the Congo is involved in processes of economic and political globalization through material resources for the production of "high tech", the Kosovo has become interesting for the related industries on the level of infrastructure. Although it might sound odd, from the viewpoint of telecommunication geopolitics, Kosovo is not primarily a contested province in Serbia, but is rather to be described as a part of Monaco. That means that in this sense Kosovo is connected to worldwide communication networks via the country code 0377, which is also Monaco's number, even though, after some political conflicts, it now officially belongs to Serbia. In the everyday reality of networks this meant that all calls from and to mobile phones both within and outside of Kosovo had to be connected through Monaco. This strange situation arose through a decision by the UNMIK (United Nations Mission in Kosovo)[6] in the course of Kosovo's "reconstruction" process. The decision implied to bring in

[5] The province is the subject of a long-running political and territorial dispute between the Serbian (and previously, the Yugoslav) government and Kosovo's Albanian population. Although de jure a part of Serbia, it has been administered by the United Nations since the end of the Kosovo War in 1999. Kosovo is governed by the UN Interim Administrative Mission in Kosovo (UNMIK) and the locally elected Provisional Institutions of Self-Government.

[6] It should be mentioned that Kosovo was the first city in Serbia to have the internet connection, because of the occupation of the United Nation army.

Alcatel (a French telecommunication company) to set up Vala900 (which is a sub-company of Monaco Telecom) for the mobile telephone infrastructure in Kosovo in 1999.[7] The use of the Monaco code was part of a package solution offered by Alcatel. Thus, because of this treaty, the mobile phone users in Kosovo, wanting to communicate locally, are still forced to make international calls – re-routed via Monaco. This means that communications in Kosovo are effectively under the control of Monaco (the Monaco Telecom) in terms of the admitted numbers of phone connections, of phone cards to be issued, and also regarding the development of the industry there at present and in future times.

Connectivity, as a decisive geopolitical paradigm, is in fact only realized after having been negotiated in global political conflicts and struggles for supremacy, which reflects the fundamental discord between economy, culture and politics today. According to the United Nations, the most important criteria for the distribution of international country codes lie in the recognition process by the International Telecommunication Union (ITU), or the UN. These criteria indirectly cooperate to allow the expansion of transnational corporations to take advantage of chaotic political situations, forming an all-important element of the development of late capitalism. Roaming technologies guarantee the continuation of communication to, from, and within Kosovo, but they take on the familiar shape of "technoscapes" (Appadurai) within the new global economic structure. Regarding mobile telecommunication, people in Monaco are as close to each other as to people in Kosovo. The Kosovo is thus partly integrated into the economy of Monaco. Here again, it becomes apparent that the space of mobile telecommunication is not simply produced through "connectivity". As Coltan in Congo was an example of how the old colonial structures persist and dictate global economic relations, the Kosovo is a representative example of geopolitical and transnational capitalism in the digital mobile network era. These are only two examples among many worldwide phenomena of mobile communication.[8] There are and will be many more inter-layered relations in daily life.

How to deal with the critical outcome of such an analysis of invisible connections? The digital networks are providing oceans of information, but although Oscar Wilde said that the true secret is not in the invisible, but in the visible, we need to discern the mechanisms of both visibility and invisibility within the system: what is to be seen and heard and what is not – and why. In the digital information era, "the meaningful is clearly marked by its fluidity."[9] However, the importance lies in an attitude that directs the fluidity with critical thinking. The comparatively easy access to information circulating at an increasing speed rate, however, implies the danger for researchers to become arrogant – to feel like we "already know".

Accordingly, it is necessary to be very careful not to content oneself with mere abstraction and linguistic formations. If one uses notions such as "flow" and "seamlessness", are they more than metaphorical elements of an administrative ideology of success? What flows, to which degree, driven by which kind of hidden force? One could also ask what happens to the seams after their erasure? Is it simply

[7] A Serbian mobile network called Mobtel operates irregularly and only in Pristina, the capital of Serbia. There was another option to bring in Deutsche Telekom instead of Alcatel, which was strongly supported by PTK (Kosovo's local public post and telecommunication company) and which proposed a better offer than Alcatel's in the long term, however political consequences did not go that way as a result of the unclear negotiations.

[8] Lisa Parks, an American artist, performed a research on issues of satellite-based and wireless communication in Slovenia and Croatia. [8]

the idealistic or positivist description of a technological system of connectivity? Is it not yet time to frame the fragmented scenes created by mobile telephony in a horizon of expectations and imaginaries? Accessibility creates new forms of control and power relations. Even so, is the mobile phone as a dispositive still able to create new and different kinds of access in the sense of an alternative social organization? As Barry has pointed out, it is important to distinguish between the idealized image of global connectivity as an imaginary and a global technoscape that means that only certain places and practices are "connected", while many others are excluded.

Conclusion

Today, almost every aspect of daily life is an integrated part of global complexities and a result of elements of transnational capitalism. It is at the same time inevitable to consider these complexities, as it is limiting many aspirations to scientific precision to time and again be condemned to start on this over-dimensioned basic level. Here, the present situation automatically offers us a great potential of choices, as it is temptingly easy to connect banal individual acts to a larger context. The mobilized condition implies difficulties to think and react concretely. Being well-informed about great numbers of global issues almost simultaneously, it is still difficult to find out how to engage oneself in those information clusters, or more simply how to raise a concrete question. Here, I would say that the kind of concretion one is likely to find in art works may help us not to be lost with abstract notions or the reality of abstraction. Alice Creischer and Andreas Siekmann translated statistic information into a visual form and shifted a level of abstraction from one field to another. HWY transferred an old model of gossip on the streets to a terrain of social telephony in order to open up a space for concrete experiences in the age of abstraction and dematerialization – abstracting visuals into a symbol, an icon, a character and dematerializing (social) relations through network connectivity. After having reached the state of a fully developed abstract thinking, Paolo Virno has pointed out "the increasing significance of sensitive experience - an importance of the aesthetic dimension, or a dimension of sensitivity in contemporary society".[10] As he emphasized, " the problem today is not the binary opposition between the abstraction and the concrete of social life, but how to derive a new 'concrete' from the reality of abstraction".[11]

Following his thought, the two art projects considered here are certainly not political activities, but produce a new concreteness within abstract conditions, producing visibility within invisible. Such a character, implying both concreteness and abstractness, in other words what Virno called "second-order sensations", certainly feeds us back into a constellation of intellectual knowledge. A "new" concreteness also has the potential to function as a catalyst to prepare for a kind of basis for thinking and acting against the geopolitical issues created by transnational capitalisms. As a consequence concreteness within art can eventually open up a space which is not glamorous or spectacular but fresh, in which social imaginaries are created that arebased on the concrete and sensitive experience, not on second-hand information.

References

[1] M. McLuhan, *Understanding Media: The Extensions of Man*, Penguin Books, New York, 1964
[2] M.M. Weber, *The Urban Place and the Nonplace Urban Realm. Explorations into Urban Structure*, Philadelphia, University of Pennsylvania Press, 1967.
[3] A. Baryy, *Political Machines. Governing a Technological Society*, The Athlone Press, London / New York, 2001.
[4] A. Appadurai, *Modernity at Large: Cultural Dimensions of Globalization*, University of Minnesota Press, Minneapolis / London, 1996. Cf. also A. Mackenzie, Moving and Imagining Moving: Infrastructural Software on the Technoscape, www.teamethno-online.org/ Issue1/Ethno_centre/Forge_study.html.
[5] Ibid.,
[6] J. Agar, *Constant Touch*, Icon Books, Cambridge, 2003. 14.
[7] Regards Croisés*: The Coltan Phenomenon*, the Pole Institute, Goma, Congo, September 2002.
[8] L. Park, "Postwar Footprints – Satellite and Wireless Stories in Slovenia and Croatia", In: exhibition catalogue *B-Zone – Becoming Europe and Beyond*, ed. by A. Franke, Kunst-Werke Institute for Contemporary Art, Berlin, 2006.308–347
[9] K. Nyíri, retrieved from http://hhobel.phl.univie.ac.at/mii/mii/node61.html. (6/20/05)
[10] PaoloVirno "Three Remarks Rearding the Multitude's Subjectivity and Its Aesthetic Component". In: *Under Pressure – Pictures, Subjects, and the New Spirit of Capitalism-*. eds by Institute für Kunstkritik Frankfurt am Main, Sternberg Press. 2008. 38.
[11] Ibid.,

Intelligent Environments 2009
V. Callaghan et al. (Eds.)
IOS Press, 2009

doi:10.3233/978-1-60750-034-6-396

Inhabiting Hybrids
On the Nature of Home Environments

Ralf HENNIG
Chair for Theory and History of Modern Architecture,
Faculty of Architecture
Bauhaus-Universität Weimar, Germany
ralf.hennig@archit.uni-weimar.de

Abstract. Our traditional understanding of dwelling stems from its classification within the private sphere, and in adherence with the latin *privatus* from *privare, to exclude*, suggests an exclusion of the public sphere. Since the middle of the 20th Century, however, this most basic relationship between the public and private has been increasingly broken down. The societal shift from the "Industrial Culture" to the "Digital Culture" is accountable for a clear transformation in the relationship between the private home and media, and with the infiltration of the public into the private has led us to a point where the borders between these two spheres are now hard to define. If, based on this societal shift, a paradigm change in architectural design and practise in the late 1990s is apparent, then now, in the process of the current change in the structure of our society, we can observe this paradigm change coming into its full fruition. Under the influence of increasing economic and technological penetration, unstoppable media linkages and improved mobility it shows that the shift of borders described above is not an isolated case. Rather, multitudinal dualisms grouped together around the concept of the private house in the course of the last view centuries attract our attention by becoming rather ambiguous. Previously clear distinctions such as inside/outside, individual/community, living/working, house/city, place/non-place, and reality vs. the virtual are becoming less distinctive, priming a more open, flowing, hybrid concept of dwelling. Using selected examples, it can be shown that current developments also have historical predecessors. Thereby we can perceive that a more or less hybrid concept of living has always existed (at least in relation to the background societal conditions and their influence on dwelling). Currently, this inherent double nature of dwelling, this union of apparently opposite elements, is being further strengthened. This has wide-reaching implications for architecture and urban development.

Keywords. Contemporary Living, Dialectics, Media, Mobility and Architecture

Introduction

"There really is no such thing as a wall separating different worlds from another. Or if there is such a wall, it is probably a flimsy one made of papier-mâché. The second we lean on it, we'd probably fall right through and end up on the other side. Or maybe its that the other side has already managed to sneak its way inside of us, and we just haven't noticed." [1]

Haruki Murakami

In his introductory passage in the catalogue of the exhibition *The Un-Private House*, Terence Riley presents the modern private home not in the usual sense of a spatial articulation of peaceful detachment, but as a space exposed to the public realm through multifarious media [2]. He describes a mode of dwelling beyond classically perceived distinctions of public and private; a dualism whose very existence forms the basis of dwelling and thereby develops its own core meaning. It occupies one side, the private, with its own contents while simultaneously separating itself from the other side, the public.

In this way, the 'well looked after' private space seems to evolve consistently through the human need for refuge, safety and protection, in contrast to the surrounding public sphere. The apartment is understood as a "receptacle for the person" [3], a segregated interior space "whose relationship to the outside world is maintained solely through strictly defined openings" [4]. The distinct, accompanying concept of privacy and its spatial-architectural analogies went through a very important phase at the end of the 19th century and the beginning of the 20th century. Pictorially, this is clearly represented in the aquarell painting *Cosy Corner* (1894) by the Swedish artist Carl Larsson as part of a series of aquarelle works inspired by his interior living spaces. The picture very accurately reflects the interpretation of the day of home, further illustrated in Larssons own words: "Here I experienced that unspeakably sweet feeling of seclusion from the noise of the world." [5].

In his reflections on radical changes in contemporary society, Riley contrasts traditional interpretations with an almost diametrically calculated concept of dwelling. He is referring to the development of the private home into "a permeable structure, receiving and transmitting images, sounds, text, and data" [2]. In this context, Riley discusses a clear transformation in the relationship between the private home and media beginning in the second half of the 20th century. The private as an opposite pole of the public seems to have had its day. The infiltration of the public into the private has reached the point where the two are now difficult to discern. As an example of this shift in borders, as well as the "natural" relationship between media and the residents of a house, Riley employed Takahide Nozawas TV GARDEN (Project, 1991), a house plan inspired by the famous stone garden of Ryoan-ji in Kyoto. 245 television screens form the outside wall of the house, allowing for a relationship between the residents and the media "equal that found 'among natural elements in the garden' " [2].

1. From Distinctions to Hybrids

If, based on such shifts of values, a paradigm change in architectural design and practise in the late 1990s is apparent, then now, in the process of the current change in the structure of our society, we can observe this paradigm change coming into its full fruition. Under the influence of increasing economic and technological penetration, unstoppable media linkages and improved mobility it shows that the shift of borders described by Riley is not an isolated case. Rather, multitudinal dualisms grouped together around the concept of the private house in the course of the last few centuries attract our attention by becoming rather ambiguous. Using the examples of previously clear distinctions, such as inside/outside, individual/community, dwelling/working, house/city, place/non-place, and reality vs. the virtual, it will be shown how such dualisms are becoming less distinctive, priming a more open, flowing, hybrid concept of dwelling.

1.1. Living vs. Working

In 1951 for example Martin Heidegger described the separation of dwelling and working as an unmistakable element of the dualities responsible for the feeling of being human [6]. And as such it is reflected in the image of a "functional city" [7,8]. But just a few decades after Heidegger's comments, the situation began a fundamental change. In the mid-1980's electronic text and data editing made headway into the working environment. Around 15 years later digital technologies led to a reintroduction of the working environment into the home. Ben van Berkels MÖBIUS HOUSE (Het Gooi, 1993-98) is an example of how originally opposite areas can be melded into one continuous space. Based on his model, the single surfaced, nonorientable form of the Möbius Strip, previously spatially and architecturally separate activities, such as dwelling and working, are realised within one building.

1.2. House vs. City

It is possible to make several generalisations: during this process the traditional distinction between house and city lost some of its credibility; that the dissolution of these two foundational values began much earlier; and that the cause of this was a medium, if but a conceivably simple one. While Frank Lloyd Wright still was embarrassingly intent on walling in his HOME IN A PRAIRIE TOWN (Project, 1900) from the surrounding city space using a diverse range of architectural techniques to create absolute privacy, at the same time however, the spread of electricity through urban areas [9] began a process of unification between the city and private homes. Light, previously limited to the secure, private sphere of the home, created an *Extension of Man* moving beyond the borders of the residence. It shines out and grasps the city, described by Marshall McLuhan's definition as a source of creation for a "space without walls", a shrinking of the inner and outer regions by means of illumination [10]. The previous differentiation of the bright, protected interiors and the dark, threatening exterior becomes obsolete [11].

This development continues to evolve in our contemporary cities when in tall urban structures, such as in Tokyo, decentralisation, density and the partial outsourcing of dwelling zones come together to create an entirely new perspective of the city as a succession of interior spaces. Within these infrastructure landscapes, dwellings are reduced to a minimum, becoming mere cocoons, a base for daily movements through the urban environment. The AURA HOUSE (Tokio, 1995-96), which would not even function without the surrounding city due to its uncompromising reduced form, is an eloquent example of this method. Alternatively, a rethink, not only of the way both systems are used but also of their spatial expression, will only become necessary in the moment when the home and the city are no longer diametrically opposed and the metropolis has become an integral part of the residential sphere. Shigeru Bans CURTAIN WALL HOUSE (Tokyo, 1995) sets a course in this direction, in that this reduction is not only visually realised, as in Ban's inspiration, Mies van der Rohe, but can also be physically experienced [12].

1.3. Place vs. Non-Place

Also in the sense of being "familiar places", the home and city are experiencing an increasing shift in meaning. For Otto Friedrich Bollnow living still clearly represented the idea of "being at home in a particular place, having roots there and belonging to that place" [13,14]. Today, one must firmly contend this statement, in that mobility has completely overtaken the idea of traditional sedentary dwelling and the classic geographical reference [15]. As a result, the 'areas of action' have taken on increasingly global dimensions, but at the same time are still shaped by a peculiar vacuum in respect to identity dividing reference areas, by a terrain of non-places apparently without identity [16,17]. The traditional equation of dwelling, place and architecture seems once and for all to be invalid. Björk further confirmed this in her answer to the question of where she hangs up her hat, capturing in words the spirit of the times: "Home is where my laptop is" [18]. In the flippancy of contemporary existence, the self is reflected not in a place or a house, but is played out in an electronic gadget.

This is all clear evidence of an increasing shift in the art dwelling from the relationship between body, place and housing. Instead of this, tiny living environments emerge which can be directly controlled and changed according to need. Dieter Hoffmann-Axthelm sees this as a minimisation of the playing field of the social construct of dwelling in which the close-up view of these aforementioned micro-worlds (mobile telephones, laptops etc.) has more meaning than the actual spatial and architectural surroundings [19]. Today, identity-establishing placing is less an issue of earthbound architectural difficulty than of ubiquitous technology [20].

1.4. Reality vs. Virtuality

This shows once again, that alredy for a long time the virtual has been an obvious and integral part of everyday reality [21]. Even so, the paradoxical separation of the two is repeatedly insisted upon in relation to apparently traditional concepts of dwelling and their spatial references. It would otherwise be impossible to explain the fact that new technologies only hesitantly find a place in the residential sphere due to their link to the aura of the virtual. Closely linked to dwelling are the anxiety and confusion surrounding the border between medial and residential space, as also occurred at the time of introduction for now banal technology such as the telephone or the television [22].

Even Gisue and Mojgan Hariri's DIGITAL HOUSE (Project, 1999) designed for the magazine *House Beautiful* still addresses this. Although it does respond to the explicit demand of integrating everyday media into its substantially architecture, thereby creating a direct symbiosis, conceptually the house operates in quasi polar opposition. This manifests itself in the form of special, isolated spaces which form a counterpart to the virtual world of digital images which significantly shape the house. “(These rooms) allow the inhabitants to unplug themselves momentarily, as they move between tasks and from the virtual to the actual world. Here, the eye takes in a layering of realities as one can look into other parts of the house, to the landscape beyond, or to the images on the walls” [2]. But that the view of the image on the wall also gives us a view into a virtual reality clearly shows how fluid the borders are indeed. Frank Eckardt comments insightfully here: “It seems hard to imagine that reality is to some extent fictional and that virtualities are not mere products of fiction, but real” [23].

The – conscious or unconscious – daily experience of the symbiosis between reality and the virtual, including the successful history of the integration of audiovisual media into the private sphere (from the ‘family cinema’, the television through to computers) is perfectly represented in Gary Changs MY OWN APARTMENT (Hong Kong, 1998). Old and new “windows” are layered on top of or behind one another, giving them all the same value. In this manner, Chang’s apartment has not only a surrounding environment like all other dwellings, but also a view out the window representative of many different perspectives of the world: the actual view out the window (of the Chinese metropolis), or “through” the widescreen TV to the fantasy world of Hollywood, the real world of the news or the electronic world of the internet. The window becomes an interface. Media function here not only as vehicles for overcoming spatial distances, but also as a critical examination, using the different ‘views’, of the communicative potential of private space. Using remote control, a “environment of your choice” becomes available [24].

1.5. Individual vs. Community

Even with the stubbornly held assumption that dwelling is a thing of the community and the familiar, the lived reality sees itself confronted with a social dissimilation of the extended family and the distinctive individualisation of society [25], which projects such as Piercy Connors MICROFLAT (Project, 2002) or Richard Hordens MICRO COMPACT HOME (Munich, 2001) permit as architectural-spatial expressions of solitary living. But even here it is media that allow for a concurrent tendency in that they open the closed apartment, the capsule of the solitary, from the inside. Peter Sloterdijk leads us to this unnavoidable fact pictorially, by revealing that all media engaged within the relative apartment are tools for group simulations, which the solo dweller uses daily to recreate the lost community in his imagination, whether through the newspaper, a book, the TV, the telephone or the internet. Media document the interconnectivity of the private subject in the societal system which evolves against all tendencies of individuality [26].

The internalisation of this fact has contributed significantly to the growth in interest of architects in the establishment of new forms of societal living. With growing intensity, spatial configurations of the behaviour of individuals vs. society are being handled differently, whether combining small living spaces with communal fittings, (BKK-3, MISS SARGFABRIK, Vienna, 1998), a layering of individual and communal forms of living, as well as their completion with additional integrated potentialities (Stücheli Architekten, KRAFTWERK 1, Zurich, 1993-2001) or loft-inspired ideas of communal living conditions (Graft, LOFT GLEIMSTRASSE, Berlin, 2003-2004 and Flöckner & Schnöll, HOUSE NEAR ADNET, 2005-2007).

Katsuhiro Miyamotos CLOVER HOUSE (Nishinomiya, Hyogo, 2006) can be seen as the most experimental realisation of a spatial concept in this area. It attempts to reduce individual requirements to a minimum by maximizing the principle of community. Traditional, clearly defined spaces are not to be found in this house. Instead, residents are forced to share the only partially divided space day and night. Missing doors, the stairway positioned in the bathroom – a provocation against traditional efforts towards intimacy – as well as a spatial concept that makes movement within the building almost visible to everyone, renders the idea of a spatially clearly defined individual retreat useless. Aside from this communal attempt of almost pathological appearance, the building of course offers strategies for providing privacy although they are extremely finely nuanced. These strategies have nothing common with the classic individual space, as shown for example by the open sleeping alcoves on the upper floor, which offer at least the suggestion of a room through the surrounding balustrades, and thereby also a certain screening effect and the possibility of privacy.

2. Looking to the past

The developmental history of dwelling demonstrates that the above mentioned contemporary phenomena of layering conflicting principles are in no way as old as they might seem. As early as the 1920s, the architects of classic modernism were able to fathom the basic dichotomy of interior and exterior in an extremely aggressive way. They experimentally linked the function and effectiveness of the new media of the day, as for example photography and film, with the architectural space. In this way they managed to blur the borders of the field, and last but not least pushed the medial properties of architecture itself into the spotlight of discussion [27].

Even the integration of work into the home environment is a re-integration, when seen as the return of a process which began almost 400 years ago: the shift of work outside of the private sphere. Up until the early 17th century, working and dwelling were synonymous with one another. The architecture historian Spiro Kostof reveals this in his reference to the widely felt presence in earlier times of the public – and in this context also work – within the private home: “The medieval town house is not only the family home, it is also a manufacturing locale, counting house, store, or shop” [28]. This layering of the most varied typologies of the day is reflected in the residents of the house. The so called great house of the middle ages was home not only to the owners and their families but also the staff, apprentices and servants.

The same can be said of the relationship between the house and the city. When McLuhan grasps media as an extension of the sensory organs, he also understands the apartment as a medium if it holds the function of an extension of the skin through clothing. Not only clothes and living quarters are a part of this extension. The city is also understood by the Alberti Generation as an expanded house. This perspective is also supported by the similarity of the old spatial classification structures in the city/communal and private area. “The city and house, house and city could be understood as an expanding or contracting interior space. The city becomes a giant inside-out house with many rooms of distinct function. Or the house becomes a miniature of the city” [11].

Also, the multi-locality and multiple new definitions of the "familiar place", due to increasing mobility, are found early in the history of dwellings: "places to take away" can be observed in the earliest stages of development in humanity. A fine example is the central pillar or holy pole of various nomadic cultures which symbolises the centre of the world. This was taken along on journeys and erected at every camp. The symbolism of the nature of a place, its structure and function, is recreated in a modified form, in a single object. This is then ascribed a special meaning much more important than the surface value of the object [29,30]. A symbolic placing is possible almost everywhere in this manner, even in the identity deprived foreignness of a non-place.

In highlighting the fluidity of the borders on reality and the virtual in the view of the image within the DIGITAL HOUSE, this view also refers to its historical predecessors, as well as the fact that the private sphere has always had a "natural fascination for the outside world" [2]. "The presence of books, maps, and works of art tempered the inward-looking nature of the private house. In the nineteenth century, a study or library – a room devoted to books, newspapers, magazines, and journals – was not uncommon in an upper-middle-class home" [2].

Also to be found in the alcove-like rooms in Miyamotos CLOVER HOUSE are resonances of very similar and easily comparable layouts to houses from 500 years ago. In principle, the open 'private' areas in the building are no different from the bays within single room houses of the middle ages, the *sala*, places for individual retreat though without being shut off from the action in the rest of the house. Separate rooms for various activities were unknown in those times. "In most instances, the inhabitants lived, slept, and ate in large, open halls that accommodated different functions principally by the rearrangement of furniture. The realization of privacy within the house was an evolutionary process that unfolded over centuries. During the renaissance and on into later eras, bourgeois and even aristocratic families continued to inhabit medieval-style halls" [2].

3. Conclusion

It is clear from the examples listed above that the declining number of opposite positions within spatial and architectural structures is in no way a phenomenon limited to current (media) discourse. In fact, numerous spatial concepts incorporating the previously opposite element, and in this sense hybrid concepts, were always part of an architectural articulation of dwelling. Variations, according to the societal conditions and their influences on dwelling, which shape the relationships of the elements and lead to changing spatial concepts, are implied here as well. Most definitely, however, this integrated double nature can be recognised at almost every point in the history of the development of dwelling. A clear split in the sense of a dualism is revealed as a purely theoretical construction, which in reality has no relevance.

One attentive look at Carl Larssons *Cosy Corner* gives proof of this: also this space should act as the embodiment of residential seclusion and provide a full separation from the public sphere. Instead, with the expansion of the true windows using portraits on the walls, innumerable images are unleashed, having a diminishing effect on the inwardness of the interior. These are also nothing but media which strengthen, with their mediative qualities, spatial connections rather than spatial differences and thereby remove previously contradictory elements from the spaces. Last but not least, they suggest the medial character of architecture itself. Architecture is always the middle ground, something which finds itself between other things [31] and with this property has always functioned as a catalyst for creating hybrid realities.

References

[1] H. Murakami, *Aftertdark*, Dumont, Köln, 2005.
[2] T. Riley, *The Un-Private House*. Museum of Modern Art, New York, 1999.
[3] W. Benjamin, *The Arcades Project*, Harvard University Press, Cambridge Mass., London, 2002.
[4] A. K. Vetter, *Die Befreiung des Wohnens: Ein Architekturphänomen der 20er und 30er Jahre*, Wasmuth, Tübingen, Berlin, 2000.
[5] M. Facos, *The Ideal Swedish Home: Carl Larsson's Lilla Hyttnäs*, in: C. Reed, *Not at Home. The Supression of Domesticity in Modern Art and Architecture*, Thames and Hudson, London, 1996, 81-91.
[6] M. Heidegger, *Bauen Wohnen Denken*, in: U. Conrads, P. Neitzke (eds.), *Mensch und Raum: Das Darmstädter Gespräch 1951*, Bauwelt Fundamente Bd. 94, Vieweg, Braunschweig, 1991, 88-102.
[7] T. Hilpert, *Die Funktionelle Stadt: Le Corbusiers Stadtvision – Bedingungen, Motive, Hintergründe*, Vieweg, Braunschweig, 1978.
[8] T. Hilpert (ed.), *Le Corbusiers „Charta von Athen": Texte und Dokumente*, Vieweg, Braunschweig, Wiesbaden, 1988.
[9] W. Schivelbusch, *Lichtblicke: Zur Geschichte der künstlichen Helligkeit im 19. Jahrhundert*, Carl Hanser, München, Wien, 1983.
[10] M. McLuhan, *Understanding Media: The Extensions of Man*, The MIT Press, Cambridge Mass., London, 1994.
[11] G. Selle, *Die eigenen vier Wände: Zur verborgenen Geschichte des Wohnens*, Campus, Frankfurt a. M., New York, 1993.
[12] R. Hennig, *Tokyo Homezooms: Die Stadt als Wohnung*, in: F. Eckardt, M. Zschocke, *Mediacity*, Verlag der Bauhaus-Universität Weimar, Weimar, 2006, 115-144.
[13] O. F. Bollnow, *Mensch und Raum*, Kohlhammer, Stuttgart, Berlin, Köln, 1990.
[14] C. Norberg-Schulz, *Genius loci: Landschaft, Lebensraum, Baukunst*. Stuttgart, Klett-Cotta, 1982.
[15] J. Urry, *Sociology Beyond Society: Mobilities for the Twenty First Century*, Routledge, London, New York, 2000.
[16] M. Augé, *Non-Places: Introduction to an Anthropology of Supermodernity*, Verso, London, 2000.
[17] M. Augé, *Orte und Nicht-Orte der Stadt*, in: Haus der Architektur (ed.), *Spaces of Solitude*, Haus der Architektur, Graz, 1997.
[18] R. Maresch, *Empire Everywhere. On the Political Renaissance of Space*, in: K. Biesenbach, A. Franke, R. Segal, E. Weizman (eds.), *Territories. Islands, Camps and Other States of Utopia*. König, Köln, 2003, 15-18. www.rudolf-maresch.de/texte/60.pdf, November 25, 2008.
[19] D. Hoffmann-Axthelm, *Wohnen als fixe Idee*, in: Daidalos, Architektur Kunst Kultur, June 1996, issue 60, *Urbane Behausung*, 30-45.
[20] D. de Kerckhove, *The Architecture of Intelligence*. Birkhäuser, Basel, Boston, Berlin, 2001.
[21] S. Weber, *Die Dualisierung des Erkennens: Zu Konstruktivismus, Neurophilosophie und Medientheorie*, Passagen, Wien, 1996.
[22] B. Colomina, *Das Wohnhaus als Schaustück*, in: R. Ferguson (ed.), *Am Ende des Jahrhunderts: 100 Jahre gebaute Visionen*, Hatje Cantz, Ostfildern-Ruit, 1999, 127-165.
[23] F. Eckardt, *Virtual Urban: The Construction of Social Life in Mediacity*. Unpublished Paper, 2007.
[24] G. Chang, *In the Age of Indeterminacy: Towards a Non-visual Pragmaticism*, in: Architectural Design, September/October 2003, issue 5, *Urban Flashes Asia, New Architecture and Urbanism in Asia*, 58-67.
[25] U. Beck, *Individualisierung, Globalisierung und Politik: Eigenes Leben in einer entfesselten Welt*, in: Arch+, Zeitschrift für Architektur und Städtebau, December 2001, issue 158, *Houses on Demand, Mass Customization in der Architektur*, 54-55.
[26] P. Sloterdijk, *Sphären: Plurale Sphärologie*, vol.. 3, *Schäume*, Suhrkamp, Frankfurt a. M., 2004.
[27] R. Hennig, *The House as a Medium: A History*, in: F. Eckardt, J. Geelhaar, L. Colini, K. S. Willis, K. Chorianopoulos, R. Hennig (eds.), *MEDIACITY: Situations, Practices and Encounters*, Frank & Timme, Berlin, 2008.
[28] S. Kostof, *A History of Architecture: Settings and Rituals*, Oxford University Press, New York, 1985.
[29] M. Eliade, *Das Heilige und das Profane: Vom Wesen des Religiösen*, Suhrkamp, Frankfurt a. M., 1990.
[30] T. Valena, *Beziehungen: Über den Ortsbezug in der Architektur*, Ernst und Sohn, Berlin, 1994.
[31] F. Heider, *Ding und Medium*, Kulturverlag Kadmos, Berlin, 2005.

Intelligent Environments 2009
V. Callaghan et al. (Eds.)
IOS Press, 2009

doi:10.3233/978-1-60750-034-6-404

Sensory Threads: Perceiving the Imperceptible

Nick Bryan-Kinns[a,1] and Demetrios Airantzis[b], Alice Angus[c], Robin Fencott[a], Giles Lane[c], Frederik Lesage[b], Joe Marshall[d], Karen Martin[c], George Roussos[b], Jenson Taylor[b], Lorraine Warren[e], Orlagh Woods[c]
[a] *Queen Mary University of London*
[b] *Birkbeck, University of London*
[c] *Proboscis, London*
[d] *University of Nottingham*
[e] *University of Southampton*

Abstract. We perceive just a tiny proportion of the phenomena that surround us everyday. Sensory Threads is a technologically mediated collective sensing expedition which allows people to explore imperceptible phenomena in the world around them. We present a description of the technical system and reflect on our design decisions. Key questions we are concerned with centre around how to represent imperceptible phenomena in real time both inside a building, and outside, and how to engender a sense of collective engagement. We also consider the value created through the multi-disciplinary work involved in constructing such an experience.

Keywords. Sensing, Collective, Interaction, Expedition, Tangible, Wireless, Soundscape, Mobile, Resonance.

1. Introduction

As we move through the world in which we live we are surrounded by a myriad of imperceptible phenomena such as high and low frequency sound and non-visible light. The Sensory Threads project considers our bodies to be a vital part of this environment. Using environmental and body sensing technologies Sensory Threads allows us to explore the imperceptible, and immerse ourselves in the complex patterns and rhythms that occur in world around us.

Sensory Threads comprises two elements: firstly a group expedition through a city in which participants are augmented with wearable technology and real-time audio feedback which creates a communally engaging experience of imperceptible phenomena; Secondly, a gallery based installation which allows for the replay of sensory experiences using a combination of tactile feedback, visuals and audio. In this paper we first describe the design of the group expedition and key design challenges. We then describe the gallery based interaction with real and recorded sensory data, and finally reflect on the design process involved in the project as a whole.

---

[1] Corresponding Author.

2. Expedition

In the expedition, groups of four people are sent on an hour long mission to explore the imperceptible city using a set of wearable sensing devices. In contrast to other technologically mediated urban experiences such as pervasive games (e.g. Uncle Roy All Around You [1]) and urban sensing experiences such as Snout [2], Sensory Threads focuses on the collective experience of a group of explorers experiencing the city in real time. There is no end 'goal' such as finding a certain location, and the motivation is less about raising awareness of environmental issues, and more on creating a novel and engaging collective experience. Indeed, Sensory Threads is a development of the Snout project and seeks to explore the collective aspects of exploration and perception.

In the expedition, each person wears a device which records data from one type of sensor (heart rate, light, sound, spatial density). Each person's individual sensor stream is sent to a 'heart' computer carried by one of the explorers. The four sensor streams are then used as input to an interactive soundscape which is produced by the heart computer. Participants listen to the soundcape using wireless headphones as they move around the city. The heart computer also records the location of the explorers using GPS which allows the system to track of where the explorers have been. Each sensor influences a different aspect of the generated soundscape. As discussed later in this paper, this creates a complex group dynamic, where participants engage with their own actions in the space as well as the communal sensing experience.

3. The Sensors

In this section we describe the technical configuration of the sensors carried by each of the explorers which are mounted on specially made costumes (see Figure 1). Figure 1a illustrates one of the hats worn by explorers which includes a sensor in the top, and technology in the bag. Figure 1b illustrates sensors which are attached to an explorer's body, and connected to technology in the shoulder bag. Each bag contains a version of the Snout Sensing Platform [2], a specially designed Linux based hardware sensing platform for participatory sensing illustrated in Figure 2. In the rest of this section we explain how the different pieces of technology interact

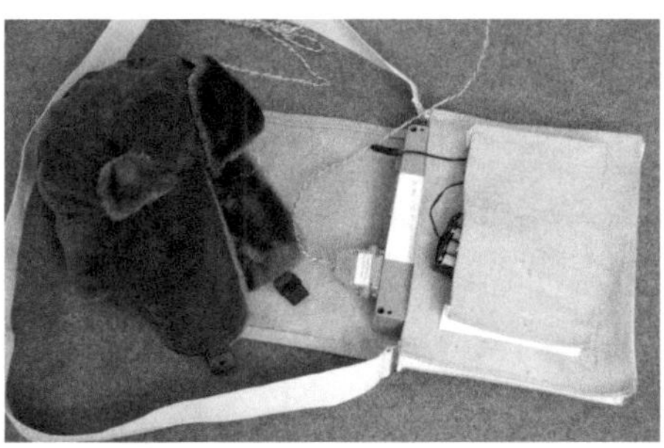

Figure 1a. Sensory Threads hat and bag, **1b**. Sensors and bag

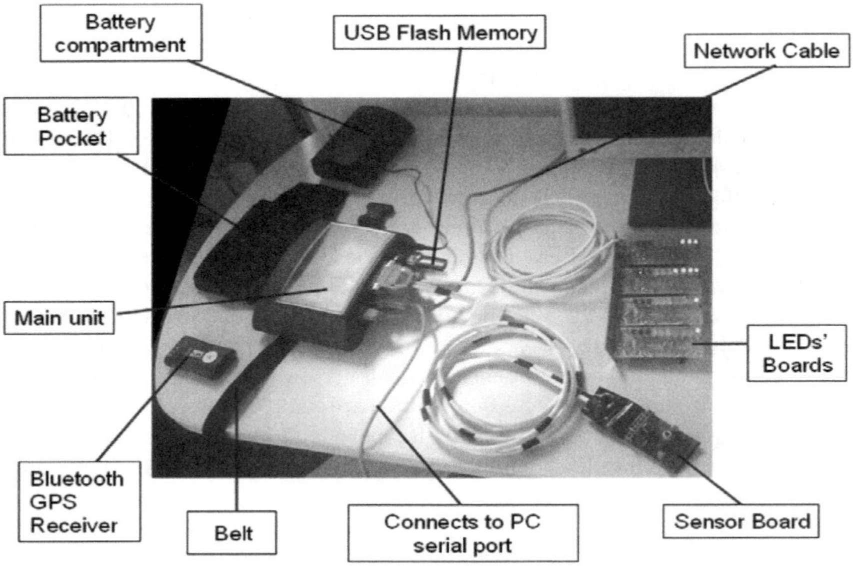

Figure 2. Snout sensing platform.

In the expedition, one explorer is designated the heart, and wears a heart rate monitoring strap as well as carrying the 'heart' computer - a small netbook style laptop in a their shoulder bag. The heartbeat of a person is intimately linked to their speed of movement, and the terrain in which they are moving, so creates an interesting bridge between the body and the environment in which it is located.

The heart computer records the sensor data from each participant, and creates the soundscape which is relayed to the explorers via wireless headphones. This creates a feedback loop whereby explorers are able to move around and hear how their actions change the soundscape. The heart computer also records the position of the group of explorers using a GPS device which it wirelessly transmits in real time with the sensor data to a server for use in the installation experience discussed later.

One of the other explorers has a noise meter on their hat (figure 1a). This detects ambient noise levels around the explorer. This is affected by many things, such as crowds, traffic, or the conversation the other explorers.

The third explorer has a light meter mounted on their hat (figure 1a) which detects levels of light falling upon the costume. This is affected by people passing by, changes in the weather, by being covered by one of the explorers, overhanging buildings and shadows, and also by changes in posture of the explorer, which may alter the shadowing of the sun or other light sources.

Finally, the fourth explorer attaches four ultrasound rangefinders to the front, left, right and back of their clothes (figure 1b). These detect the distance of the closest object in each direction. This allows detection of how cramped a space the person is exploring, or can provide a rough estimate of the density of a crowd surrounding them. It is also interesting in that it gives a very directional signal, which can differentiate between situations such as being in a narrow empty corridor (left and right sensors give close readings), and walking amongst a group of people in single file (front and back sensors give close readings).

4. Soundscape

People taking part in the Sensory Threads expedition hear an evolving, interactive soundscape which aims to create a collective experience in which participants perceive the imperceptible around them and the others in their group. The soundscape is generated in realtime using SuperCollider [3], an audio synthesis system running on the low power heart netbook.

Designing a collectively engaging soundscape involves the careful balancing of intuitiveness, responsiveness, attractiveness, and stimulation. In the rest of this section we first outline, and then discuss in more detail, a number of design 'tensions' which arose as we attempted to design a soundscape through which participants could perceive the imperceptible as an individual and a group:

Sense of identity versus collective integration. In a collectively engaging experience it is important to be able to appreciate how your actions relate to the imperceptible phenomena, and contribute to the collectively emerging shared soundscape.

Sonification versus aesthetic appeal. Conventional data sonification (see [4] for a discussion) focuses on making clear audio representations of data and typically pays little attention to the aesthetic quality of the sounds produced, whereas interactive sound art focuses on the aesthetic, typically at the expense of the representational power of audio. We strove to design and aesthetically pleasing audio representation of the data.

Recognizability versus listener fatigue. In longitudinal audio experiences there is a tension between creating sounds which participants can easily recognise and yet do not become irritating or ignored over the period of the experience. Moreover, participants' movements changes to the data readings, yet, as the readings are of imperceptible phenomena, it may be difficult for participants to grasp the connection between their actions and the phenomena that is represented.

Addressing these tensions has involved a number of research and design challenges in iteratively creating an interactive soundscape driven by four real-time wearable environmental sensor data streams as outlined below.

First, the sense of identity and collective integration is facilitated by using not just different sounds for each data stream, but also different modulations of the sounds. We used mappings of sensor data to: pitch, pulse, filter, and density of sound. These were selected and carefully refined through the iterative process to create a soundscape in which different sensor data sounds complemented each other, yet gave participants a sense of their own sensors' contribution. This sense of identity in the collective experience contributes to the emergence of mutual engagement [5] between the participants as they explore the imperceptible.

A key issue arose in the development of the soundscapes with respect to sense of identity: the impact of sensor responsiveness. For participants to gain a sense of identity with their sensor in the collective soundscape, they need to be able to appreciate how physical changes they make affect the sensor. Therefore, sensors are required whose readings may change rapidly, and the environment needs to contain sufficient potential for sensor reading change for the participants to appreciate the effect of their actions. For example, benzine sensors are probably not suitable for the collective audio environment as there may be few sources of benzine in the environment, and changes in sensor readings will be quite small. On the other hand, ultraviolet light sensors in an urban night time environment may be more appropriate as they will respond rapidly to changes in lighting e.g. streetlights, internal lighting, vehicle lighting.

Second, we paid particular attention to the overall aesthetic of the piece whilst ensuring that each data stream was directly mapped to a sound (as discussed in the first point). The overall aesthetic is ambient electronica with sounds spread across the audio spectrum to create a balanced soundscape. We worked hard to move away from jarring sounds (e.g. noise generators/ sine waves) to create a softer, less confrontational soundscape. A further consideration with selection of sounds was the mapping from sensor type to sound. For instance, it would be tempting to map a noise sensor to the volume of static noise in the soundscape, but whilst this is a literal mapping, it may be confusing as the louder the environment becomes, the louder the static noise in the soundscape would be. Instead, we argue for selecting sounds and modulations that somehow capture the essence of the phenomena being sensed. For instance, we may map sonar readings (proximal density) to intensity of a sound to create a sense of audio claustrophobia when the participants are in a densely populated area. In this way we heighten the perception of the participant by augmenting their usual senses with our audio representations of imperceptible phenomena.

Thirdly, we expect participants may be involved with the soundcape for up to one hour and so introduced some temporal development into the audio to reduce listener fatigue and boredom. In particular, we introduced a generative element to the pitch of one of the sounds. This particular sound is a medium to high pitch tone whose onset is controlled by the value of the data it represents - the higher the data reading, the faster the tone is triggered. Over time a motif is generatively evolved to replace the single tone whilst the onset of the motif is still triggered by the data. In this way we have two dimensions of representation in one sound stream: a primary representation of the sensory data (onset), and a secondary representation of the time elapsed since the experience started (increasingly complex musical motif). There are clearly issues here with selecting appropriate primary and secondary representations which we will investigate further.

Finally, as discussed in the next section, the soundscape will also be used as part of the playback of recorded sensory expeditions through auditory and tactile representations of the recorded imperceptible phenomena. This raises issues of how the piece should develop, or not, over time (our third design tension) when people playback and navigate through the experience. For example, if people navigate directly to the end of the expedition, it is not clear whether the sounds heard should be the sounds heard by the participants at the original time of the expedition, or whether the secondary representations should be relative to the time spent in playback mode. In effect, we are asking whether the sensory augmentation is always live (and so relative to the participant), or whether in playback the augmentation attempts to recreate the recorded experience. This is currently an open issue that we are investigating through our ongoing studies.

5. Playback Interface

The second part of Sensory Threads is the gallery located experience interface referred to as the *Rumbler*. This has two purposes: firstly, to relay *live* expedition experiences occurring outdoors into a gallery; and secondly, to provide a *playback* interface for journeying through time and space to explore the multi-dimensional reservoir of sensory data recorded by previous expeditions. The design uses a combination of sound, visuals and touch to create a multi-sensory representation of explorers' imperceptible experiences.

The core of the physical installation is the Rumbler - a large box made from a tea crate (3 feet tall). This box has a video screen on the top, which shows a map (illustrated in figure 3a), displaying the position currently being explored. Figure 3b illustrates the internal construction of the playback device which is encased in a tea crate during use. The box also contains a large subwoofer speaker. This is used to create very low frequency sounds which make the box resonate to create a nuanced set of vibrations when the box is touched. In this way we transform imperceptible phenomena into vibrations that are sensed by the ears (sound), and also by the body (through the resonating tea chest).This large shaking and booming box also acts to attract people's attention to the installation. Four smaller resonators are also part of the installation. These are made from hacked and repurposed computer game control pads with variable rumble support. Each of these mini-resonators represents one sensor's readings through vibration providing a physical connection to the imperceptible experiences of one explorer. Finally, a set of speakers in the exhibition space provide an audio play-back of the soundscape itself.

Figure 3a. Map display.

3b. Internals of the Rumbler.

In live mode, the box is non-interactive; the displayed map moves to the position of the latest sensor readings (which are displayed as dots on the map), the large and small resonators can be felt to respond to the sensor readings, and the soundscape can be heard as the explorers hear it.

In playback mode, the box itself becomes an interaction device. Tilting the box causes the map to move in the direction of the tilting. This allows for the exploration of new paths through the previously recorded sensor readings. The large box means that multiple people can tilt it at once engendering a new form of collective exploration of the imperceptible. Moreover, in order to feel the individual sensor experiences from the miniature resonators, two or more people must collaborate, with one tilting the large resonator whilst the other feels the mini-resonator. This is designed to encourage groups of multiple people to explore the sensor data together, in a manner analogous to the outdoor explorers.

6. Summary

Sensory Threads makes the imperceptible perceptible and creates a collective sensing experience for groups of participants. Through our design process a highly inter-disciplinary team from several university departments worked in tandem with an external arts organization - Proboscis. Members of Proboscis were the primary drivers of the conceptual side of the project and also created the physical designs of the costumes and interfaces. This interaction generated large amounts of intellectual and social capital which we will disseminate and develop through exhibitions and public expeditions. Our further work will explore our understanding and evaluation of these new forms of technologically mediated social expeditions with a view to enticing alternate views on the world beyond our perception.

Acknowledgements

Sensory Threads is part of EPSRC Creator (EP/G002088/1): New Research Processes and Business Models for the Creative Industries, http://www.creatorproject.org/.

References

[1] S. Benford, A. Crabtree, S. Reeves, M. Flintham, A. Drozd, J. G. Sheridan, and A. Dix, The frame of the game: Blurring the boundary between fiction and reality in mobile experiences. In *Proceedings of CHI 2006*, ACM Press (2006), 427-436.

[2] D. Airantzis, A. Angus, G. Lane, K. Martin, J. Taylor and G Roussos, 2008, Participatory Sensing for Urban Communities, *Urbansense08 Workshop at Sensys 2008*, Raleigh NC, USA, (2008).

[3] SuperCollider http://www.audiosynth.com

[4] T. Hermann, Taxonomy and Definitions for Sonification and Auditory Display. In *Proceedings of the 14th International Conference on Auditory Display*, Paris, France, (2008).

[5] N. Bryan-Kinns, and P. G. T. Healey, Exploring Mutual Engagement in Creative Collaborations. In *Proceedings of Creativity and Cognition 2007*, Washington, USA (2007), 223 - 232.

Special Session on Digital Lifestyles

Intelligent Environments 2009
V. Callaghan et al. (Eds.)
IOS Press, 2009

doi:10.3233/978-1-60750-034-6-413

Supporting introspective human behaviours through technologies

Dana PAVEL [a,1], Vic CALLAGHAN [a], Anind K. DEY [b] and Michael GARDNER [a]
[a] *School of Computer Science and Electronic Engineering, University of Essex, U.K.*
[b] *HCI Institute, Carnegie Mellon University, U.S.A.*

Abstract. Almost all technology supported activities we perform today involve a device with computational power able to collect data that can give information about our activities as well as, with the appropriate sensors, about our physiological status. While recording user data is not particularly novel, in our work, we concern ourselves with methods that people can use to gather and analyze data about themselves as they go about everyday work and leisure activities in order to better support self-monitoring and self-understanding. Our aim is to enable people to detect causality relationships in their behaviours either for serving their curiosity or, as we hope, for really empowering them with a tool for self-changes. In this 'work in progress' paper we describe ongoing work towards these ends. We start out by a motivation and short description of our work, followed by an exemplar scenario on 'preventive healthcare' for the system we envision. Then we describe some of the most relevant and influential related work before describing the system design and the main challenges, followed by an overview of the current status and our future vision.

Keywords. Self-monitoring, self-understanding, affective technologies, context awareness.

Introduction

Self-improvement is essential for human development and is considered as one of the higher goals of any human being [17]. Modern societies experienced a dramatic increase in the self-help market in the past years, with U.S. expected to reach a value of $14 billion by 2010 [18]. The Amazon UK store only lists more than 100,000 results under self-help books. Self-understanding plays a very big role in this process as it allows people to analyze their feelings, thinking, and behaviours. However, our attention is limited and sometimes it is hard for us to remember and, therefore, understand, why and how certain things happened. We believe that technology can help us because of its almost ubiquitous availability, continuous miniaturization, and its endless means of capturing various data that we might or might not be aware of otherwise. Technology can also help bringing together various types of data, allowing users access to more detailed views of their daily lives, making it easier for them to find relations between events. We envision a system that could, for example, help people better understand their and others' emotions, which is essential in developing social and emotional intelligence [1] or in identifying and better controlling stress factors that negatively affect their daily lives

[1] Corresponding Author: Dana Pavel, School of Computer Science and Electronic Engineering, University of Essex, Wivenhoe, Colchester, CO4 3SQ, U.K. Email: dmpave@essex.ac.uk

By combining concepts from user understanding with user-centred technologies, we set out to create an integrated system that can offer support to a user in better understanding what and why something happened as well as its physiological impact on the user. Life data collection is studied in multiple research projects but we believe that the areas of data correlation and interpretation, information visualization as well as user interaction still offer big opportunities for novel and challenging research work. In order to support this hypothesis we intend to design and build a "proof-of-concept" system which takes the form of a "companion" system that, by combining knowledge from various technological domains with user understanding, can support an individual in their process of self-monitoring and self-understanding.

In this paper we will mainly focus on presenting the system we are currently building. We start out by presenting an exemplary use case of the system we envision, followed by related work. We then set out to present our envisioned system design, followed by a description of our current status and the main challenges, before concluding the paper with our future vision.

1. A case study: Preventive Healthcare

Here is just one of the many usage scenarios we envision for such system:

Bob is 55 and he has just found out that he has high blood pressure with a risk of developing a heart condition. The visit to the doctor made him aware that he needs to make adjustments to his lifestyle if he wants to avoid any worsening of his situation. The nurse recommended some lifestyle changes but Bob found it very hard to continuously be aware of his behaviour so he decided to use the new MyRoR system that allows for automatically collecting and integrating data about his daily routines. The MyRoR system helps Bob better understand how his heart is affected by the various activities he performs during the day and supports him in making decisions about lifestyle changes. By using the MyRoR system Bob can see how his busy work schedule is affecting his heart by collecting information about his meetings, his eating habits, and other behaviours from Bob's devices (e.g., mobile phones and computers).

This scenario focuses on using our system for lifestyle management in the area of chronic diseases, a major global problem affecting a large number of people worldwide. However, the vast majority of chronic disease patients fall into the category of *low risk*, which means that, with the right support, they could learn how to better manage their disease, which could prevent or delay further deterioration. Technology-assisted lifestyle self-monitoring and self-understanding could provide timely support for chronic conditions and benefit both patients and clinicians as they can record and combine data that is sometimes forgotten or discarded.

2. Background and related work

The vision for ubiquitous computing, initially formulated by Mark Weiser in [6] was "inspired by the social scientists, philosophers, and anthropologists at PARC". The psychology-technology connections were further strengthened through user-centered areas such as affective computing, formulated by Picard [3] and captology (persuasive technologies), formulated by Fogg [5], as well as more recent work on context-awareness (defined by Dey and Abowd in [4]). Affective computing involves, among others, giving a computer an awareness of its user's emotional state. In some cases this information is used by applications to adapt their behaviours (see work by Picard *et al.* in [8] and Leon *et al.* in [14]) and in other cases this information is used with an informative goal, with data presented back to the user through various visualizations, as described by Lindström *et al.* in [9]. In our work, we are interested in emotional awareness in the context of self-understanding. In [7], Picard *et al.* make a case for a unified theory on using affect in learning as, they argue, one's emotional self awareness is very important in learning and developing an emotional intelligence, a concept described first by Salovey and Mayer [1] and later by Goleman [2]. One of the most relevant projects for us is the Affective Diary, described by Lindström, Ståhl *et al.* in [9, 10]. The Affective Diary was a very interesting user interface-focused experiment that represented abstracted physiological and activity user data in a more user friendly way involving emotion-informed shapes and colours. A user study conducted on the Affective diary showed that some people do like to look back on their daily activities, much as they would do it through a diary [10]. The study also showed that some people became quite attached to the system as it helped them look back and better understand what happened and why. This work provided us with insight as well as verified our own views on visualizations, as we believe not everybody relates the same way to certain imposed visualizations.

Fogg's book on principles of persuasive technologies [5] provides us with a significant amount of information on how technology can be used to influence human behaviours in a positive way. Many of the system and interface designs presented are informed by social psychology. Self-monitoring is one of the persuasive technology tools described in the book, as it leads to self-understanding and changing of behaviours. While we envision our system mainly as a support for remembering and reflecting over events and physical reactions, we do expect that enabling people with this type of self-awareness will result in positive behaviour changes, as it also happened in [10].

One good example of how technology can support people's self-awareness is in fitness-related self-monitoring, which became an important market with many companies, like Garmin, Polar, Suunto, *etc.* selling various types of devices. These devices employ physiological sensors and various visualization methods to help people track their fitness related history. Fitness self-monitoring is designed to help people better understand their body's reaction to exercising and, in the process, support them in making changes in their behaviour.

Interaction and visualization is very important for our project and our ideas are shaped and informed, amongst others, by work in affective HCI and empathic interfaces from Picard *et al.* [8, 11] and the work described by Lindström *et al.* in [9, 10]. User understanding work such as the Day Reconstruction Method [18] will provide us with useful insight into designing and testing such systems.

3. System design and development

This section includes a detailed look at both system design considerations and the system development. We start by presenting the system architecture and then follow with a look at each main component of the system, both in terms of design and current development status.

3.1. System architecture

The goal of our system architecture (Figure 1) is to allow for collecting a variety of (distributed) data across various input sources. This data exists in various formats, needing integration into a common data pool in order to be used for end user interaction.

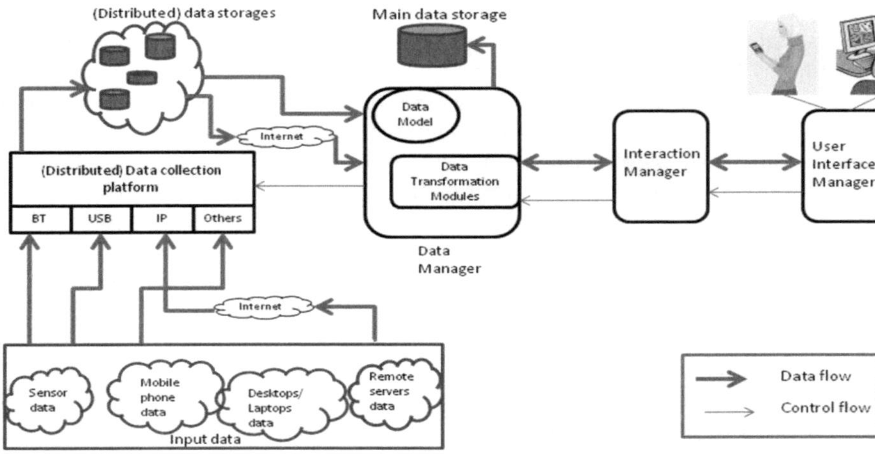

Figure 1 System architecture

It is the role of the *Data Collection Platform* to obtain data from the various input sources. Data can be collected from and can reside on various computing or sensing devices, so appropriate connectivity modules have to be provided by the platform.

In order to integrate the collected data into the system, it will need to be converted before being centrally stored and further interpreted. The *Data Manager* oversees all the data-related transformations and storage control. It includes various types of transformation modules, from input data formatting to more advanced data interpretation. The data operations are governed by the *Data Model*, containing semantic information about the collected data and the data that can be derived from it. The *Data Manager* is centralized to address potential security and privacy concerns that come with the sensitivity of the collected data.

The *Interaction Manager* coordinates various types of interactions between the system and its user(s), based on the collected data. We envision interactions for personalization, system configuration, data retrieval and new data creation.

The *User Interface Manager* is in charge of visualizing the information on a variety of different interfaces. For this, potential adaptations to the interaction or the underlying data need to be performed.

3.2. System Development

This sub-section includes a closer look at the current status of implementing the above outlined system design.

3.2.1. Data Collection Platform

The usefulness of our system relies on having relevant and rich data that can help users remember what happened during the day. To enable an almost ubiquitous user data gathering, we use mobile devices (*i.e.*, existing wearable monitoring systems and mobile phones) together with stationary devices (*i.e.*, desktops and laptops). Some examples of data considered: affective state (obtained through various means such as GSR, heart rate, voice tone level, gestures, *etc.*), location (*e.g.*, GPS, indoor infrastructure), activity (*e.g.*, Internet browsing, watching TV, talking, physical, *etc.*), messages sent/received, phone calls made/received, media created/received (*e.g.*, photos, videos), environment data, and any other information that is relevant to the user and can be collected with a reasonable amount of effort. Data is collected through various means and over multiple connectivity protocols. Sensor data can be obtained from wearables or from the environment. Computer-recorded activity data can be obtained from log files on local or remote machines.

Our strategy is to use as much off-the-shelf hardware as possible and our current experiments use a Garmin ForeRunner 305 wristwatch to gather GPS, heart rate, and interpreted GPS-based data such as distance, running pace, *etc.* We are also using the wireless Alive heart monitor [13] that provides ECG and 3D axis accelerometer. A Nokia N95 phone provides us with messaging and calling activity, images, audio and video recordings, GPS data, WLAN activity, and is also used as a sensing gateway for attached sensors, utilizing the sensor platform described by Trossen and Pavel [12]. From computers, we have been looking at various available activity monitoring platforms that collect information about messaging, communication, web browsing, *etc.*

Our ambition is to create a proof-of-concept system that whilst not presenting a complete picture of the factors affecting a person's daily experiences (as that would be unrealistic) takes a more pragmatic approach by focusing on certain data that we consider most relevant. We anticipate that other use cases developed as this research goes forward will influence what type of data is collected. It is also envisioned that the user could specify (through the user interface) which parameters they find most interesting in order to further guide the data gathering process.

3.2.2. Data Manager

Data collected from the input sources is gathered into a central database. We have chosen MySQL [15] because of its proven robustness and easiness of use.

The data collected exists in various formats and it needs to be reformatted before storing. So far, we have created data formatting modules to extract sensor data from the Alive heart monitor and from the Garmin ForeRunner 305.

Furthermore, we extract additional derived information from the raw sensor data. For instance, the ECG data of the Alive monitor is used to derive heart rate information. The accelerometer data will also be interpreted to provide the user with physical activity information.

Further interpretation, based on the Data Model, is envisioned once more data is added to the system and combined, but an appropriate balance has to be found between too much abstraction and offering transparency. As Ståhl *et al.* note [10], some people prefer to have an understanding of how abstraction is performed through access to lower level data. Also, in certain cases, when parameter changes could be due to multiple causes, it is preferred that data is not highly interpreted: *e.g.*, raised voice tone could mean the user is getting agitated (*e.g.*, angry) but also that the environmental noise or call quality forced her/him to talk louder. In these cases, it might be sensible to not interpret the data, given the ambiguity of the situation. We also expect that certain data abstractions might come directly from the user, through annotations. For example, while we might try to interpret certain input data as emotional state, it would be good to also allow the user to name that state.

3.2.3. Interaction Manager

As mentioned above, the main interactions we envision are for: personalization, system configuration, data retrieval and new data creation.

As part of the *personalization* interaction, the users should be able to customize their user interface through various means: *e.g.*, colours, images, avatars, etc. They also should be able to select which parameters are shown, which views are created (see next section) and what time range is selected. As part of the *system configuration* interaction, users have to be able to select the data to be collected and create certain privacy and access control policies that govern individual pieces of data. As part of the *data retrieval* interaction, users should be able to query the system, to see explanations for certain abstracted data (*i.e.*, what data has been used for abstractions), get support in finding causality relations (*i.e.*, why certain things happened), or get support in finding "critical" moments during the day when something special happened. As part of the *new data creation* interaction, users should be allowed to create new data through various types of annotations (*e.g.*, text, images) and also add new data into the system, such as email, images, music, *etc*.

It is worth mentioning that we do not consider real time interaction scenarios at this point, where the focus would be on alerts triggered by changes in context. Our scenarios will, for now, be focused on retrospective evaluation of collected data.

3.2.4. User Interface Manager

It is most important for such system that it uses intuitive and engaging visual interfaces that allow users to relate to the information presented and understand it. Obviously, the UI Manager is highly connected to the Interaction Manager. However, it is the job the UI Manager to select the best way of displaying information for a user.

We believe that the user should have access to both low and high level information available. For low level, the user can select which data they would like to see. We are currently envisioning the following high-level views: *emotional*, *spatial*, *activity* and *social*. As part of the *emotional* view, one of the interesting aspects is to help users find a relation between physiological data and recorded activity data. For example, by recording affective information (given by heart rate, modified skin conductivity, *etc.*) and correlating it with activity data a user could realize his bodily reaction to certain events that happened during the day, like receiving a phone call or meeting with a certain person. The *spatial* view would create a location-based picture of his activities during the selected time period. The *activity* view would emphasize the activities performed during the day. The *social* view would be built based social communication activities performed during the day, such as meetings, emails sent, sms messages sent, calls made and received, etc.

The user interface should also offer users "zoom-in" functionalities that allow seeing snapshots of various data captured at certain moments in time. Various user interface paradigms are currently explored and multiple means are considered (*e.g.*, sounds, colours, animations, *etc.*). Available graphical tools/environments like Piccolo, Alice, Scratch and Prefuse [16] are considered either for usage or for ideas.

The UI Manager will have to be aware of the technical characteristics and constraints that the display medium has and adapt accordingly. We are currently focused on a desktop-based visualization environment but we can easily foresee that in the future such system could be used on other types of devices, especially when we will be moving towards more reactive type of scenarios.

3.3. Main system challenges

A design as outlined in this paper does not come without any challenges. The following presents only a subset, albeit the most important ones from our perspective, of these challenges:

- **Data security**: Collected data in our scenarios is considered highly sensitive. Hence, data security is very important. To address this, we chose a centralized design, allowing the data to be stored securely and backed up regularly.
- **Privacy**: The sensitive nature of the data requires precautions for preserving privacy. We currently only envision a single user, this user being the sole owner of the data collected. In the future however, we envision a policy-annotated data model, also capturing multi-users cases in which the collected data has attached privacy concerns, *e.g.*, in the case of images, medical information, *etc.*. Pitfalls and negative uses of such system are left for future discussions.
- **Scalability**: Two major aspects relate to the scalability challenges, namely the size of the database and potential distribution of data sources. For the former, we rely on the scalability of commonly available database technology, handling nowadays tens of megabytes of data on single desktop machines. We intend to optimize our data model of efficient database storage by re-formatting the often XML-based input formats. As for the latter, since the design is single user centered, an explosion of devices is not expected.
- **User interface variability**: the advent of different form factors, *e.g.*, mobile devices, touchscreen PDAs, netbooks, desktops and many others poses the challenge of catering to various user interfaces. Currently however, we focus our design on desktop-based interaction with the end user, not excluding future mobile use however. In a multi-device scenario, we would need to rely on advances in interface adaptation through techniques like, *e.g.*, CCPP, UAProf.

4. Conclusions and future work

This paper presents work in progress of our system, whose main aim is to support a user's need for self-understanding through employing various sensing and sensor fusion means, reasoning over various data, and by using suitable interfaces and interactions. We focused in our presentation on an overall view of the system, starting from its architecture and main components, including development status and ideas as well as envisioned usages and main challenges. We used related work to frame our work and also show where we expect innovation to occur.

As the topic spans technical and user understanding issues, the expected results will also be split into these two categories. In the *technological* part, the expected outcome will be the design and implementation of a computer system that is able to gather and provide to its user data about their daily activities, using various input sources and appropriate interaction paradigms. The novel research results are expected to come more from the areas of data modeling, information visualization and user interactions, while the data gathering and aggregation will make use, as much as possible, of existing solutions. On the *user understanding* side the main goal is that, by allowing users to interact directly with such a system, we can gather knowledge about *how, when and by whom* such system can most effectively be used and what would be the impact on the users of having such a system available all the time. It is also interesting to identify which user parameters (as part of and in addition to affective state) are most useful in supporting self-understanding. The findings of such user studies should be fed back into the system design and should also help advance the research into supportive technologies.

Our system will also be used in a new research project starting summer 2009 funded by the UK TSB/EPSRC that investigates scenarios as the one described in Section 1 but in the larger context of infrastructure support for future healthcare.

References

[1] P. Salovey and J.D. Mayer, Emotional intelligence, *Journal of Imagination, Cognition, and Personality* **9** (1990), 185-211.

[2] D. Goleman, *Emotional intelligence*, Bantam Books, New York, 1995.

[3] R. W. Picard, Affective *computing*, MIT Press, Cambridge, MA, 1997.

[4] A. K. Dey and G. D. Abowd, Towards a Better Understanding of Context and Context Awareness, *Proceedings of HUC '99* (1999).

[5] B.J. Fogg, *Persuasive Technology: Using Computers to Change What We Think and Do,* Morgan Kaufmann, 2003.

[6] M. Weiser, The Computer for the 21st Century, *Scientific American* **265**(3) (1991), 94-104.

[7] R. Picard, S. Papert, W. Bender, B. Blumberg, C. Breazeal, D. Cavallo, T. Machover, M. Resnick, D. Roy, C. Strohecker, Affective Learning — A Manifesto, *BT Technology Journal* **22(4)** (2004), 253-269.

[8] R. Picard, Affective Computing for HCI, *Proceedings of HCI International on Human-Computer Interaction: Ergonomics and User Interfaces*, Volume I, 1999.

[9] M. Lindström, A. Ståhl, K. Höök, P. Sundström, J. Laaksolahti, M. Combetto, A. Taylor, and R. Bresin, Affective Diary - Designing for Bodily Expressiveness and Self-Reflection, *Proceedings of CHI2006* (2006), ACM Press.

[10] A. Ståhl, K. Höök, M. Svensson, A. Taylor, and M. Combetto, Experiencing the Affective Diary, *Journal of Personal and Ubiquitous Computing*, 2008.

[11] T. Bickmore, R. Picard, Towards Caring Machines, *Proceedings of CHI'04* (2004), 1489-1492.

[12] D. Trossen, D. Pavel, NORS: An Open Source Platform to Facilitate Participatory Sensing with Mobile Phones, *Proceedings of MobiQuitous 2007* (2007).

[13] Alive Technologies: http://www.alivetec.com/products.htm.

[14] E. Leon, G. Clarke, V. Callaghan, and F. Sepulveda, A User-independent Real-time Emotion Recognition System for Software Agents in Domestic Environments, *Journal of Intelligent Real-Time Automation* (2006).

[15] MySQL website: http://www.mysql.com/.

[16] GUI tools: Piccolo - http://www.piccolo2d.org/, Alice - http://www.alice.org/ , Prefuse - http://prefuse.org/, Scratch - http://scratch.mit.edu/.

[17] A.H. Maslow, A Theory of Human Motivation, *Psychological Review* **50** (1943), 370-96.

[18] D. Kahneman, A.B. Krueger, D.A. Schkade, N. Schwarz, A.A. Stone, A survey method for characterizing daily life experience: The day reconstruction method, *Science* **306**(5702)(2004), 1776-1780.

[19] Marketdata Enterprises, The U.S. Market For Self-Improvement Products & Services, September 2006, from http://www.marketresearch.com/product/display.asp?productid=1338280&g=1 [accessed 17 May 2009].

Intelligent Environments 2009
V. Callaghan et al. (Eds.)
IOS Press, 2009

doi:10.3233/978-1-60750-034-6-421

Emotion-aware intelligent environments: A user perspective

Iraitz Montalban[a,1] Ainara Garzo[a] Enrique Leon[a]
[a] *Fatronik Tecnalia, Spain*

Abstract. Evidence from areas such as neurology and psychology suggests that emotions are an important element in human decision making. The uncovered relationships between emotions and behaviour appear to be an element that may be successfully employed in human-machine interaction for adapting and optimizing the response of pervasive systems. Although initial work has been undertaken along these lines, a number of elements however technical, ethical, or social issues remain unexplored. The study presented here aims to throw light on the issue of how potential users see the prospect of a physiological emotion detection system that operates inside a domestic environment providing tele-assistance to elderly people. We present results that reveal preliminary information on the utilization, desired system response, and acceptance of such emotion detection system.

Keywords. emotion detection, ambient intelligence, pervasive computing

Introduction

Emotional intelligence is defined in Salovey and Mayer's work [1] as the subset of social intelligence that involves the ability to monitor and recognize one's own and other people's emotions and use this information to guide our thinking and actions. This kind of intelligence, which is a crucial element in human decision making, appears to be relevant in the development of natural, intuitive computer interfaces that are more easily accepted by the users [2, 3]. The utilization of emotional information in human-supporting devices like intelligent environments (IEs), might allow functionalities to reflect not only user actions but also the motivations behind them in a more faithful manner. Moreover, studies suggest that computers that generate empathy can reduce frustration and stress and impact perceptions of caring, which could be relevant in the design and implementation of health-care and assisted-living computing systems [4, 5].

Current IEs are capable of making increasingly complex decisions based on a model of user behaviour that integrates contextual, environmental and biomedical information. IEs use this model to orchestrate all domotic devices to respond to situations arising at home and adapt the ambient to assist user's specific needs. The idea behind affective pervasive computing relates to the utilization of emotional information to improve behaviour modelling inside IEs thereby further enhancing comfort, safety and energy consumption. In those situations in which IEs support the provision of tele-care services to elderly people, emotion detection may become a necessity since this age group is particularly vulnerable to the effects of negative emotional states. It has been shown that unfavourable emotional states contribute to the worsening of physical and mental disorders [6, 7, 8].

[1] Iraitz Montalban, Health and Quality of Life Unit, Fatronik Tecnalia. Parque Tecnológico E20009 San Sebastian, Spain. Email: imontalban@fatronik.com

The purpose of the study presented here is twofold. First we are interested in exploring aspects of human-machine interaction associated with affective pervasive systems that may assist in diminishing the impact of some well-known impediments to the wider adoption of assisted-living systems such as the lack of perceived usefulness [9]. Second, we aim at eliciting design guidelines that might be useful when implementing emotion-aware IEs that support elderly people at home. Although previous studies have been conducted to gauge the perceived impact of smart technology in people's lives [10, 11], it is the first time to our knowledge that this kind of analysis is directed towards the use of emotion detection in pervasive systems.

1. Background

1.1. Emotion detection

Affective Computing concerns computing systems that relate to, arise from, or deliberately influence emotion and other affective phenomena [12]. A large proportion of research projects in this field focus on the detection of human emotions by means of facial gestures, vocal utterances and physiological measures [13, 14, 15]. We are particularly interested in the latter since bodily signals associated with the autonomic nervous system are more difficult to be concealed or be purposefully controlled than facial or speech parameters. Furthermore, physiological information can be acquired in a wireless, unobtrusive, continuous manner herewith facilitating data acquisition that does interfere with people's regular activities. In this context physiological emotion detection offers a more realistic representation of inner feelings and thus remains as one of the most promising ways of detecting emotions inside pervasive environments [16].

1.2. Classification of emotional states

There are two widely accepted coexisting approaches to emotion classification that are relevant for affective computing. On the one side, a discrete or factorial approach [17] assumes the existence of a set of *Basic Emotions* that can clearly be distinguished from one another and form the basis of all other emotions we normally experience. On the other side, advocates of the dimensional approach [18] claim the existence of two (or more) major dimensions that are sufficient to describe and distinguish between different emotions, i.e. the dimension of valence with the poles positive and negative and the dimension of arousal with the poles calm and excited. Sometimes, an additional dimension of dominance with the poles strong and weak is also mentioned [19]. For the purpose of this study we are interested in the use of emotional states that a person can easily relate to and thus a discrete approach based on Ekman's work was utilized.

1.3. Assistive domotics

In the field of intelligent environments, assistive domotics appear as a feasible solution to provide elderly and disabled people with increased independence and safety. The utilization of systems that allow people to "age in place" improves well-being and reduces possible uncomfortable situation like, for example, the anxiety associated with having to move to a health care facility or being under the supervision of a personal assistant or carer. The main goal of assistive domotics is therefore to allow elder and disable people to remain safely and comfortably at home, and for that purpose they offer a variety of solutions that facilitate domestic activities. Some of these solutions involve automatic task recognition to inform a carer when something out of a normal routine occurs or continuous monitorization of the patient's physical state using physiological signals [20]. Further functionalities such as social interaction are being studied as part of in-home rehabilitation systems [21].

1.4. Artificial emotional intelligence

IEs operation relies on the acquisition of information about the events that take place inside the domestic space in order to build a model of user behaviour and preferences. This model is used to alter the environment with the intention of facilitating user activities and providing increased comfort. It is difficult however to accurately represent human behaviour as a simple relation of events and changes in the environment. Actions that make up behaviour arise from several components interacting together that require an analysis of the emotions-judgement dynamics.

In fact, as far as an artificial approach to human intelligence is concerned, the complexity of human mind and the different kinds of intelligences described in [22] are often ignored in the literature of pervasive systems. This contravenes the work of researchers in various areas such as psychology, neurology, sociology, and politics who have evidenced in recent years the strong influence of emotions in human decision making [23, 24]. We suggest that the different aspects of human mind, including the emotional elements, should be taken into account in order to establish suitable interaction mechanism and build an adequate behaviour model inside IEs.

2. Scenario-based analysis

There are two concurrent issues that are likely to have an impact on the development of IEs.

First, the impending socio-political impact of an aging population is a phenomenon already affecting industrialized countries. According to EuroStat, the percentage of people aged 65 years or over in Europe will increase from 17.1% in 2008 to 30.0% of the total population in 2060. This represents an opportunity for the IE community to develop solutions that support the provision of health services. This is indeed already happening in a number of developed countries where council houses are being equipped with domotic systems.

On the other hand, emotion detection systems have gained currency towards their widespread utilization in emerging technologies. This is mainly related to the increasing levels of customization users demand from technological solutions, the awareness about the importance of emotions as co-regulators of our actions (along with reasoning), and the sophistication of sensors employed in emotion detection systems.

We foresee that IEs that simultaneously integrate affective computing and assistive technology will become widespread in the future. In order to evaluate this idea, a focus group was organized for the purpose of collecting information about the opinion of potential users on the prospect of an affective pervasive system used in tele-assistance.

The main objective of the study was to subject the design of such hypothetical system to the scrutiny of a number of potential users.

2.1. Participants

The focus group comprised 10 elderly people (older than 65) who reside in the Basque province of Guipuzcoa in northern Spain. Two of the participants lived alone at home, six with their spouses in their own houses, one in a supervised home, and one in a gerontology centre. Some of the participants had already used tele-alarm systems and one of them received domestic assistance.

2.2. Procedure

The experiment encompassed two distinct parts. First, participants completed a questionnaire about the design and perceived usefulness of an affective wearable and also about the relevance of emotions in their daily life. For example, *"Do you think emotions influence your daily life?"* or *"Is there any emotion that you consider dangerous for your health?"* They had the opportunity to support their answers with additional comments and suggestions.

In the second part of the experiment, a presentation of slides involving various types of imagery was used to outline the functioning of the proposed system in a real-life situation. We described a scenario in which a series of daily-life events associated with negative emotions such as anger or fear took place, e.g. a simple kitchen accident. The presentation was followed by a second questionnaire that featured questions about the functional characteristics of the emotion detection system, e.g. artefacts under IE control.

2.3. An affective pervasive system for tele-assistance

The scenario that was presented to participants involved a hypothetical intelligent environment similar to Essex's iSpace where various artefacts are subject to automatic control including four variable intensity spot lights, a desk lamp, and two PC-based applications namely a word processing and a media playing program. The IE performs monitoring of contextual variables such as external and internal light and temperature levels, user's location (using pressure sensors) and current physiological and emotional state. Thanks to an uninterrupted, thorough monitoring of the users activities, the proposed system is capable of displaying signs of intelligent behaviour, e.g. turning light on in advance of the expected user action. The characteristics of the proposed system that were explicitly described to the user are:

- Capacity to learn activities and assist the user in carrying out simple actions such as turning the TV automatically upon detection of intention, e.g. when the user sits in the couch.
- Ability to identify the moment when the user wakes up using physiological and contextual information.
- Uninterrupted emotion detection (when using the affective wearable).

These functionalities would allow the system to perform actions such as greeting the user in the morning, arranging for a videoconference with a close person when sadness is detected or contacting emergency services when an abnormal physiological pattern is detected.

3. Results

3.1. Affective wearables

Since the emotion detection system needs to be provided with the user's physiological information, one or more devices providing this information should exist in the IE. We asked the discussion group about what kind of sensing devices would, in their view, be the least intrusive and most comfortable. Wrist-worn interfaces seemed to have the wider acceptance among participants in particular when they take the form of wristwatches (cf. bracelet) (see **Figure 1**).

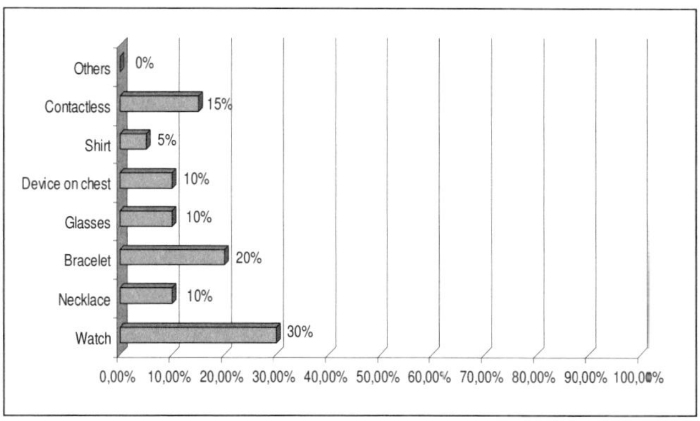

Figure 1: Answers to question "*If I had to wear such device, I would prefer this to be ..*"

The rationale behind people's selection was mainly based on the need of the wearable to be comfortable and easy to put on and take off. They also mentioned the importance of having something physical that they could touch so that they have a sensation of protection and safety. These results seem to coincide with the design of devices that involve remote physiological monitoring and that are currently available on the tele-health market such as Exmocare or Vivago.

3.2. Emotional experience

We were interested in investigating the user-need oriented approach of the system. E.g. would people actually find an affective wearable useful and acceptable? To this end, participants were inquired whether they considered emotions as being an influential element in their daily lives and whether they would like to have a system capable of automatically detecting their emotional state at home.

The group pointed out that they see emotional states influencing their daily lives (see **Figure 2**) in particular when they experience negative emotions. In this context, they argued that this system might be an effective tool to overcome their feelings of loneliness because of, amongst other things, it enables communication with family, friends or even health professionals.

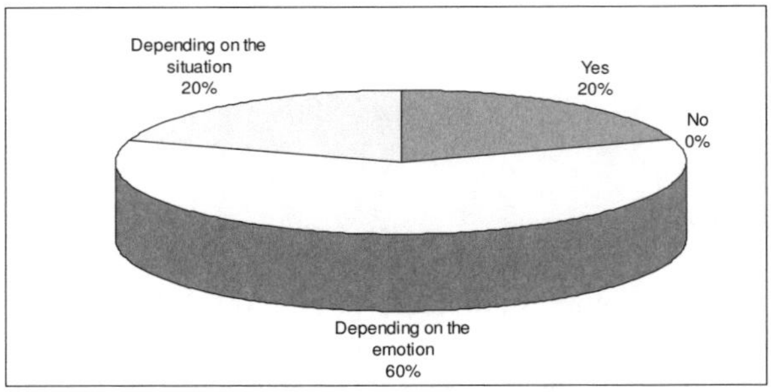

Figure 2: Answer to question "*Do you think emotions influence your daily life?*"

3.3. IE Operation

As already mentioned some sections of the survey focused on the operation of the system and the kind of response users might find useful or appropriate, that is the sort of functionalities that can realistically support user emotional and physical well-being.

There was a prevalent view that the system's functioning should depend on the type of emotion being detected and always operate under user supervision. The system however should also be capable of identifying those situations where a given emotional change represents an imminent danger to the person's health, switching from manual to automatic control when needed. In those cases where a negative emotion is detected, e.g. sadness or fear, most of the participants agreed that the provision of psychological assistance or affective support from a close person (friends, family, etc.) seems to be the most useful option (see **Figure 3**). They did not seem to be especially keen on the IE manipulating the environment.

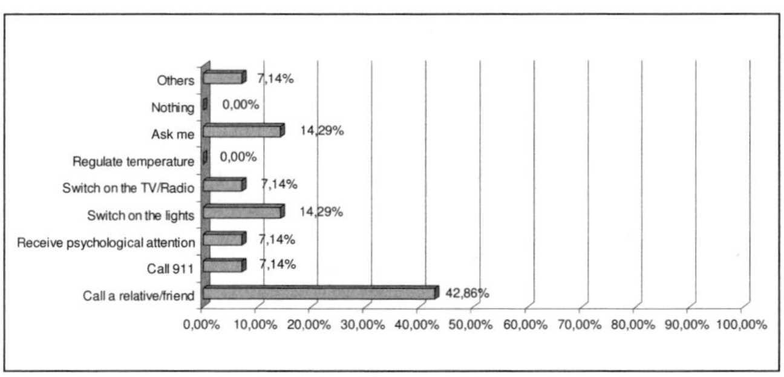

Figure 3: Answer to question "*What would you like the system to do when you feel afraid?*"

They similarly agreed that having an IE capable of coaching them to a proper emotional state, a form of biofeedback, could benefit their quality of life [6, 7, 8]. Apart from direct health related issues, socialization (calling friends or relatives) and the prospect of more natural, human-like interaction capabilities were key components for the group.

It is worth highlighting that the entirety of the group mentioned the importance of a human-like communication system, operating by means of speech interaction. We understand this as confirmation of Reeves and Nass's work regarding the preference for a human-human interaction like models [25].

3.4. Privacy and data control

One of the main concerns when handling users' private data and more in particular in those cases were psychological information is being managed, is the management of that data in a secure and confidential way. For various reasons participants were already familiar with procedures to managing medical data and therefore aware of the importance of an appropriate management of sensitive information. They understood that safeguards must be undertaken by the company implementing the system. When inquired about the use of their physiological data in real-time with no recording, 70% of them said they would not mind using such information to let someone know how they feel. This percentage however decreased to 60% when they were asked if they would mind their information being stored.

4. Conclusions

Questionnaire responses as well as the comments and suggestions stemming from group discussions support the following conclusions.

First of all, it is worth highlighting that, from a market potential point of view, the majority of participants expressed their willingness to acquire an affective pervasive system like the one presented to them. They see this kind of applications as an effective supporting tool to considerably improve their quality of live. They found particularly attractive the system's potential to ameliorate the effects of some elements associated with old age such as affective disorders and vulnerability to diseases [7, 8, 26].

It is also interesting that participants were particularly emphatic on the fact that the system must respond to an emotion only when the user purposely allows it through a question-answer interface. This conclusion which emerged from group discussions and was not part of the questionnaires seems to support the idea behind the user-is-the-king principle introduced by Essex's Intelligent Inhabited Environments Group [27]. Only when something threatens physical integrity and the user becomes unable to give an answer or perform an action should the system make decision autonomously on behalf of the user. It can thus be said that the usefulness and acceptance of this kind of systems hinges on users being in control of its operation.

The fact that people were more interested in receiving emotional support from another person rather than IE-based stimulation in the form of changes to environment is also enlightening and may be useful to the direct research efforts in affective pervasive computing.

Acknowledgements

The authors wish to thank Ingema Institute for liaising with users and assisting our team during discussion session.

References

[1] P. Salovey and J. Mayer, Emotional intelligence, *Imagination, Cognition, and Personality* (1990), 185-211
[2] G. Loewenstein, E. Weber, C. Hsee and N. Welch, Risk as feelings, *Psychological Bulletin* **127** (2001), 267-286
[3] S. Mcquiggan and J. Lester, Modeling and evaluating empathy in embodied companion agents, *Evaluating affective interactions International Journal of Human-Computer Studies* **65** (2007), 348-360
[4] K. Hone, Empathic agents to reduce user frustration: The effects of varying agent characteristics, *Interacting with computers* **18(2)** (2006), 227-245
[5] J. Klein, Y. Moon and R. Picard, This computer responds to user frustration, *CHI '99: CHI '99 extended abstracts on human factors in computing systems* (1999), 242-243
[6] D. Blazer, Depression in late life: review and commentary, *J. Gerontol A Biol Sci Med Sci* **58(3)** (2003), 249-265
[7] J. Kiecolt-Glaser, L. McGuire, T. Robles and R. Glaser, Emotions, morbidity, and mortality: new perspectives from psychoneuroimmunology, *Annual review of Psychology* **53** (2002), 83-107
[8] N. Kressin, A. Spiro and K. Skinner, Negative affectivity and health-related quality of life, *Med Care* **38(8)** (2000), 858-867
[9] M. Vastenburg, T. Visser, M. Vermaas and D. Keyson, Designing Acceptable Assisted Living Services for Elderly Users, *AmI '08: Proceedings of the European Conference on Ambient Intelligence* (2008), 1-12
[10] G. Demiris, M. Rantz, M. Aud, K. Marek, H. Tyrer, M. Skubic and A. Hussam. Older adults' attitudes towards and perceptions of "smart home" technologies: a pilot study. *Med. Inform.* **29(2)** (2004), 87-94.
[11] G. Demiris, S.M. Speedie and S. Finkelstein, Change of patients' perception of TeleHomeCare. *Telemedicine Journal and e-Health* **7(3)** (2001), 241-8
[12] R. Picard, *Affective Computing,* The MIT Press, Hardcover, 1997
[13] C. Lisetti, and F. Nasoz, Using noninvasive wearable computers to recognize human emotions from physiological signals, *Journal on Applied Signal Processing* **2004(11)** (2004), 1672-1687
[14] F. Nasoz, K. Alvarez, C. Lisetti and N. Finkelstein, Emotion recognition from physiological signals using wireless sensors for presence technologies, *Cognition, Technology & Work* **6(1)** (2004), 4-14
[15] C. Peter, and A. Herbon, Emotion representation and physiology assignments in digital systems, *Interacting with. Compututers* **18(2)** (2006), 139-170
[16] E. Leon, G. Clarke, V. Callaghan and F. Sepulveda, A user-independent real-time emotion recognition system for software agents in domestic environments, *Engineering Applications of Artificial Intelligence* **20(3)** (2007), 337-345
[17] P. Ekman, An argument for basic emotions, *Cognition & Emotion* **6(3/4)** (1992), 169-200
[18] J. Russell and A. Mehrabian, Evidence for a three-factor theory of emotions, *Journal of Research in Personality* **11(3)** (1977), 273-294
[19] M. Bradley and P. Lang, Measuring emotion: the Self-Assessment Manikin and the Semantic Differential, *Journal of behavior therapy and experimental psychiatry* **25(1)** (1994), 49-59
[20] M. Pallikonda Rajasekaran, S. Radhakrishnan and P. Subbaraj, Elderly Patient Monitoring System Using a Wireless Sensor Network, *Telemedicine and e-Health* **15(1)** (2009), 73-79
[21] M. Lew, E. Bakker, N. Sebe and T. Huang, Human-Computer Intelligent Interaction: A Survey, *Human–Computer Interaction* (2007), 1-5
[22] H. Gardner, *Frames of Mind: The Theory of Multiple Intelligences,* Basic Books, 1983
[23] Y. Hanoch, S. Wood and T. Rice, Bounded rationality, emotions and older adult decision making: not so fast and yet so frugal, *Human Development* **50** (2007), 333-358
[24] A. Damasio, *Descartes' Error: Emotion, Reason, and the Human Brain* Harper Perennial, 1995
[25] B. Reeves and C. Nass, *The media equation*, Cambridge University Press, 1996
[26] N. E. Zinberg and I. Kaufman, *Normal Psychology of the Aging Process*, International University Press, New York (1978)
[27] V. Callaghan, M. Colley, G. Clarke and H. Hagras, Embedded intelligence: research issues for ubiquitous computing, *Proceedings of the Ubiquitous Computing in Domestic Environments Conference* (2001)

Intelligent Environments 2009
V. Callaghan et al. (Eds.)
IOS Press, 2009

doi:10.3233/978-1-60750-034-6-429

Exploring Adjustable Autonomy and Addressing User Concerns in Intelligent Environments

Matthew BALL[a], Vic CALLAGHAN[a], Michael GARDNER[a] and Dirk TROSSEN[b]
[a] *University of Essex, Colchester, UK*
[b] *BT Research, Adastral Park, UK*

Abstract. Various approaches to the configuration and control of intelligent environments have been researched in the past. The majority of these however, make use of either exclusively autonomous or exclusively end-user driven techniques which, in certain situations, may be an issue. A number of users may be reluctant to allow an autonomous system to monitor and interpret every action they take while, on the other hand, some users may be unable or unwilling to program and configure such a complex (end-user driven) system alone. This work-in-progress paper outlines our preliminary work aimed at exploring a solution to this issue by investigating the possibility of creating a hybrid autonomous-agent/end-user driven system that enables the user to set the level of autonomy for any given part of an intelligent environment. The principle contributions of this paper are to expose the issues regarding intelligent environment management systems, to give a comprehensive review of related work on adjustable autonomy and to present a conceptual model and an autonomy metric that can be used as a foundation of future research into developing hybrid autonomous-agent/end-user driven systems. This work forms part of an ongoing three year research project, funded by BT, that seeks to understand and address user concerns with the aim of equipping intelligent environments with better management systems and, furthermore, making intelligent environments more commercially deployable. Given the ongoing nature of this work, we propose to report any significant progress of this research at subsequent IE conferences until this work is complete.

Keywords. Intelligent environments, hybrid management, adjustable autonomy, mixed-initiative interaction, user concerns

Introduction

With the rapid emergence of new technologies, certain fantasies of science fiction seem to be moving closer to becoming reality. It is not hard to picture a future where humans inhabit planets other than the earth. In order to survive in the harsh conditions of space, it may be necessary to create self-regulating habitats that can generate and sustain an atmosphere as well as providing a means of generating all the elements and resources we humans need to live. A key question in developing such a system is how will it be controlled? It may not be feasible for a human to be constantly present to maintain control. Consequently there is a need for the habitat to be intelligent. Recent research in Intelligent Environments (IE's) points towards this ultimate vision of space habitation [1] and in fact some organisations, NASA for example, have long been exploring how artificial intelligence and autonomous systems can be used to enhance space applications [2, 3].

In a more down to earth respect, an IE can be seen as an everyday environment, such as a home or work place, which is enriched by a number of embedded computer processors controlled by a network of intelligent agents with the aim of enhancing user experiences and improving quality of life. An IE system designed for a person's home would have to adapt and reconfigure itself both initially and over time in order to accommodate the needs and preferences of the individual user and to be able operate efficiently within the given environment. With such a dynamic nature, IE systems cannot, at least not without great difficulty, simply be designed and programmed in a structured deterministic way, as with more conventional computer systems. Instead the vision is that IE's should be programmed in dialogue with the end-user after deployment of the system. This poses the key question of how is it possible for an average user, who might not have any technical knowledge about the system nor an understanding computer programming, to program and configure (to manage) such a complex and technical system. In this work-in-progress paper we discuss the issues of IE management from a user's perspective, we review related work on adjustable autonomy and mixed initiative interaction, and we present our current work toward a solution to these issues; we propose a conceptual model for a hybrid autonomous-agent/end-user driven system that allows for varying levels of autonomy along with a metric for the numeric measurement of autonomy in an IE system.

1. Approaches to Intelligent Environment Management

There are two mainstream approaches to IE management. Firstly, an end-user driven approach can be taken. In this approach it is the responsibility of the end-user to program the IE although the user of the system may not actually have any knowledge of computer programming nor any technical knowledge of the system. The second approach is to make the system autonomous. The system then programs itself by learning from the user's behaviours and interactions with the environment in context with the current environmental state and conditions.

In an attempt to implement an effective end-user driven system, there have been various simple methods of programming developed for IE's. Alfred is a system that was developed as part of the Intelligent Room Project at MIT [4, 5]. Alfred allows the user to record macros using natural language processing and voice recognition technology. Macros can be played back by the user speaking a specified command phrase or using a pre-defined hardware trigger. Another aim of end-user driven management systems is to strive to increase the user's knowledge of the IE system. By breaking down the IE into its ubiquitous components it becomes easier for the user to understand of the inner workings of the environment. Humble's jigsaw puzzle approach [6] breaks down the IE into device components (and their corresponding functions) which are each represented by a jigsaw puzzle-like piece that can be 'snapped together' in a chain from left to right to describe the desired functionality of the system. Pervasive interactive Programming (PiP) [7] developed at the University of Essex also breaks down the system and allows the user to pick and mix from different functionalities of devices, grouping them together to form virtual pseudo-appliances known as MAps (Meta -Appliances -Applications). PiP uses a programming-by-example approach that allows the user to demonstrate the desired behaviour for any given MAp by interacting with either the physical environment itself or graphical representations of devices in the environment. The system can then generate a collection of rules (sets of actuating conditions and resulting actions) for each MAp based on these interactions of the user, effectively programming the environment.

There are many examples of autonomous approaches to IE management. Mozer's Adaptive Home [8] uses reinforcement learning and a predictive neural network to control systems such as lighting, heating and ventilation in an attempt to reduce operational costs whilst still maintaining an acceptable level of user comfort. If the system makes a false prediction and/or the user is unhappy with the systems behaviour, then the user simply corrects the system by interacting with the physical environment. The iDorm [9] developed at the University of Essex focuses on modelling user activities by employing fuzzy logic mechanisms to generate rules for system behaviour. Rules are generated in a life-long learning mode by continuously monitoring and interpreting the user's interaction with devices with respect to the current state of the environment. After an initial learning period, the system runs in its 'normal operating' mode until the system detects that the user is unhappy with the current system behaviour (i.e. the user is overriding the system rules by manually operating devices in the environment).

End-user driven and autonomous-agent driven approaches can be seen as being at two opposite ends of a scale. An end-user driven approach empowers the user, giving them complete control in managing the system while, an autonomous-agent driven system disempowers the user handing complete control over to a collection of agents. Producing a system that empowers the user might seem the logical choice; an end-user driven approach not only encourages the creativity of the user but potentially makes the user feel a lot more at ease with being completely immersed within such a complex computer system. Nevertheless, some users may lack the ability or confidence to program an IE system, even with a simplified programming interface. In this situation an autonomous system is clearly the superior choice, it greatly reduces the cognitive load placed on the user in configuring the system. In effect all that is required from the user is to carry on living within his household in the most normal manner.

The 3C model [10, 11] shown in Figure 1 is a socio-agent framework that illustrates this concept. Each quadrant represents one extreme type of usage that may be encountered as a system becomes exclusively autonomous or end-user driven given the user has a phobia (fear) or philia (love) of the system. Ideally we wish to avoid misuse and sabotage of the system and maximise creative use and symbiosis between

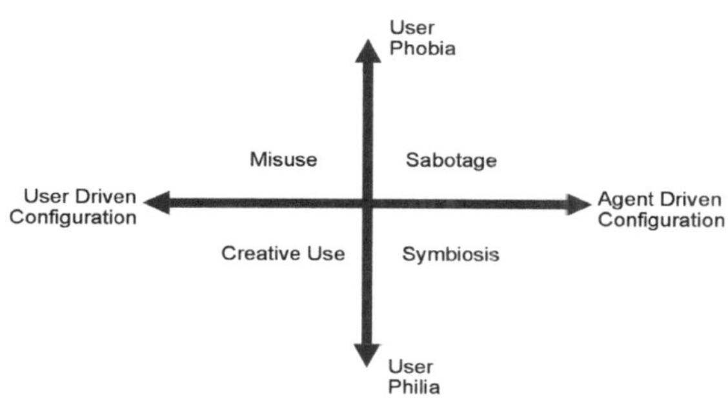

Figure 1. The Callaghan-Clarke-Chin (3C) model

the user and system. The approaches to IE management described in this section have all been either entirely end-user driven or entirely autonomous and hence maximise either creative use or symbiosis but cannot provide both (with respect to the 3C model). Maximising creative use and empowering the user with an end-user driven system may bring about a user's phobia causing the user to misuse the system, albeit perhaps unintentionally. Conversely, trying to maximise symbiosis by providing an autonomous-agent driven system may also trigger a user's phobia and cause the user to sabotage the operations within the system, again albeit perhaps inadvertently. In order to achieve complete user philia, or at least make an attempt to, we have to allow the user to choose which parts of the system they wish to control and which parts of the system they are happy to leave to be controlled by intelligent agents; we need to combine the autonomous-agent and end-user driven approaches of IE management into one single hybrid approach. By allowing the level of autonomy in the system to be variable and controllable by the user, we maximise the potential for both creative use and symbiosis throughout the system. In the next section we discuss the concepts of adjustable autonomy and mixed-initiative interaction and, furthermore, how these concepts might be applied to an IE.

2. Adjustable autonomy and Mixed-Initiative Interaction

Bradshaw [12] describes adjustable autonomy as maintaining "the system being governed at a sweet spot between convenience (i.e. being able to delegate every bit of an actor's work to the system) and comfort (i.e. the desire to not delegate to the system what it can't be trusted to perform adequately)". By altering the level of autonomy in certain ways, we allow for mixed-initiative interaction. Bradshaw also presents us with an interesting vacuum cleaner analogy to explain mixed-initiative interaction [12]. The most manual (non-autonomous) is a 'plain old' vacuum cleaner. It is directly operated by a person's arm, apart from the ongoing sweeping and sucking action of the motor, every action is taken at the initiative and direction of the user. The opposite, a fully-autonomous vacuum cleaner, would turn itself on, vacuum until it decides it's finished and then retreat back to its storage place to recharge. With this vacuum cleaner no initiative or direction is required from the user; it relies only on the initiative of agents. From this it is easy to imagine an example of a mixed-initiative vacuum cleaner; a vacuum cleaner that requires the user to switch it on, place it in a starting position and instruct it to start vacuuming. The vacuum cleaner would then autonomously move about the room ensuring every reachable spot gets cleaned and, when finished, return back to its starting position and wait to be turned off. Such a vacuum cleaner relies upon initiative and direction from both the user and agents; it relies on mixed-initiative interaction.

Mixed-initiative interaction can be achieved at varying levels. At one level users can work together with agents in a very intricate way, as in Allen and Ferguson's human-machine collaborative panning system [13]. In this system the user and the agent collaborate through a conversational dialogue in order to produce an evacuation plan for a natural disaster on an island. The user-agent collaboration is somewhat similar to the way two humans might devise a plan through a back-and-forth natural language conversation. Another possible level of human-agent interaction is through task delegation. Research at NASA has explored how life support systems and scientific equipment can be made autonomous whilst still giving the user ultimate control when needed by allowing the user to adopt or be delegated certain tasks [2]. One example presented to us is a Mars rover. Given a rover that is traversing the planet's surface autonomously, a crewmember can take control of certain parts of the rover's system to undertake certain tasks if some unanticipated event occurs. For example, a crewmember may wish to take control of the rover's visual scanning systems if the rover stumbles across something interesting. In terms of intelligent environments, both of these levels of mixed-initiative interaction could be very useful in producing a hybrid autonomous-agent/end-user driven system. At the collaborative level, agents and users could collaborate together to program behaviour rules or, moreover, to resolve conflicts in the system. The task delegation/adoption level could be used to allow the user to adopt certain programming tasks themselves while delegating others to agents. In the next section we discuss this further, presenting our current work in progress.

3. Work in Progress

Figure 2 shows a conceptual model for a hybrid autonomous-agent/end-user driven IE system, showing the major necessary components. The model consists of two functional divisions, one proactive and one reactive. The proactive division controls the system; it anticipates the user's behaviour/desires and alters the system behaviour accordingly. The reactive division handles the configuration of the system; it both learns from the user's actions and interprets user programming to construct behaviour rules (for simplicity, we use the term behaviour rules throughout this paper to refer to some description of desired system behaviour). As with the end-user driven approaches described in section one, the hybrid model provides a simple programming mechanism. This mechanism enables an end-user to program the system without the need for technical knowledge and computer programming techniques. In order to provide an autonomous learning mechanism, the hybrid model makes use of an array of

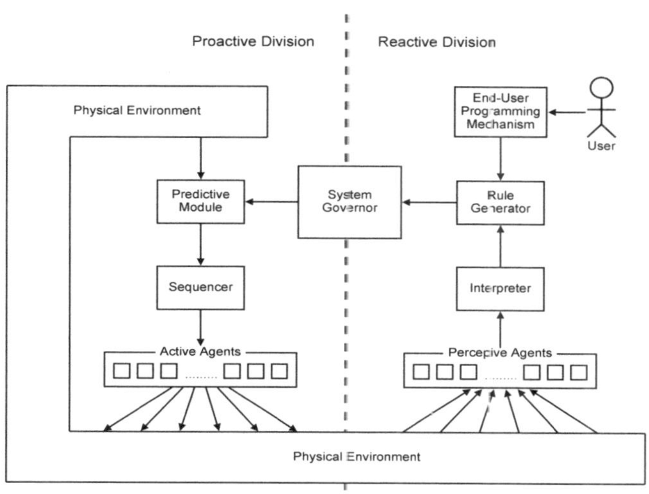

Figure 2. Conceptual model of hybrid system

perceptive agents and an interpreting component. The perceptive agents allow the system to monitor the user's actions within the physical environment which can be interpreted into a behaviour model that reflects the user's habitual activity via the interpreting component; thus, enabling the system to program itself to suit the user's needs. The rule generator is able to produce behaviour rules based on input from either end-user programming or from autonomous learning. A set of behaviour rules can then be used as an input to the central system governor. Within the proactive division, the predictive module provides the initiative for the system. Based on the user's actions in the physical environment and the behaviour rules within the system governor, the predictive module is able to anticipate the user's needs and produce a set of suitable tasks to be performed. The sequencer is in place to handle the running of tasks by driving an array of active agents working in the physical environment. The sequencer is required to enable the system to function efficiently by taking into account resource usage and avoiding potential problems such as deadlock.

The system governor is a highly integral component of the system. Part of our current research effort at Essex is in the early stages of exploring how the concerns of different stakeholders of an IE can be captured, modelled and used to govern the system. It is quite plausible that an IE will have multiple stakeholders, for example, an intelligent apartment may have multiple inhabitants, an external landlord, a health and safety regulatory body, and the system itself might even be considered a stakeholder given that it has a level of intelligence. Concerns captured by the system could represent any of a large number of things. For example, concerns could correspond to simple user preferences, energy consumption quotas, system component dependencies, health and safety restrictions, or privacy concerns. An additional key aspect of our future research will be to investigate user-agent collaborative methods of end-user programming with the possibility of varying levels of collaboration. In a concerns based system, an agent would seek to identify and capture user concerns in order to program the system in dialogue with the end-user. However, the level of collaboration could be changed so that the user received little or no input from the agent, leaving the user to specify their own concerns and program the system alone. Captured (or specified) user concerns could be used within the system governor to model behaviour rules by linking specific concerns with functions that can be performed in the physical environment by active agents. A system governed by concerns could be very useful in creating a system that allows for adjustable autonomy. Concerns of the user and those of the system itself could be used determine and refine the level of autonomy within the system. If for any given sub-system of an IE, the heating system or lighting system for example, a large number of user concerns have been captured, then the autonomous learning mechanism could be restricted from developing behaviour rules for that part of the system, leaving the end-user to drive the management. On the other hand, the automated learning mechanism could target parts of the system for which no or very few user concerns have been captured. One can imagine a sliding-scale switch (similar to a volume control) that represents the level of autonomy within a single sub-system of an IE with one end of the scale representing fully autonomous-agent driven management and the opposite end representing exclusively end-user driven. If we had a sub-system being managed solely by autonomous agents, the theoretical slider will, of course, be at the autonomous end of the scale. By restricting the automated learning mechanism and by the user collaborating towards or taking over the management instead, the slider would move somewhat further toward the opposite end of the scale. Conversely, if a given sub-system is driven exclusively by end-user management, the

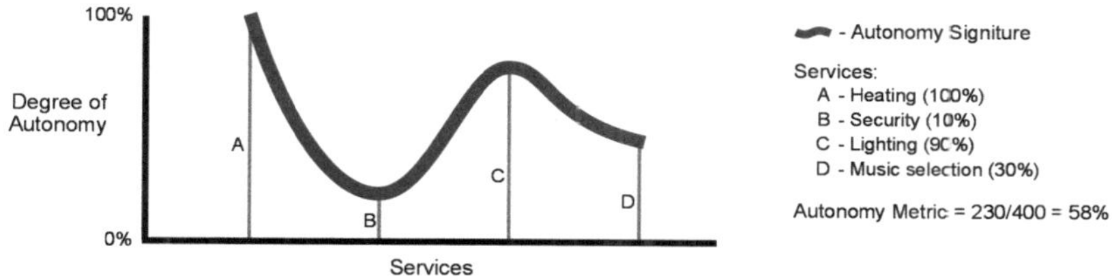

Figure 3. An illustration of autonomy metrics

theoretical slider would start at the opposite, end-user driven end of the scale. Then if the autonomous learning mechanism was introduced and/or we increase the level of input from an agent collaborating with the user, the slider will move further back towards the autonomous end of the scale. This sliding-scale switch analogy clearly has some parallels with Bradshaw's vacuum cleaner analogy for mixed-initiative interaction [12], described in section 2. At the end-user driven end of the scale, as with Bradshaw's 'plain old' vacuum cleaner, we have a system that relies on initiative and direction from the user to configure the system. Whereas, at the autonomous end of the scale, and as with Bradshaw's fully-autonomous vacuum cleaner, the system only relies on initiative and direction from intelligent agents. By allowing the agents and user to work collaboratively, adopting and delegating management tasks between them, and thus moving the theoretical slider somewhere in between the two opposing ends of the scale, we create a system that depends on initiative and direction of both the user and agents, as we also saw in Bradshaw's vacuum cleaner analogy. Given this extra dynamic of mixed-initiative interaction, it can be seen how a hybrid autonomous-agent/end-user driven system adhering our model could provide the potential for adjustable autonomy.

The same sliding-scale concept could be applied to each individual sub-system within an IE, essentially creating a theoretical mixing desk consisting of many sliding-scale switches to control the level of autonomy of the entire system. This would not only allow for a numeric measure of the total autonomy of the system, an autonomy metric, to be offered but if the amount of autonomy for each sub-system was plotted on a graph, in an ordered way, one could also produce an 'autonomy signature' for an individual user, effectively modelling a user's concerns regarding autonomy in the system. An example of this is illustrated in Figure 3. A user's autonomy signature can be seen to represent a sweet spot between the convenience of autonomous learning and the comfort of end-user programming with regards to the management of an IE system, as described by Bradshaw. Enabling this sweet spot to be found makes a higher level of IE system-philia reachable by a greater number users compared to taking an exclusively autonomous or exclusively end-user driven approach.

4. Conclusion

The vast majority of previously researched intelligent environment management systems have taken either an exclusively autonomous-agent or end-user driven approach. Although a lot of these research efforts have been fruitful, taking such an exclusive approach may cause some users to experience a phobia of the complexity and invasiveness of an intelligent environment system. In this work-in-progress paper we have sought to find a solution to this issue by investigating the potential of adjustable autonomy in intelligent environments. The principle contribution of this paper is to raise awareness of issues of intelligent environment management from a user's point of view and, moreover, to aid future researchers by giving a comprehensive review of related work on adjustable autonomy, presenting a conceptual model that builds the foundations of a hybrid autonomous-agent/end-user driven system together with a metric for measuring the autonomy, or concerns of users, both of which will the focus of the next phase of this work forming part of an ongoing three year collaborative research project between the University of Essex and BT. The project seeks to make intelligent environments more commercially deployable by exploring how user concerns can be exposed within an intelligent environment and used to accomplish better management of the system. We look forward to presenting all significant progress of this ongoing work at subsequent intelligent environment conferences.

References

[1] Clarke, G., Callaghan, V., Pounds-Cornish, A., "Intelligent Habitats and The Future: The Interaction of People, Agents and Environmental Artefacts", *4S/EASST Conference on Technoscience*, Vienna, (2000).

[2] Dorais, G. A., Bonasso, R. P., Kortenkamp, D., Pell, B., and Schreckenghost, D., "Adjustable autonomy for human-centered autonomous systems on Mars", In *Proc. Of the First International Conference of the Mars Society,* (1998).

[3] Bradshaw, J. M., Sierhuis, M., Acquisti, A., Feltovich, P., Hoffman, R., Jeffers, R., Prescott, D., Suri, N., Uszok, A., & Van Hoof, R., "Adjustable autonomy and human-agent teamwork in practice: An interim report on space applications", in *Agent Autonomy (H. Hexmoor, R. Falcone, & C. Castelfranchi Ed.),* (2003), 243–280.

[4] Gajos, K., Fox, H., & Shrobe, H., "End user empowerment in human centered pervasive computing", in *Proceedings of Pervasive 2002,* (2002), 1-7.

[5] Hanssens, N., Kulkarni, A., Tuchinda, R., and Horton, T., "Building agent-based intelligent workspaces", in *Proceedings of ABA 2002,* (2002).

[6] Humble, J., Crabtree, A., Hemmings, T., Åkesson, K.P., Koleva, B., Rodden, T., Hansson, P., "'Playing with the Bits', User-Configuration of Ubiquitous Domestic Environments", *Proceedings of UbiComp 2003,* Springer-Verlag (2003), 256-263.

[7] Chin, J., Callaghan, V., Clarke, G., "An End User Tool for Customising Personal Spaces in Ubiquitous Computing Environments", *Lecture Notes in Computer Science: Ubiquitous Intelligence and Computing*, Springer-Verlag (2006), 1080-1089.

[8] Mozer, M.C., "Lessons from an adaptive home", Smart Environments: Technology, *Protocals and Applications*, Wiley (2005), 273-298.

[9] Hagras, H., Callaghan, V., Colley, M., Clarke, G., Pounds-Cornish, A., Duman, H., "Creating an Ambient-Intelligence Environment Using Embedded Agents", *IEEE Intelligent Systems, Vol.19, No.6,* (2004), 12-20.

[10] Callaghan, V., Clarke, G.S., and Chin, S.J.Y., "Some Socio-Technical Aspects Of Intelligent Buildings and Pervasive Computing Research", *Intelligent Buildings International Journal, Earthscan, 1:1,* (2008).

[11] Chin, J., Callaghan, V., Clarke, G., "Soft-appliances: A vision for user created networked appliances in digital homes", *Journal of Ambient Intelligence and Smart Environments 1,* (2009), 69–75.

[12] Bradshaw, J.M., Feltovich P.J., Jung, H., Kulkarni, S., Taysom, W., Uszok A., "Dimensions of adjustable autonomy and mixed-initiative interaction", in *Agents and Computational Autonomy: Potential, Risks, and Solutions, (M. Nickles, M. Rovatos, and G. Weiss, Ed.)*, Springer-Verlag (2004), 17–39

[13] Allen, J., Ferguson, G., "Human-Machine Collaborative Planning", in *Proceedings of the NASA Planning and Scheduling Workshop,* (2002)

Intelligent Environments 2009
V. Callaghan et al. (Eds.)
IOS Press, 2009

doi:10.3233/978-1-60750-034-6-437

Telco@home: a seamless communication project with a user perspective

P. CASTROGIOVANNI [a], E. GUERCIO[a], A. MARCENGO[a], G. MARTINI[a], A. RAPP[b]
[a] *Telecom Italia*
[b] *Telecom Italia, Università di Torino, "Progetto Lagrange – Fondazione C.R.T."*

Abstract. Seamless communication is spreading in all areas of everyday life thanks to the greater interoperability of the consumer electronic devices. The opportunity richness that this scenario opens must be designed with the end users who will face both new opportunities but also new elements of complexity. This requires to take carefully into account their perspective in order to really help their daily lives through this new communication experience. In this paper we illustrate the design process of a seamless communication and media fruition platform for the home environment based on user meaningful service scenarios. The use of personas throughout the design phase of services has allowed us to take into account not only users actual behavior, but also their needs and desiderata in order to translate them into solutions improving their daily lives.

Keywords. HCI, Service Design, User Experience, DLNA, Digital Home, Personas

1. The "Seamless" communication paradigm

A form of seamless communication is increasingly spreading out in our society and in general communication habits since the appearance of mobile phones. What is changing, and for some aspects is continuously evolving and growing with time is the evolution of a plethora of new consumer electronic devices into communication object and the emergence of new paradigm among users. The seamless paradigm is a set of communication patterns where the user maintains a continuous session when roaming among distinct areas and/or different spaces among the same environment. This is facilitated through the usage of a set of devices available in the same environment in a "seamless" gear configuration so the user doesn't have to take any explicit action in order to accomplish his possible tasks. The user is therefore given with the opportunity of communicate, consume and share media always "at the best condition", in every moment of daily life, by removing those transition elements among the different life contexts: e.g. login on different devices or application, "identity change", sessions change, change of the communication media. In this work the designers attention is not only devoted to the basic quantitative aspects (e.g. delays, network coverage, jitters) which obviously must be well solved, but is equally focused on user acceptance issues concerning both possible services and devices. Interaction is simplified thanks to the reduction or elimination of manual configurations, context switches without user intervention ("seamless"), automatic user identification in different context and on different devices.

In order to provide the best "user experience", solutions can span without interruption from situations where all the communication is mediated by sensors/actuators available in the surrounding environment (the user has no device at hand) up to the opposite one where are used only the sensors and devices "worn" by the user. The choice about the best approach to be adopted is dynamically picked out, instant by instant, according to the service, to the context (e.g. where, time, user conditions), to the available resources (e.g. TV, displays, etc.) and to the specific user preferences. In order to "communicate", the user is able to take advantage from the surrounding environment, technologically equipped with different resources: audio/video elements (e.g. TV-set, wireless loudspeakers, microphones), sensors (e.g. proximity sensors), haptic interaction devices (e.g. gestures). Likewise the user is able to utilize sensors and devices "located on his/her own body" in those situations where the surrounding environment does not offer any elements supporting communication.

1.1. Technological enablers

The premises for enabling the previously illustrated communication paradigm lie in the current evolutionary trends. The current convergence in different technological areas, will sustain this kind of realization. From a centric approach the intelligence of service is progressively moving from the core of the network to its periphery, making use at best of the increased connectivity and processing capabilities of current user terminals. Such a shift intersects also with the connectivity trends which see continuous increase in the broadband network bandwidth, both mobile and fixed – reshaping the landscape of how communication and media production/consumption are carried out by the users. Moreover, the realization of a seamless user-experience involving all the aspects of digital media lifecycle (production, sharing, and consumption) and integrated communication – across multiple devices and multiple networks - is being tackled by standardization initiatives. Among these, promising are those related to the evolution of Consumer Electronics (CE) devices which are progressively shifting towards an interconnected and interoperability approach. The DLNA consortium [1] is among the most active in issuing a set of interoperability guidelines, pursuing a lowest-common denominator approach for empowering the sharing of digital content among a broad spectrum of CE equipments, PCs and mobile handhelds.

2. Methodology

The main ambition in the service design work is to select among the possible enabling technological solutions and derived services, those that could have the most positive rank of acceptability by the end users. However, working in a medium-long term perspective (3 to 5 years) brings some difficulties in the involvement of real users in the direct selection and evaluation of solutions and services. People poorly manage to imagine future scenarios away from technological framework in which they are immersed, finding so quite hard to find meaningful or positive aspects in the innovative perspective offered. Asking people directly what kind of future services scenarios would like the most could so lead to distorted or incomplete results [6]. Therefore we decided to take advantage from the Personas methodology [5, 7, 11, 12, 13, 14].

Personas are real users stereotypes who are described through a detailed personal card built with qualitative and quantitative data analysis. They are "used" to design medium-long term not yet available innovative services by focusing on their practical and emotional goals more than on the technological framework they are involved in. Indeed, the Personas provide the designer a clear picture of what are the desires and unmet needs of different types of users, in order to have consistent points of reference during all the service design phases. However in order to use Personas profitably they must be constructed accurately and must be reliable and based on a large amount of both qualitative and quantitative data. Personas must be sufficiently different, and characterized not only by socio-demographic data, but also by personality traits and life-styles, identifying desires and values inspiring and guiding them throughout their daily life. Otherwise the risk is to have a lack in the credibility of the characters, because not based, or with no clear connection, with the actual data [9, 12]. These aspects take often a considerable effort in terms of time and costs [e.g. 10, 12]. To maximize the cost benefits trade-off in developing the set of Personas within our research area it has been developed a Personas layering framework, which considers the single Persona as a composite entity. It consist of several layers, partly developed once and reusable in many context (the internal layer) and partly developed on the basis of the application context of the different projects requiring a user centred perspective (the context layer) [8]. In this way the process of Personas definition is articulated into two independent stages:

- the first targeted to the accurate definition of a basic set of Personas, reusable and valid for a whole research or business area. In this stage, through both quantitative and qualitative research methods, for each Persona that composes the set is created an internal layer that defines not only all the socio demographic characteristics, but also all the aspects that guide the Persona daily life that does not change through different contexts (i.e. his values and desires);
- the second is specific for each individual project that intends to reuse the basic set of Personas, and aims to define a context "layer" based on the usage context of the services under development. The context layer drives attitudes, needs and specific aims of that Persona for that context (e.g. home, car, etc.). This "layer" is built through ad hoc qualitative research techniques (ethnography, key informants interviews, scenarios, etc.) depending on the type of information crucial for the service [8].

This model can significantly lengthen the life span of the Personas set developed. This because the internal layer of all individual Personas can be reused within the same research or business area in different projects over the years maintaining its validity and constituting a solid basis for guiding the design of different services [8].

The Telco@home project has exploited the basic set of 11 Personas devised in the Research & Trends area of Telecom Italia. These Personas identified 11 different profiles for the Italian market of *"consumer and early adopter of ICT and telecommunications services"*. Among these, at first, were selected 9 Personas, according to their specific spending capacity or their influence within the household in determining the adoption of new home services. We then conducted a series of interviews with key informants, selected among the stakeholders of the home environment eco-system. This has be done in order to operate an additional Personas filtering and select only those that might actually be interested in the service solutions enabled by a seamless communication framework. For the remaining 5 Personas it was developed a specific context layer, consistent with their life values and their basic needs described in the internal layer. The context layer indeed contained all the characterizations related to the “home environment” usage context that could have been useful as reference point for the service designers during the development of the service concepts. The context layer definition has proceeded through several stages. For each Persona has been detailed a data sheet with all the specifications useful for the “home” context. Starting from this we built a scenario focused on the Persona daily life within his house, reproducing his/her daily aims, and his/her daily specific needs during his/her moving, playing, working, day in the home environment. Scenarios allows designers to imagine narrative situations in which the Personas are used as rounded characters, with specific objectives and aims, thus highlighting their unexpressed needs and their desiderata in a specific context [3, 4, 11]. With the help of non-professional actors 5 short movies based on the narrative scenario has been shot, showing moments of Personas daily life within his house.

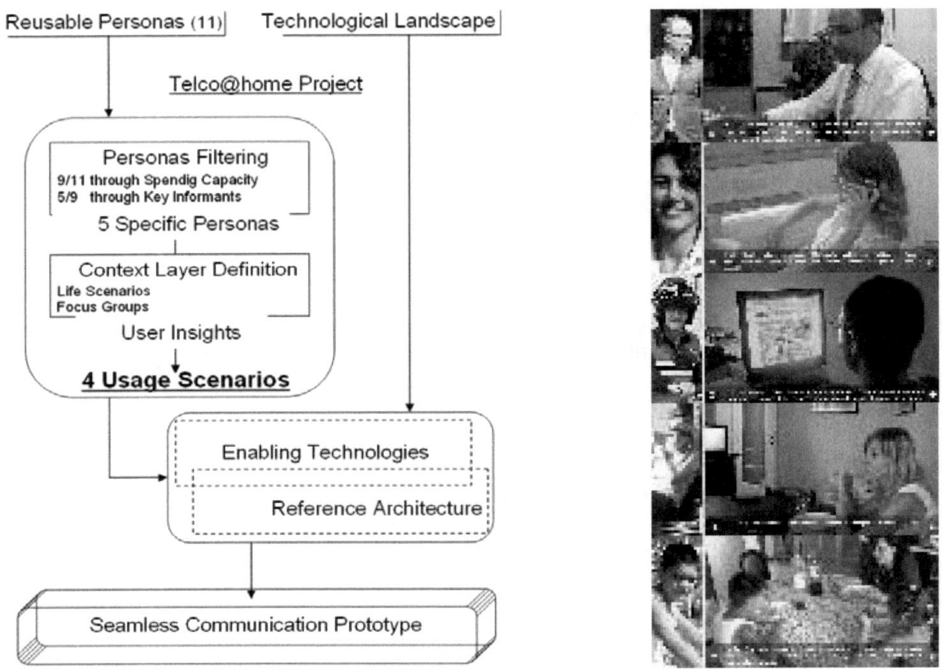

Figure 1. The personas layering framework applied to the telco@home project. From our set of 11 basic Personas, passing through the personas filtering process, 5 specific personas has been selected for this specific project. These Personas have been added with a context layer useful in order to define specific user insights. User insights have been instantiated in 4 Usage Scenarios then injected in the technological part of the project.

These clips were mainly used in the subsequent focus group validation step of the data sheet and scenarios developed in the previous phase. Five focus groups have been carried out, one for each Persona: in particular we collected in each group 6-8 people sharing the same socio-demographic characteristics of the Persona to validate (e.g. in Margherita's group we collected women, 35-45 years old , married with one child). The Focus satisfied the aim of collecting qualitative data needed to validate the assumptions made by the designers in the previous steps, integrating in this way scenarios and data

sheets with life experiences of real users. Participants of each focus have been shown, as a stimulus for the discussion, the short movie depicting the daily life of the Persona representing them; then they were asked to compare what they had seen with their actual experiences. As a result of this step we obtained a more detailed data sheet for each specific Persona able to highlight its specific needs for the home context. This card, along with the internal layer already available, provided a reference point for the developments priority for this context. Based on the data collected some unmet needs have been identified, few examples are listed below.
The need:

- to have a "zero" configuration home communication and media ecosystem
- to have an interaction as possible "hands free"
- to have personalized services for the various components of the family
- to eliminate explicit operations of login for each device or service
- to be "followed" by the services while moving through the home environment

With this insights gathered it was possible to translate them into usage scenarios that could meet the practical expectations of the end users.

3. User insight trasformed in usage scenarios

Starting from the needs gathered in the previous phase the following usage scenarios has been developed:

- <u>Communication scenario with seamless transition</u>: Gianni is talking on the cellphone while enters his house. When he sits on the sofa in front of the television the call is transferred on the screen and audio system (automatically or after vocal/GUI/gesture confirmation depending on the active profile) becoming potentially also a videocall (also depending on active profile).

- <u>Media scenario with incoming call</u>: Margherita is watching a movie when a call arrives on her cellphone. The movie (automatically or after vocal/GUI/gesture confirmation depending on the active profile) pauses and the call is potentially transferred to the audio/video media system (also depending on active profile).

- <u>Media scenario with seamless transition</u>: Gianni is watching a video clip that a friend sent to his cellphone. When he sits at his desk the video is transferred automatically on the screen of his PC (automatically or after vocal/GUI/gesture confirmation depending on the active profile) because the system recognizes it as the most suitable device for media fruition. The same scenario works from PC to the cellphone if the system recognizes that Gianni is moving outside the home environment.

- <u>Seamless multiroom transition scenario</u>: Margherita doing her housework roams through several rooms of the house while speaking with his husband about the school pick-up of their son Simone. Audio (and potentially video) call takes place without interruption of continuity through the rooms because the system tracking Margherita positioning inside the home environment dynamically select the best device available in each room.

With these usage scenarios developed it has been possible to select the opportune enabling technology frameworks (natural interaction layers, user profiling techniques, indoor positioning techniques, etc.) reflecting that in appropriate architectural choices for the service platform in order to maximize and prioritize those aspects most relevant in the value perception of the potential users.

4. Service Platform: the reference architecture

The results of service design with Personas allowed to take into account both a top-down view (considering current "off-the-shelf" available technologies) and a bottom-up view (general requirements derived from the user-driven service design phase as previously illustrated). The seamless communication and media delivery usage patterns considered in our work rely on the development and deployment of specific applications on top of a modular and adaptive service platform, integrating the home network with the external carrier network, additionally providing a common framework for integrating also CE devices.

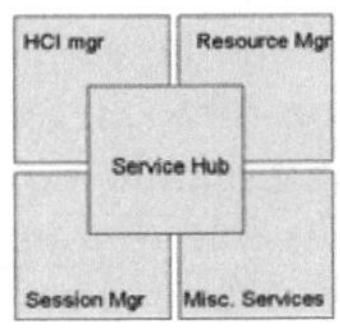

Figure 2. Services Functional Overview.

For such a realization, a residential service platform has been implemented devising it according to a reference architecture whose functional overview diagram is sketched in Figure 2 (additional details about the realization of this architecture can be found in [2]). Distinction about different responsibility areas has been carefully taken into account, leading to a separation between the service logic applications (deployed and running at the "Service Hub" level) and the ancillary modules responsible for sensing and actuating devices within the home environment (the "Resource Manager"). For the sake of the explanation, the Session manager and the Miscellaneous Services deal respectively with user service sessions (communication, media sharing) and with aspects common to all areas (e.g. identity management, authentication). Finally, the "HCI manager" deals with the multi-modal user interactions (e.g. voice, gesture, general I/O) with the rest of the system, providing integrated access modalities when the user roams among multiple environments (e.g. entering home) and/or when ambient devices become available (e.g. the user is in the range of an ambient microphone, ready for issuing vocal commands).

4.1. Technologies involved in the architectural realization

The mapping of the overall service architecture from the above described logical plane onto a physical one has required taking into account already commercially available options, in order to identify a well-founded path for enabling its realization in a future-proof home environment. As concern generic communication, all the modules are interconnected by a networked event bus, which spans multiple environments (e.g. home, outdoor, car) and is supported by different kind of networks (e.g. Wi-Fi, 3G, Ethernet LAN). The logical bus is physically implemented as an UPnP [15] infrastructure. Such a set of technologies is gaining momentum and its support is already available natively in many nowadays CE appliances and home network. The application self-discovery support and the provisioning of well defined interfaces, among applicative building-blocks, well suits with the dynamic envisaged environment where new modules (application, physical resource controllers) are time by time made available and are able to interact independently of their programming language and implementation. Another technological option proved to be well suited in this context has been the adoption of a rule engine as the enabler for ensuring the coordination among all the architectural building blocks. The "Service Hub" (Figure 2) is therefore the responsible for coordinating (by firing rules whenever proper events are emitted by other modules – e.g. a user is entering at home) the actions of the coordinating managers. Personalization and user profiling has been considered in order to ensure the possible best user experience independently of the environment (indoor, by using ambient microphones as well as outdoor, by being directly connected with Bluetooth headset to the home-based voice server).

4.2. Basic implementation example

In order to illustrate how the main architectural modules interact in a basic and very elementary usage scenario, in Figure 3 is represented a high-level interaction schema happening when a user enters home: his/her entrance is automatically detected and a welcome message is rendered by the media-center connected to the TV.

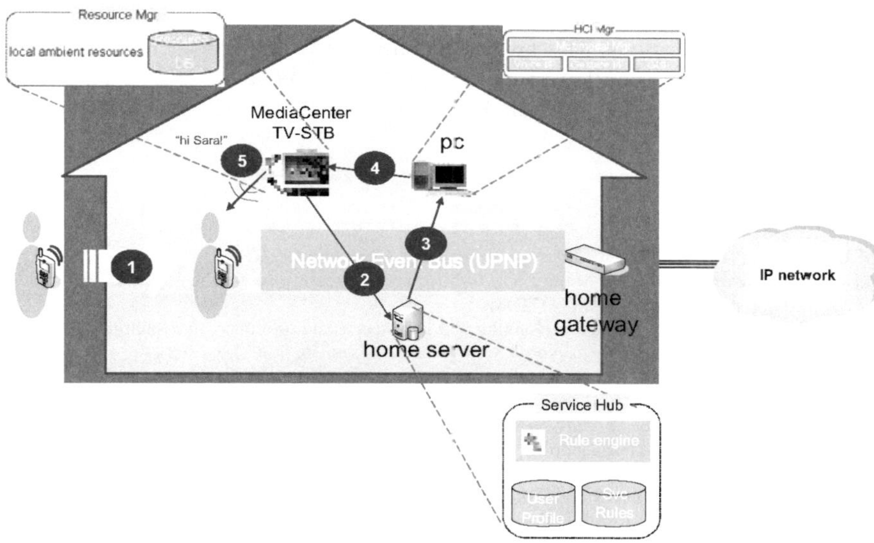

Figure 3. Architectural modules interactions involved in a basic usage scenario.

As soon as the user enters home (step 1), the proximity sensor controlled by the "Resource manager" detects his/her presence and a proper event is emitted on the networked event bus (step 2). The "Service Hub" (running on a home server) intercepts the event and fires the corresponding rules, according to context conditions and user preferences. As a consequence of the rule actions (step 3), a command is sent to the "HCI manager" in order to render the welcome message onto a proper media interface running in the living room. The "HCI manager" therefore contacts the "Resource manager" (step 4), activating its voice modules (the text-to-speech and speech recognizer) onto the proper actuator (i.e. the living-room media center) which eventually (step 5) will render the welcome message (and, for example, will be ready for receiving voice commands from the user and forward them to the "Service Hub", being this just one of the possible follow-ups of such a scenario). This very basic usage scenario shows by way of example how the previously illustrated architectural modules interact and cooperates. One additional and more complex usage scenario (e.g. involving seamless voice transition from outdoor to indoor) is fully detailed in [2].

This architecture is at the basis of the application developments and specific services realizations of the usage scenarios depicted in paragraph 3.

5. Conclusions

In this work we report the methodology and main results obtained in Telco@home, a Telecom Italia medium to long term research project. The project, whose goal was to develop a range of services and technological solutions enabling seamless communication and media fruition within the home, has been built both on a top-down stream, starting from an evolutionary technology landscape, and on a bottom up stream, considering the input from the potential users. The convergence between the service design stage, in which have been in depth investigated the unmet needs and unexpressed desiderata, then translated in usage scenarios, and the selection of enabling technologies, which led to a specific architectural solution, permitted us to prototype a set of meaningful transitions. This approach considering the end user insights a part of the service design process allowed us to prioritize the technical and service choices giving us a powerful tool in the design of service solutions for the home environment.

References

[1] DLNA, DLNA Networked Device Interoperability Guidelines, October 2006

[2] Bosco, P.G., Castrogiovanni, P., Martini, G. Architecture and realization of a residential Telco platform, *Proc. Intelligent Environment 2008,* (2008).

[3] Borglund, E., Öberg, L.-M., Scenario planning and Personas as aid to reduce uncertainty of future users, *Proc. 30th Information Systems Research Seminar in Scandinavia,* (2007)

[4] Carroll, J. M.: Five reasons for scenario-based design, *Interacting with Computers*, vol. 13(1), (2000) 43-60

[5] Cooper, A.*, The Inmates Are Running the Asylum: Why High Tech Products Drive Us Crazy and How To Restore The Sanity*, Sams, Indianapolis, 1999

[6] Guercio, E., Marcengo, A. and Rapp, A.: How to connect user research and not so forthcoming technology scenarios – The extended home environment case study, *International Journal of Social Sciences*, vol 2, Number 4, (2007) 203--208.

[7] Grudin, J., Pruitt, J., Personas: participatory design and product development: an infrastructure engagement. *Proc. Participatory Design Conference* 2002, (2002) 144-161

[8] Marcengo, A., Guercio, E., Rapp, A. Personas layering: a cost effective model for service design in medium-long term telco research project, to appear in *Proc. HCII 2009*, (2009)

[9] McGinn, J. ,Kotamraju, N., Data-driven Personas development, *Proc. CHI 2008*, (2008) 1521-1524

[10] Neiters, J. E., Subbarao, I., Iftikhar, A., Making Personas Memorable. *Proc. CHI 2007*, (2007) 1817-1823.

[11] Nielsen, L., *Engaging Personas and Narrative Scenarios*, Dept of Informatics vol. 17, PhD Series, Samfundslitteratur, Copenhagen, 2004

[12] Pruitt, J., Grudin, J.: Personas: practice and theory, *Proc. Designing for User Experiences 2003*, (2003) 1-15.

[13] Pruitt, J., Adlin, T., *The Persona Lifecycle: Keeping People in Mind Throughout Product Design,* .Morgan Kaufmann, San Francisco, 2006

[14] Sinha, R.: Persona development for information rich domains, *Proc. CHI 2003*, (2003) 830-831

[15] UPnP Forum, UPnP Device Architecture 1.0, July 2006

Special Session on Network Intelligence

Intelligent Environments 2009
V. Callaghan et al. (Eds.)
IOS Press, 2009

doi:10.3233/978-1-60750-034-6-447

Solving problems of optimization of cellular networks for mobile telephony: Towards a dynamic architecture based on agents

Chaker MEZIOUD[a] and Mohammed Khireddine KHOLLADI[b]
[a] *Department of Computer Sciences. Sciences faculty of the engineer. University Mentouri of Constantine. cmezioud@yahoo.fr*
[b] *Department of Computer Sciences. Sciences faculty of the engineer. University Mentouri of Constantine, kholladi@yahoo.fr*

Abstract. In recent years, wireless communication systems have experienced tremendous growth, especially in broadcasting, television or handheld computers to the new generation with Web access (UMTS, GPRS). Meanwhile, the techniques of radio are now crucial to a growing number of services. As a result, the size and complexity of applications increases. Current technology can not protect us from design problems. That is why we need a high-level modeling, which we will analyze the organization between the different elements of the system and the interactions between them. The interest of multi-agent systems stems from the collective behavior produced by the interaction of several autonomous entities called agents and flexible, these interactions that revolve around cooperation, competition and coexistence between these agents. However, techniques from the field, focus more on the expression of inter-agents. The expression of the mobility point of view of distributed systems is not described. A property once acquired, will allow the process to choose for themselves to move on the sites of a network to work locally on the resources and make their exchange interactions. Why we propose in this paper a formalization that uses a process algebra, which is the π -calculus to develop self-adaptive systems that can respond to the form of the problem.

Keywords. GSM, Cellular Networks, Multi Agents systems, Algebra of process, Dynamic Optimization

1. Introduction

The mobile communications industry has grown prodigiously over the past decade. It is developed beyond all expectations. Thus, at present, millions of subscribers enjoy the services offered by cellular networks. Most networks use the GSM (Global System for Mobile Communications). Cellular networks are systems with high stress factors [11]. The real-time adjustment of the solution is currently impossible. The optimization is then used to anticipate changes to be made to optimize network performance for its development and reduce the costs of its restructuring. The system must not only provide a solution, but also be able to react to failures and hazards in the readjustment of its solution, or be able to deal with problems whose data are only partially known, and for which the information arrives over time. The static design of the network in order to provide a minimum level of service at rush hour to the effect of wasting system resources when they are not well exploited. The dynamic aspect adds a new dimension to the problem of design (design) cellular networks. The detailed analysis and understanding the behavior of traffic is an essential process for the planning of mobile radio systems. As a first step, the idea led us to consider the development of a design process that can manage the changes occurring on the network during its phases of growth and maturation. The traffic demand varies over time and space. The network is about, in addition to long-term changes required by the rise of traffic on customer growth, changes in user behavior and changes in coverage. To overcome these requirements, the network has to adapt and grow. The call for a process of dynamic optimization, seems a promising outcome. This process is run periodically at points of decision, the objective of preparing the system to adapt to changes in the current period, while trying to take account of later periods, predicting areas where increased capacity is required and making intelligent changes necessary. Why we found ourselves before the need to involve multi-agent systems. The general architecture of the system proposed redevelopment is based on a set of agents of different types. Each agent is responsible for solving a problem or performing a particular task, an approach that seemed best suited as a first step. We thought thereafter that the integration of the concept of mobility, in terms of processes or interactions in the architecture of the proposed system would lead to better results. The question was to find the explicit framework for the specification and design of the system. The choice was made to the process algebra π-calculus, for its ability to dynamically change the topology of applications. In a first part of this article, we situate the context of networks of mobile telephony, his problem, and key concepts that refer to it. A brief section will be devoted to the presentation of Multi Agents. We attach particular importance to the process π-calculus, in particular to the most suitable for our study. To reach π algebra the development of the proposed approach and optimized through the integration of the concept of mobility. The last section will be the target of a conclusion and perspective.

2. Mobile Phones

We will first define the concepts of GSM mobile network, and then see its equipment and its hardware architecture.

2.1. GSM Network

A mobile network is a network that enables communication of individuals moving through a link or a radio channel. The general architecture of a GSM network [5], can be divided into three systems:

- The radio subsystem (BSS): The radio subsystem consists of several entities: mobile, the base station (BTS) controller and a base station (BSC).
- The network subsystem (NSS): plays a key role in a mobile network, its components support all the functions of monitoring and analysis of information contained in databases needed to establish connection.

- The system in operation and maintenance (OSS): it comprises three main activities of management: administration, business management and technical management.

2.2. Equipments of a network GSM

The material architecture of a network GSM, as well as the various existing streams of data between the previous equipments is illustrated by the Figure 1.

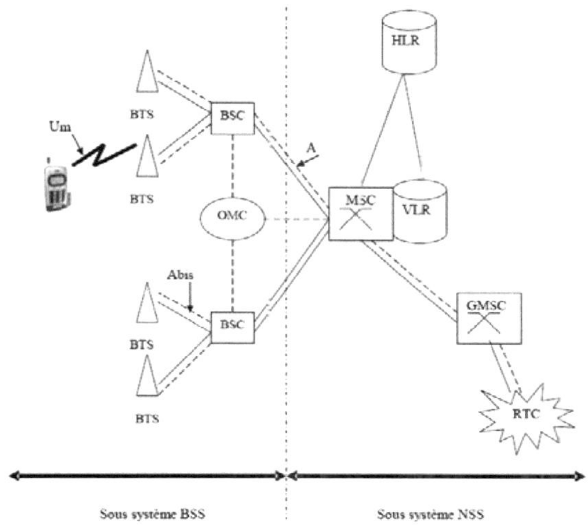

Figure 1. Material architecture of a network GSM

For our study, we will look at radio subsystem and its main entities.

2.3. Material architecture of under system radio BSS

The BSS includes the BTS, which are transmitter-receivers, but having a minimum of intelligence, and the BSC assures the control of a set of BTS.

2.3.1. Function of the BTS

The BTS is a set of transmitter-receivers called TRX. A BTS has for function the management of the transmissions radio (modulation, demodulating, equalization, coding and correction of errors). It also manages the coat connection of data for the exchange of road marking between motives and network infrastructure of the operator. Therefore, a BTS can manage at most hundred of simultaneous communications.

2.3.2. Function of the BSC

The BSC is the intelligent organ of under system radio. It has a relay role for the alarms and the statistics emanating from BTS towards the centre of exploitation and from maintenance. The BSC is a data bank for the software versions and the data of configuration downloaded by the operators on the BTS. The BSC pilots transfers between two cells (zone of the territory lit by an antenna" BTS "): it informs on one hand the new BTS who is going to take care of the subscriber "the mobile" while informing the back-end system (HLR) of the new localization of the subscriber.

Integration of the world of the agents, will allow us to conceive methods adaptive automobile, this last idea will make the objective of the next section.

3. Multi-Agents Systems

Multi-Agent Systems based on the following principle: instead of having a single agent in charge of the entire problem, we consider several agents who each have over a part of the problem. The solution to the original problem is obtained through all the individual behaviors and interactions, i.e. a collective resolution.

Called multi-agent system (or SMA), a system composed of the following elements [13]:

- An environment E, i.e. a space with a general metric.
- A set of objects O. These objects are located, i.e. that for any object, it is possible at a given time, to associate a position in E. These objects are passive, i.e. they can be collected, created, destroyed and modified by the agents.
- A set A of agents, which are individuals objects ($A \subset O$), which represent the active entities of the system.
- A set of R of relations between objects (and therefore agents) between them.
- A set of operations Op allowing agents of A to perceive, produce, consume, transform and manipulate objects from O.
- Operators responsible for representing the application of these operations and the world reaction to this attempt to change, that we call the laws of the universe.

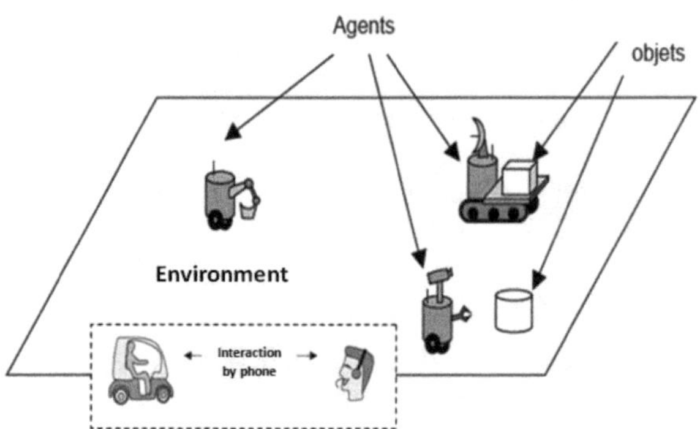

Figure 2. Example of a multi-agent system

3.1. Definition of an agent

According to an increasing number of researchers defines an agent, as being a computer system situated in an environment [7], of which it is capable of acting in perfect autonomy on its actions, with the aim of making meet the objectives of its conception, with the following characteristics:

- An agent is an entity situated in a particular environment, which perceives the state of the environment through his sensors, and which acts on its environment through its effecters.

- It is conceived to carry out specific objectives, and it has particular purposes to be affected.
- It is autonomous, since it has the control of its internal state, and its own behaviour.
- It is capable of explaining and of producing solutions for flexible problems. It needs to be at the same moment reactive (capable of answering in opportunity, in changes which arise in the environment, it is capable of acting by anticipating the future purposes).

3.2. Models of existing agents

3.2.1. Reactive Agent

Architecture of reagent agent is architecture in which the decisions of action are taken at the time of the execution, from not enough information (information got at the present moment). The execution of these actions always follows the change occurring in the environment. The mechanism of decision is often very simple, the accent being put on the robustness rather than on the exactness and the optimum of the behaviour.

Remark:

Concerning the reagent agent:

- No representation clarifies of the environment.
- No memory of its history, nor explicit purpose.
- Agents' large number (> 100), homogeneous in fine grain.

3.2.2. Deliberative Agent

This architecture contains a mechanism of decision consisting of a consideration explicit on the various possibilities of action by using, for example a generation of plans or by taking into account the utility hoped by the actions. The mechanism of decision which can be very complex, the accent is put on the optimum and on the exactness of the behaviour to the detriment of the robustness and of the time of execution.

3.2.3. Cognitive Agent

This type of agent possesses an explicit representation of its environment, so he can take into account his past, and he is complex in his conception. This type of agent when it exists in a system it is in small number.

3.3. Different types of interactions

The interaction is the mechanism which returns set existing agents in the more dynamic system, by the fact than it brings to light the mechanisms of communication and cooperation [8]. With the means of the interaction all the entities plunged into an environment, can interact according to various forms:

3.3.1. Interaction without communication

It bases itself on the inference of the actions of the others

Example:

- Use of the theory of the games with matrices of gain.
- Updating of a constraint or an updating of dependence.

3.3.2. Interaction via the communication

It is a set finished by signals without interpretation and by fixed syntax.

Example: multi-planning agents.

Example: communication by the environment via tracks (signals) which leave the agents and who can be perceived by the other agents.

3.3.3. Interaction via the sending of messages and plans

The interaction is made by sending of messages, such as calls of methods of object-oriented languages. In the sending of plans, exchanges of partial plans are made so that one a knot of exchange of the partial plans of interpretation with the other knots of the system.

3.3.4. Interaction via a blackboard

The interaction via a blackboard is a technique which proved its efficiency in the conception of the systems, and this used type of technique so that the various existing agents in a given system can to communicate itself through a common space called "blackboard", From which the mechanism and to deposit the information or the knowledge in this zone, the concerned agent will come to get back this information. We introduce this technique of communication, when all the agents are in centralized or distributed architecture. The main characteristics of this type of interaction (blackboard) are the following ones:

- No direct communication.
- Interaction via the sharing of the same space of work or system.

The figure 3 illustrates this mechanism. A system containing a set of agents based on this type of interaction possesses the following elements:

- The knowledge·
- The blackboard·
- The control mechanism.

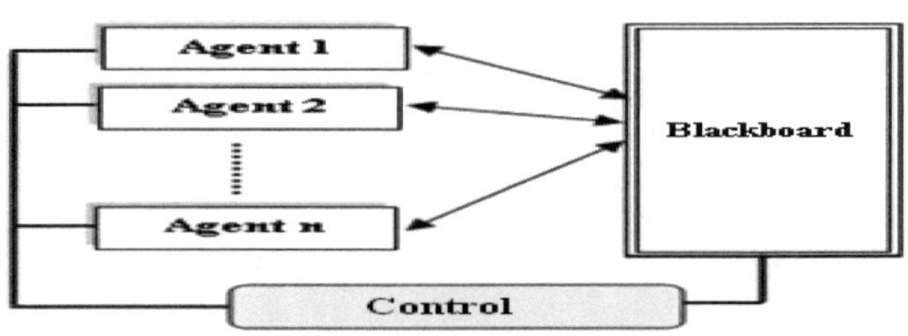

Figure 3. Agents' interaction by the blackboard

3.4. Mobile Agents

The pattern of mobility of mobile agents is derived from two different domains, the agents coming from the artificial intelligence with the multi-systems agents [3] and systems distributed with the migration of process [2]. To simplify, we can say that the plan to mobile agents is a generalization of the migration of process where the movement is for the initiative of the code. We speak then about a proactive migration. The main characteristic of a mobile agent is to have certain autonomy thanks to the proactive migration, that it is strong or weak.

4. Presentation of π -calculus

To develop safe software, it is necessary to manage at first at the good to formalize it that is why it makes use of formal languages as π -calculus. A last one who allows us to establish a mathematical model to verify certain properties expected from the software (safety, non-blocking, liveliness). The algebras of process are adequate executives for the specification and the check of reagent systems. This domain knew various approaches: CSP [1], DC [4], π -calculus [6]. The fundamental abstraction is that we are interested in the behaviour of a process only through a certain number of points of interaction called "canals". The synchronization and the communication are then expressed by internal and external laws of composition. It is necessary to note that both in CCS and π -calculus, we make no hypothesis on the relative speeds of execution of the various processes, which are thus presumed to progress each with their rhythm. π -calculus is a formal language, to argue about the communicating distributed systems. He allows furthermore describing systems of mobile processes that are systems links of communication between processes of which the processes as well as can change place in time. The purpose looked for by π -calculus is the introduction of the concept of mobility, which was non-existent in CCS. The objective is to authorize the dynamic reconfiguration of the topology of the applications.

4.1. Polyadic π -calculus

Polyadic π -calculus allows the transmission of a tuple of values during an interaction. We use in our study this version of π -calculus to benefit from an important property that is the parameterization, through the simultaneous emission of a consecutives series, in an order given to a process. Numerous software exceeds the million lines of code. It is difficult to take into account such sizes with the old formal methods. By the use of some formal techniques of π -calculus and more exactly polyadic π -calculus, the abstraction of numerous details through the parameterization allows to reduce the specification of the system to an acceptable size.
The reserved syntax is the following one:

$$P ::= 0 \mid \alpha.P \mid P \mid P \mid P+P \mid [x=y]P \mid [x \neq y]P \mid (\nu \vec{u})P \mid A(\vec{u})$$

Where prefixes α (actions) are defined as follows:

$$p ::= \tau \mid \alpha(\vec{u}) \mid \overline{\alpha}<\vec{u}>$$

With:

$\vec{u}$: Denote a list of variables also called "names".

$\alpha(\vec{u})$: reception of a list of variable u on the canal α

$\alpha<\vec{u}$: emission of a list of variable u on the canal α

4.2. π-calculus higher order

It can not only provide variables and channels but also the process [10].

Example:

P | Q avec P ≡ α (x,y,z)• 0 and Q ≡ α (u,v,R)• v (u)• R

P | Q ≡ α (x,y,S)• 0 | α (u,v,R)• v (u)• R

In the example above, the S was transferred from the process P in Q.

5. Presentation of the approach

A BTS is an element of emission and reception, having a minimum of intelligence, which has for function the management of the transmissions radios. It is the first component of the network, Person in charge on the coverage of the request of a broadcasting subscriber. So that another BTS which will be informed to take care of the receiving subscriber. The relative load of a cell corresponds to the report between the demand in traffic on this cell and its actual capacity [9]. A cell which serves many motives sees its coverage area being reduced, thus holes of cover appear and appeals will be thrown back. To avoid this type of problems, connected to the increase of the traffic, the resource BTS must be exploited in a reliable way (increase its intelligence). Cells having a load approaching the 100 % see each other applicants of help of the other nearby BST having no load "cells candidates". What can lead an automatic reorganization of the plan of frequencies, without the attribution of new cards TRX or the insertion of new BTS. A mobile becomes attached to the cell which offers him the best quality radio on the experimental canal (see figure 4: cell with intermittent line).

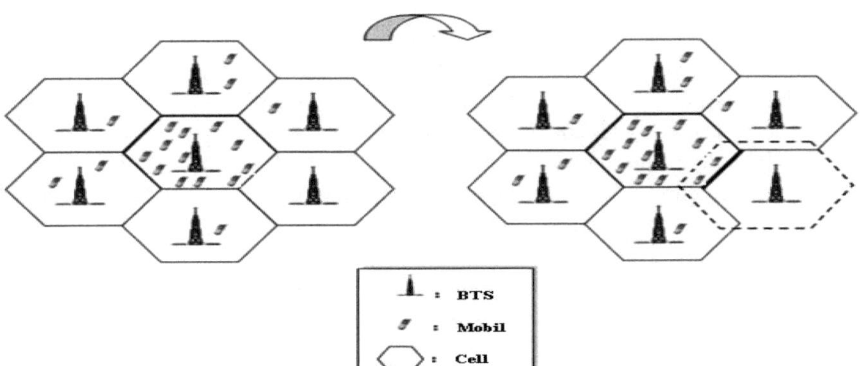

Figure 4. Process of optimization of the cellular network

When a mobile passes from a cell to the other one, he sees the pilot of the first cell weakening, and that of second to grow gradually. The affectation of an appeal of a mobile to a BTS is a process which involves several parameters (ex: azimut, tilt, power pilots) [3].

Tilt: angle of inclination of an antenna in a vertical plan. The zone covered by the antenna decreases and the intensity of the power averages received in the cell increase.

Azimut: orientation of the main lobe of the antenna in the horizontal plan. A modification of the angle azimut can be useful further to an effect of mask connected to the landscape or to the buildings (problem of interferences).

Power of the pilots: indicate to the mobile the cell with which he has to be connected (the extent of the cell). The objective of the proposed process of optimization is to supply from the beginning, a plan of expansion of the cellular network spreading out over several periods, according to the received changes. Therefore, as shows it the figure 5, the system receives as entered an initial configuration of the network and elaborates an optimized network. To maintain a collection of diversified solutions (history) will allow a better and faster adaptation of the network to the registered changes, during the next phases.

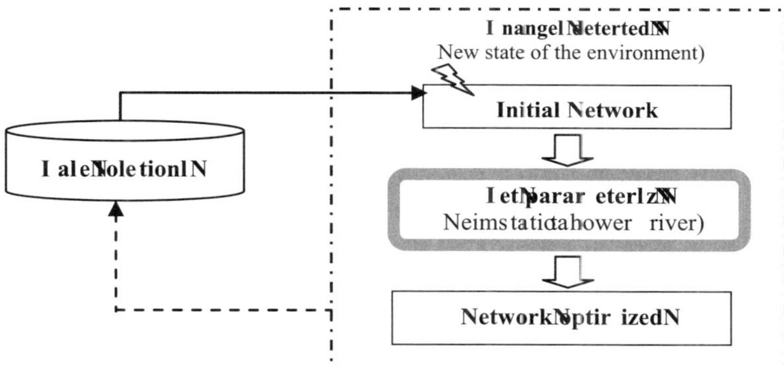

Figure 5. General principle of the process of optimization

The adjustment of the solution is begun only in the recording of the changes on the environment. The approach is defined by a succession of states of the environment E = {state 1, state 2, state n}. Every state is characterized by:

- InitialNetwork
- Network optimized
- Changes detected (New state of the environment)
- Set parameters: (Azimut, tilt, power driver)
- Base solutions

5.1. General architecture of the system

The general architecture of the system of optimization consists of agents' various types. Every agent is responsible on the resolution of a problem or the execution of a particular task.

- **Cell Agent:** this agent is in charge of by the detection of the overload of a cell (reactive agent), through the calculation of the following function:

$$L = \frac{A}{C}$$

With:
L: Load with the cell.
A: Demand in traffic on the cell.
C: Actual capacity of the cell.

If the load affects the 100 %, the cell is declared "Applicant" otherwise it is declared "Candidate" with a degree of participation (number of communications to be able to take care).

- **Supervisor Agent:** the role of this agent (deliberative agent) is to list every time which are the cells of type: "applicant" and "Candidate". After collaboration with GIS Agent, Supervisor Agent will decide what is the nearby cell (the closest in the localization of the subscriber) which has to cover the zone of overload. In addition, delegate to the Evaluator Agent the task to calculate the necessary parameters (azimut, tilt, power of the pilots). These last ones will be again sent to the Supervisor Agent to assure a remote customization of the BTS (regulation of antennas) of the concerned cell. In addition, demand for Historic Agent to make a saving of this configuration of the network (solution) according to the state registered by the environment.
- **GIS Agent:** this agent (cognitive agent) possesses a geographical representation of the region of the cellular network (line, surface, dimensions), with its various changes (in case of appearance of obstacles or new constructions).
  Remark: GIS Agent possesses a geographical representation in the form of cells in 3D, for every moment t. what we call: *cell3D - t*.
- **Evaluator Agent:** according to the dimensions of the zone to be covered, this agent takes the initiative to calculate the necessary parameters at the level of: the azimut, the tilt and powers of the pilots. It sends these parameters to Supervisor Agent.
- **Historic Agent:** this agent preservation the history of the previous solutions, according to the arisen events. What will allow the re-use of the good solutions for a better and faster adaptation of the network during the future phases.
  Remark: Once the overload is crossed, (the subscriber moved towards another cell, either decrease of the communications), the network returns again to its initial configuration.

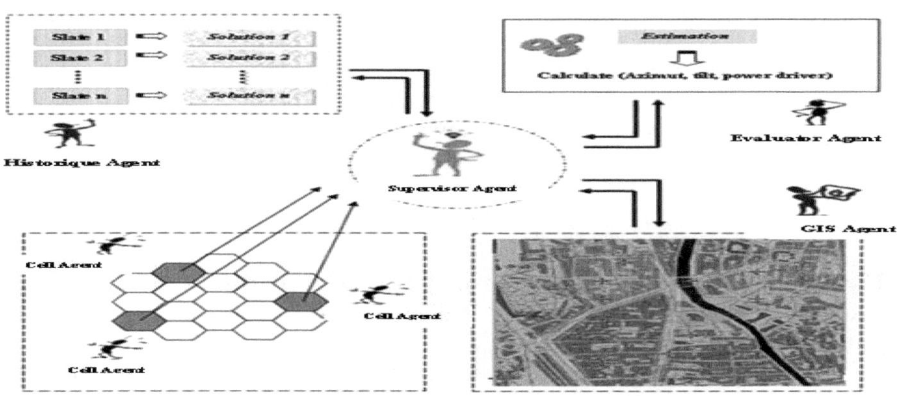

Figure 6. General architecture of the System

5.2. Dynamic Architecture

If we want to give a model of the previous architecture, in terms of process. It will be illustrated in Figure 7.

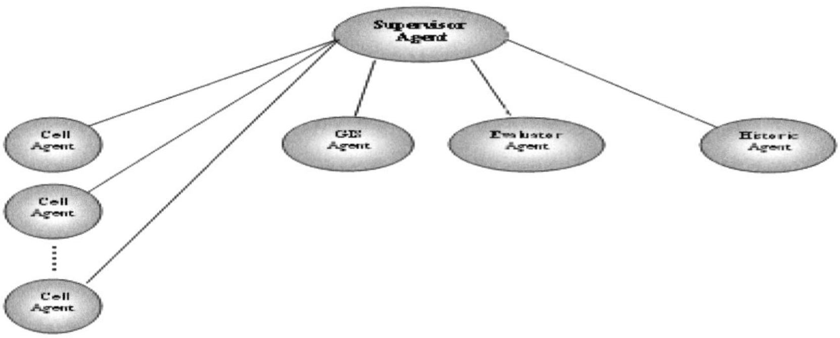

Figure 7. Modelling of the previous system

In this respect, our system configuration is described as communicating processes. These are linked by bonds (channels or ports):

```
CONFIG = ( V SA_emisport, SA_receport, CA_emisport, CA_receport ,
           GA_emisport, GA_receport, EA_emisport, EA_receport,
           HA_emisport, HA_receport)

         SA ( SA_emisport,SA_receport )     |
         CA ( CA_emisport,CA_receport )     |
         GA ( GA_emisport,GA_receport )     |
         EA ( EA_emisport,EA_receport )     |
         HA ( HA_emisport,HA_receport )     |
         COM (SA_emisport , CA_receport)    |
         COM (SA_emisport , GA_receport)    |
         COM (SA_emisport , EA_receport)    |
         COM (SA_emisport , HA_receport)    |
         COM (SA_receport, CA_emisport)     |
         COM (SA_receport, GA_emisport)     |
         COM (SA_receport, EA_emisport)     |
         COM (SA_receport, HA_emisport) )
```

With:

SA : Supervisor Agent
CA : Cell Agent
GA : GIS Agent
EA : Evaluator Agent
HA : Historic Agent

One of the issues:

1. In the event of a loss of a link (channel) between the agents. How can we intervene?
2. And if we talk in terms of value, is there a way to reduce the communication time between these agents? On the basis of π -calculus as language, in the formal specification of agents of the previous system, we will certainly lead to better results. For example: if the Agent Supervisor loses its communication link with the GIS Agent, but the expected optimization process will not be achieved. The answer to such a concern π -calculus as formal language provides a dynamic reconfiguration of π is this: The topology of applications. It means that Supervisor Agent may delegate its link to one of his agents to complete the task required (see Figure 8).

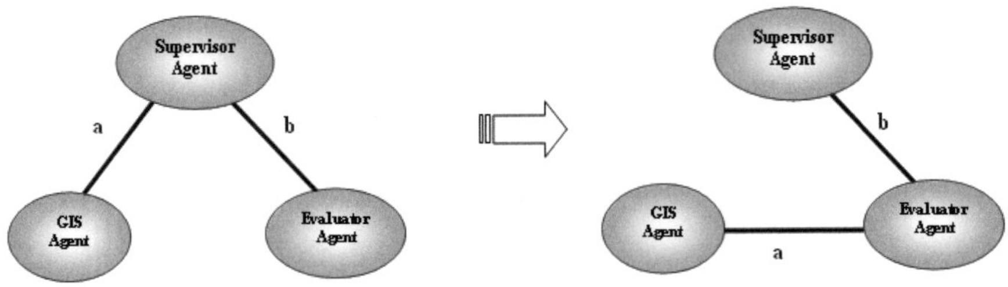

Figure 8. The mobility of links between Agents

We can translate this mobility of links in π -calculus, as follows:

SA $\equiv$ b a $\bullet$ SA' and

GA $\equiv$ a (x) $\bullet$ GA' and

EA $\equiv$ b (x) $\bullet$ a x $\bullet$ EA'

A second opportunity to be able to negotiate, it is in case the Evaluator Agent can move to the Cells Agents, which surround the overloaded cell, to intervene in every detected saturation. The nearby cells deliver their three parameters: azimuth, tilt, power signal, to be able to assure with regard to their current loads. In that case, the Evaluator Agent possesses the update to be applied and is going to move from a cell to the other one (by crossing six cells), and by getting back three parameters of every cell. As shows it the following figure:

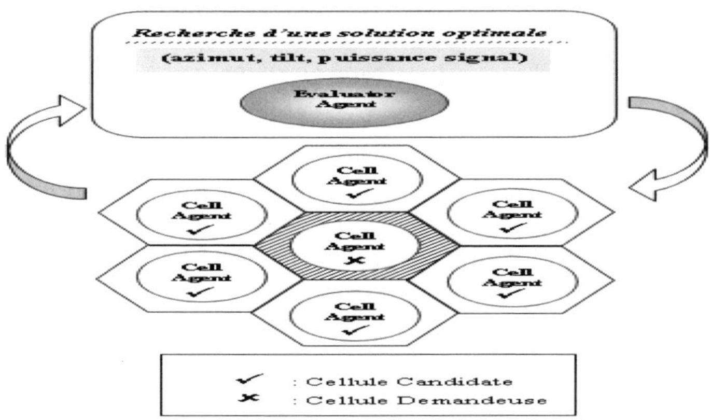

Figure 9. Movement of the Evaluator Agent

5.3. Advantages

Through this new approach of dynamic architecture, various advantages will be gained, we quote the most essential:

- The first advantage to be quoted, it is the decrease of the intensity of information exchange between the various agents.
- The second considerable advantage is the decrease of waiting times. It happens frequently that the waiting time of the answer of a request is longer than the time of treatment necessary for the realization of the service.
- We decrease considerably the cases of problems of connection (breaks of links), and in case of a break, the agent can delegate his link to another agent.

6. Conclusion and perspectives

Through this paper, we presented a new solution of a problem which enough took time researchers, in the field of optimization and which was the major concern of mobile phone operators. A solution of agents' base, which assures revisions and recycling of the network through an effective cooperation with various agents, where every agent is responsible on the resolution of a problem or the execution of a well determined task. Our work knew several stages. Having spoken about the domain of the networks of the mobile telephony and its main concepts, we thought of a presentation of domain of the multi-systems of agents and the formal language π-calculus . To arrive at the nucleus of our work that is the description of the solution proposed with its main points, in particular the presentation of the general architecture of the proposed system. We are not satisfied to us with the solutions acquired through this approach; we thought that the integration of the notion of mobility, at the level of the architecture of the proposed system, will allow ending in better results. Reason for which we appealed to the algebra of process π-calculus , for its capacity to be able to develop dynamically the topology of the applications. As perspectives, we think that the development of a software which bases itself on a method of optimization, which supports the important concepts and the techniques already revealed through our study, guide the mobile network to improve network quality optimized manually, and a reduction in the time required for this repetitive task for experts radio. The gain in performance is also reflected in the reduction for the operator investments in infrastructure. In future work we will try to propose new methods, allowing better planning for operators of mobile telephony during the installation of a new cellular network. Optimal planning, which may raise the corrections encountered, once the telephone network is operational, while monitoring the deployment of the traffic.

References

[1] C.A.R, Hoare, "Communicating Sequential Processes". Prentice Hall, 1985.
[2] D.S. Milojicic, F. Douglis, Y. Paindaveine, R.Weeler, and S. Zhou. « Process migration ». ACM Compting Surveys, 32(3) :241–299, Septembre 2000. 19.
[3] Jacques Ferber. "The multi-agent systems. Intelligence Science Articielle. Intereditions 1995. 19, 21, 44
[4] R. Milner, "Communication and Concurrency" Prentice Hall, 1989.
[5] J. CEDR, A. Petrowski, P. Siarry, E. Taillard. 'Méthaeuristiques difficult for optimization." Edition Eyrolles 2003.
[6] R. Milner, "The polyadic π-calculus : a tutorial.Logicand Algebra of Specification" . Springer-Verlag, 1993.
[7] S. Girodon. "GSM, GPRS and UMTS." June 2002.
[8] P. Godlewski, P. Martins, Mr. Coupechoux. "Cellular Concepts and Settings Radio." February 1999.
[9] R. Jennings. "On agent-based software engineering". Departement of electronic and Computer Science, University of Southampton, Southampton SO17 IBJ, UK Received 21 September 99.
[10] R. Milner, J. Parrow and D.Walker. "A calculs of mobile processes". Journal of Information and Computation. 1990.
[11] P. Godlewski, P. Martins, M. Coupechoux. Concepts Cellulaires et Paramètres Radio. Février 1999.
[12] Audrey Dupont. Étude d'une métaheuristique hybride pour l'affectation de fréquences dans les réseaux tactiques évolutifs. Octobre 2005.
[13] Ferber J., Les Systèmes Multi-Agents. Vers une intelligence collective. Interéditions, 1995.

Intelligent Environments 2009
V. Callaghan et al. (Eds.)
IOS Press, 2009

doi:10.3233/978-1-60750-034-6-460

Perceptual Evaluation of Radio Signal Quality Degradation

Sergey ZABLOTSKIY [a,1], Thomas MÜLLER [b] and Wolfgang MINKER [a]
[a] *Institute of Information Technology, University of Ulm, Germany*
[b] *Daimler AG, Ulm, Germany*

Abstract. In this paper we present an approach, which avoids expansive and time consuming subjective assessment of audio quality degradation, caused by different nature disturbances during the transmitting and receiving of stereo audio signal through the radio channel. This approach is based on the basic version of PEAQ (Perceptual Evaluation of Audio Quality) method, optimized generally for audio codec testing. The MOV (Model Output Variables) vector of the PEAQ method is transformed to the transmitted audio quality degradation scale, using the combination of neural networks and genetic algorithms.

Keywords. Perceptual evaluation, PEAQ, radio signal, audio quality degradation, neural network, genetic algorithm

Introduction

The manufacturers of radio receivers and other radio equipment have to estimate the quality of the new product or test exemplar and compare it with existent equipment. Among other things the common listening comprehension of the perceived degradation with respect to the original (reference) audio signal has to be taken into consideration, because humans with their own listening comprehension are supposed to be the main end-users of the designed equipment. Since any high-quality reliable subjective assessments are very expensive and time consuming it is strongly desirable to have a tool for automatic perceptual evaluation of audio quality degradation. This is a fundamental idea behind the PEAQ method, as specified in ITU-R BS.1387 recommendation [1]. The measurement method in this recommendation is applicable to most types of audio signal processing equipment, both digital or analog. However it is expected, that many applications will focus on audio codecs. Test results, obtained with the help of the software PQevalAudio, compliant with the basic model of PEAQ [2], disagree with the Mean Opinion Score (MOS) of the the test persons. The Objective Difference Grade (ODG) of this software, after appropriate linear rescaling, is always significantly smaller than MOS. This implies that the PQevalAudio estimates the quality of the received (degraded) radio signal to be permanently lower than it seems to be for subjects from the test group. One of the obvious reasons is that the human requirements for audio files (signals), degraded by audio coding (recoding), are significantly higher than the requirements for files, degraded by the entire transmitting-receiving process.

[1] Corresponding Author

The output of the software is not only final ODG value, but are also MOV's combined using a neural network to give an ODG value [2]. Our idea is to create another neural network [3] and train it on the basis of our own subjective estimations set to be able to use the whole algorithm for automatic perceptual evaluation of transmitted through the radio channel audio quality degradation.

1. Alignment of Reference and Received Audio Signals

All test audio files were divided into two unequal parts. The smaller one consists of artificially simulated audio signals, degraded by the additionally applied noise signals of different types, which heard to sound more or less real comparing with the radio noise. The second part of the test audio material was obtained under conditions, maximally close to the real situation - the reference short audio files were captured from different Internet radio stations with acceptable quality, which were aired at the same time (with a small time delay) in our local area. Degraded audio files were captured from the corresponding radio stations in different conditions: inside the buildings and outside, in the driving car.

PQevalAudio software assumes two input audio signals (reference and degraded) to be time and gain aligned. Therefore all the files were aligned even before the subjective assessment stage to be accurate, when finding the dependency between MOS and MOV's.

1.1. Variable Delay Compensation

The reference and degraded files, transmitted through the radio channel, have not only the constant delay between each other, but also the variable delay changing through the entire audio signal. This delay should also be compensated before performing subjective estimations and processing.

Constant delay is compensated, calculating the maximum value of the cross-correlation function. The corresponding value of the sample shift is taken as the constant delay and compensated. The variable delay compensation is an increasingly complex process. Both reference and degraded stereo files are converted into monaural ones and then divided into blocks of chosen length (2205 samples blocks were chosen for a 44,1 kHz sample rate). For each pair of blocks the mean delay is found. This delay vector is then filtered by the use of digital filter described by the coefficients of the symmetric Hanning window, normalized by the sum of its elements. The Hanning window vector length was set to 16 covering 0.8 seconds of the audio file. The symmetric Hanning window with variable length is used to avoid loosing of audio information during filtering at the beginning and end of the file.

The result delays vector is then linearly interpolated for all samples in the file. This means, that for each sample of the degraded file the necessary shift is known, which is finally performed by the use of cubic interpolation. For the most of the received files the variable delay seems to have the linear or close to linear dependency from the time. An example is shown in Figure 1.

Sometimes due to the strong sudden noise or other rapidly changed environmental conditions there are areas of the variable delay graph, where the curve seems to be either randomly changing or its shape differs significantly from the other main part of the

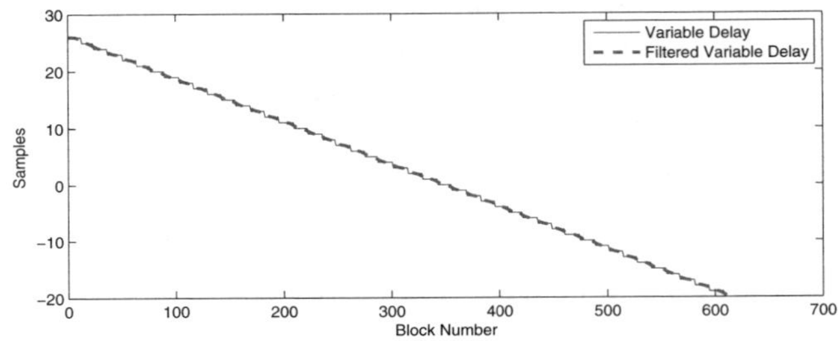

Figure 1. Variable delay between reference and degraded files.

graph. Computationally evaluated, the advanced algorithm using the linear approximation of the variable delay vector for the described areas is able to align such files more properly. This means that the average difference between reference and degraded files after variable delay compensation with the use of approximation is usually not larger (mostly significantly smaller) than the average difference between these files after variable delay compensation without approximation of such areas. This is statistically proved by the use of least square method for linear dependency approximation, calculated on all delays data out of such "untrusted" areas. These areas are automatically recognized by the algorithm with the help of assigned acceptable level of the delays standard deviation at the small period of time. The curves, showing the variable delay with and without approximation, are presented in Figure 2.

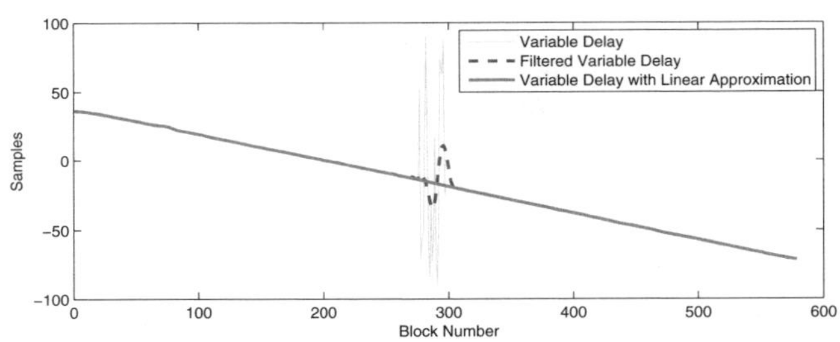

Figure 2. Variable delay between reference and degraded files with and without approximation.

In some specific cases the graph of the variable delay seems to change randomly. It may be statistically shown, that in this case it is better to avoid filtering of such unstable data. It seems to be preferable to replace the delays vector by the zero-vector. The recognition of such case is automatically performed by the algorithm and only the threshold needs to be set properly. We assigned it to 0.1, i.e. the acceptable number of "trusted" data should not be less than 10% of all block delays data. If we chose 0.05 as a threshold, we would get the approximation graph, shown in Figure 3. However the average difference in this case is larger than the average difference, if we would prefer to take a zero-vector instead of the applying of approximation.

The final advanced variable delay compensation algorithm, suggested in this work, has shown its acceptable alignment capability on the huge amount of audio signals captured in the real conditions without the necessity of any additional manual adaptation.

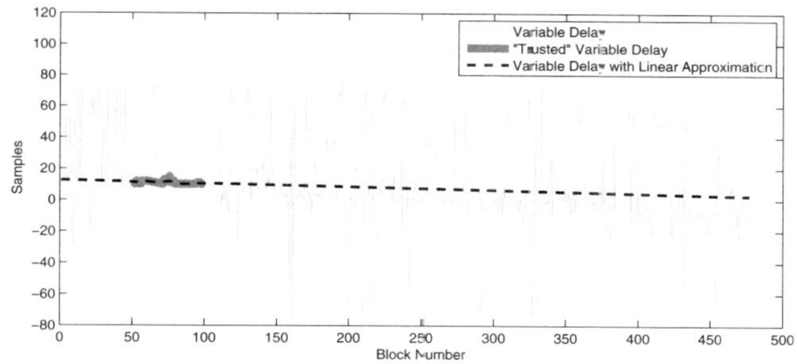

Figure 3. Variable delay between reference and degraded files (threshold = 0.05).

Once the pair of reference and degraded files are time aligned the gain alignment algorithm needs to be applied.

1.2. Gain Alignment

As a first step the monaural files have been created from reference and degraded binaural audio signals by the averaging left and right channels accordingly. This should take into account, that the most of the receivers switch the audio to mono in the case of poor radio signal, i.e. both left and right channels are the same. Therefore processing on the stereo signal may lead to a wrong gain calculation because of the reference and degraded files difference, caused even only by the switching to monaural signal, which can be quite pure itself. However, as a result of wrong gain applying the loudness of gain-aligned audio signals can strongly differ, which is undesirable. The back effect can also take place, if the gain, figured out on the stereo files, is more accurate than the one, calculated on the base of monaural files. However, this effect will be referred to the receiver inaccuracy.

The gain itself is calculated as the absolute values average of all samples of the monaural files. The sample values of the file, yielding a higher gain, are linearly reduced according to the gain difference. Then, the proportional normalization is applied for both files to bring the loudness level to the acceptable value. The variable gain, if it exists, is not compensated in our approach, but is referred also to the inaccuracy of the receiver.

2. Subjective Assessments

The files, simulated and captured in real situations, after time and gain alignment have to be estimated by the subjects from the test group. They should listen at first the reference and corresponding degraded audio files, and then estimate the degradation of the second file with respect to the reference one. In our case each test person has estimated 58 pairs of files, given for every pair only one value from the interval from 0 to 10, according to Table 1.

All pairs of files and appropriate MOS values have been divided in two sets: training set used for model (neural net) creation and the test set (10 pairs from 58). The data from the test set are not used for network modeling to be honest in evaluating of approximation results.

Table 1. Subjective estimation scale.

Grade	Subjective impression
0	Very strong reception distortion because of the low level and/or irritant presence *Program content is not/almost not understandable*
2	Strong reception distortion because of the low level and/or irritant presence *Program content is in common understandable, irritative noise*
4	Almost acceptable reception distortion because of the low level and/or irritant presence *Program content is mostly good understandable, especially when concentrating*
6	Audible reception distortion because of the low level and/or irritant presence *Noise is (always) audible, also at the usual loudness*
8	Still audible reception distortion because of the low level and/or irritant presence *Reception distortion is audible when concentrating or at the high loudness*
10	There is no audible reception distortion because of the low level and/or irritant presence *Reception distortion is inaudible even concentrating or at the high loudness*

3. Neural Network Training

We have modified the standard approach for neural network training [4] using the genetic algorithm [5]. Genetic algorithms are global optimization stochastic algorithms, which do not need the knowledge about the function and its derivatives. Only required for optimization are the values of the optimized function in the points, which are calculated by the genetic algorithm [6,7].

In our approach the genetic algorithm is applied two times within each iteration (so called generation [3]). Firstly it is used to optimize the weights of all neural nets in the current generation. As an optimum we suppose the minimal value of the mean squared error (MSE) between the neural network output and the corresponding MOS values from a training set. Secondly the genetic algorithm is used to determine the new generation of the neural nets. In order to apply the optimization algorithm to a network structure its binary representation is used. The training is iterated until the stop conditions are satisfied or the break is performed manually. It is also possible to stop the process of adaptation and continue to optimize the weights of the best found net by the use of genetic algorithm with different parameters and number of generations.

4. Results

The MSE of the difference between the output of the found neural network and MOS values, calculated on the training data set, is equal to MSE=1.040 and calculated on the test data set is even smaller MSE=0.971. The result approximation is at least much closer to the MOS, than linearly rescaled ODG software output (MSE for the difference between rescaled ODG and MOS is equal to 5.428). The improvement of the algorithm is seen in Figure 4, there MOS, rescaled ODG values and our algorithm outputs for the test set data are shown.

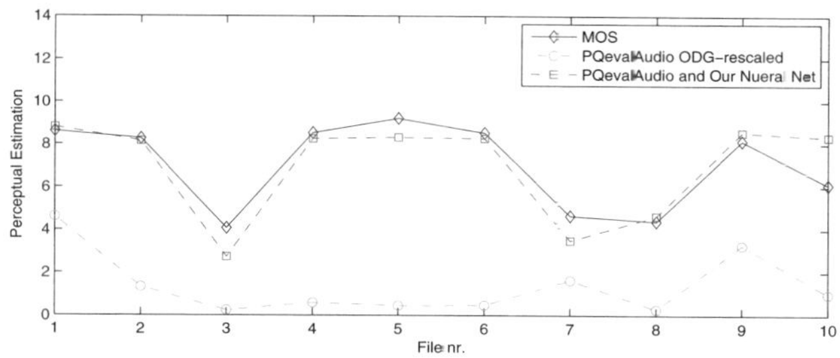

Figure 4. The algorithms comparison.

5. Conclusion and Future Directions

The neural network in combination with the PQevalAudio software can be used for the perceptual evaluation of the audio quality degradation, transmitted through the radio channel. This approach is obviously not as precise as the subjective assessments. However it can be used with the certain accuracy for the mean opinion score approximation.

The accuracy of the MOS approximation can be significantly improved by the use of described algorithms in combination, trained on the considerably greater amount of data and estimated by a higher number of people. Since this algorithm showed good results on the quite small data set, it seems to be worthy to create a more powerful training set for getting more accurate approximation of MOS and saving consequentially expenses for the subjective assessments later.

Another direction to improve the MOS approximation could be the invention of the new grade scale, different from the scale presented in Table 1. It should be found more detailed or clear description of each grade to be easier and understandable for test persons. Some accuracy may be lost because of the great value of the people opinion standard deviation in the data set.

References

[1] *ITU-R Recommendation BS.1387, Method for Objective Measurements of Perceived Audio Quality*, Dec. 1998.

[2] P. Kabal, *An Examination and Interpretation of ITU-R BS.1387: Perceptual Evaluation of Audio Quality*, Department of Electrical & Computer Engineering, McGill University, Canada, 2002.

[3] J.A. Anderson, *An Introduction to Neural Network*, The MIT Press, 1995.

[4] M.T.Hagan, *Neural Network Design (Electrical Engineering)*, PWS Pub. Co, 1995.

[5] D.E. Goldberg, *Genetic Algorithms in Search, Optimization, and Machine Learning*, Addison-Wesley Professional, 1989.

[6] J.H. Holland, *Adaptation in Natural and Artificial Systems: An Introductory Analysis with Applications to Biology, Control, and Artificial Intelligence*, The MIT Press, 1992.

[7] R.L.Haupt, *Practical Genetic Algorithms*, Wiley-Interscience, 1997.

Intelligent Environments 2009
V. Callaghan et al. (Eds.)
IOS Press, 2009

doi:10.3233/978-1-60750-034-6-466

Localized In-Network Detection and Tracking of Phenomena Clouds using Wireless Sensor Networks

Raja BOSE [a] and Abdelsalam (Sumi) HELAL [b,1]
[a] *Nokia Research Center, Palo Alto, U.S.A.*
[b] *Mobile & Pervasive Computing Laboratory, University of Florida, U.S.A.*
{raja.bose@nokia.com, helal@cise.ufl.edu}

Abstract. Phenomena clouds are characterized by non-deterministic, dynamic variations over time, of their shape, size and direction of motion along multiple axes. In the past, the utility of phenomena detection and tracking has been limited to applications such as tracking oil spills and gas clouds. However, through our collective experience over the years in a completely different deployment domain (Smart Spaces), we have discovered great utility and value in applying this concept to accurately and efficiently observe other types of phenomena. In this paper, we propose distributed sensor network algorithms which utilize localized in-network processing to simultaneously detect and track multiple phenomena clouds in a sensor space. Our algorithms not only ensure low processing and networking overhead but also minimize the number of sensors which are actively involved in the detection and tracking processes at any given time. We validate our approach using both real-life smart home applications as well as simulation experiments. We also show that our algorithms result in significant reduction in resource usage and power consumption as compared to contemporary stream-based approaches.

Keywords. Wireless Sensor Networks, phenomena detection and tracking, phenomena clouds, distributed event processing.

Introduction

Contemporary wireless sensor network (WSN) research done in the area of detection and tracking has primarily concentrated on and proposed distributed algorithms for, observing motion of objects whose shape and size are invariant. In contrast, phenomena clouds such as oil spills and gas clouds not only exhibit motion but are also characterized by non-deterministic variation of their shape and size, over time. However, the utility of phenomena cloud detection and tracking is not restricted only to application domains involving gas clouds or oil spills. In fact, they can also be utilized in situations where the quality of data originating from individual sensors cannot be trusted in isolation. In such cases, the raw sensor data originating from the system is typically extremely noisy which makes it very difficult to distinguish actual events from random stimuli. Hence, a quorum of multiple sensors which are located in close proximity to each other is required to reduce the probability of false positives. Through

[1] Corresponding Author.

our collective research and systems experience over the years in building Smart Spaces at University of Florida's Mobile and Pervasive Computing Laboratory, we have found great utility in applying the phenomena cloud concept for efficiently and accurately monitoring various events in the space. The remainder of this paper is organized as follows. Section 1 describes phenomena clouds and analyzes their structure. Section 2 describes the detection and tracking algorithms in detail. It also describes an interesting real-world application of phenomena detection and tracking in a smart space. Section 3 provides evaluation and analysis of the performance of our approach. Section 4 covers related work. Section 5 concludes this paper and describes future work.

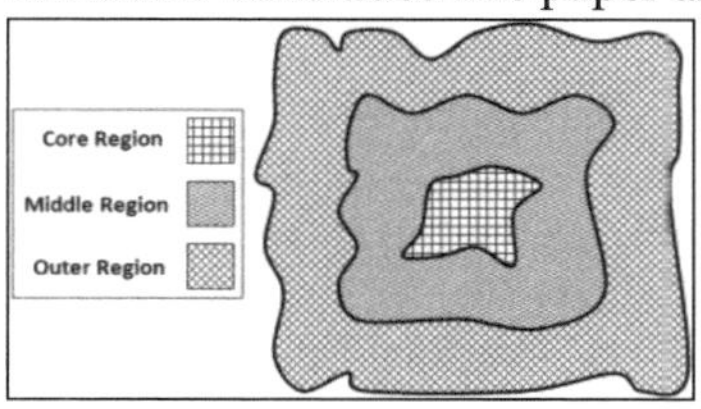

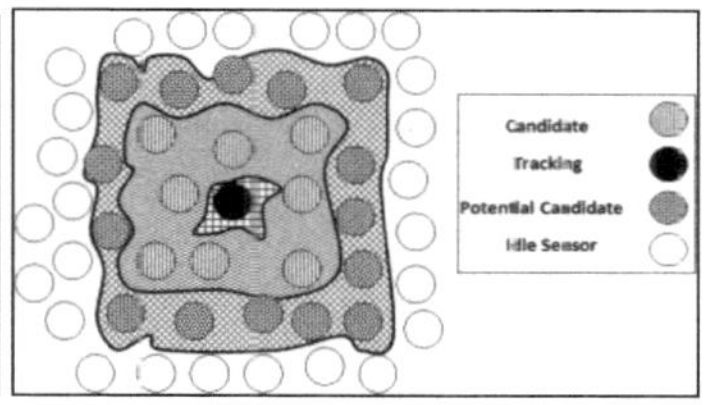

Figure 1. Dissection of a Phenomenon Cloud; Figure 2. Classification of Participating Sensors

1. Phenomena Clouds

A phenomenon cloud can be defined as a manifestation of a number of simultaneous events reaching "critical mass" and spanning a contiguous space. The shape, size and direction of movement of such phenomena clouds cannot usually be modeled accurately in real-time by sensor networks, which largely consist of low-end nodes with limited processing capabilities. Examples of such phenomena include gas clouds, flooding, oil spills, or even movement of tourists in a museum. A phenomenon cloud can exhibit non-deterministic behavior over time making it difficult to anticipate its path and motion.

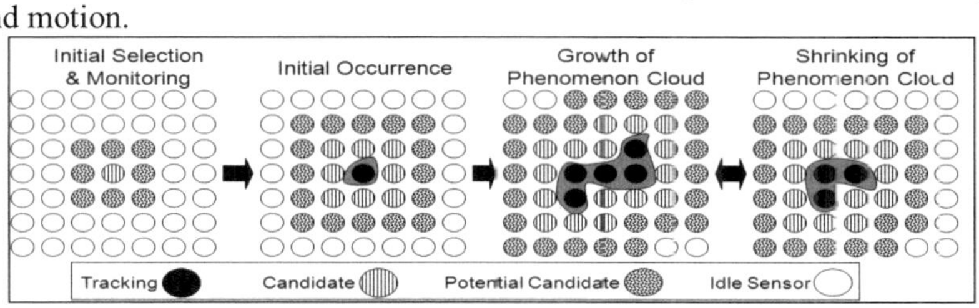

Figure 3. Detection and Tracking of a Phenomenon Cloud

We represent a phenomenon cloud as a 5-tuple, P = $<a, b, p_T, m, n>$. The lower and upper bounds of the range of sensor values which constitute a phenomenon are denoted by 'a' and 'b' respectively. p_T is the threshold probability, m is the observation count and n is the minimum quorum. We refer to a sensor's reading lying in the range [a, b] with probability greater than p_T during the last 'm' observations (that is, in a sliding window of size m) as satisfying the *Probability-Condition*. We define a sensor's neighborhood as the set of sensors immediately surrounding that sensor. We further state that a sensor is said to participate in a phenomenon cloud (or satisfy the *Phenomenon-Condition*) given by P = $<a, b, p_T, m, n>$, if it satisfies the *Probability-Condition* and at least 'n' sensors in its neighborhood also satisfy the *Probability-Condition*. This criterion ensures that a sensor must have a sufficient number of neighboring sensors in agreement with it before it can claim the existence of a phenomenon cloud, thereby reducing the occurrence of false positives. We define *Phenomenon-Set* as the set of sensors satisfying the *Phenomenon-Condition.*

2. Detection and Tracking of Phenomena Clouds

In this section we describe the main concepts of the phenomena cloud detection and tracking process in detail including an interesting real-world application.

2.1. Classification of Sensors

Sensors are classified into different categories according to the roles they play in the detection and tracking process. Figure 2 shows the phenomenon cloud depicted in Figure 1 superimposed over a group of sensors. Sensors are classified according to the region where they are located, which determines their role in detection and tracking of a cloud. The different categories are: (1) **Candidate Sensor**: A candidate sensor is one which is actively monitoring its readings to determine if it will become part of a phenomenon cloud or not. Candidate sensors make up the Middle region of a phenomenon cloud. A sensor becomes a candidate if it has been selected as such by the query processor as part of the initial detection phase or it has transitioned from the potential candidate stage. The role of a candidate sensor is to receive notifications from its neighboring sensors whenever they satisfy the *Probability-Condition.* Based on the number of such neighbors it decides whether it is eligible to become a tracking sensor; (2) **Potential Candidate Sensor**: All sensors which are immediate neighbors of candidate sensors but are not candidates themselves are called potential candidate sensors. These sensors also monitor their readings to enable a neighboring candidate sensor to check the validity of its observations. The role of a potential candidate sensor is to notify its neighboring candidate sensors whenever its readings satisfy the *Probability-Condition.* Potential candidate sensors form the fringes of detection and make up the Outer region of the phenomenon cloud; (3) **Tracking Sensor**: A tracking sensor is a sensor which has already detected a phenomenon event and is now actively engaged in tracking it. A candidate sensor becomes a tracking sensor after it satisfies the *Phenomenon-Condition.* Tracking sensors make up the Core region. The *Phenomenon-Set* is the collection of all tracking sensors hence, each cloud that a user observes through the sensor network, consists of sub-sets of tracking sensors from the *Phenomenon-Set*; (4) **Idle Sensor**: All sensors which do not belong to any of the above three categories are called idle sensors. These sensors are not engaged in phenomenon detection or tracking and do not perform any monitoring whatsoever.

Each sensor node keeps track of which category each of its neighboring sensors falls in. This is done in a peer-to-peer fashion, where a sensor transitioning from one category to another, notifies the other sensors in its neighborhood via a 1-hop broadcast. The categories a sensor and its neighbor fall into determine their mutual responsibilities towards each other. Table 1 lists the actions a sensor node performs with respect to a neighborhood node, based on which category each of them belongs to.

A set of rules govern the transition of a sensor from one category to another. These rules are executed in-network and control the entire detection and tracking process: (**R1**): Candidate → Tracking: If a sensor satisfies the *Phenomenon-Condition* then it transitions into the tracking category. Once a sensor is in the tracking category, it becomes a member of the *Phenomenon-Set*; (**R2**): Potential Candidate → Candidate: A potential candidate sensor will transition to a candidate sensor if any of its neighbors transitions into a tracking sensor. This rule corresponds to the fact that whenever a phenomenon cloud moves or expands and a new sensor becomes part of its core region, the phenomenon front also moves or expands; (**R3**): Idle → Potential Candidate: An idle sensor transitions into a potential candidate if any of its neighbors becomes a candidate sensor; (**R4**): Tracking → Candidate: A tracking sensor will transition down to the candidate category; if it is unable to satisfy the *Phenomenon-Condition*. In such a case, the sensor will cease to be a member of the *Phenomenon-Set*; (**R5**): Candidate → Potential Candidate: A candidate sensor will transition to a potential candidate sensor if none of its neighbors are tracking sensors; (**R6**): Potential Candidate → Idle: A potential candidate transitions into an idle sensor if all its neighbors are either potential candidates or idle, that is none of its neighbors are in the candidate category.

2.2. Detection and Tracking Process

The detection and tracking algorithm runs in-network in a distributed manner where each sensor node performs its tasks governed by the rules described above. The entire process (Figure 3) is executed autonomously without involvement of any centralized authority. The main steps of the detection and tracking process are:

1) Initial Selection of Candidate Sensors: A phenomenon cloud can manifest itself in multiple locations simultaneously hence, monitoring one particular location is not adequate. However, in the interest of conserving network resources and power, some specific sensors are directly chosen to be candidates. For example, we make use of this criterion in the Smart Floor application described later on in this section. Sensors located near doorways are selected as initial candidates so that whenever a person enters the room, the system is immediately able to pick up their presence and commence the detection and tracking process to monitor their movement.

2) Monitoring for Initial Occurrences: At the beginning of every epoch, each potential candidate node monitors its readings and sends a 1-hop broadcast message every time the *Probability-Condition* is satisfied. In order to enable sensor nodes to receive alert broadcasts from multiple neighbors simultaneously during the same epoch, a slotted approach is used to ensure collision avoidance similar to what is described in [5]. Each epoch is sub-divided into multiple sub-epochs and each node only broadcasts alerts during its assigned sub-epoch. The candidate sensor node aggregates alerts received via broadcasts from its neighbors and determines if it satisfies the *Phenomenon-Condition.* A candidate sensor satisfies the *Phenomenon-Condition* if its readings satisfy the *Probability-Condition* and it also receives broadcast alerts from at least 'n' neighbors which have also satisfied the *Probability-Condition* in same epoch.

3) Notification of Initial Occurrence: If a candidate node has satisfied the *Phenomenon-Condition,* it notifies the query processor residing in the base station that it has detected presence of a phenomenon cloud. The query processor adds the candidate node to the *Phenomenon-Set* and the candidate sensor transitions to a tracking sensor role using rule R1.

4) Growth of Phenomenon Cloud: The candidate sensor also broadcasts an alert about its change of state. As soon as the neighborhood sensors receive the alert, they transition to the candidate category using rule R2. Each of these sensors in turn, broadcasts its change of state and this causes all their respective neighbors which had been idle till now, to transition into potential candidate category (rule R3). In this

manner, the detection mechanism gets distributed and propagated in-network, without involvement of the centralized query processor, as the phenomenon cloud grows with time. Each sensor node keeps track of its neighborhood via the broadcast alerts that it receives and determines the actions to be undertaken with respect to a specific neighbor.

5) Shrinking of Phenomenon Cloud: The phenomenon cloud shrinks when sensors falling in the tracking category determine that they can no longer satisfy the *Phenomenon-Condition.* According to Table 1, after a sensor transitions into tracking, its neighbors will only send it alerts if their readings fail to satisfy the *Probability-Condition.* A tracking sensor is no longer participating in the observation of the phenomenon cloud if it determines that less than 'n' of its neighbors currently satisfy the *Probability-Condition.* In such a case, the tracking sensor node notifies the query processor which removes the tracking sensor from the *Phenomenon-Set.* The affected sensor transitions into a candidate (R4) and notifies the other sensors in its neighborhood of this role change, which in turn transition into their new roles.

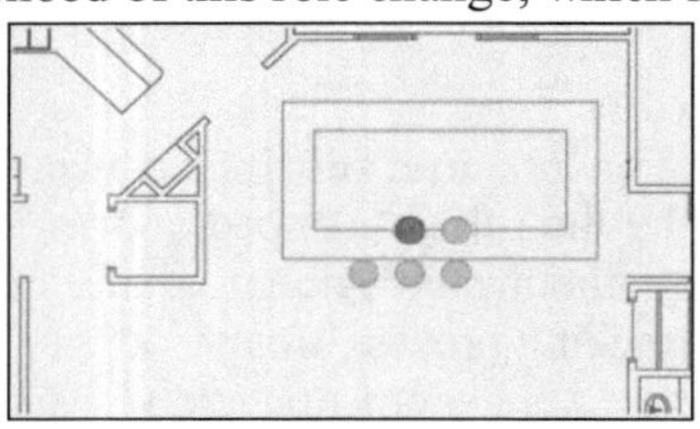

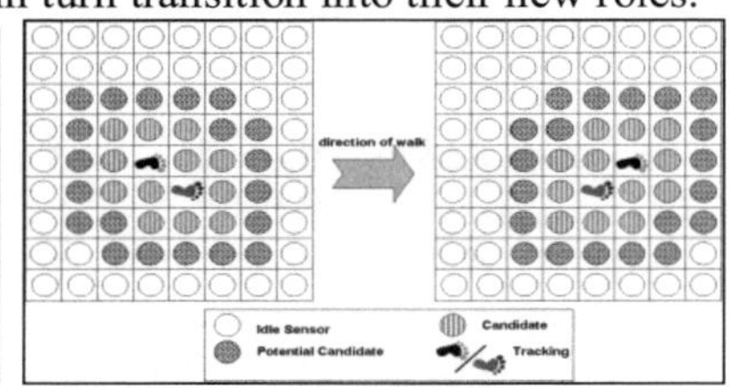

Figure 4. Ripple Effect of a Foot Step on the Smart Floor; Figure 5. Walking Motion as a Phenomenon

2.3. A Practical Application of Phenomena Detection and Tracking

The application that we describe is the Smart Floor of the Gator Tech Smart House [3]. The Smart Floor consists of a grid of piezoelectric force sensors deployed under the raised floor tiles of the house. Each tile has a sensor connected to an Atlas Platform [4] node placed below its center. The floor allows monitoring of a resident's movement and location without encumbering them with tags. Due to random vibrations individual sensor tiles sometimes output large readings even when nobody is stepping on them. This results in a very noisy sensory environment where one cannot distinguish between a genuine step and random spikes by relying on individual sensors alone. We observed that when a person steps on a tile not only does this result in that tile's sensor registering a strong reading but some of its neighboring tiles also output significantly large readings. Figure 4 shows an actual screenshot of this phenomenon in the Smart Floor where red dots indicate tiles registering readings of higher magnitude and green indicates tiles with lower magnitude. We used this to describe walking as a phenomenon by defining a step in terms of a phenomenon cloud (Figure 5), in order to reduce the number of false positives and provide accurate location information. Since our approach does not rely on modeling to track the movement of a phenomenon hence, this makes it suitable for observing phenomena such as walking where it is extremely difficult to accurately model the path that a person will take.

3. Performance Evaluation

We evaluate and analyze the performance of our algorithm using two sets of experiments. In the first set of experiments we study the effectiveness of our phenomenon detection and tracking mechanism in a real-world sensor deployment namely, the Smart Floor described previously. We observed the effect of phenomenon definition parameters (p_T, m and n) on the detection efficiency of our technique. We varied the values of each of these parameters and studied their effect by logging the number of false positives, false negatives/misses and correct detections of a human step.

Figure 6 shows the effect of varying parameter 'n' which determines the minimum quorum of neighboring sensors required to conclusively determine the occurrence of a phenomenon. Since the Smart Floor is deployed as a rectangular grid of sensors, the value of 'n' varies from 0 to 8. We observe that for n=0 (which corresponds to the naïve case) the number of false positives is extremely high since the system is entirely relying on outputs from single sensors to determine the occurrence of a footstep event. As we increase the value of 'n', the number of false positives comes down sharply since now multiple neighboring sensors need to agree on the occurrence of a phenomenon. We also notice that as 'n' increases, the number of misses also increase, thereby reducing the number of correct detections. This is due to the fact that walking is essentially a transient event where a footstep has to be detected by a specific sensor within a very small time window. For large values of 'n', the number of misses is very high since the quorum requirements become too stringent. Figure 7 shows the effect of varying the threshold probability p_T. We observe that as threshold probability increases the number of false positives decreases since it filters out random spikes. Random spikes typically result in only a few readings of significant magnitude within a fixed size sliding window hence, there is a sharp drop in the number of false positives even when we only increase p_T from 0.1 to 0.2. However making the probability requirement more stringent also results in an increase in the number of false negatives/misses. This is due to the fact that since we are using a sliding window of fixed size, as the number of readings in the window that are required to lie within the phenomena-defined bounds [a, b] in order to satisfy the *Probability-Condition* increases, the chance of the *Probability-Condition* getting satisfied decreases. Figure 8 shows the effect of varying the sliding window size 'm'. We observe that if the sliding window size is too low, this results in a large number of false positives despite having a high probability threshold. This is due to the fact that in case of sensors which have a high sampling rate even random spikes can result in a fairly large contiguous set of significant readings. Since the system essentially uses the threshold frequency ($p_T m$) to evaluate whether a sensor satisfies the *Probability-Condition*, for small window sizes the corresponding threshold frequency is also low even if threshold probability p_T is kept high. Hence, there is a high probability that random spikes get mistaken for actual footsteps. Increasing the sliding window size raises threshold frequency which results in a moderate increase in the number of misses.

In the second set of experiments we study the system resource and power consumption characteristics of our approach and compare it with that of a stream-based approach. We simulate the movement of phenomenon clouds over 100 epochs on a rectangular grid of sensors of sizes varying from a 50 x 50 grid to a 400 x 400 grid. The detection and tracking strategies that were simulated in the experiments for purposes of comparison are as follows: **StreamPDT**: Stream-based system where phenomena detection and tracking is performed by a centralized query processor, and; **DistPDT**: The phenomenon detection and tracking system described in this paper.

We observe that in the case of StreamPDT the number of update messages is directly proportional the size of the sensor grid (Figure 9). This is due to the fact that stream-based algorithms use centralized processing as opposed to in-network processing. Therefore, these mechanisms require inputs from all the sensors in the grid. The number of update messages sent by DistPDT shows negligible increase as sensor grid size varies. In fact, DistPDT requires transmission of between 78% to 99% fewer update messages than StreamPDT. This is due to the fact that in DistPDT, all the processing is done in-network and update messages are only sent to the base station query processor when a phenomenon cloud grows, shrinks or moves that is, when sensors move in or out of the *Phenomenon-Set*. Therefore, regardless of the increase in size of the grid, the number of updates required by the query processor from the DistPDT mechanism does not change significantly, thereby reducing the query processor's work load and avoiding potential bottlenecks. Figure 10 shows the average number of sensors involved in the real-time tracking of phenomenon clouds. Since StreamPDT requires inputs from all sensors to be streamed up to the query processor, the number of active sensors is proportional to increase in grid size. For DistPDT, the number of active sensors is anywhere from 30% to 98% less than StreamPDT. This is due to the fact that, the DistPDT mechanism tries to localize the process of detection and tracking to areas of the grid, where phenomena clouds have been observed or are likely to be present, significantly reducing the number of sensors which have to be actively sampled. Due to localization of in-network processing amongst sensor nodes, the number of active sensors does not change significantly with increase in grid size. Finally, from Figure 11 we observe that DistPDT has 60% to 98% lower energy consumption than StreamPDT which makes our approach more energy-efficient than stream based approaches.

4. Related Work

Nile-PDT [1] is a centralized phenomena detection and tracking framework developed by Purdue University. The drawback of their approach is that it takes a streaming database view of the process. It does not consider any mechanisms for controlling the flow of data at the source sensors themselves or address power consumption and network bandwidth issues inside the sensor network. Furthermore, it requires all sensors to pump readings to the query engine to allow it to choose phenomenon candidates, which can lead to potentially massive scalability issues. McErlean et al. [6] propose distributed event detection and tracking algorithms for moving objects using WSNs. Their approach assumes the prior availability of optimal ad-hoc routing mechanisms and is primarily designed for detecting individual discrete objects, as opposed to phenomenon clouds whose shape and size cannot be defined in exact terms. Chintalapudi et al. [2] utilize image processing and classifier techniques to determine if a sensor lies at the edge of the phenomenon or not. However, their approach requires simplistic assumptions regarding the shape of the edges which is not always feasible.

5. Conclusions and Future Work

In this paper, we described localized in-network algorithms for real-time detection and tracking of phenomena clouds using wireless sensor networks. We also validated our approach through real-world and simulation-based experiments. As part of future work, we are looking at ways to better organize the *Phenomenon-Set* to enable updating and lookup of specific clouds and their characteristics if possible, in constant time.

6. References

[1] M. Ali et al., Detection and tracking of discrete phenomena in sensor-network databases, In Proc. 17th International Conference on Scientific and Statistical Database Management (SSDBM), 2005.

[2] K. Chintalapudi et al., Localized Edge Detection in Sensor Fields, AdHoc Networks Journal, 2003.

[3] A. Helal et al., Gator Tech Smart House: A Programmable Pervasive Space, IEEE Computer, Mar. 2005.

[4] J. King et al., Atlas – A Service-Oriented Sensor Platform, In Proc. of 1st IEEE International Workshop on Practical Issues in Building Sensor Network Applications, 2006.

[5] S. Madden et al., TAG: a Tiny AGgregation Service for Ad -Hoc Sensor Networks, In Proc. of 5th Annual Symposium on Operating Systems Design and Implementation, 2002.

[6] D. McErlean et al., Distributed Detection and Tracking in Sensor Networks, In Proc. 36th Asilomar Conference on Signals, Systems and Computers, 2002.

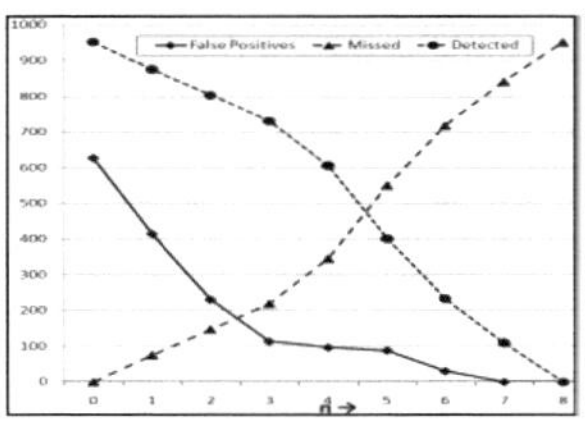

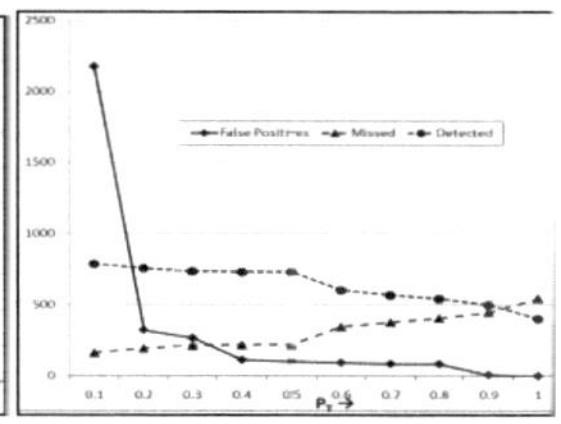

Figure 6. Effect of varying 'n' with p_T=0.4 and m=150; Figure 7. Effect of varying p_T with n=3 and m=150

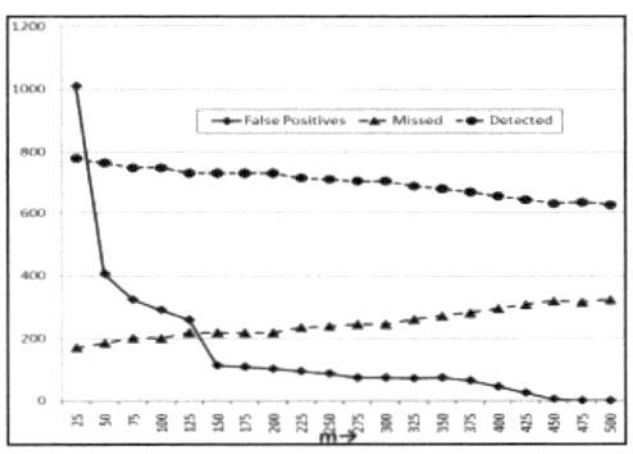

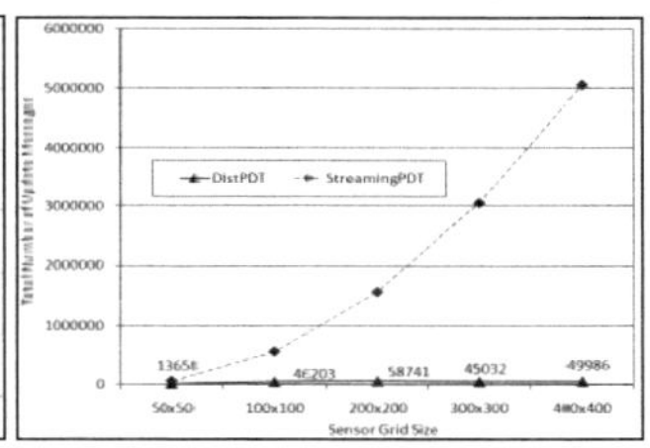

Figure 8. Effect of varying 'm' with n=3 and p_T=0.4; Figure 9. Number of Update Messages

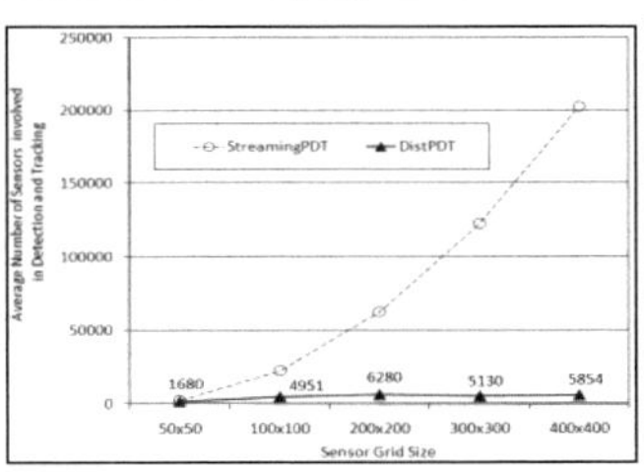

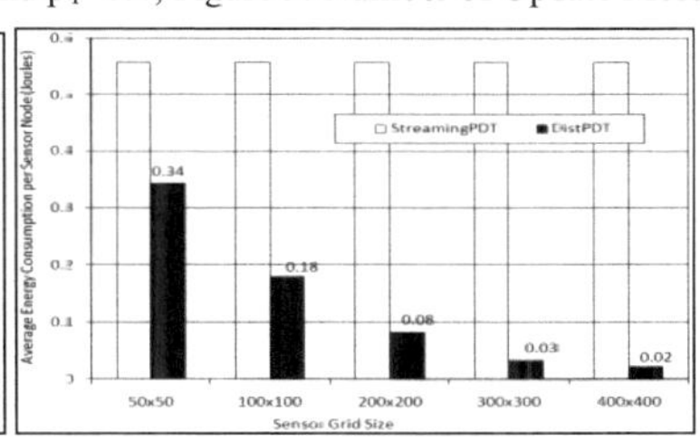

Figure 10. Average Number of Active Sensors Required; Figure 11. Average Energy Consumption per Node

Sensor Node ↓	Neighbor		
	Potential Candidate	Candidate	Tracking
Idle	None	Not Applicable	Not Applicable
Potential Candidate	None	Send alert whenever readings satisfy *Probab. Condition*	Not Applicable
Candidate	Receive alerts from neighbor whenever its readings satisfy *Probab. Condition*	Send alerts/ receive alerts whenever their readings satisfy *Probab. Condition*	Send alerts whenever readings do not satisfy *Probability Condition*
Tracking	Not Applicable	Send alert when readings satisfy *Probab. Condition*	Send/receive alerts when *Probab. Condition not satisfied*

Table 1. Actions Taken by a Sensor Node with respect to its Neighbors which are not Idle

Intelligent Environments 2009
V. Callaghan et al. (Eds.)
IOS Press, 2009

doi:10.3233/978-1-60750-034-6-474

Echo State Network for Occupancy Prediction and Pattern Mining in Intelligent Environments

Sawsan M. Mahmoud [a], Ahmad Lotfi [a], Nasser Sherkat [a], Caroline Langensiepen [a], and Taha Osman [a]

[a] *School of Science and Technology , Nottingham Trent University, Nottingham, UK*

Abstract. Pattern analysis and prediction of sensory data is becoming an increasing scientific challenge and a massive economical interest supports the need for better pattern mining techniques. The aim of this paper is to investigate efficient mining of useful information from a sensor network representing an ambient intelligence environment. The goal is to extract and predict behavioral patterns of a person in his/her daily activities by analyzing the time series data representing the behaviour of the occupant, generated using occupancy sensors. There are various techniques available for analysis and prediction of a continuous time series signal. However, the occupancy signal is represented by a binary time series where only discrete values of a signal are available. To build the prediction model, recurrent neural networks are investigated. They are proven to be useful tools to solve the difficulties of the temporal relationships of inputs between observations at different time steps, by maintaining internal states that have memory. In this paper, a special form of recurrent neural network, the so-called Echo State Network (ESN) is used in which discrete values of time series can be well processed. Then, a model developed based on ESN is compared with the most popular recurrent neural networks; namely Back Propagation Through Time (BPTT) and Real Time Recurrent Learning (RTRL). The results showed that ESN provides better prediction results compared with BPTT and RTRL. Using ESN, large datasets are learnt in only few minutes or even seconds. It can be concluded that ESN are efficient and valuable tools in binary time series prediction. The results presented in this paper are based on simulated data generated from a simulator representing a person in a 1 bed room flat.

Keywords. Sensor network, Time-series mining, Activity monitoring, Echo state network, intelligence environment

1. Introduction

The Sensor network has become one of the most important technologies for the 21st century. It is a network consisting of spatially distributed independent devices using different sensors to monitor physical or environmental conditions at different locations. Sensor networks have been used in many applications like environmental monitoring building and structures monitoring, military sensing, physical security traffic surveillance, video surveillance, distributed robotics and similar [1]. The main goal of a sensor network is to

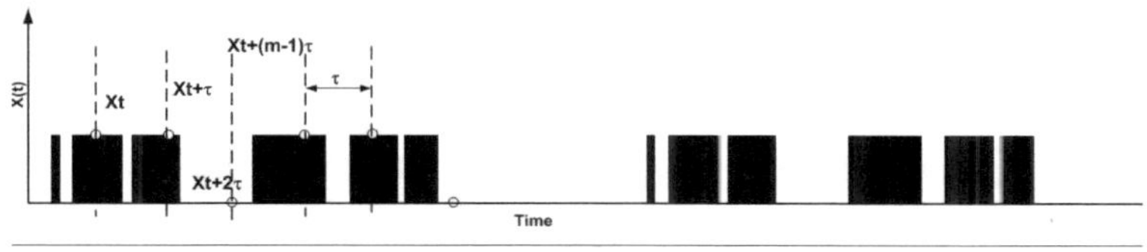

Figure 1. Discrete values of time series data collected from a door sensor

collect information in an intelligent environment. Sensor data from such an environment can be represented and mined as sequences or as time series data. These sequences are represented by a series of sensor values. All the sequences are ordered in time and occur sequentially one after another. However, for some applications it is not only important to have a sequence of these events, but also a time when these events occur.

The sensory data investigated in this paper represents the movement pattern of an occupant in an ambient intelligent environment. They are sequences of an ordered set of movements between one room and another inside a certain property, i.e. when the sensor is an on or off. The problem arising here is how one can process this huge amount of time series data and predict the next step in the series in order to extract important daily patterns from them. Figure (1) illustrates sensory data collected from a door sensor. This signal is a binary time series data where series $x(t)$, $x(t+\tau)$, $x(t+2\tau)$, ... $x(t+(m-1)\tau)$ can be used as input variables to forecast the target variable $x(t)+m\tau$, for all $t = 1, 2, \ldots\ n$ and a time delay length (τ).

To learn the pattern of the data series, Recurrent Neural Networks (RNNs) are used in which recurrent loops provide the network with some memory and thus with the ability to deal with the related time data. More specifically, we use the Echo State Network (ESN) approach. ESN is an efficient way to use RNNs where can obtain a computational power comparable to state of art of RNNs with a much simpler training algorithm and can be guaranteed to find the global optimum. It has shown that ESN learning algorithm can successfully used in an intelligent environment. The paper is organized as follows: section 2 briefly introduces ESN. Experimental results of ESN application in an intelligent environment are discussed in section 3 Finally, pertinent conclusions are drawn in section 4.

2. Echo state Network

In this section, the recurrent neural network, Echo State Network (ESN) is described. It was developed recently by Jaeger [2]. The basic architecture of ESN is illustrated in Figure (2) which consists of three layers. These include input, hidden and output layer. The input layer is connected to the hidden layer. Both the input and hidden layer are fully connected to the output layer. On the other hand, the output layer is backward connected to the hidden layer only. It is a discrete- time, continuous state where the activation function for all neurons is the sigmoid function [3].

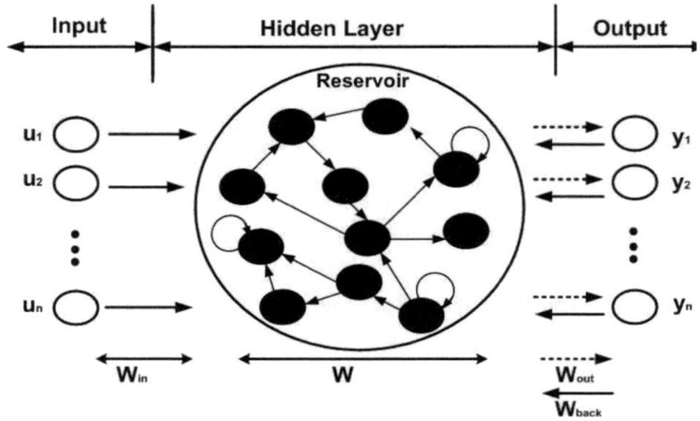

Figure 2. Structure of an Echo State Network approach. Only the output weights W$_{out}$ are adapted, all other weights (input, reservoir and feedback) are chosen randomly.

An ESN consists of a reservoir of conventional processing elements, which are recurrently interconnected with untrained random weights, and a readout (output) layer, which is trained using linear regression methods. The key advantage of the ESN is its ability to model systems without the need to train the recurrent weights [4]. For training an ESN with an input $u(n)$, a reservoir state $x(n)$ with M processing elements, and an output $y(n)$, the equations are calculates as follows:

$$x(n+1) = tansig(w_x.x(n) + w_{in}.u(n) + v(n+1)) \tag{1}$$

$$y(n) = w.x(n) \tag{2}$$

where $x(n)$ denotes the hidden layer or the internal state. The input and output to the ESNs are denoted by $u(n)$ and $y(n)$ respectively. tansig denotes hyperbolic tangent sigmoid function which is applied element wise, $v(n+1)$ is an optional noise vector. w_x, w_{in} and w are respectively the internal connection weights of the reservoir, the input weights to the reservoir and the readout (output) weights from the reservoir[5].

The ESN approach differs from other methods in that a large RNN is used (on the order of 50 to 1000 neurons) and in that only the synaptic connections from the RNN to the output neurons are updated i.e. weights coming from the hidden layer (also called reservoir) to the output layer are updated in order to achieve the learning task. As a result, large datasets are learnt in only few minutes or even seconds [2]. Also, there are neurons in the reservoir connected in loops [see Figure 2], therefore the past states 'echo' in the reservoir. The convergence of training in ESN is much faster than other RNN. This has made of ESN as an attractive model for a wide range of signal processing and control applications (e.g. time series prediction, pattern generation, event detection and classification and nonlinear control). For instance, in prediction of chaotic time series, ESN has proven to be a very efficient and valuable tool. The prediction is accomplished using a black box model, i.e. it only depends on past data since no further information is used.

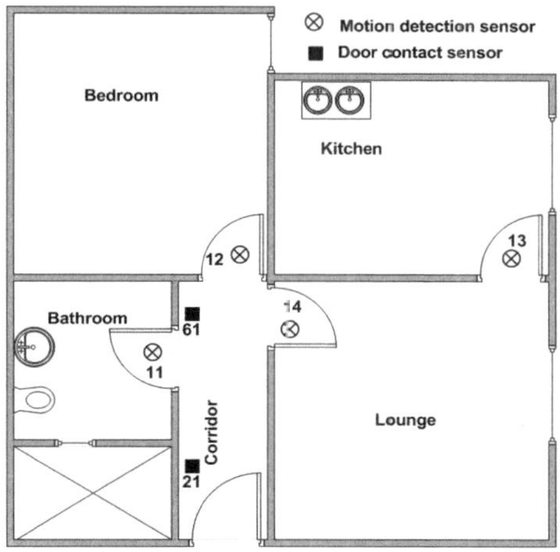

Figure 3. The flat layout

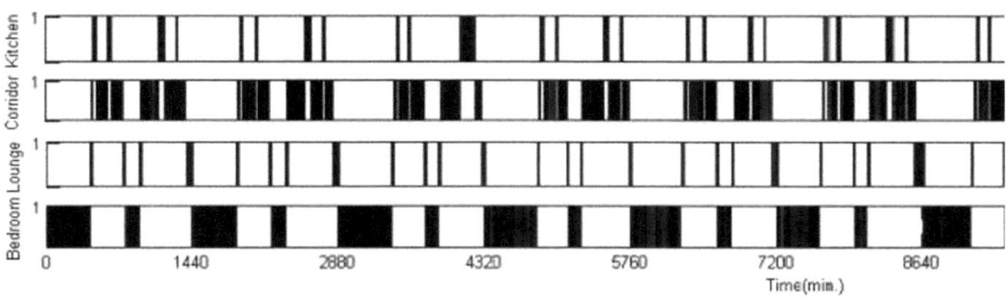

Figure 4. The occupancy Chart

In addition, no explicit model is given in order to create a new situation [6,7].

In this paper, ESN is used as a model to predict and extract behavioural patterns while keeping learning complexity at a low level. In addition, ESN is a very good choice for the modelling because in the methodology of the sensor networks, the new data are arriving at any time, whilst other approaches need all data input at the same time steps in order to compute the output.

3. Experiment Results

In our experiment results, ESN with different reservoir sizes are compared with the most popular recurrent neural networks: Back Propagation Through Time (BPTT) and Real Time Recurrent Learning (RTRL).

3.1. Intelligent Environment and Data Collection

In this section, sensor data collected from a smart environment are considered. The data collection system consists of an array of motion sensors which collect information us-

Table 1. Raw Sample of Sensor Data

Date	Time	Sensor ID	Sensor Value
14/05/2008	08:01:34	12	1
14/05/2008	08:01:35	12	0
14/05/2008	08:05:14	12	1
14/05/2008	08:05:15	12	0
14/05/2008	08:05:33	12	1
14/05/2008	08:05:34	12	0
14/05/2008	08:05:36	12	1

ing passive infra-red (PIR) sensors and door switches. In these situations, these sensors and door switches are used to record the behaviour of an elderly person, and allow the carer to observe any changes to patterns or specific incidents such as going outside at odd times. Our dataset is based on a single inhabitant living in a flat. The layout of the environment where the sensory data is collected is shown in Figure(3). The environment equipped with sensors will return the occupancy chart which records the daily activities as illustrated in Figure (4). This chart represents a single occupant only. The collected sensory data are discrete i.e. binary representing presence or absences from the environment. When the person moves from one room to another, the status of the sensor will vary. The environment consists of a lounge, kitchen, corridor, and bedroom. Therefore four sensors are deployed all around that observe the inhabitant motion. In addition, simulated data [1] have been created by a generator to validate our approach.

Each time stamped data item is characterized by specific properties. In table 1, a sample of raw data collected from a door sensor is illustrated, named as sensor 12. Our initial investigation is based on the data collected from a simulator based on the environment reported above. The model has been trained based on 10 days of data and test the model on 3 days of activities.

These datasets have been trained in our prediction tools to forecast multi-step ahead. In section 3.2, the prediction is observed and compared with test data in order to report the results which include the accuracy and error in the observations.

3.2. Results

In our experiments, instead of using a separate ESN for each sensor, all available sensors are connected at the same time as inputs to these networks and compute the prediction of these sensors reading using the combined datasets from the single input prediction. The advantages of using just one ESN for all sensors are to reduce the amount of memory and computation time. In this case, the number of input and output units depends on the number of sensors, which is driven by the actual sensor value at time t. The output unit is the value of the same sensor at time $t + \tau$ with different hidden units (reservoir) sizes. A number of parameters are used in ESN learning algorithm. These parameters are: number of neurons in the hidden layer (N), the Root Mean Square Error (RMSE)

[1]Simulated datasets have been created using a simulator based on MATLAB developed by Javad Mohammad, a PhD student in the School of Science and Technology of Nottingham Trent University

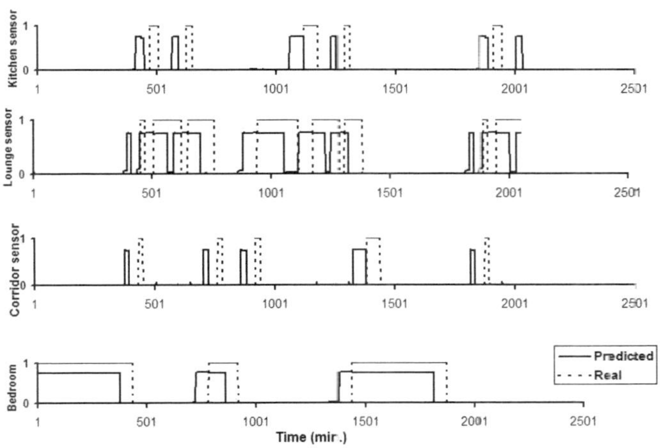

Figure 5. ESN results of 60 minute step ahead prediction of all sensors training datasets using 50 hidden neurons

for training and testing datasets, number of epochs and time required for training. To train ESN, simulated data generated by simulator were used. These data were split into training and test, e.g. the samples of 10 days are used as the training set and the samples of 3 days as the testing set. The analysis results of the echo state network for each sensor using 50 hidden neurons are depicted in Figure (5). In this figure a sample of two days is shown. This approach RMSE of about 5% for each sensor to predict 60 minutes step ahead.

Different sizes of reservoir (number of hidden neurons) are used to test the performance of ESN. It was observed that in ESN many datasets are trained in only few minutes or even seconds (see Figure (6)). Thus, the convergence of training in ESN is much faster than other RNN. Table (2) compares the results of all sensor datasets using ESN with the other recurrent neural networks techniques used in time series prediction. These techniques are back propagation through time and real time recurrent learning. ESN prediction results are better as compared with BPTT and RTRL in that the training time is significantly shorter. While the other approaches suffer from slow convergence as the number of neurons are increased.

4. Conclusions

The results presented in this paper show already that ESN is a very promising approach for a binary datasets collected from smart environments. Datasets investigated here are based on a single inhabitant environment equipped with appropriate motion sensors and door switches. Those sensors and door switches are used to record the behaviour of the occupant, and allow the carer to observe any changes to patterns. In addition, the neural network techniques have been compared to show their ability in prediction of binary time series data. It can be concluded that using large number of hidden neurons in ESN yielded a good results in terms of the error and time required for training and testing.

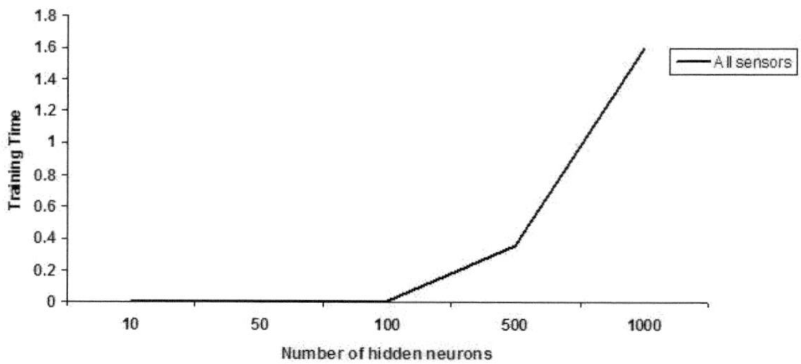

Figure 6. The training time (sec.) of all sensor datasets using different reservoir sizes (hidden neurons)

Table 2. Prediction results of all sensor datasets using ESN, RTRL and BPTT

Method	No. of hidden neurons	Training RMSE	Testing RMSE	Time(Sec.)
ESN	10	0.0556	0.0556	0.011581
ESN	50	0.0556	0.0556	0.051948
RTRL	10	0.0987	0.0964	281.823111
RTRL	50	0.0731	0.0740	1541.042739
BPTT	10	0.0759	0.0766	12.731490
BPTT	50	0.0803	0.0811	218.098591

In contrary to ESN, for other RNNs such as RTRL and BPTT, increasing the number of hidden (internal) units yields increasing the training/testing time.

A further direction for investigation is to implement ESN approach in a multiple occupancy situation, i.e. more than one occupant in a flat/home. This can be done by adding a different sensor to the network that can distinguish between occupants This task is complex, as not only must monitor the occupant, but it must also predict whether he/she alone or has visitors in a specific time. In addition, our experiments were done with simulated data, so the next step is obviously to implement ESN technique on-line with real data collected from sensors to extract the daily behaviour patterns.

References

[1] Stipanciev D., Bodroti L. and Stula M., Environmental Itelligence Based on Advanced Sensor Networks, IEEE on systems, signals and image processing, 6th EURA SIP Conference, June (2007), pp. 209–212.

[2] Herbert Jaeger and Harald Haas, Harnessing Nonlinearity: Predicting Chaotic Systems and Saving Energy in Wireless Communication, Appril, VOL 304, SCIENCE, (2004).

[3] Alexandre Devert, Nicolas Bredeche and Marc Schoenauer, Unsupervised Learning of Echo State Networks: A Case Study in Artificial Embryogeny, Artificial Evolution, Vol. 4926, (2008), pp. 278–290.

[4] Mark D. Skowronski and John G. Harris, Minimum mean squared error time series classification using an echo state network prediction model, IEEE International Symposium on Circuits and Systems, (2006).

[5] Zhiwei Shi and Min Han, Support Vector Echo-State Machine for Chaotic Time-Series Prediction,IEEE Transactions on Neural Networks, March, Vol. 18, Issue: 2, (2007), pp. 359–372.

[6] Sven Hellbach, Śoren Strauss1, Julian P. Eggert, Edgar Kórner and Horst-Michael Gross1, Echo State Networks for Online Prediction of Movement Data - Comparing Investigations , (2008).
[7] Obst, O., Wang, X.R. and Prokopenko, M. Using Echo State Networks for Anomaly Detection in Underground Coal Mines, Proceedings of the 7th international conference on Information processing in sensor networks, (2008).

Intelligent Environments 2009
V. Callaghan et al. (Eds.)
IOS Press, 2009

doi:10.3233/978-1-60750-034-6-482

Mining Purchase History to Predict Adoption of Mobile Computing

Derek STANFORD[a,1]
[a] *Globys Corporation*

Abstract. Mobile phones can provide consumers with constant, easy access to the internet, digital content, and a variety of mobile computing services. To explore how consumers choose to begin using these services, we examine purchases made by customers of a mobile carrier in the United States in 2008. We identify and quantify factors associated with adoption of mobile internet and other mobile services. We present measures of customer volatility and results from predictive models based on logistic regression, and we discuss impacts on customer retention and churn. Our results provide insight into mechanisms of consumer demand for mobile computing.

Keywords. Mobile, Telecom, Predictive, Retention, Churn

Introduction

Mobile phones have become a ubiquitous device for many consumers, providing a computing platform which is consistently present with its owner at any time of day and at almost any location. Because of this, the mobile phone presents an ideal interface for people to interact with intelligent environments. In this study, we examine how mobile phone users begin to adopt mobile data and internet services.

Our questions of interest in this study focus on two aspects of the adoption of mobile computing: volatility of service adoption, and prediction of service adoption based on past purchases. Volatility refers to the rate at which customers churn into and out of the service; high volatility would mean that customers who sign up tend to try it out temporarily and then drop it. Prediction based on other purchases can provide insight into the kinds of customers who are likely to need and use mobile computing services.

1. Motivation

Because cellular carriers routinely process large amounts of customer billing and activity data, there is wide interest in methods which can deliver competitive advantages from analysis of these datasets. Our goal here is to characterize customer volatility and develop purchase prediction models using customer billing history.

[1] Corresponding Author, dstanford@globys.com.

2. Data

Our data consist of billing history for 800,000 customers of a U.S. cellular carrier. Billing history offers a summarized form of monthly activity for each customer. This does not provide individual call details, such as would be shown in a call data record (CDR), but it is more readily available. For volatility analysis, we examine whether each customer subscribed to mobile computing services (mobile internet, mobile email, or a data plan) in January 2008 and again in July 2008. The predictive models presented in this paper are based on monthly purchases from January 2008 through September 2008 for a randomly selected subset of 200,000 customers.

3. Results

3.1. Volatility

We use several measures to assess volatility. First, we examine customers who ceased or began their service with this carrier during the study period. We determine the percentage of customers in each of these groups who subscribe to mobile computing services, and we compare them to the percentage of subscribers among customers who were present for the whole study period. Then, for customers who were present through the entire study period, we determine the percentage who added or dropped the service, as well as the percentage who maintained or never purchased the service.

Table 1 displays the percentage of subscribers for each service within each of three groups: customers who were present through the study period, customers who were lost, and new customers. For all three services, customers who are lost subscribe at a lower rate than those who are retained (all three comparisons significant at the 0.01 level); this suggests that subscribers to mobile computing services are less likely to leave the carrier. For mobile internet and mobile email, new customers tend to subscribe at slightly higher rates than customers who leave (both comparisons significant at the 0.01 level); however, new customer subscription rates are lower than rates for retained customers (all three comparisons significant at the 0.01 level). This is consistent with the idea that some new customers prefer to begin with a smaller set of services before expanding to mobile computing. The cause of this behavior is not discernable from this data; it may be due to increased price sensitivity among customers who move between carriers or who are new to cellular service.

Table 1. Percentage of customers subscribing to mobile computing services among those who retained, ceased, or began their service with this carrier during the study period.

Service Type	Retained Customers, Percent Subscribing	Lost Customers, Percent Subscribing	New Customers, Percent Subscribing
Mobile Internet	12.6%	10.9%	11.9%
Data Plan	12.5%	10.4%	10.1%
Mobile Email	20.2%	14.5%	15.6%

Table 2 displays customer purchase behavior for only those customers who were present through the whole study period. We can see that the ratio of customers who add or drop a service to those who maintain their subscription ranges from 0.45 to over 1.0. This is a high level of volatility. For comparison, we include results for the purchase of mobile phone insurance; this product shows low volatility, with a ratio of new customers to maintaining customers of only 0.05.

Table 2. Percentage who added, dropped, maintained, or never subscribed to each service between January 2008 and July 2008, only considering customers who were present through the entire study period.

Service Type	Percent who Added	Percent who Dropped	Percent who Maintained	Percent who Never Subscribed
Mobile Internet	3.9	5.7	8.6	81.7
Data Plan	6.3	6.7	6.2	80.8
Mobile Email	8.0	10.8	12.2	69.0
Mobile Phone Insurance	1.6	1.6	30.7	66.0

3.2. Prediction

We built logistic regression models to predict the probability of adoption of various mobile computing services based on past purchases. In this paper we present results from two models: purchase of mobile internet service, and purchase of a data plan. Each model was built using 100,000 customers as a training set; a separate set of 100,000 customers was used for validation. We developed 36 potential predictors based on billing history, as well as examining many interaction terms. Our final model for mobile internet contained 51 terms, and our final model for the data plan contained 39 terms. A full discussion of the logistic regression modeling process is beyond the scope of this paper; here we present only a small selection of relevant results.

Table 3 displays details for several predictors from our models. We find that business customers and customers with an unlimited calling plan are more likely to purchase mobile internet, while customers on plans with a night/weekend discount (e.g., free calling on nights and weekends) are less likely. Customers with an unlimited calling plan or a family calling plan are more likely to purchase a data plan, while prepaid or pay-as-you-go customers are less likely. Recall that a 1 unit change in log-odds is equivalent to a multiplicative impact of exp(1), or about 2.72, on the odds. For example, presence of an unlimited calling plan is associated with an increase in the odds of mobile internet purchase by a factor of 3.5.

Table 3. Selected results from logistic regression models for predicting customer purchases. Significance levels are based on the Chi-squared test of change in deviance for adding the predictor as a covariate in the final model.

Model	Predictor	Logistic Regression Coefficient (change in log-odds)	Significance Level
Mobile Internet	Unlimited Calling Plan	1.26	<0.0001
Mobile Internet	Business Customer	1.24	<0.0001
Mobile Internet	Plan with Night/Weekend discount	-0.62	<0.001
Data Plan	Family Calling Plan	0.29	<0.0001
Data Plan	Unlimited Calling Plan	0.24	<0.0001
Data Plan	Prepaid/Pay-as-you-go	-0.26	<0.01

These results are consistent with the hypothesis that customers who are less sensitive to price, such as business customers and those who have already purchased unlimited calling plans, are more likely to purchase mobile computing services. Similarly, customers who are more sensitive to price, such as those on prepaid plans or those who seek night/weekend discounts, are less likely to adopt mobile computing services.

References

[1] S.Y. Hung, D.C. Yen, and H.Y. Wang, Applying Data Mining to Telecom Churn Management, *Expert Systems with Applications* 31 (2006), 515-524.
[2] N.K. Joshi and M.A. Khan, Application of Data Mining in Telecom Industry, *Proceedings of the International Conference on Technology and Business Management* (2009), 1233-1236.
[3] P. McCullagh and J.A. Nelder, *Generalized Linear Models (2nd Edition)*, Chapman & Hall, London, 1989.
[4] M.C. Mozer, R. Wolniewicz, D.B. Grimes, E. Johnson, and H. Kaushansky, Predicting Subscriber Dissatisfaction and Improving Retention in the Wireless Telecommunications Industry, *IEEE Transactions on Neural Networks* 11-3 (2000), 690-696.
[5] M. Pagani, Determinants of Adoption of Third Generation Mobile Multimedia Services, *Journal of Interactive Marketing* 18-3 (2004), 46-59.
[6] R Development Core Team, *R: A language and environment for statistical computing*, R Foundation for Statistical Computing, Vienna, Austria, 2008.
[7] D.C. Stanford, Purchase Prediction from Billing Data, Globys Technical Report TR2009-02, 2009.
[8] J. Wareham, A. Levy, and K. Cousins, Wireless Diffusion and Mobile Computing: Implications for the Digital Divide, *Proceedings of ECIS* (2002), 1308-1319.

Posters

Intelligent Environments 2009
V. Callaghan et al. (Eds.)
IOS Press, 2009

doi:10.3233/978-1-60750-034-6-489

Maximizing Ridesharing Matches for Dynamic Carpooling

David THALER and Ankur TEREDESAI[1]
Institute of Technology, University of Washington, Tacoma

Abstract. Ubiquitous availability of web-based communications and presence information through portable data and GPS enabled mobile phones makes it possible to envision a system for dynamic carpooling to enhance flexibility in making carpool arrangements successful. However, a critical challenge is to design an algorithm that appropriately matches all travelers (riders and drivers). This paper introduces a dynamic ridesharing system that seeks to locate and optimize as many matches as possible, and then rank them by quality. This is a work-in-progress and current efforts address globally matching travelers so as to minimize the number of passengers without rides.

Keywords. Dynamic carpooling, travel planning, alternative transportation

Introduction

Carpooling is a cost-effective way to reduce carbon emission, reduce traffic, and ease parking constraints. For these reasons, governments and institutions often encourage carpooling with outreach, ride matching and preferential parking. Unfortunately, carpools are often hard to arrange. For a carpool to be formed, it is usually necessary for both the rider and the driver to be going from about the same place, to about the same place, at about the same time, and for them to be able discover this. Also, the rider needs a way to get back, so those same conditions usually apply to the return trip. At some locations, such as at an urban-university or a large corporation, the problem is simplified somewhat by the circumstance that one trip endpoint is shared by all of the members of that community. However, even if a carpool can be formed, it introduces inflexibility into the schedules of the participants. Focus group research indicates that this inflexibility is a major reason for people to discontinue participation in vanpools[1]. One approach to dealing with these difficulties is automated dynamic ride matching[2]. In this approach, a database and suitable communications technologies are used to find possible ride share opportunities, often on a day-of-travel basis, and then facilitate contact between the matched parties. This can introduce flexibility into carpooling arrangements for people who have irregular schedules or changes in their schedule.

This project will demonstrates a dynamic ride matching system based within the University of Washington, Tacoma community. It uses a web interface to communicate with travelers about their travel plans and any matches found in the system. In comparison to existing approaches to this problem, this work:

- Uses an algorithmic approach to matching riders that maximizes matches.
- Presents the resulting matches ranked by quality.

This work is still in progress, and in the next phase of the work this project will be extended to limit the likelihood of leaving certain passengers unmatched due to mismatching of the available drivers and passengers. Specifically:

- Measures will be developed to assess the quality of a set of matches. These measures will emphasize leaving as few passengers as possible without rides.
- An algorithm will be developed to consider groups of travelers so as to make the best global match of drivers and passengers over the group.

1. Dynamic Ridesharing

Dynamic ridesharing is a concept developed in response to the difficulties in forming carpools by traditional means. In this concept, travelers enter their travel plans into a database. The trips are then matched with compatible trips from the database. Results are communicated to users through a web interface.

The matching is done in one of two ways. Matching algorithms can be used to select compatible trips. A difficulty with this approach is that to work properly, algorithms need to deal with both geography and user preferences. In response to these difficulties, recent applications have relied on a data visualization approach. In this method, all trips in an area are presented on maps. Travelers are then invited to select trips that are compatible and contact the users who are making those trips.

2. Methodology

This work offers a baseline implementation of the dynamic ridesharing concept. Its principal difference from previous work is that it uses a new rule to match travelers. In this project, matches are judged by the ratio of the distance traveled to the distance that the driver would have traveled otherwise. Thus, matches of equal quality lie along an ellipse. The matches are presented in ranked order. These are relatively loose criteria, and some false positives occur. However, since the matches are presented with maps, this is acceptable. Travelers will simply identify them visually and not use them. Thus, the approach used here is a bit of a hybrid between the algorithmic and visualization-based approaches discussed earlier.

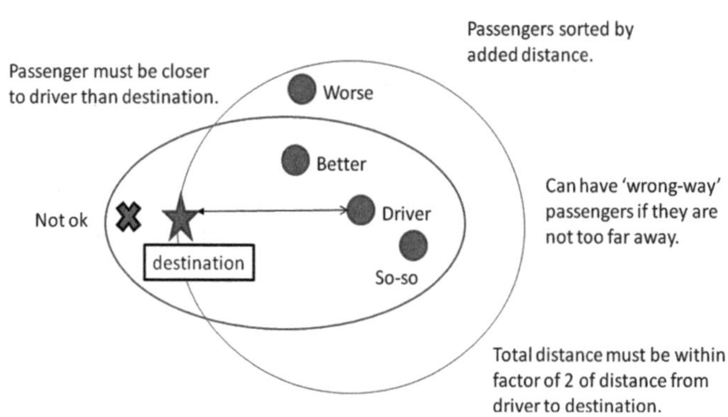

Figure 1. The matching rule.

An important point about the matching process is that it may result in sets of matches that are not globally optimal. Specifically, for a given set of trips, it may be possible to match all passengers to drivers under the constraints, yet it may not happen, resulting in stranded passengers. In figure 2, we have four travelers, all going to the same far-away location. Suppose that the constraint for the matching is a simple distance constraint, indicated by the circles in the figure. It is clearly possible to match both riders with both drivers without violating the constraint. However, if the order in which the travelers register their trips is Passenger 1, Passenger 2, Driver 1, Driver 2, then Passenger 2 will be paired with Driver 1 resulting in Passenger 1 being stranded.

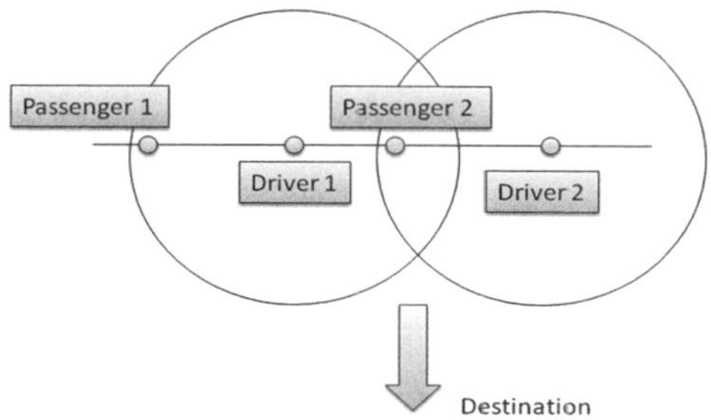

Figure 2. A possible mismatch.

This problem is inherent in any approach to ride matching that chooses the best match possible for each traveler at the time that they register a trip. Visualization-based approaches will always have this issue. Only the algorithmic approach has the potential to address this issue. In the next phase of this work, we will explore using an assignment algorithm to create globally optimal assignments of passengers and drivers. This will require developing a measure of the quality of a group of matches. The measures developed will emphasize minimizing the number of passengers who do not get rides.

3. Implementation

As currently implemented, this system consists of several components. Information about the travelers, trips and locations is stored in a database, implemented on the MySQL platform. Communication between the matching system and travelers is carried out through a web interface, implemented as a set of Java Server Pages. These pages handle the collection of trips, as well as providing updated information to travelers about any new matches. Program code that accesses the database handles data validation and conversion. Currently, the matching of travelers is accomplished by a query against the database. It says that a passenger may be routed with a driver if:

- They are going in the same direction.
- Their travel time windows overlap.
- The passenger is closer to the driver than the destination. That is the driver cannot be routed past the destination and then back.
- The total distance from the driver to the passenger to the destination is at most twice the distance from the driver to the destination.

If any matches are found, then they are sorted by the added distance and the top five are presented. Contact information is provided for the matching travelers. If drivers are receiving the matches, they get maps and location information as well. The maps are provided from Google through the Google Map API. Distances are figured on a straight-line basis, so some anomalies occur, for instance routes that cross water. Clearly, this part of the system could use improvement. However, it is worth noting that at present matches are simply presented to travelers, who then choose which travelers to contact from among any matches that they have. Thus, this is really a problem of having a few false positives, given the current communication cycle.

In the next phase of this work, it will include an algorithm for making the best global assignment of a group of passengers to a group of drivers. This will require developing measures of the quality of a set of matches. The ellipse rule is a step in this direction, in that it allows a measure of the quality of one match.

4. Related Work

The dynamic ride matching concept was the subject of federally-funded research in the 1990's at the University of Washington Seattle. In the Seattle Smart Traveler[2] (SST) program, people at the University of Washington could co-ordinate travel to and from the Seattle campus by a web-based ride matching system. This work identified scale-dependence as a key aspect of dynamic rideshare systems. There is some probability that two travelers will be compatible. Thus, the number of matches scales as the number of pairs of travelers, which is quadratic in the size of the population. Although this project was reasonably successful, its funding was not extended.

Today there are several ventures in this area. GoLoco.org is a national operation whose application allows the formation of groups. This is a step towards introducing social networking concepts into alternative transportation. Goose Networks is a Seattle company that offers a ride matching web application. Its product is integrated with transit planning. This is an important step towards integrated transportation routing.

5. Conclusion and Further Work

This project demonstrates an implementation of a dynamic ridesharing system. As currently implemented, this system seeks to locate all possible matches. In the process, it does produce some false positives. At this point, this is acceptable, since the matches found are ranked by a quality measure and presented visually with maps. Thus, the system uses a hybrid of algorithmic and visualization based matching.

In the next phase of this project, we will seek to minimize the number of passengers who do not get rides by globally matching groups of riders and drivers. This will require developing a new quality measure suitable for sets of ride matches.

References

[1]Y.B. Yim, A. Khattak. Personalized Demand Responsive Transit Systems. *Paper UCB-ITS-PWP-2000-22. Institute for Transportation Studies, University of California Berkeley* (2000)

[2]D.J Dailey, D. Loseff, D. Meyers, Seattle Smart Traveler: Dynamic Ridematching on the World Wide Web. *Transportation Research Part* C, **7** (1999), 1-16.

Intelligent Environments 2009
V. Callaghan et al. (Eds.)
IOS Press, 2009

doi:10.3233/978-1-60750-034-6-493

Cipo_09 music box

hybrid robotic <organism> - [laterna]

DAFLOS E. KOSTAS
Adjunct lecturer, Patras School of Architecture, PhD candidate
N.T.U.A. Greece

Abstract. The CIPO artwork program are interactive action-based installations, that investigate through robot agents, the relationship between subjects, body and space. The interminglement of spectators within the digital framework transforms the space to an experimental place. The CIPO program involves the physical viewer participation and the live energy of the human presence; it agitates the spectators to perform into an active relation with subjects and objects in place. Cipo_09 art objects are (3) three similar interactive handmade music boxes bring sound events. Cipo_09 music boxes have been drawn such as unhistoric impromptu instruments, which appropriate the concept and sounds of old music boxes from the 19th century. Different sound events created by human presences, are transcribed through cipo_09 hybrid objects to open sound scenarios.

Keywords. Music box, robotic, interactive instrument, hybrid, sound installation

Introduction

The CIPO installations have been hosted (2003-) in diverse spaces [1] producing interactive real environments, within the framework of independent art events and art-technology festivals. They reinforce thoughts that a diverged and disorganized merge of material parts and media in combination with the human can compose different alternatives for the imagination, by breaking up the stereotypes [2]. CIPO program wants to realize a class of communication between automated objects, subjects and space.

The cipo_09 artwork: a/ takes on the concept of old musical boxes in Europe, from the 19th century, and b/ works up the concept of the nomadic practice of mobile, ephemeral musical events, taking place in urban public spaces, as well as music objects in Greece (20th century) that are called <laterna> [Greek: *λατέρνα*] and the shape of those mechanical automated instruments.

The old musical boxes reproduce programmed performances of popular music from digital data on analogical mediums [3]. These mediums were such as marked metallic discs, cylinders and perforated paper discs and strips. The sounds from the musical boxes combined with instrumental sounds from elementary percussion instruments, bells and miniatures of musical instruments, were enclosed together in the assembly of wooden cases [4]. Mechanical parts close to the technology in the period of the telegraph and the phonograph, and micro material (reeds, foils, membranes, air columns) were linked by automated clock mechanisms which were motivated to start by the spectators with his/her contribution.

1. Description of the cipo_09 music box

Cipo_09 interactive installation (3 music boxes) is based on the articulation of modern and contemporary technologies. Human presence interacts on the internal environment of the cipo_09, generating responses from the 3 "organisms". These hybrid organisms are inspired and shaped from the old musical boxes of the 19th century as well as the "laterna" of the 20th century. These objects produce mixes of sound events (disable-enable interrupts, performances) via robotic technology (sensors, motors, cameras), as well as reproductions of musical compositions that are created in real time randomly from the audience movements.

The responses of the three cipo_09 instruments are composed from the interference of bodies (virtual and real) and their interaction into a common distributed body. The music results from stored lulling melodies [5], waltz etc, that are redrawn randomly [6] by the audience, produce new conditions of listen perceptions destroying the basic melodies, very close to parody.

1.1. The relation of cipo_09 music box with the musical boxes of the 19th century

The cipo_ 09 music boxes work up the function, the typology and melodies from the following three handmade mechanical musical boxes, also appropriating their sounds [7]:

- **caixa de musica – orquestra**, (end of the 19th century) / dimensions: 46x28x20 cm / performance duration: 51 sec/ [metallic cylinder, (comb) steel foils, 3 bells, 2 miniature drums, clock mechanism].
- **la radieuse,** (end of the 19th century) / dimensions: 70x33x126 cm / performance duration: 94 sec/ theme title: ´´Mimosa Valsa de Noronha´´/ [metallic discs of diameter 56 cm - 800 kg, (comb) steel foil with 85 endings, 6 bells, crank, slot machine].
- **kalliope** (calliope), (1890-1900) / dimensions: 65x58x26 cm / performance duration: 62 sec/ theme title: ´´Bonher Perdu´´/ [metallic disc, (comb) steel foil, 5 bells, crank].

1.2. The separation of the music box cipo_09 borrowing from Kafka's torture machine

In cipo_09 music box three separated cases are linked, each one of them with a different function, inspired from the descriptions of the fantastic torture machine in Franz Kafka's novel «in der Strafkolonie» edited in 1919 [8]. Franz Kafka writes about a fantastic torture machine which has three different parts with mechanisms that engrave the human body. Respectively, cipo_09 music box produces sound environments from the body presence through a series of successive process.

The three separated cases are:

The ´´recorder´´ is the case of communication and dialogue with the environment. Has a dimension of 17x24x40 cm, it communicates through 1 sound sensor & 1 movement sensor. It includes 1 microprocessor unit /robot & 1 camera /robot and is interconnected with the case of the ′′designer′′, the case of ′′audition′′, and the pc-computer.

Its processes boot from the computer and the robot unit. Recorded information is related with the ′′organism′′ behavior and recent information concerns its interaction with the external stimulations. The feedback is transmitted to the ′′designer′′ and the ′′reproducer′′. The human interventions are captured analogical and then digitalized and linked to digital sound files with a pc program. Then they can be transmitted to the ′′listening′′ case as an analogue form of signal. By means of a sound sensor they return as digital signals to the microprocessor/robot unit, activating the ′′designer′′, producing feedback responses.

The conceptual form of the ′′designer′′ is the case which produces natural sounds. It contains a motor, microphones, foil arms, and percussion instruments (bells, metal dishes). Internally the case of the designer has installed microphones which are connected with the pc. The ′′designer′′ has the dimensions of 50x24x40 cm and is interconnected with the case of the ′′recorder′′. The sounds are derived from feedback stimulation that comes from the ′′recorder′′ and executed in real time with contact clapping of the arms that are leaded from a motor mechanism. The influences of the human presence break in the process, designing the sound of the environment and recalling again and again different sound files that compose sound "objects", musical phrases and melody fragments.

The ′′reproducer′′ has the character of the sound insulated case that allows connections with the internal ′′auditions′′. It contains sound boxes connected with the computer, one sound sensor that communicates with the microprocessor/robot unit. Has the dimensions of 17x24x40 cm and is interconnected with the case of the ′′recorder′′ and the computer. This part is an enclosed internal environment that remains relatively isolated and unaffected from the external environment as well as from the rest parts of the disposition. The variations of sounds that are reproduced in the pc are broadcasted in this theca.

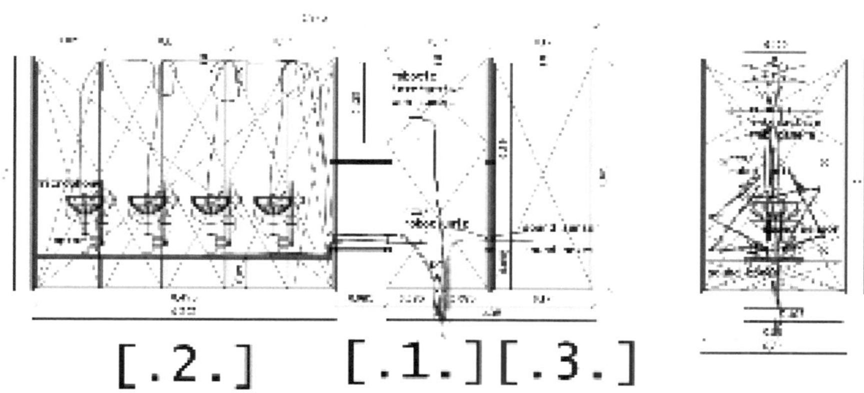

Figure 1. [.1.] theca of the ′′recorder′′, [.2.] theca of the ′′designer′′, [.3.] theca of the ′′listening′′

Figure 2. cipo_09 / music box – laterna

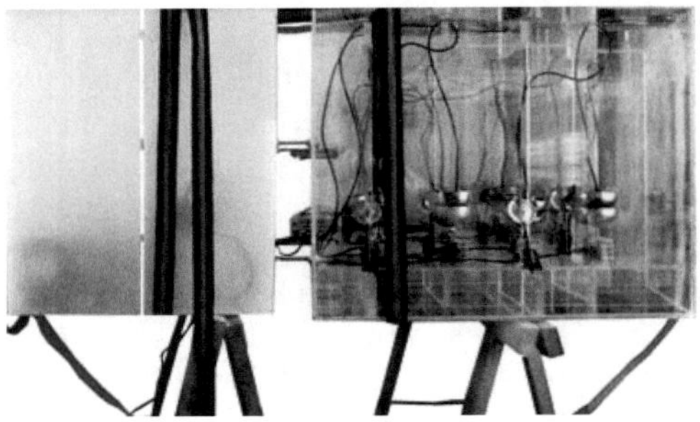

Figure 3. cipo_09 / music box - laterna

References

[1] D. Tercio, *TeDance, Perspectives on Technologically Expanded Dance*, fMH, Portugal, 2008, *K. Daflos., c(2)ipo_06 music box, p.228-231*
[2] P. K. Feyerabend, *Against Method*, 1975
[3] A. Moles, *Theorie de l'information et perception esthetique*, Denoel, Paris, 1972
[4] B. Serexhe, P. Weibel, *Wolfang von Kempelen, Man-[in the]-machine,* ZKM Book, Berlin, 2007
[5] Th. W. Adorno, *Quasi una Fantasia: Essays on Modern Music*, Frankfurt, 1963
[6] M. Solomos, *Iannis Xenakis,* Editions, 1996
[7] L. Cangueiro, *Instrumentos de Musica Mecanica*, Quinta do Rei – Lazer e Cultura, Lda, 2007
[8] F. Kafka, *in der Strafkolonie*, 1919

Doctoral Colloquium

Intelligent Environments 2009
V. Callaghan et al. (Eds.)
IOS Press, 2009

doi:10.3233/978-1-60750-034-6-499

Internalizing Unknown Objects by Means of Perception and Communication in Multi-Agent Systems

Author: PhD Student Nikolaos DIPSIS
Supervisor: Dr Kostas STATHIS
Department of Computer Science
Royal Holloway, University of London
March 2009, UK
nikolaos@cs.rhul.ac.uk

Abstract

Very commonly, multi-agent systems built for ubiquitous computing and ambient intelligence applications require from their members to perform collaborative tasks or to attempt to communicate regarding potentially unknown objects in their environment. The specific class of this type of systems that constitutes the domain for the proposed research defines multi-agent systems utilizing agents that encompass high-level symbolic name worlds that are linked to their environment via low level sensory input. A successful outcome when attempting collaborative tasks in such systems is always dependent on the ability of the agents to refer to the correct objects in their communication. In my research I will pursue an approach towards confronting the above problem and propose a solution. This solution will be applied in this category of multi-agent systems enabling them to deal with the imperative to verify that all agents refer to the correct object in order for the outcome of a collaborative task upon it or the communication regarding it to be successful.

Introduction

Computer scientists, sociologists, psychologists and engineers have been researching towards an application of a feasible solution to the problem of creating mirrors of real objects to a constructed high-level world of a machine while at the same time establishing the connections between them. Most commonly the term "Symbol Grounding"[2] is preferred by the researchers in order to categorize the above issues that deal with human or "intelligent" machine perceptions. There is a plethora of approaches and categorizations of the problem besides the one of the "Symbol Grounding" which was formulated by Harnad [2]. The Anchoring approach [1] is a notable one while others employ theories from semiotics [4].

This fundamental problem of Computer Science can emerge in various applications and systems, as many as the numerous approaches and proposed solutions towards it [see "Theoretical Foundations"]. The artificial perception is a widely researched area and depending on the application, it may appear in different forms. In this paper we present and discuss a new approach towards a form of the artificial perception problem. My research is focused on multi-agent applications that require effective communication and collaborative activity among the agents with regards to potentially unknown objects in their environment. A fundamental issue when designing such systems deals with intrinsic differences in object perception between the different agents participating in collaborative activity. It is imperative for all agents to refer to the correct objects in order for the outcome of a collaborative task upon them or the communication regarding them to be successful. This research aims to introduce a new technique that will attempt to allow the agents to communicate successfully regarding unknown physical objects in their environment, learn new ones and perform collaborative tasks upon them. This technique will be applied to a multi-agent system situated in an unknown, dynamic environment in which the agents are required to communicate regarding the unknown objects and perform collaborative tasks upon them. At this point it would be useful to present a more explanatory presentation of the theoretical foundations and the areas that affect the above problem.

1. Theoretical Foundations

An artificial agent, a machine able to perceive the environment and create mirrors of the perceived environment in a high-level symbolic world, should establish a link between the physical environment and its perception of the world. Various issues arise when designing agents that are capable of perception. An important one has to do with the fact that the limitations of perception define the creation of the high-level world in the agents' internal state. Also, many issues, as it will be argued later on in this report, deal with the actual link between a physical perceived object and its mirror in the high-level symbolic world.

It is essential at this point to familiarize the reader with a few notions defining a symbol and a symbolic world. Newell [6] in his "physical symbol system hypothesis" states that physical symbol systems are essential for the existence of intelligence. These systems are able to store, manipulate and interpret symbolic structures according to a set of specified rules. The symbols according to him are patterns that provide a distant access to a structure (Newell [6]). They are internal representations that can be accessed from an external structure and the relation between the symbols meaning to the outside world is regarded to be of high importance. Similarly and following the same school of cognition that assumes symbols as internal representations, Harnad [2] defines a symbol as an arbitrary category name. Following these definitions of symbols as internal representations, a problem rises with regards to their meaning, their connection to the outside world and the means of linking them to real world objects.

Harnad [2] is responsible for the provision of the classic formulation of the Symbol Grounding Problem. His formulation of the "Symbol Grounding" concept was a milestone in the machine perception research. He used the Chinese Room Argument (Searle 1980) to introduce the symbol grounding problem. An agent is able to manipulate high-level symbols but there is no indication that the agent actually has access to the symbols meaning. According to Searle it is like someone who is expected to learn Chinese just by using a Chinese to Chinese dictionary. In both cases, the agent and the person who does not speak Chinese will fail. The physical shape and properties of the symbol usually provide no relation to the object they refer to. Harnard [2] attempted to solve this problem by proposing a model. In his model, the manipulated by an agent symbols would become grounded by establishing a relationship with the perceptual data that they denote. His bottom-up approach was defined by categorizing the low-level perceptual data. Vogt [3][5] provided with a solution attempting to connect the approach proposed by Harnad [2] with the semiotic definition of symbols. Steels and Vogt [14] conducted experiments in which artificial and autonomous agents were grounded to their environment by means of vision and this grounding would enable the creation of meanings and language through adaptive language games. Coradeschi and Saffiotti [1] in their approach to solve the problems of connecting the sensory input to high-level names-symbols conceived the "Anchoring Problem". It illustrates the grounding of object names to sensory data and maintaining this mapping to take into account the dynamic changes of sensory input. Although the symbol grounding problem considers all kinds of symbols, Anchoring focuses on connecting object names with visual objects in the agents' physical environment.

The above approaches either (a) investigate perception from a theoretical point of view (e.g. Harnad [2], Saffioti [1]) to provide a solution to the general problem of machine perception and symbol grounding, or (b) they focus on more specific problems such as the creation of a common, uniformed grounding framework between multiple agents (Vogt [3][5][14]). A variation of (b) will be proposed in this work to provide a solution that seeks to enable the members of a multi-agent system to perform meaningful communication regarding the unknown objects that they perceive in their environment.

2. Problem Overview

The topic of machine perception and the various problems revolving around grounding symbols of high-level agent worlds to real objects have been widely researched. Harnards symbol grounding [2], Saffiotis Anchoring [1] and several others such as Clancey [10] attempted to provide with solutions and foundations towards confronting the artificial perception issues. These solutions mainly focus on the problem of agent perception per se. There are more aspects to this problem though, especially when designing multi-agent systems that are dependent on the perception in order to achieve their goals and perform their tasks successfully. These systems often require from agents to perform collaborative tasks on environment objects; these tasks require either communication between agents about the external objects or a common perception framework verifying that each agent performs the right action on the right object. In order to achieve the above though, the agents need to be able to successfully communicate to each other the objects that each one of them individually perceives. In situations that the physical objects in the multi-agent environment are pre-configured and stored in the high-level world of each agent, the potential communication regarding them would be feasible with the addition of a simple communication system. The main requirement of these systems would be the application of one of the existing perception theories, such as the symbol grounding or the Anchoring solutions from Harnard and

Saffioti respectively. As we can see in Figure 1, if the high-level symbol/name worlds would consist of preexisting symbols/names that share the same attributes, then the communication between the agents regarding the objects that the names refer to would be a relatively easy task by utilizing theories from existing literature.

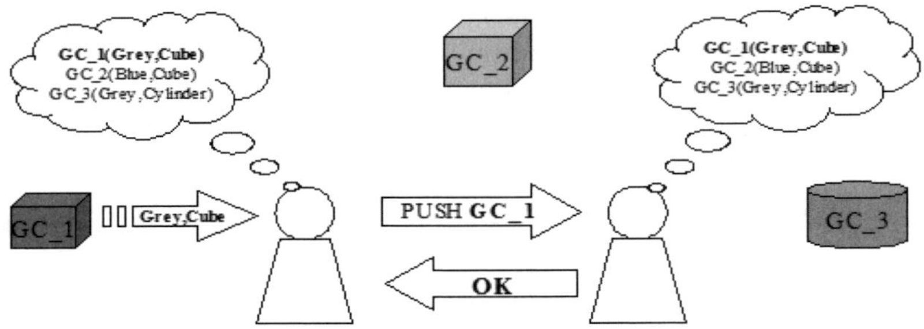

Figure 1 Successful communication regarding a known object

The problems start rising when the multi-agent system is introduced to an unknown environment containing unknown objects.

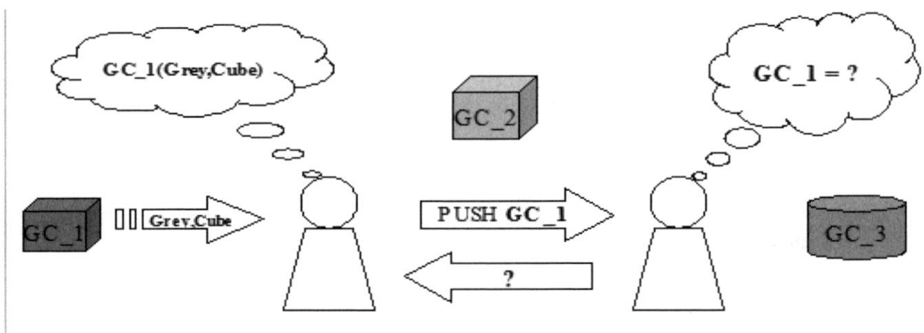

Figure 2 Attempt to communicate regarding an unknown object

In many cases the multi-agent systems are situated in unknown environments that consist of unknown to the agents objects. There are two main issues that need to be addressed for the successful completion of collaborative tasks in this type of systems. The first needs to address the problem of internalizing new objects based on the perception of each individual agent. The second issue refers to the ability of the agents to meaningfully communicate to each other the symbols that were created from their individual perception mechanisms in order to refer in a communicable manner to physical objects in their environment. Figure 2 illustrates a simple example of this problem. The first agent perceives an object and creates a high-level symbol for it. Then it requests from the second agent to perform an action upon the object. The second one has knowledge neither of the object that the first agent refers to nor of the symbol\name that the first assigned to it.

The scope of this research covers various types of artificial multi-agent systems that share a number of common characteristics. More specifically it encapsulates all multi-agent systems that share the following characteristics which from now and on we will conventionally refer to as "Scope Conditions":

i) The system should consist of multiple agents.
ii) The agents should be sharing the same physical environment.
iii) The agents should follow the design pattern duality of a high-level symbolic name world coupled by low level sensory data inputs.
iv) The agents should have identically structured high-level symbolic name worlds.
v) The agents should have identical physical means of perception for their shared environment. This includes the sensors and the mechanisms of receiving the low level data that will bestow meaning to the high-level symbolic names.
vi) The agents should be able to communicate with each other.
vii) The agents should be sharing common communication semantics that will allow their interaction and the manifestation of the proposed solution.
viii) The agents should share a set of primitives for their perception. This set will constitute of symbolic level attributes for perceived objects such as shapes and colors.

3. Importance

From the above, it is clear that the successful outcome of the collaborative tasks in multi-agent systems situated in unknown environments is impossible unless the following two issues are addressed:

1. Perception for internalizing objects. In the context of this paper, the "object internalizing" will be defined as the process of creating a new and meaningful name\symbol in an agents high-level name\symbol world. By meaningful we refer to names\symbols that are linked to an external object by a re-usable correspondence mechanism. This correspondence mechanism might differ in the various approaches (symbol grounding, Anchoring).

2. Meaningful agent communication regarding a potentially unknown to the agents environment.

Every multi-agent system that requires from its members to perform collaborative tasks or to attempt to communicate regarding objects in an unknown environment demands a solution to the aforementioned issues by any means. Thus the importance of this problem is deemed critical to any such design. My research intends to benefit collaborative multi-agent applications that require object perception, effective communication and collaborative activity among the agents with regards to potentially unknown objects in their environment. I will propose an alternative approach towards confronting this fundamental problem.

4. Proposed Solution

We are working towards a solution to the problem of collaborative activity upon unknown objects. This solution should fulfill the two fundamental requirements that were identified in the previous ("Importance"):

1. Perception: Object internalizing (as it is defined in the current context) and
2. Meaningful agent communication regarding the environment.

In order to fulfill the requirements, we will propose a technique that will revolve around a set of two capabilities that will be introduced in this research:

1. Perception Grounded Communication.
2. Virtual Anchoring for Perception.

4.1. Perception Grounded Communication

The main idea behind the Perception Grounded Communication (PGC) capability is to homogenize the way agents perceive external objects with the way they communicate regarding them. In the context of this report, the object internalization was previously defined as the process of creating a new and meaningful name/symbol in the agents high-level name/symbol world. The Perception Grounded Communication capability enables each agent to internalize new objects both by communication and perception as it is illustrated in figure 3.

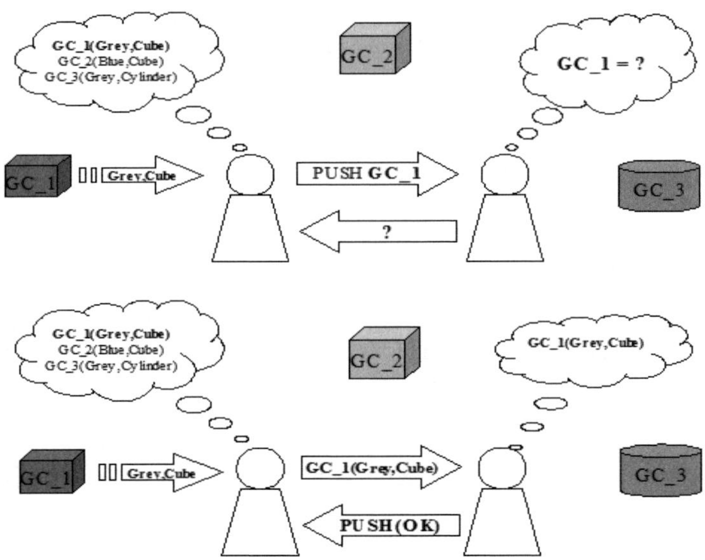

Figure 3 Successful communication regarding unknown object

Essentially, this work introduces the PGC capability in order to allow each agent to communicate the names of its individually meaningful high-level name world to other agents in a meaningful to them manner. The main idea behind the Perception Grounded Communication capability is that a new name may be created in an agents high-level name world by communicating percepts i.e. the physical attributes of the corresponding object. Figure 4 illustrates the main idea behind this technique.

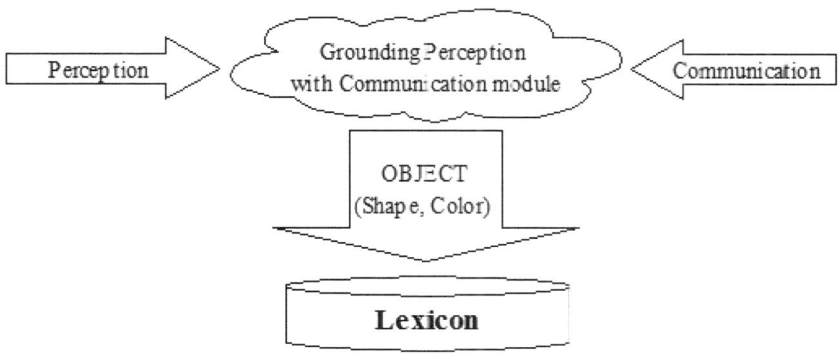

Figure 4 Perception Grounded Communication

The shared set of primitives for the agent perception will constitute the background ontology behind the PGC capability.

4.2. Virtual Anchoring

The second capability introduces an approach for an object perception solution in a way that it conforms with the "Scope Conditions" of "Problem Overview". It introduces a new approach for Anchoring low-level data to high-level names (tags) based on Saffiotis Anchoring solution that allows the attribution of "meaning" to the high-level symbolic names. An anchor provides with a direct and maintained link between the physical object and the high-level symbolic name. This link is dependent on the perception and not the internal representation. According to Saffioti, an updated relationship between the name and the physical object should be maintained. Essentially Saffiotis solution to the Anchoring problem is portrayed by the challenging task of creating and maintaining a correspondence between the high-level, abstract name and the low-level perceptual data. The proposed Anchoring process in Saffioti's paper [1] is comprised of a Symbolic Name System, a Perceptual System, and a Predicate Grounding Relation between the names and the perceptual data.

The new capability that will be a part of the researched set of capabilities, proposes a more generalized and differentiated form for an Anchoring solution. Based on Saffiotis Anchoring, the "Virtual Anchoring" or VA capability could be viewed as a more generalized and portable solution introducing at the same time new features. The idea behind the VA capability is to provide with a solution for a variety of systems and environments, real and virtual alike. The common perquisite for these environments is to encompass the notions of external world object, internal world name and a correspondence function between the two. The proposed new version of Anchoring features a number of differences in comparison to Saffiotis solution:

1. The main feature of our our proposed adaptation of Safiotis Anchoring is the ability to utilize any type of data input (sensory or other) regarding an external object and attribute it to a high-level name/tag via a correspondence function. Saffiotis Anchoring was tailored to visual sensory data while our approach may utilize any type of data (sensor) input.

2. The term Virtual refers to the ability of VA to be applied to virtual environments as well as to real ones. Saffiotis Anchoring is mainly intended for real world environments and this fact alone ties the process of Anchoring to the notion of maintenance of the correspondence function.

3. Saffiotis Anchoring is not a one-shot process and it takes into account a continuous flow of low-level data input. The difference in our adaptation is that there is a control mechanism for the maintenance function. This mechanism utilizes the maintenance function according to the needs of each task that requires VA by adjusting the number of maintenance repetitions.

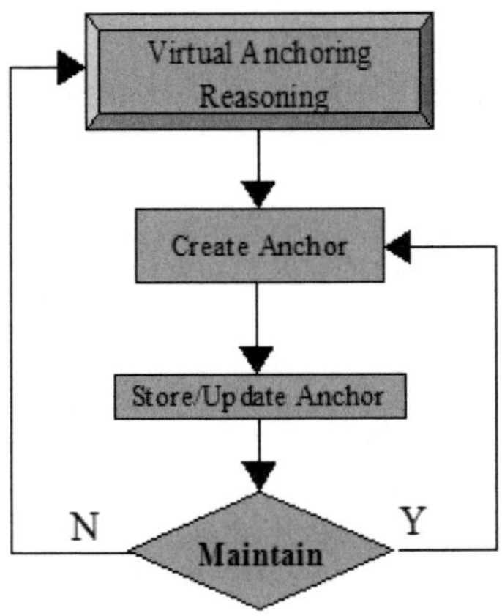

Flowchart 1 Virtual Anchoring

4.3. Achieving Meaningful Communication

The "Virtual Anchoring" capability will enable the agents to internalize previously unknown objects and the "Perception Grounded Communication" capability will allow each agent to communicate the internalized names of its individually meaningful high-level name world to other agents in a meaningful to them manner as we have seen in [*4.1*]. Thus, the agents are able to communicate successfully regarding previously unknown objects in their environment and perform collaborative tasks upon them.

5. Existing Solutions – Comparison - Evaluation

Previously we defined two capabilities: VA and PGC. The Virtual Anchoring could be viewed as a generalized and portable adaptation of Saffiotis Anchoring, maintaining the advantages of Anchoring as a perception mechanism while at the same time introducing new ones. The Virtual Anchoring extends the scope of the portability of Anchoring because:

1. By definition it can be applied to virtual systems as well.
2. It may internalize an object by utilizing any type of data input.

Furthermore, the VA mechanism benefits from the addition of intelligence and it can actually modify its performance and priorities internally. This will improve the performance of the proposed system dramatically since it will allow a determination of flexible perception and action task strategies. Also, the Virtual Anchoring will be using the necessary system resources and only. For example when a request for a task to internalize a new object is issued, the control mechanism will utilize the maintenance function accordingly and usually with fewer repetitions. In a scenario in which the agent performs an action on an object, the repetitions of the maintenance function need to reiterate until the action is complete. The Anchoring solution is a simple yet effective approach that presents great flexibility.

The second proposed capability (PGC) unifies the way agents anchor to the way they communicate regarding objects. This homogenization presents great potential for the purposes of cooperative Anchoring. It is a very beneficial addition to the Anchoring process since it provides a common framework of communication for each agent's anchors. It also simplifies the design of cooperative multi-agent systems. In comparison with Vogts Lexicon Creation [3] the simplification lies in the fact that while Vogt needed to perform the "Language Games" in order to achieve the shared and communicated grounding, the required communication semantics in the proposed solution may be as simple as a basic "reply-request" protocol.

An Anchoring approach to cooperative robotics was employed by Saffioti and Leblanc [18] in a ubiquitous robotic environment which is called PEIS (Physically Embedded Intelligent Systems). Anchoring was used as the mechanism of identifying objects in the environment that were pre-existing in a shared memory between the agents and the environment itself. The robots would employ Anchoring in order to verify that they refer to the same object along with various sources of information deriving from the ubiquitous environment including the id of the observed object itself. The results where successful yet the problem was different than the one studied in this paper. In our case there is absolutely no knowledge of the external world and the communication regarding objects for the cooperative activities. There is no blackboard and the sole information source for each agent is derived from the perception and homogenization techniques of our proposed set of capabilities. Despite the fact that the two problems, environments and systems differ, both attempt an Anchoring solution to a specific area of communicative robotics. The proposed in this paper solution theoretically could perform cooperative activity in unknown or real world environments without the perquisite of pre-defined tags.

Another benefit of the set of capabilities is the fact that it increases geometrically the speed and quality of the internalizing process since the agents may internalize new objects by direct and instant communication with other agents. The existence of more agents would consequently result to more "ground coverage" and significantly less time in internalizing all the new objects in the environment since every agent will learn what all the other agents perceive by requesting this information.

6. Experiments Applications

It has been established previously that any multi-agent system that requires from its members to perform collaborative tasks or to attempt to communicate regarding objects in an unknown environment would benefit from the proposed set of capabilities. We have chosen the Golem platform[15] for the experiments and the development of the applications. Currently we are investigating which model of agency will be used for our experiments and the implementation of a cooperative agent activity application. For the initial experiments I will be focusing in creating an agent architecture within the Golem platform that will be utilizing the proposed set of capabilities. We anticipate to utilize the KGP model of agency[19] for the more complicated application implementations. In sort, the application of the above setup benefiting from the proposed solution will be a multi-agent system situated in an unknown, dynamic environment implemented in the Golem platform, in which the agents are required to communicate regarding the unknown objects and perform collaborative tasks. The first stage of the experiments will involve a simulation of a "Guided Herd of Robots" application in which one "Leader" agent will be instructing the herd of agents to perform actions on objects in the dynamic environment.

7. Epilogue – Additions to the Set of Capabilities

This research mainly involves issues in multi-agent systems that require from their members cooperative and communicative perception of physical objects. The solution that was briefly outlined is intended for application on agents with a limited number of sensors to perceive simple objects. An extension of the work involves a larger number of sensors and perceived attributes of the physical objects. From the current research, a number of problems appear when the number of sensors and percepts increase. Some of these problems have been recorded to be storage capacity issues, communication issues in large multi-agent systems, latency, differences in perception, dysfunctional sensors, and some percepts being of no use or misleading. In the future we will attempt to provide new additions seeking to enable the agents to "choose" and utilize from experience a minimized set of attributes when perceiving or communicating an object, thus minimizing the chances of presenting the above problems. The new capability will allow the communication of super-classes from which the agents may create internal objects that refer to external ones in their environment. Also we plan to attempt more complicated forms of communication that will involve expressions of similarity (e.g. bring me the white object that is "like a ball") between agents.

References

[1] Coradeschi, S. and Saffiotti, A., 2003. An introduction to the Anchoring problem. In *Robotics and Autonomous Systems* 43(2-3):85–96. Special issue on perceptual Anchoring.

[2] S. Harnad, 1990. The Symbol Grounding Problem. In *Physica* D, pp. 335-346.

[3] Vogt, P. 2000. *Lexicon Grounding on Mobile Robots*. PhD Dissertation, Vrije Universiteit Brussel.

[4] Chandler D. 1994. Semiotics for beginners. http://www.aber.ac.uk/media/Documents/S4B/semiotic.html.

[5] P. Vogt, 2002. Anchoring Symbols to Sensorimotor Control. In *Proceedings of Belgian/Netherlands Artificial Intelligence Conference* BNAIC'02.

[6] Newell, A. 1980. Physical symbol systems. In *Cognitive Science* 4:135–183.

[7] Hume David. A Treatise of Human Nature. Chapter I, 4, 6.

[8] Peirce, C. 1931. Collected Papers, volume I-VIII. *Cambridge Ma: Harvard University Press*. (The volumes were published from 1931 to 1958).

[9] Berkeley George in "Principles of Human Knowledge, 3"

[10] Clancey 1997. *Situated Cognition*.

[11] Mariarosaria Taddeo and Luciano Floridi, December 2005. Solving the Symbol Grounding Problem: a Critical Review of Fifteen Years of Research. In *Journal of Experimental & Theoretical Artificial Intelligence*, Volume 17, Issue 4, pages 419 - 445

[12] Vogt P., 2002. *The Physical Symbol Grounding Problem.* University of Maastricht, Infonomics, Holland.

[13] Vogt P., 2003. *Anchoring of Semiotic Symbols*. University of Maastricht, Infonomics, Holland.

[14] Steels, L. and Vogt, P. 1997. Grounding adaptive language game in robotic agents. In Husbands, C., and Harvey, I., eds., *Proc. of the 4th European Conference on Artificial Life*. London: MIT Press.

[15]Stefano Bromuri and Kostas Stathis, Situating Cognitive Agents in GOLEM. In the proceedings EEMMAS 2007, Dresden, Germany, October 2007.

[16] Lego Co. *Mindstorms Robotics Manual*. http://www.**legomindstorms**.com

[17] Foundation for Intelligent Physical Agents. www.**fipa**.org/

[18] K. LeBlanc and A. Saffiotti. Issues of Perceptual Anchoring in Ubiquitous Robotic Systems. *Proc. of the ICRA-07 Workshop on Omniscient Space. Rome, Italy, 2007.*

[19] Antonis C. Kakas, Paolo Mancarella, Fariba Sadri, Kostas Stathis, and Francesca Toni. The KGP model of Agency. In Proceedings of the 16th European Conference of Artificial Intelligence (ECAI'04), pages 33-37, Valencia, Aug. 2004.

Intelligent Environments 2009
V. Callaghan et al. (Eds.)
IOS Press, 2009

doi:10.3233/978-1-60750-034-6-510

The Legal Status of Profiles

Niels VAN DIJK[1]
Institute for Law, Science, Technology & Society (LSTS)
Vrije Universiteit Brussel (VUB), Belgium

Abstract. The making of digital copies is the fundamental manner in which information technologies function. This has transformed copyright in the dominant legal form for the world of digital technologies and into a fundament for the modern knowledge economy. We are today confronted with the introduction and implementation of a new generation of information processing technologies under the header of Ambient Intelligence. Profiling is one of the enabling technologies behind Ambient Intelligence. These technologies provide a continuous and real-time production of profiles, which are themselves in a constant state of flux. Determining the legal status of profiles shows the increasing challenges of imposing the old intellectual rights scheme, based on presuppositions about original expressions of ideas, on these new information technologies.

Keywords: Ambient Intelligence, Profiling, Databases, Copyright, Idea-Expression Dichotomy, Originality

Introduction

This paper will analyze how intellectual rights relate to profiling processes. It will focus especially on the legal status of profiles. First an articulation of the steps of the technological process of profiling will be undertaken. Then the objects that are relevant from the perspective of intellectual rights will be identified, which are databases, computer programs and profiles. The questions that need to be answered and the aspects that need to be taken into account in order to determine the legal status of profiles are analyzed. The exploration in this article will be cartographical; an attempt is made to draw a preliminary map of the terrain, hoping to identify the tensions and problems and to provoke some discussion.

[1] Corresponding Author: Niels van Dijk, PhD Student at Institute for Law, Science, Technology & Society (LSTS), Vrije Universiteit Brussel (VUB), Pleinlaan 2, 1050, Brussels, Belgium, e-mail: nvdijk@vub.ac.be

1. The Technologies

We are today confronted with the introduction and implementation of a new generation of information processing technologies under the header of Ambient Intelligence [1]. In order to determine how intellectual rights relate to Ambient Intelligence we have to make an analysis of the relevant technological processes. Profiling is an important enabling technology behind Ambient Intelligence [2]. The technological process of profiling can be split up in separate segments which form an iterative loop [3] [4]. These segments will be analyzed in order to determine what legal statute is applicable. They are:

- Specification of the Problem Domain and Goals of Analysis
- Data Collection: The target dataset or *database* for analysis is formed by selecting the relevant *data* in the light of existing domain knowledge.
- Data Preparation: The data are pre-processed for removing noise and reducing complexity by eliminating attributes. Biases may be generated in the process.
- Data Mining: analysis of the data with the *algorithm* or *heuristics* chosen to suit the data, model and goals
- Interpretation: the mined patterns are evaluated on their "usefulness" by the analysts
- Application of Profiles to Users
- Institutional Decisions and Policies upon Profile Application.

Data mining provides patterns that describe relationships between a set of data. As we can see from the definition from Fayyad et al these patterns are interesting when they are valid for future data, novel, understandable and useful for the purposes of the user. When these patterns refer to people they can be called *profiles*.

2. Intellectual Rights in Profiling Processes

In order to assess the legal status of information in profiling technologies, the relevant legal objects need to be identified in these subsequent steps of the technological process. We can then determine which legal regimes are applicable [5]. We can identify three such objects:

- Databases
- Computer programs
- Profiles

The collection of data and their pre-processing often renders a database. The legal status of a database is relatively clear since the EU Database Directive. As a legal object a database is defined as "a collection of independent works, data or other materials arranged in a systematic way or methodical way and individually accessible by electronic or other means (art 1 sub. 2 Directive 96/9/EC). There are two kinds of intellectual rights that can be vested in a database. Creativity in the arrangement or selection of data is protected by copyright. Substantial investment in creating the database is protected by the *sui generis* database right of Directive 96/9/EC.

The collection, preparation and mining of data will often be executed by software (or heuristics in the case of data mining). In an environment of ambient intelligence the profiling stages of interpretation, profile application and decision making will also be executed by (autonomically computing) software. The legal status of *computer software* is complicated. Software can be protected either by copyright, patent or trade secret. If it has the form can be legally classified as an "original" "expression in any form of a computer program" it will be protected by copyright according to Directive 91/250/EC. Software can also be protected by patents in some circumstances. This is the case when the functionality it provides can be classified as "innovative" if it would have been hardware. Lastly, software can be protected as a trade secret when it is part of a secret process of production. The kind, scope and length of protection of software that enables profiling or autonomic computing will thus depend on the specific applicable legal regime.

3. The Profile

The most speculative question pertains to the legal status of the *profile* itself. No research has been done on this topic yet and no legislation or jurisprudence can give a direct answer to this question. In order to make this analysis we have to answer the question: What is a profile? It turns out that very different answers are given to this question depending on the field of occupation of the responder. Relevant for our purposes is to determine whether profiles can be protected by an intellectual right, in particular copyright. This means that we have to first interrogate the profile from a copyright perspective. Important questions we will have to answer are:

1. What is the expressive form of a profile?
2. Does a profile itself have the form of a database?

A basic principle of copyright is that it neither protects the ideas that underlie a work nor the contents or materials used. The protection rather extends only to the expressive form given to those ideas and the form in which the contents are composed. The question then becomes: What is the expressive form of a profile? The difficulty here is that there is an ambiguity in the interpretation of profiles. In its most basic sense a profile is the result of the technological process of profiling. Profiling is defined as the "process of 'discovering' correlations between data in data bases that can be used to identify and represent a human or nonhuman subject (individual or group), and/or the application of profiles (*sets of correlated data*) to individuate and *represent* a subject or to *identify* a subject as a member of a group or *category*" [6, p. 39]. A profile, in this sense, is defined as 'a set of correlated data that identify and represent a data subject' [7, p. 13]. A profile can thus be described both as a correlation of data or a category of identification or representation. These descriptions can have different contradictory consequences for qualification in intellectual rights.

When we start with the description of a profile as a *category* of representation, we can ask whether this category constitutes an "idea" in the sense of copyright. Or are these profiles themselves "expressions" of underlying ideas or mathematical concepts. What would be the expressive elements in profiles that would constitute the own intellectual creation of the author?[2] Classically speaking, a category seems similar or close to an idea, in which case the profile would be excluded from copyright protection.

---

2 The question is similar in cases of computer-generated art like creations of fractal Mandelbrot sets. In these cases one can also ask whether these constitute ideas or mathematical formulas or whether the specific input of its creator gives the sets creative expressive elements [8].

Profiles are also described as a *correlation of data*. In this description the compositional aspect of profiles is emphasized. We just saw that way in which the contents are composed in a work can be protected by copyright. In the WIPO Treaty on copyright is stated that copyright protection on literary and artistic works extends to compilations of data "which by reason of the selection or arrangement of their contents, constitute intellectual creations" (art. 5). In the header of this article these compilations of data are also called "databases". This might imply that profiles could themselves legally be qualified as databases. Within Europe this might mean that the Database Directive 96/9/EC is applicable, which defines a database as "a collection of independent works, data or other materials arranged in a systematic way or methodical way and individually accessible by electronic or other means" (Art. 1(2)). We must thus determine whether the correlation of data in a profile can be seen as:

1. a selection or arrangement of contents,
2. constituting an intellectual creation.

4. A Selection or Arrangement of Contents

In order to determine the first point it could be important to distinguish between profiling results and the representation of this output. The output of data mining, the profile, is often a structured decision procedure for assigning new data to an appropriate class. Depending on the function of the algorithm used and the complexity of the results, a certain mode of representation can be chosen. Representation allows an explanation of how the profiles were constructed in a form that is understandable for humans. In case more deterministic algorithms are chosen, possible modes of representation are, decision tables, decision trees, sets of classification rules (like Amazon's slogan "people who have bought this item also bought ..." or "if user X satisfies A and B, then he should be classified in class C") or association rules. Some algorithms like neural networks however, just render a real number output that can just be further computed. The construction process is here a black box [9]. This last case will not classify as a selection or arrangement of contents.

When we describe a profile itself as a set of rules, at first sight it might unlikely constitute a collection that can be protected by copyright. They rather themselves resemble classical algorithmic steps that are excluded from copyright protection. When we represent the same output by decision tables or decision trees however, profiles do seem to arrange data in a systematic way or methodical way required by the database directive. These contrary results point towards the same ambiguity as discussed above in case of the idea/expression classification. In line with Hugenholtz [10] we could say that this question will not be solved by turning to the traditional copyright concept of the "work". Instead drawing a line between idea and expression in case of new technologies like profiles will be a matter of what he calls "legal politics".

5. Originality

If we assume for the moment that profiles do constitute protectable "compilations of data", the next question is whether the "selection or arrangement" of data in a profile constitutes "an intellectual creation". This confronts us with the issue of the originality of profiles. A work is considered original for copyright standards when its form has a personal component that refers to its author. In the Directives on the legal protection of computer programs and databases the criterion of originality used is that the work must be the "author's own intellectual creation". This means that the work must be the result of a significant personal intellectual activity of its maker. Gotzen claims that when computers programs are used, one can only speak of an own intellectual activity when the resulting work is sufficiently determined by the human spirit [11]. This condition of being a product of the spirit (*corpus mysticum*) can be found back in the French and German legal concepts of work as "*oeuvre de esprit*" and "*gedankliche Vorstellung*". The relation between the human spirit and the work is thus of importance in order to be eligible for copyright protection. When profiling software is used this implies that the software functioned as a tool used to deliberately create the concrete profile. The question is whether the resulting profile can reasonable be foreseen and determined by human spirit to constitute the "own" intellectual creation of the author.

The answers to these questions will depend on the kind of data mining methods used for the construction of the profile - probabilistic or deterministic algorithms - and on the fact whether the profiling process is supervised or fully automated. When probabilistic algorithms like neural networks, naïve Bayes classifiers or fuzzy rule induction are used these results are non-deterministic and unpredictable. In this case no copyright protection is possible. When deterministic algorithms like regression, factor analysis or clustering are used they will always produce the same result when applied to the same data. In this case one has to determine whether the form of the resulting profiles is still sufficiently determined by the human spirit of the profiler to constitute his creation.

Whether the created profile can be foreseen or determined by human spirit can also depend on the profiling process being supervised or automated. In the first case human intervention can occur at several steps in the profiling process. First, "domain experts" have to specify the domain of analysis and the goals of profiling. Second, the expert has to select the data to be used in profiling by choosing the relevant input variables. Third, the expert can select the fields or attributes that are most relevant, instead of using all the collected data. Fourth, the expert has to choose the kind of algorithm to be used for data mining and can intervene in the data mining process itself with heuristics. Fifth, the resulting profiles will have to be interpreted. These interventions show that the skills and cognitive abilities (domain knowledge and bias information) of the profiling expert can thus be of great influence on the outcome [12].

It remains to be determined whether these interventions are sufficiently creative to classify as "original". The concepts of creativity and originality have not been uniformly interpreted by courts of the different EU member states to yet provide a clear answer. Important criteria for creativity seem to be the selection and exclusion of elements during the profiling process. This presumes that the maker has a choice. The extent to which the author can make use of this choice can be important for determining the copyrightability [13].

In Ambient Intelligence things will be different. Ambient Intelligence relies on profiling technologies and autonomic computing, a combination which we might call "autonomic profiling." In this case there is no human intervention in the profiling process. The six steps in the profiling scheme above will probably have all been automated by a hierarchical network of self-governing systems [14]. The concrete profile would be a work autonomically created by the intelligent system. This would imply that no human can be identified as its author and that it doesn't receive any protection by copyright. This is different in the UK where article 9 (3) of the Copyright,

Designs and Patents Act (CDPA) states that in "the case of a literary, dramatic, musical or artistic work which is computer-generated, the author shall be taken to be the person by whom the arrangements necessary for the creation of the work are undertaken." The European Commission has however declared that this "skill and effort" criterion of originality in the CDPA is not in accordance with the EU Directive 91/250/EC on the legal protection of computer programs.[3]

As a final note, it needs to be mentioned that when profiles turn out not to be copyrightable, they can always be protected by know-how protection. This regime will only protect the right holder against certain specific illegal actions by employees (trade secret), competitors (unfair competition law) or other legal subjects. A trade secret offers a company protection by making disclosure by employees an offence of criminal law.

6. Conclusion

Legal concepts like originality and the distinction between abstract idea and expressive form are central to the field of intellectual rights. They originated in specific political and technological contexts in the seventeenth century. These legal concepts arose in direct response to the drastic changes caused by the development of technologies like the printing press. Author rights where introduced as countermeasures against the strong monopolistic powers of publishers. The nature of challenges posed by the present technologies is very different. The autonomic profiling technologies behind Ambient Intelligence produce a continuous flux of profiles. Determining the legal status of profiles shows the increasing challenges of imposing the old scheme of intellectual rights, based on outdated presuppositions, on these new information technologies. An analysis of profiles shows that they fall between being an idea and an expression and that the notion of originality becomes more and more problematic due to the increasing amount of technological mediations in creating an original work.

References

[1] E. Aarts, S. Marzano, The New Everyday. Views on Ambient Intelligence. *010 Publishers*, Rotterdam (2003)

[2] W. Verhaegh, E. Aarts, J. Korst (eds.), Algorithms in Ambient Intelligence, Series: Philips Research Book Series , Vol. 2, 2004

[3] U.M. Fayyad, G. Piatetsky-Shapiro, P. Smyth, From Data Mining to Knowledge Discovery, *A.I. Magazine* (1996)

[4] B.H.M. Custers, The Power of Knowledge; Ethical, Legal, and Technological Aspects of Data Mining and Group Profiling in Epidemiology, Tilburg: Wolf Legal Publishers, 2004

[5] N. van Dijk, Intellectual Rights in Profiling Processes, In: B. Custers (ed.), 7.16: Profiling in Financial Institutions, FIDIS Future of Identity in the Information Society, 2009 (forthcoming)

---

[3] The Commission "had to take issue with the UK implementation because this latter Member State traditionally only requires skill and labour and permits copyright to protect computer generated works. The Commission has noted that as a result of the adoption of Directive 96/9/EC on the legal protection of databases6 the UK now provides for a legal definition of originality for the purposes of a literary work consisting of a database. A similar clause for computer programs is still lacking. It remains to be seen whether this will lead to an over-extensive protection of computer programs in the UK." See: http://eur-lex.europa.eu/LexUriServ/LexUriServ.do?uri=COM:2000:0199:FIN:EN:PDF

[6] M. Hildebrandt, Defining profiling: a new type of knowledge?, in M. Hildebrandt, S. Gutwirth (eds.), Profiling the European Citizen. Cross Disciplinary Perspectives, Springer, Dordrecht, 2008
[7] M. Hildebrandt, J. Backhouse, 7.2: Descriptive Analysis and Inventory of Profiling Practices, FIDIS Future of Identity in the Information Society, 2005
[8] D. Glasser, Copyrights in computer-generated works: whom, if anyone, do we reward?, *Duke L. & Tech. Rev. 0024* (2001)
[9] B. Anrig, W. Browne, M. Gasson, The role of algorithms in profiling, in: M. Hildebrandt, S. Gutwirth (eds.), Profiling the European Citizen, Cross Disciplinary Perspectives, Springer, Dordrecht, 2008
[10] P.B. Hugenholtz, Auteursrecht op Informatie, Amsterdam University Press, Amsterdam, 1989
[11] F. Gotzen, Auteursrecht, Manama Intellectuele Rechten, KUB, 2009
[12] A. Canhoto, J. Backhouse, General description of the process of behavioural profiling, in: M. Hildebrandt, S. Gutwirth (eds.), Profiling the European Citizen. Cross Disciplinary Perspectives, Springer, Dordrecht, 2008
[13] J.O. Kephart, D.M. Chess, The Vision of Autonomic Computing, *Computer* (2003)
[14] M. Buydens, La protection de la quasi-création, Larcier, Brussels, 1993

Intelligent Environments 2009
V. Callaghan et al. (Eds.)
IOS Press, 2009

doi:10.3233/978-1-60750-034-6-517

Real time adaptivity from Cybernetics to Intelligent Environments: *Rewriting the History of Ubiquitous Computing.*

Katja DE VRIES[1]
PhD-student at the Vrije Universiteit Brussel,
Center for Law, Science, Technology & Society Studies

Abstract. The historical framework in which a technology is placed can affect the direction of legal, societal and philosophical thought about it. It is explored in which way "Ambient Intelligent" or "Intelligent Environments"-technologies are similar or different from the technologies which arose during the mechanical and the cybernetic revolution. The findings are applied to a possible new understanding of privacy: the protection of a "time of one's own" instead of "a private space of one's own".

Keywords. Historical perspective, Intelligent Environments, Legal Philosophy, Cybernetic Revolution, Mechanical revolution, Legal protection of "time of one's own"

Introduction

Research into technology that is capable to anticipate user demands and preferences in a personalized way (see for current applications, e.g., [1]) holds the promise of becoming a very profitable field of research. Already in 1998 the executive vice-president of Philips predicted that *pre-sponsiveness* [2] would become booming business. GPS-systems which predict where a car-driver will go [3], smart electricity devices suggesting the consumer a personalized electricity scheme or a smart kitchen appliance recommending recipes: the field of possible applications seems to be vast. From a legal-philosophical perspective this makes one wonder which legal issues could be at stake in such scenarios.

1. Positioning this paper – what is it that legal philosophers do?

Law is a linguistic practice: qualifying factual matters in legal terms is its core practice. The way in which a case is resolved will depend largely on the legal terms in which it is framed. However, legal concepts are not pre-given, static entities but have to be reinvented in interaction with the concrete cases upon which the law has to act. For example, an apparently straightforward legal notion like "theft" is subject to permanent

[1] Corresponding Author: Katja de Vries, Vrije Universiteit Brussel, Center for Law, Science, Technology & Society Studies, Pleinlaan 2, 1050 Brussel, Belgium; E-mail: edevries@vub.ac.be.

reinvention as it is exposed to new factual cases. Thus, lawyers have had to face questions such as whether "stealing" electricity or virtual goods can qualify legally as "theft", i.e., whether "theft" is only possible with tangible objects. In other words, legal practice can be characterized as a practice of *naming*: a practice of finding or inventing the appropriate legal terms to frame an event. The question guiding every legal practitioner is the question of how to name what it is – legally spoken – that is happening. The concepts created by legal practice do not have the pretension to be philosophically true concepts but they must be *functional* in a legal dispute: e.g., a notion of "theft" that is too vague, too limited or too indiscriminating will quickly be overruled or forgotten. A good legal concept has to be like a reliable and multifunctional tin-opener: it must have the ability to articulate many different situations in a legally productive way.

The practice of legal conceptualisation is guided by concrete problems and the need to solve these cases within a reasonable period of time: a lawyer is not a philosopher [4, 5]. Even Plato, the father of Western philosophy, already knew that to be a judge is something quite distinct from being a philosopher: for a judge is no philosopher who can take as much time as he wants to reach the ultimate truth[2]. Both in ancient Greece as well as in our modern times lawyers are always restricted by the water-clock[3].

This makes the practice of the *legal philosopher* a strange hybrid. The trade of the legal philosopher, like the trade of the legal practitioner, is to come up with productive ways of legal qualification. Yet, what makes the legal philosopher different is that he is not always bound by the necessity to solve a concrete case but that he sketches future legal pathways – anticipating possible cases to come. Especially with regard to larger societal and technological developments it can be productive to complement the piece-meal legal tinkering with a more overarching legal outlook. When confronted with the eternal question – "How to put legal terms to what is happening?", the legal-philosopher acts like a strategist who tries to think beyond the particular battle that has to be fought today towards the possible battles of tomorrow.

2. Retelling the birth mythology of *UbiComp* in a legally productive way: where to begin the story?

The cloud of interrelated technological visions such as *Ubiquitous* or *Pervasive Computing*, *Ambient Intelligence*, the *Internet of Things* and *Intelligent* or *Smart Environments* has provoked quite some interest among policy-makers, ethicists, lawyers and philosophers. The societal, legal and philosophical analyses of the field are innumerable and very diverse in nature. For example a very normative stance can be found in Albrecht and McIntyre [7] who point to the possible adverse effects such technologies could have on civil liberties. A more optimistic approach, focusing on the economical and societal implications, can be found in several policy papers [e.g., 8, 9].

---

[2] In Plato's *Theaetetus* [6, p. 221] Socrates asks: "Or do you think there are any teachers so clever as to be able, in the short time allowed by the water-clock, satisfactorily to teach the judges the truth about what happened to people who have been robbed of their money or have suffered other acts of violence, when there were no eyewitnesses?".

[3] The length of speeches in the Athenian law courts was limited by a water-clock.

While some authors draw up a broad inventory of all the ethical, societal, economical and legal issues which might be at stake [e.g., 10], others analyse the impact on specific ethical assets such as freedom and privacy [11] or sketch concrete scenarios of possible societal effects of technologies which fall within the Ambient Intelligence vision [12]. The multiplicity and diversity of approaches is, for instance, also nicely reflected in a special issue of the *International Review of Information Ethics* on the ethical challenges of Ubiquitous Computing [13].

Even though all of the aforementioned analyses are of a diverse nature, there seems to be a great consensus about the way in which these technological visions are framed historically and theoretically. Most authors begin their narrative in the early nineties of the twentieth century with the vision of *Ubiquitous Computing* (*UbiComp*) as developed by Mark Weiser, who was at that time the chief scientist at the XEROX Palo Alto Research Center in California. Weiser's vision of *UbiComp* involved computing which is no longer restricted to the enclosed world of a desktop computer [14, 15] but which is brought into the world by integrating sensors and microprocessors with everyday objects. After the introduction of the canonized birth myth of *UbiComp* the focus tends to shift to one of the visions which sprang forth from it. The later in time the vision was developed the more elaborate the list of characteristics seems to become. Recurrent characteristics are, for instance, pervasiveness, interactivity, interoperability, adaptivity, the capacity to anticipate, embeddedness, mobility, context awareness, personalization, and being turned 'on' permanently [e.g., 16]. Thus, for example, the *Ambient Intelligence* (*AmI*) vision developed by Philips in the late nineties of the twentieth century, can be defined as a combination of *UbiComp* and Intelligent User Interfaces [11]. Though I do not dispute that there might be reasonable grounds to stick to this way of depicting the history of the conglomerate of technological visions like *UbiComp*, *AmI* and *Intelligent Environments*, it could nevertheless be illuminating to have a closer look at how their emergence relates to this other grand technological vision which caused a philosophical and societal stir from the 1940s on: *cybernetics* (see for one of the seminal books of the father of cybernetics: [17]; philosophical and historical interpretations of cybernetics can be found, e.g., in: [18-22]). Once more I have to underline that my attempt to present an alternative history does not pretend to be in any way intrinsically superior to the traditional depiction – this paper is much more modest in its ambitions! – but that it merely tries to create a productive way of framing these visions within a legal context. After all, the frame in which a painting is moulded *can* make a difference. The discourse from which one begins could guide one into a certain direction of thought. An example of how legal thought could be affected by the historical framing is presented in the fourth section of this paper.

3. Cybernetics as an illuminating precursor of Intelligent Environments: real-time negative feedback

Although there is an abundance of interesting issues which could be discussed with regard to cybernetics, I will focus in this paper on the conception of rational behaviour within cybernetic thought as emerging from negative feedback loops. To grasp the importance of the notion of negative feedback one can compare the ideas of the seventeenth century mechanical revolution with that of the twentieth century cybernetic revolution.

In the seventeenth and eighteenth century the material world was – to put it in the terminology of the famous German sociologist Max Weber – "disenchanted" by the effacement of the difference between organic and inorganic systems: the scientific world marvelled at striking similarity between, for example, the mechanical duck-automaton of Vaucanson (1738) and Harvey's hydraulic explanation of the workings of human blood-circulation in his *De motu cordis* (1628). However, what classical mechanics could not erase was the need for a transcendental explanation of rationality and the ability to adapt in a rational way to the environment: the workings of a duck-automaton or a hydraulic system do not adapt themselves over time to changes in the environment.

It is only with the advent of twentieth century cybernetic notions like *negative feedback-machine* or *iterative mechanics* that transcendental explanations of rational adaptation to one's surroundings become superfluous and the disenchantment of the world proceeds to a new level. As the title of Norbert Wiener's most famous book exemplifies [23] cybernetics bereaves notions like 'communication', 'control' and 'goal-rationality' from their privileged transcendental position outside mechanics. Thus, viewed from this perspective one can maintain that whereas a rock has no rationality because it cannot adapt itself to its environment, there is only a difference in terms of complexity between the rationality of a thermostat – adapting itself to the surrounding temperature – and human rationality. In this vain the cybernetic movement tried to explain very disparate processes in terms of negative feedback loops: from autonomic bodily processes, such as the control of the amount of oxygen in the blood in order to obtain a homeostatic state of an optimal concentration of blood gases, to the conscious control of a human person tasting and adjusting the amount of salt in a dish [24]. Both a thermostat, adjusting to the temperature of the environment, and a human, adjusting the amount of salt in a dish, are informational systems *steering* themselves through an environment which they perceive ('cybernetics' derives from the Greek word *kybernētēs*, "steersman", and is etymologically very closely related to, e.g., "government"). From the cybernetic perspective rationality is no longer to be understood as the dealing with stable knowledge but as the resilience and adaptivity of an informational system towards an unknown future. The big difference between representational information science and cybernetics is clearly expressed by Andrew Pickering:

> Mainstream informatics presumes a very familiar ontology. The world is a regular, law-like place that can be known more or less exhaustively. It is a place that can therefore be controlled and dominated through knowledge. That is the logic behind the creation of bigger databases and faster information systems. Of course, this ontology does recognise the existence of the unknown, but only as something to be conquered, to be drawn into the realm of the known. Cybernetics turned this picture inside out and exemplified a different and much less familiar ontology. [...] that there exists in the world a class of 'exceedingly complex systems,' including the brain, the firm and the economy, which are in principle unknowable. However much data we gather on them, we can never know them completely, they can always surprise us. Such systems can never be dominated by knowledge, and instead we have to learn somehow to cope with them. And cybernetics was, then, the science of dealing with the unknown, the science of adaptation—an extremely odd sort of science. [21, p. 5]

Within cybernetic systems the *timing* of informational loops is of crucial importance. In socialist Chile of the 1970s the cyberneticist Stafford Beer designed a system which would control the entire economy based on continuous, real-time streams of information on the performance of all economical actors [21, 25]. This *Cybersyn* system was never put into operation due to the coup in 1973 by Pinochet, but it is a nice example of the idea that (human) rationality can be enhanced when the informational loop can be made shorter (in time) and more all-encompassing (in scope).

On the one hand the *AmI* or *Intelligent Environments* revolution which we are witnessing today continues according to the lines set out in the mechanical revolution and the cybernetic revolution. Yet, it *is* a revolution. However, what is it that is so revolutionary compared to the previous revolutions? In the first place the world of 'numb' or 'non-informational' objects is seriously diminished: one could imagine a smart environment wherein not only a human person adjusts the amount of salt in a pot of spaghetti through a cybernetic feedback loop of tasting, but wherein the pot of spaghetti itself adapts towards its environment (the temperature, the person who is cooking, etc.) as well. Secondly, the notion of memory and learning plays a much more prominent role: whereas a 'classical' thermostat has no memory, a 'smart' thermostat might actually 'remember' and anticipate situations instead of adapting to the environment instantaneously. In this way adaptation becomes less of a 'jolting' and more of a 'smooth' process. Finally, a third striking characteristic of the present informational revolution is that it often is very human-centred. Contrary to the classical thermostat – whose environment is the temperature – or Beer's *Cybersyn* project – which adapts itself to industrial and economic output data – a smart shower, for instance, might adapt itself to its users: "*An example of a learning heuristic is time sensitive adjustment to temperature of the water: after X minutes lower the temperature to Y where X and Y are input explicitly by the user or by the shower remembering how the user adjusted the temperature during the most recent shower*". [26, p. 2]

4. Why is it important from a legal-philosophical perspective to place the *AmI* revolution in a longer tradition of disenchanting mechanical revolutions? Human rights and limits to anticipation.

Given that the *AmI* revolution will be characterized by (1) its ubiquitous informational mobilization of objects which used to be informationally 'dumb', (2) its ability for adaptation over time (memorization used for anticipation), and (3) its focus on the co-ordination and management of particular users or citizens, new types of informational constraints can become imposed on humans. Given such an understanding of the *AmI* revolution it is plausible that statistical proactive profiling could become very important in an *AmI* world to come. At the moment such techniques are applied in particular in banking (credit scoring) and in internet commerce (*Amazon* recommendation and collaborative filtering algorithms, see [27]) but they could easily find application in other domains (healthcare, policing, domestic appliances, etc.). Now how could this way of putting things affect a legal analysis of these kinds of technologies? One aspect which becomes more pronounced by an understanding of *AmI* as a third technological revolution, after the first (mechanical) and the second (cybernetic) revolution, is that the lawyer can use the cybernetic discourse to discuss the scope and timing of different informational loops. Whereas classical privacy law – springing forth from an age of mechanical distribution of information by means of newspapers and pictures – focuses on the protection of the autonomy of the individual within a certain private, spatially defined, sphere (e.g., 'home' or 'the family') the new informational revolution might call for the need to reflect upon the possibility of protecting individual autonomy with regard to *time*: how much anticipation based on previous behaviour of one's own or that of 'similar' individuals can be tolerated in a constitutional democracy that protects the autonomy of it's citizens? (see on profiles, e.g., [28-30]) To my knowledge the ideas and machines which have sprung forth from the cybernetic revolution of the 1940s have never lead to a legal dispute wherein cybernetics itself became a matter of dispute: cybernetics and human law are two fields that have rarely met before. Yet, at the dawn of the *AmI* revolution, with its promise of ubiquity, complexity with regard to timing (memory-anticipation) and individual-centeredness, new questions arise. For example: are there limits to the use of "proactive computing" (a term coined by IBM: [31]) and "intention and preference machines" (a term coined by the Microsoft researcher E. Horvitz [32])? Can one speak of "one's own time" – wherein one should not be anticipated all the time – in the same way as classical privacy law gives a privileged protection to certain private spaces "of one's own"? For instance, one could wonder whether a personalized GPS-system which recommends certain routes to a car driver – while using only fully anonymized data – still could be privacy intrusive in the sense of timing: pre-empting the choice of the driver. During the doctoral colloquium of the IE'09 conference I hope to elaborate on such questions and provoke a fruitful discussion around these issues.

References

[1] G. Uchyigit and M. Y. Ma, *Personalization Techniques and Recommender Systems*, World Scientific, [s.l.], 2008.

[2] R. Pieper, From Devices to "Ambient Intelligence": the Transformation of Consumer Electronics (keynote address), presented on the *Digital Living Room Conference*, Laguna Beach, 1998.

[3] J. Krumm and E. Horvitz, Predestination: Where Do You Want to Go Today? Predicting driver destinations could help target location-based services, *IEEE Computer Magazine* **40** (April 2007), 105-107.

[4] Y. Thomas, Le sujet de droit, la personne et la nature. Sur la critique contemporaine du sujet de droit, *Le debat: histoire, politique, societé* **100** (1998), 85-107.

[5] L. De Sutter, *Deleuze: la pratique du droit*, Michalon, Paris, 2009.

[6] Plato, *Theaetetus. Sophist*, Harvard University Press, Cambridge, Mass., 2002.

[7] K. Albrecht and L. McIntyre, *Spychips. How majar corporations and government plan to track your every move with RFID*, Nelson Current, Nashville, 2005.

[8] G. Santucci and S. Lange, *The Internet of Things in 2020. A Roadmap for the Future* (report), European Commission / EPoSS, 2008.

[9] P.-J. Benghozi, S. Bureau, and F. Massit-Folléa, *The Internet of Things. What Challenges for Europe?*, Vox Internet, Paris, 2008.

[10] J. Bohn, V. Coroamă, M. Langheinrich, F. Mattern, and M. Rohs, Social, Economic, and Ethical Implications of Ambient Intelligence and Ubiquitous Computing, in: W. Weber, J. Rabaey, and E. Aarts, (eds.), *Ambient Intelligence*, Springer, Berlin, 2005, 5-29.

[11] P. Brey, Freedom and Privacy in Ambient Intelligence, *Ethics and Information Technology* **7** (2005), 157-166, 2005.

[12] D. Wright, S. Gutwirth, M. Friedewald, E. Vildjiounaite, and Y. Punie, *Safeguards in a World of Ambient Intelligence*, Springer, [s.l.], 2008.

[13] D. J. Phillips and K. Wiegerling, (eds.), Ethical Challenges of Ubiquitous Computing, special issue of the *International Review of Information Ethics* **8** (2007).

[14] M. Weiser, The Computer for the 21st Century, *Scientific American* **265** (1991), 66-75.

[15] M. Weiser, R. Gold, and J. S. Brown, The origins of ubiquitous computing research at PARC in the late 1980s, *IBM Systems Journal* **38** (1999), 693-696.
[16] E. Aarts and B. de Ruyter, New research perspectives on Ambient Intelligence, *Journal of Ambient Intelligence and Smart Environments* **1** (2009), 5-14.
[17] N. Wiener, *The human use of human beings: cybernetics and society*, Sphere Books, London, 1968.
[18] F. J. Crosson and K. M. Sayre, *Philosophy and cybernetics: essays delivered to the Philosophic Institute for Artificial Intelligence at the University of Notre Dame*, University of Notre Dame Press, Notre Dame, 1967.
[19] J. Johnston, *The Allure of Machinic Life. Cybernetics, Artificial Life, and the New AI*, MIT Press, London, 2008.
[20] D. A. Mindell, *Between human and machine: feedback, control, and computing before cybernetics*, Johns Hopkins University Press, Baltimore, 2002.
[21] A. Pickering, *The Science of the Unknowable. Stafford Beer's Cybernetic Informatics* (working paper from the series of Working Papers from the Centre for STS Studies), University of Aarhus, 2006, 3-33.
[22] M. Triclot, *Le moment cybernétique: la constitution de la notion d'information*, Champ Vallon, Seyssel, 2008.
[23] N. Wiener, *Cybernetics: or control and communication in the animal and the machine*, MIT Press, New York, 1948.
[24] J. Voss, *Fanfares for Effective Freedom* (art-work/video, 25 min.), 2008. Exhibited at the Brussels Biennial 2008. Retrieved 26th of May 2009, from http://measurestaken-ffef2.blogspot.com/2008/10/normal-0-21-microsoftinternetexplorer4.html.
[25] E. Medina, Designing Freedom, Regulating a Nation: Socialist Cybernetics in Allende's Chile, *Journal of Latin American Studies* **38** (2006), 571-606.
[26] E. G. P. Van Doren, *Adaptivity of ambient intelligence to fulfil consumer needs* (U.S. Patent, nr. 2007/0143233 A1), Koninklijke Philips Electronics, N.V., Filing date: Oct 12, 2004; Publication date: June 21, 2007.
[27] G. Linden, B. Smith, and J. York, Amazon.com Recommendations: Item-to-Item Collaborative Filtering, *IEEE Internet Computing*, **7** (Jan./Feb. 2003), 76-80.
[28] B. H. M. Custers, *The Power of Knowledge. Ethical, Legal, and Technological Aspects of Data Mining and Group Profiling in Epidemiology*, Wolf Legal Publishers, Nijmegen, 2004.
[29] G. Elmer, *Profiling machines: mapping the personal information economy*, MIT Press, Cambridge, Mass., 2004.
[30] M. Hildebrandt and S. Gutwirth, *Profiling the European Citizen. Cross-Disciplinary Perspectives*, Springer, [s.l.], 2008.
[31] R. Want, T. Pering, and D. Tennenhouse, Comparing autonomic and proactive computing, *IBM Systems Journal* **42** (2003), 129-135.
[32] E. Horvitz, Machine Learning, Reasoning, and Intelligence in Daily Life: Directions and Challenges (keynote address), in *Proceedings of Artificial Intelligence Techniques for Ambient Intelligence*, Hyderabad, India, 2007. Available at: http://research.microsoft.com/~horvitz/AmbientAI_Keynote.pdf.

Subject Index

Author Index